SAP HANA® Security Guide

Jonathan Haun

SAP HANA® Security Guide

Rheinwerk
Publishing

Editor Meagan White
Acquisitions Editor Hareem Shafi
Copyeditor Melinda Rankin
Cover Design Graham Geary
Photo Credit iStockphoto.com/532957089/© Aslan Aphan
Layout Design Vera Brauner
Production Marissa Fritz
Typesetting III-satz, Husby (Germany)
Printed and bound in the United States of America, on paper from sustainable sources

ISBN 978-1-4932-1441-9

1st edition 2017

Library of Congress Cataloging-in-Publication Control Number: 2017005860

Contents at a Glance

Dear Reader,

"If you have built castles in the air, your Work need not be lost; that is where they should be. Now put the foundations under them."

—Henry David Thoreau, *Walden*

Your SAP HANA system is your castle, your kingdom. Beware any who should dare trespass there! From rock-hard foundations to impenetrable moats, between these pages you'll find everything you need to defend your turf.

Silliness aside, in your hands you hold the complete guide to SAP HANA security. With case studies, sample code, and detailed instructions, author-extraordinaire Jonathan Haun has shown you how to defend the turrets and raise the drawbridge (so to speak!). Whether you're new to security in SAP HANA, or looking to get a refresher on encryption or auditing, this book has it all!

As always, your comments and suggestions are the most useful tools to help us make our books the best they can be. Let us know what you thought about *SAP HANA Security Guide*! Please feel free to contact me and share any praise or criticism you may have.

Thank you for purchasing a book from SAP Press!

Meagan White
Editor, SAP PRESS

meaganw@rheinwerk-publishing.com
www.sap-press.com
Rheinwerk Publishing · Boston, MA

Contents

Preface

SAP HANA is used to power SAP applications and host data from a variety of sources. The applications it powers and the data it hosts are often critical to an organization's operations. Failure to properly secure an SAP HANA environment often can lead to system instability and a lack of data integrity; therefore, SAP HANA security must be given the proper attention and scrutiny.

Purpose

This book was written with the goal of educating readers about SAP HANA security. We focus on key aspects of the SAP HANA security model, including user provisioning, role creation, privilege assignment, encryption, auditing, and authentication. We also discuss the tools used to create and maintain an SAP HANA security model. Such information is critical for SAP HANA security architects to implement security models for their organizations. This information is also necessary for organizations to protect the data hosted within SAP HANA and to maintain the reliability of systems that rely on SAP HANA.

Who Should Read This Book

This book will help security teams, BASIS teams, security consultants, and anyone looking for a one-stop guide to implementing an SAP HANA security model.

We recommend the following prerequisites for readers of this book:

- General knowledge of SAP HANA Studio
- General knowledge of SQL
- Experience working in areas of database administration
- Experience working with database objects such as tables, views, and stored procedures

Each chapter is structured to offer background and theory for specific security-related concepts. Many chapters conclude with a case study—centering on the fictitious E-Corporation—for a "real-world" application of the topics covered in the book.

Our goal is to provide you with technical knowledge and a unique perspective on how security has been implemented in the field based on real customer engagements.

Structure of This Book

The book is structured into 18 chapters. The Introduction and Chapters one through four introduce SAP HANA, SAP HANA security, SAP HANA Studio, privileges, and database objects. Chapters four, five, and six introduce users and roles. Chapters seven through eleven discuss the various privilege types within SAP HANA. The remaining chapters discuss SAP HANA authentication, encryption, lifecycle management, audit policies, security troubleshooting, and general recommendations for securing your SAP HANA environment.

Introduction

SAP HANA represents the next evolution of data management for many organizations. It also powers critical applications used to manage an organization. This makes SAP HANA a valuable asset for many organizations. Because of its importance, it must be secured. In the Introduction, we provide an overview of SAP HANA's hardware and software layers. We introduce basic concepts of SAP HANA security and list several reasons that securing your SAP HANA environment is important.

Chapter 1: Managing Security with SAP HANA Studio

This chapter introduces SAP HANA Studio, a key tool used to manage SAP HANA security. We explain how to navigate SAP HANA Studio perspectives. We also provide a detailed workflow to help identify key security management areas within SAP HANA Studio, including the security console and SQL console.

Chapter 2: Introduction to SAP HANA Privileges

This chapter introduces the key privilege types available within SAP HANA. We provide a summary of each privilege type, including system, object, analytic, package, and application privileges. We also discuss how SAP HANA validates the assignment of privileges for users and roles.

Chapter 3: Catalog Objects

This chapter explains the role catalog objects play within an SAP HANA system. We review the process for creating standard and repository-based schemas. We also review the process used to create other standard and repository-based catalog objects. It's important to understand the nature of catalog objects, because it pertains to object privileges and the overall SAP HANA security model architecture.

Chapter 4: User Accounts

Authentication and authorization center on user accounts. Every individual and application that interacts with SAP HANA requires a user account. This chapter will provide detailed information related to the type of user accounts, the creation of user accounts, and how privileges are granted and revoked from user accounts. It also discusses how roles are granted to user accounts. In conclusion, we provide a case study to review a programmatic approach to provisioning users from an external source.

Chapter 5: Database Roles

When granting privileges, we should always avoid granting them directly to users, which can lead to significant inconsistencies within a security model. As an alternative, we can grant privileges to roles, and roles can then be granted to one or more users, thus providing consistency. In this chapter, we explore multiple options used to create roles. We also discuss the different ways that privileges can be granted and revoked from roles and how roles can be nested to simplify the management of a security model.

Chapter 6: Repository Roles

In addition to creating standard database roles, we can also define roles within the SAP HANA development repository. Using repository-based roles can overcome many of the issues associated with standard database roles. In this chapter, we discuss the reasons to use repository-based roles. We also review the syntax needed to define repository roles within design-time scripts. As an alternative to defining scripts, we also review the SAP HANA Web-Based Development Workbench editor GUI that can be used to create repository-based roles. We also discuss how repository-based roles are granted to existing users and roles. In conclusion, we walk through a case study in which we discuss common roles implemented at E-Corporation.

Chapter 7: System Privileges

System privileges govern our ability to perform specific actions within the SAP HANA system. These actions are typically related to administrative and development roles. In this chapter, we explore the system privileges available within SAP HANA. We demonstrate how system privileges are granted using SQL, SAP HANA Studio, the SAP HANA Web-Based Development Workbench security manager, and within repository-based roles. We close the chapter with a case study outlining several commonly used administrative roles and their required system privileges.

Chapter 8: Object Privileges

Object privileges play an important role in the development of any SAP HANA security model; they define the types of SQL script actions a user can perform on a catalog object. SAP HANA hosts multiple types of catalog objects. In this chapter, we look closely at object privileges. We demonstrate how we can grant object privileges to users or roles using SQL statements, SAP HANA Studio, or within repository-based roles. We close the chapter with a case study reviewing the workflow E-Corporation used to add object privileges to a few existing repository-based roles.

Chapter 9: Package Privileges

SAP HANA is a development platform, in addition to its data-management functions. To facilitate application development, application code storage, security, and application lifecycle management, SAP HANA provides a repository, organized into packaged. To secure the repository at the package level, we must implement package privileges. In this chapter, we start by discussing the SAP HANA development repository. We then review the various privileges that can be granted for packages and how they're granted to grantees. Finally, we walk through a case study in which E-Corporation identifies and resolves the gaps in their existing package hierarchy and package privilege design.

Chapter 10: Analytic Privileges

Analytic privileges are used to grant or restrict access to data hosted within the SAP HANA system. In this chapter, we provide an overview of analytic privileges. We discuss the differences between static analytic privileges and dynamic analytic privileges and discuss how classic XML-based analytic privileges are being replaced with newer SQL-based analytic privileges. We demonstrate how to manage and create static and dynamic privileges and review the process used to troubleshoot a grantee's effective analytic privileges. Finally, we discuss the processes available to grant analytic privileges.

Chapter 11: Application Privileges

SAP HANA is an application development platform in which web-based applications can be developed and hosted. At times, these applications also need their own security models based on application privileges. In this chapter, we provide an overview of application privileges within SAP HANA, how they're created, and how they're granted to roles using a variety of options. We also provide a summary of **Privileges on Users** and how it's used to grant the ATTACH DEBUGGER privilege to another grantee.

Chapter 12: Authentication

For authorization mechanisms to work properly, the SAP HANA system must first properly identify each user. To identify users, SAP HANA supports several authentication mechanisms. In this chapter, we walk through the details of SAP HANA's internal basic authentication system and its configurable password policy settings. We also discuss the various external providers that are supported for seamless authentication with the SAP HANA system. Finally, we walk through the process by which E-Corporation defined a stored procedure to add a SAML identity to existing user accounts within SAP HANA.

Chapter 13: Certificate Management and Encryption

In addition to authorization and authentication, we also need to use encryption to protect our SAP HANA system. In this chapter, we review SSL certificate management within SAP HANA. We also discuss the options for encryption communication between client applications and the SAP HANA server. Finally, we discuss the options necessary to encrypt the SAP HANA data and log volumes.

Chapter 14: Security Lifecycle Management

SAP HANA is a development platform, and security administrators will discover that security-related development artifacts can be transported easily between different

SAP HANA instances. In this chapter, we outline the best practices and options available to use this transportation mechanism. We start by discussing ways to maintain a consistent security model. We then review the steps necessary to define a delivery unit containing security-related artifacts. Then, we review the steps necessary to access the SAP HANA application lifecycle management tool. Finally, we discuss additional features within SAP HANA application lifecycle management that can benefit the lifecycle management of security artifacts.

Chapter 15: Auditing

Auditing allows organizations to configure rules that record important activities conducted within the SAP HANA system. In this chapter, we discuss why we need auditing within SAP HANA. We also discuss the steps required to enable auditing and define policies to record critical activities. Finally, we walk through a case study in which we create auditing rules to track important changes within E-Corporation's SAP HANA landscape.

Chapter 16: Security Tracing and Troubleshooting

In the real world, most security models are quite complex. SAP HANA offers security trace options and system views to help administrators manage their security model. This chapter outlines steps required to enable a security-related authorization trace and review the trace file results. In addition, we review the various system views that provide details about the effective rights granted to individual users. We close the chapter with a case study in which E-Corporation queries system views to troubleshoot authorization issues within its environment.

Chapter 17: Security Recommendations

Knowing how to configure and implement security within SAP HANA is vital, and guidelines based on established best practices can help. This chapter provides several recommendations for securing an SAP HANA system based on the principals learned throughout this book. We discuss recommendations related to password authentication, encryption, high-level privileges, the SYSTEM account, escalation vulnerabilities, appliance handover, and audit policies.

Chapter 18: SAP HANA 2.0 Security

SAP HANA 2.0 has incorporated several changes to SAP HANA security. This chapter provides an overview of the key differences. These key changes are related to authorization, encryption, classic XS engine applications, and the new SAP HANA 2.0 Cockpit.

Acknowledgments

I would like to dedicate this book to God, for the blessing of wisdom and knowledge you have bestowed upon me. To my family and loved ones, thank you for your support and understanding during the endless hours and many weekends that were committed to the completion of this project. To Samantha Haun, Addison Haun, and Mason Haun: Without your thoughtfulness and support, this book would not have been possible. Completing 18 chapters on my own was only possible because you were willing to sacrifice our precious family time. I cherish and love every moment with you and thank for your support.

Also, I'd like to thank our customers for trusting me with their SAP HANA initiatives. Without these experiences from the field, this book wouldn't be possible.

I'd also like to recognize Protiviti and show my appreciation for the use of its SAP HANA environments hosted within its Data and Analytics SAP HANA Center of Excellence. Without Protiviti's support, some of the content within this book could not have been created.

My thanks to Roy Wells, my coworker and friend who helped me pioneer many of these security concepts over the years of implementing SAP HANA solutions with our customers. Your wisdom and guidance over the years heled make this book a reality.

Finally, my sincere and utmost thanks go to everyone at Rheinwerk Publishing, especially Hareem Shafi and Meagan White. This book truly took a hard-fought battle to complete, and their patience, dedication, and guidance helped me through this process while seeing another publication dream become reality.

Introduction

SAP HANA represents the next evolution of data management for many organizations. Data has become a valuable asset and thus must be secured.

Most organizations see their data as an asset: It helps them conduct business, identify trends, manage operations, and anticipate change. Over the decades, the volume of data produced by computer systems has increased substantially. As these volumes have increased, so has the need for computer systems powerful enough to process that data. For many organizations, SAP HANA is a powerful and important tool that helps them manage and process large volumes of data.

SAP HANA hosts data and operates applications that are critical to an organization. If the data that it hosts is lost or the applications that it operates aren't available, an organization can be subject to substantial financial loss. Therefore, security is one of many important aspects required to ensure the integrity of the data and applications that rely on SAP HANA.

Throughout this book, we'll walk you through the key concepts of the *SAP HANA security model*, at its core comprised of users, roles, and privileges. We must also take steps to secure its data using encryption, authentication, and operating system controls. We must also understand the various tools used to manage security and we must track changes using auditing. Before we dive into the security model, let's first look at an overview of SAP HANA.

Overview of SAP HANA

Some consider SAP HANA just another database, but SAP HANA offers much more than its database services. SAP HANA is a next-generation data appliance. It can play many roles throughout an organization; to be more precise, it can facilitate many solutions, including those in which SAP HANA is used to manage data for an application and those in which it's used to manage data and analytics. The first step in understanding SAP HANA security is to understand its architecture. To do so, we must first examine both the software layers and hardware layers of SAP HANA.

Software Layers and Features

At its core, SAP HANA acts as a database. However, it's also an application development environment, and it has layers that facilitate multidimensional models. It offers a predictive analytics engine and even an *online transaction processes (OLTP)* engine. Let's not forget that it can also act as an unstructured data processor, full-text search engine, data federation engine, and data integration tool. Because of these capabilities, securing an SAP HANA system requires knowledge of components well beyond standard *relational database management system (RDBMS)* objects and their security.

At a high level, Figure 1 depicts the software features and layers of the SAP HANA appliance. These layers allow it to facilitate more than just standard database processing. Security within SAP HANA must address each of these layers. The SAP HANA in-memory database layer contains multiple query processing engines, such as the calculation engine, OLAP engine, row engine, and join engine. This layer also contains the row store tables, columnar store tables, and the new smart data access logical database tables. There are also engines designed to manage text processing and text search.

The SAP HANA software appliance layer, which includes the SAP HANA in-memory database layer, also includes the SAP HANA *extended application services, classic model* (XS) engine to enable SAP HANA as a development platform. There are also embedded features such as the Predictive Analytics Library (PAL), Business Function Library (BFL), planning engines, rules engines, and geospatial engines. SAP HANA supports real-time replication of data using replication agents and data integration using smart data integration (SDI). It also offers a more robust and sophisticated SAP HANA *extended application services, advanced model* (XSA) application server that is capable of supporting more complex coding languages and application process isolation. In total, these layers build upon each other to form the SAP HANA appliance. Because SAP HANA is a robust data and application platform, securing this data and application appliance can be a challenging endeavor.

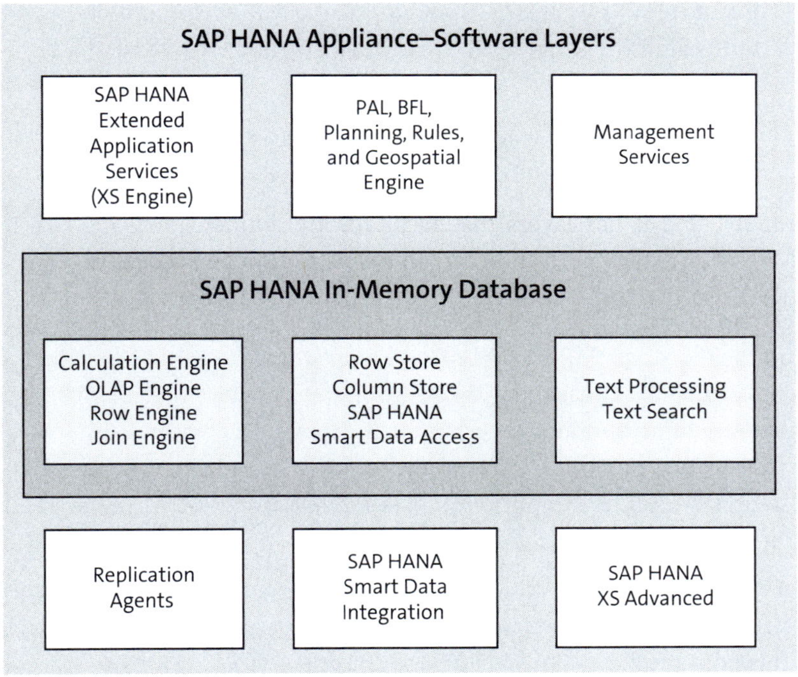

Figure 1 High-Level Overview of the SAP HANA Software Appliance Layers

Hardware Layers and Features

Understanding the hardware components of SAP HANA is also fundamentally important in understanding what SAP HANA is and how it is secured. With SAP HANA, data is stored in dynamic random-access memory (DRAM) and within the central processing unit (CPU) cache. This allows the software to deliver exceptional performance, because data is stored close to the CPU. Traditional databases store and access data on disk drives that are architecturally further away from the CPU and slower in accessing data for a variety of technical reasons.

Each server is also configured with multiple CPU sockets, each with multiple CPU cores. Multiple CPU sockets and cores allow the software to process multiple requests concurrently. For example, when data is stored in a column store, the software can reduce the processing of each column of data into one or more parallel requests.

Because there are multiple CPU cores available, each request can be processed by one or more CPU cores in parallel. The net result is more data being processed at the same time for an individual query.

Because DRAM is volatile or erased when the server loses power, it's important that the data in DRAM be backed up to nonvolatile storage layers both automatically and periodically. The SAP HANA appliance manages these periodic snapshots of memory to disk automatically. The SAP HANA in-memory database stores data in two primary persistent locations: First, a mirror image of the in-memory data is routinely synchronized and stored in the */hana/data* file path. Second, all transactions are recorded within the redo logs. SAP HANA is *ACID-compliant*—a term that describes a database that has atomicity, consistency, isolation, and durability. ACID compliance guarantees that each database transaction is reliable, even if the server loses power. The redo logs help to facilitate this ACID compliance, and the redo logs are stored in the default path of */hana/log*. It's important that security administrators understand this, because these locations might need to be encrypted.

The amount of RAM supported on a single SAP HANA appliance is finite, and organizations often need to store more data in-memory than is supported on a single host. To overcome this limitation, SAP HANA can be scaled out to run on multiple servers that act as a single instance, acting as a single appliance when scaled over multiple nodes while giving users a single point of access. When distributed on multiple nodes, the core software engines are active on each node and used to manage the distributed data in memory.

In the multinode or scale-out SAP HANA appliance, all nodes share a single logical persistent storage layer. This ensures that the in-memory data of each node is written to the same shared persistent storage layer during regular in-memory data snapshots and backups. Figure 2 depicts the SAP HANA appliance running as a single instance distributed over multiple nodes.

Each SAP HANA node communicates over dedicated redundant network links. From a security standpoint, the communications between each SAP node must be secured. In addition, the data stored in the persistent layers might also need to be encrypted. Fortunately, because the SAP HANA scale-out cluster acts as a single instance, users, roles, and privileges are centrally managed for all server nodes.

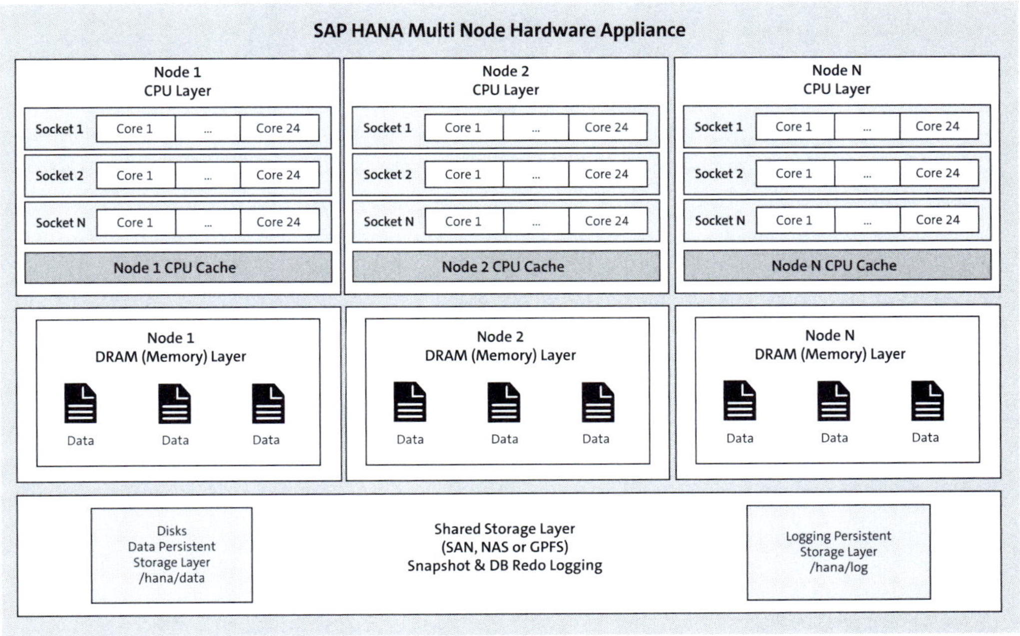

Figure 2 SAP HANA Scale-Out Appliance with One or More Nodes

SAP HANA Hardware Selection

A variety of server hardware vendors provide prebuilt certified systems to run SAP HANA. Each hardware vendor is required to undergo a strenuous certification processes to ensure that its hardware platform meets or exceeds the standards set by SAP. A certified SAP HANA appliance will only run on the following CPU modes:

- Nehalem Intel X7560
- Westmere Intel E7-2870, E7-4870 or E7-8870
- Ivy Bridge v2 Intel E7-2880/2890 v2, E7-4880/4890 v2, E7-8880/8890 v2
- Haswell v3 Intel E7-8880 v3, E7-8890 v3 or E7-8880L v3
- Broadwell v4 Intel E7-8880 v4, E7-8890 v4, E7-8894 v4

For a complete listing of certified servers by vendor, refer to the SAP HANA product availability matrix (PAM), available at *http://scn.sap.com/docs/DOC-52522*.

In addition to using the prebuilt certified SAP HANA systems, customers can design their own certified systems using the Tailored Datacenter Integration (TDI) program. This program allows customers to use their own internal network infrastructure and storage infrastructure to build a fully supported SAP HANA system. However, customers can only use servers or compute nodes listed on the SAP HANA PAM. For more information, please visit *http://www.saphana.com/docs/DOC-4380* and *https://help.sap.com/viewer/c4d7c773af4a4e5dbebb6548d6e2d4f4/1.0.12/en-US/0b15a92d554c4941a452c9ca127f8c70.html*.

SAP HANA 1.0 SPS 12 and SAP HANA 2.0 SPS 00

When we reference SAP HANA in this book, we're talking about the security features and functionality of SAP HANA 1.0 SPS 12 or SAP HANA 2.0 SPS 00. There were some significant security changes in SAP HANA 2.0, and we attempt to identify these throughout the relevant chapters.

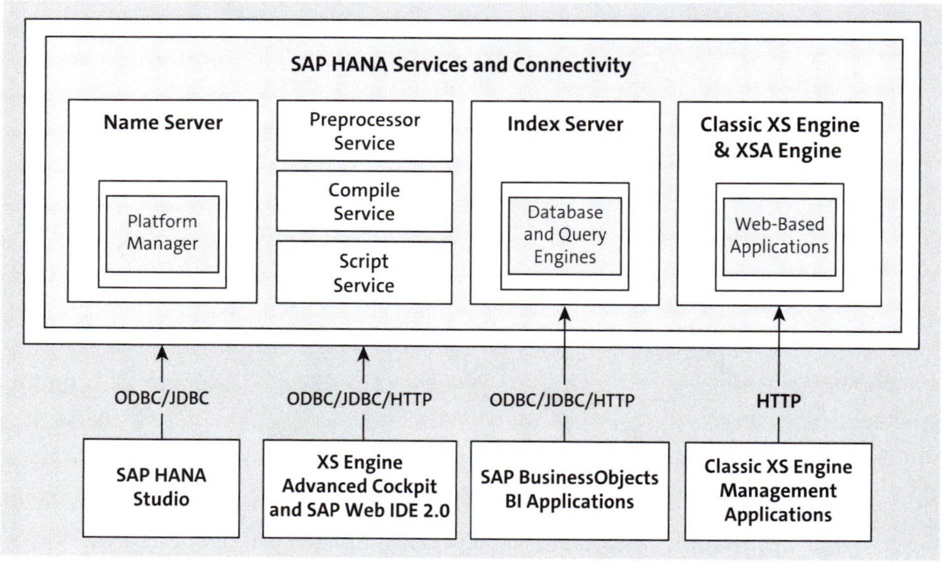

Figure 3 SAP HANA Services and Connectivity Overview

At a high level, Figure 3 depicts the basic service architecture of SAP HANA, including the standard connectivity or communications protocols. The SAP HANA system is comprised of several core services, such as the name server, preprocessor server, compile server, script server, index server, XS engine, and XSA engine. Each service provides one or more of the many features available within the SAP HANA platform. Interservice communications are secured automatically within SAP HANA. The index server is predominantly responsible for the core security model elements, such as users, roles, and privilege verification. It's also responsible for the core RDBMS catalog objects and their security. Both the XS engine and the XSA engine also have security that extends through to the index server.

To better understand the functions of each SAP HANA service, let's review what each is responsible for within the platform and how each relates to security.

Index Server

The core service of the platform is the *index server*, responsible for all database, data storage, and data processing tasks. When data is stored in-memory, it resides within the index server process. This includes data stored in row or columnar store tables. When a SQL or MDX query is executed by a BI application, the index server processes the query and returns the results. It's responsible for queries executed in the OLAP engine, calculation engine, join engine, and row engine. Overall, it's the most important service in the platform.

The index server manages many of the objects within the security model, such as users, roles, authentication, audits, catalog objects, and the development repository. It's responsible for most of the security within SAP HANA.

XS Engine

The *XS engine* acts as a web application server; it's used to manage and processes application code deployed to the SAP HANA platform. Applications such as the *SAP BusinessObjects Lumira server* reside in the XS engine. Developers can also devise custom applications using JavaScript and HTML5 code and operate them in the XS engine.

The XS engine hosts many applications used to manage security within SAP HANA. It also provides applications that aid in the lifecycle management of SAP HANA.

XSA Engine

Introduced in SAP HANA 1.0 SPS 11, the *XSA engine* is a robust web application server and is used to manage and process application code. However, its overall architecture is very different from the XS engine. Applications such as the SAP HANA 2.0 Cockpit and SAP Web IDE 2.0 are hosted within this service. It can be installed with your SAP HANA instance or it can be installed on SAP HANA, express edition, where it can run as a separate standalone application server. Each XSA application is assigned a child process and TCP/IP connectivity port. This allows an individual application to crash without crashing the entire XS engine. XSA also supports advanced programing languages, which can result in applications that are more sophisticated.

Applications such as the SAP HANA 2.0 Cockpit and SAP Web IDE 2.0 can also be used to manage many aspects of the SAP HANA security model.

Name Server

The *name server* is responsible for managing the topology of the SAP HANA architecture. With an SAP HANA scale out, the name server keeps track of which services are active and where data tables reside in the cluster.

The name server configuration file contains global password policy configurations. The global password policy is used to define how SAP HANA manages password authentication throughout a scale-out landscape.

Preprocessor Server

The preprocessor server helps the index server process text-based searches. This includes features such as sentiment analysis, text analysis, full text search, and fuzzy search of both structured and unstructured text. This service does not play a major role in securing SAP HANA.

Compile Server

The compile server is responsible for helping the index server compile L language–based procedures. It was removed from the index server in SAP HANA SPS 06 to prevent compiling tasks from crashing the index server. However, the exact reasons it was isolated from the index server have never been officially published by SAP. This service does not play a major role in securing SAP HANA.

Script Server

The script server is responsible for helping SAP HANA process operations that require the *Application Function Library* (AFL), which includes BFL and PAL. Developers or applications using SAP HANA for predictive modeling will use this service. This service does not play a major role in securing SAP HANA.

Outside of its core services, several external applications can also access SAP HANA. Figure 3 depicts a few common clients and their communication protocols. The communications between these clients and the core SAP HANA server is particularly important in the realm of security. SAP HANA supports secure communication with all client applications. SAP HANA Studio, the SAP HANA 2.0 Cockpit, and SAP Web IDE 2.0 can use Open Database Connectivity (ODBC), Java Database Connectivity (JDBC), or Hypertext Transfer Protocol (HTTP) to communicate with the SAP HANA system. Each of these communication paths supports strong encryption. Many BI applications also support ODBC and JDBC connectivity. For applications hosted in the XS engine, SAP HANA supports secure communication over HTTP or secure HTTPS.

In the next section, we'll provide a basic introduction to SAP HANA security.

Introduction to SAP HANA Security

At its core, SAP HANA security consists of users, roles, and privileges. User accounts are created and assigned one or more roles, and roles are created and assigned one or more privileges. The combination of roles and privileges determines what a user account is authorized to do within the SAP HANA platform. Figure 4 provides a high-level overview of the relationships among users, roles, and privileges.

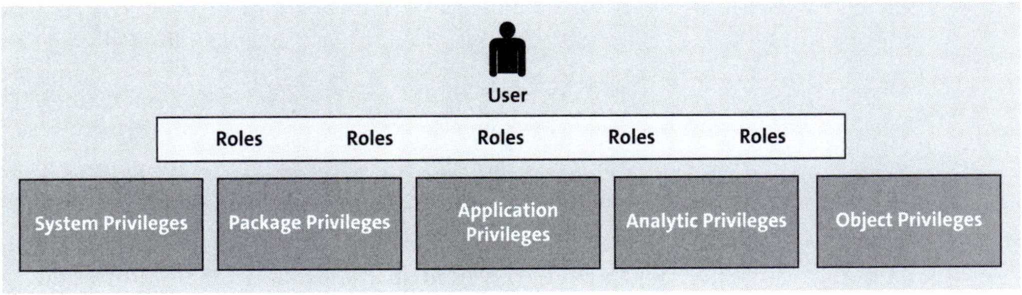

Figure 4 Overview of Users, Roles, and Privileges

Privileges are categorized into system, package, application, analytic, and object groupings. Each category controls a specific area within the SAP HANA architecture. However, a user account can't interact with the SAP HANA system until it's authenticated. Typically, a password is provided for authentication, but SAP HANA also supports several third-party authentication mechanisms.

Outside of the core areas of users, roles, and privileges, security administrators must also focus on encryption, audit policies, user provisioning, lifecycle management, and security model troubleshooting. Throughout this book, we'll introduce these key concepts and immerse you in the knowledge necessary to master the SAP HANA security model.

Importance of Securing Your SAP HANA System

As indicated in the section "Overview of SAP HANA", SAP HANA often hosts critical data for an organization. It also often operates applications that are vital to the organization. Databases like SAP HANA often contain master sources of data, such as customer, product, and financial data, sales orders, and bills of materials. If the integrity of these systems were compromised, organizations would suffer substantial financial loss or lose their advantage over competitors.

Therefore, it's important for organizations to implement a proper security model within their SAP HANA systems. Of equal importance is for an organization to invest in training for resources that will manage the security model and access the system. SAP HANA can only be secure when its administrators and users can adhere to all aspects of its security model.

The following are four key reasons that organization need to secure their SAP HANA systems:

1. Organizations should provide privacy to protect data that is stored and accessed within the SAP HANA system. This includes the use of encryption to secure the data in-memory and on disk. It also includes encryption to secure the communication of data between a client and the SAP HANA server. Authorization and authentication also play an important role in maintaining the privacy of data. In general, only authorized individuals should be granted access to an organization's data.
2. Organizations must ensure the integrity of the data hosted within the SAP HANA system. When financial transactions are recorded, they should be protected from unauthorized changes. Data integrity is protected by allowing only authorized individuals to make changes to the data and through auditing, encryption, and strong password authentication policies.
3. Organizations must also ensure the availability of the SAP HANA system. Security is an important component of maintaining a system's availability. Both trusted and unauthorized users can lead to poor database availability. A security model

can govern access among trusted users, those that have been explicitly granted privileges within the database. However, organizations must ensure that users' access is limited to their areas of responsibility. We must also ensure that they are trained well for their level of access. Unauthorized users are those outside the organization that are not explicitly granted privileges within the SAP HANA system. They often gain access through unscrupulous or unauthorized means and intend to steal data or disrupt the operations of the database. The security model can both govern authorized access and prevent unauthorized access.

4. When an organization collects sensitive data from customers, it must protect that data. Organizations that fail to protect customer data often have their reputations tarnished. When customers are unwilling to trust an organization with their sensitive data, they often choose to conduct business with the organization's competitors. Organizations can also be subject to major fines if they can't secure sensitive customer data.

As you can see, there are several reasons that an organization should prioritize, emphasize, and scrutinize their SAP HANA security models. Throughout this book, we'll help you learn how to implement a security model, identify risky privileges and provide best practices when applicable.

Summary

We're now ready to embark on a journey through the SAP HANA security model, starting with an overview of SAP HANA Studio (Chapter 1), a tool used to manage many of the SAP HANA security artifacts. We'll then provide a high-level overview of the various privileges within SAP HANA (Chapter 2). Because database objects are key object within security, we provide details about the common catalog or database objects SAP HANA supports (Chapter 3). We then explore the management of users and roles (Chapters 4, 5, and 6). To further your understanding of privileges, we take a deep dive into system, object, package, analytic, and application privileges (Chapters 7, 8, 9, 10, and 11). We'll also discuss the various authentication mechanisms supported within SAP HANA (Chapter 12). We complete our journey with a discussion of encryption (Chapter 13), security lifecycle management (Chapter 14), auditing (Chapter 15), security tracing (Chapter 16), our recommendations for securing the system (Chapter 17), and security changes in SAP HANA 2.0 (Chapter 18).

Chapter 1

Managing Security with SAP HANA Studio

In this chapter, we'll introduce SAP HANA Studio and many of the workflows necessary for using it to manage a security model.

Since its inception, most of the SAP HANA security model has been developed and maintained using *SAP HANA Studio*, a client tool that's installed on an SAP HANA developer or administrator's workstation. It's used for both administration and content development within the SAP HANA system. Given its importance in the realm of SAP HANA security, the goal of this chapter is to introduce you to the various security workflows and security options managed by SAP HANA Studio.

Web-Based Alternatives to SAP HANA Studio

As SAP HANA has evolved, new web-based administration consoles have been developed and hosted in the XS engine. Future versions of the SAP HANA 2.0 Cockpit, running in the XSA engine, will eventually replace the classic XS engine applications and most of the functionality in SAP HANA Studio. Although these web-based consoles do currently allow you to manage some of SAP HANA's security model, SAP HANA Studio still predominates security management today. In Chapter 6, we'll show you how to manage repository roles using SAP HANA Web-Based Development Workbench editor.

Use of SAP HANA Studio will be prominent throughout this book. It's important that you have a basic understanding of it and its security related interfaces. In this chapter, we'll provide an overview of SAP HANA Studio, introducing the security console and SAP HANA Studio's various perspectives, including the key perspectives used to manage security. We'll also introduce the SQL console, in which security-related SQL commands are executed, and we'll list the key user interfaces in SAP HANA Studio used to manage security-related items.

1.1 SAP HANA Studio Overview

SAP HANA Studio is a client tool that we use to interact with an SAP HANA system and manage security. One of the first dependencies in managing security in SAP HANA requires the installation and configuration of SAP HANA Studio. This section will provide the basic knowledge necessary to use SAP HANA Studio. We'll begin by demonstrating how to launch SAP HANA Studio and configure a connection, then show you how to navigate the tool by pointing out key security management areas.

Whether you're installing or upgrading SAP HANA Studio, we recommend that the installed version match that of the SAP HANA system in which you plan to implement security. Each patch version of SAP HANA Studio supports either a full installation or an update of an existing SAP HANA Studio installation. As a result, only one download and installation is required to support the appropriate version of the SAP HANA appliance being used. From an operating system standpoint, SAP HANA Studio version 2.3.15 for SAP HANA 2.0 SPS 00 supports the operating systems listed in Table 1.1.

Supported Operating System	Version(s)
Windows XP	32 bit and 64 bit
Windows Vista	32 bit and 64 bit
Windows 7	32 bit and 64 bit
Windows 8	32 bit and 64 bit
SUSE Linux 11 x86 (or higher)	64 bit
Red Hat Enterprise Linux (RHEL) 6.5	64 bit
Mac OS 10.9 or higher	64 bit

Table 1.1 Supported Operating Systems for SAP HANA Studio

Additional References

The installation of SAP HANA Studio is beyond the scope of this book. For more information on the installation of SAP HANA Studio, please download the SAP HANA Studio Installation and Update Guide from *http://help.sap.com/hana_appliance#section2.*

1.1.1 Getting Started with SAP HANA Studio

Before you can begin managing security within SAP HANA, you must first learn how to open SAP HANA Studio and connect to your SAP HANA system, as we'll discuss in this section.

SAP HANA Studio Initial Launch

Once SAP HANA Studio is installed on a Windows operating system, an **SAP HANA Studio** icon will appear in the start menu. Click the icon to launch the application. Once launched, you'll see a splash screen like that in Figure 1.1.

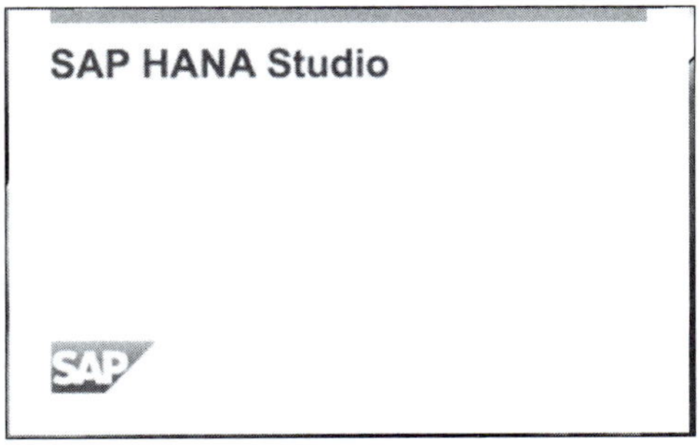

Figure 1.1 SAP HANA Studio Splash Screen

Next, you'll see a window (Figure 1.2) requesting that you specify a workspace. *Workspaces* are local system file locations that contain copies of project and other development code managed by SAP HANA Studio. The default location will be within your Windows user profile directory. We recommend that you use this default location in most cases.

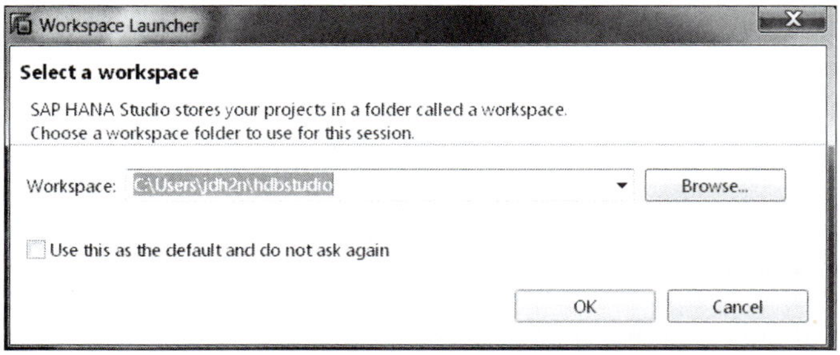

Figure 1.2 Select Workspace

If this is the first time you've launched SAP HANA Studio, you'll see a welcome screen (Figure 1.3). To close this screen, click the white **X** icon on the **Welcome** tab located near the top left of the window.

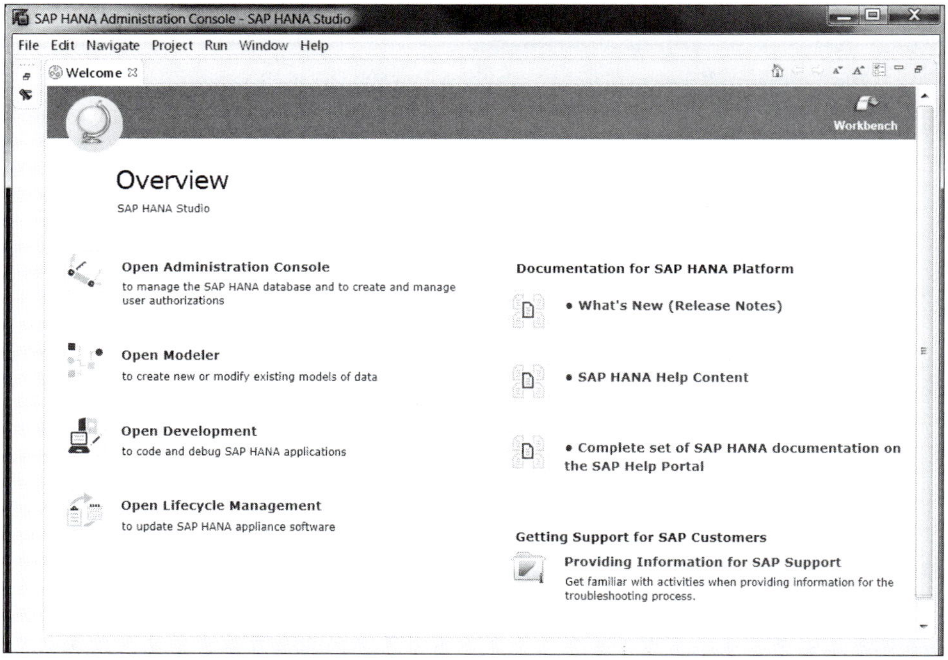

Figure 1.3 SAP HANA Studio Welcome Screen

Once the welcome screen is closed, you'll see the default SAP HANA Studio windows from the administration console perspective (see Figure 1.4).

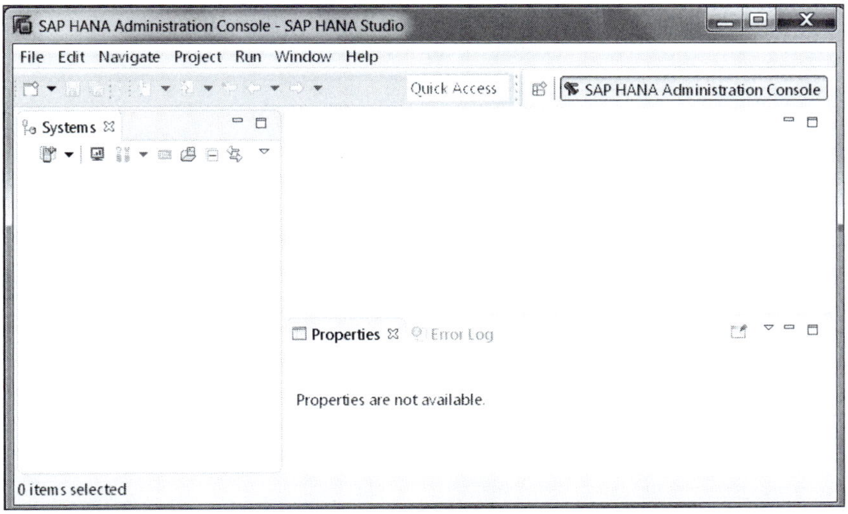

Figure 1.4 Default SAP HANA Studio Perspective

Connecting to SAP HANA

Before you can interact with an SAP HANA system, you must first add or configure a connection. Before we walk through the process, there are four important pieces of information you'll need to properly make the connection:

1. *The host name or IP address of your SAP HANA system.* Your administrator will be able to provide this information.
2. *The instance number of the SAP HANA system.* Each SAP HANA instance has its own unique instance number. This number is used to determine the TCP/IP port used to connect to the SAP HANA system. In the background, this number is concatenated with the pattern 3XX15, where XX is replaced with the two-digit instance number you provide. SAP HANA Studio will establish communications with SAP HANA using this port. For example, if you provide instance number 00, SAP HANA Studio will establish communication with SAP HANA using port 30015.
3. *The mode.* The mode is used to indicate if the SAP HANA instance is set up as a single tenant or container database or multiple tenant or database. If you aren't sure, ask your administrator if the database is set up with multiple tenants.
4. *A user name and password to authenticate with the system.* To properly interact with all security features in the system, this account will need to be configured with the proper privileges. If this is the first time you're accessing the system, you'll likely use the default built-in SYSTEM account.

To add a system to SAP HANA Studio, right-click anywhere in the **Systems** window pane. From the context menu (Figure 1.5), choose **Add System**; a new window will appear in which you can define the connection details for the system.

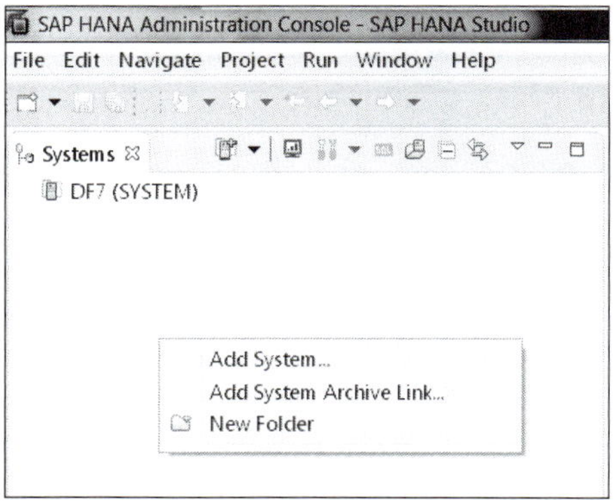

Figure 1.5 Adding System via Right-Click Context Menu

Alternatively, you can also click the **Add System** icon, at the top right of the **Systems** tab. Click the button outlined in Figure 1.6 and choose the **Add System** option.

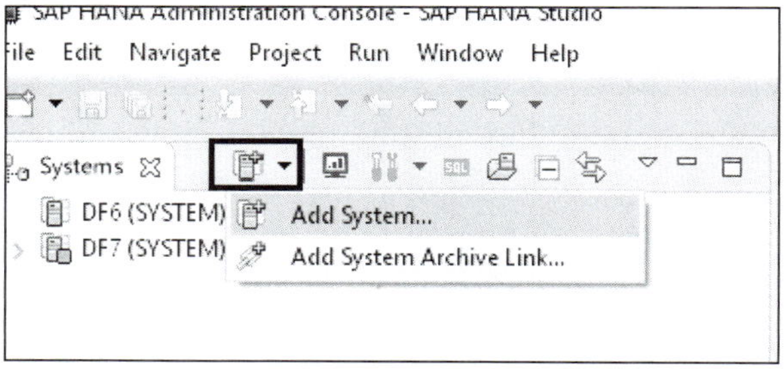

Figure 1.6 Adding System via Add System Button

A window labeled **Specify System** will now appear (see Figure 1.7). Enter three critical items to connect to an SAP HANA instance—**Host Name**, **Instance Number**, and **Mode**—and click **Next**.

Now, the **Connection Properties** window will appear (see Figure 1.8). There are two connection options. Choose **Authentication by current operating system user** if your administrator has configured Windows Active Directory Kerberos authentication. To instead specify a standard database user, select the **Authentication by database user** option. You can now enter a **User Name** and **Password**.

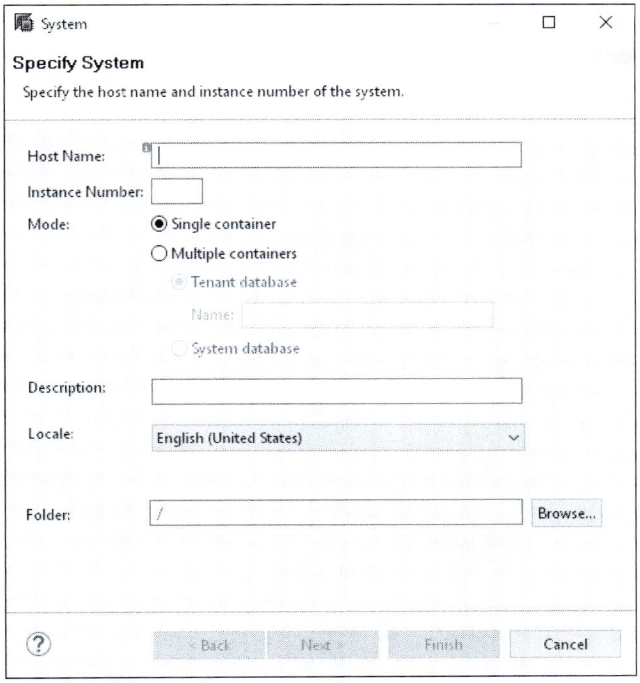

Figure 1.7 Specify System Window

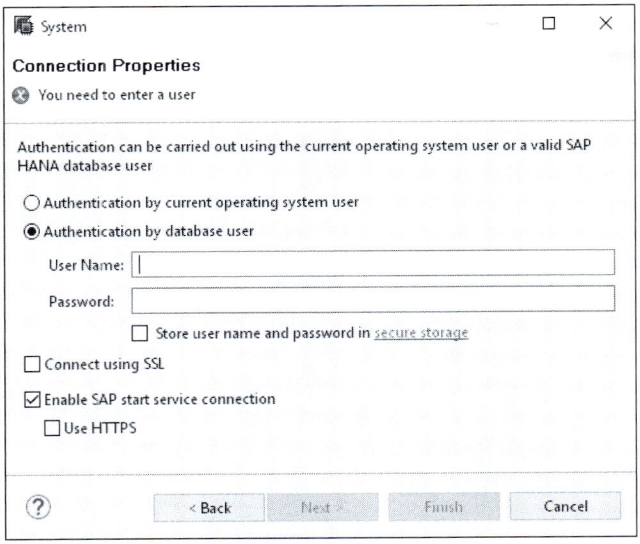

Figure 1.8 Connection Properties Window

If you want to store these credentials, select the checkbox next to **Store user name and password in secure storage**. This will save the password in an encrypted local storage container, and you won't be asked to provide a password again until the password expires.

If you want to connect using an encrypted Secure Socket Layer (SSL), select the checkbox labeled **Connect Using SSL**.

To allow SAP HANA Studio to interact with the SAP start service, check the **Enable SAP start service connection** box, which will allow SAP HANA Studio to perform functions that require operating system-level access. To ensure that this connection also uses SSL, check the **Use HTTPS** checkbox.

After you click **Next**, the window shown in Figure 1.9 will open. This final window allows you to define any additional Java Database Connectivity (JDBC) connection options. If you want to define additional options, simply type them into the **Option** field.

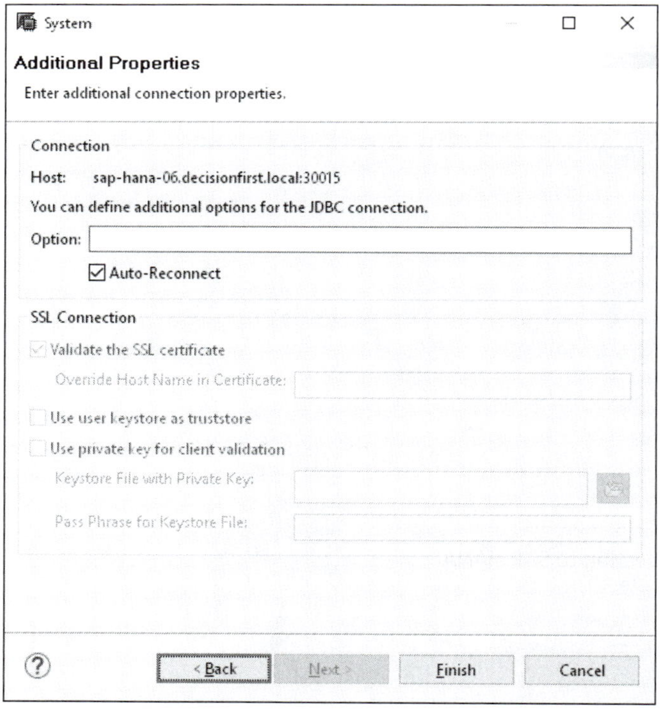

Figure 1.9 Additional Connection Properties

There is also an **Auto-Reconnect** checkbox; select it if you want SAP HANA Studio to automatically reconnect to your SAP HANA system if your connection fails.

If you chose to use SSL to connect, additional SSL options will be available in the **SSL Connection** area. Use these options to properly connect to your SAP HANA system using SSL. If you uncheck the **Validate the SSL certificate** option, SAP HANA Studio won't validate that the identity of the server matching that host name value in the SAP HANA Studio certificate trust store. Use this option with caution, because man-in-the-middle attacks are still possible even when the connection is encrypted. The **Use user keystore as truststore** checkbox allows a user to use a local maintained certificate trust store; for example, the user can import a self-signed certificate into a user trust store. This is considered a more secure connection option when well-known root certificate issuers aren't providing the certificate. If your administrator requires private keys or certificates to validate your connection, configure the requested options after checking the **Use private key for client validation** checkbox.

If you don't need to configure any additional connection or SSL options, click **Finish**.

If you don't receive any warnings or errors, you can assume that you've properly connected to your SAP HANA system. You will also see your SAP HANA system listed in the **Systems** tab. The connection name is a mixture of the SAP system ID (SID) and the user account used for authentication. If there are no issues with the system, a green dot or icon will appear, as shown in Figure 1.10. You also should be able to expand the system tree by clicking the black triangle to the left of the system name, which will reveal five top-level folders (see Figure 1.10).

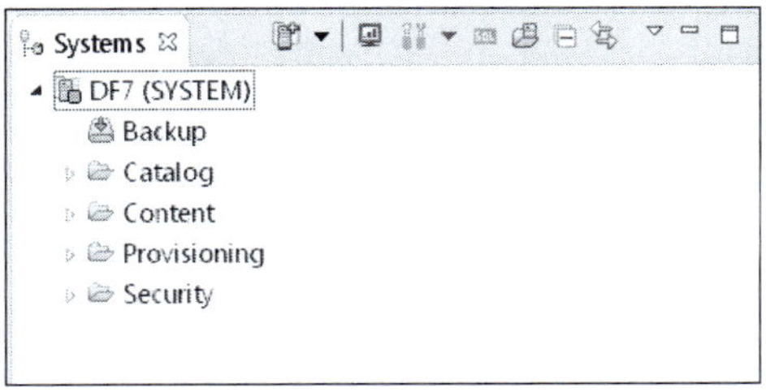

Figure 1.10 Successful Connection to SAP HANA

1.1.2 Navigating SAP HANA Studio

In this section, we'll provide several tips for navigating SAP HANA Studio. We'll start with an overview of the **Systems** window, then discuss the options available in the menu bar. Finally, we'll show you how to manage windows and tabs.

Navigating the Systems Window

Once you've established a system, you'll see that a folder hierarchy is available under the system (see Figure 1.11). There are five subfolders available, and each offers a different area to manage for your SAP HANA system. In some cases, expanding these top-level folders will reveal additional folders that extend a few more hierarchical levels down. In this section, we'll discuss the **Backup**, **Catalog**, **Content**, **Provisioning**, and **Security** top-level folders, which are used to manage the SAP HANA system.

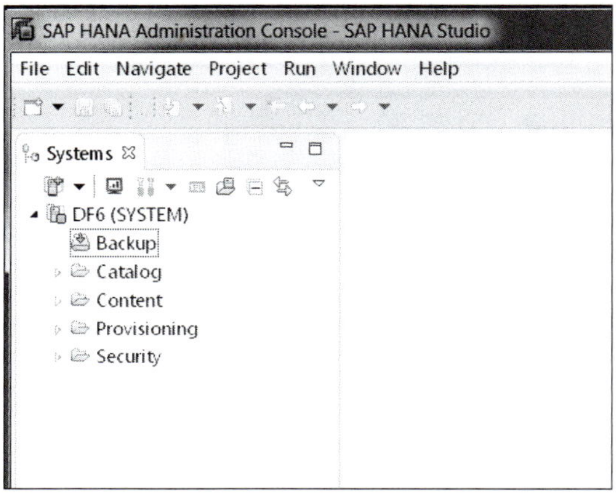

Figure 1.11 Default List of Folders Available under SAP HANA System

Backup

The folder doesn't contain any subfolders initially. Right-click the **Backup** folder to see three options. Use the **Open Backup Console** option to launch the backup console, use the **Back Up System** option to start the system backup dialogs, and use the **Manage Storage Snapshot** option to manage storage snapshots. Because none of these items are relevant to security, we won't go into any further detail here, but we encourage you to right-click the **Backup** folder to practice this common form of navigation within SAP HANA Studio.

Catalog

When you expand the **catalog** folder, you'll see schemas within your SAP HANA system. The list will be limited to only those schemas that your user account has access to. *Schemas* are top-level database object containers that contain additional database objects. To see the objects managed by a schema, expand a schema in the hierarchy tree. Now, look for the schema named **SYSTEM** and expand it to review the various database objects it contains (see Figure 1.12). In Chapter 3, we'll go into more detail about some of these objects and how they relate to security. As you'll discover, database objects play an important role in the development of an SAP HANA security model.

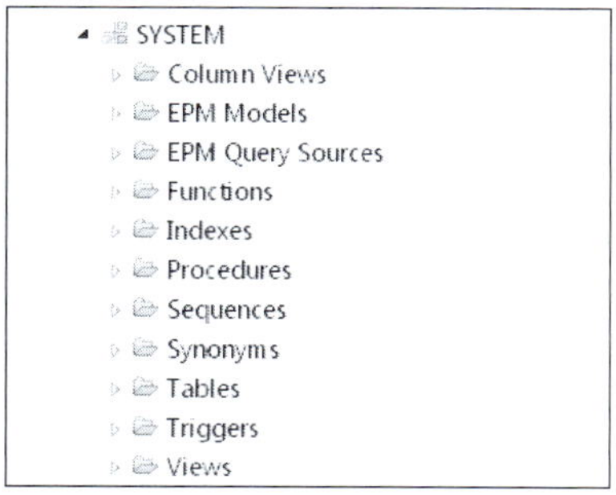

Figure 1.12 Various Schema Subobjects Available to Manage

Right-clicking the **Catalog** folder will reveal several menu options (see Figure 1.13). In particular, note the **Open SQL Console** option, which launches the SQL console tab, which can be used to issue commands specific to querying data, creating objects, managing the system, and a variety of other tasks. Also note the **Refresh** option, which can refresh the list of available subcatalog objects within the node. The remaining options aren't particularly relevant right now, but it's important to understand how right-clicking in SAP HANA Studio can invoke additional tasks or windows.

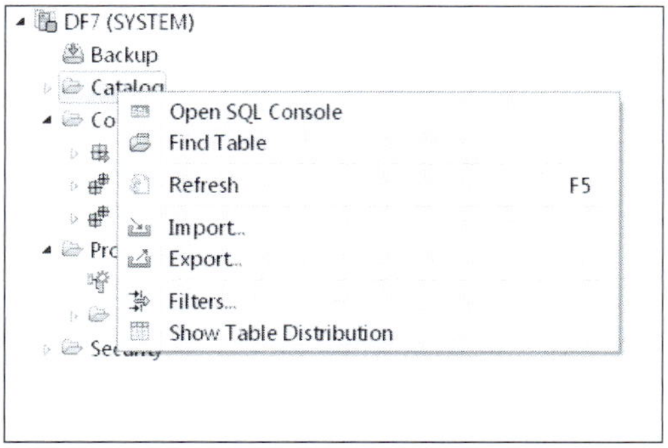

Figure 1.13 Right-Click Context Menu for Catalog Folder

Content

Expanding the **Content** folder will reveal all the top-level packages in the system. *Packages* are used to organize development objects and other subpackages. A combination of development objects and subpackages make up the logical development content repository within SAP HANA. Figure 1.14 depicts the default packages available in an SAP HANA system. Developers and security administrators will create additional packages to support developed content. In Chapter 9, we'll go into more detail about how to secure the package hierarchy and how to properly leverage development content to devise a security model.

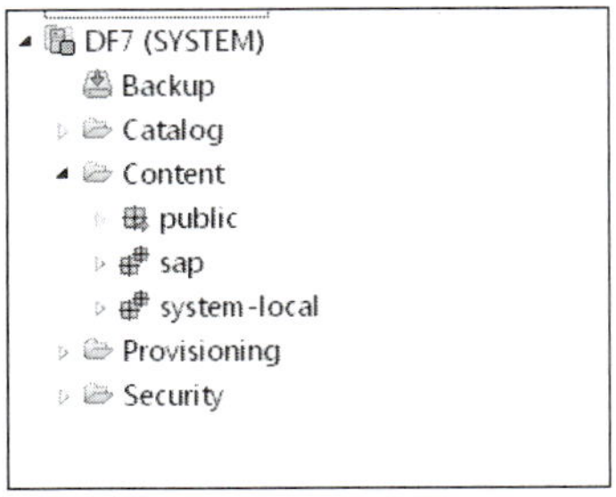

Figure 1.14 Default Packages in SAP HANA

Right-clicking the **Catalog** folder reveals a menu with several additional options (see Figure 1.15). Note the option to create a new package or subpackage by choosing **New** then **Package**.

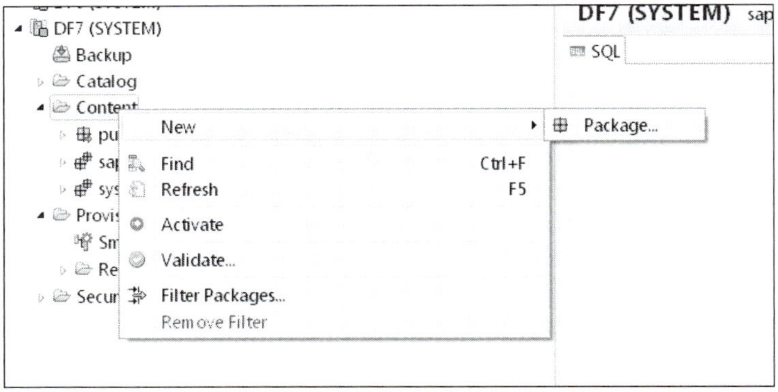

Figure 1.15 Right-Click Context Menu for Content Folder

Provisioning

Expanding the **Provisioning** folder will reveal options for managing smart data access and other remote sources. These items are beyond the scope of this book, but if you're using these features, note that they can be managed here.

Security

Expanding the **Security** folder will reveal three additional items (see Figure 1.16): The **Security**, **Users**, and **Roles** nodes are each used to manage a different aspect of SAP HANA security.

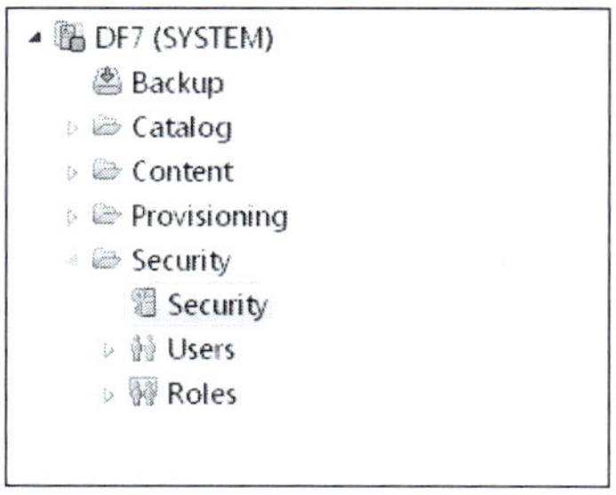

Figure 1.16 Security Folder and Its Contents

Double-click the **Security** node, located below the **Security** folder, to launch the security console. You can also right-click the **Security** node and choose **Open Security Console** from the context menu to perform the same action. Once launched, the security console window will appear on the right side of the screen (see Figure 1.17).

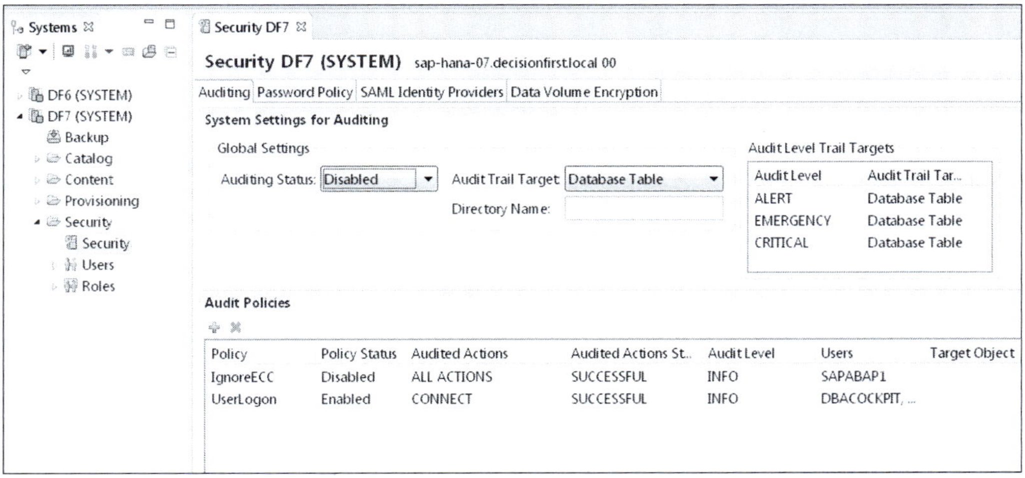

Figure 1.17 SAP HANA Security Console

There are four main tabs in the security console: **Auditing**, **Password Policy**, **SAML Identity Providers**, and **Data Volume Encryption**. Each tab offers a different area of security that can be managed, as described in Table 1.2.

Tab	Description
Auditing	Security administrators use this tab to manage auditing within the SAP HANA system. Auditing is used to track or record configurable actions in the SAP HANA system.
Password Policy	Security administrators use this tab to configure the password policies for the system, including items such as the minimum password length and complexity and options for account lockout policies and durations. They can also define password blacklists to prevent users from using certain words or phrases in their password.
SAML Identity Providers	Security Assertion Markup Language (SAML) is a supported form of third-party authentication. Security administrators can use this tab to configure the cryptographic library and the identity provider that SAP HANA will support and trust for authentication.
Data Volume Encryption	Data volume encryption allows administrators to encrypt the volumes stored on the operating system. It's used when data needs to be protected and the file system needs to be protected from unauthorized access.

Table 1.2 Tabs Available in Security Console

The **Users** node, located below the **Security** folder, allows you to list, create, and search for user accounts. To view the list of users in the system, expand the **Users** node by clicking the rotating triangle (greater than sign) to the left of users. A paginated list of users defined in the system will appear nested under the **Users** node. As shown in Figure 1.18, right-click the **Users** node for a menu that allows you to create a new user (**New User**), create a restricted user (**New Restricted User**), refresh the users list (**Refresh**), find a particular user (**Find User**), or filter the user list based on defined filter criteria (**Filters**).

The **Roles** node, located below the **Security** folder, allows you to list, create, and search for roles defined in the system. To view the list of roles in the system, expand the **Roles** node by clicking the rotating triangle to the left. A paginated list of roles defined in the system will appear. As shown in Figure 1.19, right-click the **Roles** node for a menu that allows you to create a new role (**New Role**), refresh the users list (**Refresh**), find a specific role (**Find Role**), or filter the roles list based on defined filter criteria (**Filters**).

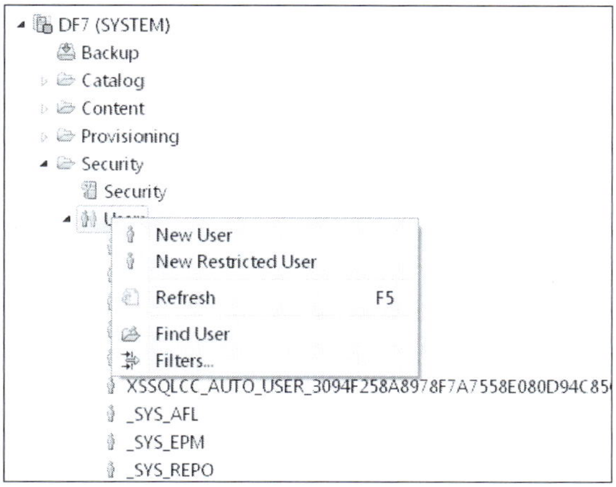

Figure 1.18 Right-Click Context Menu for Users Node

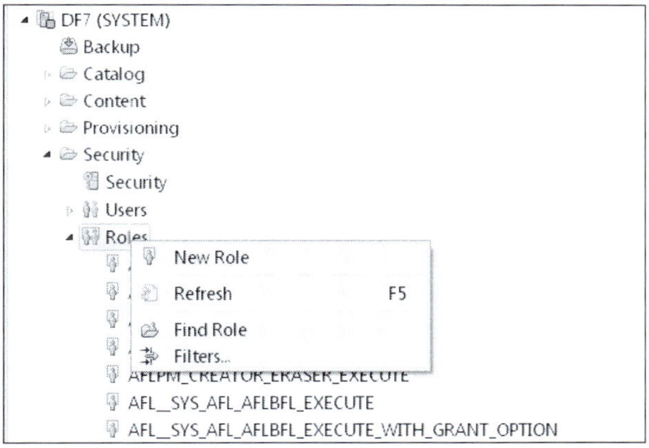

Figure 1.19 Right-Click Context Menu for Roles Node

Using the Menu Bar File Options

A feature common to most graphical applications running on a graphical, window-based operating system is the menu bar (see Figure 1.20). Here, we're most interested in the **File** menu options. To see these options, click **File**. For managing security, especially note the **New**, **Import**, and **Export** options. We'll discuss these options in more detail in later chapters.

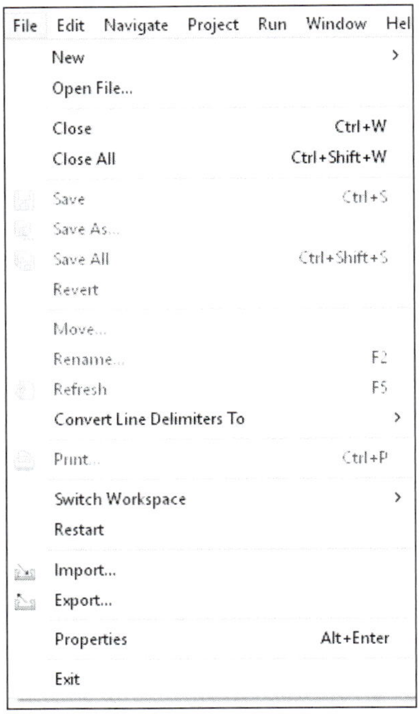

Figure 1.20 Menu Bar and File Menu Options

Another important option in the menu bar is **Window**. The **Window** menu (see Figure 1.21) provides options to manage navigation, windows, and perspectives used in SAP HANA Studio. Managing and changing perspectives, windows, and views is an important skill necessary to master the use of SAP HANA Studio. We'll show you how to manage perspectives in Section 1.3.

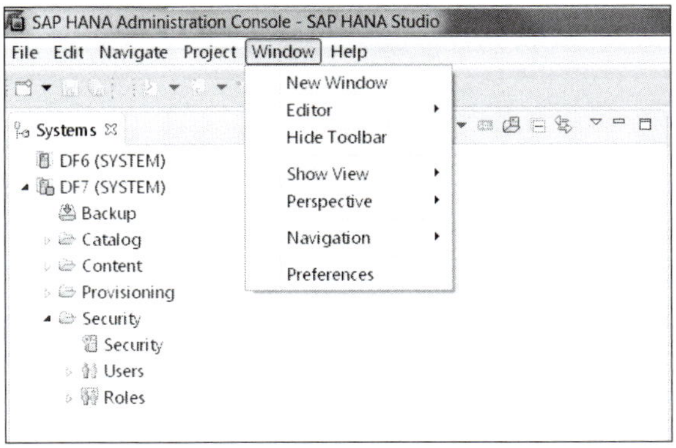

Figure 1.21 Window Menu Options

Managing Windows and Tabs

Another important workflow in SAP HANA Studio is the process of maximizing and minimizing windows. SAP HANA Studio's interface is comprised of several stacked tabs and windows. For example, the **Systems** tab is a window on the left side of the default perspective. To its right will be an editor area window in which a variety of different management or development windows can be launched. At the bottom of the editor window is a series of stacked tabs and windows containing items such as properties, error logs, and other potentially desired windows.

All these windows can be expanded or rearranged by clicking and then dragging the borders surrounding each window. They can also be minimized by clicking the minus icon (-) located in the top-right-hand corner of each window. Once minimized, the window will seem to disappear, but it's only been collapsed to a new bar located either to the extreme right or extreme left of the interface. Within this bar, a series of icons will appear, representing the windows that were minimized. There's also a **Restore** icon, as shown in Figure 1.22, which can restore the window to its previous state. You can also click any icon in this bar to temporarily pop open the related minimized window.

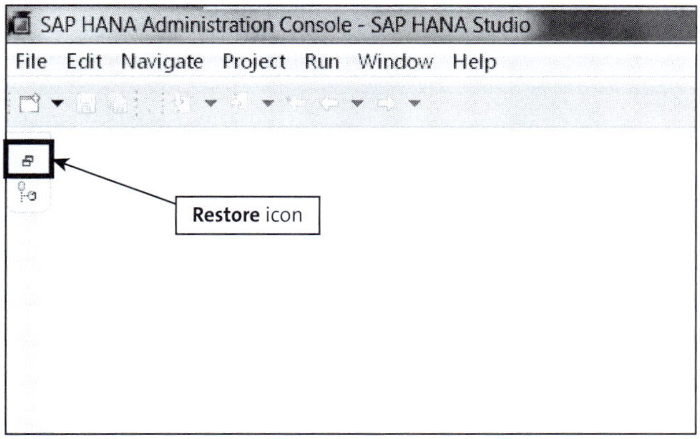

Figure 1.22 Restore Icon

Once you've returned to the default window view, you'll see a **Maximize** icon to the right of the minimize icon, highlighted in Figure 1.23.

Click this icon to maximize the window—that is, expand it to full size. This will also cause all other windows and tabs to minimize. To return the window to its normal state, click the **Restore** button at the top right of the maximized window.

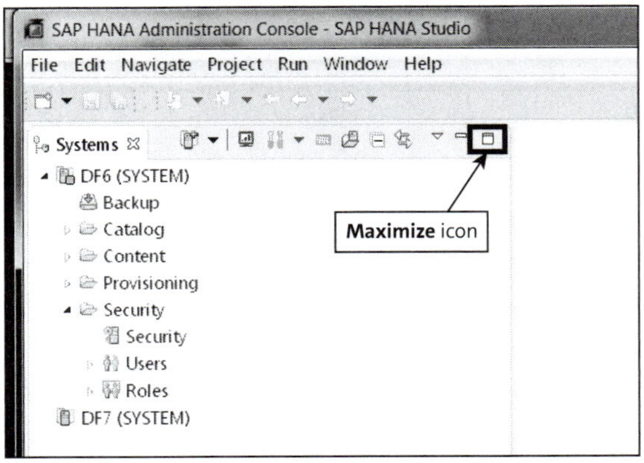

Figure 1.23 Maximize Icon

You also can maximize the view of your windows by double-clicking its corresponding tab heading. This will expand the tab into a maximized window, as shown in Figure 1.24. Double-click the tab heading a second time to return to the normal view. For example, double-click the **Systems** tab to maximize it in the window, and double-click it again to restore it to its default location.

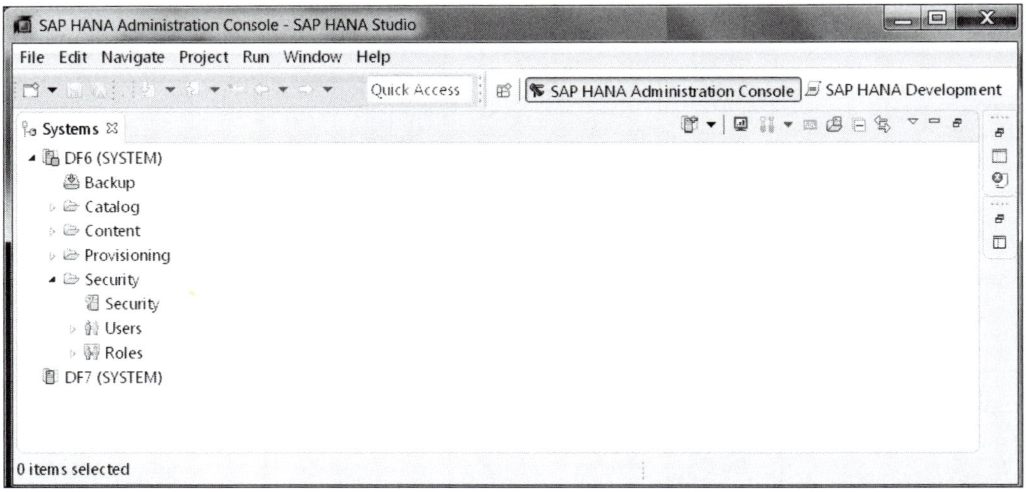

Figure 1.24 Fully Maximized Systems Tab in Window

You should now have a better understanding of how to manage the tabs and windows in SAP HANA Studio. We encourage you to take a few moments to practice by resizing, minimizing, maximizing, and restoring windows.

1.2 The Administration Console

The administration console in SAP HANA Studio offers several tabs that each contain a series of administrative and monitoring features. For security purposes, we'll be most concerned with the **Configuration** tab in this console, which allows administrators to access the all the configuration parameters for the SAP HANA system. Administrators will use this tab to configure a variety of security settings for SAP HANA. Therefore, it's important that we introduce you to the workflows necessary to access the administrative console.

To open the administration console for a given system, click the **Administration** button, shown in Figure 1.25, revealing a pop-up menu. To open the administration console, click the **Open Default Administration** option in the pop-up menu (see Figure 1.25). Alternatively, you can double-click the top-level system node in the **Systems** tab located in the left pane (**DF6 (SYSTEM)** in Figure 1.25).

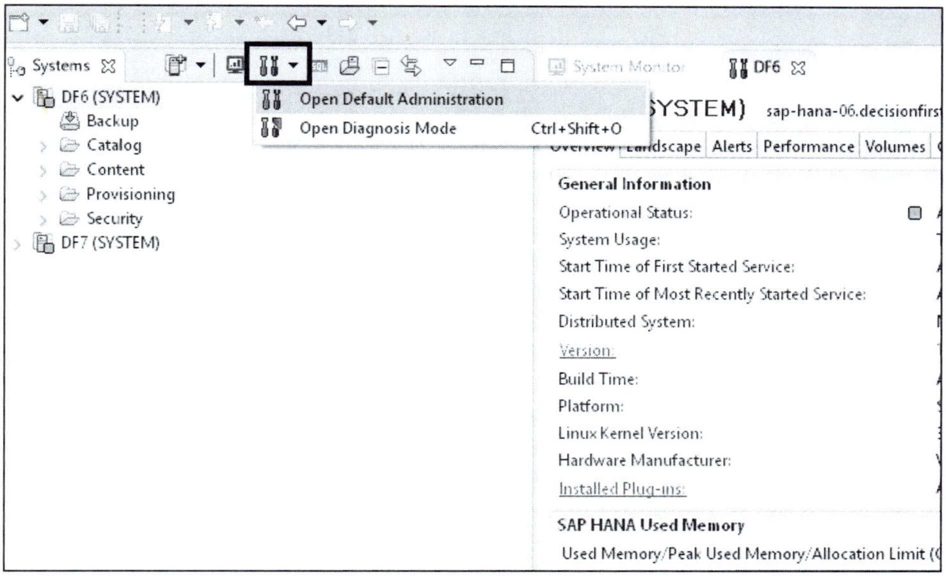

Figure 1.25 Open Default Administration Option

The administration console should open to the **Overview** tab, which contains real-time information about the SAP HANA system you're connected to. For example, you can see the current memory, CPU, and disk utilization for the system. To the right of this tab, you'll see several other tabs, including the **Configuration** tab (see Figure 1.26), where you can manage the INI file settings.

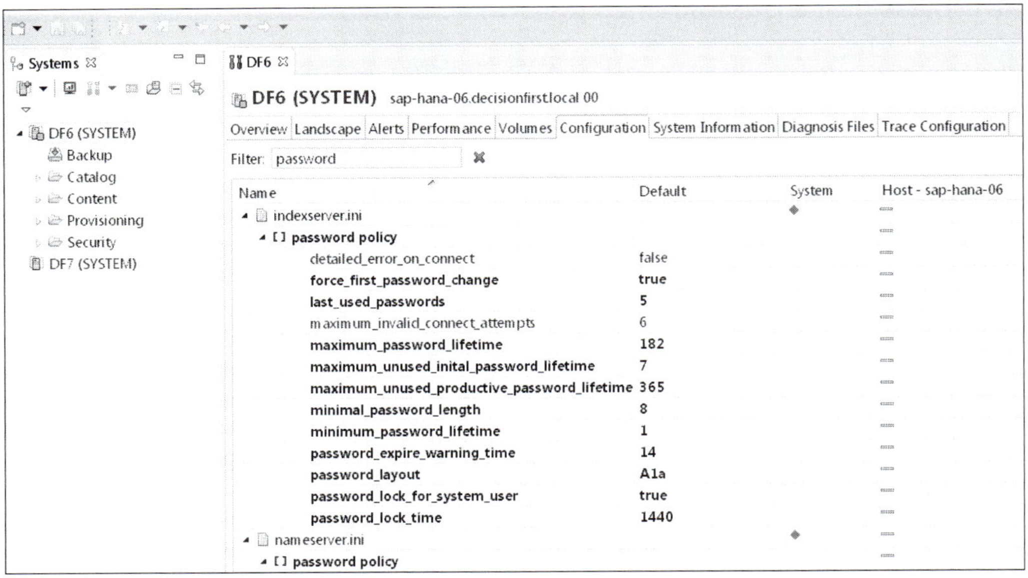

Figure 1.26 Configuration Tab

With the **Configuration** tab open, you'll see a series of files with the .ini extension. Each file represents a particular parameter file that contains configuration information for the SAP HANA system. To view the options available for each file, click the arrow beside each node to expand the navigation tree and reveal additional options.

At the top of the **Configuration** tab, you'll see the **Filter** bar. You can use the **Filter** bar to locate specific settings within .ini files quickly by name. For example, enter "password" to see all settings containing the word password.

1.3 Managing Perspectives in SAP HANA Studio

Perspectives essentially define window layouts in SAP HANA Studio. As we've discussed, we can change the layout of windows by resizing, minimizing, and maximizing them. However, each perspective defines which windows will be visible, essentially functioning as predefined window layouts necessary to perform specific tasks. Because they relate to specific tasks, SAP HANA Studio is equipped with several default perspectives; some are specific to SAP HANA development and administration, whereas other are more specific to application development in the Eclipse workbench. Figure 1.27 contains a list of the perspectives that are available.

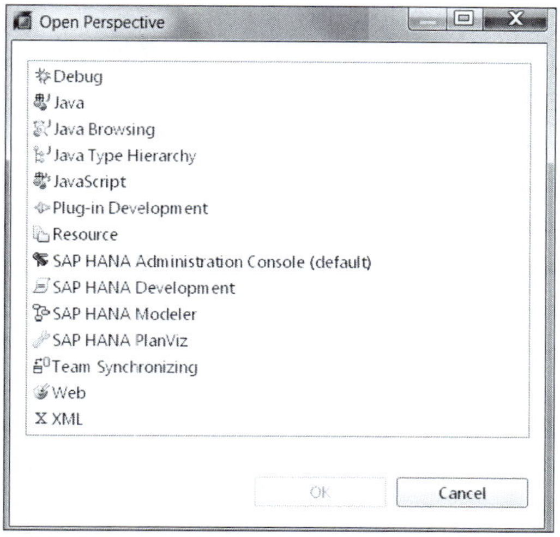

Figure 1.27 List of Perspectives Available in SAP HANA Studio

For the purposes of this book, we'll focus on the SAP HANA administration console (default), SAP HANA development, and SAP HANA modeler perspectives. This section will explain how to switch between those perspectives and why each perspective is important for security.

1.3.1 Administration Console Perspective

The *administration console perspective* is the default perspective in SAP HANA Studio. To switch to the administration console perspective, go to the **Window** menu and select **Perspective • Open Perspective • SAP HANA Administration Console** (see Figure 1.28).

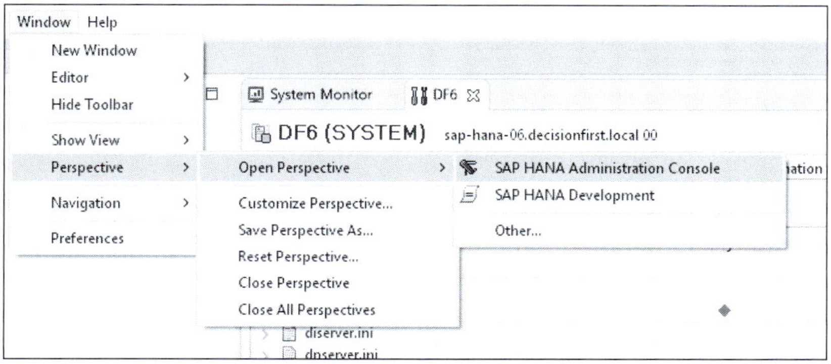

Figure 1.28 Accessing Administration Console

The administration console perspective defaults to the **Systems** window to the left and an empty editor window occupying the center and right side of interface. At the bottom of the empty editor window are a series of stacked tab windows:

- The **Properties** tab provides additional information for objects selected in other windows. You can assume that an object has no additional properties if the statement **Properties Are Not Available** is visible here.
- The **Error Log** window captures any errors generated from executed actions from plugins used in other windows. For example, if we attempt to activate code and it has errors, the activation errors will appear in this tab.
- The **Job Log** contains information related to any current or historical task that we execute. For example, if we attempt to import a delivery unit, the real-time and historical status of that task will be visible here.

We routinely use this perspective to manage security content available under the **Systems** node. For example, management of the security console, users, and roles are available under the **Security** folder found under the **Systems** node in this perspective. We also use this perspective to launch the administration console, which contains the **Configuration** tab. The Configuration tab can be utilized to configure several security related settings. However, as you'll discover, these items are also available in other SAP HANA-related perspectives. Therefore, you shouldn't assume that this is the only way to access the **Systems** tab and administration console.

1.3.2 Development Perspective

The *development perspective* contains a selection of programing- and development-related windows and tabs that are often used to develop applications in SAP HANA. However, security administrators can also use this perspective to define repository roles, repository schemas, and other repository-based database objects. We'll discuss these objects in more detail in later chapters. For now, note how to access the development perspective and how to locate the **Project and Repositories** tab in which these objects are created.

To switch to the development perspective, go to the **Window** menu and select **Perspective • Open Perspective • SAP HANA Development** (see Figure 1.29). If the development perspective is missing from the list, choose **Window • Perspective • Open Perspective • Other**. A new window will appear with a complete list of perspectives. Choose **SAP HANA Development** to open the development perspective.

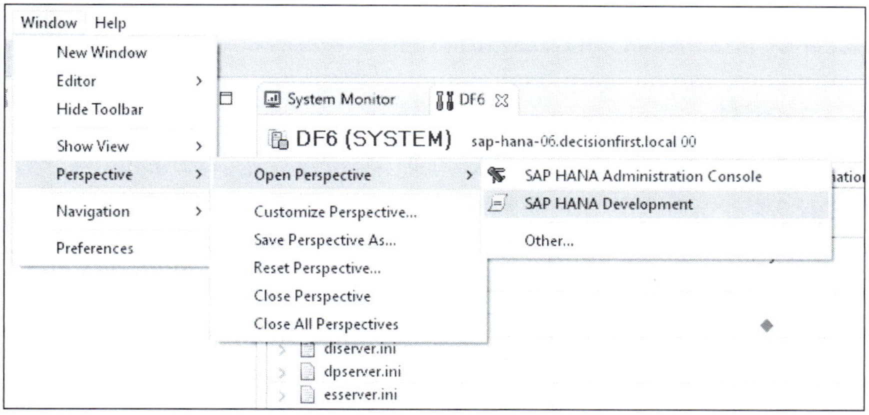

Figure 1.29 Opening Development Perspective

The development perspective offers multiple windows and tabs to help with application development. You'll see that the **Systems** tab is now accompanied by the **Repositories** and **Project Explorer** tabs (see Figure 1.30).

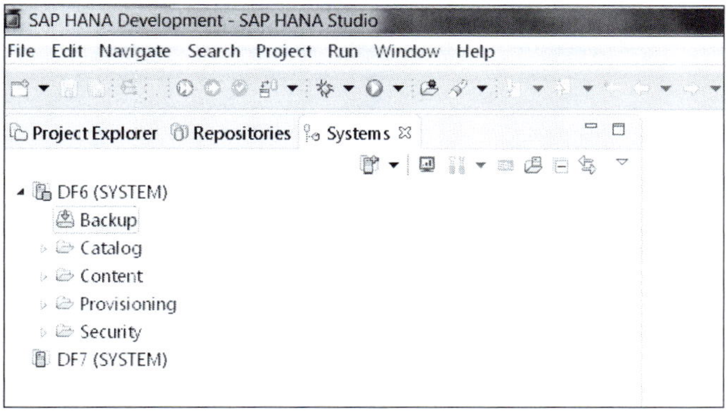

Figure 1.30 Project Explorer, Repositories, and Systems Tabs

The **Systems** tab here provides the same security options as it did in the administration console perspective.

The other two tabs are typically used for SAP HANA code development. Although SAP HANA is an in-memory database, it's also a development platform. SAP HANA Studio provides an interface for developing applications and interfaces for maintaining the database components of the system. Experienced database administrators might not assume this, but there are aspects of the security model that are managed in these application development-related tabs. Let's take a moment to discuss how to access these tabs and use them to define security objects.

Accessing the Repositories Tab

Switch to the development perspective and click the **Repositories** tab to the left of the **Systems** tab. Within this tab, expand your system to reveal a default container and top-level packages (see Figure 1.31).

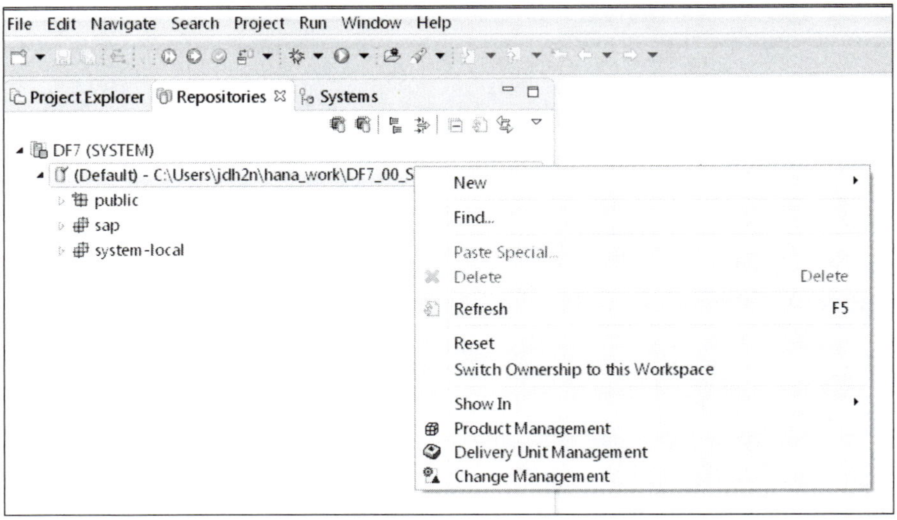

Figure 1.31 Repositories Tab and Package Hierarchy

Packages organize development content in a hierarchical tree and can contain multiple levels of subpackages to logically organize development content. However, before we can begin managing content in the package hierarchy, we need to create a repository workspace, as discussed next. (In Chapter 9, we'll explore this development repository further.)

Creating a Local Repository Workspace

A *repository workspace* is a connection between the online SAP HANA repository and your local file system. Before we can begin developing content, we must set up an area on the file system, local to SAP HANA Studio, where we can store offline versions of repository objects.

To create a repository workspace, switch to the development perspective and click the **Repositories** tab, then right-click your system node and choose **Create Repository Workspace** (see Figure 1.32).

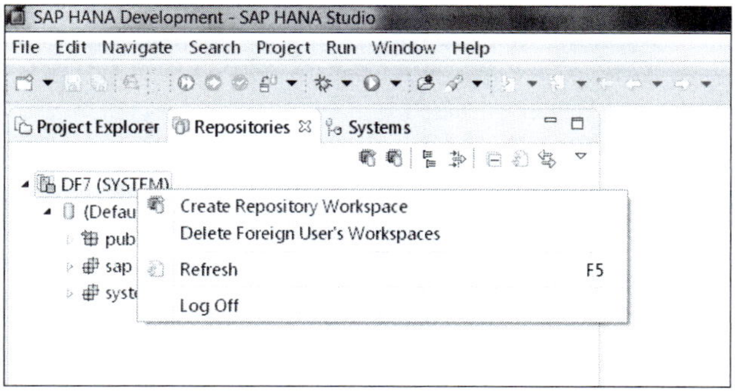

Figure 1.32 Creating Repository Workspace

As shown in Figure 1.33, a new window appears, allowing you to define the location of the repository workspace in your local file system. We recommend using the default setting, because it specifies a location that is unique to your operating system's user profile and SAP HANA instance. Each operating system user and SAP HANA instance requires its own unique folder on your local filesystem. Choose **Finish** to complete the setup of the repository workspace.

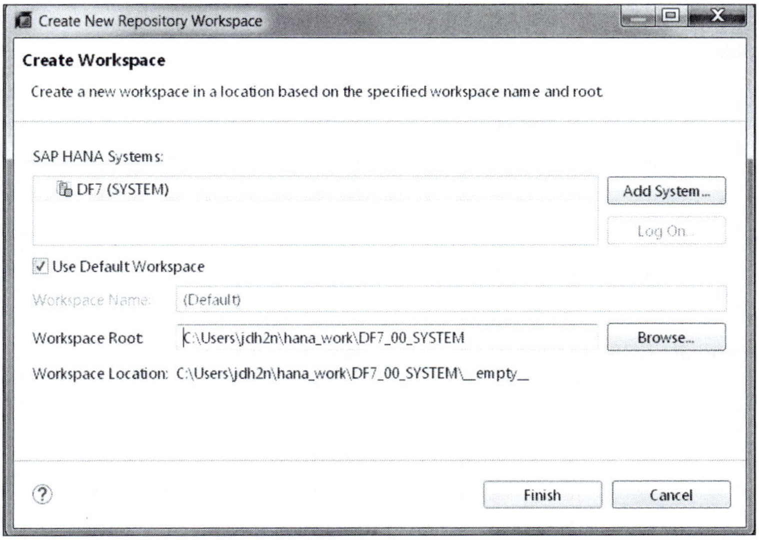

Figure 1.33 Defining File System Location of Repository Workspace

Navigating Packages in the Repository Workspace

You can now manage packages and development content within the repository workspace. To create a new top-level package, right-click the default node in the **Repositories** tab and choose **New • Repository Package** (see Figure 1.34).

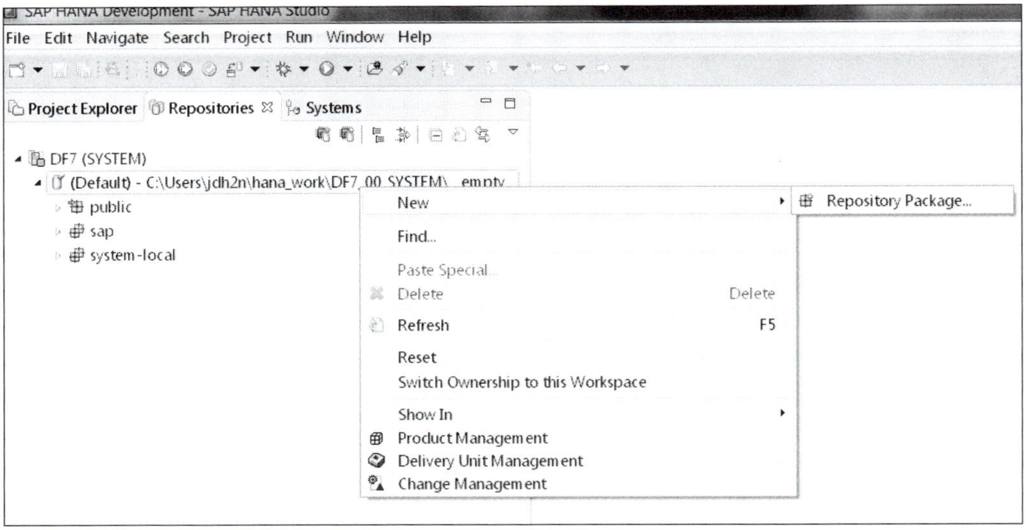

Figure 1.34 Creating New Repository Package

As shown in Figure 1.35, a **Create Repository Package** window will appear, allowing you to name the package. Start by choosing the repository workspace. If you right-clicked the default node in the previous step, this setting should already be defaulted to the correct repository workspace. Enter the package name "Security" and choose **Next**. In subsequent chapters, we'll use this package to store security-related development objects.

As shown in Figure 1.36, a new window will appear, **Edit Repository Package**. This window allows you to define additional options for the package. You can specify a description in the **Description** field and establish the account responsible for the package. We recommend you choose the **_SYS_REPO** account for packages, because that user account can't be deleted from the system. Select the checkbox next to **Structural** if the package is used only for navigation and not for storing development objects. Click **Finish** when completed. A new root-level package should appear in the package hierarchy.

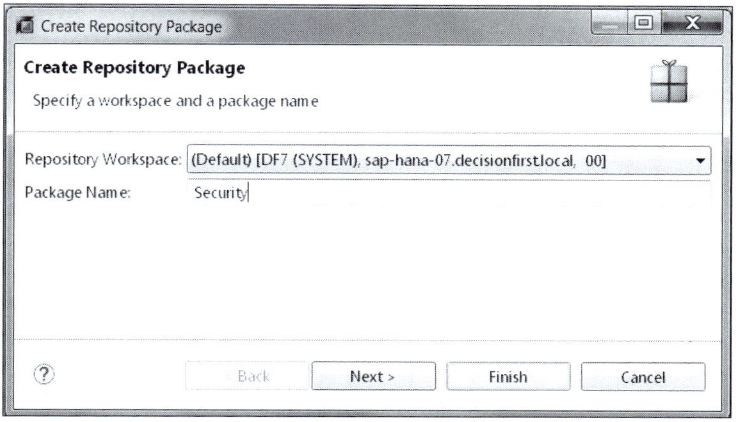

Figure 1.35 Naming Repository Package

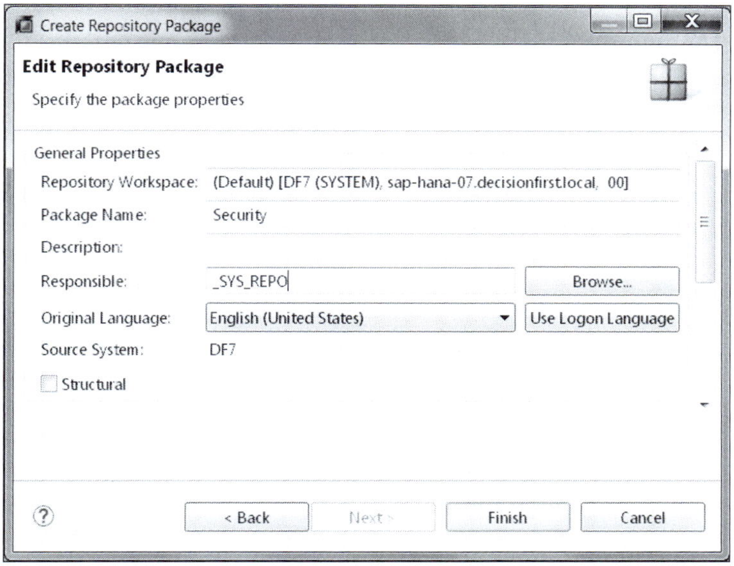

Figure 1.36 Setting Package Options

Creating Development Objects within a Package

As mentioned before, packages are used to store development objects. In Chapter 3, we'll discuss why development objects are recommended when defining a security model.

To create a new development object in the security package, right-click the package and choose **New**, then **Other**. Alternatively, click the package and press Ctrl+N. A new **Select a wizard** window will appear, like the one shown in Figure 1.37.

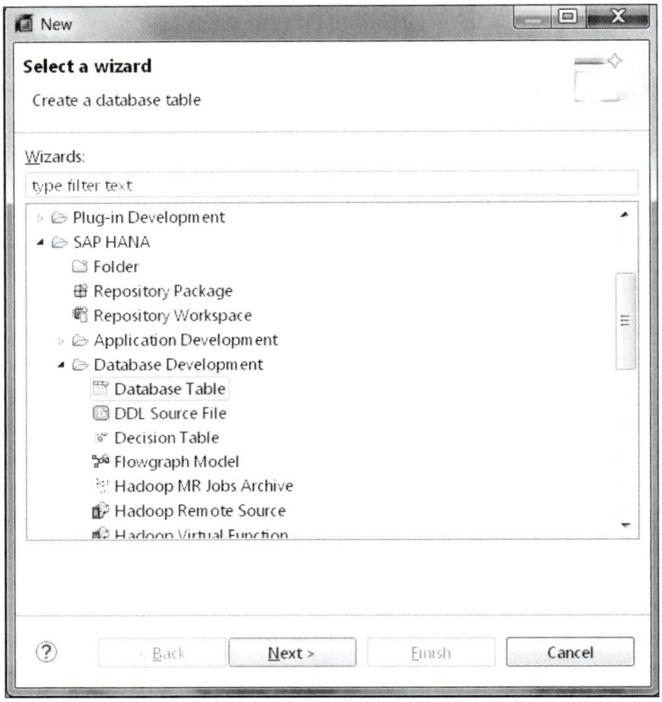

Figure 1.37 Creating New Repository Database Development Objects

In this window is a hierarchical list of folders and objects. Expand the **SAP HANA** folder and then the **Database Development** folder to reveal a variety of database objects we can create. We won't create any database objects now, but you should be familiar with the workflow necessary to create repository-based development objects. In later chapters, we'll create a variety of database development objects to complete our security model.

1.3.3 Modeler Perspective

The *modeler perspective* is used primarily to facilitate the process of developing and maintaining *information views*, metadata-rich multidimensional models that provide access to the data hosted within an SAP HANA system. They're most often used to deliver analytical solutions for organizations. This would include solutions such as reporting, self-service business intelligence, data analysis, and ad hoc queries.

To switch to the modeling perspective, go to the **Window** menu and select **Perspective • Open Perspective • Other**. A small window will appear with a list of perspectives. Select **SAP HANA modeler** from the list. SAP HANA Studio will now open a new layout appropriate for managing information views.

The default modeler perspective is organized into five main windows or tabs. Figure 1.38 shows the default modeler perspective layout.

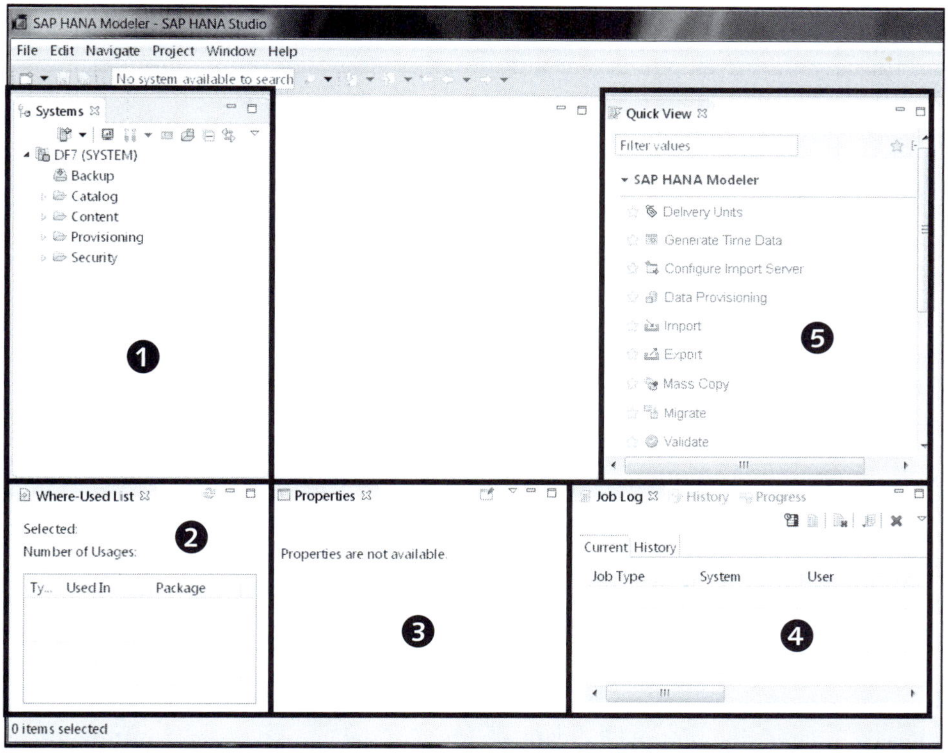

Figure 1.38 Modeler Perspective

The **Systems** tab ❶ is the same tab that was visible in other perspectives we discussed in this section. The **Where-Used List** tab ❷ contains information about where a selected modeling object is used. The **Properties** tab ❸ contains additional properties or information about a selected object. The **Job Log** tab ❹ contains an additional series of subtabs that track the status of executed tasks related to developing information views. Finally, the **Quick View** tab ❺ contains a list of shortcuts for tasks specific to managing information views.

From a security perspective, we'll predominantly use this perspective to manage data-level security in the form of an object called an *analytic privilege*. Analytic privileges are development objects that allow organizations to limit access to data or to provide role-based access to the data stored in SAP HANA. In Chapter 10, we'll discuss this topic in more detail. For now, you need to understand how to access the modeler perspective and locate the various tabs it provides.

There are also a few items in the **Quick View** tab that allow us to manage some aspects of a security model. For example, we can define *delivery units*, containers used to organize similar development objects for the purposes of importing and export content between systems. With delivery units, we can transport our security model from a development to a quality assurance SAP HANA system.

Alternative Workflow for Switching Perspectives

You may have noticed the bar containing a list of buttons at the top right of SAP HANA Studio. Each button represents a recently accessed perspective and can be clicked to switch quickly between perspectives. Figure 1.39 shows this perspective quick launch bar. Simply click the appropriate button to launch the desired perspective.

To the far left of the bar is a button that launches a window containing the master list of perspectives, which will look exactly like the one depicted in Figure 1.27. You can use that button to launch any available perspective not already listed on the frequently accessed icon bar. As you know, each perspective offers a different set of tabs related to performing a specific task. Some tabs or windows are available in all the perspectives we discussed, such as the **Systems** tab. Other tabs or windows are unique to a given perspective, such as the **Repositories** tab, which is only available in the development perspective.

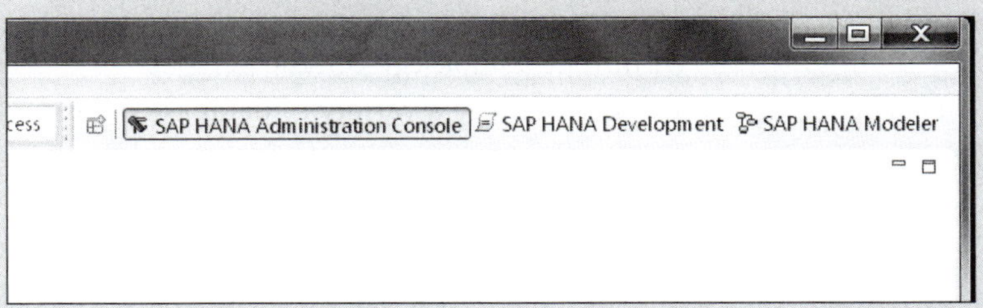

Figure 1.39 Perspective Quick Launch Bar

1.4 SQL Console

The *SQL console* allows developers and administrators to execute SQL statements. To access the SQL console, right-click a system listed in the **Systems** window and select **Open SQL Console** (see Figure 1.40).

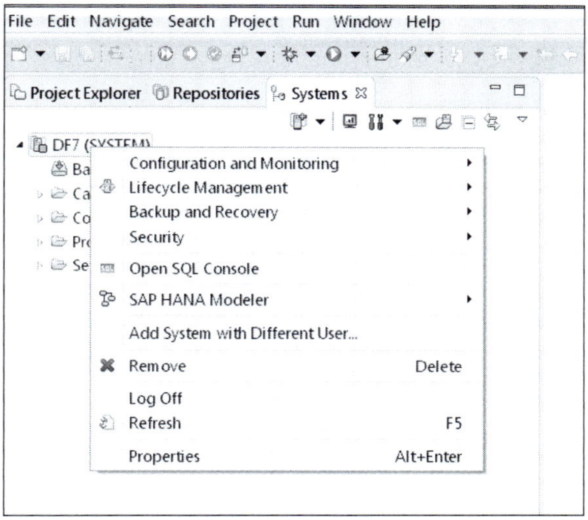

Figure 1.40 Accessing SQL Console

A new tab in the main editor window area will appear (see Figure 1.41). The SQL editor allows us to define a SQL statement and then execute that statement to perform some form of action within the database. The example SQL statement in Figure 1.41, when executed by pressing F8, will run a query that returns a list of tables hosted in the _SYS_REPO database schema. The results will appear in the **Result** tab within the SQL editor window.

The SQL console allows administrators, developers, and security admins to perform a variety of management functions within the database. From the perspective of security, we use the SQL console to create and manage a variety of database objects. We can also use it to execute commands that allow us to change system security settings. Although many of these same functions can be performed with the GUI, the SQL console offers a script-based alternative to managing some aspects of security. In chapters to come, we'll provide numerous examples of how to manage security using the SQL console.

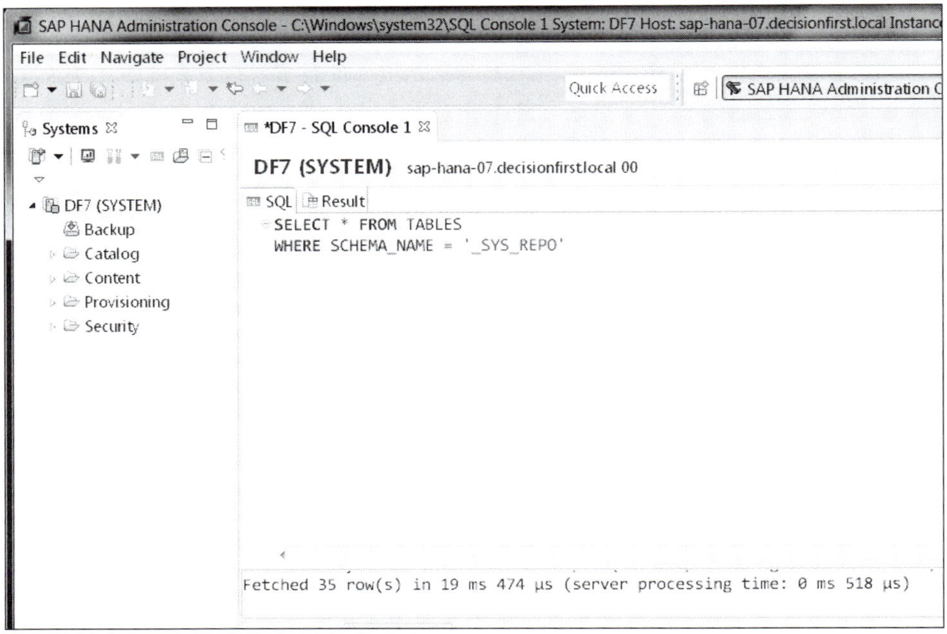

Figure 1.41 Using SQL Console

1.5 Security Settings in SAP HANA Studio

Throughout this chapter, we've provided the steps necessary to locate many of the common windows in SAP HANA Studio. In some cases, we identified how these windows were used to manage security. In this section, we'll provide you with a more comprehensive summary of how each window is used to manage security.

There are six main security functions in SAP HANA Studio: managing users, managing roles, using the security console, using the development perspective, using the SQL console, and using the system **Configuration** tab. Let's look at how to use each function to manage security.

1.5.1 User Management

In Section 1.1.2, we outlined the steps for accessing the **Users** security management area within the top-level **Security** folder. This area is available in the **Systems** tab, which is available in all three perspectives that we discussed in this chapter. This area is used specifically to list users, create users, and manage their settings via a GUI.

Administrators can also unlock users, reset their passwords, and change their roles in this area.

1.5.2 Role Management

In Section 1.1.2, we outlined the steps necessary for accessing the **Roles** security management area. This area is available in the **Systems** tab, available in all three perspectives discussed in this chapter. This area is used specifically to list roles, create roles, and manage their assigned privileges via a GUI.

1.5.3 Security Console

In Section 1.1.2, we outlined the steps necessary to open the security console. This area is available in the **Systems** tab, available in all three perspectives discussed in this chapter. The security console contains many of the commonly or frequently accessed SAP HANA security settings. It provides a GUI that allows administrators to manage auditing, password policies, SAML settings, and data volume encryption quickly. Many of these same settings are also available on the **Configuration** tab within the administration console. However, the security console offers a more convenient and easier to use GUI for managing the more frequently adjusted settings.

1.5.4 Development Perspective

It might not seem like this item belongs in this list, but we can assure you that it does. Throughout this book, security administrators will learn that using development objects to support their security model will provide numerous advantages. Multiple database objects can be created and managed as development objects, and you'll find that *repository roles* play a key role in defining a sustainable and manageable security model. Because all these items are development objects, it's important that you take some time to review the workflows for accessing the development perspective and the **Repositories** tab. In Section 1.3.2, we outlined the steps necessary to access this perspective, create a repository workspace, and create a root-level package. In Chapter 3, we'll show you how to create development objects to help manage security.

1.5.5 SQL Console

We use the SQL console to create and manage a variety of database objects. We can also use it to execute commands that allow us to change system security settings. For example, we can execute ALTER USER admin_jonathan RESET CONNECT ATTEMPTS to unlock an account that's locked out of the system or run the statement ALTER USER admin_jonathan PASSWORD P@s$wOrd1 to change a user's password.

We can also use the SQL console to configure system security parameters. For example, we can modify the maximum number of invalid logon attempts before a user account is disabled by executing the following script in the SQL console:

```
ALTER SYSTEM ALTER CONFIGURATION ('indexserver.ini', 'SYSTEM')
SET ('password_policy','maximum_invalid_connection_attempts') = '8'
```

1.5.6 Configuration Tab

The **Configuration** tab is important in SAP HANA Studio as it relates to security. In Section 1.2, we walked through the process of accessing the **Configuration** tab. As noted, the best way to get to this tab is by launching the administrative console. The **Configuration** tab gives administrators a GUI in which they can adjust system settings. We can also execute SQL commands to adjust these settings. However, with the GUI, administrators can see a complete list of the available settings and make the desired adjustments to those settings.

There are several security-related settings that can be adjusted in the **Configuration** tab, such as adjusting password policy settings, configuring encryption, configuring SSL, adjusting third-party authentication settings, and configuring auditing. As you'll discover, SAP HANA Studio also provides alternative options for adjusting some of these same settings, but the **Configuration** tab contains all possible settings in a single interface. Depending on the setting that needs to be adjusted, administrators might have to use the **Configuration** tab to make the adjustment.

1.6 Summary

This chapter provided an introduction to SAP HANA Studio and how to navigate it to access its different interfaces, windows, tabs, and hierarchy trees related to security. As you continue through this book, we'll share additional details about how to use these interfaces to build a comprehensive security model.

Chapter 2
Introduction to SAP HANA Privileges

In this chapter, we'll introduce SAP HANA privileges and define several related key terms. Privileges are a major component of SAP HANA security, because they control what operations a user can conduct.

Users can interact with SAP HANA in a variety of different ways. Some will use SAP HANA Studio to develop content and administer the system. Others might interact with business intelligence tools and query the data hosted in SAP HANA. In other cases, SAP NetWeaver uses the SAP HANA database to help operate applications like SAP Business Warehouse (SAP BW) and SAP S/4HANA. In all cases, database user accounts are required to interact with SAP HANA. These user accounts are often assigned to individual people. However, dedicated service accounts might be set up to allow an application to delegate access for multiple users to the SAP HANA system. To govern these interactions, user accounts must be assigned a variety of *privileges*.

When a user account interacts with SAP HANA, it can only perform operations and actions that have been granted via privileges. Granting privileges is a process whereby a *grantor* assigns privileges to another user account. For a grantor to grant an individual privilege, the grantor must be granted that privilege and must also have been assigned the `WITH GRANT OPTION` or **Grantable to Others** option, an additional right that allows the grantor the ability to grant the same privilege to another user. If you're using SQL to grant privileges, the `WITH GRANT OPTION` syntax will be used. If you're using the graphical user interface (GUI) in SAP HANA Studio, you'll see a checkbox labeled **Grantable to Others**.

When you first set up an SAP HANA system, the first user account available will be the *SYSTEM account*. The user name of that account is just *SYSTEM*. By default, the SYSTEM account can create users and grant privileges to other user accounts for all the default system objects, privileges, and roles.

The very first time you interact with SAP HANA, you'll most likely log on using the SYSTEM user account. If you're following best practices, you'll then create new user accounts, set up a new security model, and assign that security model to the new dedicated user accounts. Most organizations will then disable access to the SYSTEM account so that they can properly audit and associate activities with individuals.

By definition, the various operations and actions you perform in SAP HANA are organized into objects called *privileges*. Throughout this chapter, we'll introduce the five major categories of privileges available in SAP HANA, and we'll also introduce how privileges are properly granted to roles and users and how the system validates a user's access. In subsequent chapters, we'll take a much deeper dive into individual privileges and outline what each privilege authorizes; however, the goal of this chapter is to provide an overview.

2.1 Privileges within SAP HANA

The five major categories of privileges available in SAP HANA are *system*, *object*, *analytic*, *package*, and *application*. Each category contains individual privileges that can be granted to either users or roles. In the following sections, we'll look at each category in turn.

2.1.1 System Privileges

System privileges are designed to govern various system activities that a user can perform. They are predominantly used to govern administrative actives within the SAP HANA database. However, some system privileges specifically govern developer actives related to the SAP HANA development repository and development content.

To help you better understand what system privileges govern, let's review a few examples. Administrative system privileges include activities such as the ability to create schemas. Although each user account is assigned a dedicated schema, it cannot create additional schemas without first being granted the appropriate rights. Unless a user is granted the system privilege *create schema*, that user won't be able to execute SQL commands that create additional schemas. Other administrative system privileges govern the ability for a user to import and export catalog objects using SAP HANA Studio. Unless users are granted the privilege *import* or *export*, they can't conduct these actions.

As you'll discover in subsequent chapters, there are numerous system privileges that can be granted. We will go through all the different privileges in detail starting with Chapter 7. Now, in the next section, we'll look at object privileges and how they govern access to catalog objects.

2.1.2 Object Privileges

Object privileges govern a user's ability to both access and manipulate database or catalog objects. Database objects are also called *catalog objects*; some SAP HANA interfaces will call them by either name. In early versions of SAP HANA, these privileges were called *SQL privileges*. The name was appropriate because we use SQL statements to access and change catalog objects. Object privileges control the types of SQL statements that can be executed against a catalog object. The following are a few examples of the types of SQL statements that object privileges govern:

- `SELECT "column" FROM "schema"."table"`
- `EXECUTE "schema"."stored_procedure"()`
- `DROP "schema"."table"`
- `ALTER "schema"."table"`

When we grant object privileges, we're specifying the types of SQL statement commands that can be executed against a catalog object. As in the preceding examples, we can specify whether a user can execute SQL statements containing syntax like `SELECT`, `EXECUTE`, `DELETE`, or `ALTER`. In Chapter 8, we will go into more details about the different types of SQL statements that we can govern.

In recent versions of SAP HANA, object privileges can also be granted to development objects. Therefore, referring to them using the more generic term *object privileges* is a more appropriate description and name.

Managing Object Privileges Using GUIs

It's technically correct to state that object privileges govern the types of SQL statements executed against catalog objects, but administrators aren't always aware that they're issuing SQL commands when using a GUI to manage security. For example, when we add object privileges to a user via SAP HANA Studio's user administration GUI, SQL statements aren't being issued directly by the user. Instead, SAP HANA Studio converts the graphical workflow of the administrator into the appropriate SQL statements and issues them to the system in the background.

Catalog objects include items such as tables, views, stored procedures, schemas, sequences, and triggers. To properly understand object privileges, we need to separate them into two broad categories: First, we have *schema object privileges*. *Schemas* are catalog objects that logically contain other catalog objects. We can think of them as the parent object to other catalog objects. We can grant object privileges to the entire schema or to individual database catalog objects within a schema. When we grant object privileges to the schema, we are also granting those same rights to all objects within that schema. You could say that *child objects* inherit the rights granted to the *parent schema*.

However, we can also grant object privileges to individual catalog objects within a schema. In this case, we are granting *catalog object privileges* to each individual object. Security administrators might use this approach if they want to limit access to individual tables and views within a schema. Some administrators will find granting privileges to each individual catalog object to be an unscalable and tedious task. Fortunately, we also have the option to simply provide access to all objects in a schema.

Object ownership is also an important concept related to object privileges. When a user creates a catalog object, he is the owner of that object. As the owner, he has full privileged access to the object. He is also the only user that can grant rights for that catalog object to other users in the system. It is important to note that the SYSTEM database user account cannot grant rights to other users, because it doesn't own the object. The system account will have no privileges on the object until the object's owner specifically grants the necessary privileges to it. The owner must also allow the system account to grant those rights to other users via the `WITH GRANT OPTION` or **Grantable to Others** option before it can grant those catalog object rights to other users.

It's also important to understand object ownership as it relates to the deletion of user accounts. When a user account is deleted, all catalog objects that it owns are also deleted. If the user owns a schema, all objects in that schema are deleted. The same is true of any object privileges that the user has granted to other users. In Chapter 6, we will focus on strategies to help prevent cascade deletion of objects and granted privileges, but for this chapter it's important simply to understand the basic concepts of object privileges, object ownership, and user deletion.

To help further your understanding of object privileges and how users are given access to catalog objects, there are a few additional concepts to consider:

- When we create a user, the system generates a schema matching the user name. The user is the only owner of this *user schema*.
- When a user creates a schema using the `CREATE SCHEMA` SQL command, he/she is the owner of that schema.
- If a user is granted privileges to a schema, all objects in that schema inherit the same privileges. This includes the `WITH GRANT OPTION` or **Grantable to Others** option.

Object privileges play an important role in the overall SAP HANA security model. They govern access to catalog objects and the types of actions users can perform on those objects using SQL commands. In the next section, we'll look at how to govern access to the data stored or presented through catalog objects using analytic privileges.

2.1.3 Analytic Privileges

Analytic privileges govern access to data made available through SAP HANA's information views and, in some cases, catalog or database views. Information views are development and runtime objects that convert data into multidimensional models and enrich the view with metadata elements. These metadata elements include attributes, measures, hierarchies, key columns, label columns, and counters.

There are three specific types of information views, as follows:

1. *Attribute views* are a type of information view used to logically organize and manage reusable master data. They reference catalog tables and define the join relationships between those tables to produce a logical master data view.
2. *Analytic views* are a type of information view that define star schema multidimensional models. In such models, attribute views join to transaction base catalog tables to produce logical data cubes that contain attribute data columns and measures.
3. *Calculation views* are the final type of information view. They are a diverse type of information view that can express both star schema multidimensional models and complex analysis queries. They can be designed using catalog tables or other information views.

Database views are catalog objects that produce a data set when queried. However, catalog views are essentially predefined queries stored as catalog objects. They are programed using SQL statements and can express datasets based on filtering data, joining catalog tables, and joining existing catalog views. They provide basic metadata such as column names and column descriptions, but they don't offer rich metadata elements such as attributes, measures, hierarchies, and column labels.

There are two types of analytic privileges: *XML-based* and *SQL-based*. XML-based analytic privileges are the legacy type. They are used to manage access to information views and provide both simple and dynamic filtering capabilities. SQL-based analytic privileges offer the ability to govern access to both information views and catalog database views. They also offer the ability to implement more complex filter logic using subquery statements. The ability to use subquery statements overcomes some of the limitations associated with the filter logic available within XML-based analytic privileges.

XML-based analytic privileges provide a twofold level of access. First, they grant read access to the information views associated with the analytic privilege. In most security models, every information view will be associated with at least one analytic privilege. The analytic privilege is assigned to a user, subsequently granting the user read access to the data expressed through the information view. Second, data restrictions can be applied within analytic privilege to statically or dynamically filter the data based on specified filter criteria. People in the world of business intelligence call this *row-level security*. Rows of data are strategically filtered to restrict user access to data. For example, if an administrator needs to restrict data so that regional managers can only see records associated with their regions, she would use analytic privileges to do so.

SQL-based analytic privileges grant twofold access to both information views and catalog views. First, they govern read access to both types of views. They are unique in this regard, because they offer the ability to govern both information views and catalog views. Second, they offer the ability to define both simple and complex data restrictions using subquery filter logic. It's important to note that information views are automatically registered for an authorization check when they're activated. However, catalog views must be explicitly registered for an authorization check before their SQL-based analytic privileges are honored.

You should now have a basic understanding of how analytic privileges are used to govern access to both information views and catalog views. In Chapter 10, we'll explore the process for creating both XML-based and SQL-based analytic privileges in detail.

2.1.4 Package Privileges

As we stated in previous chapters, SAP HANA is a database system and a development platform, among numerous other properties. Embedded within SAP HANA is a repository used to store design-time objects used by both the database system and the SAP HANA XS engine. The hierarchy of this repository is organized into packages and their subpackages, and each package contains design-time development artifacts. To govern access to both packages and development artifacts, SAP HANA package privileges can be assigned to users and roles.

Package privileges are organized into two broad categories: Native package privileges and imported package privileges. *Native package privileges* are for packages and their child development artifacts that are developed from scratch in an SAP HANA system; we expect to create and edit native content in a development system. *Imported package privileges* represent packages and their child development artifacts that are imported into a system. These objects are created in a remote system, exported, and then imported into a different system.

SAP HANA allows security administrators to set up package privileges differently between native and imported package content. This functionality is specifically designed to help organizations facilitate proper content lifecycle management. For example, you can secure imported package content in a production system differently simply because it was imported into the production system. Although this is not a best practice, developers can be allowed to create native content in production but prevented from editing content imported from a development or quality assurance system.

Now that we've discussed how package privileges can be used to secure access to development artifacts in the SAP HANA repository, let's define application privileges.

2.1.5 Application Privileges

SAP HANA is a development platform via which web-based applications can be developed and hosted. These applications sometimes need their own unique privileges to govern actions unique to the application. Take, for example, a simple application that allows a user to enter data into a questionnaire. Some users need access simply to answer questions. These users should not have the ability to see the results of other questionnaires given to other users. However, administrative users might need the ability to see the answers given by all users. Application privileges can be developed to facilitate this custom security requirement. The SAP HANA system does not offer native privileges to manage this type of distinction, because each application is custom built to facilitate specific requirements.

2.2 Privilege Validation and Assignment

Now that we've discussed the five different types of privileges available, let's take a moment to discuss how they're assigned to user accounts and how the system validates these privileges.

2.2.1 Assigning Privileges

Figure 2.1 demonstrates how privileges should be assigned, with the user account (to which multiple roles can be assigned) at the top, roles in the middle, and the assignment of the different types of privileges at the bottom. When a user interacts with SAP HANA, the system validates the user's privileges by checking those assigned directly to that user or those inherited from an assigned role. Privileges can be assigned directly to a user account, but it's recommended that user accounts be assigned one or more roles, and roles are then assigned one or more privileges. We highly recommend that you adhere to this methodology when designing a security model.

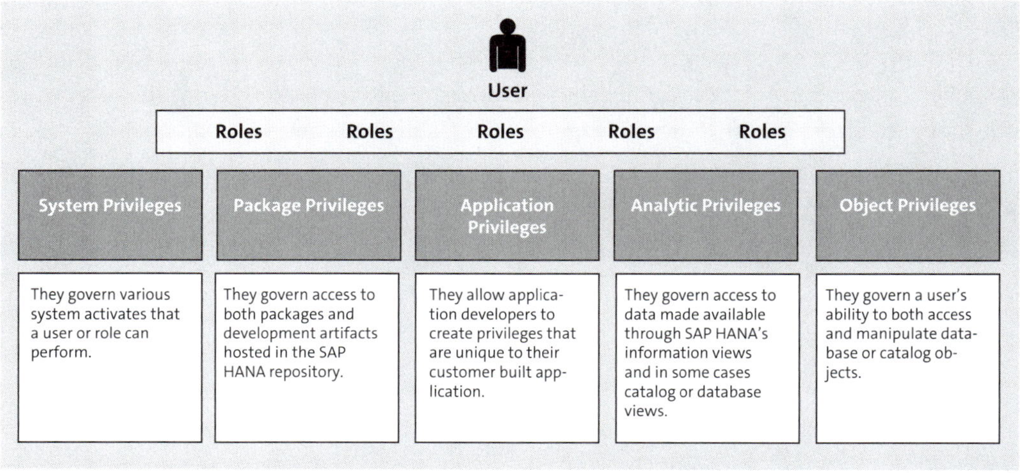

Figure 2.1 SAP HANA Privilege Assignment Hierarchy

Roles are database objects used to organize and assign privileges to one or more users. Managing privileges for each individual user account is not scalable in most large environments. Administrators prefer using roles because there are typically fewer of them to manage, they help promote a consistent application of privileges, and they can be shared by multiple user accounts. A variety of roles can be created, each role containing a variety of different privileges.

In subsequent chapters, we will discuss the processes for creating users, creating roles, and assigning privileges in detail. For now, it's simply important to understand the basic process used to grant or assign privileges to users.

2.2.2 Validating Privileges

Now that you have a basic understanding of how privileges are assigned to users, let's take a moment to discuss how these privileges are validated when a user attempts to perform an action in the system. There are two broad categories of validation that we will discuss. First, there is *basic validation*. This type of validation comes into play when a user attempts to access an object or perform an action directly. Second, we will discuss how the system validates privileges when an object references other objects. For example, how does the system fully validate a stored procedure that references other catalog objects in the system?

Basic Validation

When the system validates privileges, it checks for those assigned directly to the user and those assigned to roles that are also assigned to the user. This is basic authorization validation. SAP HANA currently only supports granting privileges, not denying them. SAP HANA simply looks at the user's privileges and those assigned to its roles. If it finds a privilege granted, it stops processing validation and assumes that it is allowed or granted. Because it does not support denied privileges, there is no need for the system to check all assigned privileges.

Validation for Catalog Objects Referencing Other Objects

Some catalog objects can be developed referencing other catalog objects, and both catalog views and catalog stored procedures represent objects that facilitate this scenario. Let's start by defining two classes of objects: First, the *parent object* contains one or more referenced objects. Parent objects are also sometimes objects with dependencies; for example, if a catalog view references three catalog tables, the view is the parent object referencing the catalog tables. Second, *referenced child objects* are the objects contained within the definition of the parent object. The parent object references these objects or is dependent on them.

The system validates privileges for parent catalog objects with dependencies using the following rules; note that catalog stored procedures have a unique option to change the default validation behavior:

1. The user account accessing the parent object must have explicit object privileges to access it. For example, if we create a catalog view that references tables in three schemas, the user account must have `SELECT` access to the catalog view regardless of the privileges specified on the referenced objects.

2. The developer that creates the parent object must have the required privileges for the child object and must have the ability to grant those privileges to other users. For example, if we create a catalog view that references tables in three schemas, the developer must have `SELECT` access to the objects in those schemas. He must also have the `WITH GRANT OPTION`/**Grantable to Others** right to delegate those privileges to other users.
3. Stored procedures created using the *definer mode* are validated using rules 1 and 2. The end user only needs to have privileges to access the stored procedure. The objects that the stored procedure references are validated against the developer's privileges during activation. Effectively, the developer is indirectly granting user access to the child referenced objects.
4. Stored procedures created using the *invoker mode* are validated differently. The end user accessing the stored procedure must have explicit catalog object privileges for both the parent object and the referenced child objects. This option changes the default behavior of dependent objects. It is used in cases in which the procedure is attempting to manipulate objects that should be validated against the executing user's privileges rather than the designer's privileges.

Validation for Packages and Development Artifacts

As we discussed, packages are nodes organized in a parent-child relationship. Together, they make up the SAP HANA repository. Each package contains a subpackage or one or more development artifacts. Package privileges are assigned at a package node. Development artifacts cannot individually or explicitly be granted privileges. However, development artifacts do inherit the privileges assigned to their parent and grandparent package nodes. When the system validates access to a development artifact, it first checks the privileges assigned to the direct parent package. If there are no privileges assigned to the direct parent, it will continue to traverse up the hierarchy, checking each grandparent node until it can validate the requested action. If no parent or grandparent node has assigned privileges for that user, the user fails the authorization and is not considered authorized to perform the requested action. This is known as the *bottom-up approach* to authorization validation.

Because SAP HANA uses a bottom-up approach, we only need to grant the user privileges on its closest desired parent or grandparent package. Therefore, there's no need to establish privileges for a given user at each level of the package hierarchy. Understanding this distinction will help you avoid overengineering the security model.

It's also important to mention that developers will likely need a combination of package, system, and object privileges to fully manage content in the package repository. For example, the REPO.MODIFY_CHANGE system privilege might need to be granted to allow the user the ability to activate content when change management is required. The user might also need the REPO.IMPORT and REPO.EXPORT system privileges to import and export repository delivery units. For the developer to access the package repository, she needs the EXECUTE object privilege for the SYS.REPOSITORY_REST stored procedure. As you can see, package privileges alone do not always provide the required access to the system. Throughout this book, we'll explore various privileges and how they're layered together in roles. For now, it's enough to know that privileges are often layered to grant complete access to some areas within SAP HANA.

2.3 Summary

In this chapter, you learned the basics of SAP HANA privileges and how those privileges are assigned to users. You also learned how the system validates those privileges. In subsequent chapters, we'll take a deeper look at each of the five privileges. We'll also explore how those privileges are assigned to both roles and user accounts. As you've seen, the key to developing a security model for SAP HANA lies in the creation of roles, the assignment of privileges to those roles, and then the assignment of users to roles.

Chapter 3
Catalog Objects

In this chapter, we'll explore the different types of catalog objects and walk through the two major options available for creating them. How you choose to create catalog objects has a profound effect on the security model structure and management processes.

Object privileges play an important role in the development of any SAP HANA security model. They define the types of SQL script actions a user can perform on a catalog object (also sometimes referred to as a *database object*). SAP HANA hosts multiple types of catalog objects. In this chapter, we'll explore the different types of catalog objects that SAP HANA hosts. We'll also explain that there are different ways to create most catalog objects: Catalog objects can be created directly using SQL CREATE statements, in which case they're called *native catalog objects*. The user issuing the SQL statement is the owner of the native catalog object. SAP HANA also supports the creation of some catalog objects as repository development artifacts, in which case they're called *repository catalog objects*. Repository catalog objects are owned by the _SYS_REPO system account.

Because the principal of object ownership is a critical concept in all security models, the acute distinction of ownership—between native and repository catalog objects—is very important. Therefore, in this chapter we'll take a detailed look at the different options for creating catalog objects. The options an organization chooses to use when create catalog objects is of critical importance to all security administrators. We'll define the different types of catalog objects, demonstrate how to create both native and repository objects, review the process for deploying repository objects, and conclude with a case study to demonstrate a real-world example.

3.1 What Are SAP HANA Catalog Objects?

Catalog objects consist of various relational database management system (RDBMS) artifacts, such as tables, views, stored procedures, triggers, sequences, and a few other items. Items such as tables both store and define the structure of the data. Other items, such as views, are used to express query logic. The following list describes the most common catalog objects available in SAP HANA:

- **Schema**
  A *schema object* is a logical organizational unit that is a parent to all other catalog objects. When other catalog objects are created, a schema must be specified. From the perspective of a security model, it's the most important catalog object. Whether to secure the entire schema or to secure the individual catalog objects within the schema is a critical choice to make.
- **Tables**
  Tables define the structure of data and store data within an RDBMS. Their structure is defined by columns, rows, and data types, and rows of data are logically stored in this table structure. Because the data contained in tables might be sensitive, it's important that organizations limit the types of SQL statements that can be executed against tables.
- **Triggers**
  Triggers are catalog objects that contain code that executes a procedure depending on a variety of events that occur within the RDBMS. They are used for a variety of purposes, ranging from database management to data integrity. Because their code can manipulate data and other catalog objects, it's important for organizations to restrict where and how they are used.
- **Views**
  Views act as logical tables. However, in SAP HANA they are not used to store data. Instead, they are defined using SQL query statements. Like tables, they offer columns and data types and can be queried. Within their definitions, their SQL query statements can perform actions such as combining tables, restricting data, and aggregating results. From a security standpoint, most catalog views need to be secured for the same reasons that we secure access to tables.
- **Synonyms**
  Synonyms are used as logical reference points to other catalog objects. They act aliases to obscure the identity of other catalog objects. Synonyms exclusively use the granted privileges of the objects they reference.
- **Sequences**
  Sequences are catalog objects used to keep track of an incremented number value by means of its definition. They can be queried in procedural code to determine the current or next value within a defined sequence. They often are used to create

unique identity columns within a table. For example, we can use a sequence to generate a new value in a primary key column, with the requirement that the value be unique for the row.

- **Procedures**
  A *stored procedure* is a catalog object that contains complex developed SQL code. It can return a dataset, much like a catalog view. However, the code can also perform tasks within the RDBMS system. These procedures support both input and output parameters, which makes them dynamic.
- **Indexes**
  An *index* is an object used to optimize the retrieval of data from a table. Although it increases the performance of some queries, it also comes at the cost of increased storage. Security administrators typically limit privileges to create and drop indexes because of the impact they have on both performance and storage cost.
- **Functions**
  Functions are custom snippets of SQL code used to perform read-only operations on data. They can be defined as single-valued input and output or table-valued input and output. Once created, they can be referenced within SQL `SELECT` statements and SQL stored procedures. Depending on the purpose of the catalog function, regulating access to these objects can be important. For example, if a function is used to apply core business logic within a SQL query, security administrators likely will need to limit the number of individuals that can alter the function.

Now that we've listed the common catalog objects used in an SAP HANA system, let's look at the options for creating them. For this discussion, we'll demonstrate the processes necessary to create a schema and the processes necessary to create a table. We'll highlight the differences based on instances in which we plan to use SQL statements and instances in which we plan to use repository objects. How you create objects is important to your security model, so pay close attention to these options while focusing on how they affect an object's ownership.

3.2 Creating and Managing Native Catalog Objects

The process used to create standard catalog objects typically involves executing a SQL statement containing a `CREATE` statement and the supporting syntax specific to the objects being created. Once a `CREATE` statement is successfully executed, a runtime version of the object will exist in the SAP HANA system. Active objects within the RDBMS catalog are called *runtime objects*. However, the design-time script will remain within the SQL console. The design-time state or *design-time objects* represent the script or code used to define an object. With SQL, if you need to save the design-time script, you'll need to save to a file system independent from the SAP HANA system.

Those familiar with SAP HANA Studio will likely be aware that some objects can be created using the GUI. Although the workflow appears graphical in nature, these GUI windows are issuing SQL statements to the system based on the options selected within the GUI. Like using SQL statements, the design-time definition of the objects isn't stored within the SAP HANA system. In fact, it's more difficult to save the script when using the GUI, because the script needs to be extracted from the GUI execution status windows. However, SAP HANA Studio allows you to copy the text of the SQL statement from the status window; if you extract the SQL statement, you can then save it to a file for safekeeping.

Regardless of the method you use to create a standard catalog object, SQL statements inevitably will be issued to the SAP HANA system. In this section, we'll introduce the basic workflows and SQL syntax needed to create a standard schema and table and discuss how they influence a security model. When applicable, we'll demonstrate how objects can be generated using SAP HANA Studio.

3.2.1 Creating Schemas

Schemas are core relational database objects used to logically store all other catalog objects. Standard catalog schemas are generated in three ways:

1. When a standard user account is created, the system automatically generates a schema for that user. The user is the sole owner of that schema, and the account owner must grant privileges to other users or roles before they can interact with the user's schema.
2. Schemas can be created using a SQL `CREATE` statement. The following SQL statements can be used to create a schema. In the first example, we can specify the owner of the schema. In the second example, the system assumes that the user executing the statement will be the owner:
   - `CREATE SCHEMA "MySchema" OWNED BY USER_NAME`
   - `CREATE SCHEMA "MySchema"`
3. The third option for creating a schema is via the SAP HANA Web-Based Development Workbench catalog editor. The SAP HANA system offers several web-based

GUIs to aid in the creation and modification of both catalog and repository-based objects. Not all objects can be created utilizing a GUI within this interface, but schemas can be. The user account used to log on to the SAP HANA Web-Based Development Workbench catalog editor will be the owner of the schema.

To access this web-based GUI, enter the correct URL into a supported web browser's address bar using the following template:

http://<sap_hana_host>:80<instance_number>/sap/hana/ide/catalog

Replace *<sap_hana_host>* with the hostname of the SAP HANA system in your environment and *<instance_number>* with the two-digit instance number corresponding to your SAP HANA system.

For secure access, use the following template:

https://<sap_hana_host>:43<instance_number>/sap/hana/ide/catalog

If you have the appropriate privileges to access the SAP HANA Web-Based Development Workbench catalog editor, you can log on to the web interface using these URLs. Once logged in, you can create a catalog schema, assuming you have the necessary system privileges.

To create a catalog schema within this interface, right-click the **Catalog** node on the left side of the window. From the context menu, choose **New Schema**. A window titled **Create new Schema** will open. Enter the name of the schema in the text box labeled **New Schema** (see Figure 3.1). If you want the exact case of the text (uppercase/lowercase) to be used in the schema name, uncheck **Case-insensitive**. Click **OK** to complete the workflow and generate the schema.

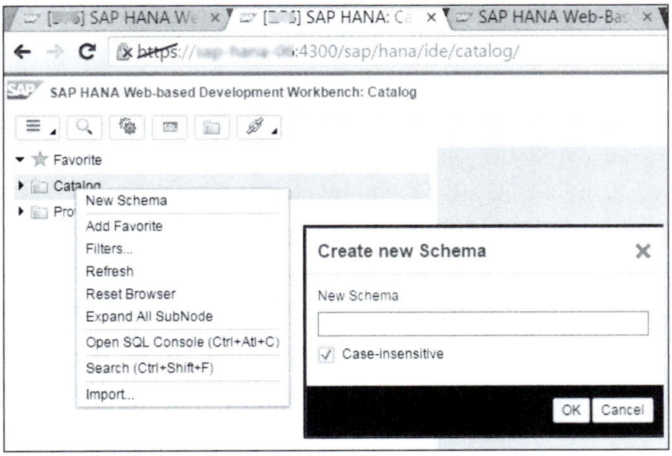

Figure 3.1 Creating Schema with SAP HANA Web-Based Development Workbench

SAP HANA Web-Based Development Workbench

For more information on accessing and using the SAP HANA Web-Based Development Workbench, please download the SAP HANA Developer Guide for the SAP HANA Web-Based Development Workbench from *https://help.sap.com/viewer/b3d0daf2a98e49ada00bf31b7ca7a42e/2.0.00/en-US.*

For a direct link to the PDF version of the guide, use the following URL: *https://help.sap.com/doc/7d957b1b6c1a4791a1212b45e9a797df/2.0.00/en-US/SAP_HANA_Developer_Guide_for_SAP_HANA_Web_Workbench_en.pdf.*

All three options will result in a schema that will be owned by the individual executing the script or completing the action within the GUI. Because standard catalog schemas are owned by standard user accounts, maintaining access to these accounts is critical. This is because only the owner of the schema can initially grant privileges on the schema's catalog objects to other users and roles. This is an important concept that needs to be understood by all security administrators.

Depending on your SAP HANA solution, a standard schema and its associated service account will likely be generated programmatically by other SAP software. For example, when we're installing an SAP NetWeaver-based solution on SAP HANA, the software provisioning manager will create a service account user and use its user schema to store the system tables, views, and other objects used by the SAP NetWeaver application. If your organization plans to provide direct access to these SAP HANA objects, maintaining access to the service account that owns this schema will be critical. At some point, the security administrator or Basis administrator will likely need to log on to SAP HANA Studio with the service account to grant privileges to other users or roles.

As mentioned before, granting privileges to a schema will inherently grant any applicable privileges to tables, views, functions, sequences, column views, and other objects associated with that schema. Some organizations might choose to grant schema privileges only to users and roles. Doing so will greatly reduce the maintenance of the security model, because all new objects will inherit the granted privileges from the schema. However, some organizations might find this too broad of a methodology and choose to secure objects individually.

Let's now look at how to create individual objects by exploring the options available when creating tables.

3.2.2 Creating Catalog Tables

There are two different methods we can use to create standard tables within SAP HANA. We can execute SQL statements using the CREATE table syntax to produce a catalog table. Such objects are owned by the user account issuing the statement. We can also use the GUI within SAP HANA Studio to define a table. Both methods issue SQL statements to the system, and the user account executing the workflow owns the object.

Let's look at how to use the CREATE SQL statement to generate a table. First, we can execute SQL statements within the SQL console. Refer to Chapter 1 if you need a refresher on how to access the SQL console within SAP HANA Studio. To create a column store table with two columns, you would execute the following SQL statement within the SQL console:

```
CREATE COLUMN TABLE "MySchema"."MyTable"
("MyColumnA" NVARCHAR(5) PRIMARY KEY, "MyColumnB" DECIMAL(26,6) );
```

To create a table using another table's definition as a template, execute the following SQL statement:

```
CREATE TABLE "MySchema"."MyCopyTable" like "MySchema"."MyTable" WITH NO DATA;
```

Creating Tables or Schemas

The complete syntax for creating tables, schemas, and other catalog objects is beyond the scope of this book. To review the full syntax and all available options, please access the SAP HANA SQL and System Views Reference Guide found at *https://help.sap.com/hana_platform* or use the following direct link to the guide in PDF format: *https://help.sap.com/doc/9b40bf74f8644b898fb07dabdd2a36ad/2.0.00/en-US/SAP_HANA_SQL_and_System_Views_Reference_en.pdf.*

The second option for creating catalog tables relies on a GUI within SAP HANA Studio. SAP HANA Studio provides an interface containing many of the standard options necessary to create a table. To access this GUI and create a table, use the following steps:

1. Open SAP HANA Studio and connect to the desired system. This workflow will work in any perspective containing the **Systems** window.
2. Within the **Systems** window, expand the system to reveal the **Catalog** node.
3. Within the **Catalog** node, expand the tree under the schema in which you want to create the table.

4. Within the schema node, right-click the **Tables** folder and choose **New Table**. A window will appear like the one shown in Figure 3.2. To properly define the table, enter a name in the **Table Name** field and define one or more columns within the **Columns** tab. When defining a column, you must provide the **SQL Data Type** and **Dimension** for applicable column types.

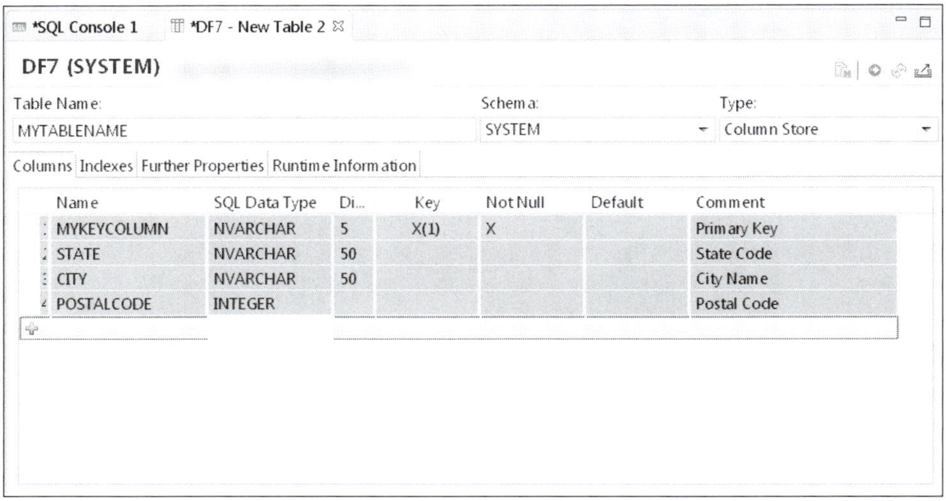

Figure 3.2 Create Table GUI in SAP HANA Studio

5. To add additional columns, click **+** within the **Columns** tab to add an additional row. Within each new row, you can define an additional column.
6. Once you've defined all the desired properties of the table, execute the object to activate it within the system. To do so, press [F8] to execute the SQL code generated by the GUI. A small window will appear at the top containing the status of the execution and the SQL code that was executed by the system. If you choose to do so, the SQL statements within this status window can be coped and saved to a local file.

It's important to note that this graphical workflow technically issues SQL statements to the system. Therefore, the table will be owned by the individual executing the workflow. From a security perspective, the owner of the table or anyone with full control of the table's schema will need to grant privileges to other users or roles to allow them access to the table. The table will also be removed from the system if the executing user is removed from the system at any time in the future.

3.2.3 Creating Other Catalog Objects

All catalog objects can be created using the SQL `CREATE` statement. The syntax in most cases follows a pattern like the following:

```
CREATE <Catalog Object Type>  <Catalog Object Name> <Options>
```

The catalog object type can be an item such as `TABLE`, `VIEW`, `PROCEDURE`, `FUNCTION`, `SCHEMA`, `TYPE`, or another catalog object. The catalog object name can be any name you choose, so long as it contains supported characters. The options will vary based on the catalog object you're creating.

For example, to create a catalog view, you can execute the following SQL code:

```
CREATE VIEW "MyView" AS
SELECT * FROM "MyTable" WHERE "State" = 'Active';
```

To create a stored procedure named `MyProcedureName` that outputs a dataset from a table, define it using the code in Listing 3.1.

```
CREATE PROCEDURE MyProcedureName(IN id INT, OUT data CUSTOMER) LANGUAGE
SQLSCRIPT
READS SQL DATA WITH RESULT VIEW ProcView AS
BEGIN
data = SELECT * FROM DMART.DIMCUSTOMER WHERE CUSTOMER_ID = :id;
END;
```

Listing 3.1 Code to Define MyProcedureName Example Stored Procedure

These are just a few examples to help demonstrate how catalog objects are created using SQL scripts. When creating objects using SQL, remember that the user executing the statement will be the owner of the object.

Creating Catalog Objects

The complete syntax for creating tables, schemas, and other catalog objects is beyond the scope of this book. To review the full syntax and all available options, please access the SAP HANA SQL and System Views Reference Guide found at *https://help.sap.com/hana_platform* or by using the following direct link to the guide in PDF format: *https://help.sap.com/doc/9b40bf74f8644b898fb07dabdd2a36ad/2.0.00/en-US/SAP_HANA_SQL_and_System_Views_Reference_en.pdf*.

For information pertaining to creating objects using the GUI within SAP HANA Studio, please access the SAP HANA Administration Guide at *https://help.sap.com/hana_platform*. Look for the sections labeled *Create a Table in Runtime or Create a View in Runtime*.

3.3 Creating and Managing Repository Catalog Objects

For many RDBMS administrators, the process of issuing `CREATE` statements is a well-known methodology used to generate database catalog objects. However, SAP HANA offers an alternative to this traditional approach. It can offer this alternative because SAP HANA is also a development environment that allows organizations to define and store both design-time and runtime versions of objects. Design-time objects are stored in the SAP HANA repository, whereas runtime objects exist within the SAP HANA RDBMS catalog.

For example, we can define a development artifact called a *repository table* within the development repository found in SAP HANA studio. Once defined and activated, a catalog table is created in a specified schema. Repository tables function exactly like tables created with a SQL `CREATE` statement. However, it's important to note that a repository table is owned by the system account _SYS_REPO and not by the developer that activates it.

_SYS_REPO is the main system account responsible for managing, generating, owning, and activating repository-based objects. This includes repository schemas, tables, roles, views, and procedures. Leveraging the use of repository objects greatly reduces maintenance within a security model, because _SYS_REPO is already the owner of these objects and many objects within the system. There will be no need to log on as the traditional object owner and grant rights to other users and roles for repository objects. Most developers have a hard time remembering that they need to grant privileges to security administrators each time they create a schema or sometimes objects within a schema. By creating repository objects, developers are decoupled from this responsibility, because their repository objects are activated as catalog objects owned by _SYS_REPO. This simplifies the process and reduces the communication that needs to be established between SAP HANA developers and security administrators

_SYS_REPO is also responsible for managing the activation of SAP HANA information views. These multidimensional views reference catalog tables and can't be activated unless the _SYS_REPO account has been granted `SELECT`, `EXECUTE`, and `WITH GRANT`

OPTION/**Grantable to others** for the object. Again, if we choose to create repository tables or schemas, the _SYS_REPO account will already have the required privileges.

In Chapter 6, we'll discuss this concept further. For now, note that most of the security model simplification is only achieved when we use both repository catalog objects and repository roles within our environment. Both objects are owned and executed by the _SYS_REPO account.

As mentioned, the designation of ownership is vital within the security model. Repository objects are owned by the _SYS_REPO system account. Therefore, we must pay close attention to the methods developers use when creating catalog objects. To further your understanding, let's look at a few examples of the process used to create both a repository schema and a repository table.

3.3.1 Creating Repository Schemas

To create a repository schema, we must first log on to an SAP HANA system and switch to the development perspective within SAP HANA Studio. As discussed in Chapter 1, we then need to access the **Repositories** tab and ensure that we have a local repository workspace defined. Once the workspace is defined, expand the package hierarchy to the desired package, then right-click and choose **New • Other.**

A window labeled **Select a wizard** will open. Within the **Search** dialog, type "schema". Choose the **Schema** object under **SAP HANA • Database Development**, then click **Next**, as shown in Figure 3.3.

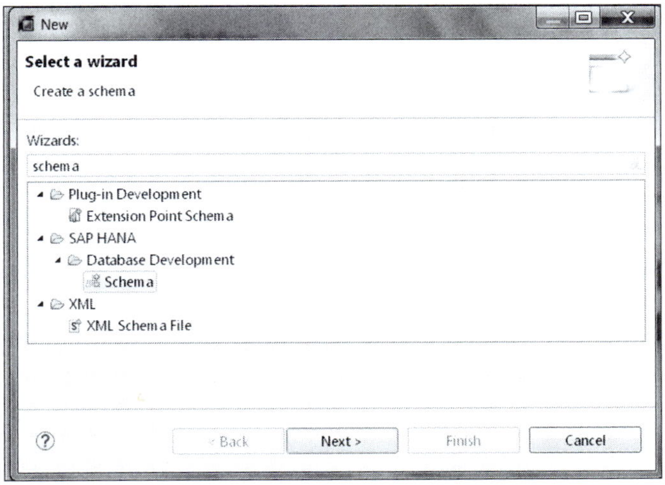

Figure 3.3 Searching for Schema Repository Objects

In the next window, labeled **New Schema**, enter a file name in the **File name** field (see Figure 3.4). The file name will become the name of the schema, so choose a name that matches the desired schema name. From the **Templates** dropdown, choose **Basic**; this will provide the basic syntax necessary to define a repository schema in the next window. Click **Next** to continue.

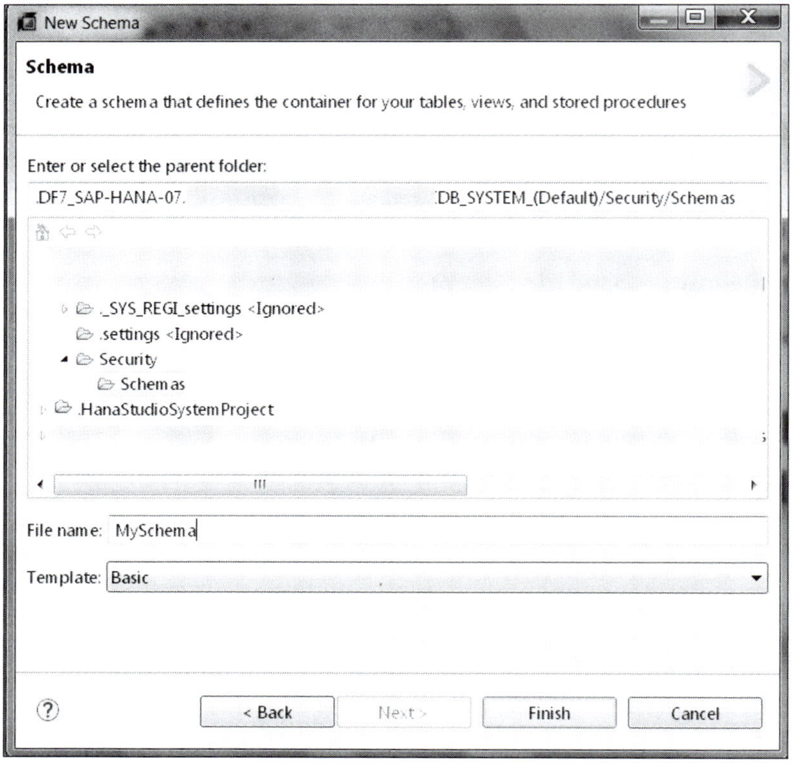

Figure 3.4 Defining Repository Schema Name and Choosing Template

A window containing the template's example text used to define a repository schema will now open, as shown in Figure 3.5. Because you chose the basic template, most of the necessary syntax has already been defined for you. Press `Ctrl`+`F3` to save and activate the repository schema. The design-time object will be saved in the SAP HANA repository, and the runtime object will be created in the SAP HANA RDBMS catalog.

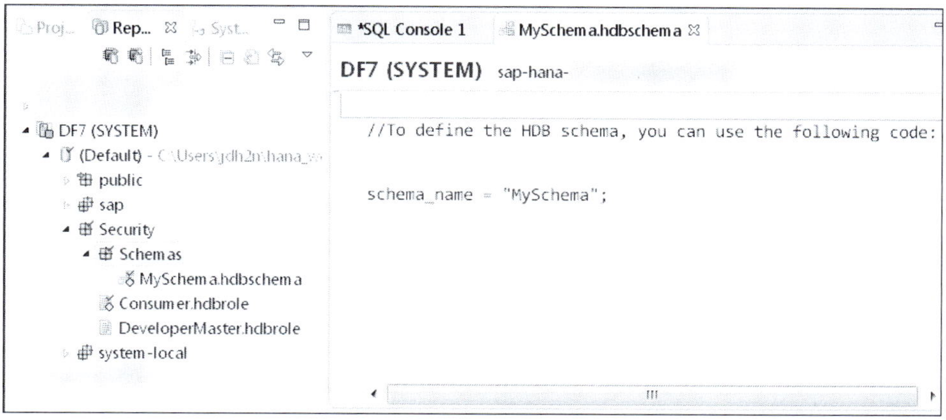

Figure 3.5 Syntax to Define Repository Schema

The syntax for creating a repository schema is very basic: The text preceded by two slash marks (//) is a comment only visible to the developer. The two slash marks tell the SAP HANA code compiler to ignore the information on that line. The core of the script is the following text:

```
Schema_name = "MySchema";
```

The text within the double quotes should match the name of the desired schema and the name given to the .hdbschema file in the repository.

Once activated, users with the CREATE ANY privilege for the schema will be able to create standard catalog objects within the schema using CREATE statements. However, we recommended that developers use the repository to create these objects. The repository schema will be owned by the _SYS_REPO user, with no need for the developer to be granted CREATE ANY on the schema. Developers only need to have access to activate objects within the SAP HANA repository; the _SYS_REPO user account creates the objects on behalf of the developer. Once again, we can simplify the security model, because developers do not need to be granted CREATE ANY privileges for a schema to create a catalog object.

Another important security aspect of a repository schema is that the _SYS_REPO account will own the schema. Thus, _SYS_REPO will have full privileges for all objects created in the schema, regardless of the method used to create them. Again, we recommend that developers use the repository to create objects. However, if for some reason they do not, then the _SYS_REPO account will already have the privileges necessary to establish repository roles that reference objects within the repository schema.

3.3.2 Creating Repository Tables

To create a repository table, first log on to an SAP HANA system and switch to the development perspective within SAP HANA Studio. As discussed in Chapter 1, you then access the **Repositories** tab and ensure that you have a local repository workspace defined. If the workspace is defined, continue to expand the package hierarchy to the desired package, then right-click it and choose **New • Other**.

A window will appear, labeled **Select a Wizard**. Within the **Search** dialog, type "database table". Choose the **Database Table** object under **SAP HANA • Database Development**, then click **Next**.

In the next window, labeled **New Database Table**, enter a file name in the **File name** field (see Figure 3.6). The file name will become the name of the table, so define a name that matches the desired table name. From the **Template** dropdown, choose **Basic**. As before, this selection will provide you with the basic syntax necessary to define a repository table in the next window. Click **Next** to continue.

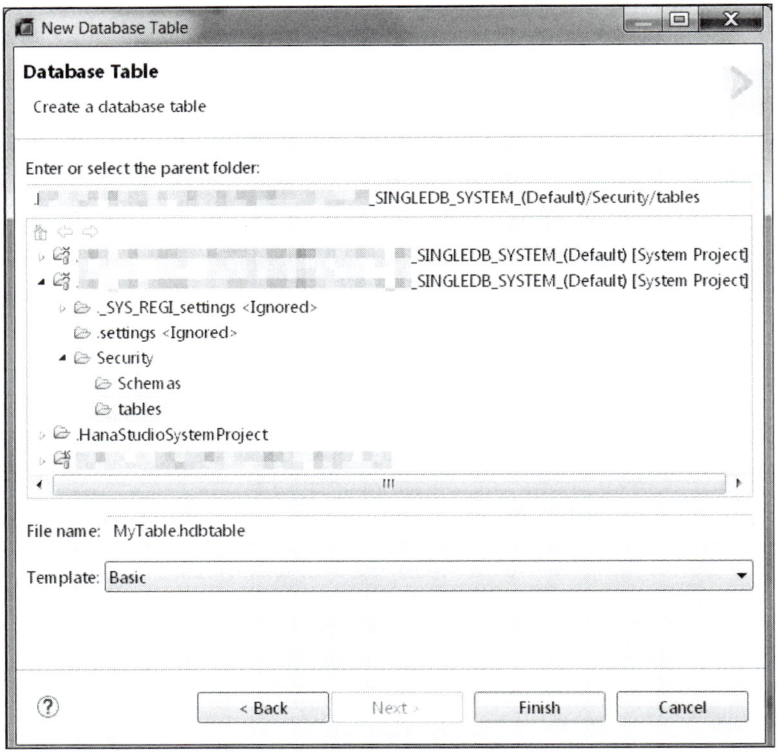

Figure 3.6 Defining Repository Table Name and Choosing Template

A window will now appear, as shown in Figure 3.7, which contains the template's example text used to define a repository table. Because you chose the basic template, several examples and comments on the syntax are included here. To define a table, simply adjust the template syntax to match your requirements.

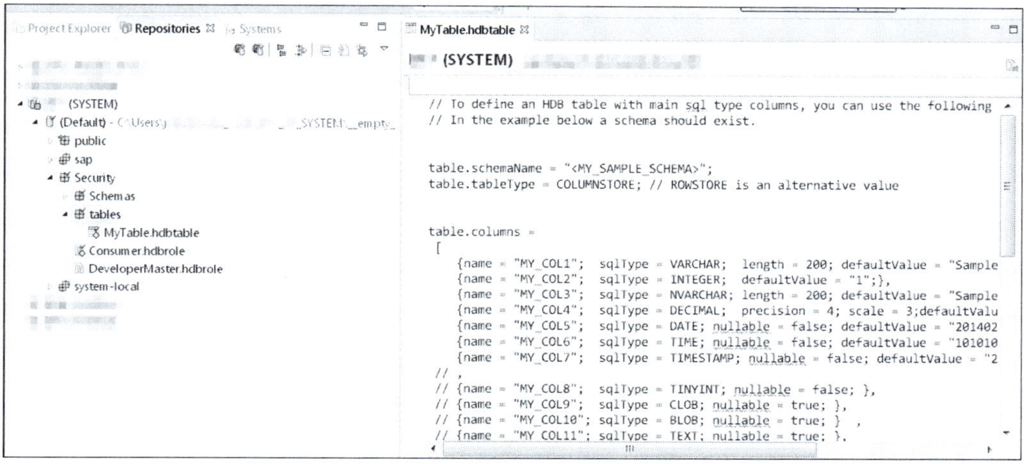

Figure 3.7 Defining Repository Table

If you've entered the correct syntax, press Ctrl+F3 to save and activate the repository table. The design-time object will be saved in the SAP HANA repository, and the runtime object will be created in the SAP HANA RDBMS catalog. Within the script, you specify the schema that will house the repository table. You will now be able to find the table within the SAP HANA catalog or within the schema node when browsing from SAP HANA Studio.

It's worth mentioning that the design-time object name and catalog object name will be different. The catalog object name will contain the name you specified for the repository object and will be prefixed with the package hierarchy name. For example, if we created the design-time repository table, named MyTable, in a package hierarchy of `myco.app.tables`, the name of the table would be `myco.app.tables::MyTable`. To query this table using SQL, you would execute the following SQL statement:

```
SELECT * FROM "MySchema"."myco.app.tables::MyTable"
```

Notice that the table name is prefixed with the package hierarchy name and two colons (`myco.app.tables::`). Because we used lowercase and camel case for the package name and table name, respectively, we must set the schema and catalog table name between double quotes in the SQL statement. SAP HANA is case-sensitive by default. Without the double quotes, the system would look for the object name while assuming you intended to use uppercase on all objects, and thus would fail to find the objects, because they were created with lowercase or camel case.

SAP HANA Repository Catalog Objects

For more information on the process used to create and manage repository tables and other repository-based objects, access the SAP HANA Developer Guide found at *http://help.sap.com/hana_platform*.

For a direct link to the PDF version of the guide, use the following URL: *https://help.sap.com/doc/fbb802faa34440b39a5b6e3814c6d3b5/2.0.00/en-US/SAP_HANA_Developer_Guide_for_SAP_HANA_Studio_en.pdf*.

Again, repository tables are owned by the _SYS_REPO system account, which will greatly simplify the setup of your security model. It will also aid in the promotion of a security model and its referenced repository objects when we need to move them into another SAP HANA environment. For example, we can define a security model in an SAP HANA development environment, within which we can create a delivery unit containing a design-time repository table, schema, and role. The delivery unit, containing a security model, can be exported to a file and later imported into a production environment. This process is only possible because we chose to define catalog objects as repository objects. In the next section, we'll take a closer look at how to deploy repository objects using a delivery unit.

3.4 Deploying Repository Objects

Chapter 14 will provide information about the processes, procedures, and steps necessary to manage a repository-based security model's lifecycle using SAP HANA application lifecycle management. In this section, we simply will introduce you to lifecycle management terms and concepts specific to catalog objects. Specifically, we'll define the terms *content vendor* and *delivery unit*. We'll also demonstrate how to package repository-based content into a delivery unit and export it to a file using SAP HANA Studio.

With most security models, there will come a point at which we need to move, share, or migrate to a new SAP HANA environment. Before we can properly do that, we need to make sure that all the objects that the model references are also available in each environment. We refer to these objects as *security model dependencies*. Security model dependencies are typically composed of various catalog objects. The makeup of a properly designed security model consists of a series of repository roles. When these repository roles reference repository-based catalog objects, we can move all parts of the model to another environment via the lifecycle management tools built into SAP HANA and SAP HANA Studio.

We've already introduced the processes necessary for creating repository schemas and tables. Assuming we develop all other objects as repository-based artifacts, moving these objects between environments will be possible. However, before we can export these objects and then import them into another environment, we must ensure that the source SAP HANA system is set up to support such activities. Two key items must be configured before we can proceed: First, we need to define the *content vendor* within our source SAP HANA system, and second, we must define a *delivery unit*.

Each SAP HANA instance must be configured with a *content vendor* before we can conduct lifecycle management activities. The *content vendor* is a value used to uniquely identify the organization or system that generated a delivery unit or exported content. The typical format of its value looks similar to that of a domain name used in an email address, but it can take on other supported formats. For example, the value can be something like `mycompany.com` or `MyCompanyName`. We don't recommend using spaces between characters, because some SAP HANA interfaces don't support them when specifying the content vendor name.

The simplest way to establish a content vendor within an SAP HANA system is to ask your SAP HANA administrator to execute an `ALTER SYSTEM` SQL statement. Our first example will set the content vendor to `'mycompany.com'`, as follows:

```
ALTER SYSTEM ALTER CONFIGURATION ('indexserver.ini', 'SYSTEM')
   SET ('repository', 'content_vendor') = 'mycompany.com'
WITH RECONFIGURE;
```

The second example will set the content vendor to `'MyCompanyName'`:

```
ALTER SYSTEM ALTER CONFIGURATION ('indexserver.ini', 'SYSTEM')
   SET ('repository', 'content_vendor') = 'MyCompanyName'
WITH RECONFIGURE;
```

For this statement to work in your environment, simply change `mycompany.com` to a value appropriate for your organization. Make sure you include the `WITH CONFIGURE` statement to activate the change without needing to restart the system. There are a few other ways to change the content vendor using a GUI; however, we find that running this SQL statement is the simplest and most direct way to implement the setting.

Once a content vendor is defined, we can then define a delivery unit. A *delivery unit* is a logical object that can be configured with one or more repository packages. As mentioned in Chapter 2, a package is a logical organization unit used to store development artifacts. The main purpose of a delivery unit is to create bundles of packages containing repository objects so that we can transport them to another SAP HANA system.

To create a delivery unit, access SAP HANA Studio and switch to the SAP HANA modeler perspective. In the default layout of this perspective, there will be a **Quick View** tab or window on the right side of the interface. Within this area, you'll see an option labeled **Delivery Units**; click it to open the **Delivery Units** management window. Figure 3.8 shows both the **Quick View** window on the right and the **Delivery Units** management window on the left.

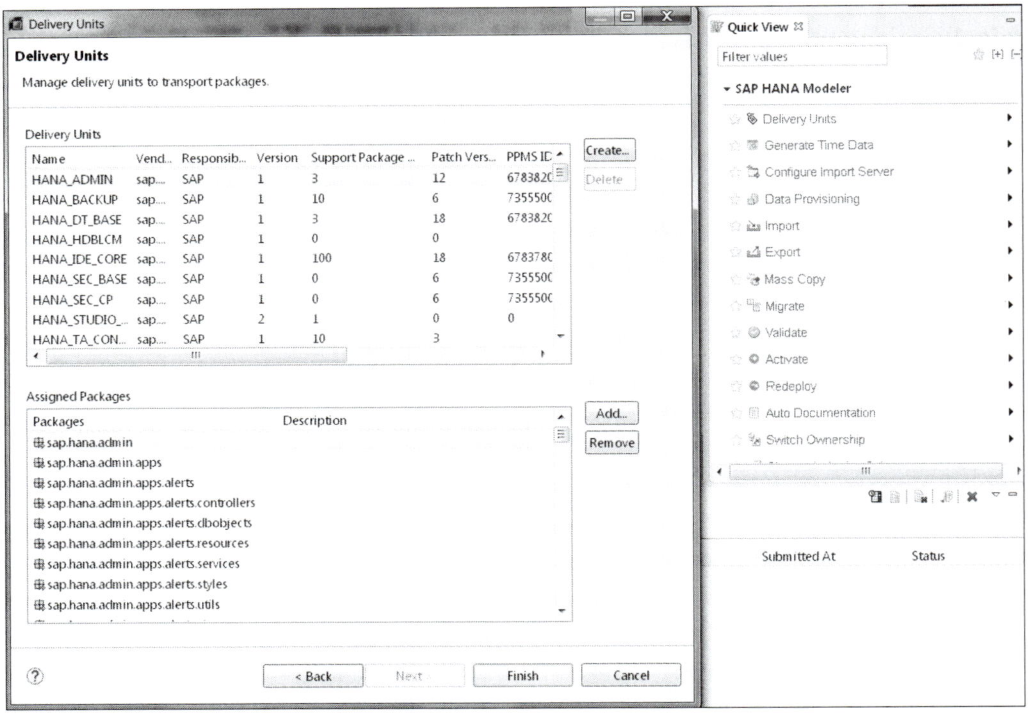

Figure 3.8 Quick View Window and Delivery Units Management Window in SAP HANA Studio

In the **Delivery Units** management window, click the **Create** button located to the right of the **Delivery Units** section. A window titled **New Delivery Unit** will open. Enter a name in the required **Name** field. All other information is optional, but Figure 3.9 shows an example of the settings to use to initialize the delivery unit. Click **OK** to create the delivery unit.

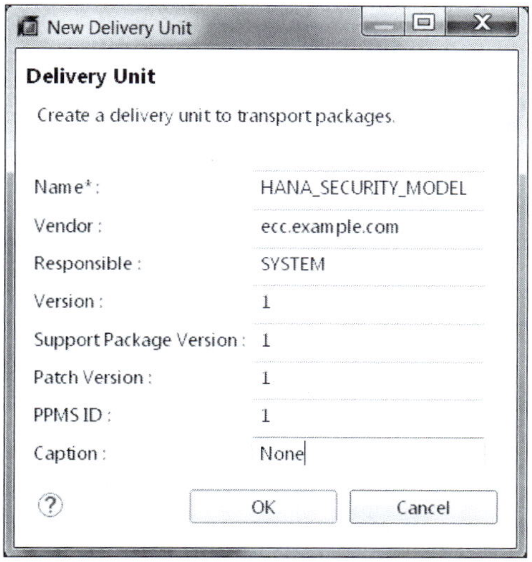

Figure 3.9 New Delivery Unit Configuration Window

We now need to assign packages to this delivery unit. After clicking **OK** in the **New Delivery Unit** configuration window, you should have been returned to the **Delivery Units** management window. To assign packages to our newly created delivery unit, first select the delivery unit within the **Delivery Units** section. To the right of the **Assigned Packages** section, click the **Add** button. A new window will appear, titled **Assign Packages** (see Figure 3.10).

To assign packages to the delivery unit, select the highest node level that contains all the appropriate packages, subpackages, and development artifacts. Make sure that the **Select all sub-packages under the selected nodes** checkbox is selected to ensure that all assigned subpackages are included within the delivery unit. Click **Finish** to complete the process. In Figure 3.11, the delivery unit named **HANA_SECURITY_MODEL** has been assigned the **Security**, **Security.Schemas**, and **Security.tables** packages. Click **Finish** to close the **Delivery Units** management window.

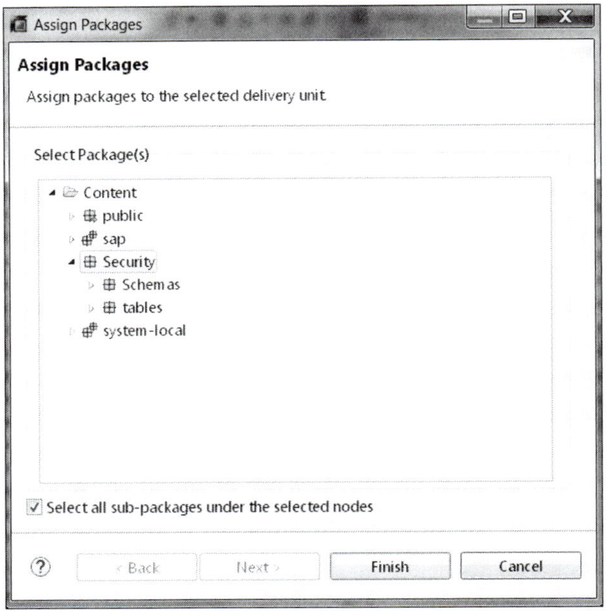

Figure 3.10 Assign Packages Window

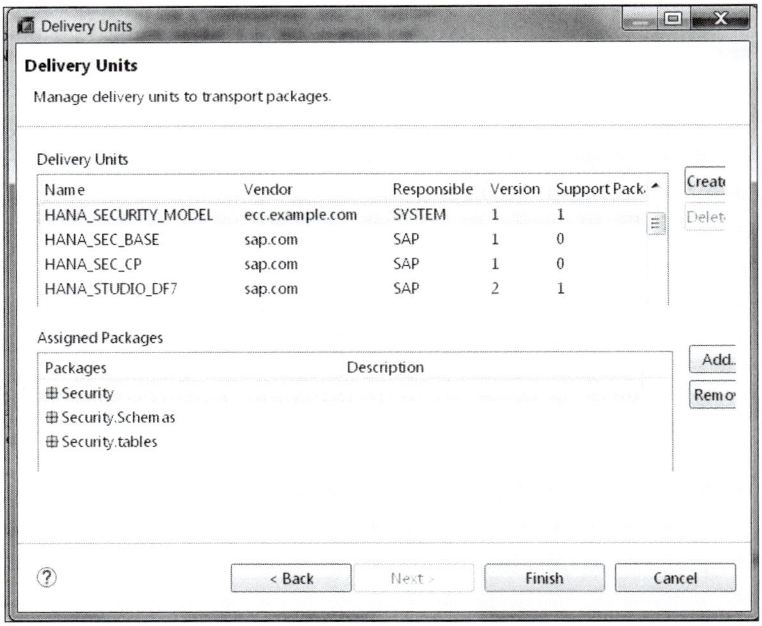

Figure 3.11 Packages Assigned to HANA_SECURITY_MODEL Delivery Unit

Managing Delivery Units and Establishing a Content Vendor Value

For more information and for alternative options available to manage a delivery unit or for alternative options for setting the content vendor, please refer to the SAP HANA Application Lifecycle Management Guide located at the following URL: *http://help.sap.com/hana_platform#section5.*

To access the guide directly in PDF format, visit *http://help.sap.com/hana/SAP_HANA_Application_Lifecycle_Management_en.pdf.*

Now that we've defined a delivery unity, we can use SAP HANA Studio to export our security model to a file. We can use this file as an import source, or we can share the file with others. To export the delivery unit, open SAP HANA Studio, then select **File • Export** from the menu bar.

A window titled **Export** will appear. Within the search box titled **Select and Export Destination**, enter "delivery unit". This will filter the available selections down to the desired option. Under the **SAP HANA Content** node, choose **Delivery Unit**. Click **Next**.

Select the SAP HANA system that will be the source of the delivery unit and click **Next**. Within the **Select Delivery Unit** window, use the dropdown menu titled **Delivery Unit** to choose the **HANA_SECURITY_MODEL** delivery unit. In the **Export Location** area, choose **Export to Client** and enter the folder location path and desired file name. Typically, the default file name is an acceptable name. Figure 3.12 shows the **Select Delivery Unit** window. Click **Next** to export the delivery unit to the specified file path.

The delivery unit file should now exist under the specified file path. Delivery unit files use a file extension of *TGZ*, commonly used on UNIX and Linux systems for files containing a compressed archive. Therefore, the delivery unit file in fact is a compressed archived containing all the SAP HANA development artifacts associated with the exported delivery unit. This file can be used as a source and imported into another SAP HANA system or even the same SAP HANA system. In most instances, these files provide an excellent backup mechanism for the content we create in the SAP HANA repository.

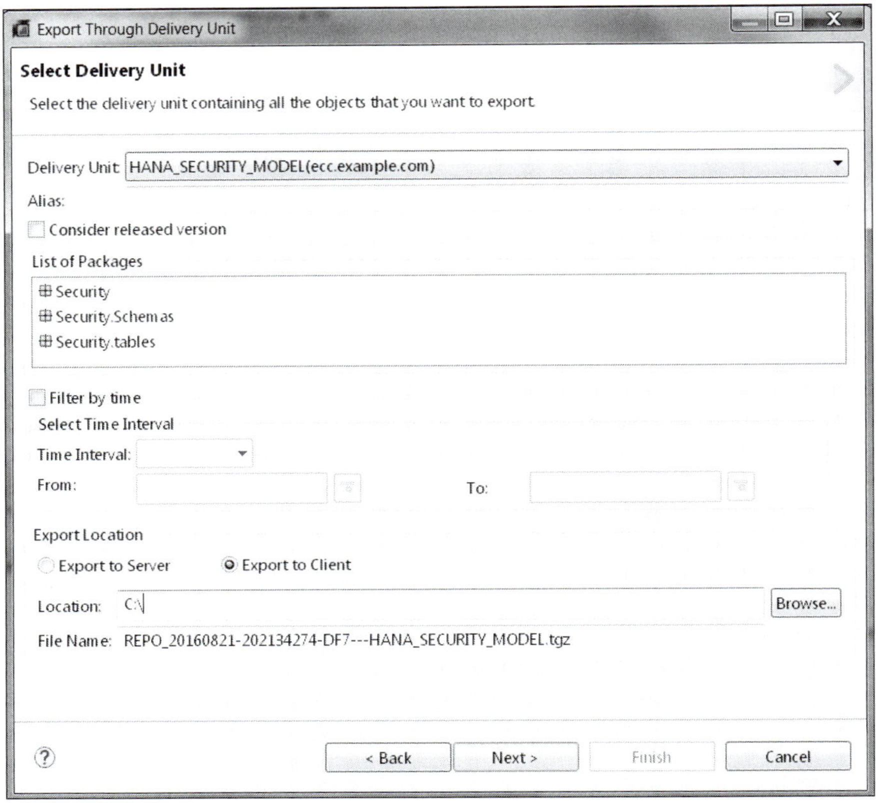

Figure 3.12 Delivery Unit Export Options Window

To import a delivery unit file, open SAP HANA Studio and log on to the desired SAP HANA system. From the menu bar, select **File • Import**. A window titled **Import** will appear. In the **Select an Import Source** search bar, type "delivery unit". Select **Delivery Unit** below the **SAP HANA Content** node, and click **Next**. A window will appear, containing the text **Target System** below the title **Import Through Delivery Unit**. In this window, select the system into which you want to import the delivery unit, and click **Next**. As shown in Figure 3.13, a **Select File** window will appear.

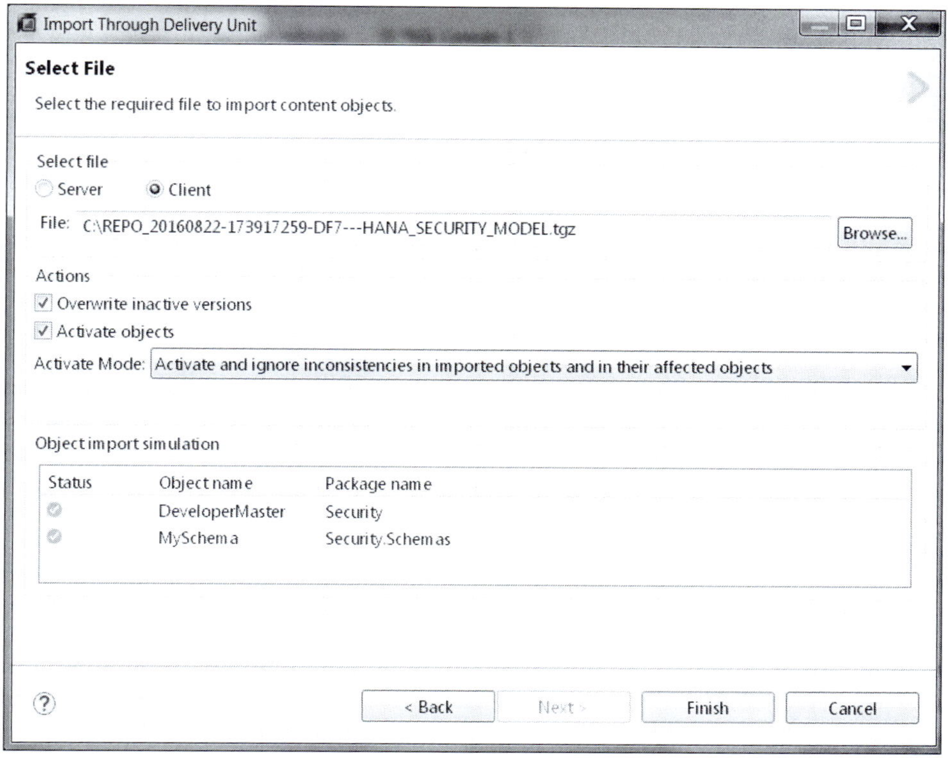

Figure 3.13 SAP HANA Delivery Unit Import Wizard Options

To import a file saved to your local file system, select the radio button labeled **Client** in the **Select file** area. Choose **Browse** to locate the file on your file system. In the **Actions** area, we typically recommend that both of the options **Overwrite inactive versions** and **Activate objects** are checked. This will both overwrite inactive versions in the target and active the newly imported content. The default **Activation Mode** of **Activate and ignore inconsistencies in imported object and in their affected objects** should be selected. The **Object import simulation** area will provide the expected import **Status** for the listed **Object name** and **Package name**. Click **Finish** to complete the import process. The status of the import process will be listed in the **Job Log** window. For more information about the **Job Log** window, see Chapter 1.

3.5 Case Study

E-Corporation is the world's largest robotics manufacturer and a large multinational conglomerate. The company has a large SAP ERP implementation and has recently purchased SAP HANA to facilitate a high-performance sales analytics data mart that combines data from multiple core SAP Business Suite systems and data from a few subsidiaries that are using non-SAP applications to manage their sales operations.

The new E-Corporation analytics project is still in its early phases. Developers are just starting to analyze and profile data from the various source systems. However, the director of analytics for E-Corporation is aware that extremely sensitive data will be hosted in the SAP HANA system. Because the data is sensitive in nature, implementing a sound security model is of the utmost importance. To help the E-Corporation team implement a sound security model, the company has contracted an SAP HANA security expert from a trusted consulting partner.

During initial project meetings, the security consultant recommends that E-Corporation start planning for the security model during the development phase. The security consultant knows that the development team needed to create several catalog tables and a few schemas to house the data from the various sources, and he highly recommends that the company begin the development process by creating two repository-based schemas to host the staging and data mart tables. The consultant also recommends that E-Corporation create repository-based tables to help simplify the development and management of a security model.

Before activating any repository-based objects, the security consultant recommends defining a package hierarchy to store the core repository objects that will be used to define the security model. (Chapter 1 provides the necessary information for creating packages and a package hierarchy.) Knowing that package privileges are critical to the security of the security model itself, the consultant recommends defining a top-level package named **Security**, followed by a subpackage named **Schemas** and another named **Roles**. Figure 3.14 shows the complete package hierarchy as viewed in the **Systems** tab of SAP HANA Studio.

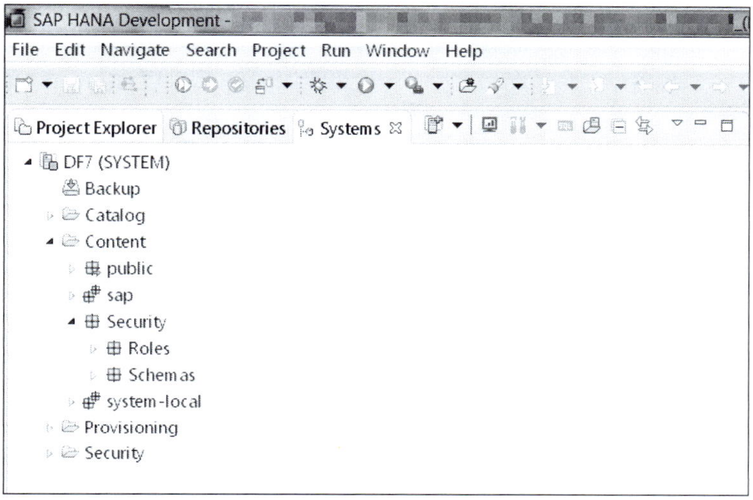

Figure 3.14 E-Corporation's Initial Package Hierarchy

E-Corporation decides to create two repository schemas (using the steps outlined in Section 3.3.1). The first schema will be named `StagingMart` and the second schema named `SalesMart`. The repository schemas will be activated within the SAP HANA package named `Security.Schemas`. The syntax for creating each repository schema is listed in Table 3.1.

Schema Name	Repository Schema Syntax
StagingMart	schema_name = "StagingMart";
SalesMart	schema_name = "SalesMart";

Table 3.1 Repository Schema Names and Syntax

Figure 3.15 shows what will be present in the package hierarchy. Under the subpackage **Schemas** will be two objects, both with the *.hdbschema* file extension. Each object or file is preceded by the name of the file and then the name of the schema.

Now that the schemas are in place, the developers can create tables to store the data. The security consultant recommends that the developers use repository-based tables, for two reasons. First, the developers won't need the CREATE ANY object privilege for the two schemas, which simplifies the security model. Second, repository tables can be promoted easily with the security model to other SAP HANA environments in order to support sound lifecycle management.

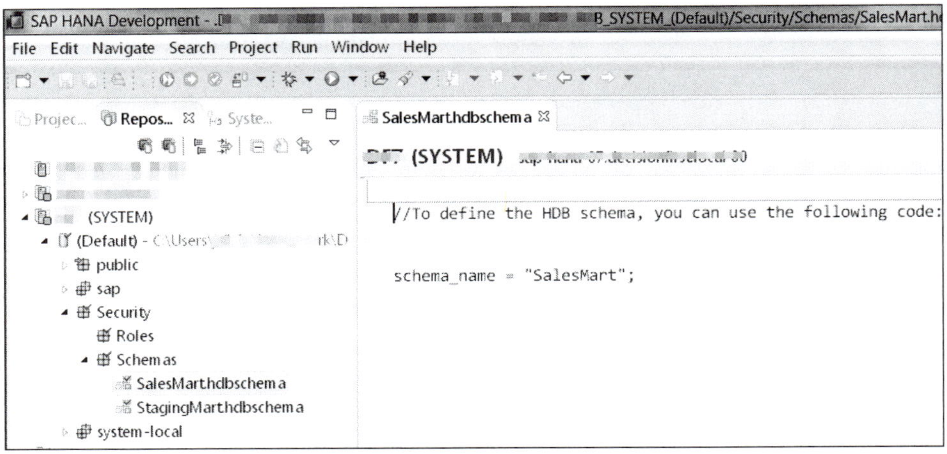

Figure 3.15 Development Repository Schema Artifacts and Corresponding Script Syntax

Because the tables created by the developers are expected to be secured in such a way that developers can frequently make changes, the security consultant recommends that E-Corporation create a new package hierarchy to store development artifacts that will be used by the development team for the sales analytics project. It's best to set up a separate package hierarchy in these instances, because it can be secured independently from the top-level security package. The consultant recommends that a top-level package named `e-corp` be created, and within it, the subpackage named `sales`. Within the `sales` package, he recommends that a package named `tables` be created. Figure 3.16 shows how the package hierarchy will appear within the **System** tab in SAP HANA Studio.

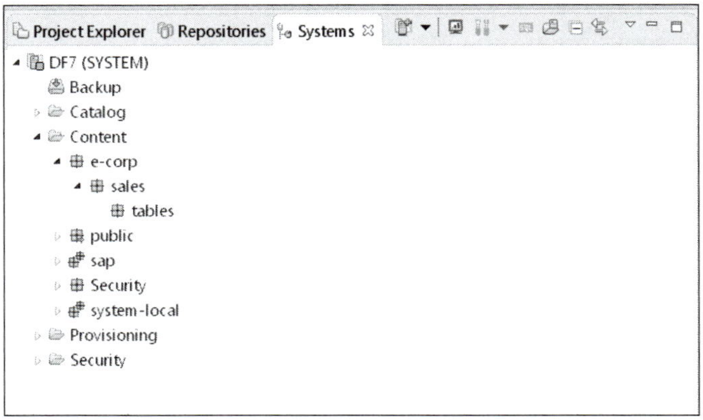

Figure 3.16 E-Corporation's Package Hierarchy

E-Corporation creates the STG_CUSTOMERS table (Listing 3.2) and the STG_PRODUCTS table (Listing 3.3) in the StagingMart schema (following the steps in Section 3.3.2). The repository tables are created within the e-corp.sales.tables package. The repository object type will be a database table or an HDBTABLE file.

```
// To define an HDB table with main SQL type columns, use the following code.
// In the following example, a schema should exist.
table.schemaName = "StagingMart";
table.tableType = COLUMNSTORE;
table.columns =
 [
    {name = "CustomerID";  sqlType = BIGINT;  comment = "Customer ID"; },
    {name = "CustomerName";  sqlType = NVARCHAR; length = 255; comment =
 "Customer Name";},
    {name = "CustomerAddressLine1";  sqlType = NVARCHAR; length =
 255; comment = "Customer Street Number and Name";},
    {name = "CustomerCity";  sqlType = NVARCHAR;  length = 255; comment =
 "Customer City";},
    {name = "CustomerLatt"; sqlType = DECIMAL; precision = 26; scale =
 6; comment = "Customer Location Latitude";},
    {name = "CustomerLong"; sqlType = DECIMAL; precision = 26; scale =
 6; comment = "Customer Location Longitude";}
];
table.primaryKey.pkcolumns = ["CustomerID"];
```

Listing 3.2 STG_CUSTOMERS Syntax

```
table.schemaName = "StagingMart";
table.tableType = COLUMNSTORE;
table.columns =
 [
    {name = "CustomerID";  sqlType = BIGINT;  comment = "Customer ID"; },
    {name = "CustomerName";  sqlType = NVARCHAR; length = 255;
comment = "Customer Name";},
    {name = "CustomerAddressLine1";  sqlType = NVARCHAR;
length = 255; comment = "Customer Street Number and Name";},
    {name = "CustomerCity";  sqlType = NVARCHAR;  length = 255;
comment = "Customer City";},
    {name = "CustomerLatt"; sqlType = DECIMAL; precision = 26;
scale = 6; comment = "Customer Location Latitude";},
```

```
    {name = "CustomerLong"; sqlType = DECIMAL; precision = 26;
scale = 6; comment = "Customer Location Longitude";}
];
table.primaryKey.pkcolumns = ["CustomerID"];
```

Listing 3.3 STG_PRODUCTS Syntax

Once the two repository table scripts are activated, two new tables will be visible within the `StagingMart` schema. The names of the tables are shown in Figure 3.17, in the **Systems** tab, under **Catalog • StagingMart • Tables**. Notice how the name of the runtime version of each table includes the repository package hierarchy name and two colons.

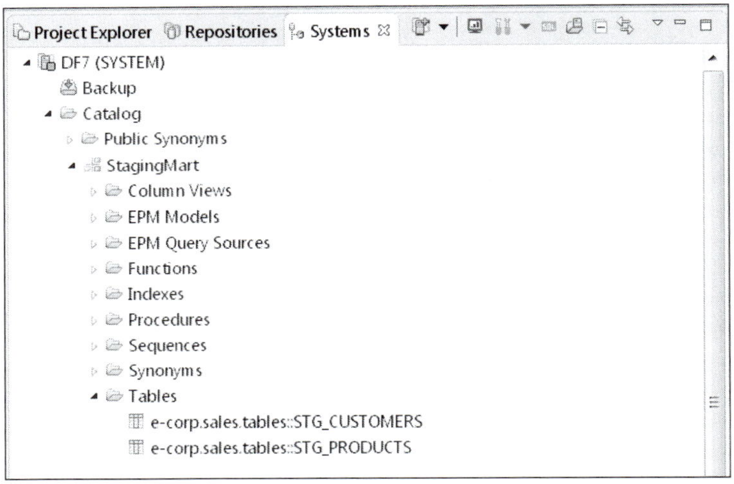

Figure 3.17 Repository Tables Created in StagingMart Schema

SAP HANA requires unique object names for all runtime versions of objects created within the repository. To achieve this requirement, the package hierarchy name is automatically included as a prefix for every catalog object created within the repository.

E-Corporation now has two design-time and runtime versions of each schema and table. The foundation for a sound security model has been implemented. Developers that have been granted privileges for these objects can now begin loading data into these SAP HANA tables. Security administrators can relax, knowing that their security model can be transported and backed up.

3.6 Summary

In this chapter, you learned about catalog objects. How you choose to create catalog objects is one of the most important factors that effects the type of security model and security process that will be implemented. If you create standard catalog objects, then developers and security administrators constantly will need to follow tedious processes for the model to be maintained. However, if you choose to create repository-based catalog objects, then developers mostly can be decoupled from the security model maintenance process. In addition, the security model and its dependent catalog objects can be transported easily to another system or into a backup file.

In the next chapter, we'll dive deeper into the security model by exploring the processes necessary for provisioning users. We'll also discuss the processes necessary to assign privileges and roles to a user account.

Chapter 4
User Accounts

In this chapter, we'll provide a complete overview of user accounts, including the processes used to provision, maintain, grant privileges to, and grant roles to user accounts.

Before a person, application, or service can interact with the SAP HANA system, it must be *authenticated*. To authenticate with SAP HANA, the person, application, or service must issue credentials. These credentials are typically validated in the form of a *user account* and a *password*. The authentication process is designed to uniquely identify the person, application, or service, because SAP HANA supports *authorizations* for each individual user account. *Authorization* is the process whereby SAP HANA determines the types of actions that the user account can perform, and these authorizations come in the form of granted privileges.

In Chapter 2, we introduced the concept of privileges and the different types of privileges within SAP HANA. Privileges can be granted to user accounts or they can be granted to roles, and roles can then be granted to one or more user accounts. Inevitably, privileges authorize a user account to perform specific actions within SAP HANA, and so there exists an important relationship between privileges and the user accounts that they are assigned to.

This chapter will introduce you to the process of creating user accounts, managing user accounts, assigning privileges to user accounts, and assigning roles to user accounts. As you will discover, there are multiple ways to perform these actions, such as via SQL statements or GUIs.

4.1 What Are User Accounts?

A *user account* is essentially an object in the SAP HANA system that stores a user name, password, and other attributes pertaining to the user account. User names can be defined with any alpha character from A–Z or numbers 0–9, and they also support the use of an underscore. Most special characters, such as a period, colon, equal sign, space, comma, and many others, are not supported within a user name. By default, passwords must be defined based on the system's configured standards for complexity. User accounts also contain other attributes, such as email address, SAML identity, Kerberos identity, locale, statement memory limit, and time zone. There are three different types of user accounts we can create, as we'll explore in the following subsections.

4.1.1 Standard User Accounts

A *standard user account* is one that is assigned the public role by default. When we use GUI interfaces within SAP HANA, a standard user account is created, and when we issue a CREATE USER SQL statement, a standard user account is created. Standard users have minimal access to SAP HANA by default. Each standard user account is provided a user schema. The user will have the CREATE ANY object privilege for its home schema. Any object created within that home schema will be owned by the user, which therefore will have full control of those objects. However, the standard user will also have any of the privileges assigned to the *public role*, which grants access to several individual catalog objects within SYS and other _SYS_* schemas. When queried or executed, most of these catalog objects provide metadata pertaining to other objects within the system. For example, without the public role, a user would not be able to access SAP HANA Studio.

Standard user accounts are created for a variety of purposes. There are three subtypes of standard user accounts that we can create, each of which has a different purpose:

1. **Individual accounts**
   These accounts are set up to support an individual person. For example, each individual in an organization is assigned an account so that he or she can query SAP HANA information views.
2. **Service accounts**
   Service accounts are used by software applications to delegate access to the SAP HANA system. For example, an external reporting system uses a dedicated service account to query SAP HANA information views. In this case, access to SAP HANA is delegated via a single standard SAP HANA user account. Every user in the reporting system authenticates using the shared service account credentials.
3. **Application accounts**
   Applications sometimes need dedicated accounts to perform actions within SAP HANA system. For example, when we install SAP S/4HANA, the SAP NetWeaver

application server will need a dedicated SAP HANA account to supply the application with the necessary SAP HANA access and a schema for storing the application's tables.

4.1.2 Technical User Accounts

Technical user accounts are essentially standard user accounts—but they're set up with the express purpose of supporting administrative and developer users within the SAP HANA landscape. As we've noted before, if we delete a user account in SAP HANA, all objects that user account owns and all privileges it grants are also removed. To avoid this potential disaster, we recommend that all administrative users be given special use accounts that will, by policy and procedure, never be deleted from the system. Such accounts technically can still be deleted from the system, but a special naming convention should be implemented for these accounts to help avoid any accidental deletions. For example, we can create the account TECH_JHAUN to facilitate the implementation of a security model. As other technical user accounts are needed, they will also be prefixed with TECH_ to identify their importance. This should signal to other administrative users that these accounts should never be deleted from the system.

It's best to use repository objects when developing catalog objects in SAP HANA, because those objects are owned by the built-in technical user, called _SYS_REPO. This account technically never can be deleted from the system. The same is true of our security model. If we're using repository-based roles, their privileges will be granted as for the system account _SYS_REPO. You might ask, if we're using these best practices, then why would we need to create technical user accounts?

In the current landscape, you should set up a technical user account to support users performing administrative tasks within SAP HANA. Our security model should strive to ensure that all objects and privileges are owned and granted by _SYS_REPO. There still are specific use cases in which a schema and other catalog objects can't be created in the development repository. In such cases, we need technical user accounts to preserve any privileges granted to other users or roles.

Some organizations might choose to use the built-in SYSTEM account to perform administrative actions. The SYSTEM account can't be deleted and therefore can serve as an excellent technical user account. However, when an organization chooses to use this account, it loses accountability, or the ability to audit administrative activity. If multiple individuals are using the same SYSTEM account to perform administrate activities, it will be very difficult—if not impossible—to identify which individual performed a specific action. Therefore, from a security audit standpoint, we don't recommend that organizations use the SYSTEM account in this fashion.

4.1.3 Restricted User Accounts

Unlike standard and technical user accounts, a restricted user account is technically very different, because it has a unique process for creation, it can't be granted the public role in SAP HANA 1.0, it doesn't have `CREATE ANY` privileges granted for its own schema, and it's denied ODBC/JDBC access by default. Restricted users typically only have limited HTTP or HTTPS access to the system. They're ideally intended to support user access to custom applications developed in the SAP XS engine. However, they can be used for the express purpose of providing extremely limited access to an SAP HANA RDBMS. Although this is not a requirement, the security administrator will need to grant privileges that are typically granted through the PUBLIC role to the restricted users before they can use the RDBMS.

It's important to note that restricted users can't be converted to standard users or vice versa in SAP HANA 1.0. However, in SAP HANA 2.0, we can convert restricted users to standard users or vice versa. (For more information, see Chapter 18.)

Restricted user access is limited to such a degree that they can't use a SQL console or SAP HANA Studio until additional privileges or roles are granted to the account. For example, to allow the restricted user basic SQL statement query access via ODBC or JDBC, we must perform the following steps:

1. Enable the user property **ODBC/JDBC Access**. This can be completed in SAP HANA Studio user management or by issuing the following SQL statement: `ALTER USER <USER> ENABLE CLIENT CONNECT`.
2. Grant the RESTRICTED_USER_ODBC_ACCESS role.
3. Grant the RESTRICTED_USER_JDBC_ACCESS role.
4. Grant `SELECT` on the catalog objects containing the data

If that same user requires minimal SAP HANA Studio access, that user would need `SELECT` granted on the `SYS.M_SERVICE` system table in addition to the previous steps. This level of access would only allow the user to log on to SAP HANA Studio, use the SQL console, and execute a SQL `SELECT` statement.

Restricted users can be created in two ways: We can issue a special SQL `CREATE` statement, or we can use the SAP HANA Studio GUI. To create a restricted user using a SQL statement, use the following syntax:

```
CREATE RESTRICTED USER <USER> PASSWORD <PASSWORD>
```

Replace `<USER>` with a desired user name and `<PASSWORD>` with the desired initial password.

Alternately, we can use SAP HANA Studio. To access the restricted user GUI, go to the **Systems** tab, expand the **Security** node, and right-click the **User** node. From the context menu, choose **New Restricted User** (see Figure 4.1). A new editing window will appear that allows you to define the restricted user account.

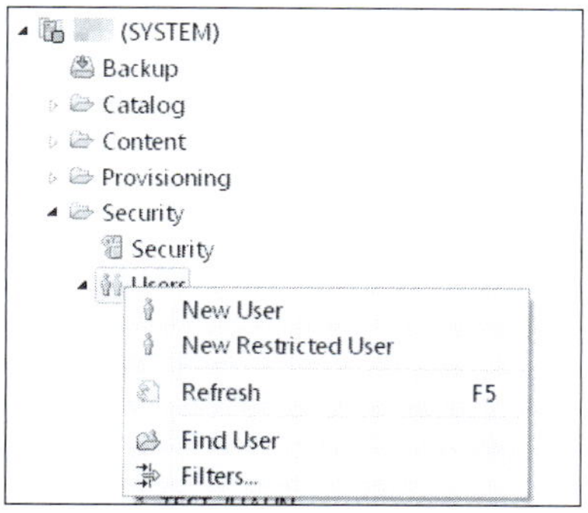

Figure 4.1 Creating Restricted User via SAP HANA Studio

In the next sections, we'll provide more details about the process to create standard, restricted, and technical user accounts. We'll review the SQL statement and SAP HANA Studio options.

4.2 Creating and Managing User Accounts

At a high level, there are three different ways to create user accounts within SAP HANA. We can use SQL statements based on the `CREATE USER` or `CREATE RESTRICTED USER` syntax or use one of two different GUIs. SAP HANA Studio provides a GUI for creating user accounts, and another GUI for creating user accounts is hosted in the SAP HANA XS engine, within the SAP HANA Web-Based Development Workbench security manager. In this section, we'll discuss the three different options to provision and manage user accounts and how we can use system views to query the system for details about user accounts. In conclusion, we'll discuss the options for and ramifications of deleting user accounts.

4.2.1 Creating and Managing Users with SQL Statements

Using SQL, we can create, alter, and drop user accounts. We can also specify additional properties for the user, such as adding third-party authentication identities, email addresses, and limitations for memory utilization. Let's look at a few example SQL statements.

Creating user accounts using SQL statements involves issuing `CREATE USER` or `CREATE RESTRICTED USER` statements. To create a standard user, issue the following statement:

```
CREATE USER <USERNAME> PASSWORD <PASSWORD>
```

Replace `<USERNAME>` with the desired user name and `<PASSWORD>` with the desired password. It's often best to wrap the specified password in double quotation marks to allow for special characters.

We can also create restricted users using SQL. To create a restricted user named REPORTSERVICE, use the following SQL statement:

```
CREATE RESTRICTED USER REPORTSERVICE PASSWORD "@134545DdfSD34";
```

To create the user JONATHAN with SAML authentication enabled for the SAML provider `ac_saml_provider`, use the following SQL statement:

```
CREATE USER JONATHAN PASSWORD "Password1" WITH IDENTITY ANY FOR SAML PROVIDER
TEST_SAML_PROVIDER;
```

To create a user with an X509 certificate authentication identity, use the following SQL statement, with your own required details:

```
CREATE USER JONATHAN PASSWORD "Password1" WITH IDENTITY 'C=US, ST=GA,
L=Atlanta, O=ecorp.com, CN=JONATHAN'
ISSUER 'C=US, ST=GA, L=Atlanta, O=ecorp.com, CN=Root CA' FOR X509;
```

We can also use SQL to manage user accounts, such as deleting a user account with a `DROP USER` statement. For example, to delete the user account JONATHAN, use the following SQL statement:

```
DROP USER JONATHAN;
```

To change a user account's properties, we can issue `ALTER USER` statements. For example, to force the user account JONATHAN to change its password at their next logon, use the following SQL statement:

```
ALTER USER JONATHAN FORCE PASSWORD CHANGE;
```

The ALTER USER syntax can also be used to unlock a user account that was disabled due to multiple failed logon attempts. The syntax to reset the number of invalid connection attempts and activate a user account is as follows:

```
ALTER USER JONATHAN RESET CONNECT ATTEMPTS;
```

To enable an account that was explicitly disabled by the administrator, use the following syntax:

```
ALTER USER JONATHAN ACTIVATE;
```

To disable SAML authentication for the user, use the following syntax:

```
ALTER USER JONATHAN DISABLE SAML;
```

To enable Kerberos and add a Kerberos identity, use the following syntax:

```
ALTER USER JONATHAN ADD IDENTITY 'testkerberosName' FOR KERBEROS;
ALTER USER JONATHAN ENABLE KERBEROS;
```

It's sometimes necessary to modify a user account to prevent the system's default settings from expiring passwords of a specific age. To prevent a user account's password from expiring, use the following syntax:

```
ALTER USER JONATHAN DISABLE PASSWORD LIFETIME;
```

To limit the amount of system memory in gigabytes that an individual user account can consume with a given SQL statement, use the following syntax:

```
ALTER USER JONATHAN SET PARAMETER STATEMENT MEMORY LIMIT = 5;
```

To disable an individual user's memory restrictions, use the following syntax:

```
ALTER USER JONATHAN CLEAR PARAMETER STATEMENT MEMORY LIMIT;
```

4.2.2 Creating and Managing Users in SAP HANA Studio

We can also create and manage user accounts in SAP HANA Studio. To access the user management GUI, start by switching to the administration console perspective. Under the **Systems** tab, located on the left side of the screen, expand the **System** node and then the **Security** node to reveal the **Security**, **Users**, and **Roles** nodes. Expand the **Users** node to reveal user accounts defined in the system.

To create a user account, right-click the **Users** node and choose **New User**. A tabbed window labeled **New User** will appear in the right-hand window (see Figure 4.2).

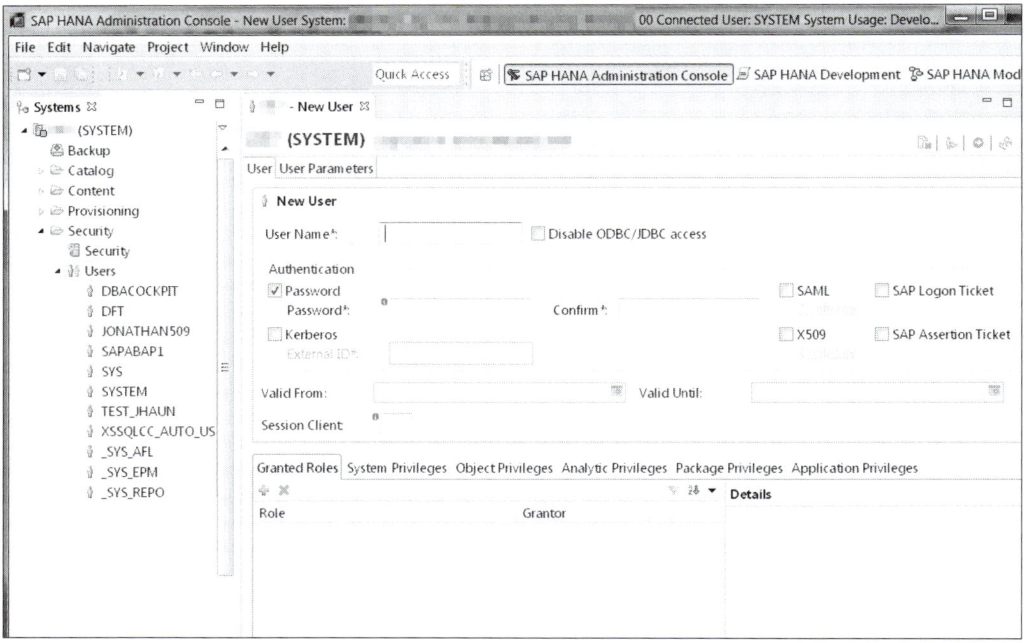

Figure 4.2 New User in SAP HANA Studio

To specify the name of the user account, enter the desired name in the mandatory **User Name:** field. In the authentication section, enter the desired password in the **Password:** field. Confirm the password in the **Confirm:** field. Specify a valid date and time using the **Valid From:** and **Valid Until:** fields. At a minimum, you must specify a user name and password for each new user account; all other elements are optional.

To define third-party authentication information, look for the checkboxes labeled **SAML**, **SAP Logon Ticket**, **X509**, and **SAP Assertion Ticket**. If the third-party authentication option can be configured further, you'll see a blue **Configure** link just below the checkbox.

At the bottom of the **New User** tab, you'll see six tabs: **Granted Roles**, **System Privileges**, **Object Privileges**, **Analytic Privileges**, **Package Privileges**, and **Application Privileges**. Click each tab to see options to grant or revoke the applicable privileges. In

Chapter 4 and Chapter 5, we'll provide more details about how to use these tabs to grant privileges. Note that it's better to grant roles to a user than to specify individual privileges for each user.

Once you've defined the required options, press F8 or CTRL+S, or click the **Save** or **Execute** icons, to activate the new user account. Check the status bar at the top of the new user window to validate that the user account was created. If there were any issues creating the account, red text will appear, containing a summary of the issue. If the account creation process was successful, the status window will read **User <'Account Name'> Created**.

When a user account is disabled or deactivated due to multiple failed logons, SAP HANA Studio user management provides an interface to re-enable the account. This same interface can also be used to explicitly disable the user account.

To access this interface, double-click a user account listed in the **users** node. The **User Account Management** tab will appear, much like the **New User Account** window discussed earlier. At the top-right-hand side of the interface, note the icon in the shape of a standing person, with an arrow pointing either left or right beside it (see Figure 4.3).

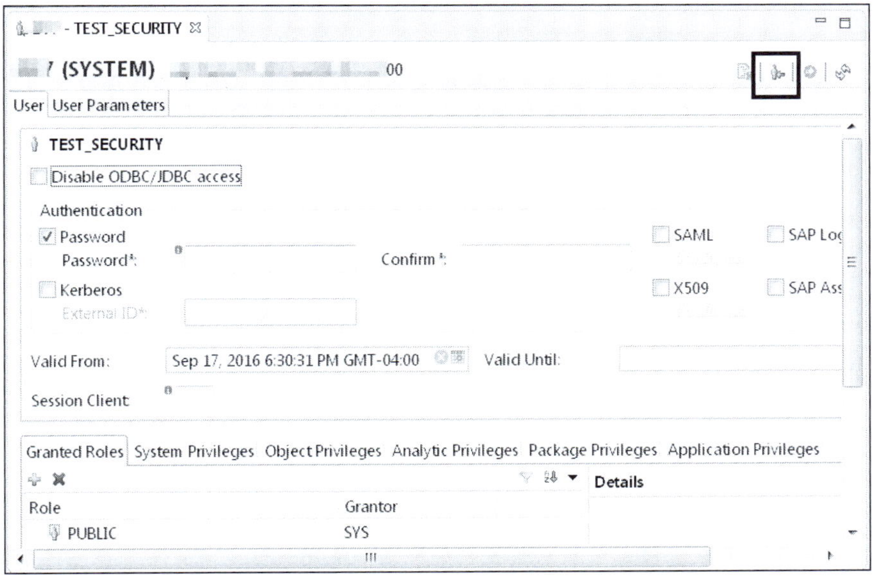

Figure 4.3 Interface to Enable or Disable User Account

If the account is currently disabled, clicking this icon will enable the account. If the account is currently active, clicking this icon will disable the account.

4.2.3 Creating and Managing Users with SAP HANA Web-Based Development Workbench

The SAP HANA Web-Based Development Workbench security manager, hosted within the XS engine, provides a GUI to create users, create roles, or manage security.

You can access the SAP HANA Web-Based Development Workbench via a supported Internet browser. The following URL can be customized to match the details of your environment:

http://<sap_hana_host>:80<instance_number>/sap/hana/ide/security

Replace <sap_hana_host> with the hostname of the SAP HANA system in your environment and <instance_number> with the two-digit instance corresponding to your SAP HANA system (e.g., *http://sap-hana.myhost.com:8000/sap/hana/ide/security*).

For secure access, use *https://<sap_hana_host>:43<instance_number>/sap/hana/ide/security* (e.g., *https://sap-hana.myhost.com:4300/sap/hana/ide/security*).

To use the SAP HANA Web-Based Development Workbench security manager, the user account first will need to be granted one of the roles listed in Table 4.1. Users only need one of the two roles to access the security manager.

Role Name	Summary
sap.hana.ide.roles::SecurityAdmin	Within the SAP HANA Web-Based Development Workbench, the user will only be able to access the security manager; the security manager provides interfaces to create and manage users and roles.
sap.hana.ide.roles::Developer	This role grants a higher level of privileges for users that need full access to the SAP HANA Web-Based Development Workbench. It grants access to the editor, catalog, and security interfaces. It's considered the parent to the sap.hana.ide.roles::SecurityAdmin role.

Table 4.1 Roles Required to Use Security Manager

Additional Privileges Needed to Use the Security Manager

Note that the roles in Table 4.1 simply allow the granted user access to the GUI. To manage a security model, additional privileges and roles will need to be granted. For example, the user will need the system privilege `USER ADMIN` to crate users and the system privilege `ROLE ADMIN` to create roles. To grant privileges to a user or role, the account accessing the security manager will also require privileges to grant the privileges to other users or roles.

To create a user within the security manager, expand the **Security • Users** nodes located on the left side of the interface. Right-click the **Users** node and choose **New User**. A tab labeled **New User** will appear to the right side of the browser window (see Figure 4.4).

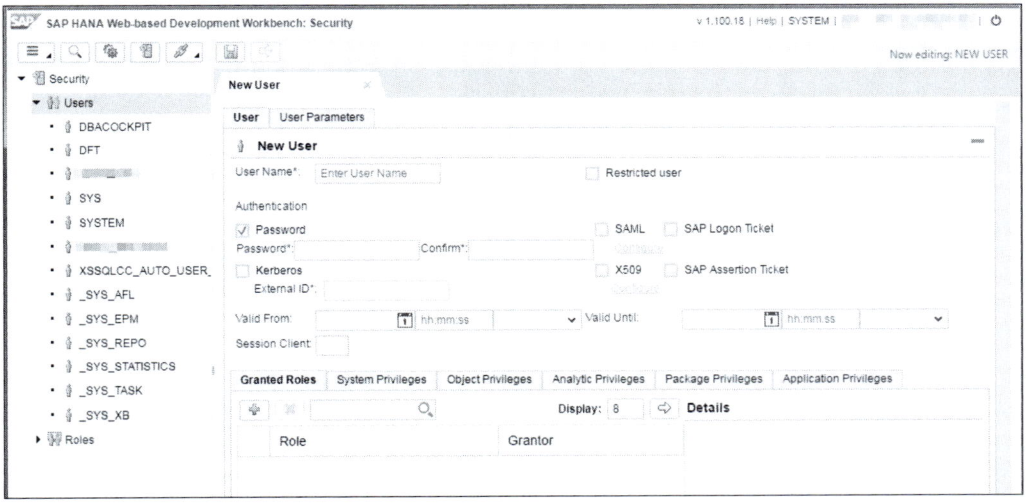

Figure 4.4 New User Tab in Security Manager

To specify the name of the user account, enter the desired name in the mandatory **User Name:** field. In the **Authentication** section, enter the desired password in the **Password:** field. Confirm the password in the **Confirm:** field. Specify a valid date and time using the **Valid From:** and **Valid Until:** fields. At a minimum, you must specify a user name and password for each new user account; all other elements are optional.

To define third-party authentication information, look for the checkboxes labeled **SAML**, **SAP Logon Ticket**, **X509** or **SAP Assertion Ticket**. If the third-party authentication option can be configured further, you'll see a grey **Configure** link below it.

At the bottom of the **New User** tab, you'll see six tabs: **Granted Roles**, **System Privileges**, **Object Privileges**, **Analytic Privileges**, **Package Privileges**, and **Application Privileges**. Click each tab to see options to grant or revoke the applicable privileges (discussed in more detail in Chapter 5 and Chapter 6). Note that it's better to grant roles to a user than to specify individual privileges for each individual user.

To activate the new user, click the disk icon located at the top of the security manager screen. Clicking the icon will save and activate the changes. Note that the activation status window is located at the bottom of the interface and has a black-colored background. If there are any errors encountered during activation, red text will appear, indicating the issue.

In the next section, we'll discuss the how we can use SQL statements and system views to view all users provisioned in the system.

4.2.4 User Account System Views

There are two main system views that we can query to view and locate user accounts defined in the system. These read-only views are very when we need to locate users based on their configured attributes and when we need to programmatically provision user accounts.

The first system view can be found in the SYS schema and is named `USERS`. To query the view directly, issue the following SQL statement in a SQL console:

```
SELECT * FROM "SYS"."USERS";
```

Most user attributes are found in this system view. Using SQL statements, we can use the attribute columns to filter the list according to the attributes we need to isolate to find the user account. Table 4.2 defines the columns available in this system view.

View Column Name	Column Comments or Description
USER_NAME	Name of the user
USER_ID	ID of the user
USER_MODE	Mode of the user: `LOCAL/GLOBAL/EXTERNAL`
EXTERNAL_IDENTITY	External identity of the user
CREATOR	Creator of the user
CREATE_TIME	Creation time
VALID_FROM	Start time of user's validity
VALID_UNTIL	End time of user's validity

Table 4.2 Columns Available in SYS.USERS View

View Column Name	Column Comments or Description
LAST_SUCCESSFUL_CONNECT	Time of the last successful connection of the user
LAST_INVALID_CONNECT_ATTEMPT	Time of the last invalid connection attempt
INVALID_CONNECT_ATTEMPTS	Number of invalid connection attempts since last successful attempt
ADMIN_GIVEN_PASSWORD	Specifies if the password was given by an administrator or by the user himself: TRUE/FALSE
PASSWORD_CHANGE_TIME	Time of last password change; NULL if password lifetime won't be checked for this user
PASSWORD_CHANGE_NEEDED	Specifies if user is forced to change his password himself: TRUE/FALSE
USER_DEACTIVATED	Specifies if user is deactivated: TRUE/FALSE
DEACTIVATION_TIME	Time given with explicit deactivation command for this user
IS_PASSWORD_ENABLED	Specifies if authentication using password is enabled: TRUE/FALSE
IS_KERBEROS_ENABLED	Specifies if authentication using Kerberos is enabled: TRUE/FALSE
IS_SAML_ENABLED	Specifies if authentication using SAML is enabled: TRUE/FALSE
IS_X509_ENABLED	Specifies if authentication using an X.509 certificate is enabled: TRUE/FALSE
IS_SAP_LOGON_TICKET_ENABLED	Specifies if authentication using an SAP logon ticket is enabled: TRUE/FALSE
IS_SAP_ASSERTION_TICKET_ENABLED	Specifies if authentication using an SAP assertion ticket is enabled: TRUE/FALSE
IS_RESTRICTED	Specifies if user was created as a restricted user: TRUE/FALSE

Table 4.2 Columns Available in SYS.USERS View (Cont.)

View Column Name	Column Comments or Description
IS_CLIENT_CONNECT_ ENABLED	When TRUE, the user can connect using the ODBC/JDBC protocols. When FALSE, the user cannot use the ODBC/ JDBC protocols to connect to SAP HANA.
HAS_REMOTE_USERS	Specifies if user has remote identity mapping: TRUE/ FALSE

Table 4.2 Columns Available in SYS.USERS View (Cont.)

The second system view also can be found in the SYS schema and is named USER_ PARAMETERS. To query the view directly, issue the following SQL statement in a SQL console:

```
SELECT * FROM "SYS"."USER_PARAMETERS";
```

This view returns a record for each combination of user and user parameter. For example, if the user has an email address and a statement memory limit defined, there will be two records returned for the user account. If the user has four parameters defined, there will be four records returned. Understanding the table's cardinality as it relates back to SYS.USERS will be important when defining custom programs that provision user accounts. Table 4.3 defines the columns available in this system view.

View Column Name	Column Comments or Description
USER_NAME	Name of the user
PARAMETER	Name of the parameter
VALUE	Parameter value

Table 4.3 Columns Available in SYS.USER_PARAMETERS View

The two views can be joined together to produce a listing of user attributes and their defined parameters. For example, the SQL statement in Listing 4.1 will return all user attributes, the email address parameter, and the defined memory statement limit for the user account.

```
SELECT
U.*,
E."VALUE" as EMAIL_ADDRESS,
M."VALUE" AS STATEMENT_MEMORY_LIMIT
```

```
FROM "SYS"."USERS" U
LEFT OUTER JOIN "SYS"."USER_PARAMETERS" E
ON (U.USER_NAME = E.USER_NAME and E.PARAMETER = 'EMAIL ADDRESS')
LEFT OUTER JOIN "SYS"."USER_PARAMETERS" M
ON (U.USER_NAME = M.USER_NAME and M.PARAMETER = 'STATEMENT MEMORY LIMIT')
```

Listing 4.1 Example SQL Statement for User Attributes and Email Address

In addition to using SQL, we can also preview these system views using SAP HANA Studio. To do so, expand **Systems • Catalog • SYS • Views** to see a list of system views defined. Right-click the **Views** node and choose **Filters...**, then enter the filter pattern "USER" and click **OK**. A list of views containing the phrase "USER" will appear. Right-click the desired view and choose **Open Data Preview** or **Open Content** to query the view (see Figure 4.5).

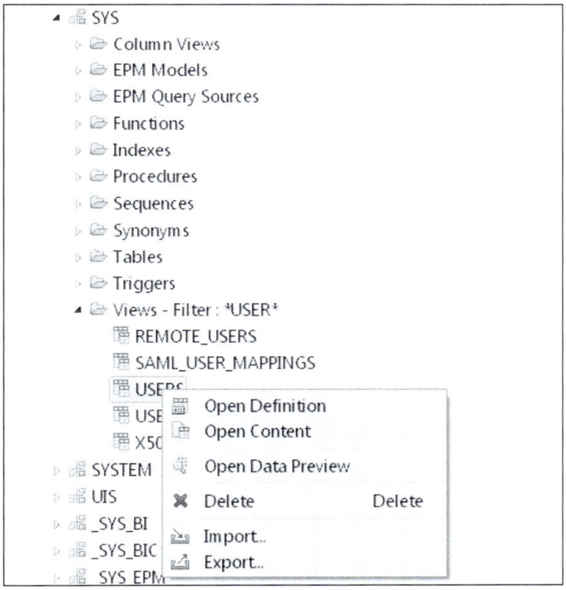

Figure 4.5 Using SAP HANA Studio to View User Account System Views

4.2.5 Deleting User Accounts

Deleting user accounts is accomplished using the DROP USER SQL statement, SAP HANA Studio, or the SAP HANA Web-Based Development Workbench security manager. The process may be very easy to execute, but the ramifications of deleting some user accounts can be profound.

When we delete user accounts, we must remember that the system will remove objects those users have created and privileges they've granted, so we need to use care. In this section, we'll review the options for deleting user accounts and discuss the ramifications for objects owned by the users and privileges that were granted by the users.

Deleting User with SQL

To delete a user account with SQL, issue the `DROP USER` statement. The following SQL statements can be used to delete a user account:

```
DROP USER my_user;
DROP USER my_user CASCADE;
DROP USER my_user RESTRICT;
```

In the last two statements, note the `RESTRICT` and `CASCADE` options. If no option is specified, the system defaults to the `RESTRICT` option.

The `RESTRICT` option will prevent the deletion of the user account if other user accounts own objects within schemas also owned by the to-be-deleted user. The `RESTRICT` option will also prevent the deletion if the to-be-deleted user has created objects in a schema that it doesn't own. The command will only execute if the following two conditions are true:

1. The to-be-deleted user owns all the objects in schemas that it owns. No other user can own objects in this user's schemas.
2. All the user's objects are in a schema that it owns. The user can't have objects in a foreign schema owned by another user.

The `CASCADE` option will remove all objects owned by the user and revoke all privileges granted by the user. It will perform the following actions:

- All schemas owned by the user will be deleted.
- All objects in all schemas owned by the user will be deleted, including objects created by other users.
- All objects that reference catalog objects owned by the deleted user will be deleted.
- All public synonyms owned by the deleted user will be deleted.
- All privileges granted to objects deleted will be revoked.

- All privileges granted by the deleted user will be revoked.
- *Note*: User accounts created by the deleted user are not affected.
- *Note*: Database roles created by the deleted user are not affected. However, privileges granted within those roles by the deleted user will be revoked.
- *Note*: Audit policies created by the deleted user are not affected.
- User accounts will be deleted, even if they have an active session.

Given the ramifications of using the CASCADE option, user accounts should only be deleted with this option if the user account isn't used to create meaningful catalog objects or isn't used to set up security. As mentioned earlier, technical user accounts should be created for this reason, and such accounts should never be deleted from the system.

Deleting Users with SAP HANA Studio

SAP HANA Studio offers a user management area to help administrators delete user accounts. To access the user management GUI, start by switching to the administration console perspective. In the **Systems** tab, located on the left side, expand the **System** node and then the **Security** node to reveal the **Security**, **Users**, and **Roles** nodes. Expand the **Users** node to reveal user accounts defined in the system.

To delete a user account, right-click it in the list and choose **Delete**. A confirmation window containing two delete options will appear (see Figure 4.6). As with the DELETE USER SQL syntax, we must choose one of two delete options (**Restrict** or **Cascade**).

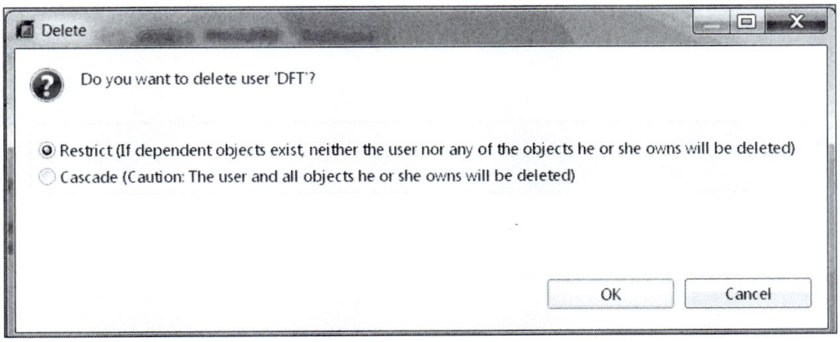

Figure 4.6 Delete User Confirmation and Options Window in SAP HANA Studio

The default **Restrict** option will prevent the account deletion if any dependent objects owned by the user or any foreign objects not owned by the user exist in schemas owned by the deleted user. The **Cascade** option will delete the user and all its objects, as well as any privileges granted by the user. Select and option by choosing the radio button to its left. With the desired option selected, click **OK** to execute the delete action. If no errors appear, the account was deleted successfully. Next, we'll look at the workflow to delete users in the SAP HANA Web-Based Development Workbench security manager.

Deleting Users with SAP HANA Web-Based Development Workbench

As mentioned previously, the SAP HANA Web-Based Development Workbench security manager provides an interface for creating and managing both user accounts and roles. The following example URLS can be used as templates when constructing the links specific to your environment:

http://<sap_hana_host>: 80<instance_number>/sap/hana/ide/security

https://<sap_hana_host>: 43<instance_number>/sap/hana/ide/security

Once you have access and if your account has the appropriate privileges, you will be able to delete user accounts. To delete users via the security manager, expand the **Security** node, followed by the **Users** node. A list of users within the system will appear. Right-click the user account that you want to delete, and choose **Delete**. A pop-up confirmation and options window titled **Delete User** will appear (see Figure 4.7).

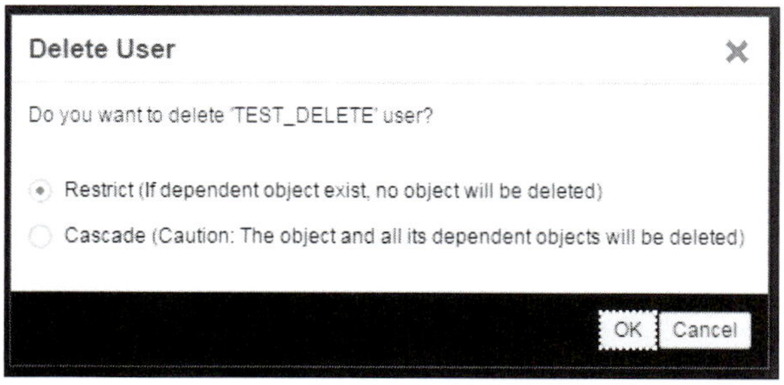

Figure 4.7 Delete User Confirmation and Options Window in SAP HANA Web-Based Development Workbench

Choose the **Restrict** or **Cascade** option, then choose **OK** to delete the user account. The two options work exactly as described in the previous two sections. The window will disappear, and the delete action status will appear in the bottom window frame with a black-colored background. If any errors are encountered, red text will appear with the error message. If there are no issues deleting the account, a message will appear that ends with the word **Succeeded**.

4.3 Granting and Revoking Privileges

Although we recommend that you never maintain privileges on a user-by-user basis, there are instances in which you need to assign privileges to individual user accounts. You might need to assign them to temporarily test a scenario or perhaps change a service account's privileges. There are three different interfaces we can use to grant and revoke privileges to a user account: SQL statements, SAP HANA Studio user management, or the SAP HANA Web-Based Development Workbench security manager. Let's look at all three options and how to use each. Then, we'll discuss how to use system database views to list all the privileges assigned to a given user account.

4.3.1 Granting and Revoking Privileges with SQL

Using the SQL console and SQL statements, we can both grant and revoke privileges for user accounts. When granting privileges to some objects, we need to be aware of the type of object. Specifically, we will need to use a different syntax for repository-based objects, because they're owned by the `_SYS_REPO` system account. With this account, there's no way to log on as `_SYS_REPO`, so we have no way to delegate grant and revoke privileges to other users in the system. For example, you can't log on as `_SYS_REPO` and grant `SELECT` to another user while including the `WITH ADMIN OPTION` statement or the `WITH GRANT OPTION` statement. Because of this, we must use a series of system-delivered stored procedures to grant privileges for repository objects owned by `_SYS_REPO`. These stored procedures are activated in the `_SYS_REPO` schema and can be called directly, assuming you have the `EXECUTE` privilege for the procedures. Let's look at some example SQL statements that show how to grant privileges based on the privilege type.

System Privileges

We can grant system privileges using the `GRANT` SQL syntax. The following three SQL statements are separated by a semicolon after each:

```
GRANT <SYSTEM_PRIVILEGE> TO <USER>;
GRANT <SYSTEM_PRIVILEGE> TO <USER> WITH ADMIN OPTION;
GRANT DATA ADMIN, EXPORT, IMPORT TO JONATHAN WITH ADMIN OPTION;
```

The first statement provides a generic template with variables. The variables are indicated by text within angle brackets (e.g., <USER>). The variables will need to be replaced with items unique to your environment. The <SYSTEM_PRIVILEGES> variable can be replaced with a comma-separated list of system privileges, as indicated in the third example. The second SQL statement includes the `WITH ADMIN OPTION` at the end of the statement. This option allows the grantee to subsequently grant the same privilege to another user and is typically reserved for user accounts or roles that manage security models. The final statement provides a full example in which we grant three different system privileges to the user JONATHAN. It includes the `WITH ADMIN OPTION`, which allows the account JONATHAN to grant the same privileges to other users or roles.

We can also revoke system privileges using the `REVOKE` SQL syntax. The following statements demonstrate the `REVOKE` syntax:

```
REVOKE <SYSTEM_PRIVILEGE> FROM <USER>;
REVOKE DATA ADMIN, EXPORT, IMPORT FROM JONATHAN;
```

The first statement provides a generic template with variables. The variables are indicated by text within angle brackets (e.g., `<USER>`). The variables will need to be replaced with items unique to your environment. The `<SYSTEM_PRIVILEGES>` variable can be replaced with a comma-separated list of system privileges, as indicated in the second example. The second statement provides a full example in which the listed system privileges are removed from the user account JONATHAN.

Catalog Schema Privileges

If a schema is owned by a standard database user, we can use one of the following SQL statements to grant one or more privileges to a user account:

```
GRANT <SCHEMA_PRIVILEGE> ON SCHEMA <SCHEMA_NAME> TO <USER>;
GRANT <SCHEMA_PRIVILEGE> ON SCHEMA <SCHEMA_
NAME> TO <USER> WITH GRANT OPTION;
GRANT SELECT, EXECUTE, DROP ON SCHEMA "MySchema" TO JONATHAN;
```

The `<SCHEMA_PRIVILEGES>` variable can be replaced with a comma-separated list of schema object privileges, as indicated in the third statement. When included, the `WITH GRANT OPTION` clause at the end of the statement allows the user to subsequently grant the same privilege to another user.

To remove the privileges, use the following syntax:

```
REVOKE <SCHEMA_PRIVILEGE> ON SCHEMA <SCHEMA_NAME> FROM <USER>;
REVOKE SELECT, EXECUTE, DROP ON SCHEMA "MySchema" FROM JONATHAN;
```

The <SCHEMA_PRIVILEGES> variable can be replaced with a comma-separated list of schema object privileges, as indicated in the second statement.

Please note that GRANT and REVOKE statements won't work on repository-based schemas. Such schemas are owned by the system account _SYS_REPO and must be granted using a special stored procedure. In the next section, we'll provide example SQL statements for such cases.

Repository Schema Privileges

When a schema is created in the SAP HANA development repository, it will be owned by the system user _SYS_REPO. We call these types of schemas *repository schemas*. In such cases, we can't use the standard GRANT and REVOKE SQL syntax to manage permissions for a given user account. Instead, we must use a specific stored procedure to grant and another to revoke repository schema privileges.

To grant repository schema privileges, we need to execute a stored procedure in the _SYS_REPO schema named GRANT_SCHEMA_PRIVILEGE_ON_ACTIVATED_CONTENT. To use this procedure, the security administrator must have the object privilege EXECUTE on the stored procedure. This procedure has three input parameters. The first parameter can accommodate a comma-separated array of schema privileges. The second parameter can accommodate a single schema name. The third parameter can accommodate a user name or role name.

In the following example, we need to replace the variable <OBJECT_PRIVILEGES> with one or more schema privileges; replace the variable <SCHEMA_NAME> with the case-sensitive name of our schema, and if the name is lowercase or mixed-case, include double quotes around the name; and replace <USER_NAME> with the name of a user defined in the SAP HANA system:

```
CALL "_SYS_REPO"."GRANT_SCHEMA_PRIVILEGE_ON_ACTIVATED_CONTENT"
('<OBJECT_PRIVILEGES>','<SCHEMA_NAME>','<USER_NAME>');
```

The following SQL statement represents a complete example based on objects in a demo environment; multiple schema privileges are granted to the user JONATHAN against the schema "MySchema":

```
CALL "_SYS_REPO"."GRANT_SCHEMA_PRIVILEGE_ON_ACTIVATED_CONTENT"
('SELECT, EXECUTE, UPDATE, CREATE ANY' ,'"MySchema"', 'JONATHAN');
```

To revoke repository schema privileges, we need to execute a stored procedure in the _SYS_REPO schema named REVOKE_SCHEMA_PRIVILEGE_ON_ACTIVATED_CONTENT. This procedure has three input parameters, which are identical to those the preceding procedure used to grant privileges. The following SQL statements are used to call the stored procedure equipped to revoke repository schema privileges; the second statement provides an example revoking privileges previously granted to the user account JONATHAN:

```
CALL "_SYS_REPO"."REVOKE_SCHEMA_PRIVILEGE_ON_ACTIVATED_CONTENT"
('<OBJECT_PRIVILEGES>','<SCHEMA_NAME>','<USER_NAME>');
CALL "_SYS_REPO"."REVOKE_SCHEMA_PRIVILEGE_ON_ACTIVATED_CONTENT"
('SELECT, EXECUTE', '"MySchema"', 'JONATHAN');
```

Catalog Object Privileges

If a catalog object is owned by a standard database user, we can use one of the following SQL statements to grant catalog object privileges to a user or role. The <OBJECT_PRIVILEGE> variable can be replaced with a comma-separated array of privileges. The `WITH GRANT OPTION`, when specified, allows the grantee the ability to subsequently grant the same privileges to other users in the system:

```
GRANT <OBJECT_PRIVILEGE> ON <OBJECT_NAME> TO <USER>;
GRANT <OBJECT_PRIVILEGE> ON <OBJECT_NAME> TO <USER> WITH GRANT OPTION;
GRANT SELECT, INSERT, UPDATE, DELETE ON “MySchema”.”MyTable” TO JONATHAN WITH
GRANT OPTION;
```

To revoke the privileges, we can use one of the following statements:

```
REVOKE <OBJECT_PRIVILEGE> ON <OBJECT_NAME> FROM <USER>;
REVOKE SELECT, INSERT, UPDATE, DELETE ON “MySchema”.”MyTable” FROM JONATHAN;
```

Repository Object Privileges

When a catalog object is created in the SAP HANA development repository, it will be owned by the system user `_SYS_REPO`. We call these types of objects *repository catalog objects*. In such cases, we can't use the standard `GRANT` and `REVOKE` SQL syntax to manage permissions for a given user account. Instead, we must use a specific stored procedure to grant and another specific stored procedure to revoke repository catalog object privileges.

To grant repository catalog object privileges, we need to execute a stored procedure in the `_SYS_REPO` schema named `GRANT_PRIVILEGE_ON_ACTIVATED_CONTENT`. To use this procedure, the security administrator must have the EXECUTE object privilege for the stored procedure. This procedure has three input parameters: The first parameter can accommodate a comma-separated array of schema privileges; the second parameter can accommodate a single schema name; and the third parameter can accommodate a user name or role name. In the first example ahead, we need to replace the <OBJECT_PRIVILEGES> variable with one or more schema privileges; replace the <OBJECT_NAME> variable with the case-sensitive and fully qualified name of our catalog object, and if the name is lowercase or mixed case, include double quotes around the schema and catalog object name; and replace <USER_NAME> with the name of a user defined in the SAP HANA system.

```
CALL "_SYS_REPO"."GRANT_PRIVILEGE_ON_ACTIVATED_CONTENT"('<OBJECT_PRIVILEGES>',
'<OBJECT_NAME>','<USER_NAME>');
CALL
"_SYS_REPO"."GRANT_PRIVILEGE_ON_ACTIVATED_CONTENT "('SELECT, EXECUTE',
'"StagingMart"."e-corp.sales.tables::STG_CUSTOMERS"', 'JONATHAN');
```

To revoke repository catalog object privileges, we need to execute a stored procedure in the _SYS_REPO schema named REVOKE_PRIVILEGE_ON_ACTIVATED_CONTENT. This procedure has three input parameters, which are the same as those used in the previous procedure to grant the privileges. The following SQL statements call the stored procedure equipped to revoke catalog object privileges; the second statement provides an example specifically revoking catalog object privileges previously granted to the user account JONATHAN.

```
CALL
"_SYS_REPO"."REVOKE_PRIVILEGE_ON_ACTIVATED_CONTENT "('<OBJECT_PRIVILEGES>',
'<SCHEMA_NAME>','<USER_NAME>');
CALL "_SYS_REPO"."REVOKE_PRIVILEGE_ON_ACTIVATED_CONTENT"('SELECT, EXECUTE' ,
'"StagingMart"."e-corp.sales.tables::STG_CUSTOMERS"' , 'JONATHAN');
```

Structured Privileges

Structured privileges are a special type of object used to force the system to provide additional access restrictions against a column view or catalog view. In Chapter 3 and Chapter 10, we introduced analytic privileges, which are used with SAP HANA information views to provide data access to an activated information view. Technically, analytic privileges are a type of structured privilege, but most GUIs refer to structured privileges as analytic privileges. Repository-based analytic privileges are owned and managed by the system account `_SYS_REPO`. However, structured privileges can be owned by any user with the required system privileges.

If a structured privilege is owned by a standard database user, then we can use the `GRANT STRUCTURED PRIVILEGE` SQL syntax to grant such privileges to a user account. To grant a structured privilege, you must be its owner, because there is no `WITH ADMIN OPTION` to allow another user to grant this privilege. Note that this this syntax will not work on repository-based analytic privileges. In the following example, replace the `<STRUCTURED_PRIVILEGE_NAME>` variable with the name of the structured privilege:

```
GRANT STRUCTURED PRIVILEGE <STRUCTURED_PRIVILEGE_NAME> TO <USER_NAME>;
```

As an example, we'll walk through the process of creating a catalog view and a structured privilege and the process for granting the privilege to a user. Start by using the SQL statement in Listing 4.2 to create a standard catalog view.

```
CREATE VIEW "MySchema"."MYVIEW" ( "MYKEYCOLUMN",
     "STATE",
     "CITY",
     "POSTALCODE" ) AS select
     TO."MYKEYCOLUMN",
     TO."STATE",
     TO."CITY",
     TO."POSTALCODE"
FROM "SYSTEM"."MYTABLENAME" TO
WITH STRUCTURED PRIVILEGE CHECK;
```

Listing 4.2 SQL Code to Create MYTABLE View

We'll then create a structured privilege referencing the view, which will apply a filter on the `STATE` column. The following SQL statements will create a structured privilege that will filter the `STATE` column to `TN`, then, after the privilege name, the `FOR SELECT` syntax is used to indicate that the privilege should be applied when querying the view:

```
CREATE STRUCTURED PRIVILEGE "MyStructuredPriv"
FOR SELECT ON "MySchema"."MYVIEW" WHERE "STATE" = 'TN';
```

We'll then grant the structured privilege to the user JONATHAN. Once granted, the user will only see value from the view where `"STATE" = 'TN'`:

```
GRANT STRUCTURED PRIVILEGE "MyStructuredPriv" TO JONATHAN;
```

To revoke the structured privilege, we use the REVOKE STRUCTURED PRIVILEGE SQL syntax. The following SQL statements provide first a generic and then a specific example of the SQL syntax:


```
REVOKE STRUCTURED PRIVILEGE <STRUCTURED_PRIVILEGE_NAME> FROM <USER>;
REVOKE STRUCTURED PRIVILEGE "MyStructuredPriv" FROM JONATHAN;
```

Remote Sources

To grant access to a remote source or a smart data access federated database connection, issue a SQL statement based on the following example:

```
GRANT <SOURCE_PRIVILEGE> ON REMOTE SOURCE <SOURCE_NAME> TO <USER>;
```

The variable <SOURCE_PRIVILEGE> can be replaced by a comma-separated array of privileges specific to remote-source objects. The <SOURCE_NAME> variable can be replaced by the name of the remote source.

To remove remote-source privileges, use the REVOKE SQL statement. The following SQL statement will remove the privileges specified in the <SOURCE_PRIVILEGE> variable array:

```
REVOKE <SOURCE_PRIVILEGE> ON REMOTE SOURCE <SOURCE_NAME> FROM <USER>;
```

Repository Analytic Privileges

When we create a standard analytic privilege, it's owned by the system user _SYS_REPO. Analytic privileges are a type of structured privilege, but we can't use the standard GRANT and REVOKE SQL syntax to assign analytic privileges to a user. Instead, we must use a specific stored procedure to grant and another specific stored procedure to revoke analytic privileges for users.

To grant an analytic privilege to a user, we must execute the stored procedure GRANT_ACTIVATED_ANALYTIC_PRIVILEGE stored in the _SYS_REPO schema. To use this procedure, the security administrator must have the EXECUTE object privilege for the stored procedure. The procedure provides two input parameters: The first parameter should contain the name of the analytic privilege, and the second input parameter will contain the name of the user. The following SQL statements provide the syntax used to execute the stored procedure, and then a specific example:

```
CALL "_SYS_REPO"."GRANT_ACTIVATED_ANALYTICAL_PRIVILEGE"
('<ANALLYTIC_PRIVILEGE_NAME>','<USER_NAME>');
CALL "_SYS_REPO"."GRANT_ACTIVATED_ANALYTICAL_PRIVILEGE"
('"e-corp.sales.security/ap_sales_reporting_region"','JONATHAN');
```

To revoke an analytic privilege from a user, we must execute the stored procedure REVOKE_ACTIVATED_ANALYTIC_PRIVILEGE stored in the _SYS_REPO schema. It uses the same two input parameters. The following SQL statements provide the syntax used to execute the stored procedure and a specific example:

```
CALL "_SYS_REPO"."REVOKE_ACTIVATED_ANALYTICAL_PRIVILEGE"
('<ANALLYTIC_PRIVILEGE_NAME>','<USER_NAME>');
CALL "_SYS_REPO"."REVOKE_ACTIVATED_ANALYTICAL_PRIVILEGE"
('"e-corp.sales.security/ap_sales_reporting_region"','JONATHAN');
```

Application Privileges

When we create an application privilege, it's owned by the system user _SYS_REPO. To grant or revoke application privileges, we must use a specific stored procedure. The following SQL statements demonstrate the syntax used to grant an application privilege and a specific example:

```
CALL "_SYS_REPO"."GRANT_APPLICATION_PRIVILEGE"
('<APPLICATION_PRIVILEGE_NAME>','<USER_NAME>');
CALL "_SYS_REPO"."GRANT_APPLICATION_
PRIVILEGE"('"sap.hana.admin::Administrator"','JONATHAN');
```

The next statements provide the syntax used to revoke an application privilege and a specific example:

```
CALL "_SYS_REPO"."REVOKE_APPLICATION_PRIVILEGE"
('<APPLICATION_PRIVILEGE_NAME>','<USER_NAME>');
CALL "_SYS_REPO"."REVOKE_APPLICATION_
PRIVILEGE"('"sap.hana.admin::Administrator"','DFT');
```

Package Privileges

To grant access to a package in the SAP HANA repository, issue a SQL statement based on the following; the second statement provides a specific example:

```
GRANT <PACKAGE_
PRIVILEGE> ON <"package.subpackage"> TO <USER> WITH GRANT OPTION;
GRANT REPO.READ, REPO.EDIT_NATIVE_OBJECTS ON "e-
corp" TO JONATHAN WITH GRANT OPTION;
```


The variable `<PACKAGE_PRIVILEGE>` can be replaced with a comma-separated array of package privileges, and the `<"package.subpackage">` variable can be replaced with the case-sensitive name of the package and subpackage hierarchy. Each node of the package hierarchy should be separated by a period. The `WITH GRANT OPTION` allows the grantee to grant the same privileges to other users.

To remove remote source privileges, use the `REVOKE` SQL statement. The following SQL statement will remove the privileges specified in the `<PACKAGE_PRIVILEGE>` variable array; the second statement provides a specific example:

```
REVOKE <PACKAGE_PRIVILEGE> ON <"package.subpackage"> FROM <USER>;
REVOKE REPO.EDIT_NATIVE_OBJECTS ON "e-corp" FROM JONATHAN;
```

4.3.2 Granting and Revoking Privileges with SAP HANA Studio

As an alternative to using SQL statements, the user accounts management area within SAP HANA Studio allows you to both grant and revoke privileges for a given user account. Most will find it easier to use SAP HANA Studio than to memorize and type SQL statements.

To access the user management area, start by switching to the administration console perspective. On the **Systems** tab, located on the left side, expand the **System** node, then the **Security** node, to reveal the **Security**, **Users**, and **Roles** nodes. Expand the **Users** node to reveal user accounts defined in the system. To manage a user account, double-click the account name in the list to open the **User Management** tab on the right side. This same tab is present when creating a user account.

Figure 4.8 shows the user management interface within SAP HANA Studio. Just below the user account options section, you'll see several tabs. Each tab represents an interface via which specific types of privileges or roles can be granted or revoked.

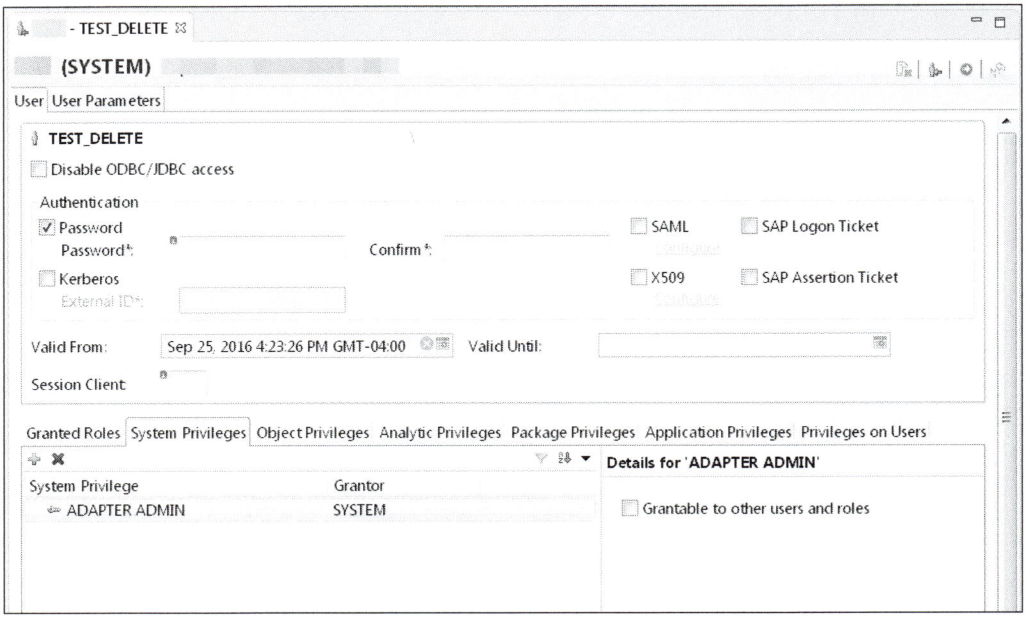

Figure 4.8 Managing Privileges Assigned to User Account in SAP HANA Studio

The first tab is **Granted Roles**. Use this tab to grant or revoke roles assigned to the user account. In Section 4.4.2, we'll discuss how to use SAP HANA Studio to grant and revoke role assignments for user accounts, but for now note that the process is similar to how we grant and revoke privileges, a process that we'll discuss next.

System Privileges

Let's first review the workflows necessary to grant and revoke system privileges. The second tab in the **User Management** window is named **System Privileges**. Use this tab to grant or revoke system privileges.

To grant a system privilege, click **+** to open a search dialog box. To view all system privileges, enter the search string "**" to list them all. To search for a specific system privilege, enter a portion of the system privilege name to search for possible matches. Next, select one or more system privileges. To select multiple items, hold down the `Ctrl` key and click each desired item. To select a list of items, click the first item, hold down the `Shift` key, and then select the last item. Once the desired items are selected, click **OK**; the search dialog will close. Your selected system privileges should now appear in the **System Privileges** tab (see Figure 4.9).

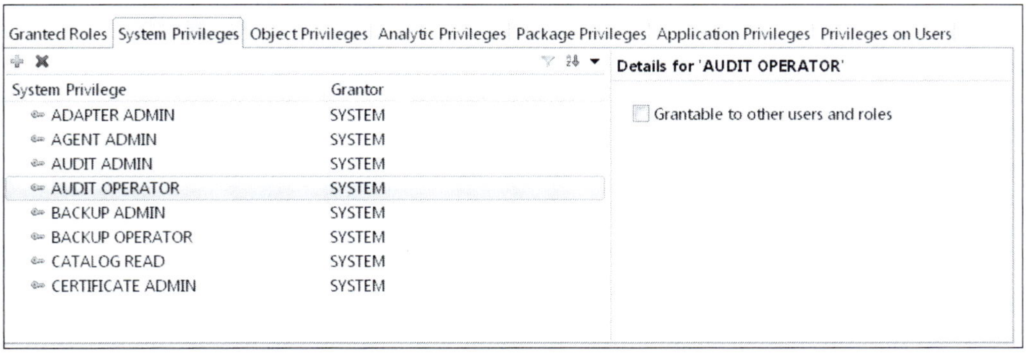

Figure 4.9 List of Selected System Privileges

To assign the **Grantable to other users and roles** privilege, first select a system privilege from the list. To the right, you'll see a frame containing the details for the selected system privilege. Select the **Grantable to other users and roles** checkbox; this will allow the user to grant the same privilege to another user or role. Repeat this process for each system privilege in the list.

Once you've added all the desired privileges to the list, save or activate the changes to implement them. Saving and activating have the same outcome, allowing you to choose either method. To save the changes, press `Ctrl`+`S`; to activate the changes, press `F8`. Either way, the changes will be saved and activated within the system. SAP HANA Studio will execute the required SQL statements in the background to grant the selected system privileges.

To revoke a system privilege, click an assigned system privilege from the list and then choose the red **X** above the list to revoke the privilege. Repeat the process for each system privilege you want to revoke. Once you've removed all the desired privileges, press `Ctrl`+`S` or `F8`. The removed privileges will be revoked, and the user object will be updated.

Object Privileges

The third tab in the user management interface is named **Object Privileges**. The process for granting or revoking object privileges is like the process used for system privileges. To grant an object privilege, click **+** to open a search dialog box. Enter the search string "**" to list all objects in the system. To search for a specific object, enter a portion of the object's name to search for possible matches.

The search dialog will return multiple types of objects, including all types of catalog objects, repository-based catalog objects, schemas, repository-based schemas, remote sources, column views, and many more.

As with system privileges, the interface allows you to select multiple items. Click **OK** once the desired objects are selected. The search dialog will close and the selected catalog objects will appear in the list. Figure 4.10 provides an example of several types of selected objects. The list contains the object name and the user account used to grant the object privilege.

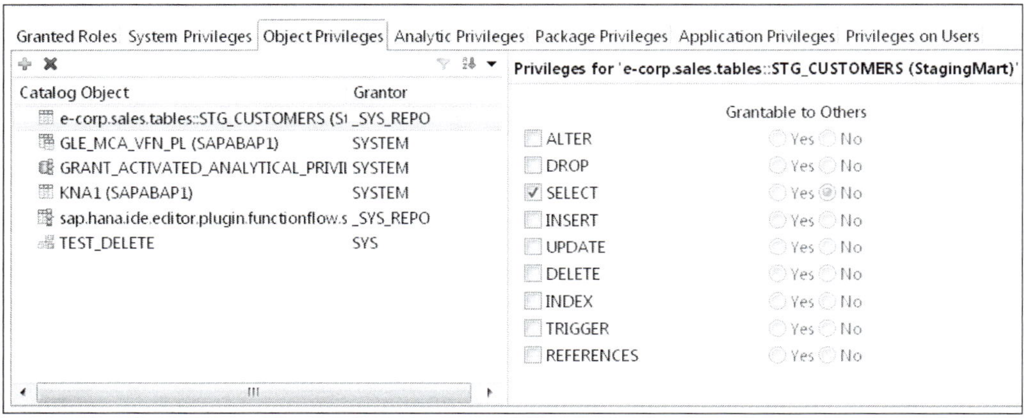

Figure 4.10 List of Selected Objects and Their Privileges in SAP HANA Studio

To view a list of available privileges for a given object, first select the object in the list. To the right of a selected object, you'll see a frame containing a series of checkboxes, privileges, and **Yes** or **No** radio buttons. To grant a privilege, select the checkbox next to the privilege name. To allow the privilege to be **Grantable to Others**, click the **Yes** radio button to the right of the given privilege. As you click through each object in the left frame, privileges applicable for the selected object will appear in the right frame.

To save the changes, press Ctrl+S or press F8. The changes will be saved and activated within the system.

When using SAP HANA Studio, there's no need to determine if the object is owned by _SYS_REPO, nor do we need to use a special interface to assign privileges owned by _SYS_REPO. SAP HANA Studio will execute the required SQL statements in the background to grant the selected object privileges. When the object is owned by the system account _SYS_REPO, SAP HANA Studio also will execute the necessary stored procedures in the background. You'll notice that the repository objects will always list the grantor as _SYS_REPO. When the object is owned by a standard user account, SAP HANA Studio will execute the standard GRANT and REVOKE statements. You'll notice in these instances that the grantor is the user account currently authenticated within the SAP HANA Studio connection.

To revoke an object privilege, click an assigned object privilege from the list and then click the red **X** above the list to revoke the privilege. Repeat the process for each system privilege you want to revoke. Once you've removed all the desired privileges, press [Ctrl]+[S] or press [F8]. The removed privileges will be revoked and the user object will be updated.

Analytic Privileges

The forth tab in the user management interface is **Analytic Privileges**. The process for granting or revoking analytic privileges is like the process used for other privileges discussed in this section. To grant an analytic privilege, click **+** to open a search dialog box. To view all objects in the system, enter the search string "**". To search for a specific analytic privilege, enter a portion of its name to search for possible matches. The search dialog will return both analytic privileges and structured privileges. Analytic privileges are those owned by the system account _SYS_REPO; structured privileges are owned by the user account that created them.

As with other privileges, the interface allows you to select multiple items. Click **OK** once the desired objects are selected. The search dialog will close, and the selected **Analytic Privileges** and their **Grantor** will appear in the list. There are no further options that need to be configured for analytic privileges; they're either granted when listed or revoked when not listed.

When using SAP HANA Studio, there's no need to determine if the analytic privilege is owned by _SYS_REPO or if we need to use a special interface to assign privileges owned by _SYS_REPO. SAP HANA Studio will execute the required SQL statements automatically in the background to grant the selected analytic privileges. If the object is owned by the system account _SYS_REPO, the system will execute the necessary stored procedures in the background. You'll notice that repository objects will always list the grantor as _SYS_REPO.

To revoke an analytic privilege, simply select it from the list and click the red **X**. To save the changes, press [Ctrl]+[S] or press [F8]. The changes will be saved and activated within the system.

Package Privileges

The fifth tab in the user management interface is **Package Privileges**. The process for granting or revoking package privileges is like the process used for other privileges discussed in this section. To grant a package privilege, click **+** to open a search dialog box. To view all packages in the system, enter the search string "**". To search for a specific package, enter a portion of the package's name to search for possible matches. Select one or more packages and click **OK**. The search dialog box will disappear, and a list of selected packages will appear (see Figure 4.11).

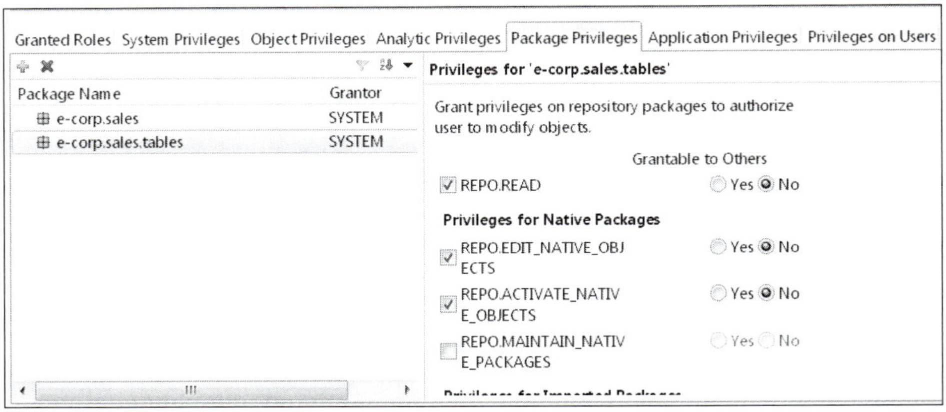

Figure 4.11 Assigning Package Privileges to User in SAP HANA Studio

To assign privileges to a selected package, look for the frame on the right side, containing checkboxes, privileges, and **Yes** and **No** radio buttons. To assign privileges, select the checkbox beside each listed privilege's name. To allow the user to assign the same privilege to others, select the **Yes** radio button in the column labeled **Grantable to Others**.

To revoke a package privilege, simply select it from the list and choose the red **X** to remove it from the list. To save the changes, press Ctrl+S or press F8. The changes will be saved and activated within the system.

4.3.3 Granting and Revoking Privileges with SAP HANA Web-Based Development Workbench

The SAP HANA Web-Based Development Workbench security manager, hosted within the XS engine, provides a GUI you can use to create users, create roles, or manage security.

You can access the web-based development workbench via a supported Internet browser. The following two URLs can be customized to match the details of your environment:

http://sap-hana.myhost.com:8000/sap/hana/ide/security

http://<sap_hana_host>: 80<instance_number>/sap/hana/ide/security

In the last example, replace <sap_hana_host> with the hostname of the SAP HANA system in your environment and <instance_number> with the two-digit instance corresponding to your SAP HANA system.

For secure access, the following examples should help you construct the correct URL:

https://<sap_hana_host>: 43<instance_number>/sap/hana/ide/security

https://sap-hana.myhost.com:4300/sap/hana/ide/security

Once you have access to SAP HANA Web-Based Development Workbench, expand the **Security** node on the right side of the window. Expand **Users** to reveal a list of user accounts. Double-click a user to open the management interface for the given user. With the selected **User Management** window open, you can begin granting and revoking privileges.

The process for granting and revoking a user's privileges in SAP HANA Web-Based Development Workbench is almost identical to the process outlined for SAP HANA Studio. Because there is tremendous overlap in the workflows, we won't go into the same level of detail in this section; refer to Section 4.3.2 for additional details. In this section, we will simply highlight the basic workflow and point out any significant differences.

If there are any activation issues, warning messages will appear in the status frame at the bottom of the **User Management** window. The status frame has a dark background color, and error messages will appear in red-colored text. Errors are generated only during an attempt to activate or save changes.

System Privileges

To add a system privilege, click **+** and search for the desired system privilege. Choose **Grantable to Other Users and Roles** to the right of each listed system privilege as needed.

To revoke a system privilege, select the privilege from the list and click the red **X**. To save your changes, press `Ctrl`+`S`. Alternatively, locate the **Save** icon, resembling a floppy disk at the top left and click it to save and activate the privilege.

Object Privileges

To add an object privilege, click **+** and search for the desired objects. A search dialog will appear, allowing you to search for an object. Unlike in SAP HANA Studio, SAP HANA Web-Based Development Workbench provides additional search options based on the object type, which likely will make it easier to pinpoint specific objects by type. This is the only noticeable difference between using SAP HANA Studio or SAP HANA Web-Based Development Workbench.

Select the desired objects and choose **OK**. A list of selected objects will appear. To the right of each object is a list of applicable privileges that can be granted. The **Grantable to Others** option is also available.

To revoke an object privilege, select the object from the list and click the red **X**. To save your changes, press [Ctrl]+[S] or the disk icon to save and activate the privilege.

Analytic Privileges

To add an analytic privilege, click **+** and search for the desired analytic privilege. To revoke an analytic privilege, selected the privilege from the list and click the red **X** to remove the analytic privilege. To save your changes, press [Ctrl]+[S] or click the disk icon to save and activate the privilege.

Package Privileges

To add a package privilege, click **+** and search for the desired package hierarchy level. To revoke a package privilege, selected the package hierarchy level from the list and choose the red **X** to remove it. To save your changes, press [Ctrl]+[S] or click the disk icon to save and activate the privilege.

4.3.4 Effective Privileges System View

Periodically, we need to query the system to view the privileges that have been granted to a specific user. Such a database view is included in the `SYS` schema. The name of the view is `EFFECTIVE_PRIVILEGES`, and it will list all privileges currently granted directly and indirectly to a specified user account. The view must be filtered to a single user account before it will execute. Listing 4.3 provides an example of the SQL code required to query this view.

```
SELECT
"USER_NAME", "GRANTEE", "GRANTEE_TYPE", "GRANTOR", "GRANTOR_TYPE",
"OBJECT_TYPE", "SCHEMA_NAME", "OBJECT_NAME", "COLUMN_NAME", "PRIVILEGE",
"IS_GRANTABLE", "IS_VALID"
FROM "SYS"."EFFECTIVE_PRIVILEGES"
WHERE "USER_NAME" = '<USER_NAME>';
```

Listing 4.3 SQL Code Executed against EFFECTIVE_PRIVILEGES View

The <USER_NAME> variable should be replaced with an active user account name. The view won't execute unless the WHERE clause contains a filter on USER_NAME. For a complete list of additional filters, please refer to the SAP HANA Reference Guide, found at *https://help.sap.com/hana/SAP_HANA_SQL_and_System_Views_Reference_en.pdf.*

One advantage of using SAP HANA Web-Based Development Workbench is that administrators don't need to install SAP HANA Studio to grant or revoke privileges. The search window for object privileges also has additional object-type search filters that will help to locate some objects more quickly. In the next sections, we'll discuss how to grant roles to a user account.

4.4 Managing User Role Assignments

Roles are a special type of database object that can be used to define a specific set or collection of privileges. They are reusable objects that can be granted to multiple users or even to other roles. Roles are typically named and configured to support specific functions or tasks within the SAP HANA platform. In Chapter 5 and Chapter 6, we will discuss the processes and workflows necessary for creating roles, but for now, we'll discuss how they can be granted to user accounts.

When granting a role, we're essentially assigning all the privileges within the role to a specified user. Any future updates to the role will automatically be granted to all users that are assigned the role. To grant a role to a user account or another role, the user performing the action must have the ROLE ADMIN system privilege. Alternatively, a user can also grant access to a specific role if the user was granted that same role with the WITH ADMIN OPTION or the **Grantable to other users and roles** option.

There are three basic interfaces we can use to both grant and revoke roles: a SQL console to issue SQL statements, SAP HANA Studio, or SAP HANA Web-Based Development Workbench.

4.4.1 Granting and Revoking Roles with SQL

When granting roles to a user, we must first determine the role type. If the role was created by a standard user account or provisioned by the system during installation, we refer to it as a *standard role*. These roles often are created using the CREATE ROLE SQL syntax. Standard roles can be granted and revoked with the GRANT and REVOKE SQL statements.

Alternatively, if the role was created as a development artifact and owned by the system account _SYS_REPO, we refer to it as a *repository role*. Repository roles can only be granted or revoked using a special stored procedure. Let's look at the two different options.

Standard Roles

Granting standard roles to a user account with SQL is performed using a syntax that is like that used when granting privileges (see Section 4.3.1). To grant a role to a user, we must use a GRANT SQL statement. The following three examples SQL statements demonstrate the syntax necessary for granting roles to a user, the syntax including an additional option, and an example:

```
GRANT <ROLE_NAME> TO <USER>;
GRANT <ROLE_NAME> TO <USER> WITH ADMIN OPTION;
GRANT MODELING, DBA_COCKPIT, CONTENT_ADMIN TO JONATHAN WITH ADMIN OPTION;
```

The variable <ROLE_NAME> can be replaced with a comma-separated list of roles. The <USER> variable can be replaced with either a user account or another role name. The WITH ADMIN OPTION can be used to allow a user account the ability to grant the specified role to another user or role even if that user doesn't have the ROLE ADMIN system privilege.

To revoke a role using SQL we must issue a REVOKE SQL statement. The following two example SQL statements demonstrate the syntax for removing or revoking a role from a user account.

```
REVOKE <ROLE_NAME> FROM <USER>;
REVOKE ROLE_ADMIN FROM JONATHAN;
```

Repository Roles

When a role is created in the SAP HANA development repository, it's owned by the system user _SYS_REPO. These are repository roles. We can't use the standard GRANT and REVOKE SQL syntax to assign repository roles to a user; instead, we must use a specific stored procedure to grant and another specific stored procedure to revoke repository schema privileges.

The first stored procedure is stored in the schema _SYS_REPO and is named GRANT_ACTIVATED_ROLE. To use this procedure, the security administrator must have the EXECUTE object privilege for the stored procedure. The procedure has two input parameters: The first input parameter requires the name of one repository role and doesn't support multiple repository roles; the second input parameter requires the name of a single user account. The following SQL statement uses variables for the role name and user name parameters:

```
CALL
"_SYS_REPO"."GRANT_ACTIVATED_ROLE"('<REPOSITORY_ROLE_NAME>', '<USER_NAME>');
```

The following example demonstrates the execution of the procedure with sample parameters:

```
CALL
_SYS_REPO"."GRANT_ACTIVATED_ROLE"('sap.hana.ide.roles::Developer',
'TEST_USER');
```

The second stored procedure is stored in the schema _SYS_REPO and is named REVOKE_ACTIVATED_ROLE. To use this procedure, the security administrator must have the EXECUTE object privilege for the stored procedure. The procedure has two input parameters: The first input parameter requires the name of one repository role and doesn't support multiple repository roles; the second input parameter requires the name of a single user account. The following SQL statement uses variables for the role name and user name parameters:

```
CALL
"_SYS_REPO"."REVOKE_ACTIVATED_ROLE"('<REPOSITORY_ROLE_NAME>', '<USER_NAME>');
```

The following statement demonstrates the execution of the procedure with sample parameters:

```
CALL "_SYS_REPO"."REVOKE_ACTIVATED_
ROLE"('sap.hana.ide.roles::Developer','TEST_USER');
```

Full SQL Syntax

The complete available syntax necessary for granting and revoking privileges and roles and for creating and managing user accounts is beyond the scope of this book. To review the full syntax and all available options, please access the SAP HANA SQL and System Views Reference Guide found at *https://help.sap.com/hana_platform* or via the following direct link to the guide in PDF format: *http://help.sap.com/hana/SAP_HANA_SQL_and_System_Views_Reference_en.pdf.*

Search for the sections pertaining to GRANT, REVOKE, CREATE USER, ALTER USER, and DROP USER statements.

Let's now look at how to use SAP HANA Studio to grant a role to a user account.

4.4.2 Granting and Revoking Roles with SAP HANA Studio

The **Users** node in SAP HANA Studio will allow you to both grant and revoke roles for a given user account. Most will find it easier to use SAP HANA Studio than to memorize and type SQL statements. In this section, we'll review the process for granting and revoking roles in SAP HANA Studio.

To access the **Users** node in SAP HANA Studio, first switch to the administration console perspective. On the **Systems** tab, located on the left, expand the **System** node. Expand the **Security** node to reveal the **Security**, **Users**, and **Roles** nodes. Expand the **Users** node to reveal user accounts defined in the system. To manage a user account, double-click the account name in the list to open the **User Management** tab on the right side; this same tab is present when creating a user account.

Figure 4.12 shows the user management interface in SAP HANA Studio. Just below the user account details section, you'll see several tabs. Each tab represents an interface in which a specific type of privileges or roles can be granted or revoked. The first tab is **Granted Roles**.

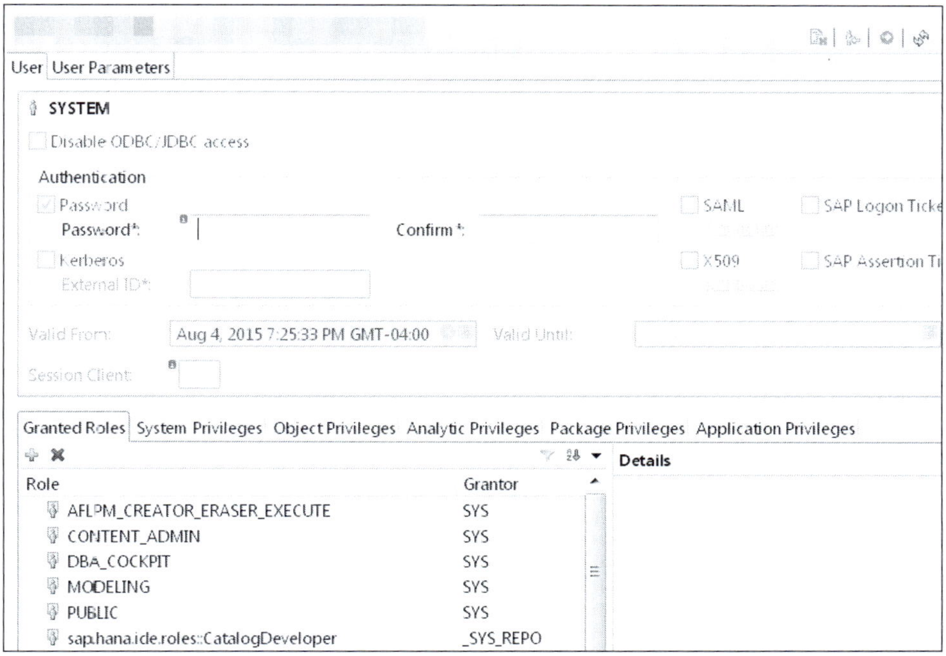

Figure 4.12 Granted Roles Configuration Tab in SAP HANA Studio

Much like granting and revoking privileges, the process required to grant a role involves clicking **+**, searching for one or more existing roles, then adding the roles to the list. Once a role is added to the list and the changes are saved, the user account will be granted the assigned roles and all the privileges granted to those roles. When applicable, the **Details** frame of the **Granted Roles** tab will contain the **Grantable to other users and roles** option; check the box next to this option to allow the user account the ability to grant the assigned role to other users. When this option is checked, the user will be able to grant the specified role even if that user doesn't have the `ROLE ADMIN` system privilege.

To revoke a role, select the role from the list and then click the red **X** icon to remove the assigned role from the list. Click the **Save** icon, resembling a floppy disk, located on the main SAP HANA Studio icon bar, to save and activate the changes.

When you click the **Save** icon, SAP HANA Studio will execute the appropriate SQL statement in the background to grant or revoke the role. Standard roles will be granted using the basic GRANT and REVOKE SQL syntax. The grantor in these cases will be the account used to authenticate with the system in SAP HANA Studio. Repository roles will be granted and revoked using the applicable stored procedures in the _SYS_REPO schema. The grantor in these cases will be the system account _SYS_REPO.

In summary, granting roles with SAP HANA Studio eliminates the need to memorize and compose SQL statements. SAP HANA Studio will automatically execute the appropriate SQL in the background based on the type of role.

4.4.3 Granting and Revoking Roles with SAP HANA Web-Based Development Workbench

As we mentioned previously (see Section 4.2.3 and Section 4.3.3), the SAP HANA Web-Based Development Workbench security manager, hosted within the XS engine, provides a GUI that you can use to create users, create roles, or manage security.

You can access the SAP HANA Web-Based Development Workbench security manager by filling in the following two URLs with the details of your environment:

http://<sap_hana_host>:80<instance_number>/sap/hana/ide/security

https://<sap_hana_host>:43<instance_number>/sap/hana/ide/security

Once you have access, expand the **Security** node on the right side of the window, then expand **Users** to reveal a list of user accounts. Double-click a user to open the management interface for the given user. With the selected **User Management** window open, you can begin granting and revoking roles using the tab labeled **Granted Roles**.

The process for granting and revoking roles in SAP HANA Web-Based Development Workbench is identical to the process outlined for SAP HANA Studio (see Section 4.4.2). Because there is tremendous overlap in the workflows, we won't go into the same level of detail in the section. Remember that if there are any activation issues, warning messages will appear in the status frame at the bottom of the **User Management** window.

4.4.4 Effective Roles System View

Periodically, we need to query the system to view the roles that have been granted to a specific user. Such a database view is included in the SYS schema. The name of the view is EFFECTIVE_ROLES. The view will list all the roles currently granted directly and indirectly to a specified user account. The view must be filtered to a single user account before it will execute. Listing 4.4 provides an example of the SQL required to query this view.

```
SELECT
"USER_NAME", "GRANTEE", "GRANTEE_TYPE", "GRANTOR", "ROLE_NAME", "IS_GRANTABLE"
FROM "SYS"."EFFECTIVE_ROLES"
WHERE ("USER_NAME" = '<USER_NAME>');
```

Listing 4.4 SQL Code Executed against EFECTIVE_ROLES View

The variable `<USER_NAME>` should be replaced with an active user account name. The view won't execute unless the `WHERE` clause contains a filter on `USER_NAME` column. For a complete list of additional filters, please refer to the SAP HANA Reference Guide found at *https://help.sap.com/hana/SAP_HANA_SQL_and_System_Views_Reference_en.pdf*.

In conclusion, the workflows and steps necessary to grant and revoke roles using the SAP HANA Web-Based Development Workbench security manager is very similar to the processes used in SAP HANA Studio. One advantage of using SAP HANA Web-Based Development Workbench is that administrators don't need to install SAP HANA Studio to grant or revoke roles. In the next section, we'll discuss a case study and demonstrate the process for provisioning users programmatically.

4.5 Case Study: Provisioning Users with SQL Scripts and Stored Procedures

E-Corporation has designed a sales analytics data mart. The data mart is hosting data that must be restricted on a user-by-user basis. E-Corporation has already created SAP HANA information views and analytic privileges to facilitate part of this requirement and has configured SAML authentication within SAP HANA. However, for the solution to work on a user-by-user basis, each user accessing SAP HANA will need his own individual user account and SAML identity. E-Corporation will need to provision and configure over five thousand individual user accounts to accommodate this requirement.

The administration team has determined that manually creating five thousand user accounts isn't feasible. Therefore, the team needs a solution to programmatically create these accounts and maintain their properties. They currently have a Lightweight Directory Access Protocol (LDAP)–based user directory system that contains all the user accounts that require access to the SAP HANA system. The LDAP system administrator was able to extract the basic user account information form the LDAP system into a comma-separated values (CSV) flat file.

The SAP HANA administrator now has a list of five thousand users and their basic attributes. He can use this list to programmatically provision and configure the accounts to support SAML authentication.

Before the SAP HANA administrator can import the CSV file into the SAP HANA system, he must create a table to store the data. Based on advice from the E-Corporation security consultant, the administrator will create a new repository schema and repository-based table to facilitate the imported LDAP user list. Using a dedicated schema and table to host security-related data and programs would help to simplify the process of restricting access to the schema, table, procedures, and future support objects.

This case study will walk you through the technical aspects of the solution. We'll start by reviewing the processes needed to import the LDAP user list into an SAP HANA table, then we'll review the processes necessary to create repository-based stored procedures that will programmatically provision, deactivate, and delete user accounts imported from the LDAP system.

4.5.1 Creating a Repository Schema

Before creating a repository schema, the administrator has decided to create a few new package hierarchy levels to store the new development objects for his user-provisioning program. E-Corporation already has a root package named **Security**. The new program will require a schema, table, and series of stored procedures. The repository schema development artifact will be stored in a subpackage named **Schemas**, the repository stored procedure development artifacts will be stored in a subpackage named **Provisioning**, and the repository table development artifacts will be stored in a subpackage named **Tables**. Figure 4.13 shows how the completed package hierarchy should be configured.

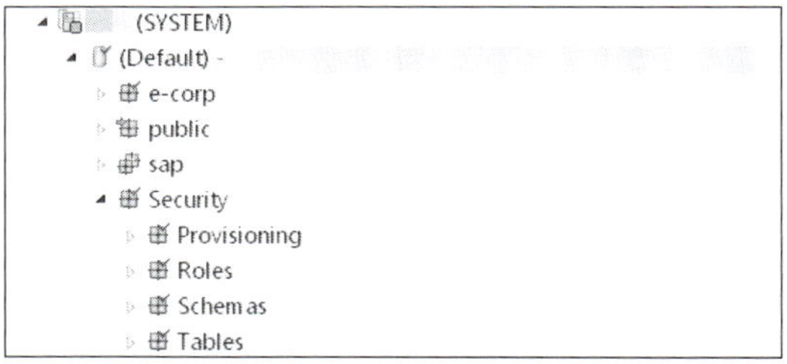

Figure 4.13 Package Hierarchy to Store Security-Related Development Content

To create the package hierarchy, log on to SAP HANA Studio and switch to the development perspective. On the left side, choose the **Repositories** tab. Within your defined repository workspace, expand the package hierarchy to reveal the root-level package node named **Security**; right-click the **Security** node and choose **New • Repository Package** to define each subpackage shown in Figure 4.13. For example, enter "Security.Tables" in the **Package Name** field to create a new **Tables** subpackage.

To create a repository schema within the package hierarchy, right-click the **Schemas** package and choose **New**. From the pop-up menu, choose the bottom option, **Other**. In the search window that opens, search for the development object named "schema". Under **SAP HANA • Database Development**, choose **Schema** and click **Next**.

A window named **New Schema** will appear. Near the bottom of the window, enter "security_tables" in the **File Name:** field. In the **Template:** field, choose **Basic** from the drop-down menu. Click **Finish** to save the file, and open the security_tables.hdbschema configuration file on the right.

Using the following syntax, define the repository schema that will be used to stored repository-based catalog objects related to managing SAP HANA security. Activate the design-time script by pressing `Ctrl`+`F3`.

```
//To define the HDB schema, use the following code:
schema_name = "security_tables";
```

4.5.2 Creating a Repository Table

With the `security_tables` schema defined, we can now create a repository-based table to host the LDAP data imported from the CSV file. To create a repository table, right-click the **Security.Tables** package and choose **New • Other**. Search for "table". From the search results, choose **SAP HANA • Database Development**, then **Database Table**, and click **Next**.

A window named **New Database Table** will appear. Near the bottom of the window, enter the lowercase name "adusers" in the **File Name:** field. In the **Template:** field, choose **Basic** from the drop-down menu. Click **Finish** to save the file, and open the adusers.hdbtable configuration file on the right.

Using the repository table's definition syntax, define a table containing four columns: `USER_NAME`, `AD_USER_NAME`, `EMAIL_ADDRESS`, and `ACCOUNT_STATUS`. Listing 4.5 contains the syntax required to define the repository table. Activate the design-time script by pressing `Ctrl`+`F3`.

```
table.schemaName = "security_tables";
table.tableType = COLUMNSTORE;

table.columns =
 [
    {name = "USER_NAME";  sqlType = NVARCHAR;  length = 256;
comment = "User Name in SAP HANA System"; },
    {name = "AD_USER_NAME";  sqlType = NVARCHAR;  length = 256;
comment = "User Name in AD System"; },
    {name = "EMAIL_ADDRESS";  sqlType = NVARCHAR;  length = 256;
comment = "Email address from AD System"; },
    {name = "ACCOUNT_STATUS";  sqlType = NVARCHAR;  length = 1;
comment = "A for Active, D for Disabled"; }

];

table.primaryKey.pkcolumns = ["USER_NAME"];
```

Listing 4.5 Repository Table Syntax

Once the repository table script is activated, table `Security.Tables::adusers` will appear in the `security_tables` schema. We're now ready to load our CSV data into this table.

4.5.3 Importing a CSV File into a Table

As you might recall, the LDAP system administrator provided a CSV file containing a list of over five thousand users. We now need to import this list of users into the SAP HANA table we crated in the previous section.

Before importing the file, we need to place the file somewhere on the local Windows-based system running SAP HANA Studio. With the file in place, we can import the data into SAP HANA. To do so, start SAP HANA Studio and switch to the administration console perspective. From the menu, choose **File • Import**. An **Import** window will appear. Select the **SAP HANA Content • Data from Local File** option from the **Select an Import Source:** window. In the **Target System** window, choose the SAP HANA system containing the table we created in the previous section. Click **Next** to define the file import properties.

In the **File Import Properties** window, we need to define the format of the provided CSV file, which is formatted to support easy import into the SAP HANA system. The first row contains the column heading names, and the remaining rows contain a comma-separated list of user account attributes. Each row represents an individual user account and its attributes. Figure 4.14 shows a sample of the first few rows of data contained in such a file.

```
USER_NAME,AD_USER_NAME,EMAIL_ADDRESS,ACCOUNT_STATUS
G5456784,jonrob01,john.roberts@e-corp.com,A
G3457543,davwel02,david.wells@e-corp.com,A
G5655643,scogol11,scott.goldburg@e-corp.com,A
G4787634,ellald34,elliot.aldersons@e-corp.com,A
H3456643,angmos33,angie.moss@e-corp.com,A
C7878777,gidgod01,gidill.goddard@e-corp.com,A
F3455900,krigor02,kristaina.gordon@e-corp.com,A
S0000543,darald02,darlene.aldersons@e-corp.com,A
```

Figure 4.14 CSV File Contents

The import properties should be defined to match the configuration options shown in Figure 4.15.

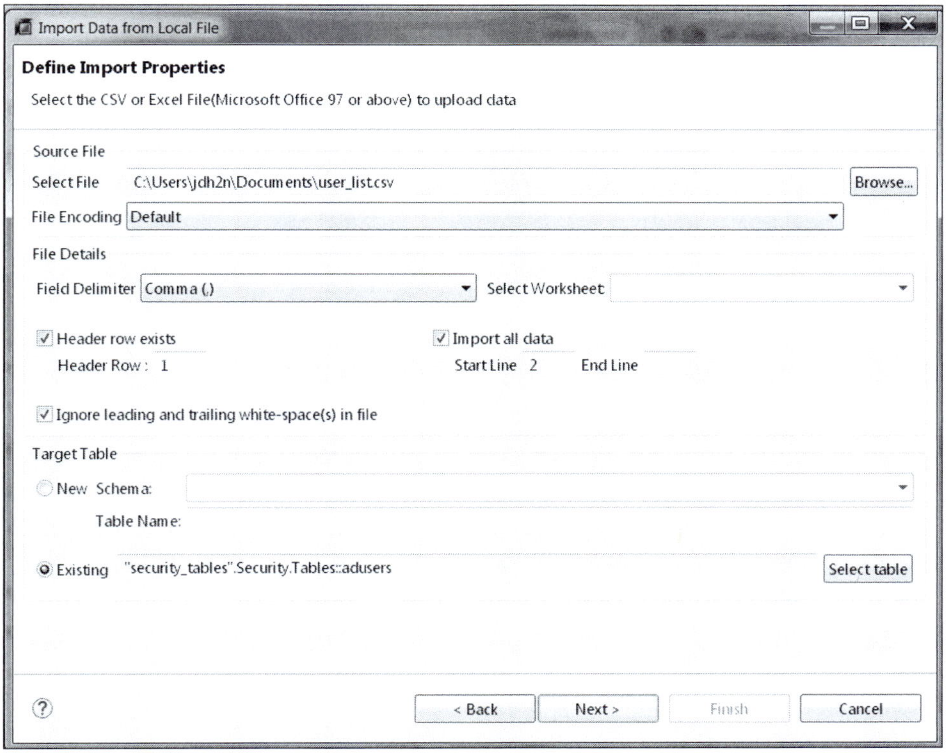

Figure 4.15 Defining CSV File Import Properties

The **Source File** option will be unique to your environment. It should contain the local file path and filename based on the provided CSV file. **File Delimiter** will be **Comma(,)**. The **Header row exists** and **Import all data** checkboxes should be checked. Under **Target Table**, select the **Existing** radio button; the case-sensitive table name will be **"security_tables".Security.Tables::adusers"**. Click **Next** to continue to the next option.

The **Manage Table Definition and Data Mappings** window will appear. Start the mapping process by dragging the **Source File** column name on the left to its matching **Target Table** column name on the right. Because the CSV file column header names match the names of the column in the table we created, the mapping process should be simple. Continue the process by matching each source and target column. Figure 4.16 provides an example of the process, with all four columns mapped to their target equivalents.

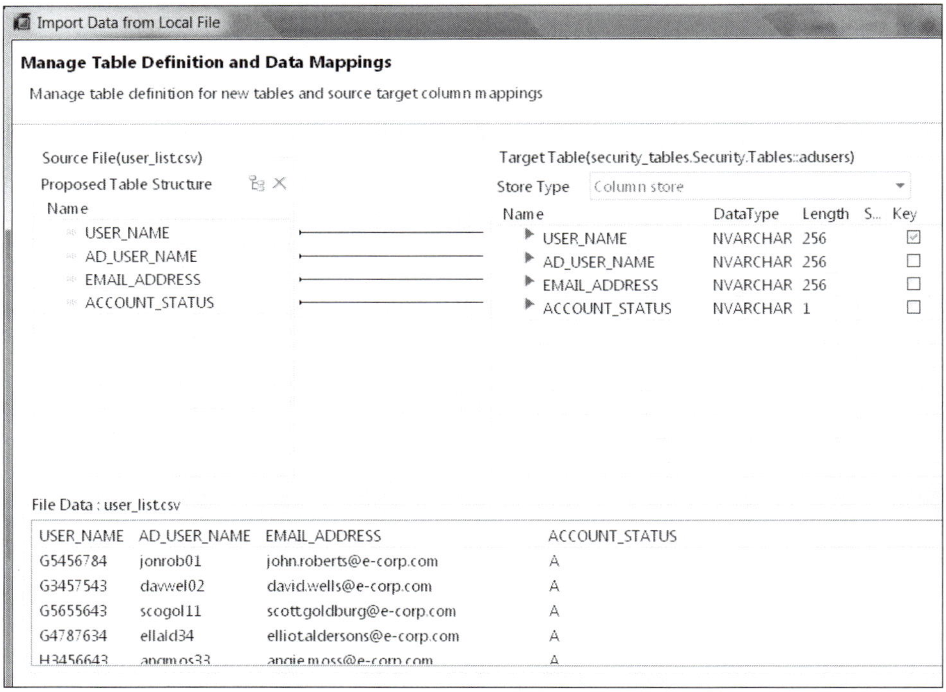

Figure 4.16 Mapping Source CSV File Columns to SAP HANA Table Output Columns

Once all the columns are properly mapped, click **Next** to preview the source and target data. Figure 4.17 shows the source and target data preview. If data already exists in the target, you'll see records in the output column named **Data from Existing Table**. If the import file contains users that already exist in the target table, delete them from the target table before importing the data. Click **Finish** to import the data into the table.

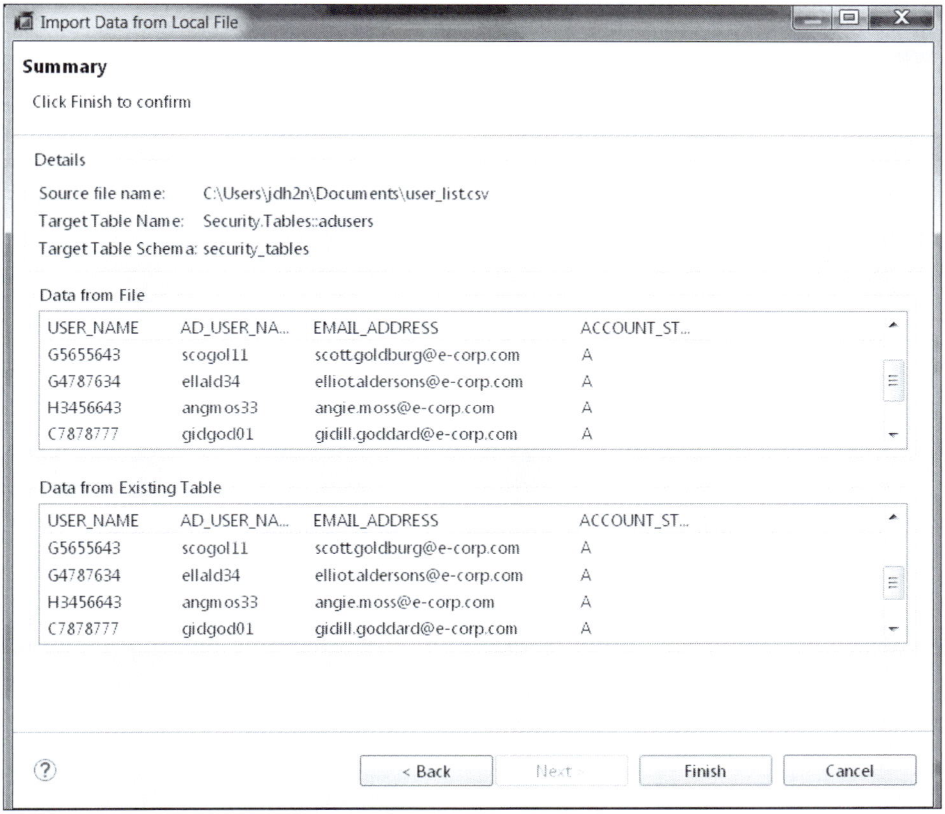

Figure 4.17 Summary Windows with Preview of Current Source and Target Data

4.5.4 Creating Repository Stored Procedures

With the data imported into table `Security.Tables::adusers`, we're now ready to develop a stored procedure to provision user accounts based on the user accounts listed in our table.

Note the following basic requirements for the stored procedure and for the process needed to create users programmatically at E-Corporation:

1. The procedure will create a user account with an account name based on the value in the USER_NAME column in the table.
2. The account password will need to be complex and randomly generated.
3. Users will never use the combination of the user name and password to manually authenticate with the SAP HANA system. Therefore, they will never need to know their passwords.
4. User accounts will be authenticated using a configured SAML provider and SAML identity.
5. The user account password will be set to never expire. However, an additional stored procedure will be created to randomly reset the user account password. The procedure will be executed every 90 days.
6. We'll need to configure and enable SAML for each user account listed in the table.
7. We'll need to add user email addresses to the user properties. This will help administrators contact users and will also allow the system to send emails to individual users when applicable.

Based on these requirements, we need to create two independent repository-based stored procedures. The first procedure will be named CREATE_AD_USERS and will provision a user listed in the table, add a SAML identity, enable SAML, and add an email address.

To create the first repository-based stored procedure using the development perspective and **Repositories** tab, right-click the **Security.Provisioning** package and choose **New • Other.** Search for "procedure". From the search results, choose **SAP HANA • Database Development**, then choose **Stored Procedure**, and click **Next.**

A window named **New Stored Procedure** will appear. Near the bottom of the window, enter "create_ad_users" in the **File Name:** field. In the **File Format:** field, choose **Text (.hdbprocedure)** from the drop-down menu. In the **Target Schema:** field, enter "security_tables", using all lowercase letters. Click **Finish** to save the file, and open the **CREATE_AD_USERS.hdbtable** configuration file on the right.

Define the CREATE_AD_USERS repository-based stored procedure using the syntax listed in Listing 4.6. Activate the design-time script by pressing Ctrl+F3.

```
PROCEDURE "security_tables"."Security.Provisioning::CREATE_AD_USERS" ()
  LANGUAGE SQLSCRIPT
  /* Procedure invoker must have privileges to create users */
  SQL SECURITY INVOKER
```

```
  AS
   BEGIN
/*Use a Cursor for future use. The following only
loops one time based on each record from SQL statement */

 DECLARE CURSOR c_users_list FOR
/* Get Active Users from table that are not currently
provisioned in HANA */
/* We need to escape the single quote mark around
SAMUSER and EMAILADDRESS with three single quote
marks ''' a total of 4 are needed */

SELECT
UT.AD_USER_NAME,
upper(UT.USER_NAME) as HANAUSER,
'''' || UT.AD_USER_NAME || '''' as SAMUSER,
CAST(ROUND(RAND() * 100000000,0) as NVARCHAR(50)) as RAN_NUMBER,
'''' || UT.EMAIL_ADDRESS || '''' as EMAILADDRESS
FROM  "security_tables"."Security.Tables::adusers" UT
WHERE upper(UT.USER_NAME) NOT IN
    (SELECT upper(USER_NAME) FROM "SYS"."USERS")
    and UT.ACCOUNT_STATUS = 'A';

 FOR cur_row as c_users_list DO
    --- Create Users with generic complex random password
    EXEC 'CREATE USER ' || cur_row.HANAUSER
        || ' PASSWORD "asdfSAD!' || cur_row.RAN_NUMBER || '"';
    --- Update user account so the password will not expire
    EXEC 'ALTER USER ' || cur_row.HANAUSER || ' DISABLE PASSWORD LIFETIME' ;
    --- Add SAML identity to user account
    EXEC 'ALTER USER ' || cur_row.HANAUSER || ' ADD IDENTITY '
        || cur_row.SAMUSER || ' FOR SAML PROVIDER TEST_SAML_PROVIDER';
    --- Enable SAML Authentication for the user account
    EXEC 'ALTER USER ' || cur_row.HANAUSER ||' ENABLE SAML';
    --- Add Email Addres to user account
    EXEC 'ALTER USER ' || cur_row.HANAUSER
        || ' SET PARAMETER EMAIL ADDRESS = ' || cur_row.EMAILADDRESS ;
```

```
 END FOR;

END;
```

Listing 4.6 Syntax of Stored Procedure to Create Users

Repeat the process to create another stored procedure, UPDATE_USER_PASSWORDS. This procedure can be executed periodically to change all the passwords of the users listed in the table. The password will be different for each user, because we append a random number generator to the end of each password string (see Listing 4.7).

```
PROCEDURE "security_tables"."Security.Provisioning::UPDATE_USER_PASSWORDS" ( )
  LANGUAGE SQLSCRIPT
  /* Procedure invoker must have privileges to create users */
  SQL SECURITY INVOKER
  AS
   BEGIN
/*Use a Cursor for future use. The following only
loops one time based on each record from SQL statement */

 DECLARE CURSOR c_users_list FOR
/* Get Active Users from table that are currently
provisioned in HANA */
/* We need to escape the single quote mark around
SAMUSER and EMAILADDRESS with three single quote
marks ''' a total of 4 are needed */

SELECT
UT.AD_USER_NAME,
upper(UT.USER_NAME) as HANAUSER,
'''' || UT.AD_USER_NAME || '''' as SAMUSER,
CAST(ROUND(RAND() * 100000000,0) as NVARCHAR(50)) as RAN_NUMBER,
'''' || UT.EMAIL_ADDRESS || '''' as EMAILADDRESS
FROM  "security_tables"."Security.Tables::adusers" UT
WHERE upper(UT.USER_NAME) IN
    (SELECT upper(USER_NAME) FROM "SYS"."USERS");

 FOR cur_row as c_users_list DO
    ---
 Update Users from security table with a new generic complex random password
```

```
    EXEC 'ALTER USER ' || cur_row.HANAUSER
        || ' PASSWORD "WxgT67e#21^' || cur_row.RAN_NUMBER || '"';

  END FOR;

END;
```

Listing 4.7 Syntax of Repository Stored Procedure to Update User Passwords

4.5.5 Executing the Repository Stored Procedure

To execute the stored procedure, open a SQL console. If your account has the USER ADMIN system privilege, you can execute the procedure to programmatically create or update the user based on the user records imported into the table from a CSV file. The syntax necessary to execute the two procedures is provided in the following two SQL statements:

```
CALL "security_tables"."Security.Provisioning::CREATE_AD_USERS";

CALL "security_tables"."Security.Provisioning::UPDATE_USER_PASSWORDS";
```

To validate that the users have been created, execute the SQL code in Listing 4.8.

```
SELECT
CASE WHEN U.USER_NAME is null
    THEN 'Not Created' ELSE 'Created'
    END as CREATION_STATUS,
UT.USER_NAME as REQUESTED_HANAUSER,
U.USER_NAME as PROVISIONED_HANAUSER

FROM  "security_tables"."Security.Tables::adusers" UT
LEFT OUTER JOIN "SYS"."USERS" U
    on (upper(UT.USER_NAME) = upper(U.USER_NAME));
```

Listing 4.8 SQL Code to List Users Not Created by Provisioning Process

Users listed in the table that are not provisioned in SAP HANA will show **Not Created** in the CREATION_STATUS column; execute the CREATE_AD_USER procedure again to create the missing user accounts. You'll also see the user accounts listed in SAP HANA Studio's **Security** area or in the SAP HANA Web-Based Development Workbench security manager.

4.6 Summary

The process of creating and managing user accounts can be accomplished with SQL statements, SAP HANA Studio, or SAP HANA Web-Based Development Workbench. All three interfaces also allow you to grant and revoke both privileges and roles that can be assigned to a user account. With all three options, we always must be aware of the impact of deleting user accounts from the system. We must be especially mindful if the user account was used to manage the SAP HANA system or develop content in the SAP HANA system.

Chapter 5
Database Roles

In this chapter, we'll present a complete overview of standard roles, including the processes used to provision roles, maintain roles, and grant privileges to roles.

Roles are objects that aid in the creation of a security model. The bulk of the security model development process involves defining roles, assigning privileges, and assigning roles to user accounts. In this chapter, we'll define standard database roles, which are created using the `CREATE ROLE` SQL syntax. Based on best practices, standard database roles shouldn't be used in SAP HANA; we'll discuss why shortly. However, there are instances in which we must use them. In this chapter, we'll start with an overview of the role creation and deletion process, then review the options to manage privilege assignments to roles. Finally, we'll explore how roles can be assigned to other roles.

5.1 What Are Roles?

A *role* is essentially an object in the SAP HANA system that contains a collection of granted privileges. A role can be granted to a user, causing the user to inherit all the privileges assigned to the role, and privileges can be granted to a role directly. In these instances, `GRANT` statements are used to assign individual privileges to the role. However, existing roles can also be granted to a role. In these cases, the role will contain its privileges plus any privileges in the attached role. We often refer to these as *nested roles*, because the parent role's privileges are extended to the child role.

Roles aid in the creation of a security model because they allow administrators to create a reusable collection of privileges. Without roles, administrators would need to grant individual permissions to each individual user account. If the SAP HANA environment had hundreds of users, each with a diverse level of access, administrators would find it difficult to manage SAP HANA security. With roles, the security administrator should only be concerned with granting roles to users.

Because roles are reusable, a single role can be granted to hundreds of users. This methodology helps the administrator in several ways. First, a user account needs only a few roles granted. Second, updates to a role are automatically cascaded to each user assigned the role. Third, roles support the creation of a consistently implemented security model. Therefore, roles are fundamentally important to the creation of a security model; in fact, we might argue that roles are the key object we produce when creating a security model.

The SAP HANA system is delivered with several base roles that are created by the system during installation. Most experts agree that you should avoid assigning these roles to users, because they often grant a high level of access to the SAP HANA system. Administrators can review the privileges granted to these roles to determine privileges assigned to specific activities within SAP HANA. As a rule of thumb, new custom roles should be created based on the requirements of each organization.

Table 5.1 provides an overview of each of the standard database roles delivered with an SAP HANA system.

Role Name	Description
MODELING	The modeling role allows a user to create information views or models within SAP HANA Studio. By default, this role has the full access analytic privilege `_SYS_BI_CP_ALL` granted. Users with this level of access have full data (row-level) access to all information view data within SAP HANA. The role also has full native object root package privilege access. Because of this, it should only be used as a template when access to data is important. It also has a high level of access to the _SYS_BIC and _SYS_BI schemas, in which information views are published. This role is not capable of assigning any of its privileges to other users.

Table 5.1 Default Standard Database Roles Delivered with SAP HANA

Role Name	Description
CONTENT_ADMIN	This role has all the privileges necessary for an SAP HANA modeler to manage and produce information views or models within SAP HANA Studio. It can also assign these privileges to other users and roles. In general, it has all the privileges assigned to the modeling role, plus a few extra. However, this role allows these privileges to be granted to other users. This role also allows a user to import and export content within the SAP HANA package repository. It provides full access to both imported and native development artifacts. This role has very high privileges and should not be granted to an actual user. It's best used as a template to help an administrator understand the various rights and privileges required by an SAP HANA modeler and security administrator.
PUBLIC	This role is the default role assigned to all standard users within SAP HANA. It contains a variety of SELECT and EXECUTE object privileges on tables, views, and procedures found in the SYS schema. Many of the stored procedures in the SYS schema are used to create database objects or list SAP HANA content. Without access to these procedures, tables, or views, a user would have extremely limited rights within SAP HANA and SAP HANA Studio. Only the system can grant the PUBLIC role to a user. Security administrators are not permitted to GRANT or REVOKE this role. Additional privileges can be both granted and revoked from the PUBLIC role. This allows the administrator to establish a baseline set of privileges for all standard users.
MONITORING	This role contains all the privileges necessary to query system metadata and system state tables. As its name implies, this role grants the privileges needed to monitor the system. It grants the DBA_COCKPIT role and the CATALOG READ system privilege and grants SELECT on the _SYS_STATISTICS schema.
RESTRICTED_USER_JDBC_ACCESS	This role provides the absolute minimum privileges necessary to connect to SAP HANA using JDBC. It's often granted to restricted users so they can connect to SAP HANA via JDBC.
RESTRICTED_USER_ODBC_ACCESS	This role provides the absolute minimum privileges necessary to connect to SAP HANA using JDBC. It's often granted to restricted users so they can connect to SAP HANA via ODBC.

Table 5.1 Default Standard Database Roles Delivered with SAP HANA (Cont.)

Role Name	Description
SAP_INTERNAL_HANA_SUPPORT	This role provides a minimal level of access for an SAP support engineer to review information about a customer's system, including trace log management. It doesn't provide access to any of the customer's data. It's similar to the monitoring role, with only a few differences.

Table 5.1 Default Standard Database Roles Delivered with SAP HANA (Cont.)

There are two main issues with the usage of standard database roles when developing a security model: The first is an organization's ability to maintain a consistent security model between environments, and the second is an organization's ability to manage the user accounts that grant privileges to other users and roles—for example:

- **Consistency issues**

  Most organizations likely will maintain multiple related SAP HANA systems to facilitate lifecycle management practices. One characteristic of a lifecycle management practice is that it's a process in which content is developed in a particular environment and then promoted to a test environment, followed by a production environment. The process isn't limited only to SAP HANA application development artifacts; we can also include the development lifecycle of a security model in this process. In particular, a security model can be created in a development environment and then promoted to a test and production environment for the purposes of validation. This practice is important, because each environment requires security, and we need to test our security changes outside of a production environment.

  When we use standard database roles, the design-time scripts used to create roles, grant privileges, and revoke privileges must be maintained outside of the SAP HANA system in the form of text files containing SQL scripts. To promote these roles and their privileges, we must execute identical SQL scripts in each environment. In addition, we must also manually preserve each version of the role within SQL scripts in instances in which we need to revert a change. Because the design-time versions of our roles are decoupled from the SAP HANA system, management of this process is manual and prone to inconsistencies between environments. Fortunately, SAP HANA offers an alternative to standard database roles. Such roles are called repository-based roles and aren't subject to this issue. We'll discuss repository roles in more detail in the next chapter.

- **Grantor issues**
  Standard database roles are also subject to grantor issues. When a user account grants privileges to another user or role, it becomes the grantor. As discussed in Chapter 4, technical user accounts should be created for each security administrator to avoid the cascade deletion issue common to deleting user accounts. Deleting user accounts that have granted privileges will revoke any privileges that they have granted to a standard role. Therefore, the use of standard roles in a security model will require an extra level of discipline, because we must make sure that all security changes are implemented with technical user accounts and that these accounts are never deleted. This can make the security model management process more difficult than usual. Again, fortunately, repository-based roles aren't subject to this issue (see Chapter 6 for more information).

5.2 Creating and Managing Roles

At a high level, there are three different ways to create and manage roles within SAP HANA: via SQL statements based on the `CREATE ROLE` syntax, in SAP HANA Studio, or in the SAP HANA Web-based Development Workbench security manager. In this section, we'll discuss the three different options used to provision and manage standard roles.

5.2.1 Creating and Deleting Roles with SQL Statements

We can create and drop roles with SQL statements. Creating global roles using SQL statements involves issuing a `CREATE ROLE` statement. Users must have the system privilege `ROLE ADMIN` to create and delete standard roles. To create a standard role, use the following syntax:

```
CREATE ROLE <ROLENAME>
```

Replace `<ROLENAME>` with the desired role name. Role names can contain most characters, including spaces and special characters. For example, we can create the My Role Has a Long Name? role based on the following SQL statement:

```
CREATE ROLE "My Role Has a Long Name?";
```

As of SAP HANA SPS 11, roles can also be created with a schema prefix. The name of a given role must be unique within the global system namespace or schema-specific namespace, but the same role name can exist in the global and schema namespaces simultaneously. Technically, the schema prefix differentiates the roles within the system, even when their display names appear to overlap. Schema-prefixed roles will also be deleted from the system if the associated schema is deleted from the system. To create a role with a schema name prefix, issue the following two SQL statements:

```
CREATE ROLE <MY_SCHEMA_NAME>.<ROLENAME>;
CREATE ROLE "MySchema"."DATABASE ADMIN USER 2200";
```

Replace <MY_SCHEMA_NAME> with the name of an existing schema.

We can also use the DROP ROLE SQL syntax to delete a role, as follows:

```
DROP ROLE <ROLENAME>;
DROP ROLE <MY_SCHEMA_NAME>.<ROLENAME>;
```

Replace <ROLENAME> with the name of an existing standard role and replace <MY_SCHEMA_NAME> with the name of an existing schema.

When a role is dropped from the system, it will be revoked from any user or role that was previously granted the deleted role, as will all the privileges associated with the role. In general, you should avoid deleting roles from the system when they're currently associated with users or other roles.

Starting with SAP HANA SPS 12, a new system view was created in the SYS schema to help identify the user accounts associated with a specified role. The name of the view is EFFECTIVE_ROLE_GRANTEES. The following SQL statement queries this view:

```
SELECT * FROM EFFECTIVE_ROLE_GRANTEES WHERE ROLE_NAME = <ROLE_NAME>;
```

Replace <ROLE_NAME> with the name of a role defined within the system. The view must be filtered based on the ROLE_NAME column. Therefore, the WHERE clause in this SQL statement is mandatory.

5.2.2 Creating and Deleting Roles with SAP HANA Studio

We can also create and delete roles with SAP HANA Studio. To access the user management area, start by switching to the administration console perspective. On the **Systems** tab, located on the left, expand the **System** node, then the **Security** node, revealing the **Security**, **Users**, and **Roles** nodes. Expand the **Roles** node to reveal roles defined in the system.

To create a role, right-click the **Roles** node and choose **New Role**. A **New Role** tab will open on the right (see Figure 5.1).

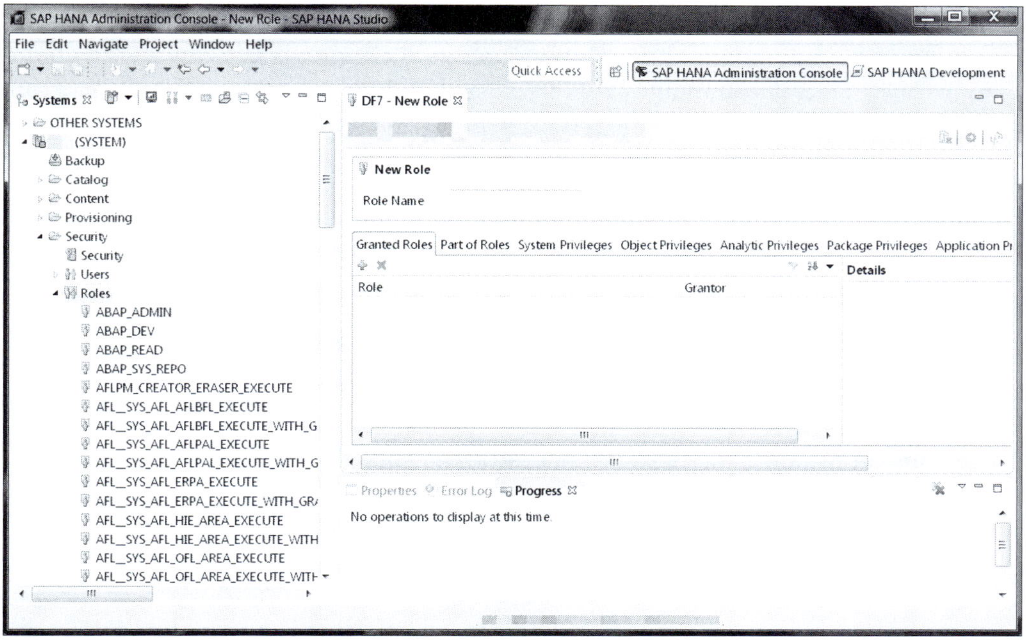

Figure 5.1 New Role Tab in SAP HANA Studio

To specify the name of the role, enter the desired name in the mandatory **Role Name** field; all other configuration options are optional. At the bottom of the **New User** tab, you'll see seven tabs: **Granted Roles, Part of Roles**, **System Privileges, Object Privileges, Analytic Privileges**, **Package Privileges**, and **Application Privileges**. Click each tab to reveal new options to grant or revoke the privileges applicable to the tab name.

Once you've defined the required options, press F8, press Ctrl+S, or click the **Save** or **Execute** icons to activate the new role. Check the status bar at the top of the **New Role** window to validate that the role was created. If there were any issues creating the role, red text will appear with a summary of the issue causing the activation to fail. If the account creation process was successful, the status window will read **Role <'role Name'> Created**.

To delete a role with SAP HANA Studio, locate the **Security** node in the **System** tab and expand it to reveal the **Security**, **Users**, and **Roles** nodes. Expand the **Roles** node to reveal roles defined in the system. Right-click a role and choose **Delete**, or select the role and press the Delete key. In the confirmation window that appears, click **OK** to permanently delete the role.

When a role is deleted from the system, it will be revoked from any user or role that was previously granted the deleted role, as will all the privileges associated with the role. In general, you should avoid deleting roles from the system when they're currently associated with a user. Query the system view `EFFECTIVE_ROLE_GRANTEES` to identify any users or roles currently assigned a role.

5.2.3 Creating and Deleting Roles with SAP HANA Web-Based Development Workbench

The SAP HANA Web-Based Development Workbench security manager, hosted within the XS engine, provides a GUI to create and delete roles.

You can access SAP HANA Web-Based Development Workbench via a supported Internet browser. Use the following URLs, customized to match the details of your environment:

http://sap-hana.myhost.com:8000/sap/hana/ide/security

http://<sap_hana_host>: 80<instance_number>/sap/hana/ide/security

Replace <sap_hana_host> with the hostname of the SAP HANA system in your environment. Replace <instance_number> with the two-digit instance number corresponding to your SAP HANA system.

For secure access, customize the following URLs:

https://<sap_hana_host>: 43<instance_number>/sap/hana/ide/security

https://sap-hana.myhost.com:4300/sap/hana/ide/security

To use the SAP HANA Web-Based Development Workbench security manager, the user account first will need to be granted one of the roles listed in Table 5.2. Users only need one of the two roles listed to access the security manager.

Role Name	Description
`sap.hana.ide.roles::SecurityAdmin`	Within the SAP HANA Web-Based Development Workbench, a user will only be able to access the security manager, which provides interfaces to create and manage users and roles.

Table 5.2 Roles Required for SAP HANA Web-Based Development Workbench Security Manager

Role Name	Description
`sap.hana.ide.roles::Developer`	This role grants a higher level of privileges for users that need full access to SAP HANA Web-based Development Workbench. It grants access to the editor, catalog, and security interfaces and is considered the parent to the sap.hana.ide.roles::SecurityAdmin role.

Table 5.2 Roles Required for SAP HANA Web-Based Development Workbench Security Manager (Cont.)

Additional Privileges to Use Security Manager

It's important to note that the roles in Table 5.2 simply allow the granted user access to the security interface. To manage a security model, additional privileges and roles will need to be granted. For example, the user will need the `ROLE ADMIN` system privilege to create and drop roles. To grant privileges to a user or role, the account accessing the security manager will also require privileges to grant the privileges to other users or roles.

To create a role within the SAP HANA Web-Based Development Workbench security manager interface, expand the **Security • Users** nodes located on the left. Right-click the **Roles** node and choose **New Role**. A **New Role** tab will open on the right (see Figure 5.2).

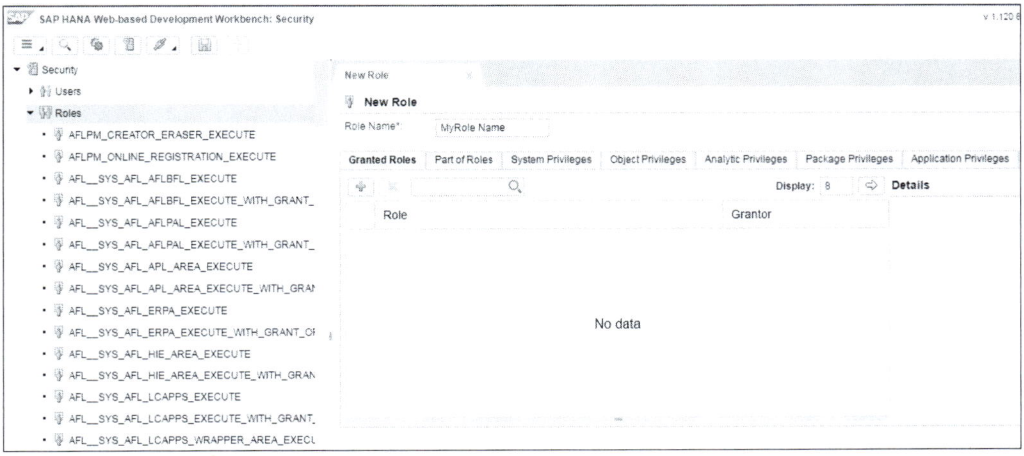

Figure 5.2 New User Area in SAP HANA Web-Based Development Workbench

To specify the role name, enter the desired name in the mandatory **Role Name** field. At the bottom of the **New User** tab, you'll see seven tabs: **Granted Roles**, **Part of Roles**, **System Privileges**, **Object Privileges**, **Analytic Privileges**, **Package Privileges** and **Application Privileges**. Click each tab to reveal new options to grant or revoke privileges applicable to the tab name.

To activate a new role, click the disk icon located in the icon bar. Clicking the icon will save and activate the changes. Note that the activation status window is located at the bottom of the interface window and has a black-colored background. If any errors are encountered during activation, red text will appear indicating the issue.

To delete a role with the SAP HANA Web-Based Development Workbench security manager, locate the **Security** node on the right and expand it to reveal the **Security** and **Roles** nodes. Expand the **Roles** node to reveal roles defined in the system. Right-click a role and choose **Delete**. In the confirmation window that appears, click **OK** to permanently delete the role.

When a role is deleted from the system, it will be revoked from any user or role that was previously granted the deleted role, as will all the privileges associated with the role. In general, you should avoid deleting roles from the system when they're currently associated with a user. Query the system view `EFFECTIVE_ROLE_GRANTEES` to list any users or roles currently assigned a role.

In the next section, we'll discuss how privileges are granted and revoked from a role.

5.3 Granting and Revoking Privileges

As discussed in Chapter 4, we don't recommend assigning individual privileges to individual user accounts as the basis for a security model. Roles should be created, and privileges should then be assigned to roles. Once a role is configured with the applicable privileges, it should then be granted to one or more user accounts. In the following sections, we'll look at the different methodologies for granting privileges to roles and then provide instructions for doing so with SQL, SAP HANA Studio, and SAP HANA Web-Based Development Workbench.

5.3.1 Methodologies for Granting Privileges to Roles

Using a role-based security model methodology is generally more scalable in environments with a large quantity of user accounts and a diverse mixture of access requirements. Roles should be created based on common access requirements and common user functions. For example, we might create a role named PUBLIC_DATA_ACCESS. Such a role can grant basic SELECT access to database tables, column views, and standard views that are deemed accessible by all defined user accounts. We can create another role named SECURE_DATA_ACCESS that grants limited access to tables, column views and views that contain confidential data. Such a role might also incorporate a structured privilege that filters the results based on a defined level of data access.

Generally, we recommend that two broad categories of roles be created. First, there are roles that accommodate both basic catalog object and schema-level access. These roles focus on providing SELECT and EXECUTE access to specific catalog objects or perhaps an entire schema. For example, we might create a role named DATA_MART_READ_ONLY. This role will provide SELECT access to all objects in the schema named DATA_MART. It's very common for each schema to have a dedicated set of roles, with each role providing a different level of access to the schema. For example, we can define the following roles in which each role grants a higher level of privileges to the schema name used in the prefix:

- DATA_MART_READ_ONLY
- DATA_MART_POWER_USER
- DATA_MART_SEC_ADMIN
- DATA_MART_OWNER

Second, we recommend creating roles based on functional activities. For example, developers would be granted privileges to work in the SAP HANA package repository. A role named ECORP_INFORMATION_MODELER might be created for users that will create information views. Security administrators would be granted privileges to manage security. For example, the ECORP_SECURITY_ADMIN role would be created for individuals that plan to manage security. Finally, the BACKUP_MONITOR and BACKUP_ADMIN roles could be created and granted to individuals that manage backups.

These categories provide a nice delineation, but there will likely be some overlap between the types of privileges we grant within either type of role. However, we should still try to avoid granting the same privileges to multiple roles. One easy way to do this is by granting roles to roles. SAP HANA supports granting privileges to roles and existing roles to roles. Nesting roles within roles, when implemented properly, can greatly reduce maintenance on a security model. For example, we can grant the role DM_READ_ONLY to the role ECORP_INFOMRATION_MODELER. In this case, we can ensure that the developers also have SELECT access to the data mart schema even if we don't explicitly grant those privileges in the ECORP_INFOMRATION_MODELER role, ensuring that the information modeler has a basic level of access to the data mart schema.

Figure 5.3 illustrates how we can nest roles to simplify the security model design.

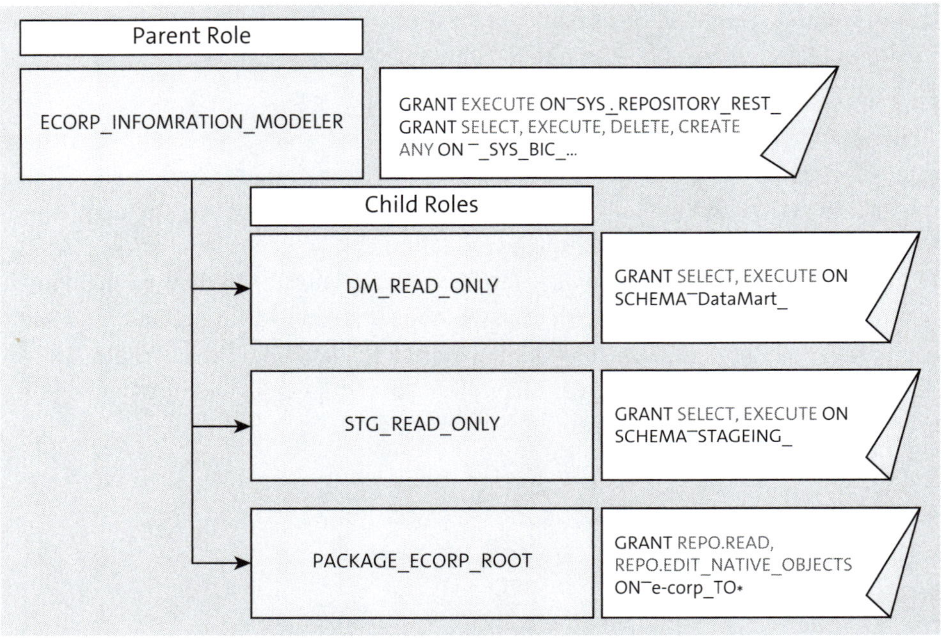

Figure 5.3 Child Roles Nested within Parent Role

The ECORP_INFORMATION_MODELER parent role has been granted the DM_READ_ONLY, STG_READ_ONLY, and PACKAGE_ECORP_ROOT child roles to provide access to the schemas and packages used by the information modeler. The diagram only depicts a few example privileges granted to the roles, shown to the right of each role name. In a true security model, we'd expect each role to be granted several different privileges.

5.3.2 Granting and Revoking Privileges with SQL

Using the SQL console and SQL statements, we can both grant privileges to and revoke them from roles. When granting privileges to specific objects, we need to first recognize the object type. Specifically, we need to use a different syntax for repository-based objects than for standard catalog objects. Repository-based objects are owned by the _SYS_REPO system account. With this account, we have no way to delegate grant and revoke privileges to other users in the system. For example, you can't logon as _SYS_REPO and grant `SELECT` to another user while including the `WITH ADMIN OPTION` or `WITH GRANT OPTION` statement options. Because of this, we must use a series of system-delivered stored procedures to grant privileges for repository-based objects owned by _SYS_REPO. These stored procedures are activated in the _SYS_REPO schema and can be called directly, assuming you have the `EXECUTE` privilege for the procedures. Standard catalog objects can be granted or revoked using the standard SQL `GRANT` or `REVOKE` statements. Let's look at a series of SQL statements used to grant privileges based on the object and privilege type.

System Privileges

We can grant system privileges to roles using the `GRANT` SQL syntax. The following three SQL statements are separated by concluding semicolons:

```
GRANT <SYSTEM_PRIVILEGE> TO <ROLENAME>;
GRANT <SYSTEM_PRIVILEGE> TO <ROLENAME> WITH ADMIN OPTION;
GRANT DATA ADMIN, EXPORT, IMPORT TO ROLE_SEC_ADMIN WITH ADMIN OPTION;
```

The first statement provides the general syntax, with variables indicated by text within angle brackets (<>). The variables need to be replaced with items unique to your environment. The <SYSTEM_PRIVILEGES> variable can be replaced with a comma-separated list of system privileges, as indicated in the third SQL example. The <ROLENAME> variable will be replaced with the name of an activated role within the system.

The second SQL statement includes the `WITH ADMIN OPTION` at the end of the statement. This option allows the grantee of the role to subsequently grant the same privilege to another user or role. It's typically reserved for user accounts or roles that manage security models. The final SQL statement provides a full example in which we grant system privileges to the role ROLE_SEC_ADMIN. It includes the `WITH ADMIN OPTION`, which allows the role grantee to grant the same privileges to other users or roles.

We can also revoke system privileges using the `REVOKE` SQL syntax, as follows:

```
REVOKE <SYSTEM_PRIVILEGE> FROM <ROLENAME>;
REVOKE DATA ADMIN, EXPORT, IMPORT FROM ROLE_SEC_ADMIN;
```

The first statement provides the general syntax, and the second SQL statement provides a full example in which the listed system privileges are removed from the role ROLE_SEC_ADMIN.

> **Note**
>
> As we continue through this section, the same rules will apply to the each of the examples: The first and/or second example is a generic template that contains variables within angle brackets that need to be replaced with items unique to your environment, and the final SQL statement will provide a full example.

Catalog Schema Privileges

If a schema is owned by a standard database user, we can use the following syntax to grant one or more privileges to a role:

```
GRANT <SCHEMA_PRIVILEGE> ON SCHEMA <SCHEMA_NAME> TO <ROLENAME>;
GRANT <SCHEMA_PRIVILEGE> ON SCHEMA <SCHEMA_
NAME> TO <ROLENAME> WITH GRANT OPTION;
GRANT SELECT, EXECUTE ON SCHEMA "MySchema" TO MYSCHEMA_READONLY_ACCESS;
```

The <SCHEMA_PRIVILEGES> variable can be replaced with a comma-separated list of schema object privileges, as indicated in the example.

To remove the privileges, use the following syntax:

```
REVOKE <SCHEMA_PRIVILEGE> ON SCHEMA <SCHEMA_NAME> FROM <ROLENAME>;
REVOKE SELECT, EXECUTE ON SCHEMA "MySchema" FROM MYSCHEMA_READONLY_ACCESS;
```

Note that `GRANT` and `REVOKE` statements won't work on repository-based schemas, which are owned by the system account _SYS_REPO and must be granted using a special stored procedure. In the next section, we'll provide example SQL statements.

Repository Schema Privileges

When a schema is created in the SAP HANA development repository, it's owned by the system user _SYS_REPO; these are repository schemas. In such cases, we can't use the standard `GRANT` and `REVOKE` SQL syntax to manage permissions for a given role. Instead, we must use a specific stored procedure to grant and another to revoke repository schema privileges.

To grant repository schema privileges, we need to execute a stored procedure in the _SYS_REPO schema named `GRANT_SCHEMA_PRIVILEGE_ON_ACTIVATED_CONTENT`. To use this procedure, the security administrator must have the `EXECUTE` object privilege on the stored procedure. This procedure has three input parameters: The first parameter can accommodate a comma-separated array of schema privileges, the second parameter can accommodate a single schema name, and the third parameter can accommodate a role name.

In the following example, we need to replace <OBJECT_PRIVILEGES> with one or more schema privileges; <SCHEMA_NAME> with the case-sensitive name of the schema, enclosed in double quotes if lowercase or mixed case; and <ROLENAME> with the name of a role defined in the SAP HANA system. To execute a stored procedure, use the SQL CALL function followed by the name of the stored procedure:

```
CALL "_SYS_REPO"."GRANT_SCHEMA_PRIVILEGE_ON_ACTIVATED_CONTENT"
('<OBJECT_PRIVILEGES>','<SCHEMA_NAME>','<ROLENAME>');
```

The following SQL statement provides a full example; multiple schema privileges are granted to the MYSCHEMA_ADMIN role within the MySchema schema:

```
CALL "_SYS_REPO"."GRANT_SCHEMA_PRIVILEGE_ON_ACTIVATED_CONTENT"
('SELECT, EXECUTE, UPDATE, CREATE ANY' ,'"MySchema"', ' MYSCHEMA_ADMIN');
```

To revoke repository schema privileges, we need to execute a stored procedure in the _SYS_REPO schema named REVOKE_SCHEMA_PRIVILEGE_ON_ACTIVATED_CONTENT. This procedure has three input parameters, which are the same as those for the previous procedure used to grant the privileges—for example:

```
CALL "_SYS_REPO"."REVOKE_SCHEMA_PRIVILEGE_ON_ACTIVATED_CONTENT"
('<OBJECT_PRIVILEGES>','<SCHEMA_NAME>','<USER_NAME>');
CALL "_SYS_REPO"."REVOKE_SCHEMA_PRIVILEGE_ON_ACTIVATED_CONTENT"
('SELECT, EXECUTE, DROP, CREATE ANY', '"MySchema"'; 'MYSCHEMA_ADMIN');
```

Catalog Object Privileges

If a catalog object is owned by a standard database user, we can use the following SQL syntax to grant catalog object privileges to a role. The <OBJECT_PRIVILEGE> variable can be replaced with a comma-separated array of privileges. The WITH GRANT OPTION, when specified, allows the grantee the ability to subsequently grant the same privileges to other users in the system. The example assumes that the schema is not repository-based:

```
GRANT <OBJECT_PRIVILEGE> ON <OBJECT_NAME> TO <ROLENAME>;
GRANT <OBJECT_PRIVILEGE> ON <OBJECT_NAME> TO <ROLENAME> WITH GRANT OPTION;
GRANT SELECT, INSERT, UPDATE, DELETE ON "MySchema"."MyTable" TO MYSCHEMA_
ADMIN WITH GRANT OPTION;
```

To remove the privileges, use the following syntax:

```
REVOKE <OBJECT_PRIVILEGE> ON <OBJECT_NAME> FROM <ROLENAME>;
REVOKE SELECT, INSERT, UPDATE, DELETE ON "MySchema"."MyTable" FROM MYSCHEMA_
ADMIN;
```

Repository Object Privileges

When a catalog object is created in the SAP HANA development repository, it's owned by the system user _SYS_REPO. We call these repository catalog objects. In such cases, we can't use the standard GRANT and REVOKE SQL syntax to manage permissions on a given user account. To accommodate, we must use a specific stored procedure to grant and another to revoke repository catalog object privileges.

To grant repository catalog object privileges, we need to execute a stored procedure in the _SYS_REPO schema, named GRANT_PRIVILEGE_ON_ACTIVATED_CONTENT. To use this procedure, the security administrator must have the object privilege EXECUTE on the stored procedure. This procedure has three input parameters: The first parameter can accommodate a comma-separated array of schema privileges, the second parameter can accommodate a single schema and object name, and the third parameter can accommodate a role name.

In the following example, we need to replace <OBJECT_PRIVILEGES> with one or more schema privileges; replace <OBJECT_NAME> with the case-sensitive and fully qualified name of our catalog object, enclosed in double quotes if the name is lowercase or mixed case; and replace <ROLENAME> with the name of a role defined in the SAP HANA system:

```
CALL "_SYS_REPO"."GRANT_PRIVILEGE_ON_ACTIVATED_CONTENT"
('<OBJECT_PRIVILEGES>','<OBJECT_NAME>','<ROLENAME>');
CALL
"_SYS_REPO"."GRANT_PRIVILEGE_ON_ACTIVATED_CONTENT "('SELECT, EXECUTE',
'"StagingMart"."e-corp.sales.tables::STG_CUSTOMERS"', 'STAGING_READ_ONLY');
```

To revoke repository catalog object privileges, we need to execute a stored procedure in the _SYS_REPO schema named REVOKE_PRIVILEGE_ON_ACTIVATED_CONTENT. This procedure has three input parameters, which are identical to those used in the previous procedure to grant the privileges. Use the following syntax to call the stored procedure equipped to revoke catalog object privileges previously granted:

```
CALL
"_SYS_REPO"."REVOKE_PRIVILEGE_ON_ACTIVATED_CONTENT "
```

```
('<OBJECT_PRIVILEGES>','<SCHEMA_NAME>','<ROLENAME>');
CALL "_SYS_REPO"."REVOKE_PRIVILEGE_ON_ACTIVATED_CONTENT"('SELECT, EXECUTE' ,
'"StagingMart"."e-corp.sales.tables::STG_CUSTOMERS"' , 'STAGING_READ_ONLY');
```

Structured Privileges

Structured privileges are a special type of object used to force the system to provide additional access restrictions against a column view or catalog view. In Chapter 2, we introduced analytic privileges, which are used with SAP HANA information views to provide data access to an activated information view. Technically, analytic privileges are a type of structured privilege, but most GUIs refer to them as analytic privileges. Repository-based analytic privileges are owned and managed by the system account _SYS_REPO. However, structured privileges can be owned by any user with system privileges.

If a structured privilege is owned by a standard database user, we can use the GRANT STRUCTURED PRIVILEGE SQL syntax to grant such privileges to a user account. To grant a structured privilege, we must own the structured privilege, because there is no WITH GRANT OPTION to allow another user to grant this privilege. Note that this this syntax won't work on repository-based analytic privileges. In the following example, replace the <STRUCTURED_PRIVILEGE_NAME> variable with the name of the structured privilege:

```
GRANT STRUCTURED PRIVILEGE <STRUCTURED_PRIVILEGE_NAME> TO <ROLENAME>;
```

Now, we'll walk you through the process of creating a catalog view and structured privilege and the process of granting the privilege to a user. Start by using the SQL code in Listing 5.1 to create a standard catalog view.

```
CREATE VIEW "MySchema"."MYVIEW" ( "MYKEYCOLUMN",
     "STATE",
     "CITY",
     "POSTALCODE" ) AS select
     T0."MYKEYCOLUMN",
     T0."STATE",
     T0."CITY",
     T0."POSTALCODE"
FROM "SYSTEM"."MYTABLENAME" T0
WITH STRUCTURED PRIVILEGE CHECK;
```

Listing 5.1 CREATE VIEW SQL Code

We then create a structured privilege referencing the view, which will apply a filter on the column named STATE. The following SQL statement will create a structured privilege that will filter the STATE to the value TN; after the privilege name, use the FOR SELECT syntax to indicate that the privilege should be applied when querying the view:

```
CREATE STRUCTURED PRIVILEGE "MyStructuredPriv"
FOR SELECT ON "MySchema"."MYVIEW" WHERE "STATE" = 'TN';
```

We then grant the structured privilege to the user JONATHAN. Once granted, the user will only see value from the view where "STATE" = 'TN':

```
GRANT STRUCTURED PRIVILEGE "MyStructuredPriv" TO ROLE_STATE_TN;
```

To revoke the structured privilege, use the REVOKE STRUCTURED PRIVILEGE SQL syntax:

```
REVOKE STRUCTURED PRIVILEGE <STRUCTURED_PRIVILEGE_NAME> FROM <ROLENAME>;
REVOKE STRUCTURED PRIVILEGE "MyStructuredPriv" FROM ROLE_STATE_TN;
```

To allow other users or roles to grant the structured privilege, you can include the WITH GRANT OPTION. For example, to allow the role ROLE_SEC_ADMIN the ability to grant the structured privilege to other users, you must include the WITH GRANT OPTION, as in the following:

```
GRANT STRUCTURED PRIVILEGE "MyStructuredPriv" TO ROLE_SEC_ADMIN WITH GRANT
OPTION;
```

Remote Sources

To grant access to a remote source or a smart data access federated database connection, issue a SQL statement as follows:

```
GRANT <SOURCE_PRIVILEGE> ON REMOTE SOURCE <SOURCE_NAME> TO <ROLENAME>;
```

The <SOURCE_PRIVILEGE> variable can be replaced with a comma-separated array of privileges specific to remote source objects, and the <SOURCE_NAME> variable can be replaced with the name of the remote source.

To remove remote source privileges, use the REVOKE SQL statement. The following statement will remove the privileges specified in the <SOURCE_PRIVILEGES> variable array:

```
REVOKE <SOURCE_PRIVILEGE> ON REMOTE SOURCE <SOURCE_NAME> FROM <ROLENAME>;
```

Repository Analytic Privileges

When we create a standard analytic privilege, it's owned by the system user _SYS_REPO. Analytic privileges are a type of structured privilege, but we can't use the standard GRANT and REVOKE SQL syntax to assign analytic privileges to a user. Instead, we must use a specific stored procedure to grant and another to revoke analytic privileges for users.

To grant an analytic privilege to a user, we must execute the stored procedure GRANT_ACTIVATED_ANALYTIC_PRIVILEGE, stored in the _SYS_REPO schema. To use this procedure, the security administrator must have the EXECUTE object privilege on the stored procedure. The procedure provides two input parameters. The first parameter should contain the name of the analytic privilege, and the second input parameter will contain the name of the user:

```
CALL "_SYS_REPO"."GRANT_ACTIVATED_ANALYTICAL_PRIVILEGE"
('<ANALLYTIC_PRIVILEGE_NAME>','<ROLENAME>');
CALL "_SYS_REPO"."GRANT_ACTIVATED_ANALYTICAL_PRIVILEGE"
('"e-corp.sales.security/ap_sales_reporting_region"','ROLE_REGION');
```

To revoke an analytic privilege from a user, we must execute the stored procedure REVOKE_ACTIVATED_ANALYTIC_PRIVILEGE, stored in the _SYS_REPO schema. It uses the same two input parameters:

```
CALL "_SYS_REPO"."REVOKE_ACTIVATED_ANALYTICAL_PRIVILEGE"
('<ANALLYTIC_PRIVILEGE_NAME>','<ROLENAME>');
CALL "_SYS_REPO"."REVOKE_ACTIVATED_ANALYTICAL_PRIVILEGE"
('"e-corp.sales.security/ap_sales_reporting_region"','ROLE_REGION' );
```

Application Privileges

When we create an application privilege, it's owned by the system user _SYS_REPO. To grant or revoke application privileges, we must use a specific stored procedure, as follows:

```
CALL "_SYS_REPO"."GRANT_APPLICATION_PRIVILEGE"
('<APPLICATION_PRIVILEGE_NAME>','<ROLENAME>');
CALL "_SYS_REPO"."GRANT_APPLICATION_PRIVILEGE"
('"sap.hana.admin::Administrator"','ROLE_APP');
```

Use the following syntax used to revoke an application privilege:

```
CALL "_SYS_REPO"."REVOKE_APPLICATION_PRIVILEGE"
('<APPLICATION_PRIVILEGE_NAME>','<ROLENAME>');
CALL "_SYS_REPO"."REVOKE_APPLICATION_PRIVILEGE"
('"sap.hana.admin::Administrator"','ROLE_APP');
```

Package Privileges

To grant access to a package in the SAP HANA repository, issue a SQL statement as follows:

```
GRANT <PACKAGE_PRIVILEGE> ON <"package.subpackage"> TO <ROLENAME> WITH GRANT
OPTION;
GRANT REPO.READ, REPO.EDIT_NATIVE_OBJECTS ON "e-corp" TO ROLE_ECORP_PKG_ROOT_
ADMIN WITH GRANT OPTION;
```

The <PACKAGE_PRIVILEGE> variable can be replaced with a comma-separated array of package privileges, and the <package.subpackage> variable can be replaced with the case-sensitive name of the package and subpackage hierarchy. Each node of the package hierarchy should be separated by a period. The `WITH GRANT OPTION` allows the grantee to grant the same privileges to other users.

To remove remote source privileges, use the `REVOKE` SQL statement. The following example SQL statement will remove the privileges specified in the <PACKAGE_PRIVILEGE> variable array:

```
REVOKE <PACKAGE_PRIVILEGE> ON <"package.subpackage"> FROM <ROLENAME>;
REVOKE REPO.EDIT_NATIVE_OBJECTS ON "e-corp" FROM ROLE_ECORP_PKG_ROOT_ADMIN;
```

Full SQL Syntax

The complete available syntax necessary for granting and revoking privileges and creating and managing roles is beyond the scope of this book. To review the full syntax and all available options, see the SAP HANA SQL and System Views Reference Guide found at *https://help.sap.com/hana_platform* or at the following direct link to the guide in PDF format: *http://help.sap.com/hana/SAP_HANA_SQL_and_System_Views_Reference_en.pdf*.

Search for the sections pertaining to the `GRANT`, `REVOKE`, `CREATE ROLE`, and `DROP ROLE` statements.

5.3.3 Granting and Revoking Privileges with SAP HANA Studio

We also can use the role management area in SAP HANA Studio to both grant and revoke privileges for a given standard role. Most will find it easier to use SAP HANA Studio than to memorize and type SQL statements. In this section, we'll review the process for granting and revoking system, object, analytic, and package privileges.

To access the **role** management node, start by switching to the administration console perspective. On the **Systems** tab, located on the left, expand the **System** node. Locate the **Security** node and expand it to reveal the **Security**, **Users**, and **Roles** nodes. Expand the **Roles** node to reveal roles defined in the system. To manage a role, double-click the role name in the list to open the **Role Management** tab on the right. This same tab is present when creating a role.

Figure 5.4 shows the role management interface within SAP HANA Studio. Just below the role name, you'll see several tabs, each of which represents an interface in which specific types of privileges or roles can be granted or revoked.

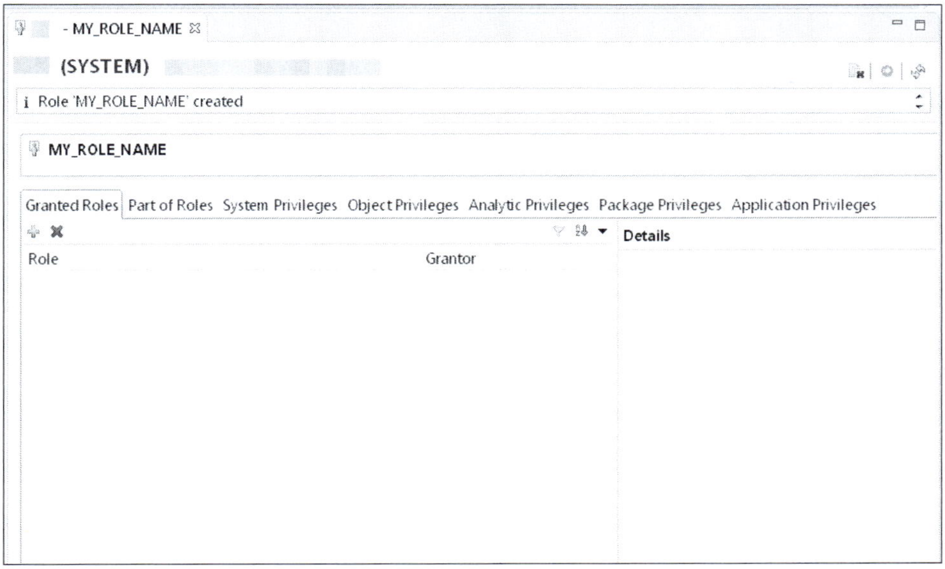

Figure 5.4 Managing Privileges Assigned to Roles in SAP HANA Studio

Granted Roles

The first tab is **Granted Roles**. Use this tab to grant or revoke additional roles to the given role. In Section 5.4.2, we'll discuss how to grant and revoke role assignments to roles in SAP HANA Studio, but for now, note that the process is similar to that for granting and revoking privileges. Now, let's look at how to use SAP HANA Studio to grant or revoke a role's privileges.

Part of Roles

If the active role is granted to other roles, the roles it's assigned to will appear in the **Part of Roles** tab. This is a read-only tab; the listed roles can't be removed from or added to this tab.

System Privileges

Now, let's discuss the process and review the workflows necessary to grant and revoke system privileges. The third tab in the **Role Management** window, **System Privileges**, lets you grant or revoke system privileges.

To grant a system privilege, click **+** to open a search dialog box. To view all system privileges, enter the search string "**". To search for a specific system privilege, enter a portion of the system privilege name to search for possible matches. Select one or more system privileges within the list. To select multiple items, hold down the `Ctrl` key and click each desired item. To select multiple consecutive items, click the first item in the list, hold down the `Shift` key, and then select the last item in the list. One the desired items are selected, click **OK**, and the search dialog will close. Your selected system privileges should now appear in the **System Privileges** tab (see Figure 5.5).

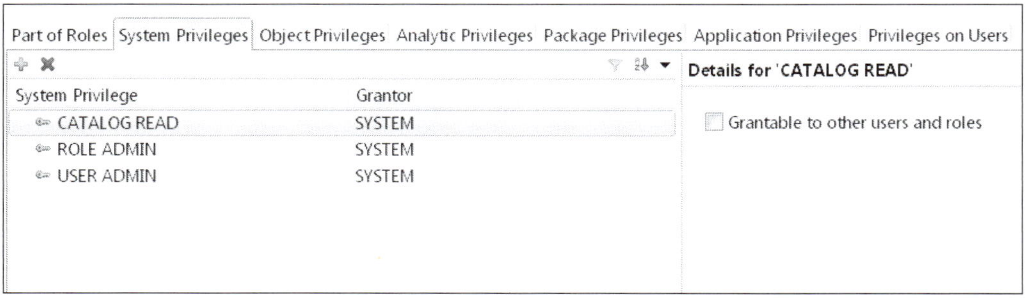

Figure 5.5 List of Selected System Privileges

To assign the **Grantable to Other Users and Roles** privilege, select a system privilege from the list. To the right, you'll see another frame containing the details for the selected system privilege. Check the **Grantable to Other Users and Roles** box to allow the role grantee to grant the same privilege to another user or role. Repeat this process for each system privilege in the list.

Once you've added all the desired privileges to the list, save or activate the changes to implement them. Saving and activating have the same outcome, so choose either one. To save the changes, press Ctrl+S, and to activate the changes, press F8 key. Either way, the changes will be saved and activated in the system. SAP HANA Studio will execute the required SQL statements in the background to grant the selected system privileges.

To revoke a system privilege, click an assigned system privilege from the list and then click the **X** icon above the list to revoke the privilege. Repeat the process for each system privilege you want to revoke. Once you've removed all the desired privileges, press Ctrl+S or press F8. The removed privileges will be revoked.

Object Privileges

The fourth tab in the user management interface is **Object Privileges**. The process for granting and revoking object privileges is like the process used for system privileges. To grant an object privilege, click **+** to open a search dialog box. To view all objects in the system, enter the search string "**" to list them all. To search for a specific object, enter a portion of the object's name to search for possible matches.

The search dialog will return multiple types of objects, including all types of catalog objects, repository-based catalog objects, schemas, repository-based schemas, remote sources, column views, and many more.

As with system privileges, the interface allows you to select multiple items. Click **OK** once the desired objects are selected. The search dialog will close, and the selected catalog objects will appear in the list. Figure 5.6 shows a few types of selected objects; the list contains the object name and the user account used to grant the object privilege.

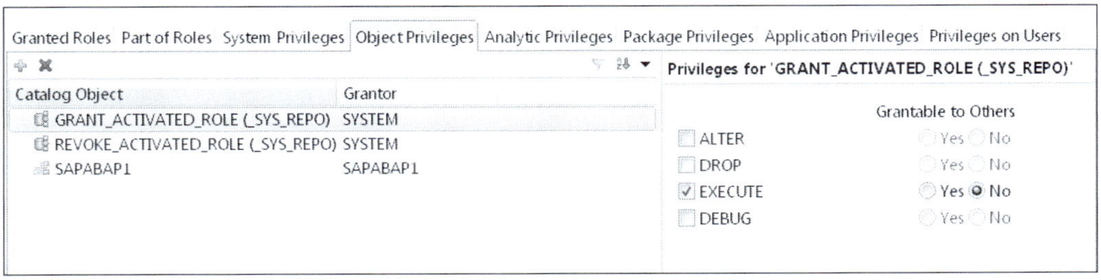

Figure 5.6 Selected Objects and Their Privileges in SAP HANA Studio

To view a list of available privileges for a given object, select the object in the list. To the right of the selected object is a frame containing a series of checkboxes, privileges, and **Yes** or **No** radio buttons. To grant a privilege, select the checkbox next to the privilege name. To allow the privilege to be **Grantable to Others**, click the **Yes** radio button to the right of the given privilege. As you click through each object in the left frame, privileges applicable for the selected object will appear in the right frame.

To save the changes, press [Ctrl]+[S] or press [F8]. The changes will be saved and activated within the system.

When using SAP HANA Studio, there's no need to determine if the object is owned by _SYS_REPO, nor do we need to use a special interface to assign privileges owned by _SYS_REPO. SAP HANA Studio will execute the required SQL statements in the background to grant the selected object privileges. If the object is owned by the system account _SYS_REPO, SAP HANA Studio will execute the necessary stored procedures in the background. You'll also notice that repository objects will always list the grantor as _SYS_REPO. When an object is owned by a standard user account, SAP HANA Studio will execute the standard GRANT and REVOKE statements, and the grantor will be the user account currently authenticated within the SAP HANA Studio connection.

To revoke an object privilege, click an assigned object privilege from the list and then click the **X** icon above the list to revoke the privilege. Repeat the process for each system privilege you want to revoke. Once you've removed all the desired privileges, press [Ctrl]+[S] or press [F8]. The removed privileges will be revoked.

Analytic Privileges

The fifth tab in the user management interface is **Analytic Privileges**. The process for granting and revoking analytic privileges is like the process used for other privileges already discussed in this section. To grant an analytic privilege, click **+** to open a search dialog box. To view all objects in the system, enter the search string "**". To search for a specific analytic privilege, enter a portion of the analytic privilege's name to search for possible matches. The search dialog will return both analytic privileges and structured privileges. Analytic privileges are those owned by the system account _SYS_REPO. Structured privileges are owned by the user account that created them.

As with other privileges, the interface allows you to select multiple items. Click **OK** once the desired objects are selected. The search dialog will close, and the selected analytic privileges and their grantors will appear in the list. There are no further options that need to be configured with analytic privileges. They are either granted when listed or revoked when not listed.

When using SAP HANA Studio, there's no need to determine if the analytic privilege is owned by _SYS_REPO or if we need to use a special interface to assign privileges owned by _SYS_REPO. SAP HANA Studio will execute the required SQL statements automatically in the background to grant the selected analytic privileges. If the object is owned by the system account _SYS_REPO, the system will execute the necessary stored procedures in the background. You'll notice that repository objects will always list the grantor as _SYS_REPO.

To revoke an analytic privilege, simply select it from the list and click **X**. To save the changes, press [Ctrl]+[S] or press [F8]. The changes will be saved and activated within the system.

Package Privileges

The sixth tab in the user management interface is **Package Privileges**. The process for granting and revoking package privileges is like the process used for other privileges already discussed in this section. To grant a package privilege, click **+** to open a search dialog box. To view all packages in the system, enter the search string "**". To search for a specific package, enter a portion of the package's name to search for possible matches. Select one or more packages and click **OK**. The search dialog box will disappear, and a list of selected packages will appear (see Figure 5.7).

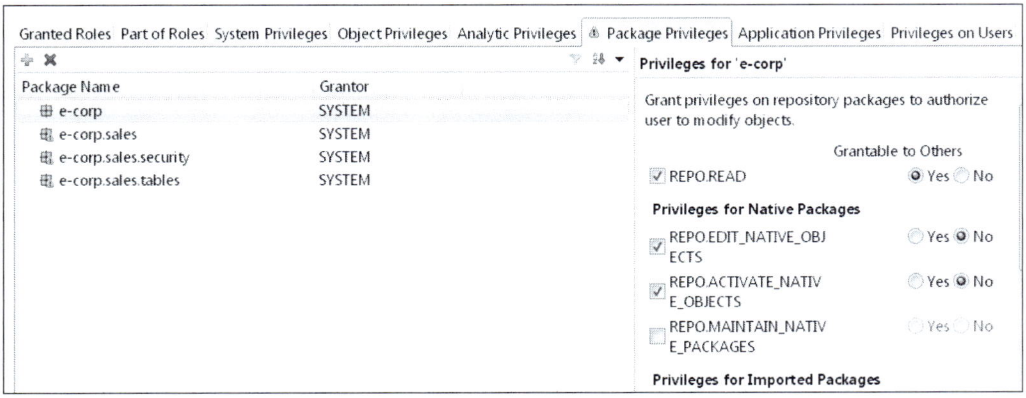

Figure 5.7 Assigning Package Privileges to Roles in SAP HANA Studio

To assign privileges to a selected package, look for the frame on the right with checkboxes, privileges, and **Yes** and **No** radio buttons. To assign package privileges, select the checkbox beside each listed privilege's name. To allow the user to assign the same privilege to others, select the **Yes** radio button in the column labeled **Grantable to Others**.

To revoke a package privilege, simply select it from the list and click **X** to remove the privilege from the list. To save the changes, press Ctrl+S or press F8. The changes will be saved and activated within the system.

5.3.4 Granting and Revoking Privileges with SAP HANA Web-Based Development Workbench

The SAP HANA Web-Based Development Workbench security manager, hosted within the XS engine, provides an interface to create users, create roles, or manage security.

You can access SAP HANA Web-Based Development Workbench via a supported Internet browser. The following two URLs can be customized to match the details of your environment:

http://sap-hana.myhost.com:8000/sap/hana/ide/security

http://<sap_hana_host>:80<instance_number>/sap/hana/ide/security

In the last example, replace <sap_hana_host> with the hostname of the SAP HANA system in your environment. Replace <instance_number> with the two-digit instance corresponding to your SAP HANA system.

For secure access, the following examples should help you construct the correct URL:

https://<sap_hana_host>: 43<instance_number>/sap/hana/ide/security

https://sap-hana.myhost.com:4300/sap/hana/ide/security

Once you have access to the SAP HANA Web-Based Development Workbench security manager, expand the **Security** node on the right, then expand **Roles** to reveal a list of roles defined in the system. Double-click a role to open the management interface for the given role. With the selected **Role Management** window open, you can begin granting and revoking privileges.

The process for granting and revoking a role's privileges in the SAP HANA Web-Based Development Workbench security manager is almost identical to the process outlined in Section 4.3.2 for SAP HANA Studio. Because there is tremendous overlap in the workflows, we won't go into the same level of detail in this section; we'll simply highlight the basic workflow and point out any significant differences.

If there are any activation issues, warning messages will appear in the status frame at the bottom of the **User Management** window. The status frame has a dark background color, and error messages will appear in red-colored text. Errors are only generated during an attempted activation or attempt to save changes.

System Privileges

To add a system privilege, click **+** and search for the desired system privilege. Choose **Grantable to other users and roles** to the right of each listed system privilege as needed.

To revoke a system privilege, selected the privilege from the list and click **X**. To save your changes, press Ctrl+S or click the disk icon at the top left to save and activate the privilege.

Object Privileges

To add an object privilege, click **+** and search for the desired objects. A search dialog will appear. The SAP HANA Web-Based Development Workbench security manager provides additional search options beyond those available in SAP HANA Studio, based on the object type. This added feature will likely make it easier to pinpoint specific objects by type. This is the only noticeable difference between using SAP HANA Studio and the SAP HANA Web-Based Development Workbench security manager.

Select the desired objects and choose **OK**. A list of selected objects will appear. To the right of each object is a list of applicable privileges that can be granted. In addition, the **Grantable to Others** option is also available.

To revoke an object privilege, selected the object from the list and choose the **X**. To save your changes, press Ctrl+S or click the disk icon at the top left to save and activate the privilege.

Analytic Privileges

To add an analytic privilege, click **+** and search for the desired analytic privilege. To revoke an analytic privilege, selected the privilege from the list and click **X** to remove the analytic privilege. To save your changes, press Ctrl+S or click the disk icon at the top left to save and activate the privilege.

Package Privileges

To add a package privilege, click **+** and search for the desired package hierarchy level. To revoke a package privilege, selected the package hierarchy level from the list and click **X** to remove it. To save your changes, press Ctrl+S or click the disk icon at the top left to save and activate the privilege.

5.4 Managing Nested Roles

There are three basic interfaces we can use to grant and revoke nested roles or roles granted to other roles: a SQL console to issue SQL statements, SAP HANA Studio, or SAP HANA Web-Based Development Workbench. We'll discuss these options ahead.

5.4.1 Granting and Revoking Roles with SQL

When granting roles to another role, we must first determine the role type. If the role was created by a standard user account or if the role was provisioned by the system during installation, we refer to the role as a *standard role*. These roles often are created using the CREATE ROLE SQL syntax. Standard roles can be granted and revoked with the GRANT and REVOKE SQL statements.

Alternatively, if the role was created as a development artifact and owned by the system account _SYS_REPO, we refer to the role as a *repository role*. We will discuss the process for nesting repository roles in Chapter 6.

Granting standard roles to a user account with SQL is performed using a syntax that is like that used when granting privileges. To grant a role to another role, we must use a GRANT SQL statement, as follows:

```
GRANT <EXISTING_ROLENAME> TO <TARGET_ROLENAME>;
GRANT <EXISTING_ROLENAME> TO <TARGET_ROLENAME> WITH ADMIN OPTION;
GRANT MODELING, DBA_COCKPIT, CONTENT_ADMIN TO MY_ROLE_NAME;
```

The <EXISTING_ROLENAME> variable can be replaced with a comma-separated list of existing roles, and the <TARGET_ROLENAME> variable can be replaced with the name of the target role. The WITH ADMIN OPTION, when included, allows the existing role to be granted to other users or roles.

To revoke a role using SQL, we must issue a REVOKE SQL statement, as follows:

```
REVOKE <EXISTING_ROLENAME> FROM <TARGET_ROLENAME>;
REVOKE MODELING, DBA_COCKPIT, CONTENT_ADMIN FROM MY_ROLE_NAME;
```

5.4.2 Granting and Revoking Roles with SAP HANA Studio

We also can use the role management area in SAP HANA Studio to both grant and revoke roles for another role. Most will find it easier to use SAP HANA Studio than to memorize and type SQL statements.

To access the **Role** management node in SAP HANA Studio, first switch to the administration console perspective. On the **Systems** tab, located on the left, expand the **System** node, then the **Security** node, revealing the **Security**, **Users**, and **Roles** nodes. Expand the **Roles** node to reveal roles defined in the system. To manage a role, double-click the role name in the list to open the **Role Management** tab on the right. Note that this same tab is present when creating a role.

Figure 5.8 shows the **Role Management** tab in SAP HANA Studio. Just below the role name details section, you'll see several tabs, each of which represents an interface in which specific types of privileges or roles can be granted or revoked. The first tab is **Granted Roles**.

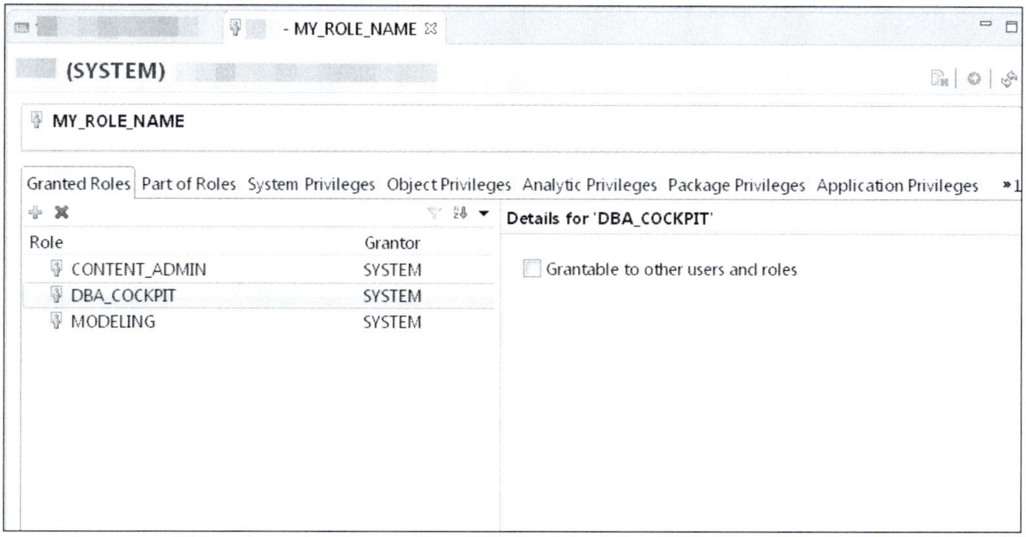

Figure 5.8 Granted Roles Configuration Tab in SAP HANA Studio

Much like granting and revoking privileges, the process required to grant a role involves clicking **+**, searching for one or more existing roles, and then adding them to the list. Once a role is added to the list and the changes are saved, the role will be granted the assigned roles and all the privileges granted to those roles.

When applicable, the **Details** frame of the **Granted Roles** tab will contain the **Grantable to other users and roles** option. Select the checkbox next to this option to allow the role's grantees the ability to grant the assigned role to other users or roles. When this option is checked, the role's grantees will be able to grant the specified role even if they don't have the `ROLE ADMIN` system privilege.

To revoke a role, select the role from the list and then click the red **X** icon to remove the assigned role from the list. Click the disk icon in the icon bar to save and activate the changes.

When clicking the **Save** icon, SAP HANA Studio will execute the appropriate SQL statements in the background to grant or revoke the role. Standard roles will be granted using the basic `GRANT` and `REVOKE` SQL syntax. The grantor in these cases will be the account used to authenticate with the system in SAP HANA Studio.

5.4.3 Granting and Revoking Roles with SAP HANA Web-Based Development Workbench

As mentioned earlier, the SAP HANA Web-Based Development Workbench security manager, hosted within the XS engine, provides an interface to create users, create roles, or manage security.

In summary, you can access the SAP HANA Web-Based Development Workbench security manager by updating the following two URLs to match the details of your environment:

http://<sap_hana_host>: 80<instance_number>/sap/hana/ide/security

https://<sap_hana_host>: 43<instance_number>/sap/hana/ide/security

Once you have access to the SAP HANA Web-Based Development Workbench security manager, expand the **Security** node on the right side of the window. Expand **Roles** to reveal a list of roles. Double-click a role to open the management interface for the given role. With the selected role management window open, you can begin granting and revoking roles using the **Granted Roles** tab.

The process for granting and revoking roles in the SAP HANA Web-Based Development Workbench security manager is identical to the process outlined for SAP HANA Studio. Because there is tremendous overlap in the workflows, we won't go into the same level of detail in the section. See Section 5.4.2 for additional details. Remember that if there are any activation issues, warning messages will appear in the status frame at the bottom of the role management window.

5.5 Summary

The process of creating and managing roles can be accomplished using SQL statements, SAP HANA Studio, or the SAP HANA Web-Based Development Workbench security manager hosted in the XS engine. We can also use all three interfaces to grant and revoke both privileges and roles. In the next chapter, we'll will explore repository-based roles, which are an alternative to standard roles and in most cases provide advantages over standard roles.

Chapter 6
Repository Roles

In this chapter, we'll provide a complete overview of repository roles, including the processes used to create, maintain, and grant privileges to repository roles.

Roles are objects that aid in the creation of a security model. The bulk of the security model development process involves defining roles, assigning privileges to roles, and assigning roles to user accounts. However, SAP HANA offers a unique type of role called a *repository role*, which we'll explore throughout this chapter. We'll start by defining repository roles and discussing their importance, then we'll review the options for creating and managing repository roles. As with standard roles, we must also review the process for granting and revoking privileges and roles to repository roles. Because of the importance of repository roles, we'll outline an basic repository role structure example. Finally, we'll demonstrate the process for creating a basic security model with repository roles.

6.1 What Are Repository Roles?

In Chapter 5, we discussed standard roles and the process used to create them. For those with experience creating roles in other RDBMS, creating standard SAP HANA roles is very similar. During the process, we issue statements to generate a *runtime* version of the role, meaning that the object only exists in an active state within the RDBMS. Once the standard role is created, it's instantly available for use.

Once a role is created, we issue a series of GRANT statements to assign privileges to the role. To remove privileges from the role, we issue REVOKE statements. As each individual command is issued, the runtime version of the role is immediately updated. With this process, we don't have the ability to easily roll back changes or promote changes seamlessly to upstream SAP HANA environments. For example, if we make a change in a development environment, we need to make the same change in a test environment and possibly a production environment by issuing the same commands. This process historically has been very cumbersome to manage, a problem that often requires third-party software to remedy. Without software to help, the SQL scripts issued to create, alter, grant, or revoke roles would all need to be manually retained and executed sequentially in each upstream environment.

Repository-based roles can overcome many of the limitations attributed to standard database roles. Repository roles are defined and saved in the SAP HANA development repository or package hierarchy. They can be defined using an SAP HANA-specific script language or using SAP HANA Web-Based Development Workbench editor. In either case, we can save a design-time version of the role within a development artifact, meaning that the role and its granted privileges can exist as a separate object, independent of the runtime version. Once the design-time version of the role is activated, a matching runtime version is created in the SAP HANA RDBMS. This feature of SAP HANA allows us to implement change management, rollback, and transportation of roles between environments.

In addition to these benefits, repository roles also help simplify the management of our SAP HANA security model. To illustrate these benefits, let's first discuss the importance of the _SYS_REPO system account. We'll then discuss how repository roles help us avoid issues related to the grantor of privileges and roles. Finally, we'll outline the overall benefits of repository roles.

6.1.1 User Account _SYS_REPO and Repository Roles

As we've established, when we use the SAP HANA development repository to define repository-based objects and roles, the runtime versions of these objects will be owned or granted by the _SYS_REPO system account. You must understand the importance of this, because it has a profound impact on how we establish a security model in SAP HANA.

Recall that catalog objects created using the SQL CREATE statement will be owned by the user issuing the statement. The owner therefore must grant privileges to other users or roles if they require access to their catalog objects. The owner must also grant privileges to security administrators if they're expected to facilitate access to the owner's objects. This is required because of the how standard RDBMS catalog security operates in a multiple user account environment. By design, no single user is automatically granted privileges to objects owned by other users without some form of action by the owner or security administrator.

Although this is a very secure methodology, it often leads to a near-unmanageable security model in practice. Object owners must work closely with security administrators and follow strict procedures to help maintain a security model. Security administrators must rely on each other to revoke any roles they granted, because only the grantor can revoke a granted role. This, among other requirements, makes security management of standard catalog roles and objects very difficult without an external software system delegating, managing, controlling, and tracking the process.

To simplify this mechanism within SAP HANA, we would need to logically devise a system in which a single user owns all objects and that same user grants all privileges. This user should also be set up in such a way that it can never be deleted from the system. Ideally, this special user would delegate the actions of the developers to prevent their accounts from owing objects. It would also delegate the actions of security administrators to prevent their accounts from being listed as the grantors of privileges.

Some might assume that this is an unlikely solution in a multiple user environment. Luckily, SAP HANA has already incorporated this solution into the SAP HANA development repository. The _SYS_REPO system user, in this case, becomes both the owner of all repository objects and the grantor of all privileges defined within a repository role. With SAP HANA, we have a single system user account managing this process while avoiding most of the pitfalls of security management in a multiple-user RDBMS environment.

If we follow the repository-based model when creating objects, developers only need the ability to create repository objects, and security administrators only need the ability to create repository roles and grant them to others. We'll also be able to segregate these actions within the system, because the repository-based model offers a delineation between those that can define roles and those that can grant them to others.

In contrast, when we use standard roles and catalog objects, the definer and grantor of roles must have the `ROLE ADMIN` system privilege. This privilege should only be granted sparingly and only to security administrators. Not having a clear delineation also forces security administrators to define all roles and work closely with the developers while doing so. This dependency often proves to be inefficient and prone to error.

The _SYS_REPO account therefore is very important to the structure of our security model. We should strive to set up a security model that ensures that this account owns all catalog objects and grants privileges to repository roles.

6.1.2 Grantor and Privileges

When we issue a `GRANT <PRIVILEGE>` SQL statement using a standard user account, that user account becomes the grantor of the privilege. The grantor is an important function within a security model. When a privilege is granted to a role or user, only the grantor can revoke the privilege. If there are multiple security administrators operating within an SAP HANA environment, this can be difficult to manage.

For example, if one security administrator grants a privilege to a role, only that administrator can revoke the privilege. If that security administrator is not available the following day and the privilege must be revoked, there's no other user account in the system that can revoke that privilege. This can be problematic, and it also introduces risk, because key individuals must be present always to manage changes to the security model.

Some organizations will try to solve this problem by creating a dedicated account that's shared by multiple administrators. Such a decision isn't recommended, because there are few options to properly audit an individual's activities when shared accounts are used. In other words, someone can make an important change that affects the security of the system without there being any record of the actual person that performed the change.

When we use repository roles, we don't need to be concerned with these issues. With repository roles, privileges are always granted using the _SYS_REPO system account. There's also no need to be concerned about multiple users managing security. A repository role can be updated by anyone with access to the package where it resides in the SAP HANA repository. Each time a repository role is activated, the privileges within it are granted with _SYS_REPO as the grantor. If a privilege is removed from the repository role definition, it will be revoked. Because _SYS_REPO is the original grantor, it has full access to revoke the privilege.

Another important requirement for grantors entails that we understand the privileges the grantor needs before it can grant privileges. There are two ways that an account can serve as the grantor. First, the grantor must have been granted the same privilege with `WITH GRANT OPTION`. Second, it must own the object. If it doesn't own the object, the owner must first grant the security administrator the necessary privileges.

As mentioned before, this makes management of a security model based on standard catalog objects and standard roles very difficult.

If we use repository objects, again, we don't encounter this issue. The repository objects will be owned by _SYS_REPO. If we reference repository objects in a repository role, _SYS_REPO will already be the owner and the natural grantor of the privileges. Now, let's look at how repository roles can help with the grantor of roles.

6.1.3 Grantor and Roles

Just as the security manager account can grant individual privileges, it can also grant existing standard roles to other users or roles. However, before a security account can grant a standard role, it must meet one of two preconditions: 1) It must be directly or indirectly granted the role and the `WITH ADMIN OPTION` must be set for the granted role; or 2) it must have the system privilege `ROLE ADMIN`. This system privilege allows the assignee to grant or revoke any existing standard role to another user or role. The `ROLE ADMIN` privilege allows the security administrator to both create and grant roles. This might not be an issue for some organizations, but those that require segregation of duties will find it difficult to prevent the creator from also being the grantor of the role. Some organizations will insist that the model allow one group to create the roles and another group to be responsible for assigning them.

Repository roles are granted using the `"_SYS_REPO"."GRANT_ACTIVATED_ROLE"` stored procedure and are revoked using the `"_SYS_REPO"."REVOKE_ACTIVATED_ROLE"` stored procedure. Repository roles themselves are created within the SAP HANA package hierarchy, and design-time objects can be secured independently from the stored procedures just mentioned. Therefore, organizations that require a segregation of duties have a solution: Repository role creation can be isolated from the privileges required to grant a repository role. Now, let's look at a summary of the benefits of repository roles.

6.1.4 Why Use Repository Roles?

Overall, repository roles help organizations achieve a security model in the following ways:

- As we've established, the definition of the repository role is stored in the SAP HANA development repository in the form of a text-based script. Therefore, it can be managed independently from the runtime version of the repository role.

- Repository roles can be transported from one SAP HANA system to another using SAP HANA application lifecycle management or using the delivery unit (DU) export and import process.
- When a user is copied in SAP HANA Studio, all the user's repository roles are also copied to the target user account.
- Because they're development artifacts, the standard SAP HANA version management process applies. Each activated version is maintained in the SAP HANA database and repository, allowing each version to be retrieved and activated as needed.
- Repository roles are granted and revoked using special stored procedures, which make it easier to define accounts used by security administrators. Security administrators only need `EXECUTE` access to the stored procedures that grant repository roles or revoke them from others. They don't require the `ROLE ADMIN` system privilege that might grant too many rights in the system, nor do they need first to be granted a role and the additional `WITH ADMIN OPTION` privilege before gaining the ability to grant roles to others.
- Users only require access to the SAP HANA package repository to define a repository role and its privileges. They don't require the `ROLE ADMIN` system privilege that might grant too many rights in the system. Although they can define the repository role, they can't grant the role to others without `EXECUTE` access to the special stored procedures mentioned in the previous bullet point. This allows organizations to separate the granting and revoking processes from the repository role definition process. Developers can define repository roles and privileges for their applications without the need to also be able to grant roles and privileges to other users.
- If standard database objects are used in the system, the object's owner only needs to grant privileges using `WITH ADMIN OPTION` or `WITH GRANT OPTION` to the _SYS_REPO user account. Without repository roles, the owner would need to grant privileges to existing security administration users or roles each time an object is created.
- If repository-based objects are used in the system, the _SYS_REPO account will already own the objects and therefore can grant privileges to them without any further actions by the developer. This is partly why we highly recommend that developers use repository-based objects rather than catalog objects in their solutions.

Additional Comparison of Repository Roles to Standard Roles

SAP provides an additional matrix to compare the differences between standard catalog roles and repository-based roles in the SAP HANA Security Guide for SPS 12. You can download the guide at *http://help.sap.com/hana/SAP_HANA_Security_Guide_en.pdf*.

Within the document, look for Section 8.2.2.1, Catalog Roles and Repository Roles Compared.

Given the benefits of using repository roles, most will conclude that using them as the basis for a security model is a good idea. Based on our firsthand experience, a system based on repository objects and repository roles is considerably more manageable than one based on standard roles and catalog objects. With their importance established, let's now look at how they're created, how we grant privileges to them, and how they're assigned to other users or roles.

6.2 Managing Repository Roles with Design-Time Scripts

In broad terms, there are two ways to create repository roles as of SAP HANA 2.0 SPS 00. First, we can define them in SAP HANA Studio's development perspective and development repository in the form of hand-coded scripts, as discussed in this section. The scripting language is unique to SAP HANA, but it's similar to JSON scripting. For those that don't want to hand-code scripts, SAP HANA Web-Based Development Workbench editor offers a GUI that mirrors the role creation UI found in SAP HANA Studio (see Section 6.4). Most beginners will find it much easier to use SAP HANA Web-Based Development Workbench editor because there's no need to memorize the scripting language.

As we discussed in Chapter 1, SAP HANA Studio provides a development perspective, which includes a **Repositories** tab, in which connected SAP HANA systems appear. To access the development repository, expand the SAP HANA system to reveal the default container and its corresponding workspace directory. If a workspace directory isn't present, right-click the SAP HANA system node and choose **Create Repository Workspace**. (For more information, refer to Chapter 2.)

Before we create a repository role, it's important to define a unique repository package in which to store repository roles. The package should be structured in such a way that it can be completely isolated using package privileges. Only administrators assigned the responsibility of creating repository roles should have any level of access to the package. We typically recommend that a first-level package named **Security** be created. Within that package, a subpackage named **Roles** should be created to host our repository roles. Figure 6.1 shows one way to set up a package hierarchy for security-related objects such as repository roles.

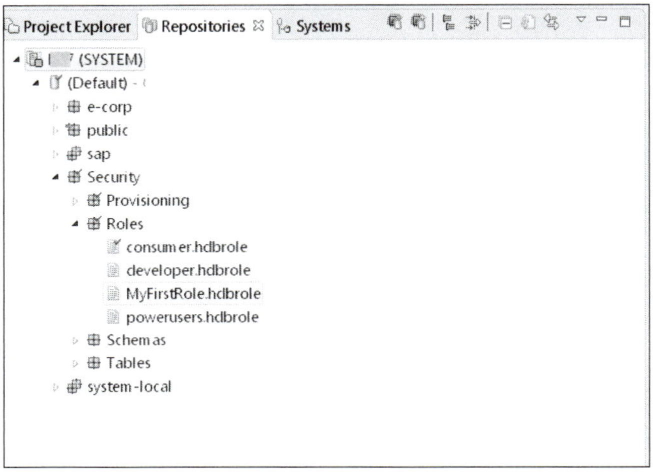

Figure 6.1 SAP HANA Package Hierarchy for Security-Related Objects

We highly recommend using this methodology, because it's critical that only security role creators have access to these objects. If a standard developer were to accidently gain edit access to this package, the developer could update the design-time repository role, activate changes, and elevate its own privileges. Therefore, it's less risky to place this package at the root level, thereby preventing accidental inheritance of package privileges. Ideally, this package will contain the base repository roles used to establish roles and privileges in the SAP HANA system. Now, let's look at the process used to create a repository role.

6.2.1 Creating Repository Roles within a Package

As mentioned before, packages are used to store repository roles. To create a new repository role in the **Security.Roles** package shown in Figure 6.1, right-click the **Roles** package and choose **New • Other**, or click the package and press Ctrl+N. A new **Select a Wizard** window will appear (see Figure 6.2).

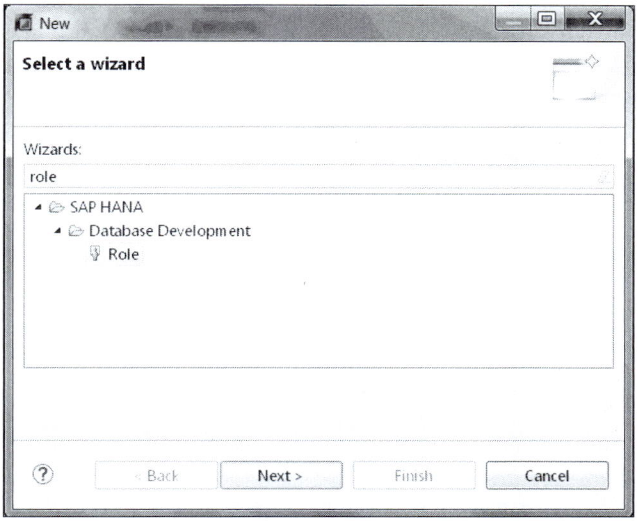

Figure 6.2 Selecting Repository Role Development Artifact

Within the window is a hierarchical list of folders and objects. Expand the **SAP HANA** folder and then the **Database Development** folder to reveal a variety of database objects we can create. Look for an object named **role**. Alternatively, you can use the filter bar just below the **Wizards** label to search for "role", which will filter the selection to any wizard containing the word role. Click **Next** to begin defining the repository role.

A window will appear titled **New Role**. Use the default workspace folder path in the **Container** field. In the **Role Name** field, enter the name of the role, which will also become the name of the .hdbrole file stored in the repository workspace folder. Click **Finish** to open the role script text editor tab.

6.2.2 Defining the Role Name Tag

The syntax of a repository role begins with the word role followed by the fully qualified repository role name. A fully qualified role name is prefixed with the complete package hierarchy name, followed by two colons and the role name. The following script represents the basic syntax of a repository role. Replace the items in angle brackets (<>) with objects unique to your environment:

```
role <package.subpackage>::<repository role name> {
}
```

For example, let's assume that we need to create a role named ExampleRole and that it will be stored in the Security.Roles package. The following script would be the beginning point for defining that repository role:

```
role Security.Roles::ExampleRole {
}
```

6.2.3 Extending Roles

Between the name of the role and our first opening bracket, we can optionally define existing roles that will extend the new repository role. This means that the privileges within the referenced roles will be granted to our new repository role, in addition to any privileges we explicitly define after the brackets. Listing 6.1 demonstrates how to include existing roles by adding `extends role`, followed by a comma-separated list of existing, fully qualified repository role names.

```
role Security.Roles::ExampleRole extends role
Security.Roles::BasicRole,
sap.hana.xs.formLogin.profile::ProfileOwner,
sap.hana.xs.selfService.user.roles::USSExecutor {
}
```

Listing 6.1 Repository Role Script with Multiple Extended Roles

6.2.4 Assigning Privileges

Each privilege is granted or assigned to a role using a special syntax. The privileges will be specified within the opening and closing curly brackets ({}). Listing 6.2 will grant schema privileges for the StagingMart and SalesMart schemas. In addition, it will grant the `CATALOG READ` system privilege, an analytic privilege, and a package privilege.

```
role Security.Roles::ExampleRole extends role  Security.Roles::BasicRole,
 sap.hana.xs.formLogin.profile::ProfileOwner,
 sap.hana.xs.selfService.user.roles::USSExecutor {
```

```
  -- Begin Schema Privileges
  catalog schema "StagingMart": SELECT, EXECUTE;
  catalog schema "SalesMart": SELECT, EXECUTE;

  -- Beging System Privileges
  system privilege: CATALOG READ;

  -- Begin Analytic Privileges
  catalog analytic privilege : "_SYS_BI_CP_ALL";

  // Begin Package Privileges
  package .REPO_PACKAGE_ROOT: REPO.READ;
}
```

Listing 6.2 Repository Role Script Granting Different Privilege Types

Each privilege line must end with a semicolon. To place comments in the script, start the comment line with two consecutive dashes or slashes (-- or //). Comments are optional, but they should be included to communicate important information about the overall script or about each script line. Again, the individual privileges must be confined within the opening and closing curly brackets. As you can see in Listing 6.2, we can define different types of privileges within the same script. In most cases, each privilege type will require a slightly different syntax.

6.2.5 Save and Activate

Once the script is complete, you need to save or activate the script. Saving will simply save the changes in the local workspace. Activation will save the script in the local workspace, deploy the script to the SAP HANA repository, and generate the runtime versions of the repository role. To save the script, click the **Save** icon, which shows a floppy disk (see Figure 6.3 ❶). You can also save by pressing [Ctrl]+[S]. To activate, click the **Activate** icon on the icon bar, which shows a green circle with an embedded white arrow pointing to the right (see Figure 6.3 ❷). You can also activate by pressing [Ctrl]+[F3].

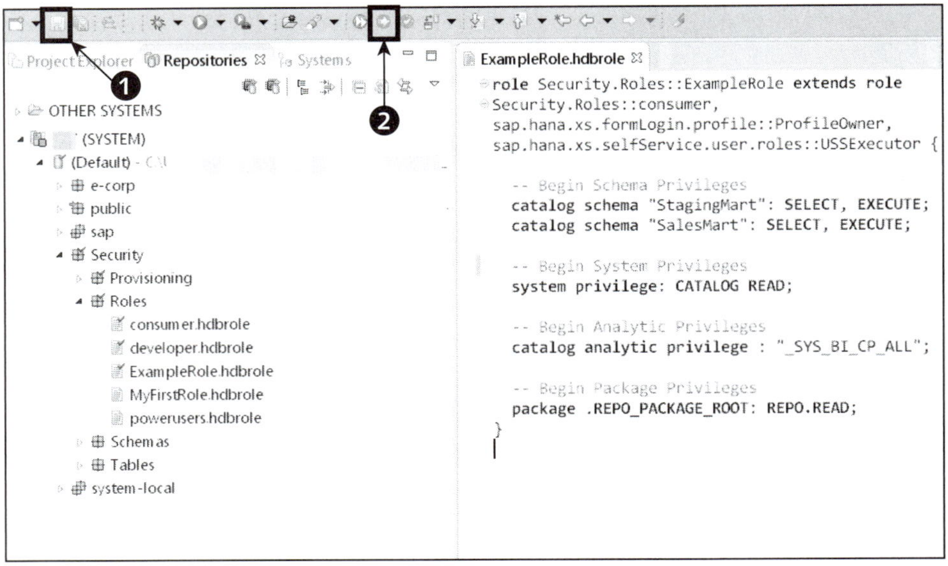

Figure 6.3 Save and Activate Icons in SAP HANA Studio

6.2.6 Runtime Repository Roles

When a repository role is activated, a runtime version of the role will be created within the SAP HANA catalog. The name of the runtime role will be constructed using a combination of the package hierarchy and repository role name. Each element will be separated by two colons. For example:

```
<package.subpackage>::<repository role name>
```

Or:

```
Security.Roles::ExampleRole
```

The role will be visible within the standard roles list found in the security manager of SAP HANA Studio. To view the repository role in the list, switch to the administration console perspective and expand the **Systems** node on the left side to reveal the **Security** node. Expand the **Security** node and then the **Roles** node to view a complete list of runtime roles within the catalog. The list will contain both standard roles and activated repository roles.

Note that repository roles can only be granted if the grantor has the `EXECUTE` privilege on the `"_SYS_REPO"."GRANT_ACTIVATED_ROLE"` stored procedure. Now, let's take a moment to look at how we define privileges for each object and privilege type.

6.3 Granting and Revoking Privileges in Design-Time Scripts

When developing repository roles with design-time scripts, you'll find that the syntax varies based on the object type or the privilege type. Figure 6.4 provides an example of a complete repository role script within SAP HANA Studio. For demonstration purposes, this role grants a variety of privileges to various design-time and runtime object types.

*webExample.hdbrole

```
role Security.Roles::webExample
        --- Include privileges from these roles (extend)
        extends role sap.hana.admin.roles::Administrator
{
-- System Privileges
system privilege: CREATE REMOTE SOURCE;

-- Catalog Object Privileges
catalog schema "_SYS_BIC", "_SYS_REPO": EXECUTE, SELECT, ALTER, DELETE;
catalog sql object "MySchema"."SAP-HANA-06_DIM_ACCOUNT", "MySchema"."TestTableTwo": SELECT;

-- Repository Object Privileges
sql object Security.Tables::adusers, e-corp.sales.tables::STG_CUSTOMERS: SELECT, ALTER, DROP;
schema Security.Schemas:security_tables.hdbschema, Security.Schemas:MySchema.hdbschema: SELECT, EXECUTE;

-- Analytic Privileges
analytic privilege : e-corp.sales.security:ap_sales_reporting_region.analyticprivilege;
catalog analytic privilege : "MyStructuredPriv";
catalog analytic privilege : "_SYS_BI_CP_ALL";

-- Package Privileges
package e-corp.sales: REPO.READ, REPO.ACTIVATE_NATIVE_OBJECTS, REPO.MAINTAIN_NATIVE_PACKAGES;
package .REPO_PACKAGE_ROOT: REPO.READ;

-- Application Privileges
application privilege: "sap.hana.security.base::DataService";

}
```

Figure 6.4 Example Repository Role Script

When using repository-based scripts, it's important to note that the _SYS_REPO system user either must own the catalog objects or must have been granted the same privileges using either `WITH ADMIN OPTION` or `WITH GRANT OPTION`. If _SYS_REPO doesn't meet these requirements, the repository role will fail to activate. In this section, we'll explore the syntax to grant privileges using design-time repository role scripts.

6.3.1 System Privileges

When defining system privileges in design-time repository-based role scripts, you must start each line with `system privilege:`. After the colon, provide a comma-separated list of system privileges. At the end of the list, include a semicolon to finish the line. If you don't want to include a comma-separated list, you can explicitly list each privilege on its own line, ensuring that each line begins with `system privilege:`.

The following snippets of code show the definition of system privileges within a repository role script. The first line includes two privileges, and the remaining two lines include only a single system privilege each:

```
system privilege: AGENT ADMIN, AUDIT ADMIN;
system privilege: AUDIT OPERATOR;
system privilege: CREATE REMOTE SOURCE;
```

As you can see, you can reuse the `system privilege:` expression multiple times within the script. You can also consolidate them all into a single line on which each privilege is separated from the next with a comma. It's important to note that the _SYS_REPO account has been granted all system privileges by default. _SYS_REPO also can grant all system privileges to other users or roles by default.

6.3.2 Schema Privileges

Schema privileges can be granted in two ways. First, we can grant schema privileges to any runtime catalog schemas active in the system. In this instance, we can reference a schema regardless of the method used to create it. Schema privileges can also be granted to design-time schema objects. In this instance, we can only reference schemas created within the repository.

Runtime Schemas

When defining runtime catalog schema privileges within design-time repository-based role scripts, you must start each line with `catalog schema`. Following this term, include the name of the schema followed by a colon. You can also include a comma-separated list of schemas if you want them all to share the same privileges. After the colon, include a comma-separated list of schema privileges. At the end of the list, include a semicolon to finish the line.

The following snippets of code show the definition of catalog schema privileges within a repository role script. The first line grants `EXECUTE` and `SELECT` on the _SYS_BIC schema. The second line grants several privileges for the MySchema schema. The third line shows the use of multiple schemas in the same line:

```
catalog schema "_SYS_BIC": EXECUTE, SELECT;
catalog schema "MySchema": CREATE ANY, DROP, ALTER, UPDATE;
catalog schema "_SYS_REPO", "_SYS_BIC": SELECT;
```

It's also important to note that the _SYS_REPO system account must have full privileges for the listed schemas or must own the schemas before such privileges can be activated within the definition of a repository role.

Design-Time Schemas

In addition to referencing runtime catalog objects, we can also reference design-time schemas. Referencing a design-time schema is only possible if the schema itself is a repository object. In most cases, we recommend that you reference the design-time version of a schema, because it helps to create a dependency chain that can be identified during lifecycle management. The privileges will be granted on the runtime version of the object once all referenced objects are activated.

When defining repository schema privileges, you must start each line with schema. This is only applicable for design-time schema objects. Following this term, include the name of the repository schema file. The name of the file will need to include the package hierarchy and a colon preceding the file name. You can specify multiple schema files in the list as well. The following example includes the fully qualified name of a design-time schema object:

```
Security.Schemas:SalesMart.hdbschema
```

After the schema file name, include a colon, then a comma-separated list of schema privileges. At the end of the list, include a semicolon to finish the line. Listing 6.3 shows two complete lines that grant the listed schema privileges. The first line references a single schema file, and the second references multiple schema files within the same line.

```
schema Security.Schemas:SalesMart.hdbschema: SELECT, EXECUTE;
schema
  Security.Schemas:SalesMart.hdbschema,
  Security.Schemas:MySchema.hdbschema:
  SELECT;
```

Listing 6.3 Repository Role Script Granting Schema Privileges

In summary, we use different syntax to program runtime schema objects and design-time schema objects.

6.3.3 Object Privileges

Object privileges can be granted in two ways. First, we can grant object privileges to any runtime catalog object. This works for both standard catalog objects and activated repository objects. Object privileges can also be granted to design-time objects listed in the repository. In this instance, we can only reference objects created within the repository. The privileges assigned to the design-time object will also be granted to the runtime version of the same object.

Runtime Objects

When defining runtime object privileges in repository role scripts, you must start each line with `catalog sql object`. Following this term, include the fully qualified name of the catalog object, followed by a colon. We can also specify a comma-separated list of catalog objects if we want them to all have the same privileges. After the colon, include a comma-separated list of object privileges. At the end of the list, include a semicolon to finish the line. It's also important to note that the _SYS_REPO system account must have full privileges for the object or own it before such privileges can be included within the definition of a repository role.

Listing 6.4 shows the definition of catalog object privileges within a repository role script. The first line references a single catalog object. The second line references two different catalog objects, each granted the listed privilege.

```
catalog sql object "MySchema"."TestTableTwo": SELECT, ALTER, DROP;
catalog sql object
  "MySchema"."DIM_CUSTOMER", "MySchema"."DIM_PRODUCT":
  SELECT, DELETE, ALTER;
```

Listing 6.4 Repository Roles Script Granting Runtime Catalog Object Privileges

We recommend that you only reference catalog objects that exist exclusively in runtime when using this syntax—that is, objects created using the SQL `CREATE` statement. It's best to use the design-time syntax for any repository-based catalog objects.

Design-Time Objects

In addition to referencing runtime catalog objects, we can also reference design-time catalog objects. Referencing design-time objects is only possible if the object itself is a repository object. In most cases, we recommend that you reference the design-time version of an object, because it helps to create a dependency chain that can be identified during lifecycle management.

To reference design-time repository objects, we need to use a different syntax. The syntax must start each line with `sql object`. In effect, we're just removing the term `catalog` from the statement used when referencing runtime objects. Following this term, include the package and object name of the design-time object. We separate the package name and object name with two colons. Unlike schemas, we don't need to include the file extension in the fully qualified name. For example, to reference repository table `STG_CUSTOMER` stored in the `e-corp.sales.table` package, you'd use the following repository table syntax:


```
e-corp.sales.tables::STG_CUSTOMERS
```

Note that the package name and object name are separated by two colons. We can also specify multiple repository objects within a comma-separated list. After the name of the repository object, we need to include another colon. After the final colon, include a comma-separated list of object privileges. At the end of the list, include a semicolon to finish the line. Listing 6.5 shows two lines of code referencing design-time object privileges within a repository role script.

```
sql object Security.Tables::adusers: SELECT, ALTER, DROP;

sql object
 e-corp.tables::STG_CUSTOMERS, e-corp.tables::STG_PRODUCTS,
 e-corp.tables::STG_EMPLOYEE:
SELECT, ALTER, DROP, DELETE;
```

Listing 6.5 Repository Role Script Granting Design-Time Catalog Object Privileges

6.3.4 Structured Privileges

As of SAP HANA 2.0 SPS 00, structured privileges can only be defined as standard catalog objects. There are no documented repository artifacts that can produce a structured privilege other than an analytic privilege. As you'll recall, an analytic privilege is a type of structured privilege that regulates access to SAP HANA information views. In generic terms, structured privileges extend beyond information views and can also provide restrictions to standard catalog views. Therefore, we only need to discuss the syntax required to include catalog-structured privileges within a repository role.

When defining runtime structured privileges within repository-based role scripts, you must start each line with `catalog analytic privilege`. Following this term, include a colon and the structured privilege name, wrapped in double quotes for case-sensitivity purposes. Include a semicolon to finish the line:

```
catalog analytic privilege : "MyStructuredPriv";
```

It's important to note that a catalog-structured privilege will be owned by the account that created it. Repository roles are activated when the system account _SYS_REPO is the grantor of privileges. Therefore, the owner of the structured privilege will need to grant _SYS_REPO the structured privilege and include `WITH GRANT OPTION`. The following example SQL statement grants the structured privilege `"MyStructuredPriv"` to the _SYS_REPO user and includes the `WITH GRANT OPTION`:

```
GRANT STRUCTURED PRIVILEGE "MyStructuredPriv" TO "_SYS_REPO" WITH GRANT
OPTION;
```

This statement must be executed by the user that owns the structured privilege or by a user that was previously granted full access to the structured privilege.

6.3.5 Remote Sources

As of SAP HANA 2.0 SPS 00, remote source catalog object privileges can't be specified within SAP HANA repository roles. We couldn't find any documentation from SAP that provides an example, nor were we able to configure such privileges using SAP HANA Web-Based Development Workbench editor. To all appearances, they aren't supported.

If you're using SAP HANA smart data access or SAP HANA smart data integration and you need to develop a security model that includes remote source privileges, we have the following recommendations:

1. You'll find that you can configure repository role privileges for individual remote source virtual tables that are published in a schema. This helps limit access to the individual remote source tables without the need for a workaround.
2. Create one or more standard roles using a technical user account, and assign the remote source privileges. Grant the roles and privileges to the _SYS_REPO system account and include the `WITH GRANT OPTION` or `WITH ADMIN OPTION`.
3. Extend the standard catalog roles within a standard repository role.

4. Preserve all SQL statements in a repository text object. This is the only way to store the SQL code in the repository. You'll likely need to use this SQL code in upstream SAP HANA environments governed by proper lifecycle management. Remember that these repository roles won't activate until the catalog roles have been created.

6.3.6 Analytic Privileges

When defining analytic privileges within repository-based role scripts, you must start each line with analytic privilege. Following this term, include a colon. After the colon, include the fully qualified name of the analytic privilege file. The file name must include the package hierarchy name, analytic privilege name, and .analytic privilege extension. The package hierarchy name and analytic privilege name will be separated by a single colon. At the end of the statement, include a semicolon to finish the line. Because all analytic privileges are owned by _SYS_REPO, there's no need to grant _SYS_REPO privileges to these analytic privilege objects. See the following example:

```
analytic privilege: <package.name> : <analytic privilege name>
<.analyticprivilege> ;
```

The following example grants the ap_sales_reporting_region analytic privilege, stored in the e-corp.sales.security package. Remember that repository package and object names are case-sensitive:

```
analytic privilege:
  e-corp.security:ap_sales_reporting_region.analyticprivilege;
```

In a final example, we'll grant the _SYS_BI_CP_ALL system analytic privilege. This special catalog analytic privilege, when granted, gives full access to all information views defined within the repository:

```
catalog analytic privilege : "_SYS_BI_CP_ALL";
```

6.3.7 Application Privileges

When defining application privileges within repository-based role scripts, you must start each line with application privilege. Following this term, include a colon. After the colon, include the name of the application privilege. The application privilege name must include the package hierarchy name, two colons, and the name of the application privilege. For case-sensitivity purposes, the name must be wrapped in double quotes. At the end of the statement, include a semicolon to finish the line.

The following example is a single line used to grant application privileges within a repository-based role:

```
application privilege: "sap.hana.security.base::DataService";
```

6.3.8 Package Privileges

When defining package privileges within repository-based roles scripts, you must start each line with `package`. Following this term, include the name of the package hierarchy node. After package name, include a single colon, then a comma-separated list of package privileges. At the end of the statement, include a semicolon to finish the line.

The following example is a single line used to grant package privileges within a repository-based role:

```
Package e-corp.sales: REPO.READ, REPO.ACTIVATE_NATIVE_OBJECTS, REPO.MAINTAIN_
NATIVE_PACKAGES, REPO.EDIT_IMPORTED_OBJECTS;
```

To grant root package privileges, use the system package value of `.REPO_PACKAGE_ROOT` to represent privileges that will be applied to all packages. The following example shows the syntax needed to grant root package privileges:

```
package .REPO_PACKAGE_ROOT: REPO.READ;
```

6.4 Managing Repository Roles with SAP HANA Web-Based Development Workbench

The SAP HANA Web-Based Development Workbench editor, hosted within the XS engine, provides an interface that you can use to manage and create repository roles. The interface looks similar to the standard role management option in SAP HANA Studio, but the role objects it creates are profoundly different. The editor creates repository-based roles. The objects created in SAP HANA Web-Based Development Workbench can be opened in the SAP HANA Studio developer perspective, which means that we can use either SAP HANA Studio or the script editor to manage repository roles.

Most will find it easier to use SAP HANA Web-Based Development Workbench editor when creating repository roles. The interface eliminates the need to memorize the exact syntax for each object type. It also helps you search for objects within the catalog or repository. In the following sections, we'll first look at accessing SAP HANA Web-Based Development Workbench and navigating its basic functionality. We'll then review the specific processes required to grant system privileges, object privileges, analytic privileges, package privileges, and application privileges.

6.4.1 Accessing and Navigating the SAP HANA Web-Based Development Workbench Editor

You can access SAP HANA Web-Based Development Workbench via a supported Internet browser. The following two URLs can be customized to match the details of your environment:

http://sap-hana.myhost.com:8000/sap/hana/ide/editor

http://<sap_hana_host>:80<instance_number>/sap/hana/ide/editor

In the last example, replace <sap_hana_host> with the hostname of the SAP HANA system in your environment and <instance_number> with the two-digit instance number corresponding to your SAP HANA system.

For secure access, the following examples should help you construct the correct URL:

https://<sap_hana_host>:43<instance_number>/sap/hana/ide/editor

https://sap-hana.myhost.com:4300/sap/hana/ide/editor

To use the editor, the user account first will need to be granted one of the roles listed in Table 6.1. Users only need one of these two roles to access the SAP HANA Web-Based Development Workbench editor.

Role Name	Summary
sap.hana.ide.roles::EditorDeveloper	Within SAP HANA Web-Based Development Workbench, users will only be able to access the editor. The editor provides interfaces to create a variety of repository objects, including repository-based roles.
sap.hana.ide.roles::Developer	This role grants a higher level of privileges for users that need full access to SAP HANA Web-based Development Workbench. It grants access to the editor, catalog, and security interfaces. It's considered the parent to the sap.hana.ide.roles::EditorDeveloper role.

Table 6.1 Roles Required to Use SAP HANA Web-Based Development Workbench Editor

Additional Privileges

Note that the roles in Table 6.1 simply allow the granted user access to the interface. The user will also need access to the package in which the repository roles are stored. To grant repository roles to other users and roles, the user will need EXECUTE access to the system stored procedure named "_SYS_REPO"."GRANT_ACTIVATED_ROLE". To revoke repository roles, the user will need EXECUTE access to the "_SYS_REPO"."REVOKE_ACTIVATED_ROLE" stored procedure.

Once you have access to the SAP HANA Web-Based Development Workbench editor, expand the **Content** node on the right side of the window. Expand **Packages** to reveal a list of packages defined in the system. As stated before, repository roles must be stored in a package that only security administrators can access. We typically create a top-level package named **Security** to host such objects.

To create a repository role, right-click the package in which you want to store it, then choose **New • Role** (see Figure 6.5).

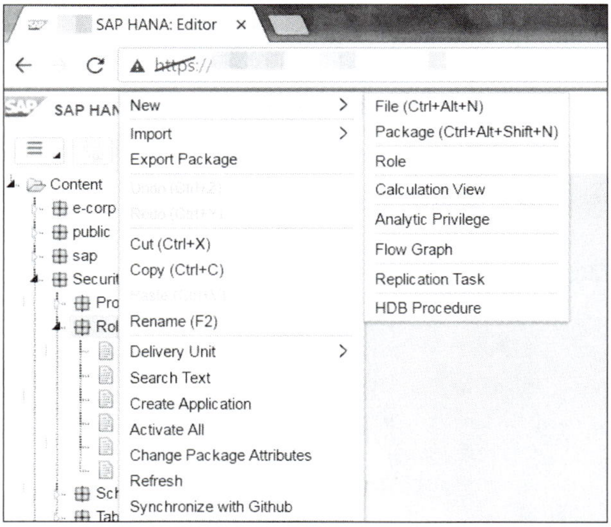

Figure 6.5 Navigating the SAP HANA Web-Based Development Workbench Editor and Creating Repository Role

A small window named **New Role** will appear. Enter the desired name of the role and click **Create**. A new tabbed window will appear in the large right-hand frame. The tab label should match the provided name of the repository role. The new window will contain a series of subtabs: **Granted Roles**, **System Privileges**, **Object Privileges**, **Analytic Privileges**, **Package Privileges**, and **Application Privileges**. Like in SAP HANA Studio, each tab allows a developer to define certain privileges.

Repository Role Scripts and SAP HANA Web-Based Development Workbench Editor

Note that repository roles created in SAP HANA Web-Based Development Workbench can also be opened and modified using SAP HANA Studio's text editor, which means that we can create a repository role using SAP HANA Web-Based Development Workbench, then open it in SAP HANA Studio to modify or change the design-time script. We can also create the repository role as a design-time script, activate the role in the repository, and then open it with SAP HANA Web-Based Development Workbench.

In relation to repository-based roles, there are three main tasks that we can perform within the SAP HANA Web-Based Development Workbench editor. We can create a new role, edit an existing role, or manage privileges assigned to an existing repository role.

We've already discussed the process for creating a repository role, so now let's discuss the process for deleting a repository-based role within the SAP HANA Web-Based Development Workbench editor. First, locate the role to be deleted in the package hierarchy. Right-click it and choose **Delete**. A **Confirmation Needed** window will appear. Choose **OK** to delete the repository role.

To edit an existing repository role within the SAP HANA Web-Based Development Workbench editor, first locate the role to be edited within the package hierarchy. Double-click it to open the role editor. Alternatively, right-click the role and choose **Open With • Role Editor** to edit the role using the GUI. This is the same process that a double-click invokes. You can also choose **Open With • Text Editor** if you want to edit the role's script, like the process used in SAP HANA Studio's development perspective.

If you opened the repository role with the role editor, we can now add or remove privileges from the role. Let's now take a closer look at the process required to grant each type of privilege.

6.4.2 System Privileges

Click the **System Privileges** tab to reveal an interface in which we can add or remove system privileges. To add a system privilege, click the large **+** button on the subtab header. A pop-up window will appear titled **Select System Privilege** (see Figure 6.6). A search box will appear in this window; enter a portion of the system privilege name to narrow the results. Alternatively, you can scroll through the unfiltered list to locate the desired system privilege. Select one or more privileges within the list. Hold down the `Ctrl` to select multiple items. The selected items are highlighted in light blue. Click the **OK** button at the bottom of the window to finalize the selection.

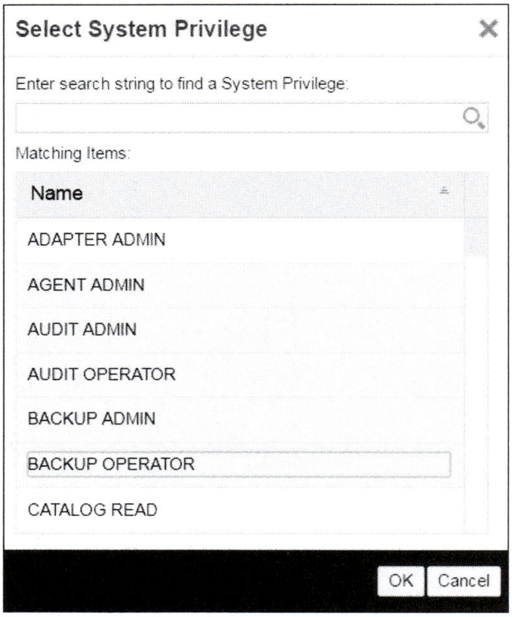

Figure 6.6 Selecting and Assigning System Privileges in SAP HANA Web-Based Development Workbench

The selected privilege will now appear in the **System Privileges** tab (see Figure 6.7).

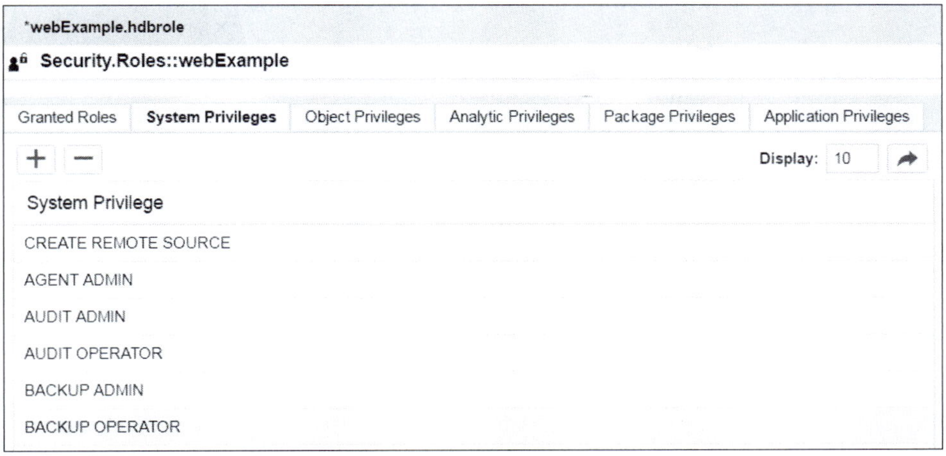

Figure 6.7 Selected System Privileges

To remove an assigned system privilege, select one from the list, then click the large – button above the list to remove it. Items in the list must be deleted one at a time.

Once you've configured the desired list of system privileges, click the **Save All** button at the top left, which shows three stacked floppy disks.

If there are any issues saving and activating the repository role, messages will appear in red text in the console window just below the opened **Repository Roles** tab. The console window has a dark background color and is located at the bottom of the opened tab. Affirmative messages will appear in white text, and error messages will appear in red text.

To close the open repository role tab, click the small **x** to the right of the tab.

6.4.3 Object Privileges

Click the **Object Privileges** tab to reveal an interface in which we can add or remove object privileges. To add an object, click the large **+** button on the subtab header. A pop-up window will appear titled **Select Object Privilege** (see Figure 6.8). The search box is divided into two broad types of objects. The top two radio buttons allow us to toggle between design-time or runtime objects. When searching for design-time objects, choose the **Design-time** radio button. When searching for runtime objects, choose the **Run-time** radio button.

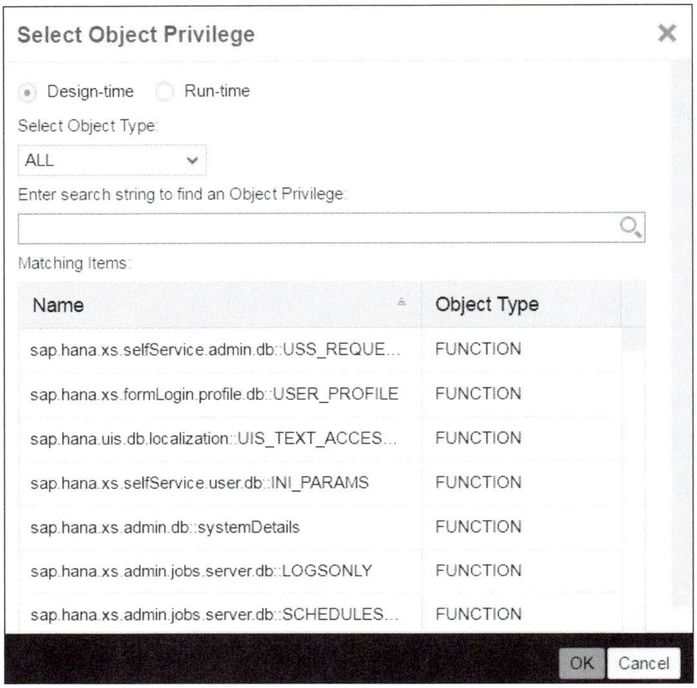

Figure 6.8 Selecting and Assigning Object Privileges in SAP HANA Web-Based Development Workbench

Below the radio buttons, there are more filter options to limit the results to a specific object type. The dropdown is titled **Select Object Type**. Use the dropdown menu to choose the specific object type you want to use to limit the search results. The default option is **All**, meaning that all objects types are considered. For example, if you want to limit the search results to just tables, choose **Table** from the dropdown list and only table objects will appear in the results.

Just below the dropdown menu, a search box will appear. In the text box, enter a portion of the object name to narrow the results. Alternatively, you can scroll through the unfiltered list to locate the desired object by name. Select one or more objects within the list. Hold down the `Ctrl` key to select multiple items. Click the **OK** button at the bottom of the window to finalize the selection.

The selected objects will now appear in the **System Privileges** tab (see Figure 6.9).

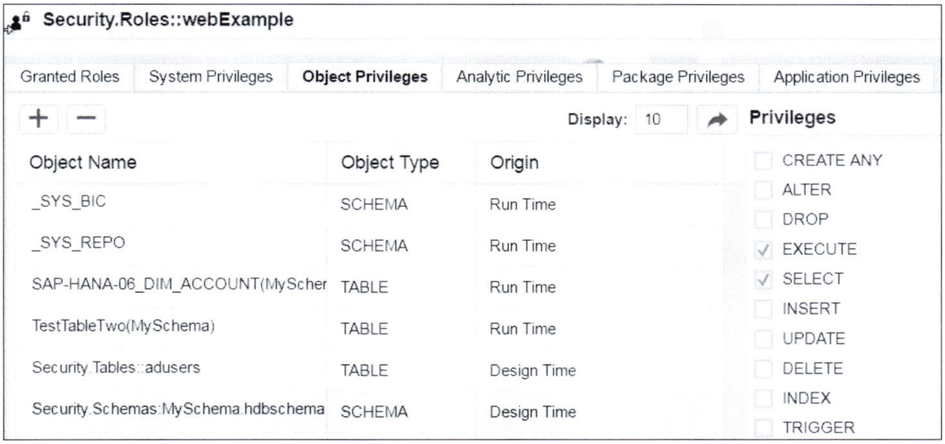

Figure 6.9 Selected Runtime and Design-Time Objects

With the objects listed, we now need to assign the various object privileges to each selected object. To specify the privileges for an individual object, click the object to select it in the list. To the right of the selected object, a series of privileges and corresponding checkboxes will appear (shown on the right in Figure 6.9).

Check the box beside each privilege to assign the selected privilege to the selected object. Repeat the process for all objects. To remove the privilege, simply uncheck the box beside the privilege you want to remove.

To remove an assigned object and all its privileges, select an object from the list, then click the large – button above the list to remove it. Items in the list must be deleted one at a time.

Once you've configured the desired list of objects and established their privileges, click the **Save All** button.

If there are any issues saving and activating the repository role, messages will appear in red text within the console window just below the opened **Repository Roles** tab. The console window has a dark background color and is located at the bottom of the opened tab. Affirmative messages will appear in white text and error messages in red text.

To close the open repository role tab, click the small **x** to the right of the tab.

6.4.4 Analytic Privileges

Click the **Analytic Privileges** tab to reveal an interface in which we can add or remove analytic privileges. To add an analytic privilege, click the large **+** button on the subtab header. A pop-up window will appear titled **Select Analytic Privilege** (see Figure 6.10).

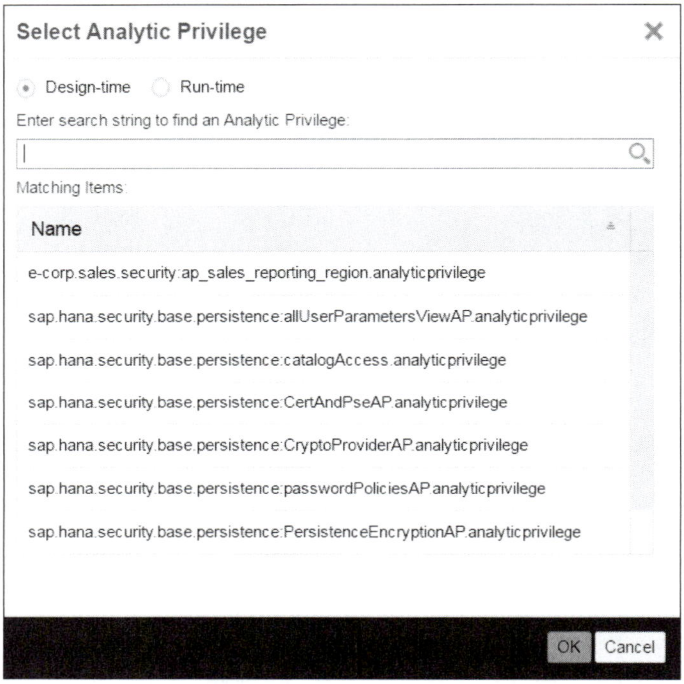

Figure 6.10 Selecting and Assigning Analytic Privileges in SAP HANA Web-Based Development Workbench

The search box is divided into two broad types of analytic privileges. The top two radio buttons allow us to toggle between design-time and runtime objects. When searching for design-time analytic privileges, choose the **Design-time** radio button. When searching for runtime analytic privileges, choose the **Run-time** radio button. Note that the runtime list also includes generic structured privileges.

A search box will appear in this window; enter a portion of the analytic privilege's name to narrow the results. Alternatively, you can scroll through the unfiltered list to locate the desired analytic privileges by name. Select one or more analytic privileges within the list, holding down the `Ctrl` key to select multiple items. Click the **OK** button at the bottom of the window to finalize the selection.

The selected analytic privileges will now appear in the **Analytic Privileges** tab (see Figure 6.11).

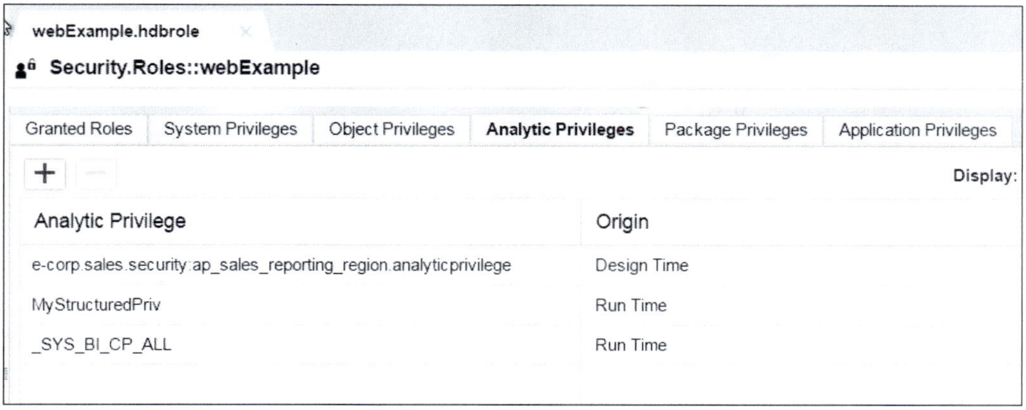

Figure 6.11 Selected Runtime and Design-Time Analytic Privileges

To remove an assigned analytic privilege, select it from the list, then click the large **–** button above the list to remove it. Items in the list must be deleted one at a time.

Once you've configured the desired list of analytic privileges, click the **Save All** button.

If there are any issues saving and activating the repository role, messages will appear in red text within the console window, which has a dark background color and is located at the bottom of the opened tab. Affirmative messages will appear in white text and error messages in red text.

To close the open repository role tab, click the small **x** to the right of the tab.

6.4.5 Package Privileges

Click the **Package Privileges** tab to reveal an interface in which we can add or remove package privileges. To add a package, click the large **+** button on the subtab header. A pop-up window will appear titled **Select Package** (see Figure 6.12).

Within the window, a search box will appear. In the text box, enter a portion of the package name to narrow the results. Alternatively, you can scroll through the unfiltered list to locate the desired package by its complete hierarchical name. Select one or more objects within the list, using the `Ctrl` key to select multiple items. Click the **OK** button at the bottom of the window to finalize the selection.

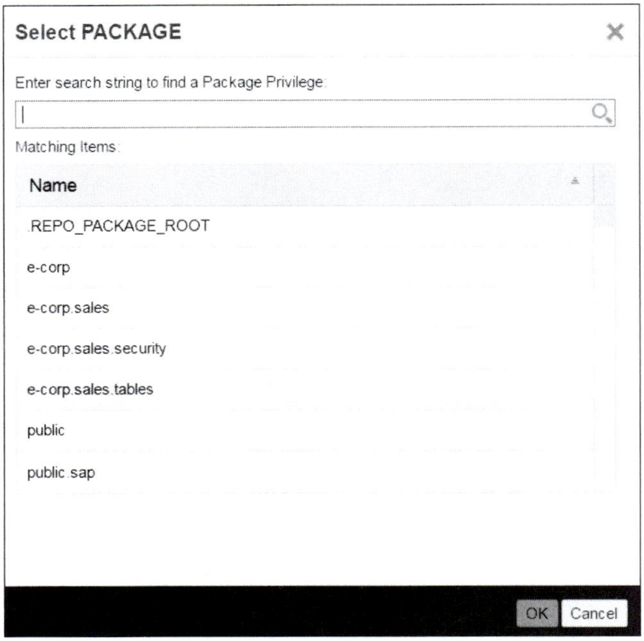

Figure 6.12 Selecting and Assigning Package Privileges in SAP HANA Web-Based Development Workbench

The selected packages will now appear in the **Package Privileges** tab (see Figure 6.13).

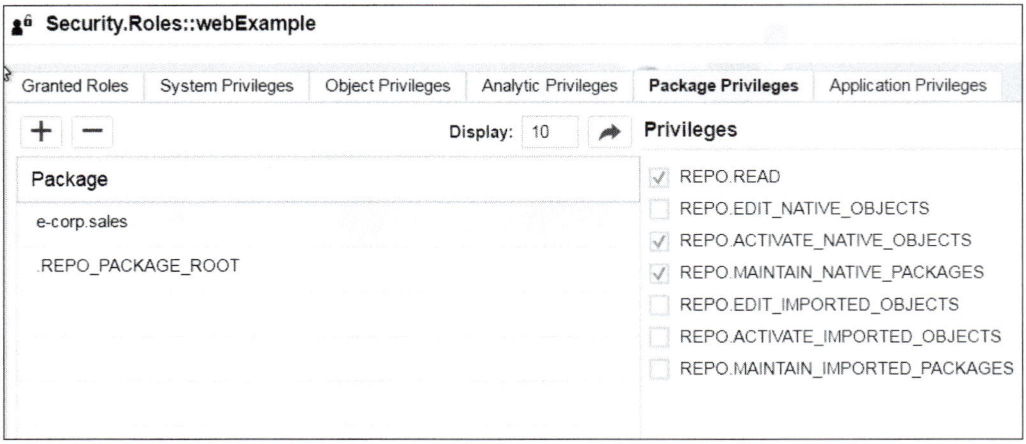

Figure 6.13 Selected Packages and Their Privileges

With the objects listed, we now need to assign the various package privileges to each selected package. To specify the privileges for an individual package, select and highlight the package within the list on the left side. To the right of the selected package, a series of privileges and corresponding checkboxes will appear (shown on the right in Figure 6.13).

Check the box beside each privilege to assign the selected privilege to the selected package. Repeat the process for all packages. To remove a privilege, simply uncheck the box beside the privilege you want to remove.

To remove an assigned package and all its privileges, select an object from the list on the left, then click the large – button above the list to remove it. Items in the list must be deleted one at a time.

Once you've configured the desired list of packages and established their privileges, click the **Save All** button.

If there are any issues saving and activating the repository role, messages will appear in red text within the console window, which has a dark background color and is located at the bottom of the opened tab. Affirmative messages will appear in white text and error messages in red text.

To close the open repository role tab, click the small **x** to the right of the tab.

6.4.6 Application Privileges

Click the **Application Privileges** tab to reveal an interface in which we can add or remove application privileges. To add an application privilege, click the large **+** button on the subtab header. A pop-up window will appear titled **Select Application Privilege** (see Figure 6.14).

A search box will appear in this window; enter a portion of the application privilege's name to narrow the results. Alternatively, you can scroll through the unfiltered list to locate the desired application privileges by name. Select one or more application privileges within the list, using the `Ctrl` key to select multiple items. Click the **OK** button at the bottom of the window to finalize the selection.

The selected application privileges will now appear in the **Application Privileges** tab (see Figure 6.15).

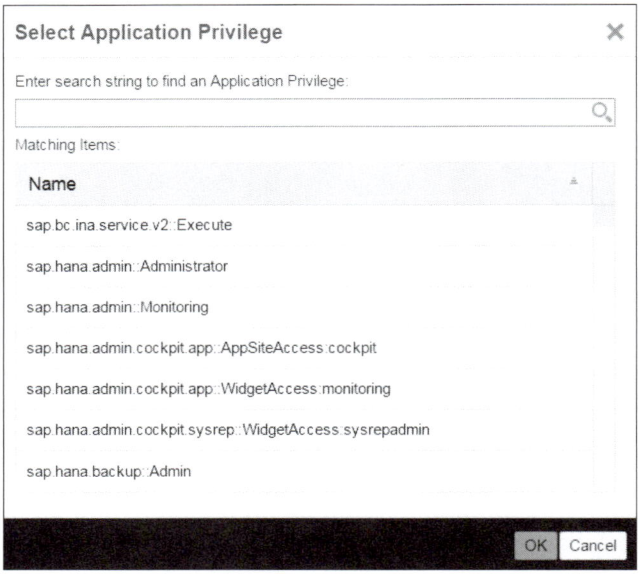

Figure 6.14 Selecting and Assigning Application Privileges in SAP HANA Web-Based Development Workbench

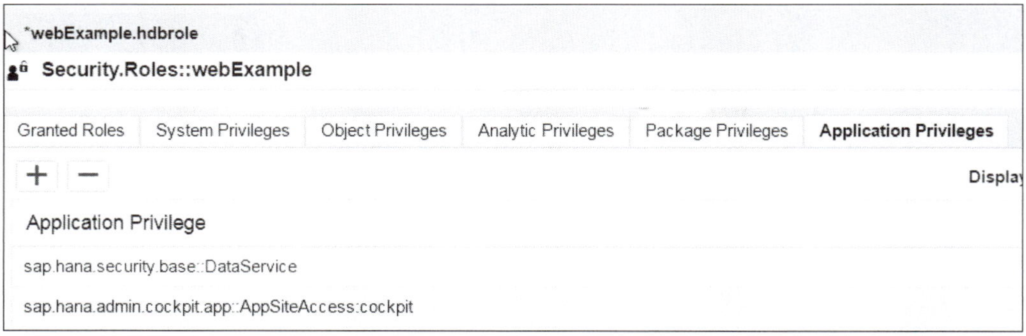

Figure 6.15 Selected Application Privileges

To remove an assigned application privilege, select it from the list and click the large – button above the list to remove it. Items in the list must be deleted one at a time.

Once you've configured the desired list of application privileges, click the **Save All** button.

If there are any issues saving and activating the repository role, messages will appear in red text within the console window, which has a dark background color and is located at the bottom of the opened tab. Affirmative messages will appear in white text and error messages in red text.

To close the open repository role tab, click the small **x** to the right of the tab.

6.5 Granting Repository Roles to Users

Unlike standard roles, repository roles require a slightly different process when assigning them to existing users or roles. Standard roles rely on specific GRANT SQL syntax. For example, GRANT <SOME PRIVILEGE> TO <GRANTEE> must be executed to assign a standard role. Repository roles are different. They're owned by the _SYS_REPO system account and therefore can only be granted by that account. Given that there is no means to directly log on as this system account, we need an alternative method to impersonate _SYS_REPO for granting actions.

To accommodate this need, SAP HANA provides special stored procedures to either grant or revoke the assignment of repository roles to other users or roles. The stored procedures can be called directly using the SQL console. They also can be automatically invoked using either SAP HANA Studio or the SAP HANA Web-Based Development Workbench security manager. Let's look at how to grant and revoke repository roles using each of the three available methods.

6.5.1 Granting and Revoking Repository Roles with Stored Procedures

Repository roles are granted using the GRANT_ACTIVATED_ROLE stored procedure in the SYS_REPO schema. For a security administrator to use the stored procedure, he must have EXECUTE rights on the procedures.

The stored procedure requires that we specify two input parameters for proper execution. The first parameter requires the name of an active repository role and the second requires the name of a grantee. The grantee can be either a user or a role. Use the following syntax:

```
GRANT_ACTIVATED_ROLE"('<Repository Name Name>','Grantee Name')
```

For example, to grant the `Security.Roles::consumer` repository role to the user account G3457543, we would execute the stored procedure in the SQL console as follows:

```
CALL "_SYS_REPO"."GRANT_ACTIVATED_ROLE"
('Security.Roles::consumer','G3457543');
```

To revoke a repository role, we need to use another stored procedure found in the _SYS_REPO schema, named `REVOKE_ACTIVATED_ROLE`. For a security administrator to use the procedure, they must have been granted `EXECUTE` rights on the procedures. It has the same two input parameters as the previous example. For example, to revoke the repository role Security.Roles::consumer from the user account G3457543, we would execute the stored procedure in the SQL console as follows:

```
CALL "_SYS_REPO"."REVOKE_ACTIVATED_ROLE"
('Security.Roles::consumer','G3457543');
```

The grant procedure is set up to execute the role granting actions as if the system account _SYS_REPO was executing the code. This insures that the grantor is not the user account executing the procedure. Therefore, we don't need to be concerned with protecting the grantor of the role. The revoke procedure performs a similar function. When executed, the procedure impersonates the _SYS_REPO user and the role is easily revoked, because _SYS_REPO was the grantor.

6.5.2 Granting and Revoking Repository Roles with SAP HANA Studio

As an alternative to using stored procedures, we can use the role management options in SAP HANA Studio to both grant and revoke repository roles. Most will find it easier to use SAP HANA Studio than to memorize and type the SQL commands and stored procedure syntax.

To access the user management options in SAP HANA Studio, start by switching to the administration console perspective. In the **Systems** tab, expand the **System** node. Locate the **Security** node and expand it to reveal the **Security**, **Users**, and **Roles** nodes. Expand the **Users** node to reveal a list of users. Double-click a user to assign a repository role.

Figure 6.16 shows the user management interface in SAP HANA Studio. Just below the user name details section, you'll see a series of tabs. The first tab is **Granted Roles**. We'll use this tab to grant a repository role to the user.

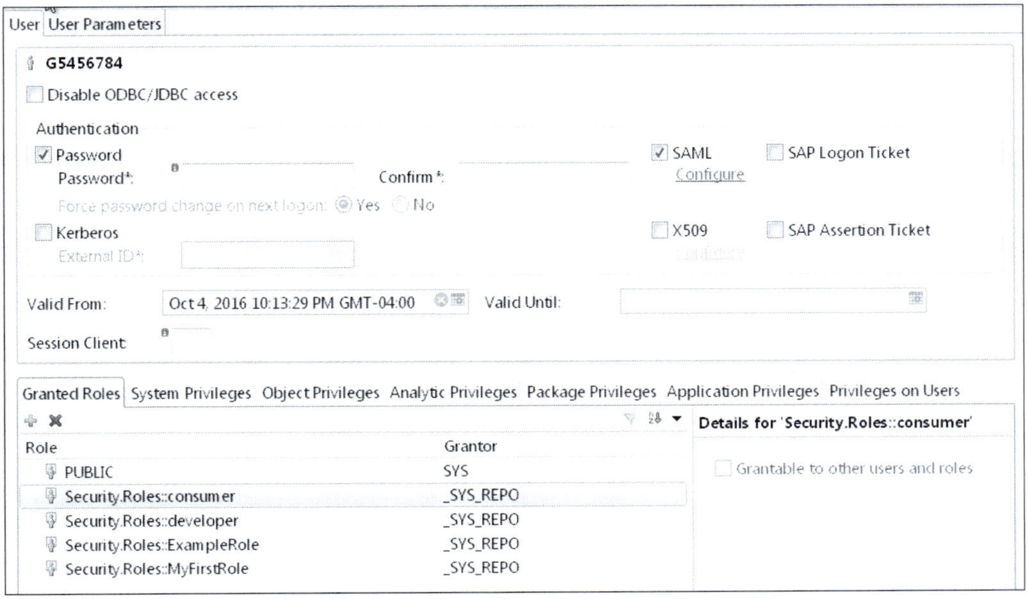

Figure 6.16 Granted Roles Configuration Tab in SAP HANA Studio

When searching for repository-based roles, you'll see that their runtime object names include the package hierarchy. For example, the consumer role stored in the `Security.Roles` package will be named `Security.Roles::consumer`. Understanding this naming convention will help you identify repository-based roles within the list.

Much like granting and revoking privileges, the process required to grant a repository role involves clicking **+**, searching for one or more existing roles, and adding them to the list. Once a repository role is added to the list and the changes are saved, the user will be granted the assigned repository roles and all the privileges granted to those repository roles. When selecting a repository role, you'll notice that the grantor is _SYS_REPO. For standard roles, the grantor will be the user account that authenticated with SAP HANA. SAP HANA Studio treats repository roles differently, because it knows that it must execute the _SYS_REPO stored procedure to grant the role to the user.

When you click **Save**, SAP HANA Studio will execute the appropriate stored procedure statement in the background to grant the repository role. The grantor will always be _SYS_REPO when this occurs.

To revoke a repository role, select the repository role from the list and then click the red **X** icon to remove the assigned role from the list. Click the disk icon located on the main SAP HANA Studio icon bar to save and activate the changes.

6.5.3 Granting and Revoking Repository Roles with SAP HANA Web-Based Development Workbench

As mentioned in Chapter 5, the SAP HANA Web-Based Development Workbench security manager, hosted within the XS engine, provides an interface that you can use to create users, create roles, or manage security.

You can access the SAP HANA Web-Based Development Workbench security manager by updating the following two URLs to match the details of your environment:

http://<sap_hana_host>:80<instance_number>/sap/hana/ide/security

https://<sap_hana_host>:43<instance_number>/sap/hana/ide/security

Once you have access to the SAP HANA Web-Based Development Workbench security manager, expand the **Security** node on the right side of the window. Expand **Users** to reveal a list of users. Double-click a user to open the management interface for the given user account. With the selected user management window open, you can begin granting and revoking repository roles using the tab labeled **Granted Roles**.

The process for granting and revoking roles in the SAP HANA Web-Based Development Workbench security manager is identical to the process outlined for SAP HANA Studio. Because there is tremendous overlap in the workflows, we won't go into the same level of detail in this section; see Section 6.5.2 for additional details. Remember that if there are any activation issues, warning messages will appear in the status frame at the bottom of the user management window.

To help demonstrate the concept of repository roles further, let's review a case study in which we'll examine how E-Corporation used repository roles to create a security model.

6.6 Case Study: Creating Basic Repository Roles

E-Corporation has recently implemented an analytic solution within the SAP HANA platform. The company has provisioned tables, loaded data with an ETL tool, and created a series of SAP HANA information views. The user community will primarily interact with the SAP HANA information views, which will be secured with an analytic privilege that limits data access by region. Each user will have her own logon to the SAP HANA system to accommodate the data security requirements. However, the users will primarily access the data via SAP BusinessObjects. The SAP BusinessObjects system has been configured to support SSO for the SAP HANA platform with SAML authentication.

In addition to the privileges needed to secure access to the information views, the security model must support power user access, developer access, and security administrator access.

E-Corporation has contacted its lead SAP HANA security consultant and requested help defining a security model to accommodate its security requirements. The consultant has determined that a series of repository roles will need to be defined. Let's look further at the consultant's decision-making process and the four repository roles recommended for this project.

6.6.1 Consumer Repository Role

The first repository role will provide a base level of access to the SAP HANA information views. The name of the repository role will be consumer. It will grant both SELECT and EXECUTE access to the _SYS_BIC and _SYS_BI schemas. This is required because SAP HANA information views and additional metadata are published to these schemas. Users will need to have SELECT access, at a minimum, to query the information views and metadata. An analytic privilege will also be granted. The analytic privileges will limit the consumer's access to a series of information views and will dynamically filter the results of the views so that each user will be limited to one or more sales regions based on his predetermined security profile.

Figure 6.17 shows the configuration of the consumer repository role script. It contains two catalog schema privileges and one analytic privilege.

*consumer.hdbrole

```
role Security.Roles::consumer

{
catalog schema "_SYS_BIC": SELECT, EXECUTE;
catalog schema "_SYS_BI": SELECT, EXECUTE;

analytic privilege : e-corp.sales.security:ap_sales_reporting_region.analyticprivilege;

}
```

Figure 6.17 Consumer Repository Role Script

6.6.2 Power User Repository Role

In addition to the standard users at E-Corporation, a small group of power users require unique permissions. They're expected to access SAP HANA Studio to query information views and tables for debugging purposes. They'll also need to access the SAP HANA packages to view the design-time versions of the SAP HANA information views. Therefore, they'll need basic access to the SAP HANA repository. To accommodate this requirement, the security consultant recommends that an additional repository role named *poweruser* be created.

The poweruser repository role will be extended by the consumer repository role. This means that it will inherit all the privileges assigned to the consumer repository role. It will grant access to the `REPOSITORY_REST` stored procedure, which is required to access the package hierarchy within SAP HANA. It will also grant `SELECT` access to the schemas housing the data used by the SAP HANA information views. Finally, it will grant `REPO.READ` access to the `e-corp` package. This will allow a power user the ability to view the configuration of each information view within the repository.

Figure 6.18 shows the configuration of the poweruser repository role script. It contains all the privileges necessary to accommodate the security requirements.

powerusers.hdbrole

```
role Security.Roles::powerusers extends role
    Security.Roles::consumer
    //This role should include all of the privilege setup in the consumer role
{

    catalog sql object "SYS"."REPOSITORY_REST": EXECUTE;
    // Necessary procedure to view repository objects in HANA Studio

// Query data found in the base tables.
    catalog schema "SalesMart": SELECT;
    catalog schema "StagingMart": SELECT;

    package e-corp: REPO.READ;

}
```

Figure 6.18 Poweruser Repository Role Script

6.6.3 Developer Repository Role

The developers at E-Corporation will require access to SAP HANA and SAP HANA Studio. They'll be responsible for creating the development artifacts used by the analytic solution. At a high level, developers require the following privileges and accesses:

- Developers will need to have at least the privileges assigned to the consumer and power user repository roles.
- They need the ability to fully manage the staging and data mart schemas. They'll be responsible for creating and managing the tables used by the solution.
- They'll require access to the SAP HANA repository, system views, application lifecycle management, delivery units, analytic privileges, and import and export interfaces.
- They'll require access to all data when querying SAP HANA information views.
- They'll require full access to the e-corp package and its child packages.
- They'll require read access to all packages and development artifacts.
- They'll require access to the SAP HANA Web-Based Development Workbench.

To accommodate these requirements, a repository role named developer will be created. Figure 6.19 shows the repository role script that will be designed to accommodate the E-Corporation requirements for developers.

```
developer.hdbrole
role Security.Roles::developer extends role
Security.Roles::powerusers,
sap.hana.xs.ide.roles::CatalogDeveloper,
sap.hana.xs.ide.roles::EditorDeveloper
{

--Begin Schema Privileges
catalog schema "SalesMart": ALTER, SELECT, EXECUTE,
                            INSERT, UPDATE, DELETE, CREATE ANY,
                            DROP, DEBUG, TRIGGER, INDEX;

catalog schema "StagingMart":   ALTER, SELECT, EXECUTE, INSERT,
                                UPDATE, DELETE, CREATE ANY, DROP, DEBUG,
                                TRIGGER, INDEX;
--Begin System Privileges
system privilege: CATALOG READ, CREATE SCENARIO, CREATE STRUCTURED PRIVILEGE,
  EXPORT, IMPORT, REPO.EXPORT, REPO.IMPORT, REPO.MAINTAIN_DELIVERY_UNITS,
  REPO.WORK_IN_FOREIGN_WORKSPACE, REPO.MODIFY_CHANGE, REPO.MODIFY_OWN_CONTRIBUTION,
  REPO.MODIFY_FOREIGN_CONTRIBUTION, STRUCTUREDPRIVILEGE ADMIN;

catalog analytic privilege : "_SYS_BI_CP_ALL";

package e-corp:
  REPO.ACTIVATE_NATIVE_OBJECTS, REPO.EDIT_NATIVE_OBJECTS,
  REPO.MAINTAIN_NATIVE_PACKAGES, REPO.ACTIVATE_IMPORTED_OBJECTS,
  REPO.EDIT_IMPORTED_OBJECTS, REPO.MAINTAIN_IMPORTED_PACKAGES, REPO.READ;

package .REPO_PACKAGE_ROOT: REPO.READ;

}
```

Figure 6.19 Developer Repository Role Script

Let's look at how the developer repository role script shown in Figure 6.19 achieves the requirements:

- By including three existing roles within the `extends role` section of the script, two requirements are achieved. Developers will gain all the privileges of the consumer and poweruser roles and will gain access to SAP HANA Web-Based Development Workbench.
- The two `catalog schema` privilege lines grant the role full access to the staging and data mart schemas.
- The items listed in the `system privilege` line grant access to the SAP HANA repository, system views, application lifecycle management, delivery units, analytic privileges, and import and export interfaces.
- The `catalog analytic privilege` line grants full query access to all SAP HANA information views.
- The first `package` line grants full access to the top-level `e-corp` package.
- The second `package` line grants read-only access to the entire package hierarchy.

As you can see, we can achieve the developer requirements by including a few existing roles and by specifying several specific privileges. Referencing existing roles is helpful, because it reduces redundancy within the custom repository roles. It also ensures that the developer will inherit the same privileges as the lower-level poweruser and consumer roles. Two of the existing repository roles also provided application privileges specific to SAP HANA Web-Based Development Workbench.

6.6.4 Security Administrator Repository Role

The final recommended repository role is one that grants privileges to a select group of security administrators. This role must provide security administrators the ability to manage users, create repository roles, and grant permissions. Figure 6.20 shows the privileges and additional roles that will be assigned to the repository role named SecurityAdmin.

As you can see in the comments within the script, the role is extended by the developer role and three additional XS engine application-specific roles. The applications in the XS engine provide interfaces useful in managing a security model. Three additional `system privilege` lines are included to grant user, role, and audit management. The `catalog sql object` lines grant `EXECUTE` privileges for a series of stored procedures that are necessary to grant and revoke privileges for objects owned by _SYS_REPO. Finally, package security lines are included to provide exclusive access to the top-level package that will be used to store security-related development artifacts.

```
*SecurityAdmin.hdbrole
role Security.Roles::SecurityAdmin extends role
Security.Roles::developer, //Same Privileges as Developer, power user and consumer
sap.hana.ide.roles::Developer, //Full Access to web-based Workbench
sap.hana.xs.admin.roles::RuntimeConfAdministrator, //Full access config. settings for SAP HANA XS application
sap.hana.xs.selfService.admin.roles::USSAdministrator // User Self-service Admin.
{
system privilege: USER ADMIN; //Create and manage user accounts
system privilege: ROLE ADMIN; //Create and manage Standard Roles
system privilege: AUDIT ADMIN; //Manage Audit Policy

// Access to stored procedures used to grant and revoke repository object privileges
catalog sql object "_SYS_REPO"."GRANT_PRIVILEGE_ON_ACTIVATED_CONTENT": EXECUTE;
catalog sql object "_SYS_REPO"."REVOKE_PRIVILEGE_ON_ACTIVATED_CONTENT": EXECUTE;
catalog sql object "_SYS_REPO"."GRANT_ACTIVATED_ANALYTICAL_PRIVILEGE": EXECUTE;
catalog sql object "_SYS_REPO"."REVOKE_ACTIVATED_ANALYTICAL_PRIVILEGE": EXECUTE;
catalog sql object "_SYS_REPO"."GRANT_ACTIVATED_ROLE": EXECUTE;
catalog sql object "_SYS_REPO"."REVOKE_ACTIVATED_ROLE": EXECUTE;
catalog sql object "_SYS_REPO"."GRANT_APPLICATION_PRIVILEGE": EXECUTE;
catalog sql object "_SYS_REPO"."REVOKE_APPLICATION_PRIVILEGE": EXECUTE;
catalog sql object "_SYS_REPO"."GRANT_SCHEMA_PRIVILEGE_ON_ACTIVATED_CONTENT": EXECUTE;
catalog sql object "_SYS_REPO"."REVOKE_SCHEMA_PRIVILEGE_ON_ACTIVATED_CONTENT": EXECUTE;

// Full Access to the package storing repository role and other security dev. objects
package Security:
 REPO.READ, REPO.EDIT_NATIVE_OBJECTS,
 REPO.ACTIVATE_NATIVE_OBJECTS, REPO.MAINTAIN_NATIVE_PACKAGES,
 REPO.EDIT_IMPORTED_OBJECTS, REPO.ACTIVATE_IMPORTED_OBJECTS,
 REPO.MAINTAIN_IMPORTED_PACKAGES;

}
```

Figure 6.20 SecurityAdmin Repository Role Script

Once the repository roles are activated and assigned to the appropriate users, E-Corporation will have the makings of a sound security model. Because the company used repository roles, the model can easily be transported to other systems and managed using lifecycle management best practices. In addition, the _SYS_REPO system account will be the primary owner and grantor of the privileges.

6.7 Summary

Repository roles offer multiple advantages when used to manage an SAP HANA security model. With few exceptions, they should be used as the basis for an SAP HANA security model. We can create repository roles using design-time scripts within SAP HANA Studio or with SAP HANA Web-Based Development Workbench.

Chapter 7
System Privileges

In this chapter, we'll explore the different system privileges that govern a broad spectrum of actions within the SAP HANA platform.

System privileges play an important role in the development of any SAP HANA security model. They govern specific actions within the SAP HANA platform: In some cases, they govern actions specific to administrators; in other cases, they govern access to actions performed by developers. Throughout this chapter, we'll explore the various system privileges that SAP HANA provides and the types of activities that they govern. We'll also review the system privileges that are included with SAP HANA 2.0, and we'll demonstrate how system privileges are granted using SQL, SAP HANA Studio, the SAP HANA Web-Based Development Workbench security manager, and within repository-based roles. We'll close the chapter with a case study outlining several commonly used administrative roles and their required system privileges.

7.1 What Are System Privileges?

System privileges govern various activities or actions that can be executed within the SAP HANA platform. Administrators must be granted system privileges to perform activities such as backups, license key management, audit management, SSL management, system configuration settings, user creation, and role creation. Developers must be granted system privileges to perform imports and exports of catalog objects and repository objects. There are also several system privileges that govern access to actions performed within the SAP HANA development repository.

System privileges are predefined and delivered with the SAP HANA system. They can't be created or customized as of SAP HANA 2.0 SP 00. To clarify the role that system privileges play in a security model, let's review each of the default system privileges and organize them into categories.

7.2 Default System Privileges

SAP HANA is delivered with multiple system privileges. To better explain how system privileges might be used within a security model, we've organized them into five broad categories: developer, security admin, system admin, environment monitoring, and environment performance. We defined these categories based on our experience, but they don't exist natively within SAP HANA. Placing the system privileges into categories will hopefully help you understand how they'll likely be granted to the repository roles devised to support your security model.

7.2.1 Developer-Related System Privileges

The following system privileges are typically required by developers. In general, these privileges only grant access to areas within SAP HANA related to the development of content. For example, a developer creating SAP HANA information views would likely need many of these system privileges in the development environment.

Create R Script

The *create R script* system privilege grants roles the ability to create a stored procedure using the R language.

REPO.EXPORT

The `REPO.EXPORT` system privilege governs access to interfaces that are used to export a *delivery unit* (DU) from an SAP HANA system to a DU export file. *Delivery units* are logical organization units that contain one or more SAP HANA development artifacts. Typically, they're exported and then imported into another SAP HANA system to transport code between systems.

REPO.IMPORT

The `REPO.IMPORT` system privilege governs access to interfaces that are used to import a DU file into an SAP HANA system.

REPO.MAINTAIN_DELIVERY_UNITS

The `REPO.MAINTAIN_DELIVERY_UNITS` system privilege governs access to interfaces used to define a DU within the SAP HANA repository.

REPO.WORK_IN_FOREIGN_WORKSPACE

The `REPO.WORK_IN_FOREIGN_WORKSPACE` system privilege grants a role the ability to take over ownership of inactive development artifact versions hosted in another user's workspace.

REPO.CONFIGURE

The `REPO.CONFIGURE` system privilege is used within SAP HANA application lifecycle management. Specifically, this system privilege allows the grantee to configure change recording when enabled.

REPO.MODIFY_CHANGE

The `REPO.MODIFY_CHANGE` system privilege is used within SAP HANA application lifecycle management. Specifically, this system privilege allows the grantee to assign objects to a change list when change recording is enabled.

REPO.MODIFY_OWN_CONTRIBUTION

The `REPO.MODIFY_OWN_CONTRIBUTION` system privilege is used within SAP HANA application lifecycle management. Specifically, this system privilege allows the grantee to assign objects to a change list when change recording is enabled.

REPO.MODIFY_FOREIGN_CONTRIBUTION

The `REPO.MODIFY_FOREIGN_CONTRIBUTION` system privilege is used within SAP HANA application lifecycle management. Specifically, this system privilege allows the grantee to modify objects to a change list when change recording is enabled. The grantee can perform the action even if it doesn't own the change list assignment.

7.2.2 Security Admin-Related System Privileges

Security administrators typically require the following system privileges. In general, these privileges grant access to actions within SAP HANA related to the management and maintenance of users, roles, auditing, and encryption.

Audit Admin

The *audit admin* system privilege governs the execution of the auditing-related SQL commands or actions performed using the various options within SAP HANA Studio or the SAP HANA Cockpit. SQL commands such as `CREATE AUDIT POLICY`, `DROP AUDIT`

POLICY, ALTER AUDIT POLICY, and SELECT * FROM SYS.AUDIT_LOG can't be executed unless a user inherently has the audit admin system privilege. This also applies to GUIs, because they execute the same SQL commands in the background when a user attempts to make changes to the various activities being audited.

Audit Operator

The *audit operator* system privilege governs access to commands that can clear the audit logs, assuming auditing is enabled. For example, it allows the SQL command ALTER SYSTEM CLEAR AUDIT LOG ALL to be executed. This also applies to similar GUI options that allow the audit log to be cleared. Note that clearing the audit log is an action that is always recorded to the audit log. It is a MandatoryAuditPolicy within the SAP HANA system; meaning that this audit policy is always active and can't be circumvented. This system privilege also provides read access to the system audit log or the execution of SELECT * FROM SYS.AUDIT_LOG SQL statement.

Certificate Admin

The *certificate admin* system privilege governs access to SQL commands and GUIs that are used to manage certificates within the SAP HANA in-database certificate store. It provides data access when executing SELECT * FROM SYS.CERTIFICATES or SELECT * FROM SYS.PSE_CERTIFICATES. It allows for the execution of CREATE CERTIFICATE, DROP CERTIFICATE, and other related in-database certificate-management commands.

Create Structured Privilege

The *create structured privilege* system privilege grants access to the execution of the SQL command CREATE STRUCTURED PRIVILEGE. Structured privileges can be implemented to restrict data-level access to catalog views and column views.

Note that this system privilege is included in the MODELING and CONTENT_ADMIN default roles. You might conclude that it's required for all roles or users creating SAP HANA *analytic privileges*, a type of structured privilege—but custom roles don't need this privilege to activate analytic privileges created using SAP HANA Studio or the web-based IDE. Activation of SAP HANA analytic privileges is controlled using package privileges, and navigation of the package hierarchy is controlled using the SYS.REPOSITORY_REST stored procedure. The runtime object type of an SAP HANA analytic privilege artifacts is a special type of structured privilege, but created by the system account _SYS_REPO. Therefore, only the _SYS_REPO system account requires the *create structured privileges* system privilege.

Credential Admin

The *credential admin* system privilege governs access to containing the CREATE CREDENTIAL, ALTER CREDENTIAL, and DROP CREDENTIAL SQL commands. Credentials are objects that store authentication information for remote sources used by SAP HANA smart data access and SAP HANA smart data integration.

Encryption Root Key Admin

The *encryption root key admin* system privilege grants access to all SQL commands related to the management of root keys used to encrypt data, logs, and applications. SQL commands such as ALTER SYSTEM APPLICATION ENCRYPTION, ALTER SYSTEM PERSISTENCE ENCRYPTION, and ALTER SYSTEM LOG ENCRYPTION are governed by this system privilege. In addition to specific SQL commands, it also grants access to use any SAP HANA–related GUI that issues the same statements on behalf of a user.

LDAP Admin

The *LDAP admin* system privilege governs the use of SQL statements that manage an SAP HANA LDAP provider, such as CREATE, ALTER, DROP, and VALIDATE LDAP PROVIDER.

Role Admin

The r*ole admin* system privilege governs access to GUI interfaces and SQL commands that CREATE, ALTER, or DROP standard roles within the system. It also governs interfaces and SQL statements that GRANT or REVOKE roles. The role admin system privilege is only applicable to standard catalog roles; it doesn't grant the same privileges to repository-based roles.

Although this is commonly granted to security administrators, it doesn't necessarily need to be when repository-based roles are used as the basis for a security model. Repository roles are granted using special stored procedures, and security administrators only need EXECUTE access for those procedures.

SSL Admin

The *SSL admin* system privilege governs access to SQL commands that establish the purpose of a SSL certificate, such as SET <STORE_NAME> PURPOSE SSL. It also grants data access to the SYS.PSES personal security environment system view.

Structuredprivilege Admin

The *structuredprivilege admin* system privilege grants the grantee the ability to CREATE, ALTER, and DROP any structured privileges defined in the system. Roles with this privilege don't need to be the owner of the structured privilege to perform the DROP or ALTER actions.

Trust Admin

The *trust admin* system privilege governs access to GUIs and commands that manage SSL certificates within the trust store or certificate store. It's used to grant access to the CREATE PSE SQL command used to create a certificate store for in-database certificate management.

User Admin

The *user admin* system privilege governs access to GUIs and SQL statements used to CREATE, ALTER, and DELETE user accounts within the SAP HANA system.

7.2.3 System Admin-Related System Privileges

System administrators typically require many of the following privileges. Some of these privileges might appear to be related to other areas, and that might be true in some cases. However, these privileges typically grant the means to perform actions that can have a profound impact on the stability and reliability of the SAP HANA system. Because these privileges garner a higher level of scrutiny, it's best to limit them to only high-level system administrators. It's also best that system auditing and critical rules be enabled before such privileges are granted to administrators.

Adapter Admin

The *adapter admin* system privilege should be assigned to roles that manage the SAP HANA *smart data integration adapter framework*. It must be granted to roles that will be responsible for issuing SQL statements such as CREATE ADAPTER, DROP ADAPTER, and ALTER ADAPTER. It also provides data access to system views such as SYS.ADAPTERS, SYS.ADAPTER_CAPABILITIES, and SYS.ADAPTER_LOCATION.

Agent Admin

The *agent admin* system privilege should be assigned to roles that manage the SAP HANA *smart data integration data provisioning agent framework*. It must be granted to roles that will be responsible for issuing SQL statements such as CREATE AGENT, DROP AGENT, and ALTER AGENT. It also provides data access to system views such as SYS.AGENTS, SYS.AGENT_CONFIGURATION, and SYS.AGENT_GROUPS.

Backup Admin

The *backup admin* system privilege governs access to commands and GUIs that allow the initiation of backup and restoration activities related to the SAP HANA system. It grants the ability to alter system configuration parameters related to backup and recovery of the system and allows for the truncation of the backup catalog and its associated files. It also grants access to query backup-related system views in the SYS schema, such as with SELECT * FROM SYS.M_BACKUP_CATALOG.

On its own, it doesn't provide access to the *backup console* area in SAP HANA Studio or interfaces within the SAP HANA Cockpit. During our testing, we identified that the CATALOG READ system privilege was also required to use the backup console. However, with both privileges granted, such roles would be able to fully manage the backup and restore processes within SAP HANA.

Backup Operator

The *backup operator* system privilege governs access to SQL commands that initiate a system backup or those that provide read access to backup specific system views. However, it doesn't provide access to change backup settings, restore the system, or execute commands that manage the backup catalog. It's most often granted to service accounts that initiate a system backup from the command line—for example, SAP HANA accounts that initiate scheduled backup jobs from the Linux cron scheduling engine.

Create Remote Source

The *create remote source* system privilege governs access to SQL commands and GUIs used to create remote sources used by SAP HANA smart data access or SAP HANA smart data integration. It also provides read-only data access to system views such as SYS.REMOTE_SOURCES and SYS.REMOTE_SOURCE_OBJECTS.

Create Scenario

The *create scenario* system privilege governs access to the execution of the CREATE CALCULATION SCENARIO SQL statement. Calculation scenarios are specialized catalog objects used by SAP HANA calculation views. SAP hasn't published significant information about calculation scenarios, but we do know that they are fundamental to the creation of SAP HANA calculation views. The _SYS_REPO system account normally creates calculation scenarios in the _SYS_BIC schema on behalf of a developer activating a calculation view, so most roles don't necessarily need this privilege.

However, if an application or highly skilled user is creating calculation views and storing calculation scenarios in a custom schema, this system privilege will be required. For example, the SAP BW service account creates calculation scenarios and column views within the SAP HANA service account schema. Therefore, the SAP BW service account requires this privilege.

Note that this system privilege is included in the MODELING and CONTENT_ADMIN default roles. You might conclude that they're required for all roles or users creating *SAP HANA information views*, but custom roles don't need this privilege to activate SAP HANA information views using SAP HANA Studio or the web-based IDE. Activation of SAP HANA information views is controlled using package privileges and navigation of the package hierarchy is controlled using the `SYS.REPOSITORY_REST` stored procedure. Run-time SAP HANA information view artifacts are created by the _SYS_REPO system account. Therefore, only the _SYS_REPO system account requires the create scenario system privilege.

Create Schema

The *create schema* system privilege grants a user the ability to execute the `CREATE SCHEMA` SQL command. The system usually creates a user schema for each standard user. However, if a user expects to create additional standard catalog schemas, he must be granted this system privilege.

Data Admin

The *data admin* system privilege governs access to several items. Like the catalog read system privilege, it grants full read-only access to all system views stored in the SYS schema.

It also allows the execution of any DDL statement. For example, the `CREATE COLUMN TABLE` command is considered a DDL statement. DDL statements can be issued towards objects in any schema, even if the grantee doesn't have `CREATE ANY` privilege access for the schema. However, this privilege doesn't grant the grantee access to issue DML statements against catalog objects that it doesn't own or otherwise have DML access to.

In addition to allowing the execution of any DDL statement, the *data admin* system privilege also grants the ability to delete any table in the system regardless of any other granted privileges. For reference, we could delete system-related tables when granted this privilege. Grantees can delete a table even if they don't own it or otherwise have the DELETE privilege granted. Therefore, this privilege should only be granted on an extremely limited basis.

Database Admin

The *database admin* system privilege grants access to all SQL commands related to the tenant database. This includes tenant database SQL commands such as CREATE, DROP, ALTER, RENAME, BACKUP, and RECOVERY. In addition to specific SQL commands, it also grants access to use any SAP HANA-related GUI that issues the same statements on behalf of a user.

Export

The *export* system privilege governs access to the exporting of catalog objects and data using the EXPORT SQL command. Based on our testing, it only applies to the issuing of the SQL command in the SQL console. In addition to the export system privilege, grantees will also need the SELECT privilege for the catalog objects they're exporting.

Note that this privilege doesn't govern access to the catalog export wizard in SAP HANA Studio. To perform a catalog export using SAP HANA Studio, the grantees only require the SELECT privilege on the schemas or tables they're exporting.

Extended Storage Admin

The *extended storage admin* system privilege grants access to manage *SAP HANA extended storage* and issues SQL commands such as CREATE EXTENDED STORAGE, ALTER EXTENDED STORAGE, and DROP EXTENDED STORAGE. It also governs read-only data access to extended storage system views such as SYS.M_ES_DBSPACES, SYS.M_ES_DELTA_MEMORY, and others. In addition to specific SQL commands, it also grants access to use any SAP HANA-related GUI that issues the same statements on behalf of a user.

Import

The *import* system privilege governs access to the importing of data into catalog tables using the IMPORT SQL command. Based on our testing, it only applies to the issuing of the SQL command in the SQL console. In addition to the import system privilege, grantees will also need the INSERT privilege on the target catalog table.

Note that this privilege doesn't govern access to *catalog import* wizard in SAP HANA Studio. To perform a catalog import using SAP HANA Studio, the grantee needs the INSERT, UPDATE, DROP, and CREATE ANY privileges on the target schema. If the schema doesn't exist, the SCHEMA ADMIN system privilege will be required as well.

INIFILE Admin

The *INIFILE admin* system privilege governs access to changes within the system settings. With this privilege, the system configuration can be changed by issuing ALTER SYSTEM ALTER CONFIGURATION SQL statements in the SQL console.

License Admin

The *license admin* system privilege governs access to UIs and SQL statements used to install and remove license keys. SQL statements such as SET SYSTEM LICENSE can only be issued in the SQL console once the license admin system privilege is granted.

Log Admin

The *log admin* system privilege governs access to the SQL command ALTER SYSTEM LOGGING. This command allows the redo logging mechanism to be enabled or disabled. When the redo logging mechanism is disabled, the RDBMS will not be able to properly recover following an index server outage. Therefore, this privilege only should be granted as needed.

Optimizer Admin

The *optimizer admin* system privilege governs access to ALTER SYSTEM SQL commands, such as ALTER SYSTEM CLEAR SQL PLAN CACHE. These commands can influence the query optimizer.

Resource Admin

The *resource admin* system privilege governs access to a variety of SQL commands and GUIs used to affect system resources, table distribution, page file data encryption keys, and table partitioning. SQL commands such as ALTER SYSTEM RECLAIM DATAVOLUME and ALTER SYSTEM RESET MONITORING VIEW are managed by this system privilege. GUIs that reset memory statistics are also allowed when this system privilege is granted.

Savepoint Admin

The *savepoint admin* system privilege governs access to the ALTER SYSTEM SAVEPOINT SQL command. Executing this command will commit all in-memory data to the data volume within the persistent storage layers of SAP HANA. By default, SAP HANA savepoints are executed automatically by the system every five minutes.

Scenario Admin

The *scenario admin* system privilege governs access to all calculation scenario–related activities, including the ability to create calculation scenarios. SAP hasn't published significant information about calculation scenarios, but we do know that they're fundamental to the creation of SAP HANA calculation views. Calculation scenarios normally are created by the _SYS_REPO account when SAP HANA information views are created.

Service Admin

The *service admin* system privilege governs access to the SQL commands and GUIs used to start, stop, kill, cancel, and reconfigure SAP HANA system services. Services include items such as indexserver, compileserver, nameserver, and xsengine.

Session Admin

The *session admin* system privilege governs access to GUIs and SQL statements used to cancel or change a user session. SQL commands such as ALTER SYSTEM CANCEL SESSION and ALTER SYSTEM ALTER SESSION can't be executed without this system privilege.

Tenant Admin

Per its documentation, the *tenant admin* system privilege governs GUIs and SQL statements used to resume and suspend a tenant database. Unfortunately, the SAP HANA documentation doesn't provide any example SQL statements that can be used to suspend or resume a tenant database, so we weren't able to fully test such functionality. We did attempt to execute ALTER SYSTEM SUSPEND TENANT <TENANT DATABASE>, but an error was returned: **ALTER TENANT deprecated and Was Never Fully Implemented**.

Table Admin

The *table admin* system privilege governs GUIs and SQL statements used to unload a columnar table into memory, unload a columnar table from memory, and perform a delta merge on a columnar table. Users granted this system privilege don't require ownership of the table or schema, nor do they require any SQL object privileges to perform the listed actions.

Trace Admin

The *trace admin* system privilege gives a role access to configure traces within the SAP HANA system. It also authorizes the ability to delete trace files from the system.

Version Admin

The *version admin* system privilege governs access to SQL statements used to manage the row-store garbage collector—for example, `ALTER SYSTEM RECLAIM VERSION SPACE`.

Workload Admin

The *workload admin* system privilege governs access to SQL statements used to `CREATE`, `ALTER`, and `DROP` workload mappings and workload classes. Workloads and workload classes can be used to govern statement execution priority, statement memory limits, or statement thread limits based on user- or application-specific information.

7.2.4 Environment Monitoring-Related System Privileges

Individuals that need to monitor the SAP HANA system will typically require the following privileges. For example, the *catalog read* system privilege is included with the MONITORING default role.

Catalog Read

The *catalog read* system privilege provides full read-only data access to all catalog views within the SYS schema. No filter restrictions will be applied to the view, and no further privileges are required to access system view data.

Monitor Admin

The *monitor admin* system privilege governs access to `ALTER SYSTEM` SQL commands specific to event management.

7.2.5 Environment Performance-Related System Privileges

For individuals using the workload-related tools to capture, compare, or test the performance of a particular workflow, the following system privileges will likely be required.

Workload Analyze Admin

The *workload analyze admin* system privilege is used to govern access to workload analysis, capture, and replay actions within the SAP HANA System.

Workload Capture Admin

The *workload capture admin* system privilege governs data access to the SYS.M_WORKLOAD_CAPTURES system view and grants the EXECUTE privilege on the SYS.WORKLOAD_CAPTURE stored procedure. Capturing workloads and replaying them will allow the administrator to view performance impacts after changes are made to the SAP HANA configuration or hardware.

Workload Replay Admin

The *workload replay admin* system privilege governs data access to the SYS.M_WORKLOAD_REPLAY_PREPROCESSES and SYS.M_WORKLOAD_REPLAYS system views. It also grants the EXECUTE privilege on the SYS.WORKLOAD_REPLAY stored procedure. Capturing workloads and replaying them will allow the administrator to view performance impacts after changes are made to the SAP HANA configuration or hardware.

7.3 Granting System Privileges

In this section, we'll review the various options available to grant and revoke system privileges: SQL commands, SAP HANA Studio, the SAP HANA Web-Based Development Workbench security manager, and repository-based role scripts or the repository-based role editor GUI.

7.3.1 Granting System Privileges with SQL

Using the SQL console and SQL statements, we can both grant and revoke privileges to roles or users. Let's look at a series of example SQL statements used to grant system privileges to both users and roles.

With system privileges, the grantee can be either a user account or a role. A sound security model will grant privileges to roles and avoid directly granting individual privileges to individual users. Technically, we can grant system privileges to a grantee using the GRANT SQL syntax. However, as we've discussed, it's best to use repository-based roles, which don't use SQL to grant system privileges; we'll review this again in Section 7.3.4. With that said, it's still important that we review the process for granting system privileges to standard users or roles. Although we've provided SQL script examples in several chapters, let's take a moment to review the SQL used to grant system privileges to a grantee. Note that a semicolon marks the end of each of the following SQL statements:

```
GRANT <SYSTEM_PRIVILEGE> TO <GRANTEE>;
GRANT <SYSTEM_PRIVILEGE> TO <GRANTEE> WITH ADMIN OPTION;
GRANT DATA ADMIN, EXPORT, IMPORT TO ROLE_SEC_ADMIN WITH ADMIN OPTION;
```

The first statement provides the general syntax, with variables indicated by text within angle brackets (<>). The variables need to be replaced with items unique to your environment. The <SYSTEM_PRIVILEGES> variable can be replaced with a comma-separated list of system privileges, as shown in the third statement. The <GRANTEE> variable will be replaced with the name of an activated role or user account within the system.

The second SQL statement includes the `WITH ADMIN OPTION` at the end, which allows the grantee of the role to subsequently grant the same privilege to another user or role. It's typically reserved for user grantees that manage security models.

The final statement provides a complete example in which we grant system privileges to the ROLE_SEC_ADMIN role. It includes the `WITH ADMIN OTPTION`, allowing the role grantee to grant the same privileges to other users or roles.

We can also revoke system privileges using the `REVOKE` SQL syntax, as follows:

```
REVOKE <SYSTEM_PRIVILEGE> FROM <GRANTEE>;
REVOKE DATA ADMIN, EXPORT, IMPORT FROM ROLE_SEC_ADMIN;
```

The first statement provides the general syntax, and the second SQL statement provides a full example, in which the listed system privileges are removed from the ROLE_SEC_ADMIN role.

7.3.2 Granting System Privileges with SAP HANA Studio

We also can use the role management options in SAP HANA Studio to both grant and revoke privileges for a given grantee. Most will find it easier to use SAP HANA Studio than to memorize and type the SQL statements. In this section, we'll review the process for granting and revoking system privileges using SAP HANA Studio.

To access the user management area in SAP HANA Studio, start by switching to the administration console perspective. In the **Systems** tab on the left side, expand the

System node and then the **Security** node to reveal the **Security**, **Users**, and **Roles** nodes. Expand the **Roles** node to reveal roles defined in the system. To manage a role, double-click its name in the list to open the **Role Management** interface tab on the right. This same tab is present when creating a role. Note that you can follow the same process to grant or revoke system privileges for a user account. Expand the **Users** node to reveal user accounts defined in the system. To manage a user, double-click the user name in the list to open the **User Management** interface tab on the right.

Figure 7.1 shows the role management interface in SAP HANA Studio. Just below the role name, you'll see several tabs; the **System Privileges** tab is used to grant system privileges to or revoke them from a user or role.

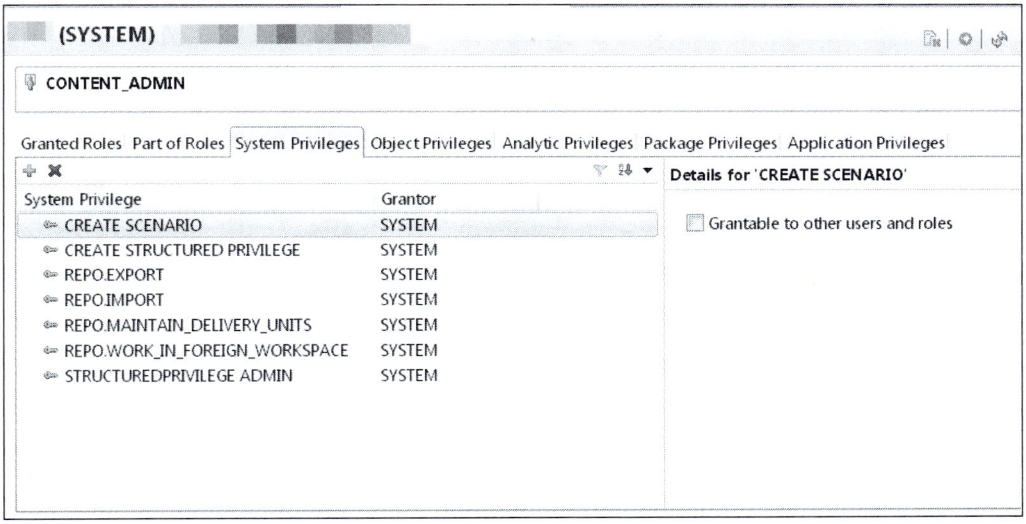

Figure 7.1 System Privileges Tab in SAP HANA Studio

Now, let's discuss the process and review the workflows necessary to grant and revoke system privileges using the **System Privileges** tab.

To grant a system privilege, click **+** at the top-left side of the open tab (see Figure 7.1). Clicking **+** will open a search dialog box. To view all system privileges, enter the search string "**". To search for a specific system privilege, enter a portion of the system privilege name to search for possible matches. Select one or more system privileges within the list. To select multiple items, hold down the `Ctrl` key and click each desired item. To select multiple consecutive items, click the first item in the list, hold down the `Shift` key, and then select the last item in the list. One the desired items are selected, click **OK** and the search dialog will close. Your selected system privileges should now appear in the **System Privileges** tab. (Figure 7.1 also shows how the selected system privileges will appear in the interface.)

To assign the **Grantable to other users and roles** privilege, select a system privilege from the list. To the right, you'll see another frame containing the details for the selected system privilege. Select the checkbox next to **Grantable to other users and roles** to allow the role grantee to grant the same privilege to another user or role. Repeat this process for each system privilege in the list.

Once you've added all the desired privileges to the list, save or activate the changes to implement them within the system. Saving or activating has the same outcome, so choose either method. To save the changes, press [Ctrl]+[S], or to activate the changes, press [F8]. The changes will be saved and activated in the system. SAP HANA Studio will execute the required SQL statements in the background to grant the selected system privileges.

To revoke a system privilege, click an assigned system privilege in the list, then click the red **X** icon above the list to revoke the privilege. Repeat the process for each system privilege you want to revoke. Once you've removed all the desired privileges, press [Ctrl]+[S]. The removed privileges will be revoked and the role will be updated. Alternatively, to activate the changes, press [F8]. The removed privileges will be revoked.

7.3.3 Granting System Privileges with SAP HANA Web-Based Development Workbench

The SAP HANA Web-Based Development Workbench security manager, hosted within the SAP HANA XS engine, provides an interface that you can use to create users, create roles, or manage security.

You can access SAP HANA Web-Based Development Workbench via a supported Internet browser. The following URLs can be customized to match the details of your environment:

http://sap-hana.myhost.com:8000/sap/hana/ide/security

http://<sap_hana_host>:80<instance_number>/sap/hana/ide/security

In the last example, replace <sap_hana_host> with the hostname of the SAP HANA system in your environment and <instance_number> with the two-digit instance number corresponding to your SAP HANA system.

For secure access, the following examples should help you construct the correct URL:

https://<sap_hana_host>:43<instance_number>/sap/hana/ide/security

https://sap-hana.myhost.com:4300/sap/hana/ide/security

Once you have access to the SAP HANA Web-Based Development Workbench security manager, expand the **Security** node on the right. Expand **Roles** to reveal a list of roles defined in the system. Double-click a role to open the management interface for the given role. With the selected role management window open, you can begin granting and revoking privileges. This GUI is almost identical to that of SAP HANA Studio. *Note*: To perform the same action for an individual user account, expand the **Users** node and double-click the desired user account.

The process for granting and revoking a role's privileges in the SAP HANA Web-Based Development Workbench security manager is almost identical to the process outlined for SAP HANA Studio. Because there is tremendous overlap in the workflows, we won't go into the same level of detail in this section; see Section 7.3.2 for additional details. Here, we'll simply highlight the basic workflow and point out any significant differences.

To add a system privilege, click **+** and search for the desired system privilege. Choose **Grantable to other users and roles** to the right of each listed system privilege as needed.

To revoke a system privilege, select it in the list and choose the red **X**. To save your changes, press Ctrl+S, or click the disk icon at the top left to save and activate the privilege.

If there are any activation issues, warning messages will appear in the status frame at the bottom of the user management window. The status frame has a dark background color. Error messages will appear in red text. Errors are only generated during an attempted activation or saving of changes.

7.3.4 Granting System Privileges with Repository Roles

When SAP HANA was initially released, assigning system privileges to standard roles was the best available option. Multiple GUIs and SQL statements were created to help organizations manage standard role granting and revoking. As SAP HANA evolved, repository roles were introduced to aid in application development efforts. Because of their numerous benefits, we highly recommend that they be used to generate a security model. Now, let's review the process for granting and revoking system privileges within repository-based roles.

Script-Based Repository Roles

In Chapter 6, we introduced repository roles and outlined the workflows required to create and manage repository roles. In this section, we'll again review the syntax necessary to assign system privileges to design-time repository-based role scripts. If you require more information about this process, please see Chapter 6.

When defining system privileges within design-time repository-based role scripts, you must start each line with `system privilege:`. After the colon, you can provide a comma-separated list of system privileges. At the end of the list, include a semicolon to finish the line. If you don't want to include a comma-separated list, you can explicitly list each privilege on its own line, with each line beginning with `system privilege:`.

The following snippets of code show the definition of system privileges within a repository roles script. The first line includes three privileges, each separated by a comma; the remaining two lines only include a single system privilege each:

```
system privilege: AGENT ADMIN, AUDIT ADMIN, AUDIT OPERATOR;
system privilege: AUDIT OPERATOR;
system privilege: CREATE REMOTE SOURCE;
```

As you can see, you can reuse the `system privilege:` expression multiple times within the script. You can also consolidate them all into a single line in which each privilege is comma-separated. It's important to note that the _SYS_REPO account has been granted all system privileges by default. _SYS_REPO also can grant all system privileges to other users or roles by default.

SAP HANA Web-Based Development Workbench Editor

The SAP HANA Web-Based Development Workbench editor, hosted within the XS engine, provides an interface that you can use to build and test development artifacts. From a security perspective, we can use this interface to create and manage repository-based roles. This interface offers all the advantages of repository-based roles without the need to define the repository roles using scripts and the SAP HANA domain-specific language. The interface isn't exclusive, meaning that you can edit repository-based roles created using scripts via a GUI. Conversely, you can edit a repository-based role's scripts, those created using a GUI, in SAP HANA Studio. This flexibility allows the security administrator to manage the repository roles using either interface.

You can access the SAP HANA Web-Based Development Workbench editor via a supported Internet browser. The following URLs can be customized to match the details of your environment:

http://sap-hana.myhost.com:8000/sap/hana/ide/editor

http://<sap_hana_host>:80<instance_number>/sap/hana/ide/editor

Replace <sap_hana_host> with the hostname of the SAP HANA system in your environment. Replace <instance_number> with the two-digit instance corresponding to your SAP HANA system.

For secure access, the following examples should help you construct the correct URL:

https://<sap_hana_host>: 43<instance_number>/sap/hana/ide/editor

https://sap-hana.myhost.com:4300/sap/hana/ide/editor

To use the workbench and define a repository role, the user account first will need to be granted one of the roles listed in Table 7.1. Users only need one of the two roles to use the workbench.

Role Name	Summary
sap.hana.ide.roles::EditorDeveloper	Within SAP HANA Web-Based Development Workbench, users will only be able to access the editor. Within the editor, users can view, edit, create, delete, or activate repository-based roles or other repository-based development artifacts found in development packages or the development repository. Users must have package privileges in addition to this role to properly access and activate a repository role or other development artifacts.
sap.hana.ide.roles::Developer	This role grants a higher level of privileges for users that need full access to SAP HANA Web-Based Development Workbench. It grants access to the editor, catalog, and security interfaces. It's considered the parent to the sap.hana.ide.roles::EditorDeveloper role.

Table 7.1 Roles Required to Use SAP HANA Web-Based Development Workbench Editor

> **Package Privileges Required to Use the SAP HANA Web-Based Development Workbench Editor**
>
> In addition to the roles in Table 7.1, a user will also need the appropriate package privileges for the package in which they plan to edit, create, or activate repository roles. This also applies to script-based repository roles created using SAP HANA Studio. For example, users will need the following package privileges to create repository roles using the SAP HANA Web-Based Development Workbench editor interface:
>
> - `REPO.READ`
> - `REPO.EDIT_NATIVE_OBJECTS`
> - `REPO.ACTIVATE_NATIVE_OBJECTS`

The SAP HANA Web-Based Development Workbench editor interface (see Figure 7.2) is very similar to the development areas within the **Repositories** tab of SAP HANA Studio. On the left side of the interface is a **Content** folder, under which is the package hierarchy.

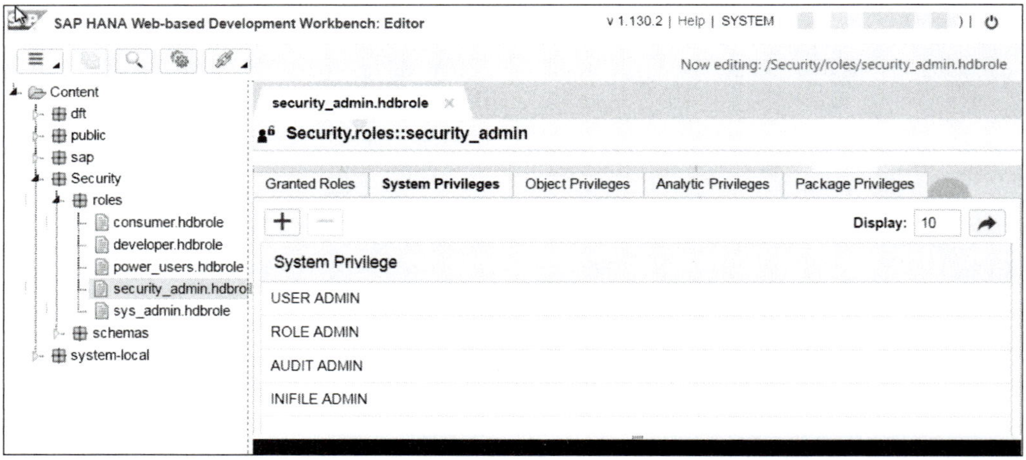

Figure 7.2 SAP HANA Web-Based Development Workbench Editor

As you expand the package hierarchy nodes, you'll likely begin seeing development artifacts, depending on what's available in your environment. To create a repository role, right-click the package in which you want to store it and choose **New • Role**. A small window will appear asking for the **Role Name**. Enter the desired name and click **OK**, and a new tab-based window will appear on the right (shown in Figure 7.2). In the figure, the tab is named **security_admin.hdbrole**. Click the **System Privileges** tab to manage and list system privileges.

In this tab, to add a system privilege, click the large **+** button on the subtab header. A pop-up window will appear titled **Select System Privilege** (see Figure 7.3). A search box will appear in this window; enter a portion of the system privilege name to narrow the results, or scroll through the unfiltered list to locate the desired system privilege. Select one or more privileges within the list, using the `Ctrl` key to select multiple items. The selected items are highlighted in light blue. Click the **OK** button at the bottom of the window to finalize the selection.

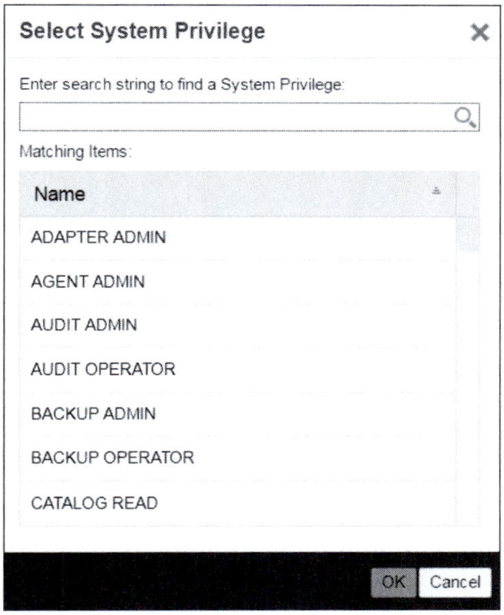

Figure 7.3 Selecting and Assigning System Privileges

The selected privileges will now appear in the **System Privileges** tab. To remove an assigned system privilege, select it from the list and click the large – button above the list. Items in the list must be deleted one at a time.

Once you've configured the desired list of system privileges, click the **Save All** button at the top left, which shows three stacked floppy disks.

If there are any issues saving and activating the repository role, messages will appear in red text within the console window just below the opened repository role tab. The console window has a dark background color and is located at the bottom of the opened tab. Affirmative messages will appear in white text and error messages in red text.

To close the open repository role tab, click the small **x** to the right of the tab.

7.4 Case Study: Security Administrator System Privileges

E-Corporation has contacted its lead SAP HANA security consultant and requested help defining a series of repository roles that will be used by its security team to manage security within the SAP HANA environment. Based on previous experience, the consultant recommends defining four repository roles for the security team to allow for a *separation of duties* within the system. This helps to reduce both fraud and negligence within the security model. The consultant suggests that the four roles be created based on the following groups:

- Admins responsible for managing users
- Admins responsible for creating roles
- Admins that manage communication and data encryption
- Admins that mange system auditing

To help E-Corporation better understand the consultant's reasoning, he provided a justification for each of the activates and why they needed to be separated. In addition, he also listed the capabilities and system privileges that were required for each of the broad activities. In this case study, we'll examine the consultant's suggestions and his justifications for each.

7.4.1 User Management Role

The first repository role recommended by the security consultant grants the necessary privileges to provision and administer user accounts. Grantees of this role will be responsible for the following tasks:

- Provisioning user account
- Resetting user account passwords
- Assigning SAML and Kerberos identities

To ensure that best practices are followed and that separation of duties is implemented properly, grantees with this role should not be able to perform the following tasks:

- Creating or updating existing roles
- Granting standard roles to users
- Granting repository roles to users
- Granting individual privileges to users
- Managing system auditing

With these requirements and restrictions defined, the security consultant recommends that the user management repository role be limited to only those system privileges required to manage users. Grantees of this role should not have the ability to assign roles to user accounts. Allowing them to assign roles would grant them the ability to both manipulate a user and assign privileges to the user. This level of access gives the grantee the ability to impersonate a user account, allowing it to perform fraudulent or malicious actions within the system. To achieve the listed requirements, the user management repository role only requires the `USER ADMIN` system privilege.

In addition to only granting the `USER ADMIN` system privilege, the following conditions must also exist for the user accounts within this repository role:

- The user account must not have the `ROLE ADMIN` system privilege, which grants the ability to create standard roles and to grant them to other users.
- The user account must not have `EXECUTE` access to the `_SYS_REPO.GRANT_ACTIVATED_ROLE` stored procedure or other stored procedures in the _SYS_REPO schema that are used to manage security. Granting such access to these procedures will allow repository roles to be granted or other privileges to be assigned.
- The user account must not have been granted any other privileges using the `WITH ADMIN OPTION` or `WITH GRANT OPTION`. This will prevent the user from granting any individual privileges to other user accounts directly. Note that a user will be able to grant others access to its own schema in SAP HANA 1.0. Starting with SAP HANA 2.0, users can be restricted from their own user schema and subsequently prevented from granting privileges to their own schema.
- The grantee must be granted the sap.hana.ide.roles::SecurityAdmin role to use web-based GUIs for managing users.
- To prevent access to the auditing mechanism, the `AUDIT ADMIN` and `AUDIT OPERATOR` system privileges must not be granted to the user.

When implemented according to these requirements, the grantee will not be able to elevate his own privileges or the privileges of another user account. In addition, because the grantee doesn't have access to manipulate the auditing mechanisms, he will be unable to cover his tracks. All actions he performs on a user account should be captured by the auditing mechanism. Now, let's look at how the role management role should be structured and why.

7.4.2 Role Management Role

The second repository role recommended by the security consultant grants the necessary privileges to provision roles and grant them to users. Grantees of this role will be responsible for the following tasks:

- Creating repository-based roles and assigning all privileges
- Creating standard roles when necessary
- Mapping LDAP groups to roles
- Managing structured privileges other than analytic privileges
- Creating analytic privileges and assigning restrictions
- Granting roles to and revoking roles from users

Grantees assigned this role shouldn't be able to create or manipulate user accounts. This will prevent such grantees from impersonating a user account, subsequently allowing them to perform fraudulent or malicious actions within the system while concealing their identity.

To ensure that best practices are followed and that a separation of duties is implemented properly, the following list contains tasks that the grantees should *not* be able to perform:

- Creating user accounts or changing user account passwords
- Granting individual privileges to users
- Managing system auditing

To achieve the listed requirements, the role management repository role requires the role admin, LDAP admin, and structuredprivilege admin system privileges. In addition to granting these system privileges, the following conditions must also exist for the user accounts within this repository role:

- The grantee must have package privileges for the package hierarchy node used to store the repository roles and analytic privileges. Grantees must be able to create, edit, and activate repository-based roles within this package.

- The grantee must have the REPO.READ package privilege on package nodes they intend to grant to repository roles using a GUI. This is only required to view them in the graphical list.
- The grantee must have the REPO.READ package privilege on packages containing information views that will be configured within analytic privileges.
- The grantee and _SYS_REPO must have SELECT access to any tables containing data-level security information—for example, tables that map user accounts to data attributes. Such tables will be used to define dynamic analytic privileges.
- The grantee must have EXECUTE privileges for stored procedures in the _SYS_REPO schema the names of which begin with GRANT_ and REVOKE_.
- The grantee must have EXECUTE privileges for the SYS.REPOSITORY_REST stored procedure. This is required to work in the SAP HANA package hierarchy or repository in which repository roles are created.
- If standard roles are used in the security model, the grantee must have been granted the grantable privileges using the WITH ADMIN OPTION or WITH GRANT OPTION. This isn't necessary if repository roles are used. In the case of repository roles, the system account _SYS_REPO must be granted the grantable privileges using the WITH ADMIN OPTION or WITH GRANT OPTION.
- The grantee must be granted the sap.hana.ide.roles::EditorDeveloper and sap.hana.ide.roles::SecurityAdmin roles in order to use web-based GUIs when creating repository roles or managing roles.
- To prevent access to the auditing mechanism, the AUDIT ADMIN and AUDIT OPERATOR system privileges must not be granted to the user.

When implemented according to these requirements, the grantee won't be able to use another user account to perform fraudulent or malicious actions in the SAP HANA system. In addition, because the grantee doesn't have access to manipulate the auditing mechanisms, he will be unable to cover his tracks. All actions he performs using his assigned account should be captured by the auditing mechanism.

7.4.3 Data and Communication Encryption Role

The third repository role recommended by the security consultant grants the necessary privileges to administer communication protocol, log volume, and data volume encryption. Grantees of this role will be responsible for the following tasks:

- Changing the root key
- Enabling persistent data volume encryption
- Enabling transaction log volume encryption
- Managing credentials used by remote sources
- Managing keystores and certificate files on the SAP HANA operating system
- Administering SSL certificates used for authentication and secure communications

Given that a high level of operating system and administrative level access is required by this role, it's likely that system administrators will be assigned this role, and individuals on the security team won't perform the listed actions. A separation of duties in this case has more to do with the amount of access required to manage end-to-end encryption. For example, a user administering a role doesn't require operating system-level access or SAP HANA INI file access to perform her functions. Therefore, she shouldn't automatically obtain administrative functionality just because she's a member of the security team.

Regardless of how an organization decides to configure encryption-related administration access, it's still important to maintain limited access to these activities. If communication encryption is disabled, it's possible for man-in-the-middle attacks to intercept data and credentials. If data volume or log volume encryption is disabled, unauthorized individuals with physical access to SAP HANA persistent storage devices might be able to access confidential or proprietary data. This is especially important when the SAP HANA system is hosted outside the physical security of an organization's internal data center or network.

With that in mind, let's look at the system privileges that are required to manage data and communication encryption. To manage all aspects of encryption, the certificate admin, encrypted root key admin, SSL admin, trust admin, INIFILE admin, credential admin, and catalog read system privileges will be required. In addition, an operating system user account will need to be used if certificates are stored on the OS file system.

7.4.4 System Auditing Role

The final repository role recommended by the security consultant grants the necessary privileges to manage auditing within the SAP HANA system. This very important role should be limited to individuals that have no other security or system administration–related privileges within the system. Grantees of this role will be responsible for the following tasks:

- Enabling or disabling auditing
- Creating audit policies to track actions within the SAP HANA system
- Clearing the audit database table, logs, or files

The audit admin and audit operator system privileges must be granted to roles that will facilitate these requirements. The ability to maintain a separation of duties with this role is critical. Grantees of this role mustn't be able to cover their tracks within the system. This means that they can't simultaneously administer users, roles, and auditing. Granting a single user all these abilities would allow that user to commit fraud or perform malicious actions without accountability.

7.5 Summary

System privileges govern access to a variety of actions within an SAP HANA system. These actions can be categorized into development, security, administration, system monitoring, and performance testing areas. System privileges can be granted to users, roles, and repository roles, but it's best to use repository roles, because the _SYS_REPO account has the necessary privileges by default to grant system privileges to other users.

Chapter 8
Object Privileges

In this chapter, we'll explore the different privileges that can be granted to catalog objects and the process we use to grant them.

Object privileges play an important role in the development of any SAP HANA security model and define the types of SQL script actions a user can perform on a catalog object. SAP HANA hosts multiple types of catalog objects. In Chapter 3, we discussed the various types of catalog objects that can be created in SAP HANA and how the way we create them affects our security model.

As a reminder, catalog objects consist of various RDBMS artifacts, such as schemas, tables, views, stored procedures, triggers, sequences, and a few other items. Items such as tables both store and define the structure of the data. Other items, such as views, are used to express query logic.

Schemas are very important in the world of catalog objects. All catalog objects are assigned to a single schema. We could say that the schema is the parent object to all other catalog objects. SAP HANA allows security administrators the option to grant privileges on a schema, in which case all objects within the schema inherit the privileges assigned to the schema. Alternatively, security administrators can assign privileges to individual objects, in which case the security administrator will need to update the security model to grant the appropriate privileges to the catalog object each time a new object is created within a schema.

In this chapter, we'll look at object privileges. We'll demonstrate how we can grant object privileges to users or roles using SQL statements, SAP HANA Studio, or within repository-based roles.

8.1 Overview of Object Privileges

When we grant privileges to a catalog object, we're essentially specifying the types of actions that we can execute against the catalog objects using SQL. Some of those actions correlate directly with the syntax we use in a SQL statement. For example, we can query a table using the following SQL statement:

```
SELECT TOP 100 "FirstName" FROM "EDW"."DimCustomer" WHERE "Status" = 'Active'
```

As you can see, this SQL statement starts with SELECT. To properly execute this SQL statement, a user or its associated role must be granted the SELECT privilege for the catalog table DimCustomer. We could also grant SELECT to the EDW schema, allowing the user or associated role to query any table in that schema.

In the following subsections, we'll explore catalog object privileges related to schemas, tables, views, stored procedures, functions, remote sources, and sequences.

8.1.1 Catalog Object Privileges

Before we explore the process for granting privileges to catalog objects, let's look at the different privileges that can be granted to each of the major types of catalog objects, starting with catalog schemas.

Catalog Schemas

Table 8.1 outlines the frequently used SQL actions related to schemas. These actions can be granted to a user or roles. In the table, we give a brief description of how each action relates to the schema and the objects associated with that schema. Keep in mind that these actions will apply to all catalog objects within the schema. Schema privileges aren't as restrictive as those applied to individual catalog objects; therefore, they should be heavily scrutinized before they're granted.

Grantable Privileges for Catalog Schema	Description of SQL Action
CREATE ANY	When granted, allows the creation of catalog objects within the specified schema. When a user creates a catalog object, he's the owner of that object and has full privileges for it. *Note*: The privilege to create a catalog object is established at the schema level only. You can't grant this privilege for each individual object type.
ALTER	Allows changes to all objects within the schema.
DROP	Allows any object within the schema to be deleted or dropped from the system.

Table 8.1 Privileges That Can Be Granted to Catalog Schema

Grantable Privileges for Catalog Schema	Description of SQL Action
EXECUTE	Allows for the execution of any stored procedure or function defined within the specified schema.
SELECT	Allows for the use of the SQL SELECT statement against any applicable object defined within the referenced schema. This statement is typically used to query tables and views, but it also allows access to a sequence.
INSERT	Allows the insertion of data into any table defined within the specified schema.
UPDATE	Allows data to be updated within any table defined in the specified schema.
DELETE	Allows data to be deleted within any table defined in the specified schema. This applies to both the DELETE and TRUNCATE SQL actions.
INDEX	Used to govern the ability to create, change, or remove an index for any table defined within the specified schema.
TRIGGER	Used to govern the ability to create triggers associated with any table defined within the specified schema.
DEBUG	Authorizes the debug functionality for any applicable object defined within the schema.
REFERENCES	Allows the grantee the ability to retrieve the name of the schema and its objects when using SAP HANA Studio or querying system views that contain basic table metadata. For example, the schema's referenced table names will return when the granted user queries the system view tables using the SQL statement SELECT * FROM SYS.TABLES.
CREATE TEMPORARY TABLE	Allows the creation of a temporary local table used by stored procedures. This privilege is independent from the CREATE ANY privilege to limit users from creating any type of object in a schema.

Table 8.1 Privileges That Can Be Granted to Catalog Schema (Cont.)

Catalog Table

Table 8.2 outlines the frequently used SQL actions related to tables that can be granted to a user or role. In addition, we give a brief description of how each action relates to tables in general.

Grantable Privileges for Catalog Table	Description of SQL Action
ALTER	Used to make DDL changes to tables—for example, to add or delete a column.
DROP	Used to remove a table from the system.
SELECT	Used in SQL statements to retrieve data from a table.
INSERT	Used to add additional data to the table.
UPDATE	Used to update existing rows within a table.
DELETE	Used to delete or truncate one or more rows within a table. This action supports both DELETE and TRUNCATE SQL statements.
INDEX	Used to govern the ability to create, change, or remove an index defined within a table.
TRIGGER	Used to govern the ability to create triggers associated with the table.
REFERENCES	Used to grant limited access to any table referenced by a foreign key constraint. For example, say we're securing a table named transactions and it has a foreign key constraint or reference to a table named customers. Granting REFERENCES to table transactions also grants limited access to table customers.

Table 8.2 Privileges That Can Be Granted to Catalog Table

Catalog Views

Table 8.3 outlines the frequently used SQL actions related to catalog views. These actions can be granted to a user or roles. Within the outline, we give a brief description of how each action relates to the view and the objects referenced by the view.

Grantable Privileges for Catalog View	Description of SQL Action
ALTER	Allows changes to the definition of a view.
DROP	Allows the view to be deleted or dropped from the system.

Table 8.3 Privileges That Can Be Granted to Catalog View

Grantable Privileges for Catalog View	Description of SQL Action
SELECT	Allows for the use of the SQL SELECT statement against the view. *Note*: Objects referenced within the definition of the view are granted as well.
INSERT	Allows data to be inserted into the view's underlying table. There are limitations to the types of catalog views that support these operations. Based on our testing, you can only INSERT data into a view if it references a single table and if no formulas or functions are applied to the columns defined within the view.
UPDATE	Allows data to be updated within the view's underlying table. There are limitations to the types of catalog views that support these operations. Based on our testing, you can only UPDATE data into a view if it references a single table and if no formulas or functions are applied to the columns defined within the view.
DELETE	Allows data to be deleted within the view's underlying table. There are limitations to the types of catalog views that support these operations. Based on our testing, you can only DELETE data from a view if it references a single table.

Table 8.3 Privileges That Can Be Granted to Catalog View (Cont.)

Catalog Stored Procedures and Functions

Table 8.4 outlines the frequently used SQL actions related to catalog stored procedures and to functions. Because these two catalog objects have the same privileges and related actions, we've combined them into a single table. These actions can be granted to a user or role. In the table, we also give a brief description of how each action relates to the stored procedure or function and the objects referenced by each.

Grantable Privileges for Procedure or Function	Description of SQL Action
ALTER	Allows for changes to the definition of the stored procedure or function using the ALTER SQL syntax.

Table 8.4 Privileges That Can Be Granted to Catalog Stored Procedure or Catalog Function

Grantable Privileges for Procedure or Function	Description of SQL Action
DROP	Allows the stored procedure or function to be deleted or dropped from the system.
EXECUTE	Allows the stored procedure or function to be executed. The actions that are executed directly depend on the SQL or SQLScript code defined within the procedure or function. *Note*: In definer mode, objects referenced within the definition of the stored procedure or function don't need to be explicitly granted to the user executing it. Those objects are accessible on behalf of the creator of the procedure or function. However, objects referenced with the invoker mode enabled must be explicitly granted to the user executing the procedure or function.
DEBUG	Allows debugging of the stored procedure or function.

Table 8.4 Privileges That Can Be Granted to Catalog Stored Procedure or Catalog Function (Cont.)

Remote Source

Remote sources are a unique type of catalog object. They're virtual tables that reference RDBMS tables through SAP HANA *smart data access* (SDA), a mechanism built into SAP HANA that supports the federation of data from a third-party or remote RDBMS. Using SDA, we can present a remote table as if it were a local table within the SAP HANA database catalog. When this table is queried within SAP HANA, the system will fetch the requested data from the remote table in real time. Because of its unique nature, special privileges are available within SAP HANA to accommodate interactions with remote sources and virtual tables. Table 8.5 lists the available privileges by name and their descriptions related to remote sources.

Grantable Privileges for Remote Source	Description of SQL Action
CREATE VIRTUAL TABLE	Grants the ability to create a virtual table within an authorized schema. The user must also have the CREATE ANY privilege or own the schema in which the virtual table is placed.
DROP	Grants the ability to delete or drop a virtual table from the system.

Table 8.5 Privileges That Can Be Assigned for Working with Remote Source

Grantable Privileges for Remote Source	Description of SQL Action
CREATE VIRTUAL FUNCTION	Grants the ability to create a function.
CREATE VIRTUAL PROCEDURE	Grants the ability to create a virtual procedure.
PROCESS REMOTE SUBSCRIPTION EXCEPTION	Allows processing exceptions for a remote subscription.
CREATE REMOTE SUBSCRIPTION	Allows for the creation of subscriptions used to capture changed data from a virtual source.
ALTER	Allows for the modification of an existing remote source configuration.

Table 8.5 Privileges That Can Be Assigned for Working with Remote Source (Cont.)

Catalog Sequence

Sequences are used to define the behavior of automatically incrementing number sequences. For example, we can define a primary key column in a table and call a sequence to retrieve the next or previous available value within the sequence. Table 8.6 lists the available privileges by name and descriptions related to a sequence.

Grantable Privileges for Sequence	Description of SQL action
Drop	Allows for a sequence to be deleted or dropped from the system.
Select	Allows the sequence to be queried—for example, to retrieve the next number in the sequence.

Table 8.6 Privileges That Can Be Assigned for Working with Sequences

8.1.2 Security Considerations for Catalog Objects

Let's take a moment to discuss a few critical security considerations when dealing with catalog objects. Some of these items were discussed in Chapter 2, but we feel that it's important to reiterate them in this chapter. When designing a security model, we need to consider the **Grantable to Others** authorization, object ownership, schema-level privileges, object-level privileges, authorizations for catalog views, authorizations for stored procedures, authorizations for functions, and repository objects.

Grantable to Others Authorization

In addition to the SQL privileges outlined in the tables in Section 8.1.1, we also must consider the authorizations required to grant privileges to other users. In most cases, a security administrator will need both a SQL privilege and the **Grantable to Others** authorization for that privilege to establish a security model. SAP HANA won't allow just any user account to grant other users access to an object. If the user is the owner of the objects, he can grant rights to other users.

However, most security administrators aren't the owners of all objects; each object has only one owner, and there are often multiple security administrators. Therefore, security administrators require both SQL access to an object and the ability to grant those same privileges to other users.

When you establish privileges for a user and a role using SAP HANA Studio, you'll notice that to the right of each privilege there are **Yes** and **No** radio buttons in a column titled **Grantable to Others** (see Figure 8.1). The **Yes** radio button must be selected to allow the assigned user or role the ability to give that same privilege to another user.

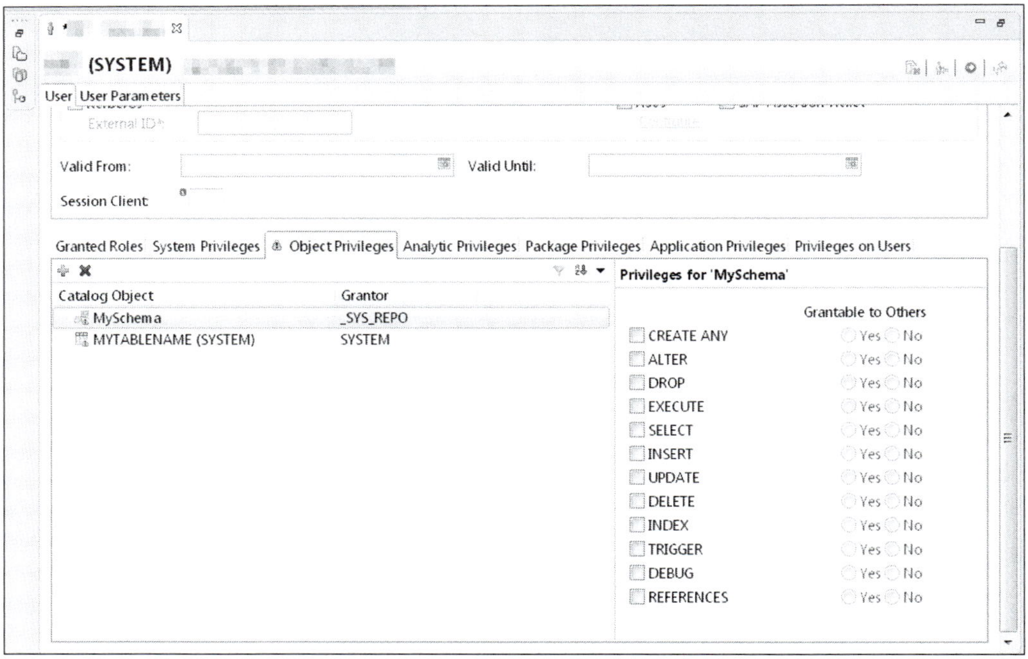

Figure 8.1 Assigning Privileges to Catalog Objects in SAP HANA Studio

Object Ownership

As discussed, the individual that creates an object is the owner of that object. She inherently has full control of the privileges for that catalog object. Depending on the setup of your security model, each time an object is created, it's likely that privileges will need to be granted to other users and roles for that object. However, authorizing privileges at the schema level might simplify this requirement. We'll discuss that in the next subsection.

Object ownership is also important in relation to the user account that creates the objects. If a user account is used to create a catalog object, most likely that user account should never be deleted, because deleting the account also deletes any catalog objects and granted privileges established by that user account. This is why special technical accounts are often created for users that create catalog objects and manage security. Hopefully, an established policy ensures that technical user accounts are never deleted. As we'll discuss shortly, as an alternative, we can create most objects as repository objects. These objects are owned by the _SYS_REPO system account and won't be deleted when a developer's account is deleted.

Authorizations at the Schema Level

When securing catalog objects, we can establish authorizations either at the schema level or, in some cases, for each individual object. It's much easier to simply establish the privileges at the schema level; when privileges are established at the individual object level, the security model has to be adjusted each time a new object is created. The owner of the object or a security administrator will likely need to update existing roles to accommodate each new object. These tasks can become tedious and are often overlooked if objects are created frequently. To simplify the security mode, privileges can be established at the schema level. In this way, all objects with a schema automatically inherit the privileges assigned to the schema.

Authorizations at the Catalog Object Level

Although it may be easier to establish privileges at the schema level, it can be less secure. If we determine that using schema-level privileges is acceptable, we do so with the understanding that all current and future objects in that schema will be accessible for the assigned users or roles. There are no mechanisms to deny privileges in SAP HANA. Therefore, if our security requirements call for two catalog tables in the same schema to have different privileges assigned to different roles, we'll likely have to establish privileges at the individual table level and forgo the use of schema-level privileges. This approach is more tedious, but it provides more granular control of privileges for objects within the same schema.

Considerations for Catalog Views

As discussed in Chapter 2, catalog views reference other catalog views or tables within their definitions. When a user queries a catalog view, he only needs the SELECT privilege on that catalog view. The system doesn't validate the privileges against objects referenced within the view.

However, the developer creating the catalog view must have the SELECT privilege and the authority to give this privilege to other users. The developer won't be able to activate the view unless she's the owner of all reference objects or has the SELECT privilege and **Grantable to Others** privilege for each referenced object. In our experience, this concept is most often not understood and implemented poorly within most security models. If your organization plans to develop catalog database views to support access to data, make sure that your developers have the appropriate privileges to activate the catalog view.

Considerations for Catalog Stored Procedures and Functions

As discussed in Chapter 2, we can choose between two security options when defining stored procedures or functions. We can establish the SQL security in *definer* or *invoker* mode.

In *definer mode*, the developer must have privileges to perform all SQL actions defined within the stored procedure or function. In addition, he must have the **Grantable to Others** privilege for each associated SQL privilege. In this way, the definer is effectively delegating those privileges to the user or role that's been granted the EXECUTE privilege against the stored procedure or function. In most cases, this is the least restrictive way to manage access to the activities performed by the stored procedure or function.

In *invoker mode*, the user or role with EXECUTE privileges against the stored procedure or function must also have the appropriate privileges to support the defined actions against each referenced catalog object. For example, if the stored procedure adds data to a table, the user first would need the EXECUTE privilege for the stored procedure. Second, he would need the INSERT privilege against the referenced catalog table. In most cases, this is the most restrictive way to manage access to the activities performed by the stored procedure or function.

Schemas, Tables, Procedures, and Views as Repository Objects

One of the most important concepts in SAP HANA security is the ability to understand the difference between catalog objects created using a SQL CREATE statement and those created using development artifacts within the SAP HANA development repository. Objects created within the SAP HANA repository are often called *repository objects*. The key differentiator between the two object types lies in the ownership of the objects, as we'll discuss.

When a user executes a CREATE SQL statement to define an object, he becomes the sole owner of the object. In most cases, he must then grant privileges to other users or roles for them to access the object he created. If the owner's user account is deleted from the system, any objects he created or privileges he granted are also removed from the system. In addition, if an organization has multiple SAP HANA environments to support proper lifecycle management, these CREATE statements must be manually executed in each environment. These situations should be avoided when establishing a security model, because the model should be able to be transported easily between SAP HANA environments.

When an object is created as a development artifact in the SAP HANA repository, the object isn't owned by the developer. It's owned by a special system account called *_SYS_REPO*. This account can't be deleted from the system and exists in all SAP HANA systems. Therefore, it's ideal when we need to transport the definition of catalog objects or a security model between two or more SAP HANA systems; it already exists in each environment and therefore can easily take ownership of these objects in each.

As discussed in Chapter 3 and Chapter 6, _SYS_REPO is responsible for activating repository-based roles, SAP HANA information views, and a few other security-sensitive objects. In an ideal security model, almost all catalog objects would be created as development artifacts specifically to ensure that _SYS_REPO is the owner of the object. When _SYS_REPO owns most objects, it's much easier to establish, transport, and maintain a security model within an SAP HANA landscape.

8.2 Granting Object Privileges with SQL

In this section, we'll review the different ways to grant object privileges to users or roles using SQL statements.

8.2.1 Securing Schemas with SQL

When we secure catalog objects, we're essentially granting SQL privileges to users, roles, or both. In Section 8.1, we outlined many of the privileges that can be granted based on the type of catalog objects we're working with. In this section, we'll demonstrate the actual process of granting those privileges to users or roles using SQL statements.

In Chapter 3, we outlined the process for creating a catalog schema. Once a schema is created, the owner of the schema will likely need to access SAP HANA Studio and grant other administrator users or security administration roles full privileges that are grantable to others on the schema. Once this is complete, the security administrators will be able to establish a security model based on the schema and its objects. Keep in mind that the schema might also be associated with a service account and not an actual human user. For example, if we set up an SAP HANA service account to manage table replication between SAP ERP and SAP HANA using SAP Landscape Transformation, then additional security settings in SAP HANA will need to be established. This assumes that users will interact with the replicated data. Once an SAP Landscape Transformation mass data transfer configuration is established, we will most likely need to log on to SAP HANA using the service account credentials and grant others access to the schema used by SAP Landscape Transformation. Remember, only the owner of the schema can grant such access.

One way for a user to grant or revoke privileges to its schema is by issuing SQL statements, which can be executed within the SAP HANA SQL console. The basic syntax of the SQL script that grants privileges is as follows:

```
GRANT <PRIVILEGE1, PRIVILEGE2,…> ON SCHEMA <SCHEMA> TO <SOME_USER or
SOME_ROLE> WITH GRANT OPTION;
```

In this syntax, the items inside the angle brackets (<>) are variables that you can adjust based on the privilege, schema, user, or role. The `GRANT` command means that we're allowing the action. A comma-separated array of privileges can also specified after the `GRANT` statement. If only one privilege is required, there's no need for an array; simply specify a single privilege by name without commas. Include `ON SCHEMA` followed by the schema name to identify the schema catalog object. Then include `TO` followed by a user or role to identify who is receiving the granted privileges.

For example, to grant the ADMIN_SEC user account the `SELECT` privilege on a user's schema, log on as the user that owns the schema, access the SQL console, and execute the following statement (assume that the account that owns the schema is named TEST_USER and that the schema name is the same):

```
GRANT SELECT on SCHEMA TEST_USER to ADMIN_SEC WITH GRANT OPTION;
```

Adding the WITH GRANT OPTION syntax is critical in this case, because we need to grant the security administrator full access to a user's schema. The user must include this statement to grant the security administrator the ability to grant the same privilege to other users or roles.

As an alternative, the schema owner can also grant privileges to existing roles. We typically recommend that the schema owner grant the privileges to existing roles, because roles can be assigned to multiple security administrator user accounts. To grant the SEC_ADMINS role SELECT rights for a user's schema, log on as the user that owns the schema, access the SQL console, and execute the following statement. Here, assume that the account that owns the schema is named TEST_USER and the SEC_ADMINS role is assigned to all security administration accounts; we can assume that this is a user schema because the user name and schema name are the same:


```
GRANT SELECT on SCHEMA TEST_USER to SEC_ADMINS WITH GRANT OPTION;
```

Now, assume that we need to give the SEC_ADMIN role full privileges for a user schema named TEST_USER. Issuing the statement in Listing 8.1 will grant all privileges to that role.

```
GRANT
ALTER, SELECT, CREATE ANY, DEBUG,
DELETE, DROP, EXECUTE, INDEX,
INSERT, UPDATE, REFERENCES, TRIGGER,
SELECT CDS METADATA, SELECT METADATA,
CREATE TEMPORARY TABLE, CREATE VIRTUAL FUNCTION PACKAGE
ON SCHEMA TEST_USER TO ADMIN_SEC WITH GRANT OPTION;
```

Listing 8.1 SQL Code to Grant Multiple Schema Privileges

Notice how we can specify multiple SQL privileges separated by commas in a single statement.

To remove the privileges, we need to issue a REVOKE statement, as follows:

```
REVOKE <PRIVILEGE1, PRIVILEGE2,…> ON SCHEMA <SCHEMA> FROM <SOME_USER or
SOME_ROLE>
```

In this syntax, the items inside the angle brackets (<>) are variables that you can adjust based on the privilege, schema, user, or role. The REVOKE command means that we're removing the action. A comma-separated array of privileges can also be specified after the REVOKE statement. Include ON SCHEMA followed by the schema name to identify the schema catalog object. Then include FROM followed by a user or role to identify from whom we are removing privileges.

To remove all privileges assigned to a role for a given schema, execute the SQL statement in Listing 8.2 as the schema owner.

```
REVOKE
ALTER, SELECT, CREATE ANY, DEBUG,
DELETE, DROP, EXECUTE, INDEX,
INSERT, UPDATE, REFERENCES, TRIGGER,
SELECT CDS METADATA, SELECT METADATA,
CREATE TEMPORARY TABLE, CREATE VIRTUAL FUNCTION PACKAGE
ON SCHEMA TEST_USER FROM ADMIN_SEC;
```

Listing 8.2 SQL Code to Revoke Multiple Schema Privileges

It's worth noting that the GRANT and REVOKE SQL statements can be issued against a user or role even if the listed privileges are already granted or not already revoked. This is helpful when we're programmatically granting or revoking privileges. There's no need to first identify which privileges are missing or which privileges are absent before executing commands; they'll execute regardless.

8.2.2 Securing Individual Catalog Objects with SQL

Tables and other catalog objects within a schema can be secured individually. We identified these other catalog objects in Section 8.1.1. In these cases, privileges are granted not at the schema level but at the individual object level. For example, let's assume that the user account JH2345 has been granted the SELECT privilege on schema CORPORATE. Another user account, GR4555, has the CREATE ANY privilege on schema COPORATE. GR4555 creates a table named CUSTOMERS in schema CORPORATE. At this point, GR4555 has all privileges on table CUSTOMERS because the account owns the table. However, JH2345 also has SELECT privileges on the table, because he was granted that privilege on schema CORPORATE.

It's important to remember this relationship between schema privileges and individual object privileges. Granting too many privileges on a schema can expose security risks for objects created within that schema. Granting too many privileges on individual objects can also lead to difficulties in maintaining the security model. Therefore, security administers often must carefully balance their use of schema privileges and individual object privileges.

Now, let's walk through the process for granting and revoking privileges for a catalog table, one of many different types of catalog objects that can be secured. However, the SQL statements and processes for securing each item is the same as those used to secure a table. The syntax for granting privileges to a table is as follows:

```
GRANT <PRIVILEGE1, PRIVILEGE2,…> ON <CATALOG OBJECT> TO <SOME_USER or
SOME_ROLE> WITH GRANT OPTION;
```


As with the syntax used for schemas, we can specify one or more privileges in a comma-separated array. The privileges that can be granted are specific to the object listed after the `ON` clause. Section 8.1.1 contains a list of the privileges that can be granted based on the object type. After the `ON` clause, we then specify the catalog object. After the `TO` clause, we list the users or roles for which we want to grant privileges.

For example, to grant `SELECT` on table `CUSTOMERS`, created in the CORP schema, to the role named QUERY_USERS, we'd issue the following SQL statement:

```
GRANT SELECT ON CORP.CUSTOMERS TO QUERY_USERS;
```

Notice that we prefixed the catalog table with the schema name. This is often required so that the system knows the exact table we are referencing.

Now, let's look at how an object owner would delegate all privileges to the security administrator group. Keep in mind that they'll likely need to delegate these privileges to other users in the future. To grant all privileges to the security administrator role named SEC_ADMIN, we'd use the following SQL statement:

```
GRANT ALTER, DROP, SELECT, INSERT, UPDATE, DELETE, INDEX, TRIGGER, REFERENCES
ON CORP.CUSTOMERS TO SEC_ADMIN WITH GRANT OPTION;
```

Note that we included `WITH GRANT OPTION`. This is required to allow the grantee the ability to grant these privileges to other users or roles. In most cases, we only specify this option if the grantee will be responsible for establishing security within the SAP HANA system.

In some instances, we also need to revoke privileges—that is, remove privileges granted to a user or role. Use the following syntax to revoke catalog object privileges from a user or role:

```
REVOKE <PRIVILEGE1, PRIVILEGE2,…> ON <Catalog Object> FROM <SOME_USER or
SOME_ROLE>
```

As with schemas, the statement starts with REVOKE followed by a list of privileges. After the ON clause, we specify the catalog object. After the FROM clause, we include the user or role to remove the privilege from.

Now, let's look at how an object owner would remove all privileges from the security administrator group, in this case named SEC_ADMIN. Use the following SQL statement:

```
REVOKE ALTER, DROP, SELECT, INSERT, UPDATE, DELETE, INDEX, TRIGGER, REFERENCES
ON CORP.CUSTOMERS FROM SEC_ADMIN;
```

Except for schemas, the syntax we use to either GRANT or REVOKE privileges for a given catalog object applies to all individual catalog object types. We can grant or revoke privileges for tables, views, procedures, functions, and sequences. Now, let's look at how to use SAP HANA Studio to grant or revoke privileges for catalog objects.

8.3 Granting Object Privileges with SAP HANA Studio

We also can perform the same actions discussed in the previous section by using the security options in SAP HANA Studio.

As discussed in Chapter 1, you can access the security options from any perspective containing the **Systems** tab. To access the **Security** node within the **Systems** tab, expand the tree under the desired system. Expand the **Security** node to reveal the **Security**, **Users**, and **Roles** nodes. When using the GUI, we effectively work backwards compared to issuing a SQL statement. The final part of the SQL syntax references a user or role, but when using the GUI, we start by choosing a user or a role from within the **Security** node of SAP HANA Studio.

For example, to modify the privileges assigned to a user, expand the **Users** node and double-click the desired user to reveal the security options. To modify the object privileges assigned to a catalog role, expand the **Roles** node. Double-click the desired role in the tree list to open the security options for the given role.

Within the GUI, locate the **Object Privileges** tab (see Figure 8.2). A list of catalog objects will appear at the bottom of the window. If no catalog objects have been assigned, the list will be empty and they can be added. To reveal the privileges, select a catalog object in the list. Privileges on the right will be visible and can be granted or revoked for the selected object.

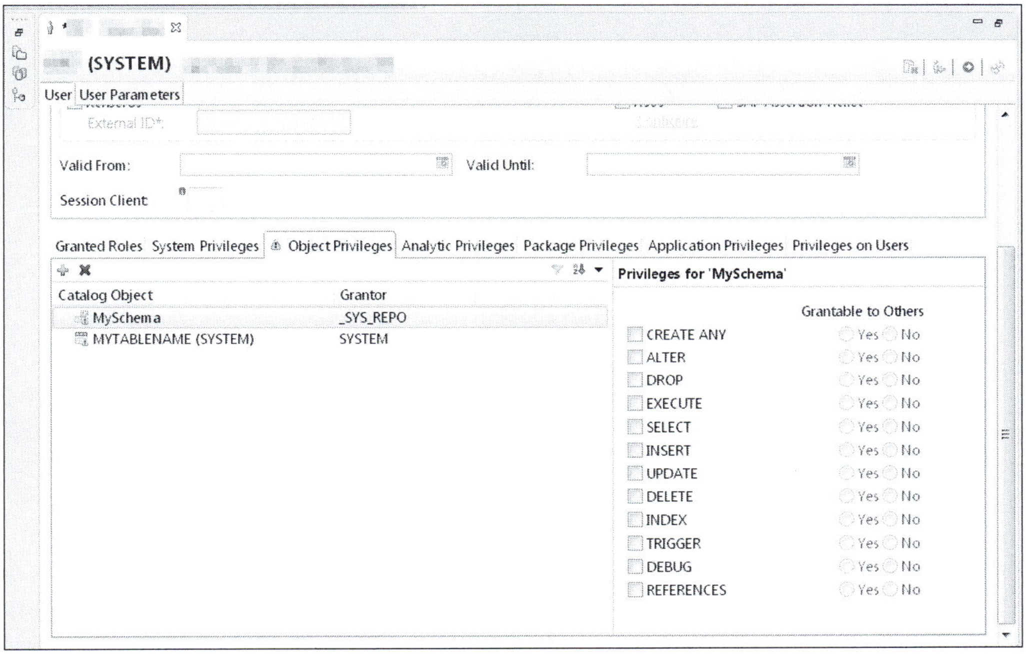

Figure 8.2 Managing Object Privileges Using SAP HANA Studio

To add additional catalog objects, locate the **+** button on the left side of the window, just under the tabs. The window is labeled **Select Catalog Objects**. A search dialog box within the window is visible, allowing you to search for the object in question. The list will include all runtime catalog objects that can be used in this interface. Select the object in question and choose **OK** to close this window and return to the window in which privileges can be assigned.

On the right side of that window, as shown in Figure 8.2, is a list of privileges. The privileges that appear are those that can be granted to the selected object for the given role or user you're editing. If you select another object in the catalog object list, you might see a slightly different list of privileges to the right. This is because the GUI only displays applicable privileges based on the selected object. To grant the privilege, select the checkbox to the left of each privilege. To allow that privilege to be assigned to other users or roles, select the **Yes** radio button within the column labeled **Grantable to Others**.

Once you've selected the desired checkboxes and radio buttons, press F8 to activate the changes. You can also click the **Save** icon on the main icon bar or press Ctrl+S to save and execute your changes.

To revoke privileges for a given user, role, or catalog object, simply uncheck the checkbox beside each privilege and save or activate; you can press F8 or Ctrl+S to save and execute the changes. To remove all privileges for a given object, simply remove the object from the catalog object list by highlighting the object and then clicking the red **X** on the bottom bar above the list.

This procedure works exactly the same way whether we're modifying a user or a standard role. If for any reason you aren't authorized to grant or revoke a privilege, look for a message in red font indicating that. The status window at the top of the tab will display any activation messages.

Administrators will find that using SAP HANA Studio is a quick and easy way to make incremental changes to a security model. There's no need to memorize a variety of SQL commands and the syntax necessary to grant privileges. However, using SQL statements can be beneficial when you need to perform mass updates on users or roles. For example, assume you need to add a new role for every user in the system and that there are four thousand user accounts. Very few administrators would have the patience or time to update four thousand users via a GUI, but a stored procedure can be created to loop through a list of current system users and assign privileges programmatically. Programmatically changing privileges is a skill that requires familiarity with both procedural SQL programing and SQL statements used to grant privileges.

Now that we've reviewed the different methods for granting privileges using either SQL statements or SAP HANA Studio, it's time to look at how we can grant the same privileges using repository-based roles.

8.4 Granting Object Privileges with Repository Roles

In Chapter 6, we introduced repository roles and the process for managing and creating them. As you recall, repository roles can be defined and managed using the role script language within an .hdbrole development artifact. Repository roles can also be defined and managed in the SAP HANA Web-Based Development Workbench editor. In this section, we'll dive deeper into the syntax and process specific to catalog object privileges using repository roles.

8.4.1 Script-Based Repository Roles

In Chapter 6, we outlined the steps and procedures necessary for creating an .hdbrole repository artifact. Within that script, we can define catalog object privileges for both individual catalog objects and for schemas. The syntax for defining privileges against individual catalog objects is as follows:

```
catalog sql object <schema>.<object>: <array of privileges> ;
```

The statement starts with `catalog sql object` and is case-sensitive. This is followed by a fully qualified catalog object name, including the schema name. After the catalog object, we include a colon, followed by a comma-separated array of privileges identified by name. The statement concludes with a semicolon.

For example, to grant the role access to execute a system stored procedure, use the following syntax:

```
catalog sql object "SYS"."REPOSITORY_REST": EXECUTE;
```

To grant privileges to multiple individual catalog objects, simply repeat the syntax for each catalog object. Each line will need to end with a semicolon, which tells the system that the statement is complete. Listing 8.3 illustrates the syntax to grant privileges for three different catalog objects.

```
catalog sql object "dev_tables"."MyTable": SELECT, DELETE;
catalog sql object "dev_tables"."MyStoredProc": SELECT, EXECUTE, DROP, ALTER;
catalog sql object "dev_tables"."MyUDFunction": SELECT, EXECUTE, DROP, ALTER;
```

Listing 8.3 Repository Role Script Granting Privileges to Three Different Catalog Objects

Now, let's look at the syntax used when privileges need to be assigned to an entire schema, as follows:

```
catalog schema <schema name>: <array of privileges>;
```

This is similar to the syntax used to grant individual catalog objects, but we start the statement with `catalog schema` followed by the name of the schema. For example, to grant multiple privileges for the schema named demo_schema, use the following syntax within the .hdbrole development script:

```
catalog schema "demo_schema": ALTER, SELECT, EXECUTE, INSERT, UPDATE, DELETE,
CREATE ANY, DROP, DEBUG, TRIGGER, INDEX;
```

To grant privileges to multiple catalog schemas, simply repeat the syntax for each schema. Remember to conclude each line with a semicolon (see Listing 8.4).

```
catalog schema "dev_tables": SELECT, EXECUTE;
catalog schema "ECCDATA": SELECT, EXECUTE;
catalog schema "_SYS_BIC": SELECT, EXECUTE;
catalog schema "SLT_ECC_ECP": SELECT, UPDATE, ALTER, DROP;
catalog schema "ECC76DATA": SELECT;
```

Listing 8.4 Repository Role Script Granting Privileges to Five Different Schemas

Figure 8.3 shows a complete repository role script within SAP HANA Studio. This repository role will grant both schema and catalog object privileges.

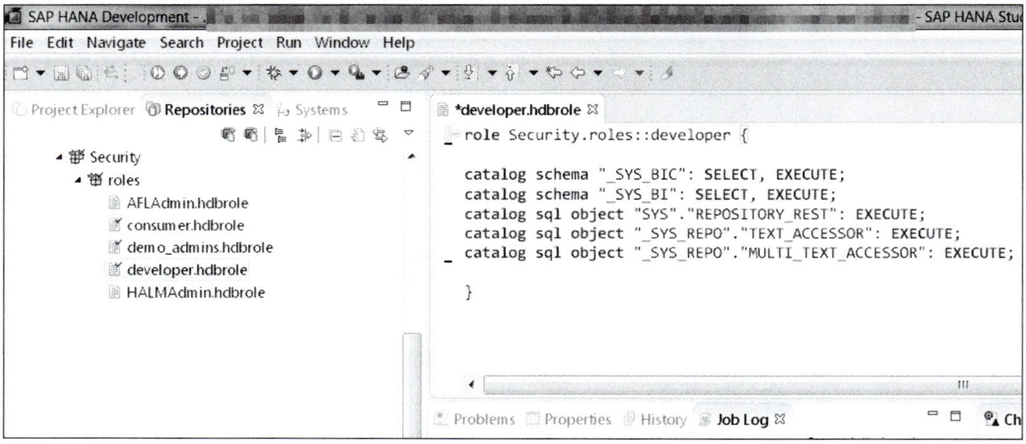

Figure 8.3 Example Repository Role Script in SAP HANA Studio

When these privileges are activated in the developer.hdbrole script, the grantee user account will be _SYS_REPO. However, before the system will allow these privileges to be activated, the owner of the catalog object must ensure that the _SYS_REPO account has complete access to the objects, including the ability to grant the privileges to other users. This is only applicable if the object itself is a standard catalog object owned a standard user account. However, if the catalog object is repository-based, it will be owned by the_SYS_REPO account, so there's no need to grant any privileges to the _SYS_REPO user. As we've indicated before, this is one reason that we recommend developers create catalog objects via the repository development process.

8.4.2 SAP HANA Web-Based Development Workbench

The SAP HANA Web-Based Development Workbench editor, hosted within the XS engine, provides an interface that you can use to build and test development artifacts. From a security perspective, we can use this interface to create and manage repository-based roles. This interface offers all the advantages of repository-based roles without the need to define those roles using scripts. The interface is not exclusive, meaning that you can edit repository-based roles created using scripts with the GUI interface, and you can edit a repository-based role's scripts, those created using a GUI, in SAP HANA Studio. This flexibility allows the security administrator to manage the repository role using either interface.

You can access the SAP HANA Web-Based Development Workbench editor via a supported Internet browser. The following URLs can be customized to match the details of your environment:

http://sap-hana.myhost.com:8000/sap/hana/ide/editor

http://<sap_hana_host>:80<instance_number>/sap/hana/ide/editor

Replace <sap_hana_host> with the hostname of the SAP HANA system in your environment and <instance_number> with the two-digit instance number corresponding to your SAP HANA system.

For secure access, the following examples should help you construct the correct URL:

https://<sap_hana_host>:43<instance_number>/sap/hana/ide/editor

https://sap-hana.myhost.com:4300/sap/hana/ide/editor

To use the workbench and define a role, the user account first will need to be granted one of the roles listed in Table 8.7. Users only need one of the two roles to use the workbench.

Role Name	Summary
sap.hana.ide.roles::EditorDeveloper	Within the workbench, users will only be able to access the editor. Within the editor, users can view, edit, create, delete, or activate a repository-based role or other repository based development artifacts found in development packages or the development repository. A user must have package privileges in addition to this role to properly access and activate the repository role or other development artifacts.

Table 8.7 Roles Required to Use SAP HANA Web-Based Development Workbench Editor

Role Name	Summary
sap.hana.ide.roles::Developer	This role grants a higher level of privileges for users that need full access to SAP HANA Web-based Development Workbench. It grants access to the editor, catalog, and security interfaces. It's considered the parent to the sap.hana.ide.roles::EditorDeveloper role.

Table 8.7 Roles Required to Use SAP HANA Web-Based Development Workbench Editor (Cont.)

Package Privileges Required for SAP HANA Web-Based Development Workbench Editor

In addition to the roles in Table 8.7, users will also need the appropriate package privileges on the package in which they plan to edit, create, or activate repository roles. This also applies to script-based repository roles created using SAP HANA Studio. For example, they'll need the following package privileges to create a repository role using the SAP HANA Web-Based Development Workbench editor interface:

- `REPO.READ`
- `REPO.EDIT_NATIVE_OBJECTS`
- `REPO.ACTIVATE_NATIVE_OBJECTS`

The SAP HANA Web-Based Development Workbench editor interface is very similar to the development areas within the **Repositories** tab of SAP HANA studio. Figure 8.4 shows the editor; on the left side, you'll see a **Content** folder with the package hierarchy below it.

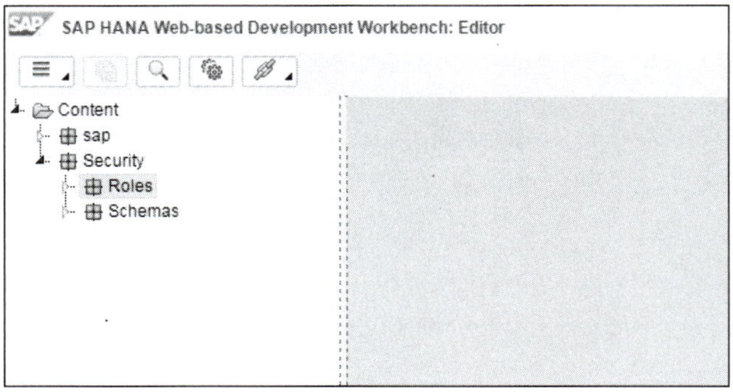

Figure 8.4 View of SAP HANA Web-Based Development Workbench Editor

As you expand the package hierarchy nodes, you'll likely begin seeing development artifacts, depending on what's available within your environment. To create a repository role, right-click the package where you want to store it and choose **New • Role**. A small window will appear asking for the **Role Name**. After entering the name, click **OK** and a new tab-based window will appear on the right (see Figure 8.5). Click the **Object Packages** tab to manage object privileges. Select or add a catalog object to manage its privileges.

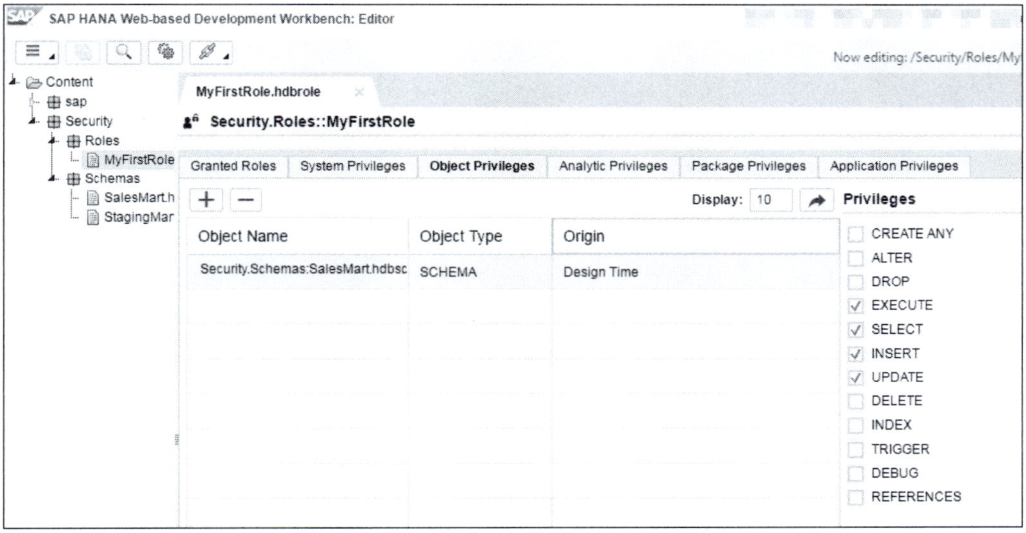

Figure 8.5 Object Privileges Tab in SAP HANA Web-Based Development Workbench Editor

To grant catalog object privileges, on the right side of the tab under the section labeled **Privileges**, select the checkbox next to each privilege name. Items that are checked will be granted; those unchecked won't be granted. When finished, click the **Save All** icon to save and activate the repository role. Security administrators won't be able to grant this repository role to other user or roles.

Users that want to avoid using SQL to grant catalog privileges or scripts to define catalog privileges in a repository role will find the workbench very useful. The GUI is very easy to use and decouples the security developer from the need to memorize SQL statements or script syntax. As you recall, there's an option in SAP HANA Studio for granting standard roles and user privileges, but SAP HANA Web-Based Development Workbench offers options to define repository-based roles. As we've mentioned throughout this book, repository roles offer numerous advantages.

So far, we've reviewed the process for granting catalog object privileges using SQL statements, SAP HANA Studio, script-based repository roles, and now GUI-based repository roles. In the next section, we'll walk through a case study to provide a real-world example of how to use catalog object privileges within a security model based on repository roles.

8.5 Case Study: Updating Repository Roles to Access Information Views

E-Corporation is in the processing of defining its security model using repository roles. Its security consultant directs the company to define a few necessary catalog object privileges within its base-level repository roles. There are three repository roles that need to be updated: consumer, power user, and developer roles. In the next three subsections, we'll provide an overview of each role and the catalog object privileges required. We'll also provide the repository role scripts that make up each of the repository roles.

8.5.1 Consumer

E-Corporation is building several SAP HANA information views to provide analytical query access to the data hosted in the SAP HANA system. When an information view is activated, its runtime catalog column view object is generated in the _SYS_BIC schema. For users to query these information views, they'll need both catalog object and analytic privileges.

The security consultant explains that it would be best for E-Corporation to simply provide the `SELECT` and `EXECUTE` catalog object privileges to the _SYS_BIC and _SYS_BI schemas. The _SYS_BI schema contains a few date- and time-based tables that users might need to query. Because total information view access is a component of both `SELECT` catalog object privileges and analytics privileges, E-Corporation can provide the bulk of its data security via dynamic analytic privileges. E-Corporation could have chosen to restrict access to individual column views within the _SYS_BIC schema, but the company determines that this would require frequent security model maintenance.

The consumer role will be created within the `Security.roles` package hierarchy. The security consultant recommends that the consumer role be set up based on the script in Listing 8.5.

```
role Security.Roles::consumer extends role
        sap.hana.xs.formLogin.profile::ProfileOwner
{
catalog schema "_SYS_BIC": SELECT, EXECUTE;
catalog schema "_SYS_BI": SELECT, EXECUTE;

analytic privilege : e-corp.sales.security:ap_sales_reporting_region.
analyticprivilege;

}
```

Listing 8.5 Consumer Repository Role Syntax

E-Corporation's security developers decide to use SAP HANA Studio to develop and activate the script-based repository role. Figure 8.6 shows how the script will look in both the package hierarchy on the left side and script editor window on the right side.

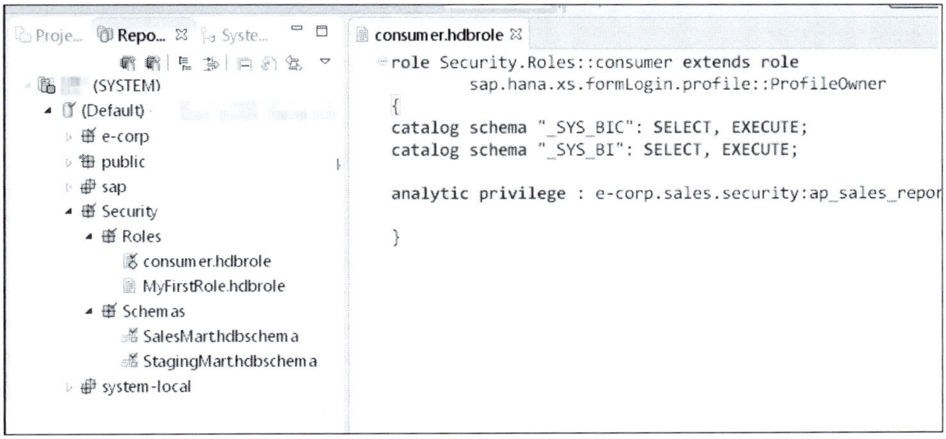

Figure 8.6 View of Consumer Role Script in SAP HANA Studio

8.5.2 Power User

The power user role will need all the privileges assigned to the consumer role, plus the ability to query the sales data mart tables and staging tables. Power users have also requested the ability to view the definition of information views defined in the `e-corp` package.

To facilitate these requirements, the security consultant recommends that the power user repository role script use the syntax in Listing 8.6.

```
role Security.Roles::powerusers extends role
    Security.Roles::consumer
    //
This role should include all of the privileges set up in the consumer role
{

    catalog sql object "SYS"."REPOSITORY_REST": EXECUTE;
    // Necessary procedure to view repository objects in SAP HANA Studio


// Query data found in the base tables
    catalog schema "SalesMart": SELECT;
    catalog schema "StagingMart": SELECT;

    package e-corp: REPO.READ;
}
```

Listing 8.6 Power User Repository Role Syntax

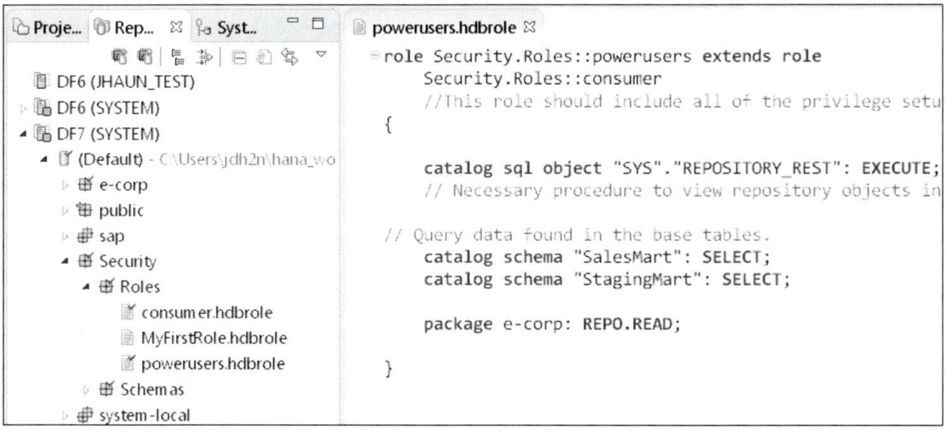

Figure 8.7 View of Power User Repository Role in SAP HANA Studio

This role grants SELECT access to the SalesMart and StagingMart schemas. In addition, it also grants access to the REPOSITORY_REST system stored procedure. EXECUTE access to this system procedure is required for the user to view and navigate the SAP HANA package hierarchy using SAP HANA Studio or other tools that provide similar access. In addition to the catalog object privileges, power users will need `READ` access to the top-level `e-corp` package node. To include the privileges assigned to the consumer role, the syntax includes the `extends role Security.Roles::consumer` syntax, as shown in Listing 8.6 and Figure 8.7. This allows the power user role to also include the privileges in the consumer role.

8.5.3 Developer

The developer repository role will contain several types of privileges. For this case study, we'll focus on those related to catalog objects.

The security consultant has identified that the developers will require a high level of access to all catalog objects that will be associated with the SalesMart and StagingMart schemas. Developers need the ability to create catalog objects and load data into these objects. Listing 8.7 contains an excerpt of the portion of the developer repository role script that grants the appropriate catalog schema privileges.

```
role Security.Roles::developer extends role
Security.Roles::powerusers,
sap.hana.xs.ide.roles::CatalogDeveloper,
sap.hana.xs.ide.roles::EditorDeveloper
{

catalog schema "SalesMart":
                    ALTER, SELECT, EXECUTE,
            INSERT, UPDATE, DELETE, CREATE ANY,
            DROP, DEBUG, TRIGGER, INDEX;


catalog schema "StagingMart":
                    ALTER, SELECT, EXECUTE,
            INSERT, UPDATE, DELETE, CREATE ANY,
            DROP, DEBUG, TRIGGER, INDEX;
```

Listing 8.7 Excerpt from Developer Repository Role Syntax

Notice that the developer role extends the power user role. Because of this, there is no need to include the privileges granted to the consumer and power users roles. As you recall, the power user role extends the consumer role. In this way, we can cascade the granting of role privileges from the consumer role, through the power user role, to the developer role. This cascading technique can be used to minimize duplication of code for each repository role.

8.6 Summary

In this chapter, you learned about the different catalog objects and their privileges. We also discussed a variety of ways that we can grant catalog object privileges to users and roles. Because of the numerous benefits of repository roles, we reviewed a case study in which catalog object roles were granted.

Chapter 9
Package Privileges

In this chapter, we'll explore the different package privileges that can be granted to the package hierarchy and the processes we use for granting them.

SAP HANA is a development platform, in addition to many of its other data-management qualities. To facilitate application development, application code storage, security, and application lifecycle management, SAP HANA provides a repository. This repository is used to store design-time objects used by both the database system and the SAP HANA extended application services, classic model (XS). The hierarchy of this repository is organized into packages and their subpackages. Each package contains design-time development artifacts. To govern access to both packages and development artifacts, SAP HANA package privileges can be assigned to users and roles.

To understand package privileges thoroughly, we must also study the makeup of the SAP HANA development repository. In this chapter, we'll start by discussing the SAP HANA development repository. We'll then review the various privileges that can be granted for packages and how they're granted. Let's first discuss how the development repository is organized and managed.

9.1 The SAP HANA Development Repository

The SAP HANA development repository is organized into major node structures called *packages*. In this section, we'll explore the hierarchical structure of this package-based repository, and we'll explain the process used to create packages. In conclusion, we'll explain the process used to create a delivery unit (DU).

9.1.1 Structure of the Development Repository

The development repository consists of packages, logical organizational units that begin with the root node, followed by the top-level nodes, then optionally a hierarchy of subpackage nodes. Figure 9.1 shows an example package hierarchy, as viewed in the **Repository** tab of the SAP HANA development perspective.

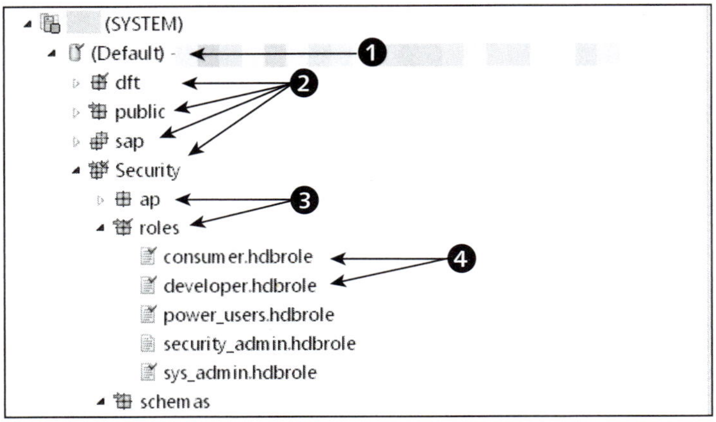

Figure 9.1 Package and Development Artifact Hierarchy in SAP HANA Repository

In Figure 9.1, the root of all the packages is at the top ❶. It's a logical location, but privileges can be applied at this level. The logical root node is named `.REPO_PACKAGE_ROOT`; we reference that name when assigning root package privileges in GUIs and via SQL commands. However, only top-level packages can exist under the root level. We can't create development artifacts directly under the root node. Beneath the root are several top-level packages ❷. Top-level packages can contain either subpackages ❸ or development artifacts. Several development artifacts are stored in the package named **roles** ❹. Privileges can only be applied at the package level; the development artifacts effectively inherit privileges from their parent or grandparent package nodes.

With this structure in mind, let's review the process for creating packages and subpackages.

9.1.2 Creating Packages and Subpackages

We can access the package hierarchy easily in two ways. When using the development perspective in SAP HANA Studio, locate the **Systems** tab or **Repositories** tab. From the **Repositories** tab, expand the **System** node and the **(Default)** container node. When using the administration console perspective, expand the **System** node and the top-level **Content** folder to reveal the package hierarchy.

To create a new top-level package in the development perspective, right-click the default node within the **Repositories** tab and choose **New • Repository Package**. Figure 9.2 shows the menus that will appear when you follow this workflow from the development perspective.

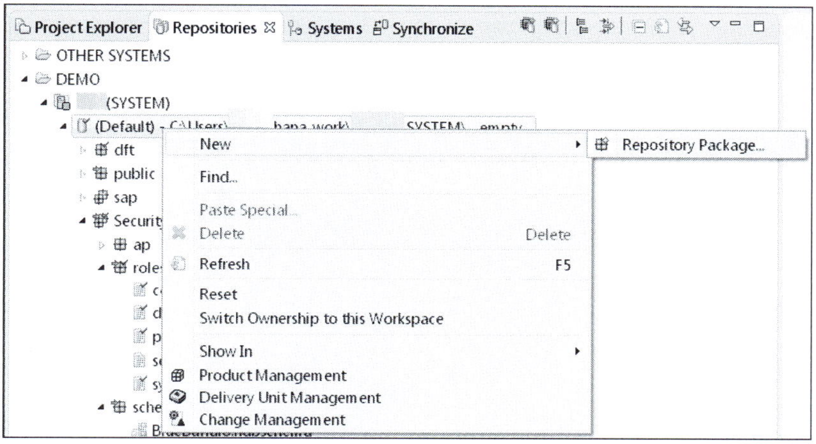

Figure 9.2 Creating New Repository Package

As shown in Figure 9.3, a **Create Repository Package** window will appear, allowing you to name the package. Start by choosing the **Repository Workspace**, which we discussed setting up in Chapter 2. If set up correctly, this option should already be defaulted to the correct repository workspace. Enter "Security" in the **Package Name:** field, and click **Next**.

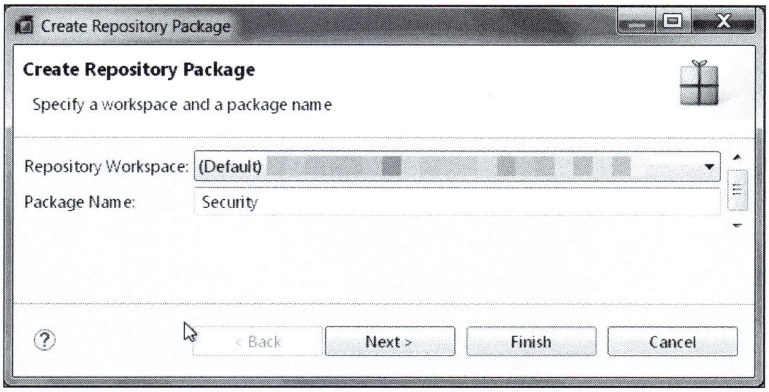

Figure 9.3 Naming Package

As shown in Figure 9.4, a new window will appear: **Edit Repository Package**. This window allows you to define additional options for the package. We can specify a description in the **Description** field and establish the account that is **Responsible** for the package. _SYS_REPO is a good choice for packages, because this user account can't be deleted from the system. Check the **Structural** checkbox if the package is used only for navigation and not for storing development artifacts. Click **Finish** when you're done. A package now should exist within the repository.

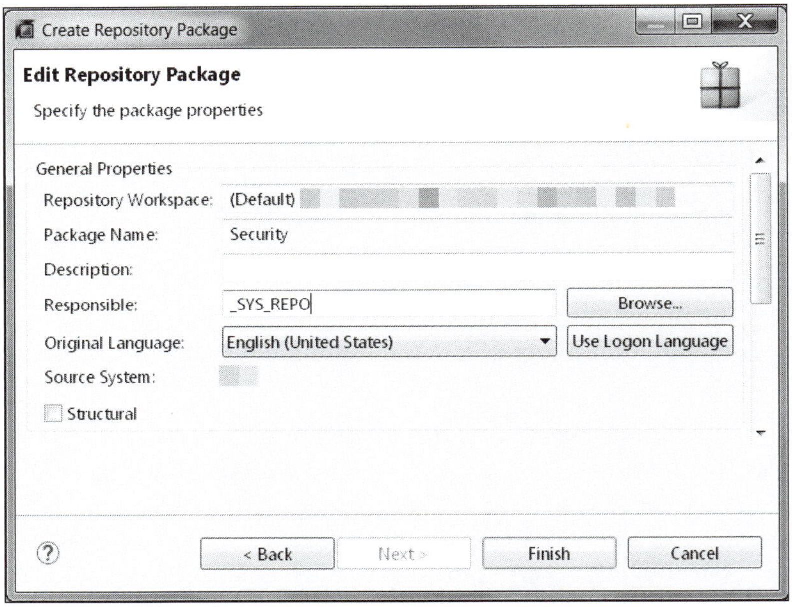

Figure 9.4 Setting Package Options

9.1.3 Overview of Delivery Units

Delivery units (DUs) play a role in the lifecycle management of packages. Before we can export content to a file or transport development content from one SAP HANA system to another, we must first assign a package or package hierarchy to a DU. A DU should contain package and development artifacts that are associated with each other. For example, a web-based application developed in the XS engine and its associated package hierarchy can be assigned to a single DU. Using a DU allows the content to be transported in an organized and consistent manner.

Once content is organized into a DU, we can export it to a compressed file, which then can be imported into another SAP HANA system for the purposes of transporting the code. Using *SAP HANA application lifecycle management*, we can also transport DUs between systems. A DU can also serve as an external code backup and can be imported back into the originating SAP HANA system if content needs to be restored.

Note that the administrator must define the vendor ID or content vendor within the system configuration before content can be assigned to a DU. This is configured in the indexserver.ini file under the `repository` option and `content_vendor` key. Specify a value that will identify your organization name; for example, you could enter a domain name, such as *e-corp.com*.

The user creating the DU must have privileges similar to those assigned to the default role sap.hana.xs.lm.roles::Administrator. Note that the system privilege INIFILE admin, found in this default role, is only necessary to define the content vendor. A custom role should be created for developers that create DUs to avoid granting them access to make configuration changes to the SAP HANA system.

9

Additional Information about Delivery Units

For additional information pertaining to the creation and management of delivery units, please review the SAP HANA Application Lifecycle Management Guide, available at *http://help.sap.com/hana/SAP_HANA_Application_Lifecycle_Management_en.pdf*.

9.2 Overview of Package Privileges

Package privileges are organized into two broad categories: *native package privileges* and *imported package privileges*. Native package privileges refer to packages and their child development artifacts that are developed from scratch in an SAP HANA system. We expect to create and edit native content in a development system. Imported package privileges represent packages and their child development artifacts that are imported into a system. These objects are created in a remote system, exported, and then imported into a different system.

As noted earlier, packages are nodes organized in a parent-child relationship. Together, they make up the *SAP HANA repository*. Each package contains a subpackage or one or more development artifacts. Package privileges are assigned for a package node; development artifacts can't be granted privileges individually or explicitly. However, development artifacts do inherit the privileges assigned to their parent and grandparent package nodes.

Inheritance can be used to simplify the design of a security model. For example, we can establish privileges for a top-level package and assume that all child objects will inherit the same privileges. There is no need to explicitly configure privileges for each child package or subpackage within the repository. This simplifies the design of repository roles, because we don't need to address package privileges each time a new package or development artifact is created.

In addition to its benefits, inheritance also introduces some risks, depending on the placement of critical development artifacts such as repository roles. For example, repository roles must be in an isolated location to prevent privilege elevation by users that don't manage roles or the assignment of privileges. Stored procedures used to provision users also need to be in an isolated location for the same reasons. Therefore, inheritance can also present challenges to a security model that leverages development artifacts.

When the system validates access to a development artifact, it first checks the privileges assigned to the direct parent package. If there are no privileges assigned to the direct parent, it will continue to traverse up the hierarchy, checking each grandparent node until it can validate the requested action. If no parent or grandparent node has assigned privileges for that user, the user fails authorization and is considered not authorized to perform the requested action.

Development artifacts use a bottom-up approach to authorization validation. Therefore, we don't have to explicitly assign privileges to each parent and grandparent package node; we only need to grant privileges on its closest desired parent or grandparent package and there's no need to establish privileges for a given user at each level of the package hierarchy. It's important to understand this point, because experienced security professionals might assume that development artifacts use a top-down approach based on inheritance and might then overengineer the security model.

Native package privileges apply to objects that are directly created, maintained, and activated within a particular originating environment. For example, if you create a repository role within a development system, it will always remain a native object within that system. The native package privileges are as follows:

- `REPO.READ`
  This package privilege grants read access to a package and its child objects. It applies to both native and imported objects.

- REPO.EDIT_NATIVE_OBJECTS
  This package privilege grants edit privileges to design-time objects within a package. It only applies to native objects or those created within an originating system.
- REPO.ACTIVATE_NATIVE_OBJECTS
  This package privilege grants the ability to create, activate, or reactivate design-time objects within a package. It only applies to native objects or those created within an originating system.
- REPO.MAINTAIN_NATIVE_PACKAGES
  This package privilege grants the ability to edit and create packages and subpackages. It only applies to native packages or those created within an originating system.

Imported package privileges are as follows:

- REPO.EDIT_IMPORTED_OBJECTS
  This package privilege grants edit privileges to design-time objects within a package. It only applies to imported objects or those imported from a DU.
- REPO.ACTIVATE_IMPORTED _OBJECTS
  This package grants that ability to create, activate or reactivate design-time objects within a package. It only applies to imported objects or those imported from a DU.
- REPO.MAINTAIN_IMPORTED_PACKAGES
  This package privilege grants the ability to edit and create packages and subpackages. It only applies to imported packages or those imported from a DU.

9.3 Granting Package Privileges

In this section, we will review four options available to grant package privileges: via SQL commands, SAP HANA Studio, the SAP HANA Web-Based Development Workbench security manager, or repository-based role scripts or the repository-based role editor.

9.3.1 Granting Package Privileges with SQL

Using the SQL console, we can grant access to a package in the SAP HANA repository. To do so, use the following SQL syntax:

```
GRANT <PACKAGE_PRIVILEGE> ON <"package.subpackage"> TO <GRANTEE> WITH GRANT
OPTION;
```

The <PACKAGE_PRIVILEGE> variable can be replaced with a comma-separated array of package privileges. The <"package.subpackage"> variable can be replaced by the case-sensitive name of the package and subpackage hierarchy. When constructing a complete package name, each node of the package hierarchy should be separated by a period. The WITH GRANT OPTION allows the grantee to grant the same privileges to other users. <GRANTEE> can either be a role or a user account. For example, you can have the following:

```
GRANT REPO.READ, REPO.EDIT_NATIVE_OBJECTS ON "e-corp" TO JONATHAN WITH GRANT
OPTION;
```

To remove package privileges, use the REVOKE SQL statement. The following SQL statement will remove the privileges specified in the <PACKAGE_PRIVILEGES> variable array:

```
REVOKE <PACKAGE_PRIVILEGE> ON <"package.subpackage"> FROM <GRANTEE>;
```

To give a concrete example:

```
REVOKE REPO.EDIT_NATIVE_OBJECTS ON "e-corp" FROM JONATHAN;
```

9.3.2 Granting Package Privileges with SAP HANA Studio

We also can use the user account or role management area within SAP HANA Studio to both grant and revoke package privileges for a given grantee. Grantees can be either roles or users. Most will find it easier to use SAP HANA Studio than to memorize and type SQL statements.

To access the user management area in SAP HANA Studio, start by switching to the administration console perspective. In the **Systems** tab, located on the left, expand the **System** node then the **Security** node to reveal the **Security**, **Users**, and **Roles** nodes. Expand the **Users** node to reveal user accounts defined in the system, or expand the **Roles** node to reveal roles defined in the system. To manage a particular grantee, double-click the account name or role name in the list to open the **Grantee Management** tab on the right.

The fifth tab in the grantee management interface is **Package Privileges**. To grant a package privilege, click **+** to open a search dialog box. To view all packages in the system, enter the search string "**". To search for a specific package, enter a portion of the package's name to search for possible matches. Select one or more packages and click **OK**. The search dialog box will disappear, and a list of selected packages will appear (see Figure 9.5).

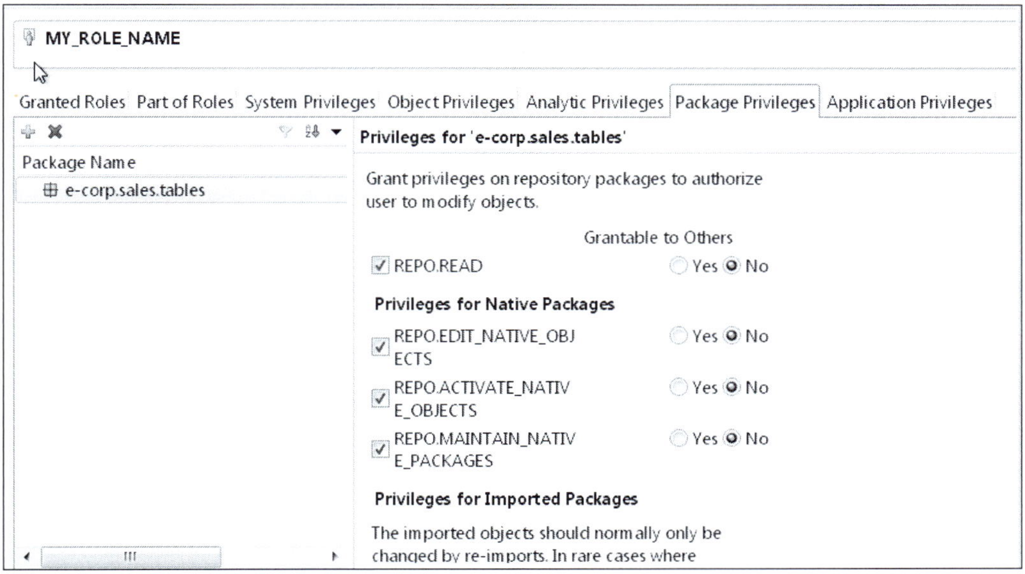

Figure 9.5 Package Privileges Management Tab

To assign privileges to a selected package, look for the frame on the right containing checkboxes, privileges, and **Yes** and **No** radio buttons. To assign privileges, select the checkbox beside each listed privilege's name. To allow a user to assign the same privilege to others, select the **Yes** radio button in the column labeled **Grantable to Others**.

To revoke a package privilege, simply select it from the list and click the red **X** to remove it from the list. To save the changes, press `Ctrl`+`S`, or to activate the changes, press `F8`. Either way, the changes will be saved and activated in the system.

9.3.3 Granting Package Privileges with SAP HANA Web-Based Development Workbench

The SAP HANA Web-Based Development Workbench security manager, hosted within the XS engine, provides an interface that you can use to assign privileges to a grantee.

You can access SAP HANA Web-Based Development Workbench via a supported Internet browser. The following two URLs can be customized to match the details of your environment:

http://sap-hana.myhost.com:8000/sap/hana/ide/security

http://<sap_hana_host>:80<instance_number>/sap/hana/ide/security

In the last example, replace <sap_hana_host> with the hostname of the SAP HANA system in your environment. Replace <instance_number> with the two-digit instance number corresponding to your SAP HANA system.

For secure access, the following examples should help you construct the correct URL:

https://<sap_hana_host>:43<instance_number>/sap/hana/ide/security

https://sap-hana.myhost.com:4300/sap/hana/ide/security

Once you have access to the security manager, expand the **Security** node on the right. Expand **Users** to reveal a list of user accounts, or expand **Roles** to reveal a list of roles. Double-click a grantee to open the management interface for the given item. With the selected grantee management window open, you can begin granting and revoking privileges. Figure 9.6 shows the **Package Privileges** management tab.

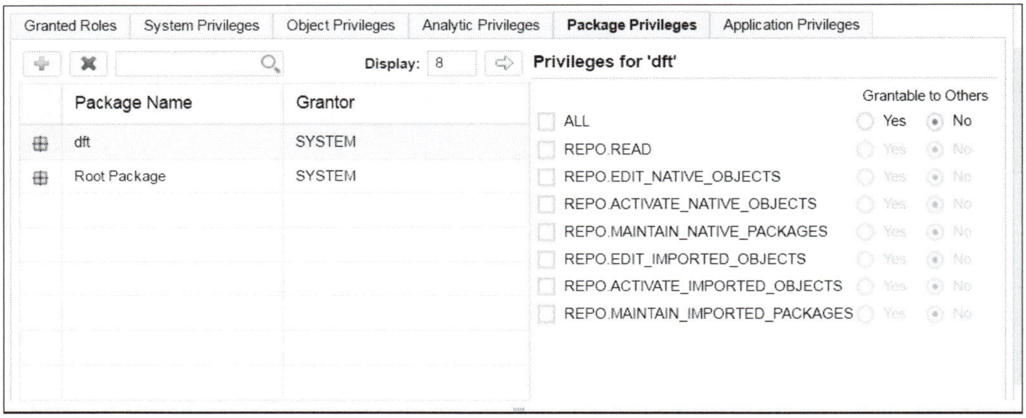

Figure 9.6 Managing Package Privileges in SAP HANA Web-Based Development Workbench

The process for granting and revoking a grantee's privileges in the SAP HANA Web-Based Development Workbench security manager is almost identical to the process outlined for SAP HANA Studio. Because there is tremendous overlap in the workflows, we won't go into the same level of detail in this section; see Section 9.3.2 for additional details. Here, we'll simply highlight the basic workflow and point out any significant differences.

To add a package privilege, click **+** and search for the desired package hierarchy level. To revoke a package privilege, select the package hierarchy level from the list and click the red **X** to remove it. To save your changes, press [Ctrl]+[S]. Alternatively, click the disk icon at the top left to save and activate the privilege.

If there are any activation issues, warning messages will appear in the status frame at the bottom of the user management window. The status frame has a dark background color. Error messages will appear in red colored text.

9.3.4 Granting Package Privileges within Repository-Based Roles

In Chapter 6, we discussed the importance of using repository-based roles as the foundation of our security model. We also thoroughly discussed the workflows for creating repository-based roles. For a complete review of repository roles, please see Chapter 6. In this section, we'll provide a summary of the workflows used to grant or revoke package privileges within repository-based roles, either via design-time script or via the SAP HANA Web-Based Development Workbench repository role management options.

Granting and Revoking Privileges with Design-Time Scripts

When defining package privileges within repository-based role scripts, you must start the line with the term package, then include the name of the package hierarchy node. After the package name, include a single colon. After the colon, include a comma-separated list of package privileges. At the end of the statement, include a semicolon to finish the line.

The following example is a single line of code used to grant multiple privileges to the `e-corp.sales` package:

```
Package e-corp.sales: REPO.READ, REPO.ACTIVATE_NATIVE_OBJECTS, REPO.MAINTAIN_
NATIVE_PACKAGES, REPO.EDIT_IMPORTED_OBJECTS;
```

The following example is a single line of code used to grant a single privilege to a single package:

```
Package e-corp.sales: REPO.READ;
```

To grant the root package privilege, use the system-defined package name value, `.REPO_PACKAGE_ROOT`, to represent privileges that will be applied to all packages. Use the following syntax:

```
package .REPO_PACKAGE_ROOT: REPO.READ;
```

Managing Repository Roles with SAP HANA Web-Based Development Workbench

The SAP HANA Web-Based Development Workbench editor, hosted within the XS engine, provides an interface to manage and create repository roles. The interface looks a lot like the standard role management options in SAP HANA Studio, but the role objects it creates are profoundly different: The editor creates repository-based roles. The objects created in the editor also can be opened in the SAP HANA Studio developer perspective, which means that we can use either the SAP HANA Studio interface or the script editor to manage repository roles.

You can access SAP HANA Web-Based Development Workbench via a supported Internet browser. The following two URLs can be customized to match the details of your environment:

http://sap-hana.myhost.com:8000/sap/hana/ide/editor

http://<sap_hana_host>:80<instance_number>/sap/hana/ide/editor

In the last example, replace <sap_hana_host> with the hostname of the SAP HANA system in your environment and <instance_number> with the two-digit instance number corresponding to your SAP HANA system.

For secure access, the following examples should help you construct the correct URL:

https://<sap_hana_host>:43<instance_number>/sap/hana/ide/editor

https://sap-hana.myhost.com:4300/sap/hana/ide/editor

Once you have access to the editor, expand the **Content** node on the right, then expand **Packages** to reveal a list of packages defined in the system. We typically create a top-level package named Security to host such objects.

To create a repository role, right-click the package in which you want to store it. From the context menu, choose **New • Role** (see Figure 9.7).

A small window named **New Role** will appear. Enter the desired name of the role and click **Create**. A new tabbed window will appear in the large right-hand frame. The tab's label should match the provided name of the repository role. The new window will contain a series of subtabs: **Granted Roles**, **System Privileges**, **Object Privileges**, **Analytic Privileges**, **Package Privileges**, and **Application Privileges**. Like in SAP HANA Studio, each tab allows a developer to define privileges specific to that tab. Let's now take a closer look at the process required to configure each of the listed privileges.

Click the **Package Privileges** tab to reveal an interface via which we can add or remove package privileges. To add a package, click the large **+** button on the subtab header. A pop-up window will appear, titled **Select Package** (see Figure 9.8).

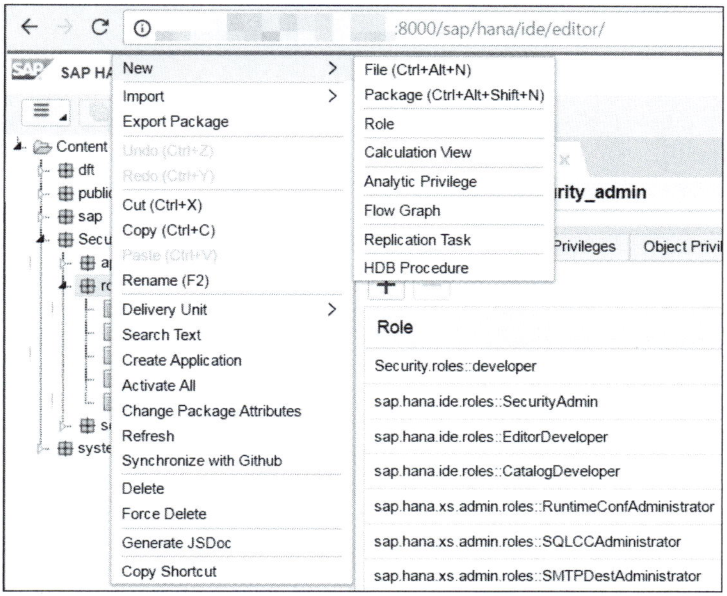

Figure 9.7 Navigating SAP HANA Web-Based Development Workbench Editor and Creating Repository Role

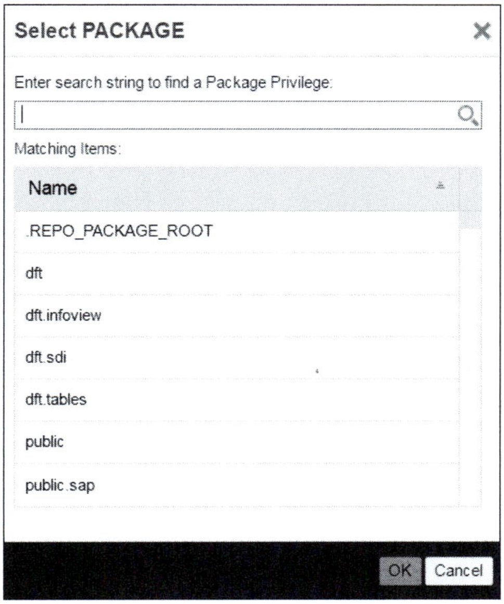

Figure 9.8 Selecting and Assigning Package Privileges in SAP HANA Web-Based Development Workbench

Within the window, a search box will appear. In it, enter a portion of the package name to narrow the results. Alternatively, you can scroll through the unfiltered list to locate the desired package by its complete hierarchical name. Select one or more objects within the list, holding down the [Ctrl] key to select multiple items. The selected items are highlighted with a light blue color. Choose the **OK** button at the bottom of the window to finalize the selection.

The selected packages will now appear in the **Package Privileges** tab (see Figure 9.9).

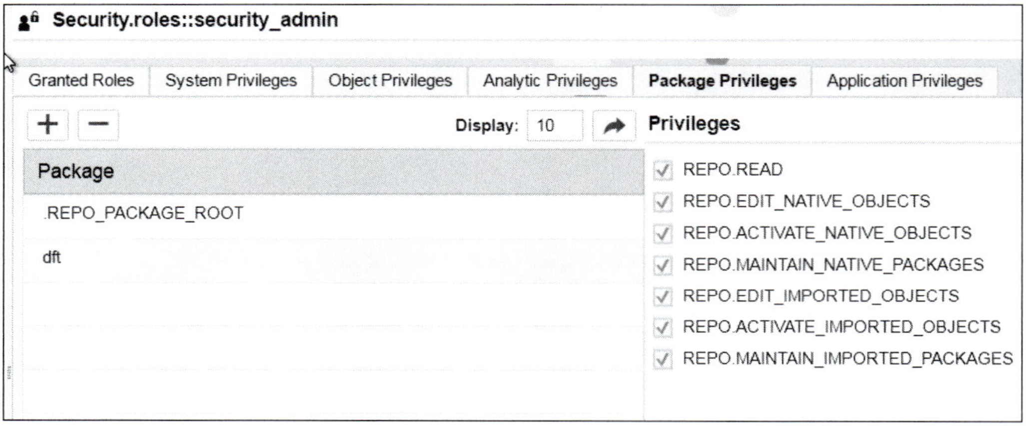

Figure 9.9 Selected Packages and Their Privileges Listed in Package Privileges Tab

With the objects listed, we now need to assign the various package privileges to each selected package. To specify the privileges for an individual package, select and highlight the package within the list on the left side. To the right of the selected package, a series of privileges and corresponding checkboxes will appear (see right side of Figure 9.9).

Check the box beside each privilege to assign the selected privilege to the selected package. Repeat the process for all packages. To remove the privilege, simply uncheck the box beside the privilege you want to remove.

To remove an assigned package and all its privileges, select an object from the list on the left side, then click the large – button above the list to remove it. Items in the list must be deleted one at a time.

Once you've configured the desired list of packages and established their privileges, click the **Save All** button at the top left, which looks like three stacked floppy disks.

If there are any issues saving and activating the repository role, messages will appear in red text within the console window just below the opened **Repository Roles** tab. The console window has a dark background color and is located at the bottom of the open tab. Affirmative messages will appear in white text, and error messages will appear in red text.

To close the open **Repository Roles** tab, click the small **x** to the right of the tab.

9.4 Case Study: Preventing Content Developers from Elevating Their Privileges

E-Corporation has several developers using the SAP HANA system to create information views and custom applications within the XS engine. The company also relies heavily on the use of repository-based roles to support its security model. Because developers and security administrators both require access to the same repository, E-Corporation management is concerned that developers might have access to the repository roles. If they were to gain access, the developers could edit the repository roles and grant their assigned roles additional privileges. In the following sections, we'll look at E-Corporation's current security model before discussing some changes the company can make to improve it.

9

9.4.1 Assessing the Current Configuration

E-Corporation requests that the company's security consultant review the security model and repository structure to make sure the company has properly secured access to its repository-based roles. To properly assess the current design, the security consultant creates a diagram to outline the current package hierarchy (Figure 9.10).

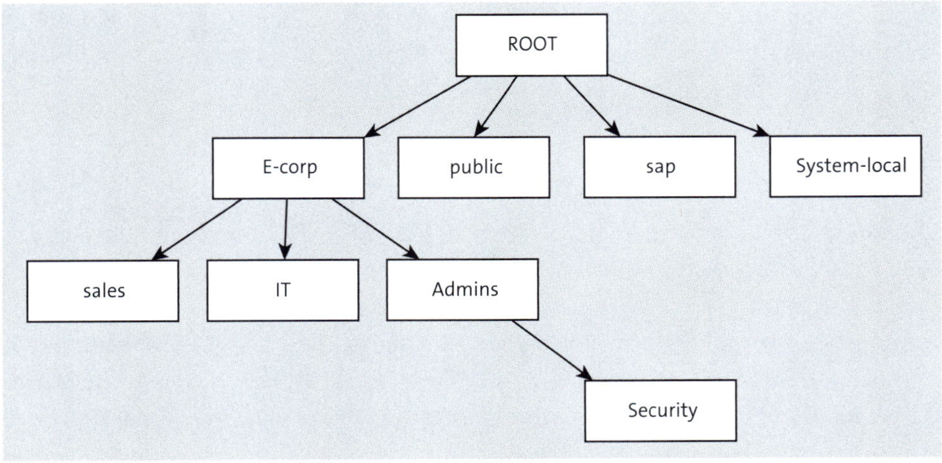

Figure 9.10 Current E-Corporation Package Hierarchy

E-Corporation currently stores all security-related artifacts, including repository roles, in the E-corp.Admins.Security package. The parent package, E-corp.Admins, contains system administration–related development artifacts. The E-corp package is configured as a structural package, which prevents development artifacts from being created directly under the E-corp top-level package.

In addition to assessing the package hierarchy, the consultant requests a listing of all roles that are assigned package privileges for the ROOT, E-corp, E-corp.Admins, and E-corp.Admins.Security nodes. Table 9.1 outlines the role types and package privileges assigned for each package node.

Role Type	Package Node	Assigned Package Privileges
System administrators	ROOT	All
Developers	E-corp	REPO.READ
System administrators	E-corp.Admins	All
Role managers	E-corp.Admins.Security	All

Table 9.1 Roles with Access to ROOT, Administration, and Security Packages at E-Corporation

Based on the provided information, system administrators have full access to all packages in E-Corporation's SAP HANA system. Developers can review all content created under the top-level E-corp node, system administrators are again granted full access to the E-corp.Admins node, and role managers are granted full package access to the E-corp.Admins.Security node. With this information, the security consultant determines that several changes could be implemented to improve the overall security of the environment, as we'll discuss next.

9.4.2 Recommendations

The consultant recommends changes to both the package hierarchy and the package privileges that are assigned the role types at E-Corporation. The predominant recommendation is that only security managers should have access to elevate the privileges assigned within repository roles. System administrators should not have access to create or edit existing repository roles because of the need for a separation of duties at E-Corporation. To achieve this, changes related to the package hierarchy and the package privileges assigned to roles are needed.

Changes to the Package Hierarchy

E-Corporation's current package hierarchy places repository roles in the E-corp.Admins.Security package. This design allows repository roles to reside in a dedicated package, but it complicates the design of the security model. As you recall, we can't explicitly deny privileges in SAP HANA, and packages inherit the privileges assigned to parent and grandparent nodes. If a role is assigned privileges at a parent or grandparent node, child nodes will inherit those privileges. We also have no option to break this inheritance or to explicitly deny a privilege on a child node. The current design grants full access to the system administrators, even though they were not explicitly granted full access on the E-corp.Admins.Security node. This is due to the inheritance of privileges assigned at the ROOT and E-corp.Admins nodes. The design also grants REPO.READ access to all developers. Although read access for developers is not a significant concern, it does highlight the importance of calculating the risk of accident privilege inheritance within the package hierarchy. For example, the security team might accidently grant the REPO.EDIT_NATIVE_OBJECTS developer role to the E-corp package node, which would grant developers edit access to the repository roles via inheritance.

The security consultant recommends a simple change to the hierarchy. Given the significance of inheritance and the probability of accidental privilege elevation through inheritance, he recommends that the Security package node move to the top level of the hierarchy. In this way, only ROOT-level package privileges will present a challenge to the security model design. Furthermore, the security consultant recommends that the Security.Roles, Security.UserProvisioning, and Security.Schemas packages be created to better organize and potentially restrict security-related development artifacts. Figure 9.11 provides an example of the recommended package hierarchy for E-Corporation.

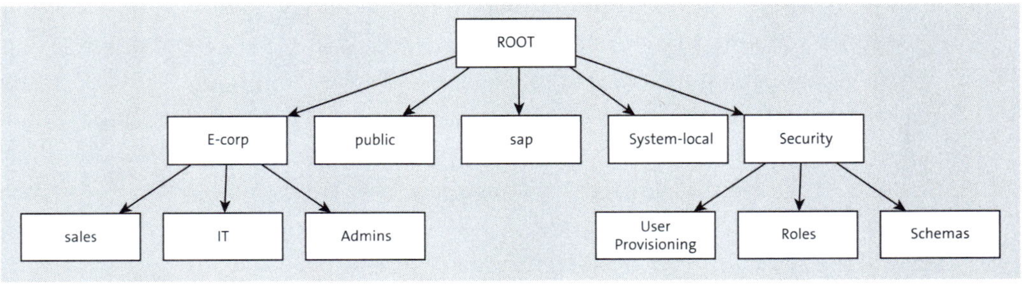

Figure 9.11 Recommended E-Corporation Package Hierarchy

Role Types and Changes to Their Package Privileges

With the `Security` package configured as a top-level package, several changes to the roles will need to be implemented, as listed in Table 9.2.

Role Type	Package Node	Assigned Package Privileges
System administrators	ROOT	REPO.READ, REPO_MAINTAIN_NATIVE_PACKAGES, REPO_MAINTAIN_IMPORTED_PACKAGES
Developers	E-corp	None
Developers	E-corp.Sales	All
System administrators	E-corp.Admins	All
Role managers	Security	All

Table 9.2 Recommended Role Types and Package Privileges for E-Corporation

Starting with the system administrators, the consultant recommends that their `ROOT`-level package privileges be limited to `REPO.READ`, `REPO`, `REPO_MAINTAIN_NATIVE_PACKAGES`, and `REPO_MAINTAIN_IMPORTED_PACKAGES`, which will allow them to add package nodes at any level without automatically being granted privileges to activate or modify existing development artifacts within existing packages. The **Grantable to Others** or `WITH GRANT` option must not be assigned to the system administrators role type, to prevent them from assigning their package privileges to other users or standard roles. System administrators can be granted full access to the `E-corp.Admins` package, because it contains their development-related artifacts. This should be the only area in which they activate or modify content.

Unless justified, it's best that the developers role not receive `REPO.READ` privileges on the top-level `E-corp` package node. Developers should only be granted privileges on the nodes containing their development artifacts. For example, for the `E-corp.sales` package node, they might have full access to create SAP HANA information views. They don't require `REPO.READ` on parent or grandparent nodes to work within their designated packages. As you recall, package privileges are evaluated from the bottom up; therefore, we don't need to grant `REPO.READ` access for each parent or grandparent level of the package hierarchy. Developers will be able to navigate the package hierarchy because of this bottom-up evaluation.

The role managers role should be granted full access to the top-level package security. This is where role managers will create development artifacts used for the security model.

Overall, the recommended changes will provide for a more secure environment. Moving the security package to the top level will reduce the likelihood of both accidental and deliberate privilege elevation within the environment. Adding a few additional subpackages within the `Security` node provides for better organization of security-related development artifacts. By preventing system administrators from having full access at the `ROOT` node, E-Corporation can better ensure that only role managers are able to manage repository roles within the environment.

9.5 Summary

Securing the package hierarchy plays an important role in any security model. Package privileges are divided into two broad categories, privileges for native content and privileges for imported content. When repository-based roles are used within the model, we must ensure that only role managers can modify repository roles. In addition, we must establish the appropriate security to support development activities within the environment. Inheritance can be both beneficial and risky when leveraged to implement package privileges.

Chapter 10
Analytic Privileges

In this chapter, we'll explore analytic privileges and how they can be utilized to secure access to SAP HANA information views and data.

Analytic privileges are used to grant or restrict access to data hosted within the SAP HANA system. They provide two levels of access. First, they provide read-only access to information views. To query an information view, you must have an associated analytic privilege; that is, users can't query an information view unless they're granted an analytic privilege referencing that information view or an analytic privilege that applies to all information views. Second, analytic privileges can be configured to restrict the data that an information view returns when queried. At a high level, they achieve this by filtering the attribute data during query execution. When using analytic privileges to filter data, each user accessing an information view will require his own unique user account, which becomes the basis for filtering the data.

In this chapter, we'll give an overview of analytic privileges and discuss the differences between static and dynamic analytic privileges. We'll also discuss how classic XML-based analytic privileges are being replaced with the new SQL-based analytic privileges, and we'll explain how to manage and create static and dynamic privileges. Finally, we'll review the process used to troubleshoot a grantee's effective analytic privileges and discuss the processes available to grant analytic privileges.

However, before we can begin discussing analytic privileges, first you need understand a few basics about SAP HANA information views, as we'll discuss next.

10.1 Overview of SAP HANA Information Views

Information view is a generic term describing any of the components used to create metadata-rich multidimensional models within the SAP HANA system. In addition to SAP HANA's ability to store data in a columnar table, we can also create information views to consolidate the complex relationships between tables and data elements. Information views are typically used to produce analytical models that aggregate quantifiable data elements by various attributes. For example, an information view for SAP ERP Controlling and Profitability Analysis (CO-PA) can be created to generate analytics for gross margin by time, material, customer, market, and region, attributes that become the basis for restricting the data using analytic privileges.

There are three main types of information views in SAP HANA: attribute, analytic, and calculation views. In this section, we'll briefly discuss these three view types and how they relate to analytic privileges.

10.1.1 Attribute Views

Attribute views are models created to produce views of master data. For example, a customer attribute view would generate columns such as customer ID, customer name, customer address line 1, customer region, customer sales region, and many more customer-related attributes. Attribute views are objects that help associated attributes with measures within analytic views. They're reusable objects that can be associated with multiple analytic views. On their own, attribute views don't create a complete multidimensional model. They simply model master data that will be used within a multidimensional model. Each column within the attribute view is a candidate for filtering with an analytic privilege. For example, we can limit the customers returned in a query based on the sales region attribute column.

Differences between SAP HANA 1.0 and SAP HANA 2.0

With SAP HANA 1.0, attribute views are created using SAP HANA Studio. Starting with SAP HANA 2.0, the XSA engine *SAP Web IDE application* will provide an updated interface for creating SAP HANA calculation views. Note that attribute views will be replaced with dimensional calculation views in the future.

10.1.2 Analytic Views

Analytic views are models that connect one or more attribute views to quantifiable transactions. Within analytic views, we define measure objects to aggregate values within specific tables. The combination of attribute views and analytic views create a complete multidimensional model. These views are capable of answering analytic questions, such as the following: What are my sales by region? Which are my top 10 customers by gross margin? What quantity did we sell in January of 2016? What is the current balance of the expense account?

Nonaggregate columns within analytic views can be filtered using analytic privileges. Analytic views also inherit the analytic privileges assigned to attribute view columns used within the definition of the analytic view.

Differences between SAP HANA 1.0 and SAP HANA 2.0

With SAP HANA 1.0, analytic views are created using SAP HANA Studio. Starting with SAP HANA 2.0, the XSA engine *SAP Web IDE application* will provide an updated interface for creating SAP HANA star join calculation views. Note that analytic views will be replaced by star join calculation views in the future.

10.1.3 Calculation Views

Historically, calculation views were the third type of information view available within SAP HANA. They were used to perform complex calculations, scripted calculations, and complex denormalizations of data. Beginning with SAP HANA 1.0 SPS 11 and SAP HANA 2.0 SPS 00, SAP has indicated that calculation views are the preferred information view for all multidimensional modeling within SAP HANA. To accommodate that direction, they introduced two new types of SAP HANA calculation views. In addition to standard calculation views, they also provide dimensional calculation views and star join calculation views. All calculation views share a common interface, and each type of calculation view is defined using options available at the initial stage of their creation. The views are as follows:

- **Dimensional calculation views**
  Fundamentally, *dimensional calculation views* are the same as attribute views. They're used to model master data and shared across multiple star join type calculation views. Attribute columns within these calculation views can be filtered using analytic privileges.
- **Star join calculation views**
  Star join calculation views are fundamentally the same as analytic views. They model transactional data and master data together to produce a complete multidimensional model. Attribute columns and dimensional calculation views used within the model can be filtered using analytic privileges.
- **Standard calculation views**
  Standard calculation views are the legacy version of the calculation view. They are used to model more advanced calculations, such as cross-fact aggregations, unions, and others that can't be solved using the star join methodology. Calculation views

can be constructed using a GUI and graphical objects. They can also be constructed using a scripting language such as SQL. Like all other information views, attribute columns defined within the calculation views can be filtered using analytic privileges.

10.2 Overview of Analytic Privileges

Analytic privileges govern access to data made available through SAP HANA's information views. There are two types of analytic privileges: *XML-based* and *SQL-based*. XML-based analytic privileges are the legacy type of analytic privilege. They're used to manage access to information views and provide both simple and dynamic filtering capabilities. SQL-based analytic privileges offer the ability to govern access to both information views and catalog database views. They also offer the ability to implement more complex filter logic using subquery statements, which overcomes some of the limitations associated with the filter logic available with XML-based analytic privileges.

10.2.1 XML-Based Analytic Privileges

Like all analytic privileges, XML-based analytic privileges provide a twofold level of access. First, they grant read access to the information views associated with the analytic privilege. Within the SAP HANA Studio GUI, we refer to them as *secured models*. In most security models, every information view will be associated with at least one analytic privilege, which will then be assigned to a role. When the analytic privilege is assigned to a role, grantees of that role will have read access to the information views.

Second, data restrictions can be applied within analytic privileges to statically or dynamically filter the data based on specified filter criteria. In the world of business intelligence, we call this *row-level security*. Rows of data are strategically filtered to restrict a user's access to specific rows of data. For example, if the security administrator needs to restrict data so that regional managers can only see records associated with their region, he'd use analytic privileges to do so.

XML-based analytic privileges provide two different types of restriction to filter data. We can define *static analytic privileges* using static filter conditions or *dynamic analytic privileges* that will dynamically look up filter conditions on a user-by-user basis. Let's look at these options in more detail.

Static Analytic Privileges

The methodology behind static analytic privileges dictates that an analytic privilege object be created for each unique filter scenario. For example, if an organization wanted to filter its information views for 10 different regions, it would need to define 10 different analytic privilege objects within the repository. It would then likely define 10 different roles for each analytic privilege and assign user accounts one or more corresponding roles for matching filter conditions. Figure 10.1 illustrates how the mapping of static analytic privileges to roles and users typically would be set up.

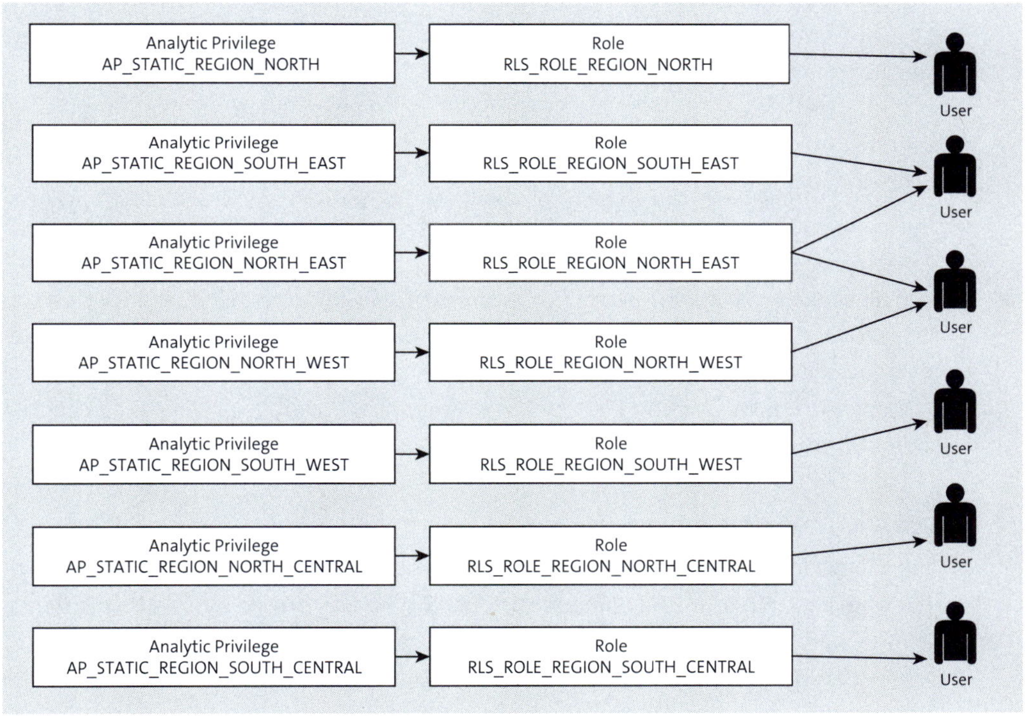

Figure 10.1 Static Analytic Privileges Mapped to Roles and Users

Let's assume that each analytic privilege filters the sales region attribute column within each assigned information view. For example, the attribute column SALES_REGION = 'NORTH' would be applied to the analytic privilege AP_STATIC_REGION_NORTH, and the SALES_REGION = 'SOUTH EAST' condition would be applied to the analytic privilege AP_STATIC_REGION_SOUTH_EAST. As shown in Figure 10.1, each filter condition would require an analytic privilege, and each analytic privilege would require a role. Each user can be granted one or more roles.

Each analytic privilege can be assigned one or more filter conditions or restrictions. When multiple conditions are configured within the same analytic privilege, they're executed using an AND condition, which means that all filter conditions or restrictions must be true. For example, if we configured an analytic privilege with the conditions SALES_REGION = 'NORTH' AND SELLING_PLANT = 'Chicago North', only data records having both restrictions would be returned when queried.

When a user is assigned one or more analytic privileges, the overall filter condition is executed using an OR condition, which means that either of the restrictions in each individual analytic privilege can be true. For example, a user is granted two roles, each with its own unique analytic privileges. The first role's analytic privilege requires the SALES_REGION = 'NORTH' restriction, and the second role's analytic privilege requires the SALES_REGION = 'SOUTH_EAST' restriction. When the user queries the assigned information view, the query would result in records with SALES_REGION of either NORTH or SOUTH_EAST.

Static analytic privileges are effective at providing data-level security. However, as you can see from Figure 10.1, each unique filter condition requires an analytic privilege object and role. When an organization requires a large quantity of restrictions on a variety of different attribute columns, a significant number of objects must be created and maintained. This proliferation of objects can produce a management issue in most SAP HANA systems. Let's look at how dynamic analytic privileges can help to solve this problem.

Dynamic Analytic Privileges

The methodology behind *dynamic analytic privileges* allows a single analytic privilege object to dynamically look up restrictions based on one or more data elements. Dynamic analytic privileges significantly reduce the number of objects required to support a large and diverse set of restrictions. Figure 10.2 provides an overview of the objects required to implement dynamic analytic privileges.

Dynamic analytic privileges work by retrieving the filter criteria from a catalog table within the SAP HANA system. The catalog table, at a minimum, must map each SAP HANA user account to a specific data element. For example, each user account is mapped to one or more regions within a table. Users with multiple data element assignments will have multiple rows defined in the table, and each row will map the user account name to a unique data element. These data elements will be dynamically generated and applied to the analytic privilege when an associated information view is queried.

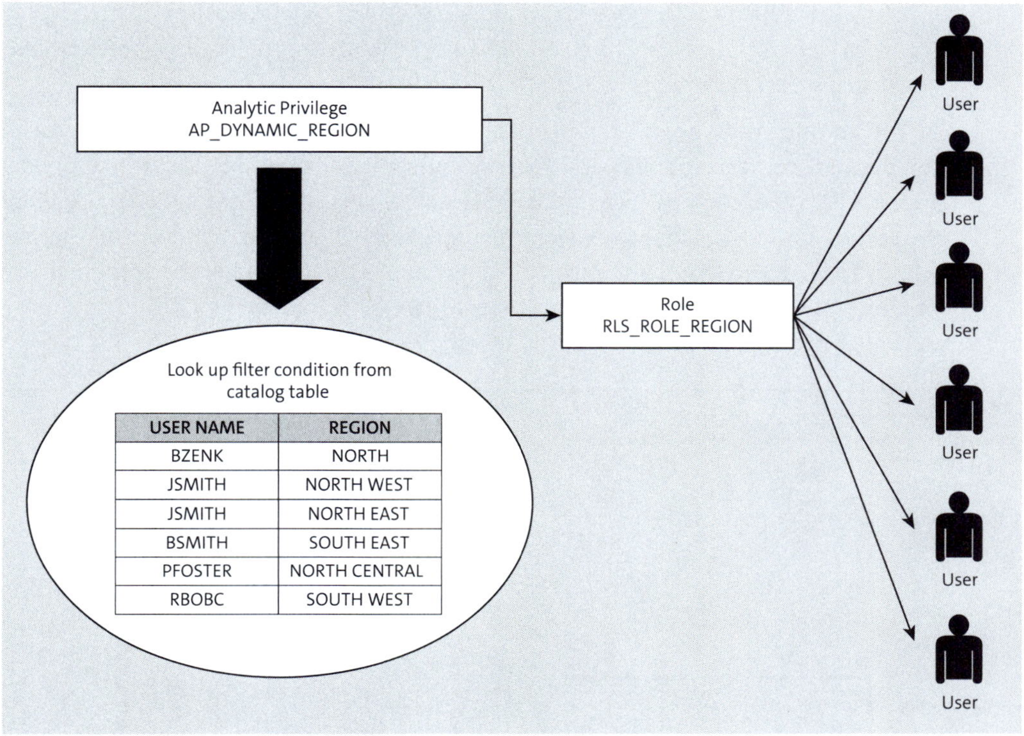

Figure 10.2 Dynamic Analytic Privilege Mapping to Roles and Users

The major benefit of dynamic analytic privileges is that they reduce the number of analytic privilege and role objects required to facilitate data restrictions. For example, in the previous region-based example, using dynamic analytic privileges would require only a single analytic privilege and role. It isn't necessary to create an analytic privilege and role for each filter condition. However, the catalog table containing the user-to-region mapping would need to be maintained. In an ideal scenario, it could be programmatically derived and refreshed from an external source.

10.2.2 SQL-Based Analytic Privileges

SQL-based analytic privileges grant access to either information views or catalog views. In this chapter, we'll only discuss the options for restricting information views using the analytic privilege objects stored in the SAP HANA repository. It's important to note that SQL based analytic privileges are a type of structured privilege. Typically, when we refer to SQL-based analytic privileges, we're referring to the graphical analytic privilege objects created in the SAP HANA repository. When working with catalog views, we typically create structured privileges or refer to the restrictions as structured privileges.

Before an information view can use SQL-based analytic privileges, it must be registered for an authorization check. When defining an information view, the option to support SQL analytic privileges must be selected. This option is found on the **View Properties** tab, in the **Apply Privileges:** dropdown. Figure 10.3 shows this option within an analytic view, highlighting the **View Properties** tab ❶ and the dropdown list in which the **SQL Analytic Privileges** option can be found ❷. You'll find the same options when working with calculation views.

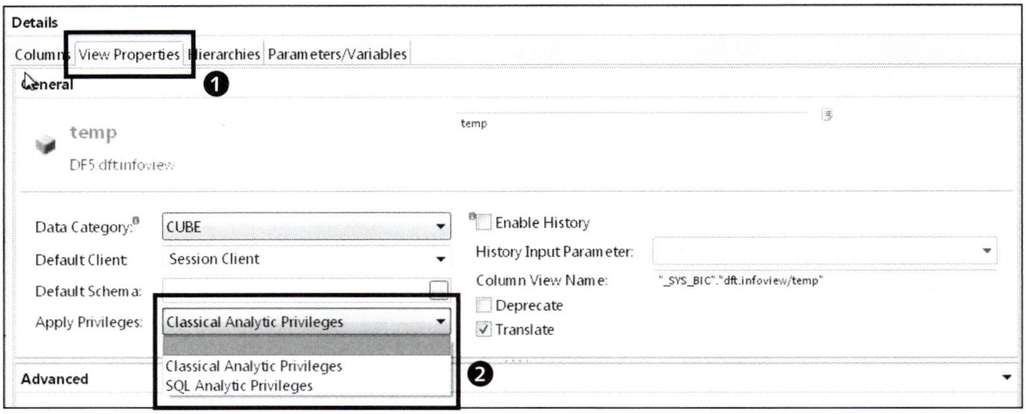

Figure 10.3 Setting SQL Analytic Privileges Option in Analytic View

SQL analytic privileges also offer the ability to define both simple and complex data restrictions using complex SQL filter logic. They support three options for defining a restriction: static, SQL expression, and dynamic.

Static Analytic Privileges

Static SQL-based analytic privileges are like their XML counterparts, and they too lead to scalability issues when an organization requires a diverse allotment of filter conditions. You can assume that all the benefits and issues associated with static XML-based privileges also apply to static SQL-based analytic privileges.

Dynamic Analytic Privileges

Dynamic SQL-based analytic privileges are also like their XML-based counterparts. However, SQL-based analytic privileges look up filter conditions as opposed to filter values. For example, dynamic XML-based analytic privileges will look up and return an array of values such as 10, 100, 300, 400, and 900. Dynamic SQL-based analytic privileges will look up and return a single string value, such as (CUSTOMER IN (10, 100, 300, 400, 900)). This string value becomes the syntax for a condition used to filter an information view. They also support more complex conditions, such as ((CUSTOMER = 900) or (PLANT = 1000)). We'll explore dynamic analytic privileges further in Section 10.5.2.

SQL Expression Analytic Privileges

Dynamic expression-based SQL analytic privileges are unique and don't have an XML-based counterpart. These types of analytic privileges are dynamic, but they don't require the use of stored procedures to look up filter conditions; the filter conditions are manually crafted into a filter expression. Filter expressions support the use of subqueries and other complex operators in their definition. For example, we can use a complex subquery expression to dynamically filter data for a given user. The following code represents such an example expression:

```
"CUSTOMERKEY" IN
(SELECT DISTINCT CUSTOMERKEY
FROM "SECURITY"."Security.ap::RLS_CUSTOMER_ACCESS"
WHERE USERNAME = SESSION_USER)
```

These expressions can be even more complex than this example, and they support a wide variety of solutions. We'll explore these further in Section 10.6.

10.3 _SYS_BI_CP_ALL: A System-Generated Analytic Privilege

Only one system-generated analytic privilege is included with SAP HANA by default: The system-generated analytic privilege _SYS_BI_CP_ALL is a special analytic privilege that provides access to all information views and all data produced by an information view configured using classic XML-based analytic privileges. When a grantee is granted this analytic privilege, it will override the restrictions of other classic XML-based analytic privileges that have been assigned to the same grantee; therefore, it should only be granted to grantees that do not require any analytic privileges.

Based on testing and research, the _SYS_BI_CP_ALL analytic privilege doesn't override SQL-based analytic privileges. When using SQL-based analytic privileges, all users require at least one custom analytic privilege referencing each information view they wand to query. To grant full access to an information view, simply reference the information view without any defined restrictions. This will grant such grantees full data access to the referenced information view, even if other SQL-based analytic privileges are granted to the same user. Now, let's look at the processes used to create analytic privileges.

10.4 Managing Static Analytic Privileges

There are two types of static analytic privileges we can create: XML-based or SQL-based. Both options are nearly identical, with a few exceptions. SAP has not officially deprecated the classic XML-based option as of HANA 2.0 SPS 00, but the documentation indicates that SAP will do so in the future. UIs refer to XML-based analytic privileges as the *classic option* as well. Therefore, we recommend that all new development be based on SQL analytic privilege workflows. In this section, we'll provide instructions for creating both types.

Converting XML-Based Analytic Privileges to SQL-Based

The SAP HANA Modeling Guide provides documentation for the steps necessary to convert XML-based analytic privileges to SQL-based analytic privileges. Look for the section titled Convert Classical XML-Based Analytic Privileges to SQL-Based Analytic Privileges in the guide, which can be found at *http://help.sap.com/hana/SAP_HANA_Modeling_Guide_for_SAP_HANA_Studio_en.pdf.*

10.4.1 Creating Static XML-Based Analytic Privileges

Analytic privileges are development artifacts and as such are created and stored in the SAP HANA repository. Typically, they're stored in a package with limited access. For example, the same package structure used to store repository roles would be an ideal location. This package structure should already be set up so that only role administrators have the proper package privileges. We can use any perspective within SAP HANA Studio that provides development-level access to the package repository, but we must have the appropriate package privileges to create and activate these development artifacts.

To create an analytic privilege, open SAP HANA Studio. Within the repository, locate a package in a secure location. Right-click the package and choose **New** followed by

Analytic Privilege.... A pop-up window will appear labeled **New Analytic Privilege** (see Figure 10.4).

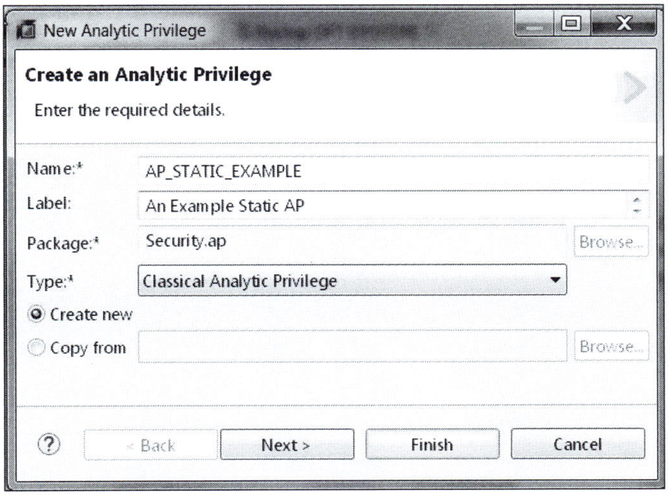

Figure 10.4 New XML-Based Analytic Privilege Window

In this window, specify the technical name of the analytic privilege in the **Name** field. The name can only contain the characters Aa–Zz and the underscore (_) special character. In the **Label** field, enter a description for the analytic privilege. The **Package** field should already contain the package name. In the **Type** dropdown, choose the appropriate option based on the referenced information views. For example, select the **Classical Analytic Privilege** option for referenced information views configured to use classical analytic privileges. Choose the **Create new** option when creating a new analytic privilege, or choose the **Copy from** option to base the new analytic privilege on an existing analytic privilege. Use the **Browse** button to specify the existing analytic privilege. Click **Next** to continue.

A new window will appear, with **Select Information Models** in the title (see Figure 10.5). In this optional step, you can preselect the information views that will be restricted within the new analytic privilege.

To select information views at this stage, locate them in the package hierarchy on the left side of the window, select them, and click the **Add** button located between the left and right sides of the window. The selected information views will appear on the right side. Click **Finish** to generate the analytic privileges. Note that you still can add or remove information views after clicking **Finish**.

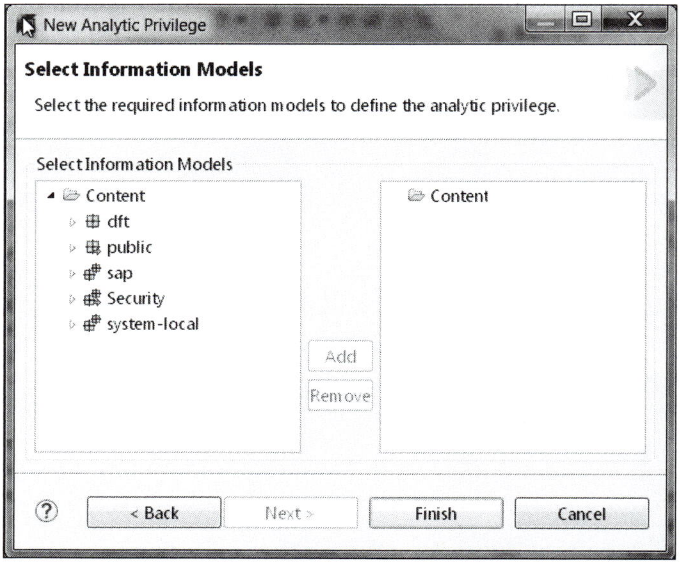

Figure 10.5 Selecting Information Views for Analytic Privileges

The XML-based or classic analytic privilege management window is organized into six main sections, as illustrated in Figure 10.6.

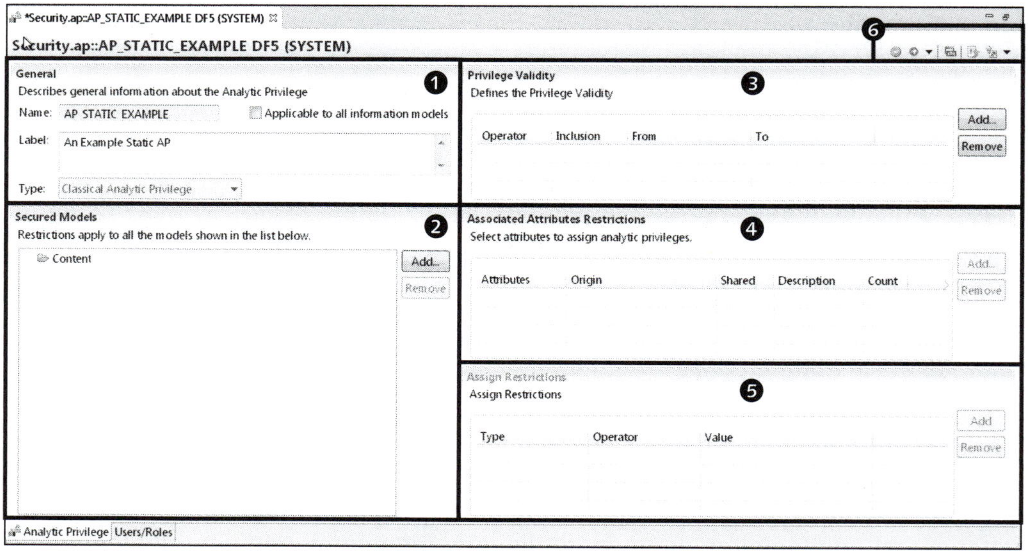

Figure 10.6 XML-Based Analytic Privilege Management Window

The **General** section ❶ provides two key options. The first option allows us to update the **Label** field, and the second option, titled **Applicable to all information models**, provides universal capabilities for the analytic privilege. When the **Applicable to all information models** option is selected, all information views will be subject to the analytic privilege restrictions. For example, if there are 12 information views activated in the system and each has an attribute column with a technical name of `CUSTOMER_REGION`, the restrictions defined within this analytic privilege will apply even if they aren't explicitly referenced within the analytic privilege.

The **Secured Models** section ❷ provides the option to add or remove referenced information models. If the **Applicable to all information models** option isn't selected, information views in this section will have query access to the referenced models and be subject to any restrictions defined.

The **Privilege Validity** section ❸ can be used to define a validity period for the restrictions. To define a validity period, click the **Add...** button, then choose an **Operator** to define the date range. Use the **From** and **To** date fields to define the date based on the chosen operator. When a validity is defined, the analytic privileges will only be applied within the date range specified. If no validity is defined, the privilege will be valid on any date. To remove the validity, select it in the list and click the **Remove** button.

The **Associated Attribute Restrictions** section ❹ is used to select the attribute columns that will be subject to the restrictions. Click the **Add...** button to select an attribute column from an information view referenced in the **Secured Models** section. If the attribute column is derived from a dimensional calculation view or attribute view, the box in the column labeled **Shared** will be checked. To remove the attribute column, select it in the list and click the **Remove** button.

The **Assign Restrictions** section ❺ provides an interface to define the filter conditions or restrictions for each column specified in the **Associated Attribute Restrictions** section. To define a filter condition, highlight an attribute column in the **Associated Attribute Restrictions** section, then, in the **Assign Restrictions** section, click the **Add...** button to define the filter condition. For static analytic privileges, choose the type **Fixed**. Select an **Operator** from the dropdown menu to define part of the filter condition. For example, choose **Equal** if the filter condition requires that the attribute column value equal the static value specified in the **Value** field. Alternatively, choose **GreaterEqual** if the value must be greater than or equal to the static value specified. The **Value** field contains the static value used in the filter condition.

Filter conditions in the static XML-based analytic privileges support the use of the **Between**, **ContainsPattern**, **Equal**, **GreaterEqual**, **GreaterThan**, **Is Not Null**, **IsNull**, **LessEqual**, and **LessThan** operators. If multiple restrictions are applied to the same attribute column, all filter conditions will be executed as true or executed using an **AND** condition. Figure 10.7 shows static restrictions configured for the example attribute **CUSTOMERKEY**. The filter conditions of **Between 0–99999** and **Is Not Null** are applied in the example.

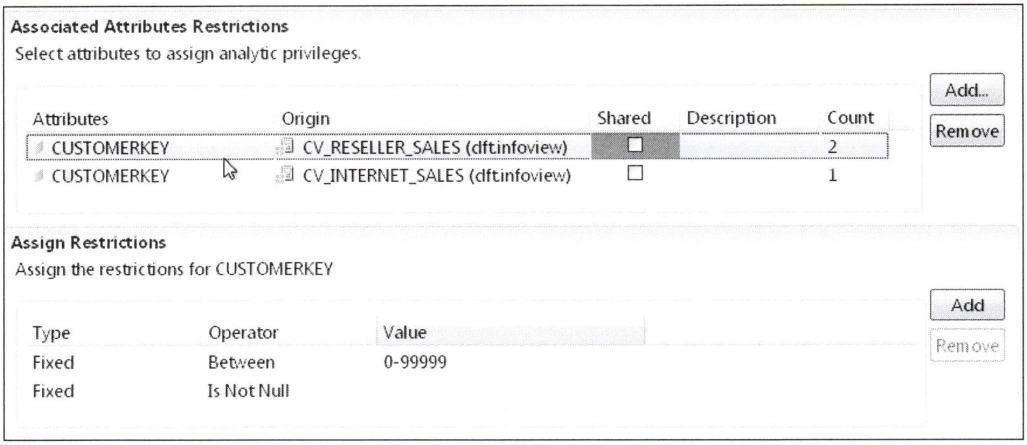

Figure 10.7 Example Restrictions Applied in an Analytic Privilege

Note that the **Count** column in Figure 10.7 and the **Associated Attribute Restrictions** section indicate that two restrictions have been applied to the attribute column, but the second row indicates that only one restriction has been applied. This is because each row in the **Associated Attribute Restrictions** section has its own corresponding restrictions set in the **Assign Restrictions** section just below it.

The icon bar section ❻ in Figure 10.6 provides icon button options—from left to right, **Save and Validate**, **Save and Activate**, **DISPLAY XML** definition, view the **Activation History**, and switch to a **Historical Version** of the analytic privileges. As you hover your mouse pointer over each icon, a disruptive text pop-up will appear. The second button, **Save and Activate**, should be used when you're ready to deploy the analytic privileges. Clicking **Save and Activate** will both save the analytic privilege within the repository and deploy it to the system for use within a role.

Once the analytic privileges are activated, their restrictions won't apply until the analytic privileges are granted to existing roles or users. If no competing analytic privileges are also applied to the grantee, queries to the referenced information views will be limited based on the defined filter conditions or restrictions.

10.4.2 Creating Static SQL-Based Analytic Privileges

The process used to create static SQL-based analytic privileges is nearly identical to that of its classic XML-based counterpart. To create a static SQL-based analytic privilege, open SAP HANA Studio. Within the repository, locate a package in a secure location. Right-click the package and choose **New** followed by **Analytic Privilege....** A pop-up window will appear labeled **New Analytic Privilege** (see Figure 10.8).

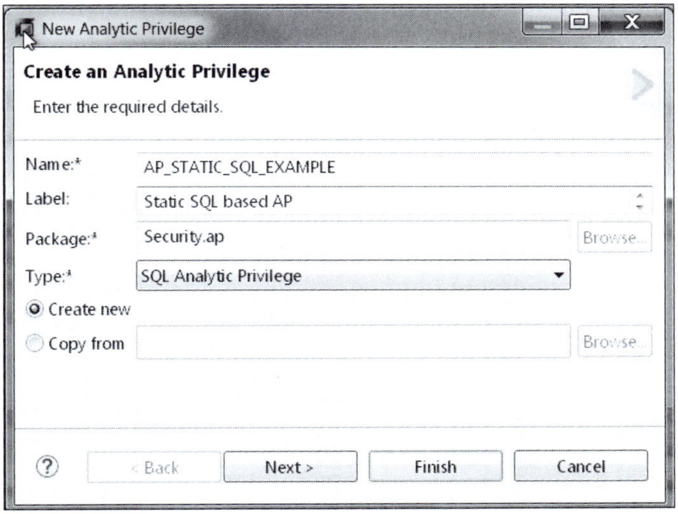

Figure 10.8 New SQL-Based Analytic Privilege Window

To specify the use of SQL analytic privileges, the **Type** dropdown must be set to **SQL Analytic Privilege.** Other than this difference, the process is identical to what was outlined in Section 10.4.1. In the **New Analytic Privilege** window, specify the technical name of the analytic privilege in the **Name** field. The name can only contain the characters A–Z, a–z, and the underscore special character. In the **Label** field, enter a description. The **Package** field should already contain the package name. In the **Type** dropdown choose the appropriate option based on the referenced information views. For example, select the **SQL Analytic Privilege** option for referenced information views configured to use SQL analytic privileges. Choose the **Create new** option when creating a new analytic privilege. Choose the **Copy from** option to base the new analytic privilege on an existing analytic privilege. Use the **Browse** button to specify the existing analytic privileges. Click **Next** to continue.

A new window will appear with **Select Information Models** in the title (see Figure 10.9). Here, you can optionally preselect the information views that will be restricted within the new analytic privilege.

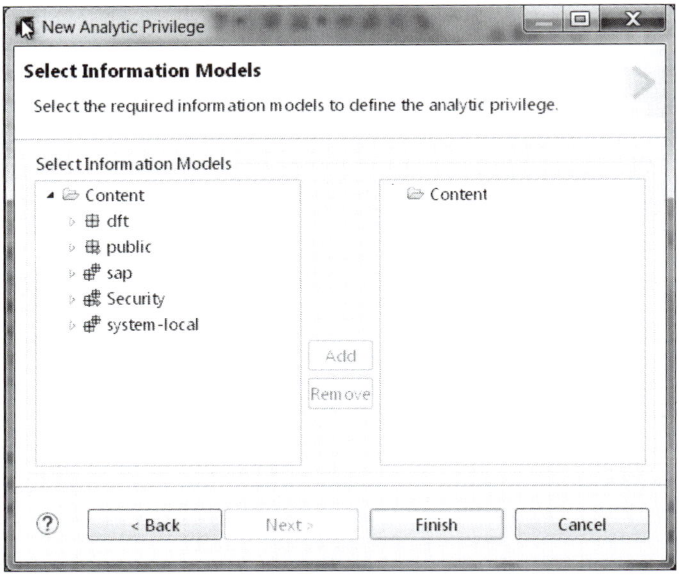

Figure 10.9 Selecting Information Views for Analytic Privileges

To select information views at this stage, locate them in the package hierarchy on the left side of the window, select them, and click the **Add** button. The selected information views will appear on the right side. Click **Finish** to generate the analytic privileges. Note that you still can add or remove information views after this step.

The SQL-based analytic privilege management window is almost identical to the window used to manage XML-based analytic privileges. One key difference is that the SQL-based analytic privilege windows has three additional options, shown in Figure 10.10 section ❶.

To configure a static analytic privilege, the **Attributes** option must be selected. Later in this chapter, we'll explore the use of the remaining two options, **Dynamic** (Section 10.5.2) and **SQL Editor** (Section 10.6), seen in section ❶.

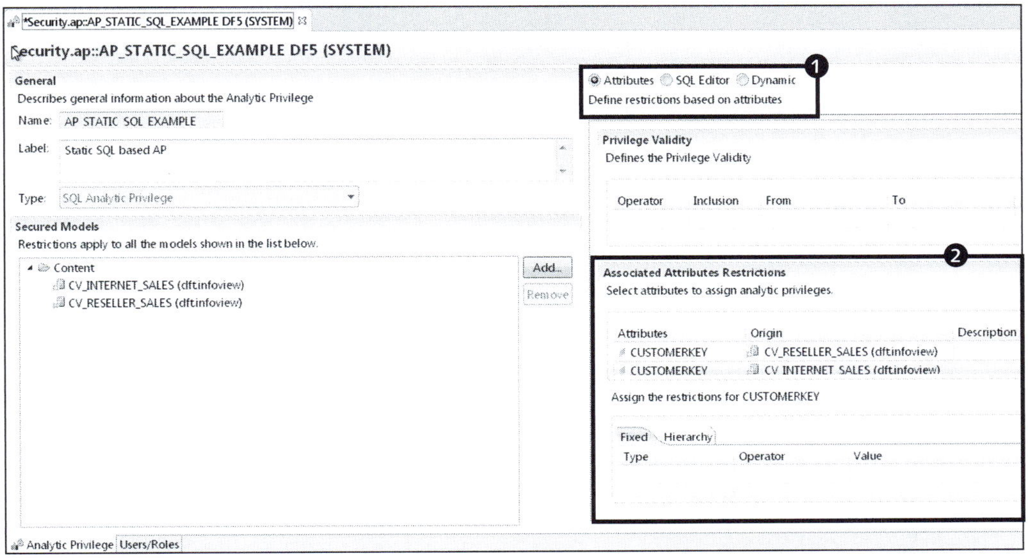

Figure 10.10 SQL-Based Analytic Privileges Management Window

With the **Attributes** option selected, the configuration for the **Secured Models** and **Privilege Validity** sections is identical to the steps provided in Section 10.4.1. However, Figure 10.10 only contains an **Associated Attribute Restrictions** section ❷, without a dedicated **Assign Restrictions** section. This is because the options to create filter conditions are embedded in the **Associated Attribute Restrictions** section. At the bottom of this section, there are two tabs. The first tab, **Fixed**, is used to define static filter conditions. This is like the options found in the XML-based management interface. The second tab, **Hierarchy**, is used to define static filter conditioning based on a calculation view's hierarchy metadata.

Note that if you reference an information view in the **Secure Models** section and fail to define any restrictions, roles granted this analytic privilege will have full query access to the referenced information view and any data it governs. This is true even when the grantee has multiple contradicting SQL-based analytic privileges also granted for the same information view. Based on testing, in such cases, the filter condition 1 = 1 is effectively derived and applied as a restriction. All other restrictions are effectively ignored, because 1 = 1 is true for all records.

10.5 Managing Dynamic Analytic Privileges

We can create either XML-based or SQL-based dynamic analytic privileges. The options are similar, but there are a few major differences. Note that SAP documentation indicates XML-based analytic privileges will be replaced in the future by SQL-based, so we recommend that all new development be based on the SQL analytic privilege workflows. In this section, we'll first provide a brief overview of XML-based analytic privileges. Then, because SQL-based analytic privileges are the recommended approach going forward, we'll provide a more through discussion covering their end-to-end creation process.

10.5.1 Dynamic XML-Based Analytic Privileges

Dynamic XML-based analytic privileges are set up within the same interface used to define static XML-based analytic privileges (see Section 10.4.1). However, to configure the analytic privileges as dynamic, we must select different options within the **Assign Restrictions** section of the management interface. Within this section, we must change the value of the **Type** column from **Fixed** to **Catalog Procedure** or to **Repository Procedure**. The **Operator** column should contain an operator that facilitates the results of the stored procedure selected in the **Value** column. In most cases, we choose the **IN** operator because the procedure will return an array of values.

Before we discuss the configuration of the stored procedure, let's review how XML-based dynamic privileges are structured. These analytic privileges are essentially configured to perform a lookup into a catalog table to retrieve an array of filter values for a given user. The lookup is based on user name, which is derived from the SAP HANA user account querying a referenced information view. The table used to store the mapping data requires a minimum of two columns: The first column will contain the user name, and the second column will contain the filter value. Table 10.1 provides an example of how this table is structured and includes some example data.

USER_NAME	FILTER_VALUE
JHARRIS01	North Central
TTIM03	South West
WTRAN05	North Central
WTRAN05	South Central

Table 10.1 Mapping to Facilitate XML-Based Dynamic Analytic Privileges

The stored procedure selected for use with the analytic privilege must be configured to return a single value or an array of values from this table. Therefore, the stored procedure's output variable must be configured as a *table type*. Table types are catalog objects that act as kinds of virtual tables. They're most often used to temporarily define the tabular output of a stored procedure. For example, we can use the following SQL code to define the table type required to accommodate the output of this stored procedure:

```
CREATE TYPE "SECURITY"."CUSTOMER_ACCESS" AS TABLE ( "CUSTOMERKEY" int);
```

The procedure itself is defined to output one or more records based on the table containing the user-to-value mappings. The SAP HANA-specific SQLScript in Listing 10.1 will create a procedure that accommodates these requirements.


```
CREATE PROCEDURE "SECURITY"."SP_RLS_
CUSTOMER" ( OUT VAL      "SECURITY"."CUSTOMER_ACCESS" )
LANGUAGE SQLSCRIPT
SQL SECURITY DEFINER
READS SQL DATA AS
BEGIN
      VAL = SELECT FILTER_VALUE FROM "SECURITY"."RLS_CUSTOMER_ACCESS"
WHERE USER_NAME = SESSION_USER;
END;
```

Listing 10.1 Stored Procedure Used with XML-Based Dynamic Analytic Privileges

In the SQLScript code, note the line that begins `VAL = SELECT FILTER_VALUE FROM`. The `SELECT` statement in this line queries the table and uses the `WHERE` clause of `USER_NAME = SESSION_USER` to refine the values returned. The `SESSION_USER` variable is known to the SAP HANA system and is replaced at runtime with the user name assigned this analytic privilege.

For example, assume that the user account WTRAN05 is used to authenticate with SAP HANA when querying an information view. WTRAN05 is granted an XML-based dynamic analytic privilege. When WTRAN05 queries an information view referenced by the dynamic analytic privilege, the filter condition within the stored procedure is changed from `USER_NAME = SESSION_USER` to `USER_NAME = WTRAN05`. All values in the table associated with WTRAN05 are returned by the table type output variable. The array of values is then passed to the execution engine and used to filter the information view. Based on Table 10.1, the values `North Central` and `South Central` will be used as the filter condition.

You should now have a basic understanding of the structure of an XML-based dynamic analytic privilege. Remember that this type of analytic privilege will be replaced by SQL-based dynamic analytic privileges. In the next section, we'll review the process used to create SQL-based dynamic analytic privileges in detail.

10.5.2 Dynamic SQL-Based Analytic Privileges

Dynamic SQL-based analytic privileges offer the ability to perform programmatic lookups of filter conditions based on a mapping between user names and filter conditions. XML-based dynamic analytic privileges required individual data values, but SQL-based dynamic analytic privileges require filter conditions, like a portion of what we might use in a SQL `WHERE` clause. The use of filter conditions supports complex and diverse filters that are dynamically generated for a given user. For example, we can reference multiple attribute columns and filter operator types in the same condition clause. In contrast, each XML-based dynamic analytic privilege restriction is limited to a single attribute column and array of filter values.

To accommodate the lookups, a table must exist that maps each user account to one or more filter conditions. Table 10.2 is a basic example of how this table and its data should be structured. The table can be more complex, but at a minimum it must adhere to this structure.

User Name	Filter Condition
JHARRIS01	("REGION" = ' North Central')
TTIM03	("REGION" = ' South West')
WTRAN05	("REGION" = ' North Central')
TIMG05	("REGION" = ' South Central')

Table 10.2 Example Mapping Used with SQL-Based Dynamic Analytic Privileges

In the table, the left column contains the user name. The user name values should exactly match configured SAP HANA user account names. The column on the right provides the filter conditions, which will be retrieved and added to the execution of the information view. They should be constructed in a way that matches an attribute column to a data value. Again, this is like how we would construct a filter within a SQL `WHERE` clause. The following syntax represents the construction of a basic single column filter condition:

```
( <"COLUMN"> operator <'VALUE'> )
```

Parenthesis are recommended around the entire condition statement. Attribute columns should be double quoted. The supported operators are `=`, `<=`, `<`, `>=`, `>`, `LIKE`, `BETWEEN`, and `IN`. The value should be single quoted if it's a string value. Single quotes are not required for number type values. Note that subquery filter conditions aren't supported in this mode.

Unlike XML-based analytic privileges, the stored procedure used to return these conditions must only support a single-valued string output variable. If multiple rows for a given user are stored in the table, the stored procedure code will need to condense them into a single value. Alternatively, the condition we store in the table can be quite complex, using a mixture of columns and operators and eliminating the need to store multiple values for a given user. For example, the following condition is also supported for a given user:


```
((REGION IN ('NE','NW','SW','NC') ) or (PLANT IN ('1001','1005','1006')))
```

Again, to accommodate the lookup of the values from within the table, we need to create a stored procedure. Ideally, we'd create a repository-based stored procedure, but catalog stored procedures are supported as well. Keep in mind that the _SYS_REPO system account will require access to the table and stored procedure. Therefore, it's best to create these objects within the repository for which _SYS_REPO will be the owner with full access. The objects will also be transportable within a delivery unit when they're created within the repository.

The structure of the stored procedure must comply with a few conditions. First, it must be configured as a `DEFINER`-based procedure. This means that the creator of the procedure will be used for validation when executed. Second, the procedure must be considered read-only. It should only return values without executing any *data manipulation language (DML)* statements. Third, it can't contain any input parameters. Fourth, the procedure can only contain a single-value output parameter with a data type of `VARCHAR` or `NVARCHAR`. Finally, _SYS_REPO must have full access to the procedure and any tables it references.

To better understand the process, let's walk through the three main steps required to implement a dynamic analytic privilege. First, we must create a table to host the user and data element mappings. Second, we must create a stored procedure to perform the lookups of the values. Finally, we'll construct a SQL-based dynamic analytic privilege.

Creating a Repository-Based Security Table

To simplify the design, we'll create a repository-based table. We can create this table using the development perspective within SAP HANA Studio. With that perspective active, locate the repositories on the left side of the perspective. Expand the **System** node and **Repository Container** node to reveal the package repository. Locate a secure package location to host the repository-based table. Right-click the desired package node and choose **New • Other**. A window titled **New** will appear. Within that window, search for "table" in the **Wizards** section. Choose **Database Table** from the list and click **Next**. A window titled **Database Table** will appear. In the **File Name** field, enter the name of the repository-based table. Click **Next** to define the table. Figure 10.11 provides an example of the script we can use to define this table.

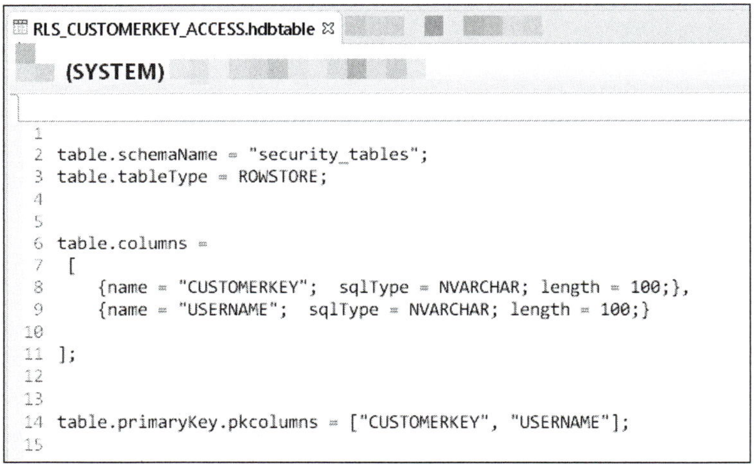


```
table.schemaName = "security_tables";
table.tableType = ROWSTORE;


table.columns =
 [
    {name = "CUSTOMERKEY";  sqlType = NVARCHAR; length = 100;},
    {name = "USERNAME";  sqlType = NVARCHAR; length = 100;}

 ];


table.primaryKey.pkcolumns = ["CUSTOMERKEY", "USERNAME"];
```

Figure 10.11 Example Repository-Based Table Definition Script

The example table is configured with two columns. The first column contains the filter conditions; in the example, the **CUSTOMERKEY** column was used. The second column is **USERNAME**.

With the table created, we must now populate it with the mapping data. There are multiple options for populating this table. We can import data from a file, insert records manually using SQL, or use supported tools to extract the data from other sources and load it into the security table. Figure 10.12 shows sample data within the table.

CUSTOMERKEY	USERNAME
(CUSTOMERKEY >= '0' and CUSTOMERKEY <= '100')	TEST_SVC3
(CUSTOMERKEY >= '1000' and CUSTOMERKEY <= '2000')	TEST_SVC3
(CUSTOMERKEY >= '5000' and CUSTOMERKEY <= '15000')	BJONES
(CUSTOMERKEY >= '1000' and CUSTOMERKEY <= '2000')	FGORE
_ALL	SYSTEM

Figure 10.12 Example Filter Conditions in Security Table

The INSERT statements in Listing 10.2 provide an example of how the data can be populated in the example table.


```
insert into "SECURITY"."Security.ap::RLS_CUSTOMER_ACCESS"
values ('(CUSTOMERKEY >= ''0'' and CUSTOMERKEY <= ''100'')','TEST_SVC3');

insert into "SECURITY"."Security.ap::RLS_CUSTOMER_ACCESS"
values ('(CUSTOMERKEY >= ''1000'' and CUSTOMERKEY <= ''2000'')','TEST_SVC3');

insert into "SECURITY"."Security.ap::RLS_CUSTOMER_ACCESS"
values ('(CUSTOMERKEY >= ''5000'' and CUSTOMERKEY <= ''15000'')','BJONES');

insert into "SECURITY"."Security.ap::RLS_CUSTOMER_ACCESS"
values ('(CUSTOMERKEY >= ''1000'' and CUSTOMERKEY <= ''2000'')','FGORE');

insert into "SECURITY"."Security.ap::RLS_CUSTOMER_ACCESS"
values ( '_ALL','SYSTEM');
```

Listing 10.2 A Series of Five SQL INSERT Statements Used to Populate an Example Table

Creating a Repository-Based Stored Procedure

To simplify the design, we'll create a repository-based stored procedure. We can create this stored procedure using the development perspective within SAP HANA Studio. With that perspective active, locate the repositories on the left side. Expand the **System** node and workspace node to reveal the package repository. Locate a secure package location to host the repository-based stored procedure. Right-click the desired package node and choose **New • Other**. A window titled **New** will appear. In that window, search for "stored procedure" in the **Wizards** section. Choose **Stored Procedure** from the list and click **Next**.

A window titled **Stored Procedure** will appear. Specify the file name of the stored procedure in the **File Name:** text box. For **File Format:**, select **Text (.hdbprocedure)**. In the **Target Schema:** text box, enter the name of the schema in which the catalog version of the stored procedure will reside. Click **Finish** to define the stored procedure code.

A SQLScript editor window will appear, and you can begin defining your stored procedure code. Figure 10.13 provides an example stored procedure that can be used to retrieve the various conditions from the table.

```
PROCEDURE "SECURITY"."Security.ap::SP_RLS_CUSTOMER_ACCESS" (OUT OUT_FILTER NVARCHAR(256))
    LANGUAGE SQLSCRIPT
    SQL SECURITY DEFINER
    DEFAULT SCHEMA "SECURITY"
    READS SQL DATA AS
    v_Filter VARCHAR(256);
    CURSOR v_Cursor FOR SELECT CUSTOMERKEY FROM "Security.ap::RLS_CUSTOMER_ACCESS"
                        WHERE "USERNAME" = SESSION_USER;
BEGIN

v_Filter := '';
FOR cur_row AS v_Cursor
    DO
        v_Filter := cur_row."CUSTOMERKEY" || ' or ' || v_Filter;
    END FOR;
    /*No Access*/
    IF v_Filter = ''
    THEN OUT_FILTER := '(CUSTOMERKEY <= 0)';
    /*Full Access*/
    ELSEIF
    v_Filter like '%_ALL or%'
    THEN OUT_FILTER := '(CUSTOMERKEY >= 0)';
    /*Conditional Access*/
    ELSE
    v_filter :='(' || TRIM( TRAILING ' or ' FROM v_Filter) || ')';
    OUT_FILTER := v_Filter;
    END IF;

END;
```

Figure 10.13 Example Stored Procedure Used with SQL-Based Dynamic Analytic Privileges

This example is programed to retrieve the filter conditions from the mapping table. If no records are found for a given user, a filter condition of `customerkey <= 0` is returned. Because all customer keys are greater than 0, this condition simply returns no data. If the value `_ALL` is found in the table, the condition `customerkey > 0` is returned, resulting in all records being returned. For users with a single condition or multiple conditions in the table, the procedure uses a cursor loop to concatenate multiple condition lines together, using an `OR` operator to divide them. Based on the example data, Figure 10.14 provides the output of the stored procedure when the example user TEST_SVC3 executes it. The output is on line **1** under the column header **out(1)**.

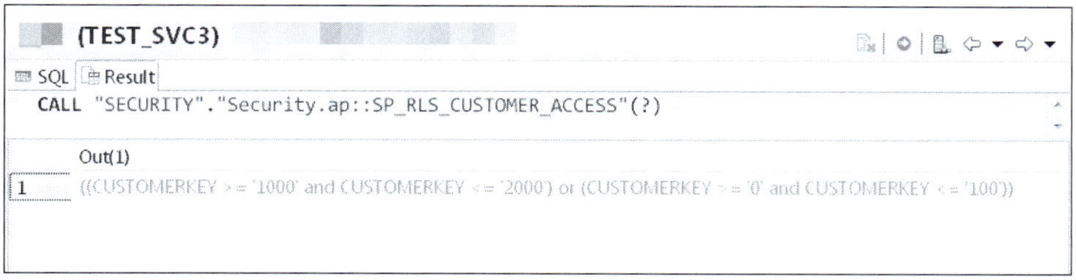

Figure 10.14 Example Stored Procedure Output When Executed by User

As you can see from the results, two different filter conditions are concatenated together using an `OR` operator. This design is an optional feature of this example. We could have simply stored this exact condition in the table and avoided the need to construct it using the stored procedure code. However, it illustrates the need to return only a single string for each user.

Also notice within the example that the cursor `v_Cursor` is based on a SQL `SELECT` statement that uses the `SESSION_USER` system variable in the `WHERE` clause to dynamically filter the security table based on the user name querying the information view. At runtime, `SESSION_USER` is replaced with the user accessing the information view. This is critical to the functionality of the dynamic analytic privileges.

When you've completed programing the stored procedure, press `Ctrl`+`F3` to save and activate the stored procedure.

Defining a SQL-Based Dynamic Analytic Privilege

To create a SQL-based dynamic analytic privilege, open SAP HANA Studio. Within the repository, locate a package in a secure location. Right-click the package and choose **New** followed by **Analytic Privilege...**. A pop-up window will appear labeled **New Analytic Privilege** (see Figure 10.15).

In this window, specify the technical name of the analytic privilege in the field labeled **Name**. The name can only contain the characters A–Z, a–z, and the underscore special character. In the **Label** field, specify a description for the analytic privilege. The **Package** field should already contain the package name. The **Type** dropdown must contain the option **SQL Analytic Privilege** because the information views are configured to use SQL analytic privileges. Choose the **Create new** option when creating a new analytic privilege, or choose the **Copy from** option to base the new analytic privilege on an existing analytic privilege. Use the **Browse** button to specify the existing analytic privilege. Click **Next** to continue.

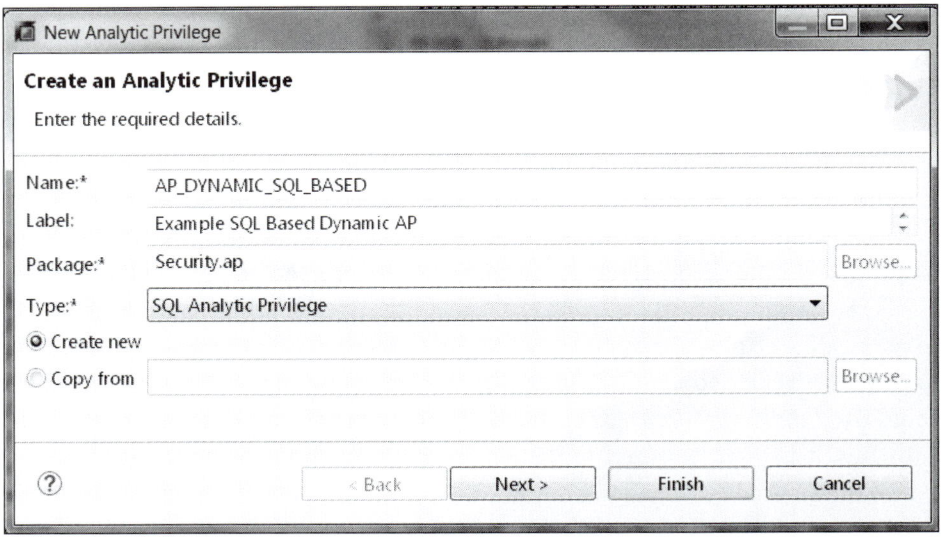

Figure 10.15 New SQL-Based Analytic Privilege Window

A new window will appear with **Select Information Models** in the title (Figure 10.16). In this optional step, you can preselect the information views that will be restricted within the new analytic privilege.

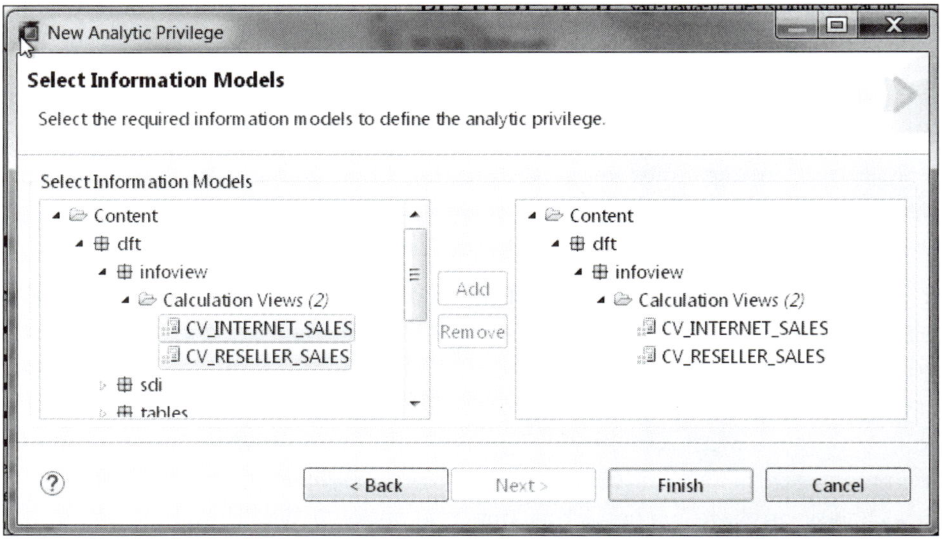

Figure 10.16 Selecting Information Views for Analytic Privileges

To select information views at this stage, locate them in the package hierarchy on the left, select them, and click **Add**. The selected information views will appear on the right side. Click **Finish** to generate the analytic privileges. Note that you still can add or remove additional information views later.

The SQL-based dynamic analytic privileges management window is divided into four main sections, as shown in Figure 10.17.

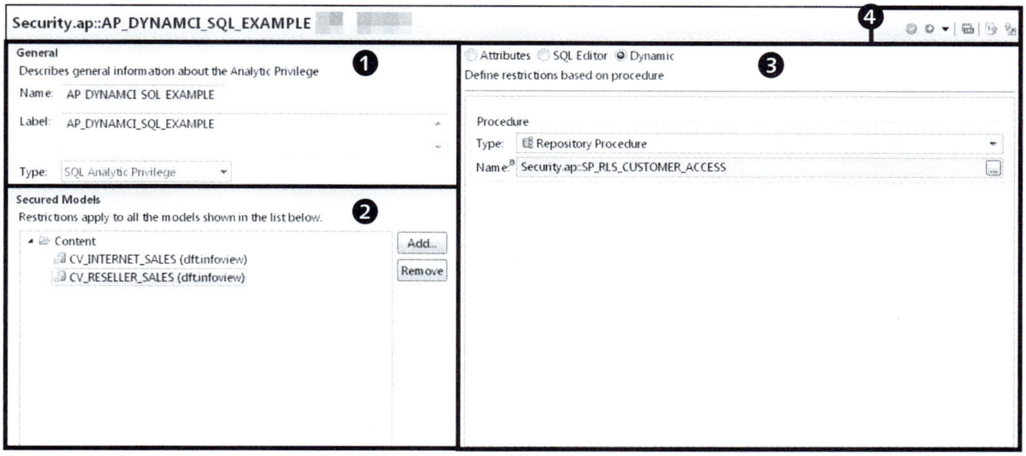

Figure 10.17 SQL-Based Dynamic Analytic Privileges Management Window

The first section, **General** ❶, contains fields for the **Name:**, **Label:**, and **Type:** of analytic privileges. The **Label** field can be updated at any time; **Name:** and **Type** filed are read-only at this point in the process.

The **Secured Models** section ❷ provides an interface to add or remove additional referenced information views. To add information views, click the **Add...** button and search for the desired information views. To remove an information view, highlight it in the list and click the **Remove** button.

The large section on the right ❸ lets you choose **Attributes**, **SQL Editor**, or **Dynamic**. Because we're defining a SQL-based dynamic analytic privilege, the **Dynamic** option must be selected. Once selected, a new interface will appear titled **Procedure** ❸; it contains two options, **Type:** and **Name:**. The **Type:** dropdown allows us to choose **Repository Procedure** or **Catalog Procedure**. Select **Repository Procedure** to leverage a design-time stored procedure. Select the option **Catalog Procedure** to use a runtime procedure. Click the ellipsis to the right of the **Name** field to search for a stored procedure by name.

The icon bar section ❹ provides icon button options—from left to right, **Save and Validate**, **Save and Activate**, **DISPLAY XML** definition, view the **Activation History**, and switch to a **Historical Version** of the analytic privileges. As you hover your mouse pointer over each icon, a tooltip will appear. Click the second button, **Save and Activate**, when you're ready to deploy the analytic privileges; this will both save the analytic privilege within the repository and deploy it to the system for use within a role.

Once the analytic privileges are activated, their restrictions won't apply until the analytic privileges are granted to an existing role or user. If no competing analytic privileges are also applied to the grantee, queries to the referenced information views will be limited based on the defined filter conditions or restrictions.

SQL-based dynamic analytic privileges can accommodate a variety of complex filter conditions and filter condition operators. They offer more flexibility than the legacy XML-based options. In the next section, we'll review options via which even more complex dynamic filter conditions can be constructed with the use of SQL expressions, including the use of subqueries.

10.6 Managing Dynamic Expression-Based SQL Analytic Privileges

SQL-based analytic privileges offer a third option for defining filter expressions. This option allows the definer to use custom SQL expressions to define the `WHERE` clause generated by the analytic privileges. When mixed with the use of filter values in a catalog table and the `SESSION_USER` system variable, they are both dynamic and flexible.

Unlike dynamic analytic privileges, expression-based SQL analytic privileges don't require a stored procedure to accommodate the dynamic lookup of the filter conditions or values. We can directly define the lookup within the SQL editor provided within the interface. In some ways, this is a more simplistic way to support complex filter conditions within SQL-based analytic privileges.

Although a stored procedure is not required, the use of a catalog table to store the mappings between user accounts and filter values is required. The structure of this table is different than that of the dynamic SQL-based analytic privileges, which requires the mapping of filter conditions to users. In fact, the structure is most like that required to support dynamic XML-based analytic privileges. Table 10.3 provides an example of the structure and data of such a table.

USER_NAME	FILTER_VALUE
JHARRIS01	North Central
TTIM03	South West
WTRAN05	North Central
WTRAN05	South Central

Table 10.3 Example Mapping Used to Facilitate Dynamic Expression-Based SQL Analytic Privileges

The USER_NAME column must contain values that matches user accounts defined in the SAP HANA system. The FILTER_VALUE column must contain individual values. This table will become the source of our subqueries defined in the SQL editor.

Based on our testing, the SQL editor supports a variety of different SQL expressions. The supported syntax seems to match anything that can be used in a SQL statement WHERE clause. However, there might be some limitations that we were unable to identify during testing and validation.

In the following statement, we can define a static filter condition. Assume that the information view has an attribute column named CUSTOMERKEY. We use the IN clause and a static string array of values:

```
("CUSTOMERKEY" in (100,200,300,400,500))
```

In the following statement, we reference two different columns in the expression. Assume that all referenced information views have attribute columns with names CUSTOMERKEY and PLANT. We use two different operators in the expression—an IN operator for CUSTOMERKEY and an = operator for PLANT:

```
("CUSTOMERKEY" in (100,200,300,400,500)) and ("PLANT" = 1000)
```

In the following statement, we reference two different columns in the expressions. Assume that all referenced information views have attribute columns with names CUSTOMERKEY and PLANT. However, as opposed to the static list of filter values, a subquery is used to lookup the filter values from two different catalog tables. We also use the SESSION_USER system variable to dynamically reference the user account column USER_NAME within the table:

```
 ("CUSTOMERKEY" in (SELECT DISTINCT "FILTER_VALUE" FROM "SECURITY".
"RLS_CUSTOMER_ACCESS" WHERE USER_NAME = SESSION_USER))
AND
("PLANT" in (SELECT DISTINCT "FILTER_VALUE" FROM "SECURITY".
"RLS_PLANT_ACCESS" WHERE USER_NAME = SESSION_USER) )
```

As you can see from these examples, we can use a variety of attribute columns, operators, and even subqueries to define filter expressions. To better illustrate these dynamic expression-based SQL-based analytic privileges, we'll walk through the process used to define them.

10.6.1 Creating a Repository-Based Security Table

The structure of the table in this example will be slightly different from the structures used in previous examples. In this case, we'll need to define three columns within the table: `USER_NAME`, `MIN_FILTER_VALUE`, and `MAX_FILTER_VALUE`. This structure can be used to support a range of values for a given user. We'll assume users are granted access to the values in the `CUSTOMERKEY` attribute column based on a range. For example, we need to support conditions such as (`CUSTOMERKEY between 0 and 1000`). To prevent a user from having more than one record in this table, the primary key of the table is based on the `USER_NAME` column only, which will make it impossible for duplicate records to exist for a given user account.

To simplify the design, we'll create a repository-based table. We can create this table using the development perspective within SAP HANA Studio. With that perspective active, locate the repositories on the left. Expand the **System** node and **Repository Container** node to reveal the package repository. Locate a secure package location to host the repository-based table. Right-click the desired package node and choose **New • Other**. A window titled **New** will appear. Within that window, search for "table" in the **Wizards** section. Choose **Database Table** from the list and click **Next**. A window titled **Database Table** will appear. In the **File Name** field, enter the name of the repository-based table. Click **Next** to define the table. Figure 10.18 provides an example of the script we can use to define this table.

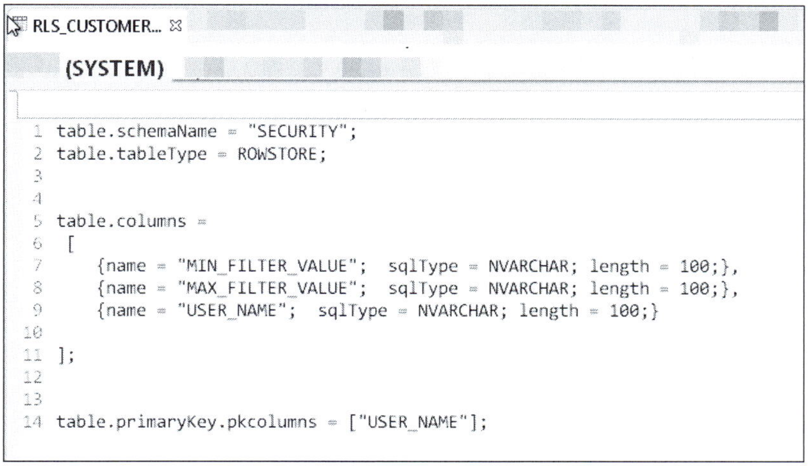

Figure 10.18 Example Repository Table Definition for Use in Dynamic Analytic Privileges

To populate example data into the table, the three SQL INSERT statements in Listing 10.3 can be issued.

```
INSERT INTO "SECURITY"."Security.ap::RLS_CUSTOMERKEY_ACCESS"
("USER_NAME","MIN_FILTER_VALUE","MAX_FILTER_VALUE")
VALUES ('TEST_SVC3','0','1000');

INSERT INTO "SECURITY"."Security.ap::RLS_CUSTOMERKEY_ACCESS"
("USER_NAME","MIN_FILTER_VALUE","MAX_FILTER_VALUE")
VALUES ('SYSTEM','0','99999999');

INSERT INTO "SECURITY"."Security.ap::RLS_CUSTOMERKEY_ACCESS"
("USER_NAME","MIN_FILTER_VALUE","MAX_FILTER_VALUE")
VALUES ('WTRAN01','5000','15000');
```

Listing 10.3 Three SQL INSERT Statements Used to Populate Example Table

Once the table is created and populated with data to support all possible users, we can define the analytic privilege. In the next section, we'll walk through the process of creating a dynamic expression-based SQL analytic privilege.

10.6.2 Defining Dynamic Expression-Based SQL Analytic Privileges

To create a dynamic expression-based SQL analytic privilege, open SAP HANA Studio. Within the repository, locate a package in a secure location. Right-click the package and choose **New** followed by **Analytic Privilege...**. A pop-up window will appear labeled **New Analytic Privilege** (see Figure 10.19).

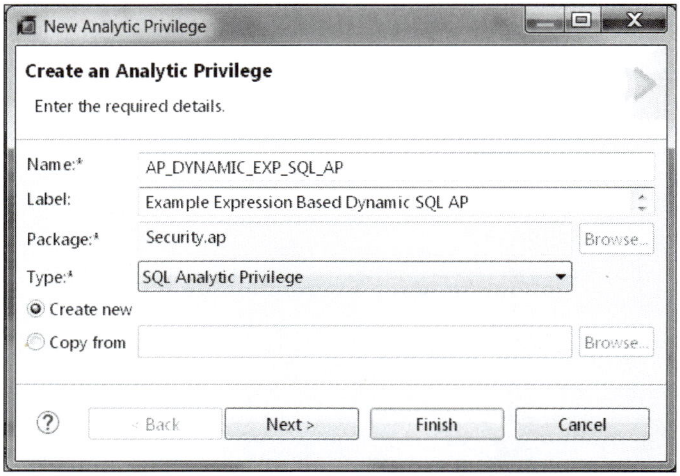

Figure 10.19 New SQL-Based Analytic Privilege Window

In this window, specify the technical name of the analytic privilege within the field labeled **Name**. The name can only contain the characters A–Z, a–z, and the underscore special character. Within the **Label** field, specify a description. The **Package** field should already contain the package name. The **Type** dropdown must contain the option **SQL Analytic Privilege** because the referenced information views are configured to use SQL analytic privileges. Choose the **Create new** option when creating a new analytic privilege, or choose the **Copy from** option to base the new analytic privilege on an existing analytic privilege. Use the **Browse** button to specify the existing analytic privileges. Click **Next** to continue.

A new window will appear with **Select Information Models** in the title (see Figure 10.20). In this optional step, you can preselect the information views that will be restricted within the new analytic privilege.

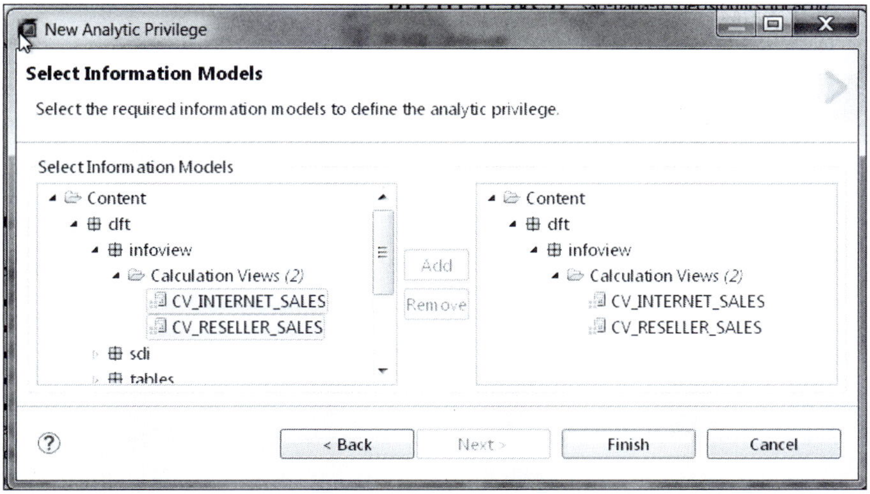

Figure 10.20 Selecting Information Views for the Analytic Privileges

To select information views at this stage, select them in the package hierarchy on the left side then click **Add**. The selected information views will appear on the right side. Click **Finish** to generate the analytic privileges. Note that you still can add or remove information views after this step.

The SQL-based dynamic analytic privileges management window is divided into four main sections, as illustrated in Figure 10.21.

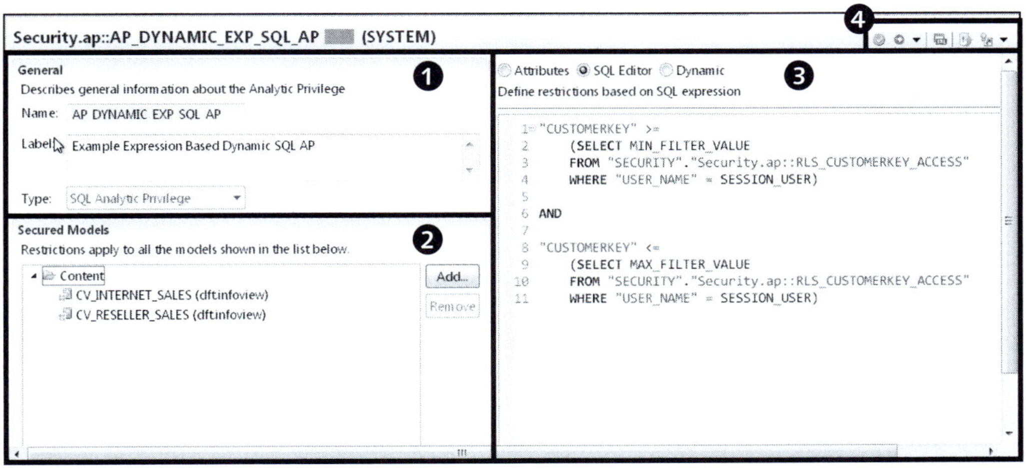

Figure 10.21 Dynamic Expression-Based SQL Analytic Privileges Management Window

The first section, **General** ❶, contains fields for the **Name**, **Label**, and **Type** of the analytic privileges. The **Label** field can be updated at any time. The **Name** and **Type** fields are read-only at this point in the process.

The **Secured Models** section ❷ provides an interface to add or remove additional referenced information views. To add additional information views, click the **Add** button and search for the desired information view. To remove an information view, highlight it in the list and click the **Remove** button.

The large section on the right ❸ allows you to choose **Attributes**, **SQL Editor**, or **Dynamic**. Because we're defining a dynamic expression–based SQL analytic privilege, the **SQL Editor** option must be selected. Once selected, a new expression editor interface will appear ❸. In this frame, we can type the desired expression.

Based on the example requirements, the expression must support the use of a range. To accommodate this, we'll use two subqueries (see Listing 10.4). The first subquery will look up the minimum filter value from the `MIN_FILTER_VALUE` column, and the second subquery will look up the maximum filter value from the `MAX_FILTER_VALUE` column.

```
"CUSTOMERKEY" >=
    (SELECT MIN_FILTER_VALUE
    FROM "SECURITY"."Security.ap::RLS_CUSTOMERKEY_ACCESS"
    WHERE "USER_NAME" = SESSION_USER)
AND
"CUSTOMERKEY" <=
    (SELECT MAX_FILTER_VALUE
    FROM "SECURITY"."Security.ap::RLS_CUSTOMERKEY_ACCESS"
    WHERE "USER_NAME" = SESSION_USER)
```

Listing 10.4 Example Complex SQL Filter Expression

In effect, we can look up the minimum and maximum values for the range and apply them to the filter expression. We can complete this even without the use of a stored procedure.

The icon bar section ❹ provides icon button options—from left to right, **Save and Validate**, **Save and Activate**, **DISPLAY XML** definition, view the **Activation History**, and switch to a **Historical Version** of the analytic privileges. As you hover your mouse pointer over each icon, a tooltip will appear. Click the second button, **Save and Activate**, when you're ready to deploy the analytic privileges. This will both save an analytic privilege within the repository and deploy it to the system for use within a role. Once the analytic privileges are activated, their restrictions won't apply until the analytic privileges are granted to an existing role or user. If no competing analytic privileges are also applied to the grantee, queries to the referenced information views will be limited based on the defined filter conditions or restrictions.

10.7 Troubleshooting Effective Analytic Privileges and Filter Conditions

The easiest method of troubleshooting the net effect of analytic privileges for a given user and information view is to query the system view SYS.EFFECTIVE_STRUCTURED_PRIVILEGES.

When querying this system view, three filter conditions within the WHERE clause must be satisfied before it will execute. The USER_NAME, ROOT_SCHEMA_NAME, and ROOT_OBJECT_NAME columns must all be specified in the WHERE clause as filter conditions. The SQL code in Listing 10.5 will check for the effective analytic privileges applied to the TEST_SVC3 user for the dft.infoview/CV_INTERNET_SALES information view.

```
SELECT *
FROM "SYS"."EFFECTIVE_STRUCTURED_PRIVILEGES"
WHERE
"USER_NAME" = 'TEST_SVC3' AND
"ROOT_SCHEMA_NAME" = '_SYS_BIC' AND
"ROOT_OBJECT_NAME" = 'dft.infoview/CV_INTERNET_SALES'
```

Listing 10.5 SQL Statement for Querying EFFECTIVE_STRUCTURED_PRIVILEGES System View

The output of the query provides some important information. The EFFECTIVE_FILTER output column will indicate the total filters applied from all restrictions. If multiple restrictions are applied, this column will have the same output value for all rows.

The STRUCTURED_PRIVILEGE_NAME output column will indicate the source of the restriction. A unique row will exist for each unique analytic privilege.

The STRUCTURED_PRIVILEGE_FILTER output column will indicate the syntax of the restriction in relation to the analytic privileges that produced the restriction. A unique row will exist for each unique analytic privilege.

The STRUCTURED_PRIVILEGE_STATUS output column will contain the value APPLIED when a restriction is found and applied. If the value NOT AUTHORIZED is returned, then the user doesn't have any analytic privileges assigned. Other values, such as NOT GRANTED,

NO MATCHING ATTRIBUTE, and NO FILTER VALUES FOUND, are also possible depending on the type of structured privilege referenced.

10.8 Granting Analytic Privileges

In this section, we'll review the options available to grant analytic privileges to and revoke them from grantees: SQL commands, SAP HANA Studio, the SAP HANA Web-Based Development Workbench security manager, and repository-based role scripts or repository-based role editor options.

10.8.1 Granting Analytic Privileges with SQL

When we create an analytic privilege, it's owned by the system user _SYS_REPO. Analytic privileges are a type of structured privilege, but we can't use the standard GRANT and REVOKE SQL syntax to assign analytic privileges to a grantee. Instead, we must use a specific stored procedure to grant and another to revoke analytic privileges for a grantee.

To grant an analytic privilege to a grantee, we must execute the GRANT_ACTIVATED_ANALYTIC_PRIVILEGE stored procedure in the _SYS_REPO schema. To use this procedure, the security administrator must have the EXECUTE object privilege on the stored procedure. The procedure provides two input parameters. The first parameter should contain the name of the analytic privilege, and the second input parameter will contain the name of the grantee. Use the following SQL syntax to execute the stored procedure and assign the analytic privilege:

```
CALL "_SYS_REPO"."GRANT_ACTIVATED_ANALYTICAL_PRIVILEGE"
('<ANALLYTIC_PRIVILEGE_NAME>','<GRANTEE>');
```

For example:

```
CALL "_SYS_REPO"."GRANT_ACTIVATED_ANALYTICAL_PRIVILEGE"
('"e-corp.sales.security/ap_sales_reporting_region"','ROLE_REGION');
```

To revoke an analytic privilege from a grantee, we must execute the REVOKE_ACTIVATED_ANALYTIC_PRIVILEGE stored procedure in the _SYS_REPO schema. It uses the same two input parameters. Use the following syntax to execute the stored procedure:

```
CALL "_SYS_REPO"."REVOKE_ACTIVATED_ANALYTICAL_PRIVILEGE"
('<ANALLYTIC_PRIVILEGE_NAME>','<GRANTEE>');
```

For example:

```
CALL "_SYS_REPO"."REVOKE_ACTIVATED_ANALYTICAL_PRIVILEGE"
('"e-corp.sales.security/ap_sales_reporting_region"','ROLE_REGION' );
```

10.8.2 Granting Analytic Privileges with SAP HANA Studio

We also can use the role management area in SAP HANA Studio to both grant and revoke analytic privileges for a given grantee. Most will find SAP HANA Studio easier to use than memorizing and typing the SQL statements and stored procedure syntax. Let's review the process used to grant and revoke analytic privileges using SAP HANA Studio.

To access the user management are, start by switching to the administration console perspective. In the **Systems** tab on the left, expand the **System** node, then the **Security** node, revealing the **Security**, **Users**, and **Roles** nodes. Expand the **Roles** node to reveal roles defined in the system, or expand the **Users** node to reveal user accounts defined in the system. To manage a grantee, double-click a user or role in the list to open the **Management** tab on the right side of the perspective.

Figure 10.22 shows the role management interface in SAP HANA Studio. Just below the role name, you'll see a series of tabs. Each tab represents an interface in which specific types of privileges or roles can be granted or revoked. In this case, we need to select the **Analytic Privileges** tab.

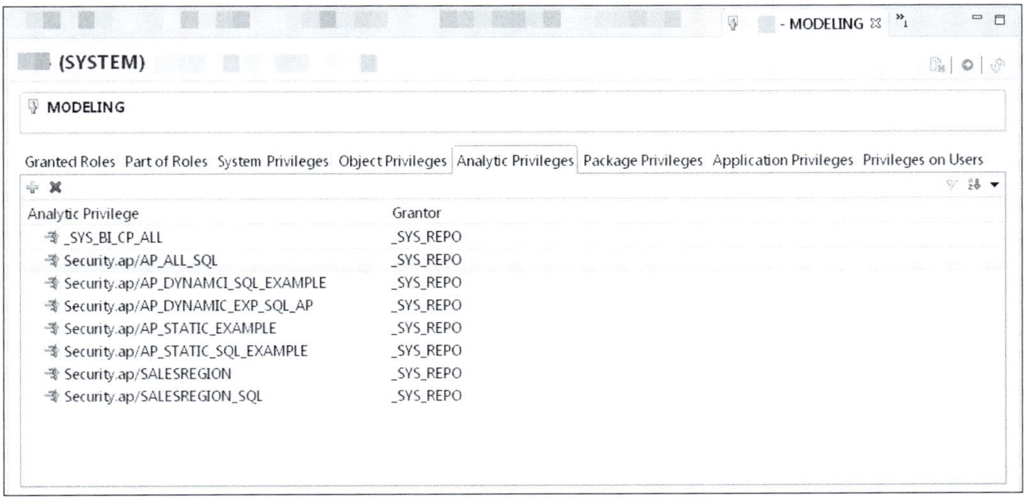

Figure 10.22 Analytic Privileges Tab in SAP HANA Studio Role Management

Using this tab, the process for granting and revoking analytic privileges is like the process used for other privileges. To grant an analytic privilege, click **+** to open a search dialog box. To view all objects in the system, enter the search string "**". To search for a specific analytic privilege, enter a portion of the analytic privilege's name to search for possible matches. The search dialog will return both analytic privileges and structured privileges. Analytic privileges are those owned by the system account _SYS_REPO. Structured privileges are owned by the user account that created them.

As with other privileges, the interface allows you to select multiple items. Click **OK** once the desired objects are selected. The search dialog will close, and the selected **Analytic Privileges** and their **Grantor** will appear in the list. There are no further options that need to be configured with analytic privileges. They are either granted when listed or revoked when not listed.

When using SAP HANA Studio, there's no need to determine if the analytic privilege is owned by _SYS_REPO or if we need to use a special interface to assign privileges owned by _SYS_REPO. SAP HANA Studio will execute the required SQL statements automatically in the background to grant the selected analytic privileges. When an object is owned by the _SYS_REPO system account, the system will execute the necessary stored procedures in the background. You'll also notice that repository objects will always list the grantor as _SYS_REPO.

To revoke an analytic privilege, simply select it from the list and click the red **X**. To save the changes, press `Ctrl`+`S`, or to activate the changes, press `F8`. Either way, the changes will be saved and activated within the system.

10.8.3 Granting Analytic Privileges with SAP HANA Web-Based Development Workbench

The SAP HANA Web-Based Development Workbench security manager, hosted within the XS engine, provides an alternative interface to create users, create roles, or manage security.

You can access SAP HANA Web-Based Development Workbench via a supported Internet browser. The following URLs can be customized to match the details of your environment:

http://sap-hana.myhost.com:8000/sap/hana/ide/security

http://<sap_hana_host>:80<instance_number>/sap/hana/ide/security

In the last example, replace <sap_hana_host> with the hostname of the SAP HANA system in your environment, and replace <instance_number> with the two-digit instance numbercorresponding to your SAP HANA system.

For secure access, the following examples should help you construct the correct URL:

https://<sap_hana_host>:43<instance_number>/sap/hana/ide/security

https://sap-hana.myhost.com:4300/sap/hana/ide/security

As a reminder, a user must be granted the sap.hana.ide.roles::SecurityAdmin role before he can access the security manager. Once you have access, expand the **Security** node on the right, then expand **Roles** to reveal a list of roles defined in the system, or expand **Users** to reveal a list of user accounts defined in the system. Double-click the desired object to open the management interface for the given grantee.

The process for granting and revoking analytic privileges in the SAP HANA Web-Based Development Workbench security manager is almost identical to the process outlined for SAP HANA Studio. Because there is tremendous overlap in the workflows, we won't go into the same level of detail in this section; see Section 10.8.2 for additional details on navigating the management interface for a given grantee. In this section, we'll simply highlight the basic workflow and point out any significant differences.

To add an analytic privilege, click **+** and search for the desired analytic privilege. To revoke an analytic privilege, select the privilege from the list and click the red **X** to remove it. To save your changes, press Ctrl+S, or click the disk icon at the top left to save and activate the privilege.

If there are any activation issues, warning messages will appear in the status frame at the bottom of the user management window. The status frame has a dark background color. Error messages will appear in red-colored text. Errors are only generated during an attempted activation or saving of changes.

10.8.4 Granting Analytic Privileges within Repository Roles

As we've noted, it's best to base a security model on the use of repository-based roles. Because of their benefits, we'll review the process for granting analytic privileges within repository-based roles. To assign analytic privileges to a repository-based role, we can choose between two options. With the first option, we can choose to modify or develop repository roles within design-time scripts. With the second, we can use the SAP HANA Web-Based Development Workbench editor to create and modify repository-based roles.

Design-Time Scripts

In Chapter 6, we walked through the process of creating repository roles in SAP HANA Studio. SAP HANA Studio provides interfaces for creating and defining repository roles using design-time scripts based on an SAP HANA domain-specific syntax. In this section, we'll review the syntax used to define analytic privileges within these design-time scripts.

When defining analytic privileges within repository-based role scripts, you must start the line with `analytic privilege`. Following this, include a colon. After the colon, include the fully qualified name of the analytic privilege file, which must include the package hierarchy name, analytic privilege name, and .analyticprivilege extension. The package hierarchy name and analytic privilege name will be separated by a single colon. At the end of the statement, include a semicolon to finish the line. Because all analytic privileges are owned by _SYS_REPO, there's no need to grant _SYS_REPO privileges to these analytic privilege objects. The syntax is as follows:

```
analytic privilege: <package.name> : <analytic privilege name>
<.analyticprivilege> ;
```

As an example, the following statement grants the `ap_sales_reporting_region` analytic privilege, stored in the `e-corp.sales.security` package; remember that repository package and object names are case-sensitive:

```
analytic privilege:
  e-corp.security:ap_sales_reporting_region.analyticprivilege;
```

For a final example, we'll grant the system analytic privilege `_SYS_BI_CP_ALL`. This special catalog analytic privilege, when granted, will give full access to all information views defined within the repository:

```
catalog analytic privilege : "_SYS_BI_CP_ALL";
```

Granting and Revoking with SAP HANA Web-Based Development Workbench

The SAP HANA Web-Based Development Workbench editor, hosted within the XS engine, provides an interface to manage and create repository roles. The interface looks similar to the standard role management options found in SAP HANA Studio, but the role objects it creates are profoundly different. The editor creates repository-based roles. The objects created here can also be opened in the SAP HANA Studio developer perspective, which means that we can use either the SAP HANA Studio or the script editor to manage repository roles.

You can access SAP HANA Web-Based Development Workbench via a supported Internet browser. The following URLs can be customized to match the details of your environment:

http://sap-hana.myhost.com:8000/sap/hana/ide/editor

http://<sap_hana_host>:80<instance_number>/sap/hana/ide/editor

In the last example, replace <sap_hana_host> with the hostname of the SAP HANA system in your environment, and replace <instance_number> with the two-digit instance number corresponding to your SAP HANA system.

For secure access, the following examples should help you construct the correct URL:

https://<sap_hana_host>:43<instance_number>/sap/hana/ide/editor

https://sap-hana.myhost.com:4300/sap/hana/ide/editor

To use the SAP HANA Web-Based Development Workbench editor, the user account first will need to be granted one of the roles listed in Table 10.4; users only need one of the two roles to access the workbench security manager.

Role Name	Summary
sap.hana.ide.roles::EditorDeveloper	Within SAP HANA Web-Based Development Workbench, a user will only be able to access the editor, which provides interfaces to create a variety of repository objects, including repository-based roles.
sap.hana.ide.roles::Developer	This role grants a higher level of privileges for users that need full access to SAP HANA Web-based Development Workbench. It grants access to the editor, catalog, and security interfaces. It's considered the parent to the sap.hana.ide.roles::EditorDeveloper role.

Table 10.4 Roles Required to Use SAP HANA Web-Based Development Workbench Security Manager

Additional Privileges Needed to Use Security Manager

It's important to note that the roles in Table 10.4 simply allow the granted user access to the interface. The use will also need access to the package in which the repository roles are stored. To grant repository roles to other users and roles, the user will need `EXECUTE` access to the system stored procedure named `"_SYS_REPO"."GRANT_ACTIVATED_ROLE"`. To revoke repository roles, they will need `EXECUTE` access to the `"_SYS_REPO"."REVOKE_ACTIVATED_ROLE"` stored procedure.

Once you have access to the editor, expand the **Content** node on the right side of the window. Expand **Packages** to reveal a list of packages defined in the system. As noted before, repository roles must be stored in a package that only security administrators can access. We typically create a top-level package named **Security** to host such objects.

To create a repository role, right-click the package in which you want to store it. From the context menu, choose **New • Role** (see Figure 10.23).

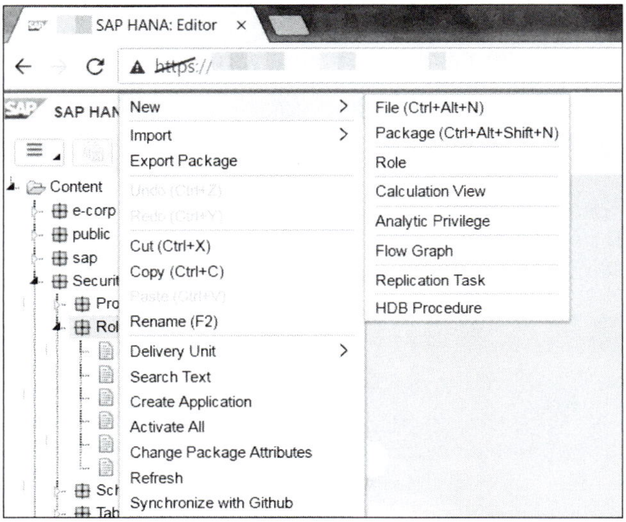

Figure 10.23 Navigating SAP HANA Web-Based Development Workbench Editor and Creating Repository Role

A small window named **New Role** will appear. Enter the desired name of the role and click **Create**. A new tabbed window will appear in the large right-hand side frame. The tab label should match the provided name of the repository role. The new window will contain a series of subtabs labeled **Granted Roles**, **System Privileges**, **Object Privileges**, **Analytic Privileges**, **Package Privileges**, and **Application Privileges**. Like in SAP HANA Studio, each tab allows a developer to define certain types of privileges.

Click the **Analytic Privileges** tab to reveal an interface in which we can add or remove analytic privileges. To add an analytic privilege, click the large **+** button on the subtab header. A pop-up window will appear titled **Select Analytic Privilege**.

The search box is divided into two broad types of analytic privileges. The top two radio buttons allow us to toggle between design-time or runtime objects. When searching for design-time analytic privileges, choose the **Design-Time** radio button. When searching for runtime analytic privileges, choose the **Runtime** radio button. Note that the runtime list also includes generic structured privileges.

A search box will appear in this window; enter a portion of the analytic privilege's name to narrow the results. Alternatively, you can scroll through the unfiltered list to locate the desired analytic privileges by name. Select one or more analytic privileges within the list. Hold down the [Ctrl] key to select multiple items. The selected items are highlighted in light blue. Click the **OK** button at the bottom of the window to finalize the selection. The selected analytic privileges will now appear in the **Analytic Privileges** tab.

To remove an assigned analytic privilege, select it from the list, then click the large – button above the list to remove it. Items in the list must be deleted one at a time.

Once you've configured the desired list of analytic privileges, click the **Save All** button at the top left. The **Save All** button icon shows three stacked floppy disks.

If there are any issues saving and activating the repository role, messages will appear in red text within the console window just below the opened **Repository Roles** tab. The console window has a dark background color and is located at the bottom of the opened tab. Affirmative messages will appear in white text, and error messages will appear in red text.

To close the open **Repository Role** tab, click the small **x** to the right of the tab.

10.9 Summary

Many organizations will need to secure access to the data hosted in their SAP HANA systems. When this need arises, analytic privileges offer multiple solutions to help. Analytic privileges govern access to data made available through SAP HANA's information views. Going forward, *SQL-based* analytic privileges will replace the legacy XML-based analytic privileges. SQL-based analytic privileges offer the ability to implement complex filter logic using subquery statements or complex filter condition statements. Like all privileges, they must be granted to a grantee before they go into effect. Ideally, we'll assign analytic privileges to repository-based roles, then grant repository roles to users.

Chapter 11
Application Privileges

In this chapter, we'll discuss application privileges and how they relate to the security model and applications developed within the SAP HANA development platform.

11

Application privileges define custom levels of access to applications developed in the XS or XSA engine. SAP HANA is an application development platform in which web-based applications can be developed and hosted. These applications sometimes need their own unique privileges to govern actions unique to the application. Take, for example, a web-based application that allows a user to respond to a series of questions. Some users need access to simply answer each question, and these users shouldn't have the ability to see the results of other questionnaires given to other users. However, administrative users might need the ability to see the answers given by all users. Application privileges can be developed to facilitate these custom application-level security requirements. Application privileges then can be granted to roles within the security model.

In this chapter, we'll give an overview of application privileges within SAP HANA, how they're created, and how they're granted to roles using a variety of options. We'll also provide a brief summary of *privileges on users* and how it's used to grant the ATTACH DEBUGGER privilege to another grantee.

11.1 Application Privileges in SAP HANA

In principal, application privileges aren't native to the SAP HANA RDBMS. They don't exist in SAP HANA unless they're developed natively or imported from a delivery unit that supports an externally developed SAP HANA application. However, when an SAP HANA system is initially deployed, the installation engine will import several SAP-developed delivery units, which represent applications hosted in the SAP HANA XS engine. Many of these imported applications have associated application privileges and repository-based roles.

In most cases, these default application privileges are delivered with corresponding repository-based roles. We typically grant the corresponding repository-based roles to other grantees and avoid directly granting these default application privileges. Most of the SAP-delivered application privileges are also not documented, but their corresponding repository-based roles are. Because they aren't well documented, it's not always clear what permissions they grant within the SAP-delivered XS engine applications.

Starting with SAP HANA 1.0 SPS 11 and SAP HANA 2.0, most of the SAP-delivered classic XS engine-based applications are in the process of transitioning to the *SAP HANA Cockpit* or *SAP Web IDE*. These web-based applications are hosted in the XSA engine. The advanced XSA engine runtime has its own role-management interface based on XSA engine application-specific roles and doesn't leverage classic SAP HANA 1.0 application privileges. Therefore, though we'll discuss application privileges in this chapter, keep in mind that they'll be obsolete at some point in the future.

11.2 Creating Application Privileges

Application privileges are defined within specific files that are stored in the SAP HANA package repository. They must be stored in a package in which the corresponding application code resides. They're defined based on a domain-specific language using a text editor. The process is similar to the one used to define repository roles within design-time scripts.

There are two different types of script files that must be created within the XS engine application package hierarchy. The first script file has a file extension of .xsprivileges and requires no file name. It's called the *application-privileges file* and it defines one or more application privileges for the associated application. The application-privileges file is stored at the top of the application's specific package hierarchy node to encompass the full scope of all subsidiary application access definitions. The application-privileges script is programed as a catalog, list, or definition of all subsidiary authorization privileges specific to the application. The script in Listing 11.1 shows how three example authorizations, `QEdit`, `QAdmin`, and `QView`, are defined.

```
{
 "privileges" :
  [
   { "name" : "QEdit", "description" : "Edit Questions" },
   { "name" : "QAdmin", "description" : "Full Access"},
```

```
    { "name" : "QView", "description" : "View Questions"},
  ]
}
```

Listing 11.1 Script to Define Example Application Authorizations

The script acts as a catalog. For each authorization, we define a line that includes the authorization name and description. Subsidiary application privilege objects will look for a corresponding entry in the file and won't activated unless a corresponding entry is found.

The second file has an extension of .xsaccess and no file name is specified. It's called the application-access file. It defines the level of access that will be granted to application code hosted in the corresponding subpackage. Each application-access file must be stored in a subpackage corresponding to the application code it governs. The application code will take precedence over application-access files hosted in the same subpackage or closest parent package. The script in Listing 11.2 shows how application privileges can be associated with application code hosted in the subpackage `dft.apps.survey.results`.

```
{
    "prevent_xsrf": true, // Prevent cross-site request forgery
    "exposed": true,      // Expose data via HTTP
    "authentication": {
        "method": "Form"
    },
    "force_ssl": true,    // Accept only HTTPS requests
    "authorization": [
        "dft.apps.survey::QView",
        "dft.apps.survey::QEdit",
         "dft.apps.survey::QAdmin"
     ]
}
```

Listing 11.2 Script to Associate Application Privileges with Custom Application Code

The script language includes a variety of keywords that enable or disable various levels of access to the package and its corresponding application code. The specified application privileges listed in brackets next to the keyword `authorization` represent the application privileges that will be applied to the subpackage node and its code.

Similar .xsaccess files are then added to other subpackages to define a complete application specific security model.

Creating Application Privileges for SAP HANA

For more information pertaining to the creation of application privileges, please review the SAP HANA Developer Guide. The sections titled Creating the Application Descriptors and Maintaining Application Security will provide additional details not covered in this section. You can download the SAP HANA Developer Guide from *http://help.sap.com/hana/SAP_HANA_Developer_Guide_for_SAP_HANA_Studio_en.pdf*.

Once application privileges are defined, they must be granted to roles, and those roles must then be granted to users. In most cases, repository-based roles are created specifically for access to an application. These roles are then extended or granted to other security model-specific repository-based roles.

11.3 Granting Application Privileges

In this section, we'll review the various options available to grant application privileges to and revoke them from grantees: SQL commands, SAP HANA Studio, the SAP HANA Web-Based Development Workbench security manager, and repository-based role scripts or a repository-based role editor GUI.

11.3.1 Granting Application Privileges with SQL

When we create an application privilege, it's owned by the system user _SYS_REPO. To grant or revoke application privileges, we must use a specific stored procedure. The SQL statements in Listing 11.3 provide a generic example of how to use the stored procedure to grant an application privilege to a grantee. Grantees can be either user accounts or existing roles.

```
CALL "_SYS_REPO"."GRANT_APPLICATION_PRIVILEGE"
('<APPLICATION_PRIVILEGE_NAME>','<GRANTEE>');
CALL "_SYS_REPO"."GRANT_APPLICATION_PRIVILEGE"
('"sap.hana.admin::Administrator"','Security.roles::ADMIN_ROLE');
```

Listing 11.3 SQL Syntax to Grant Application Privileges

Listing 11.4 provides the syntax used to revoke an application privilege.

```
CALL "_SYS_REPO"."REVOKE_APPLICATION_PRIVILEGE"
('<APPLICATION_PRIVILEGE_NAME>','<GRANTEE>');
CALL "_SYS_REPO"."REVOKE_APPLICATION_
PRIVILEGE"('"sap.hana.admin::Administrator"','ADMIN_ROLE');
```

Listing 11.4 SQL Syntax to Revoke Application Privileges

The security administrator executing these stored procedures will require the EXECUTE object privilege.

11.3.2 Granting Application Privileges with SAP HANA Studio

We also can use the management options in SAP HANA Studio to both grant and revoke application privileges for a given grantee. Most will find it easier to use SAP HANA Studio than to memorize and type SQL statements and stored procedure syntax.

To access the user or role management options in SAP HANA Studio, start by switching to the administration console perspective. In the **Systems** tab, located on the left, expand the **System** node. Locate the **Security** node and expand it to reveal the **Security**, **Users**, and **Roles** nodes. Expand the **Users** node to reveal user accounts defined in the system, or expand the **Roles** node to reveal standard roles defined in the system. To manage a grantee, double-click its name in the list to open the management interface tab on the right.

Figure 11.1 shows the SAP HANA Studio management interface with the **Application Privileges** tab selected. In the management window are several tabs. Each tab represents an interface in which a specific type of privilege or role can be granted or revoked. To manage application privileges, choose the **Application Privileges** tab.

The process for granting and revoking application privileges is similar to the process used for other privileges. To grant an application privilege, click **+** to open a search dialog box. To view all objects in the system, enter the search string "**". To search for a specific application privilege, enter a portion of the application privilege's name to search for possible matches.

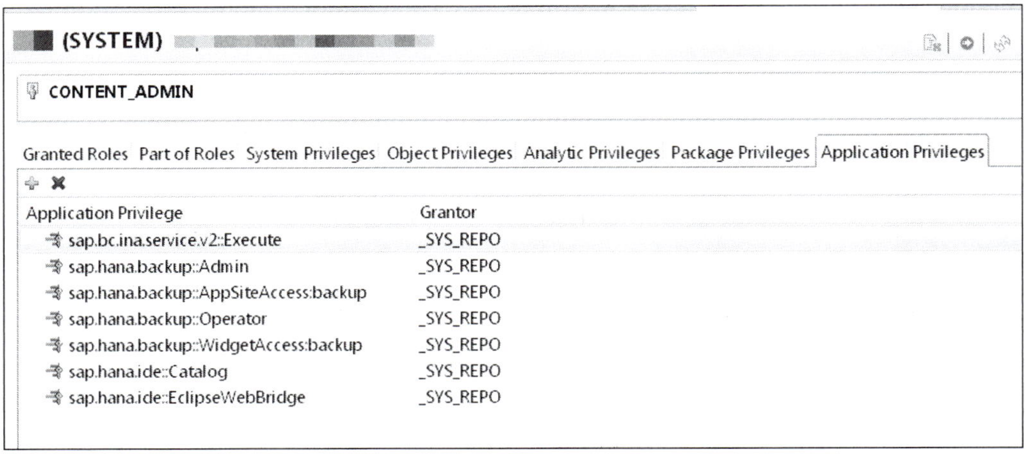

Figure 11.1 Role Application Privilege Management Tab in SAP HANA Studio

As with other privileges, the interface allows you to select multiple items. Click **OK** once the desired objects are selected. The search dialog will close and the selected application privileges will appear in the list. There are no further options that need to be configured for application privileges. They're granted when listed or revoked when not listed. All application privileges will list _SYS_REPO as the grantor. SAP HANA Studio will execute the required stored procedures automatically in the background to grant the selected application privileges. When application privileges are revoked, SAP HANA Studio will also execute the required stored procedures automatically in the background.

To revoke an application privilege, simply select it in the list and click the red **X**. To save the changes, press [Ctrl]+[S], or to activate the changes, press [F8] key. The changes will be saved and activated in the system.

11.3.3 Granting Application Privileges with SAP HANA Web-Based Development Workbench

The SAP HANA Web-Based Development Workbench security manager, hosted within the XS engine, provides an interface you can use to grant and revoke application privileges. You can access SAP HANA Web-Based Development Workbench via a supported Internet browser. The following two URLs can be customized to match the details of your environment:

http://sap-hana.myhost.com:8000/sap/hana/ide/security

http://<sap_hana_host>:80<instance_number>/sap/hana/ide/security

In the last example, replace <sap_hana_host> with the hostname of the SAP HANA system in your environment and <instance_number> with the two-digit instance number corresponding to your SAP HANA system.

For secure access, the following examples should help you construct the correct URL:

https://<sap_hana_host>:43<instance_number>/sap/hana/ide/security

https://sap-hana.myhost.com:4300/sap/hana/ide/security

As a reminder, a user must be granted the sap.hana.ide.roles::SecurityAdmin role before it can access the SAP HANA Web-Based Development Workbench security manager. Once you have access to the security manager, expand the **Security** node on the right, then expand **User** or **Roles** to reveal a list of grantees. Double-click a grantee to open its management interface. With the selected grantee management window open, you can begin granting and revoking application privileges.

The process for granting and revoking a user's privileges in the SAP HANA Web-Based Development Workbench security manager is almost identical to the process outlined for SAP HANA Studio. Because there is tremendous overlap in the workflows, we won't go into the same level of detail in the section; see Section 11.3.2 for additional details. In this section, we'll simply highlight the basic workflow and point out any significant differences.

Access the **Application Privileges** tab in the management interface. To add an application privilege, click **+** and search for the desired application privilege. To revoke an application privilege, select the privilege from the list and click the red **X** to remove it. To save your changes, press `Ctrl`+`S`, or click the **Save** icon at the top left to save and activate the privilege. If there are any activation issues, warning messages will appear in the status frame at the bottom of the user management window. The status frame has a dark background color. Error messages will appear in red text. Errors are only generated during an attempted activation or saving of changes.

11.3.4 Granting Application Privileges within Repository Roles

As we've stated before, it's best to base a security model on repository-based roles. Because of their benefits, we'll review the process for granting application privileges within repository-based roles. To assign application privileges to a repository-based role, we can either modify or develop repository roles within design-time scripts or we can use the SAP HANA Web-Based Development Workbench editor to create and modify repository-based roles.

SQL Syntax in Design-Time Scripts

In Chapter 6, we walked you through the process for creating repository roles within SAP HANA Studio, which provides interfaces for creating and defining repository roles using design-time scripts based on an SAP HANA domain-specific syntax. In this section, we'll review the syntax used to define application privileges within these design-time scripts.

When defining application privileges within repository-based role scripts, you must start each line with `application privilege`. Following this term, include a colon, then include the name of the application privilege. The application privilege name must include the package hierarchy name, two colons, and the name of the application privilege. For case-sensitivity purposes, the name must be wrapped in double quotes. At the end of the statement, include a semicolon to finish the line.

The following example shows a single line used to grant application privileges within a repository-based role:

```
application privilege: "sap.hana.security.base::DataService";
```

Granting and Revoking with SAP HANA Web-Based Development Workbench

The SAP HANA Web-Based Development Workbench editor, hosted within the SAP HANA XS engine, provides an interface to manage and create repository roles. The interface looks similar to the standard role management GUI in SAP HANA Studio, but the role objects it creates are profoundly different. The editor creates repository-based roles. The objects created in the editor can also be opened in the SAP HANA Studio developer perspective, which means that we can use either the Web-Based Development Workbench editor or the SAP HANA Studio script editor to manage repository roles.

You can access SAP HANA Web-Based Development Workbench via a supported Internet browser. The following URLs can be customized to match the details of your environment:

http://sap-hana.myhost.com:8000/sap/hana/ide/editor

http://<sap_hana_host>:80<instance_number>/sap/hana/ide/editor

In the last example, replace <sap_hana_host> with the hostname of the SAP HANA system in your environment and <instance_number> with the two-digit instance number corresponding to your SAP HANA system.

For secure access, the following examples should help you construct the correct URL:

https://<sap_hana_host>:43<instance_number>/sap/hana/ide/editor

https://sap-hana.myhost.com:4300/sap/hana/ide/editor

To use the editor, the user account first will need to be granted one of the roles listed in Table 11.1. Users only need one of the two roles to access the workbench editor.

Role Name	Summary
sap.hana.ide.roles::EditorDeveloper	Within SAP HANA Web-Based Development Workbench, users will only be able to access the editor. The editor provides interfaces to create a variety of repository objects, including repository-based roles.
sap.hana.ide.roles::Developer	This role grants a higher level of privileges for users that need full access to SAP HANA Web-Based Development Workbench. It grants access to the editor, catalog, and security interfaces. It's considered the parent to the sap.hana.ide.roles::EditorDeveloper role.

Table 11.1 Roles Required to Use SAP HANA Web-Based Development Workbench Editor

Additional Privileges Needed to Use the Editor

Note that the roles in Table 11.1 simply allow the granted user access to the interface. Users will also need access to the package in which the repository roles are stored. To grant repository roles to other users and roles, users will need `EXECUTE` access to the system stored procedure named `"_SYS_REPO"."GRANT_ACTIVATED_ROLE"`. To revoke repository roles, they'll need `EXECUTE` access to the `"_SYS_REPO"."REVOKE_ACTIVATED_ROLE"` stored procedure.

Once you have access to the SAP HANA Web-Based Development Workbench editor, expand the **Content** node on the right, then expand **Packages** to reveal a list of packages defined in the system. As stated before, repository roles must be stored in a package that only security administrators can access. We typically create a top-level package named **Security** to host such objects.

To create a new repository role, right-click the package in which you want to store it and choose **New • Role** (see Figure 11.2).

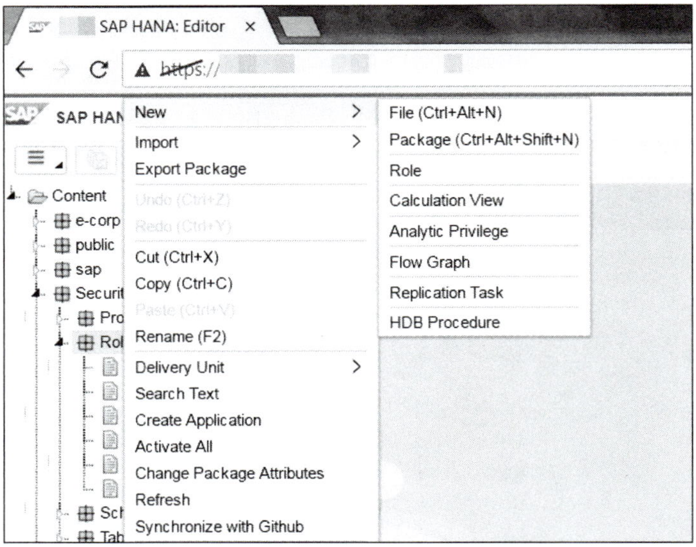

Figure 11.2 Navigating SAP HANA Web-Based Development Workbench and Creating Repository Role

A small window named **New Role** will appear. Enter the desired name of the role and click **Create**. A new tabbed window will appear in the large right-hand frame. The tab label should match the provided name of the repository role. The new window will contain a series of subtabs: **Granted Roles**, **System Privileges**, **Object Privileges**, **Analytic Privileges**, **Package Privileges**, and **Application Privileges**. Like in SAP HANA Studio, each tab allows a developer to define specific privileges.

Click the tab named **Application Privileges** to reveal an interface in which we can add or remove application privileges. To add an application privilege, click the large **+** button on the subtab header. A pop-up window will appear titled **Select Application Privilege** (see Figure 11.3).

A search box will appear in this window; enter a portion of the application privilege's name to narrow the results, or scroll through the unfiltered list to locate the desired application privileges by name. Select one or more application privileges within the list, holding down `Ctrl` to select multiple items. The selected items are highlighted in light blue. Click the **OK** button at the bottom of the window to finalize the selection.

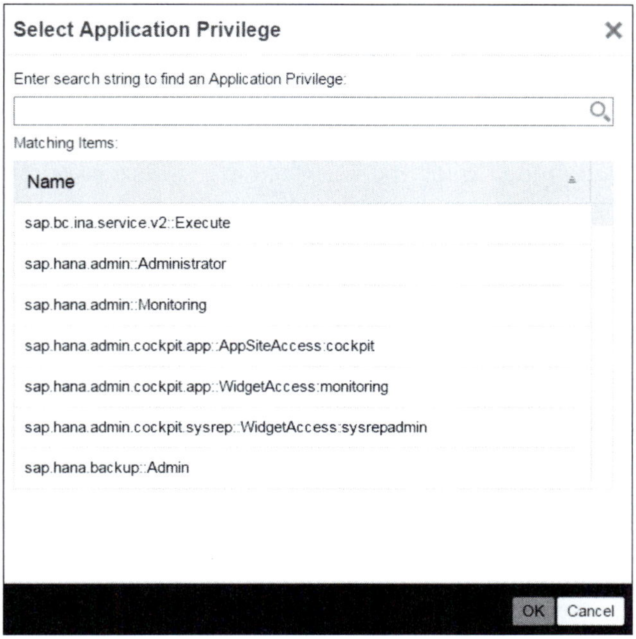

Figure 11.3 Selecting and Assigning Application Privileges in SAP HANA Web-Based Development Workbench

The selected application privileges will now appear in the **Application Privileges** tab (see Figure 11.4).

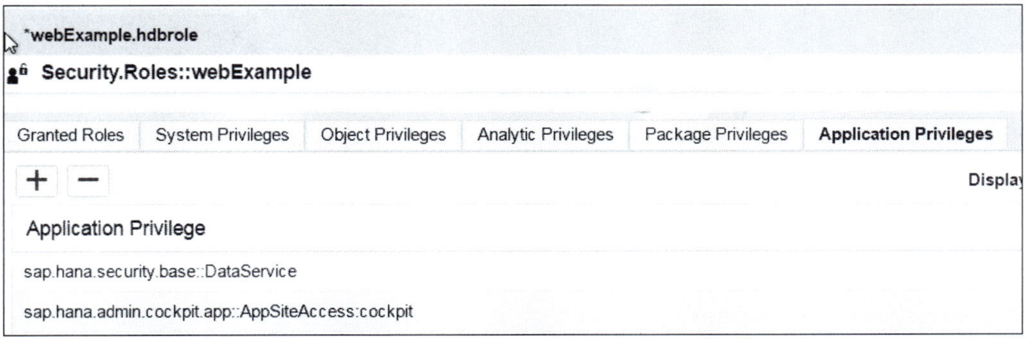

Figure 11.4 Selected Application Privileges

To remove an assigned application privilege, select it from the list, then click the large – button above the list to remove it. Items in the list must be deleted one at a time.

Once you've configured the desired list of application privileges, click the **Save All** button at the top left, which shows three stacked floppy disks.

If there are any issues saving and activating the repository role, messages will appear in red text within the console window just below the opened repository roles tab. The console window has a dark background color and is located at the bottom of the opened tab. Affirmative messages will appear in white text and error messages in red text.

To close the open repository role tab, click the small **x** to the right of the tab.

11.4 Privileges on Users

Unrelated to application privileges, an additional item named *privileges on users* can be used to grant the ATTACH DEBUGGER privilege, which has a very limited scope of usage within SAP HANA. It allows a user to grant a grantee debug access to the user's own session. This privilege only offers the ability to assign the ATTACH DEBUGGER privilege and is limited to the grantor's account.

For example, the user account SYSTEM can logon to SAP HANA Studio and grant to the user account ADMIN_MIKE the ATTACH DEBUGGER privilege but only for the user SYSTEM. In fact, SAP HANA Studio will only allow you to specify the grantor's account name under the column titled **user**. This privilege grants ADMIN_MIKE debug SQLScript code rights within the SYSTEM account's session. SYSTEM is also the only user that can grant this privilege to ADMIN_MIKE.

11.4.1 Granting Privileges on Users with SAP HANA Studio

To access the user or role management area in SAP HANA Studio, start by switching to the administration console perspective. On the **Systems** tab, located on the left side of the perspective, expand the **System** node. Locate the **Security** node and expand it to reveal the **Security**, **Users**, and **Roles** nodes. Expand the **Users** node to reveal user accounts defined in the system, or expand the **Roles** node to reveal standard roles defined in the system. To manage a grantee, double-click its name in the list to open the management interface tab on the right.

Within the management interface is a tab on the right named **Privileges on Users**. In this tab, click **+** to add your user account to the list. To the right of your user account, check the box next to **Attach Debugger**. Save your changes to grant the privilege to the grantee. Outside of your own account, no other grantees can be chosen using this interface.

Please note that the grantee also needs the DEBUG object privilege on the relevant stored procedure to debug another grantee's session.

11.4.2 Granting Privileges on Users with SQL

In addition to using SAP HANA Studio, a grantor can execute the following SQL code to grant the ATTACH DEBUGGER privilege to another grantee:

```
GRANT ATTACH DEBUGGER TO <GRANTEE>;
```

Replace the <GRANTEE> variable with the name of a grantee within your environment. When executed, the grantee will be granted access to debug the grantor's session.

11.5 Summary

Application privileges define custom levels of access to applications developed in the XS engine. Once activated, they can be granted to users or roles within the SAP HANA system. The **Privileges on Users** tab in SAP HANA Studio is used to grant the ATTACH DEBUGGER privilege to another grantee. We can also use SQL to grant the ATTACH DEBUGGER privilege.

Chapter 12
Authentication

Authentication is key in validating a user's access to the SAP HANA system. In this chapter, we'll discuss how SAP HANA supports external authentication providers in addition to its basis internal authentication mechanism.

Most of the chapters in this book spend a great deal of time discussing *authorization*, a process in which the SAP HANA system determines if a user is allowed to perform specific actions within the platform. To define allowable actions in SAP HANA, we effectively grant privileges to a user to define the individual actions a user account is authorized to perform. However, for the authorization mechanism to work properly, the SAP HANA system must first properly identify each user. The process used to identify a user is called *authentication*. SAP HANA supports several different types of authentication mechanisms, including both internal basic authentication and external authentication systems.

SAP HANA's internal basic authentication systems work through *password authentication*, meaning that SAP HANA will challenge users to supply both their user name and password—or, *user credentials*—as a form of identification. Like most authentication systems, SAP HANA assumes that the account owner is the only individual with knowledge of the credentials and therefore can prove his identity. Once an account is verified through password authentication, SAP HANA will conduct authorization checks based on the user's granted privileges or roles.

SAP HANA can also leverage many external authentication systems to support *single sign-on* (SSO), which allows a user's credentials to be challenged once by a master system and then passed to subsequent systems without the need to supply the credentials again. In the case of SAP HANA, we can configure the system to support the following external provider options: Kerberos, SAML, SAP logon or assertion tickets, and X.509 client certificates. By default, all user accounts support SAP HANA's internal basic authentication mechanism. However, each user can be configured to support one or more additional external authentication providers for the purposes of SSO.

When configuring the user account for external authentication, we must first activate the external provider and then specify mapping data. SAP HANA uses this mapping data to validate an SAP HANA user account's external identity. This also means that a dedicated SAP HANA user account is required for every internal or external user of the system. For example, we can't use SAML SSO authentication between SAP HANA and another system unless a user account exists in SAP HANA, with its SAML identity enabled and configured. Therefore, every authenticating user must be a provisioned user for all authentication scenarios.

As of SAP HANA 2.0 SPS 00, external authentication providers can't be used for password authentication. For example, you cannot logon to SAP HANA using SAP HANA Studio by supplying your credentials that are hosted in an external system, such as LDAP or Active Directory.

To better understand the authentication providers supported by SAP HANA, this chapter will walk through the details of the internal basic authentication system and its configurable settings. We'll also discuss the various external providers that are supported for SSO to the SAP HANA system.

12.1 SAP HANA Internal Authentication Mechanism

SAP HANA provides an internal basic authentication mechanism, in the form of an internal user account and password system. The internal password authentication mechanism needs to be secured in two ways: First, we need to identify the methods we use to transmit these passwords to the SAP HANA system and implement encryption to prevent others from intercepting these passwords. Second, we need to establish policies related to a user's password. The password should be sufficiently complex and changed periodically. Let's look at how to use both encryption and password policies to protect the internal SAP HANA authentication mechanism.

12.1.1 Protecting SAP HANA Passwords with Encryption

When a client application communicates with SAP HANA and when password authentication is used to authenticate the user, we often need to use encryption to prevent unauthorized individuals from intercepting the password. By default, many client applications don't use encryption when communicating with SAP HANA. However, SAP HANA supports communication encryption with the ODBC, JDBC, and HTTP protocols.

We can use ODBC, JDBC, HTTP, or HTTPS client connection protocols depending on our mode of connection. Tools such as SAP HANA Studio will use JDBC to communicate user provided authenticate credentials to the SAP HANA system. Business intelligence tools often use ODBC and JDBC as well. Users accessing applications in the XS engine will likely use HTTP or HTTPS to communicate authentication credentials to the SAP HANA system.

JDBC and ODBC client credentials can be transmitted in an encrypted format to help protect them from unauthorized access. Applications hosted in the XS engine can be accessed using the HTTPS protocol. The HTTP protocol isn't encrypted; using HTTPS will provide the necessary encryption. In general, HTTP access shouldn't be used for SSO or form-based authentication because it isn't secure. Form-based authentication, in which users enter their username and password in a form, is used by web-based applications to collect credentials for authentication. Most XS engine applications support form-based authentication by default. Many external authentication systems also rely on the HTTP protocol when communicating SSO credentials. In all cases, SAP HANA should be configured to use HTTP with SSL or HTTPS for encrypted communications over the HTTP protocol. We'll discuss how encryption is enabled and managed in Chapter 13; for now, note that we need encryption in addition to strong password policies to properly protect SAP HANA's internal authentication mechanism.

12.1.2 Configuring the Internal Authentication Password Policy

Password policy security settings within SAP HANA can be configured using a few different methods: First, we can issue `ALTER SYSTEM ALTER CONFIGURATION` SQL commands to update security settings stored in the SAP HANA INI configuration files. Second, we can use SAP HANA Studio's configuration area to directly update the individual INI settings. Third, SAP HANA Studio provides a security management area for easy access to security settings within SAP HANA. Finally, the SAP HANA Web-Based Development Workbench security manager provides an interface like the one in SAP HANA Studio.

These password policy security settings, specific to the SAP HANA internal authentication, allow for changes to password policies. There are two main configuration files that affect the password policy. If the SAP HANA system is set up as a single container system, the indexserver.ini file will be used for password policy settings. This configuration file contains settings specific to the SAP HANA index server process. Settings can be entered for an index server process on a specific server node or for all index servers in the cluster. To accommodate all servers in a cluster, the system layer should be used. To accommodate a specific host, the host layer should be used. If the SAP HANA system is set up as a multicontainer system, the nameserver.ini file will be used in the same capacity.

In this section, we'll review the password policy settings in SAP HANA and demonstrate the steps and procedures used to configure password policy settings using SQL statements, SAP HANA Studio configuration, and the SAP HANA Web-Based Development Workbench security manager.

SAP HANA offers security administrators several options to manipulate the behavior of its internal basic authentication mechanism. The specific settings allow organizations to either strengthen their password policy standards or relax them as needed. Let's look at these settings, listed by their technical names, in more detail.

minimal_password_length

The `minimal_password_length` setting governs the minimum allowed length for passwords. The system supports a length of six to 64 characters. When creating user accounts or changing passwords, the specified password must comply with the configured minimum password length. Most GUIs refer to this setting as **Minimum Password Length**.

password_layout

The `password_layout` setting governs the minimum supported complexity of the password. The setting value is based on the entered expression pattern. To define the pattern, you can choose one or more of the following character expressions:

- Lowercase letters from `a` to `z`
- Uppercase letters from `A` to `Z`
- Numerical digits from `0` to `9`
- Most special characters found on the keyboard

To define the minimum complexity expression, choose values from each of the supported characters. There's no need to choose more than one of each type, and the selected letter, digit, or special character has no impact on the exact password letters that will be allowed. For example, if the minimum password complexity requires the use of at least one uppercase letter, one lowercase letter, and one number, we could specify the expression `Aa1`, `Cz1`, or `F03`. If the complexity requires the use of at least one uppercase letter, one number, and one special character, we could specify the expression G3_. Again, the specific letter, digit, or character used isn't important. The system looks at the pattern specified to determine the minimum complexity. To disable the minimum complexity requirement, specify an empty string value as the expression. However, it's advisable that the default expression pattern of Aa1 be specified at a minimum. Most GUIs refer to this setting as **Required Character Types**.

Using Special Characters in Passwords

Although using special characters in passwords is an excellent way to increase password complexity, users might have trouble authenticating with SAP HANA from some clients. When a password contains a special character, SAP HANA requires that it's sent to the system enclosed in double quotes (e.g., "_"). If the client fails to comply with this requirement, the user might not be able to authenticate. As a result, we highly recommend checking that all required client interfaces authenticate users with special characters in their passwords before they're mandated in all passwords.

force_first_password_change

The force_first_password_change setting mandates whether a user must change his initial password before the first attempt to authenticate with the system. Most GUIs refer to this setting as **Password Change Required on First Logon**.

When set to true, the user must change the password established by the administrator before he can completely log on to the system. When set to false, the user can log on using the password created by the administrator. Note that at some point in the future the user might be forced to change his password based on other password policy settings.

On a per-user basis, we can issue the following SQL statement to require a password change before the next authentication attempt:

```
ALTER USER <USER_NAME> FORCE PASSWORD CHANGE
```

We can also create or alter user accounts on a per-user basis and disable this policy. The following SQL statements can be used to disable the policy on a per-user account basis:

```
CREATE USER <USER_NAME> PASSWORD "!niti@LPass" NO FORCE_FIRST_PASSWORD_CHANGE
ALTER USER <USER_NAME> PASSWORD "!niti@LPass" NO FORCE_FIRST_PASSWORD_CHANGE
```

When issuing the ALTER statement, we must specify a password or the statement won't execute. Depending on the configuration of the password reuse policy, a new password might be required when issuing ALTER statements.

last_used_passwords

The last_used_passwords setting governs the minimum number of times that a password must be changed before it can be used again. This setting forces users to choose a password not used in the last x number of passwords each time they change it or each time they're required to change it. The default value is five previous passwords. If the value of 0 is specified, a password can be reused at any time. Most GUIs refer to this setting as **Number of Last Used Passwords That Cannot Be Reused**.

maximum_invalid_connect_attempts

The maximum_invalid_connect_attempts setting specifics the minimum number of failed logon attempts for a given account before the system locks the account to prevent further access. Most GUIs refer to this setting as **Number of Allowed Failed Logon Attempts**.

A minimum value of 1 is required for this setting, and no maximum value is specified in the documentation. The system defaults to six invalid logon attempts before an account is locked. Once an account is locked, the user account can't authenticate with the system. The user must wait until the system unlocks the account after a configured duration or until the administrator manually unlocks the account. The system won't unlock the account if the lock indefinitely policy setting is set to true in the configuration settings. Only administrators can unlock an account when the lock indefinitely policy is enabled.

Administrators can issue the following SQL statement to unlock a user account:

```
ALTER USER <USER_NAME> RESET CONNECT ATTEMPTS;
```

To list accounts that have invalid connection attempts exceeding the configured invalid connection attempt policy, execute the SQL code in Listing 12.1.

```
SELECT
X.USER_NAME,
X.INVALID_CONNECT_ATTEMPTS,
(CASE WHEN X.INVALID_CONNECT_ATTEMPTS >= X.PASSPOL
THEN 'Locked' ELSE 'OK' END) AS ACCOUNT_STATUS
```

```
FROM
    (
SELECT USER_NAME, INVALID_CONNECT_ATTEMPTS,
(SELECT TOP 1 "VALUE" FROM "SYS"."M_PASSWORD_POLICY"
WHERE PROPERTY = 'maximum_invalid_connect_attempts')
AS PASSPOL
FROM "SYS"."USERS"
    ) X
WHERE X.INVALID_CONNECT_ATTEMPTS >= X.PASSPOL
```

Listing 12.1 SQL Code to List Account Status for Users in SAP HANA System

The number of active consecutive failed connection attempts will be reset each time a user logs on successfully. However, the system records the number of historical failed attempts issued before each successful logon. The following SQL statement will query the system view containing the failed connection attempt history preceding each successful connection attempt's timestamp:


```
SELECT * FROM SYS.INVALID_CONNECT_ATTEMPTS
```

To remove all historical data related to failed connection attempts, issue the following SQL statement per user:

```
ALTER USER <USER_NAME> DROP CONNECT ATTEMPTS;
```

password_lock_time

The `password_lock_time` setting specifies the amount of time in minutes the system will wait before it unlocks accounts that have exceeded the maximum number of failed logon attempts. Most GUIs refer to this setting as **User Lock Time**.

The default is 1,440 minutes or one day. If a value of 0 is specified, the account will be unlocked immediately and the `maximum_invalid_connect_attempts` setting will effectively be disabled.

To lock an account indefinitely, enter a value of `-1` in the file settings or choose the **Lock User Indefinitely** option found in some SAP HANA GUIs.

minimum_password_lifetime

The `minimum_password_lifetime` setting, or **Minimum Password Lifetime** in most GUIs, dictates the minimum number of days that must elapse before a user can change his/her own password. The default value is one day and a value of 0 disables this setting. It's designed to prevent users from changing their passwords several times consecutively, thereby circumventing the password reuse policy. A default value of one day will discourage consecutive password changes for most users given the required delay. The value should be increased if users aren't discouraged by the default value.

maximum_password_lifetime

The `maximum_password_lifetime` setting, or **Maximum Password Lifetime** in most GUIs, governs the age of passwords in days. The default value is 182 days and a minimum value of 1 is supported. When the password lifetime is exceeded, a user will be forced to change her password before she can successfully authenticate with the system. Passwords should be changed periodically to protect from intentional decryption or to reduce the likelihood of the password being compromised.

On a per-user basis, issue the following SQL statement to disable the password lifetime policy:

```
ALTER USER <USER_NAME> DISABLE PASSWORD LIFETIME;
```

To re-enable the policy, issue the following SQL statement:

```
ALTER USER <USER_NAME> ENABLE PASSWORD LIFETIME;
```

maximum_unused_initial_password_lifetime

The `maximum_unused_initial_password_lifetime` setting determines the validity of passwords established by the administrator in days. When an account is created or a password generated by an administrator, this setting will determine how long the password remains viable before it expires and the account is disabled. The system default value is seven days and a minimum value of one day is supported. After the duration of the configured value, a user's account will be disabled until the administrator resets the password. Note that this value was misspelled in versions of SAP HANA prior to SAP HANA 1.0 SPS 12. Most GUIs refer to this setting as **Lifetime of Initial Password**.

maximum_unused_productive_password_lifetime

The `maximum_unused_productive_password_lifetime` setting specifies the number of days before an inactive user account is disabled. Inactive user accounts are those that haven't authenticated with the system for some time. The default value is 365 days and a minimum value of one day is supported. Administrators must reset the account password once the user account expires. Most GUIs refer to this setting as **Maximum Duration of User Inactivity**.

password_expire_warning_time

The `password_expire_warning_time` setting specifies how long in days before the expiration of a password the system will notify a user. The notification is transmitted during any ODBC or JDBC successful authentication or connection attempt. It's the duty of the connecting application to send this message through to the user. If a value of `0` is specified, password expiration notifications are disabled. Most GUIs refer to this setting as **Notification of Password Expiration**.

password_lock_for_system_user

When configured with the default value of `true`, the `password_lock_for_system_user` setting will prevent the SYSTEM user account from being locked out, even if multiple consecutive invalid passwords are issued. It supersedes the `password_lock_time` and `maximum_invalid_connect_attempts` settings. Most GUIs refer to this setting as **Exempt SYSTEM User from Locking**.

detailed_error_on_connect

The `detailed_error_on_connect` setting determines the amount of failed logon information provided during authentication attempts. Most GUIs refer to this setting as **Detailed Error Information on Failed Logon**. The default value is `false`, which means that the generic **Authentication Failed** message is returned regardless of the failure reason. When `true`, a more specific message, such as **Invalid User or Password**, **User Is Locked**, **Connect Try Is Outside Validity Period**, or **User Is Deactivated** is returned. It's best to use the default value of `false` to make it more difficult for hackers to gain unauthorized access to the SAP HANA system.

12.1.3 Managing Password Policy Settings with SQL

Using SQL commands, we can directly set the value for each of the settings listed in Section 12.2.1. The syntax is based on the `ALTER SYSTEM ALTER CONFIGURATION` commands. You'll need the `INIFILE ADMIN` system privilege to modify these settings using SQL. The following generic SQL statement demonstrates the required syntax to manipulate password policy settings within SAP HANA:

```
ALTER SYSTEM ALTER CONFIGURATION ('<ini file name>', '<layer>')
   SET ('password policy', '<Setting Name>') = '<value>' WITH RECONFIGURE ;
```

The `<ini file name>` variable should be replaced with the name of the configuration file. For a single-container system, use `indexserver.ini`. For multiple container system use `nameserver.ini`. The `<layer>` variable should be replaced with `SYSTEM` or `HOST`. Use `SYSTEM` to apply the setting to all configuration files in the cluster. Use `HOST`, to apply the setting to a specific host. The `<Setting Name>` variable must contain a setting listed in Section 12.2.1. The `<value>` field should be replaced with a supported value for the given setting. Specify `WITH RECONFIGURE` to apply the setting instantly. If this setting isn't specified, the configured value won't take effect until the next reboot.

The following example SQL statement will configure the `password_layout` password policy setting with a value of `Aa1`:

```
ALTER SYSTEM ALTER CONFIGURATION ('nameserver.ini', 'SYSTEM')
   SET ('password policy', 'password_layout') = 'Aa1' WITH RECONFIGURE ;
```

To revert a setting to its default value, use the `UNSET` option within the command. The following example will revert the `password_layout` setting to its default value:

```
ALTER SYSTEM ALTER CONFIGURATION ('nameserver.ini', 'SYSTEM')
   UNSET ('password policy', 'password_layout');
```

We can use the same syntax to unset all the password policy settings listed in Section 12.2.1; simply update the variables to match your environment. Remember to specify the correct INI settings file and layer specific to your environment. Now, let's review how to change the settings using SAP HANA GUIs.

12.1.4 Managing Password Policy Settings in GUIs

SAP HANA offers GUIs in which password policy settings can be configured. SAP HANA Studio provides the configuration area and the **Password Policy** configuration tab, and SAP HANA Web-Based Development Workbench security manager also provides an interface. Let's look at these three options.

SAP HANA Studio: Configuration

Instead of using SQL commands to update the security policy settings, we can use the configuration options in SAP HANA Studio. The configuration options can be found on a specific tab. Open the administration console perspective, log on to your system, and right-click it in the **Systems** tab found on the left side of the screen, then choose **Configuration and Monitoring • Open Administration**. The **Administration** tab will open to the right, with the **Overview** tab selected by default.

Exactly five tabs to the right of the **Overview** tab, you'll see the **Configuration** tab; click it to reveal a list of INI files for the specified SAP HANA system (see Figure 12.1). You'll need the `INIFILE ADMIN` system privilege to modify these settings.

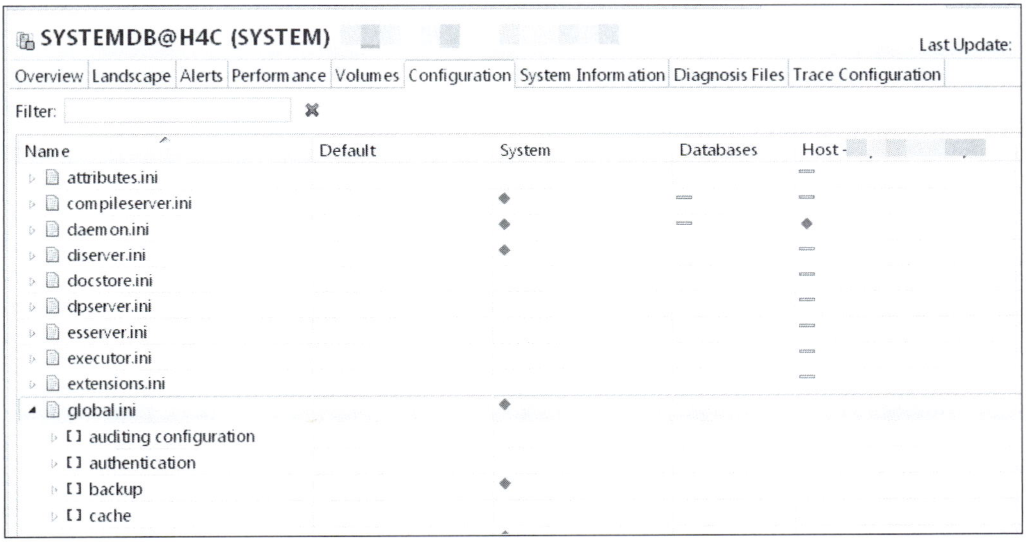

Figure 12.1 Configuration Tab in SAP HANA Studio

On the **Configuration** tab, you'll see a **Filter** box at the top left; in it, enter the search term "password" to filter all configuration settings related to the password policy. Alternatively, you can navigate the configuration file hierarchy by expanding the file nodes containing the password policy settings, **indexserver.ini** and **nameserver.ini**. For single-container systems, expand **indexserver.ini**; for multicontainer systems, expand **nameserver.ini**. Under the file node, look for the node named **password policy** and expand it to reveal the individual password policy settings. Double-click a specific setting to open its configuration window. For example, double-click the **last_used_passwords** node (see Figure 12.2). Each setting node a window in which you can change the setting's value.

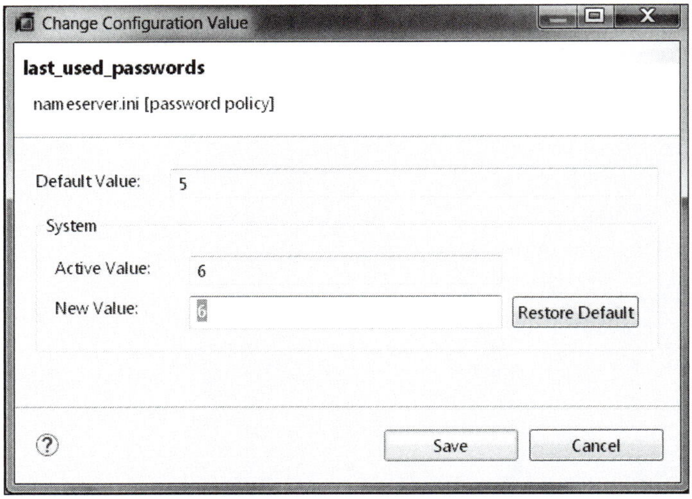

Figure 12.2 Changing Password Policy Settings for last_used_passwords in SAP HANA Studio

The interface will list the **Default** and **Active** values for the setting. In addition, there is a **Restore Default** button that can be used to quickly restore the default value for the setting. To change the configuration setting, enter the desired value in the **New Value** field and click the **Save** button. To cancel changes before they're saved, click the **Cancel** button. Password policy settings are implemented instantly within the SAP HANA system; no reboot is required for them to take effect.

SAP HANA Studio: Security Manager

SAP HANA also offers a security manager area that includes a **Password Policy** configuration tab. To access this tab, open the administration console perspective in SAP HANA Studio, log on to your system, and expand the **Systems** node. Double-click the **Security** node to open the security management interface, then click the **Password Policy** tab (see Figure 12.3). A new configuration window will appear containing options to configure the password policy.

As you can see, some of the same configuration settings listed in the previous section are available here as well. There are a few settings not available here, such as `password_expire_warning_time`, `password_lock_for_system_user`, and `detailed_error_on_connect`.

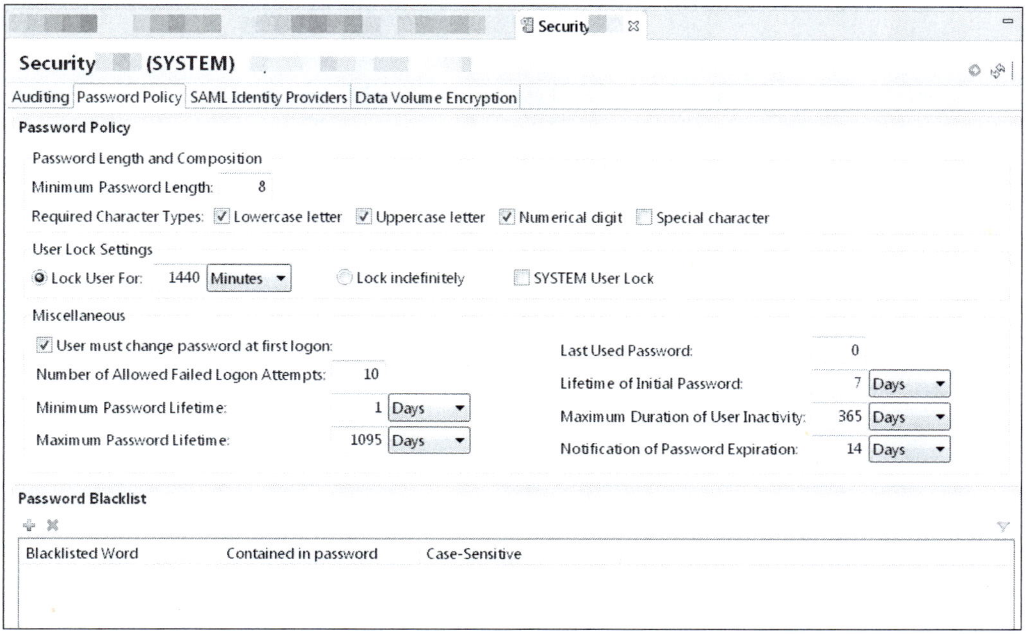

Figure 12.3 Password Policy Configuration Tab in SAP HANA Studio

Although this interface might be missing a few settings, it also offers an additional **Password Blacklist** configuration area, located at the bottom of the **Password Policy** tab (see Figure 12.4). This interface allows the administrator to define a blacklist of specific words, phrases, or password combinations that won't be accepted by the system.

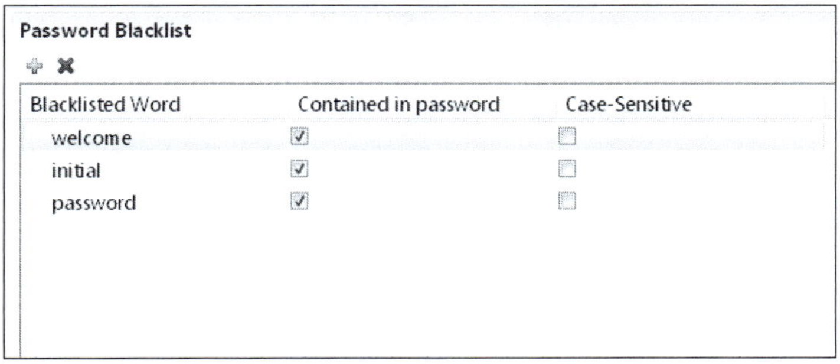

Figure 12.4 Password Blacklist Configuration

To add a blacklist item, click the **+** button just below the **Password Blacklist** title. In the columns provided, click the first cell to enter the **Blacklisted Word**. If you want the system to look for the word within the provided password, select the checkbox beside the **Contained in Password** option. For example, if the blacklisted word is welcome, the password welcome1234 wouldn't be accepted because it contains the word welcome. If this option isn't checked, the system will only prevent the exact word as listed in the first cell. Using the same example, the password welcome1234 would be acceptable because it isn't an exact match for welcome. If the word should be evaluated using the exact case of the entered text, select the **Case-Sensitive** checkbox. For example, if the option is selected, then Welcome would be accepted if the provided blacklisted word is welcome.

We can also execute the following SQL statement to view a list of configured blacklisted password words defined in the system:

```
SELECT * FROM "_SYS_SECURITY"."_SYS_PASSWORD_BLACKLIST"
```

SAP HANA Web-Based Development Workbench Security Manager

The SAP HANA Web-Based Development Workbench security manager, hosted within the SAP HANA XS engine, provides an interface to manage security settings, including password policies.

You can access the SAP HANA Web-Based Development Workbench security manager by updating the following two URLs to match the details of your environment:

- *http://<sap_hana_host>:80<instance_number>/sap/hana/ide/security*
- *https://<sap_hana_host>:43<instance_number>/sap/hana/ide/security*

Once you have access to the SAP HANA Web-Based Development Workbench security manager, expand the **Security** node on the left. Figure 12.5 shows the **Security Console** interface and the **Password Policy** tab.

Click the **Security** icon ❶ shown in Figure 12.5. The **Security Console** tab ❷ will open. This tab contains all the same options available in SAP HANA Studio, including a **Password Blacklist** area, located at the bottom of the **Security Console** tab.

SAP HANA also supports a few external or third-party authentication providers for SSO to the system. In the next section, we'll review these external providers in more detail.

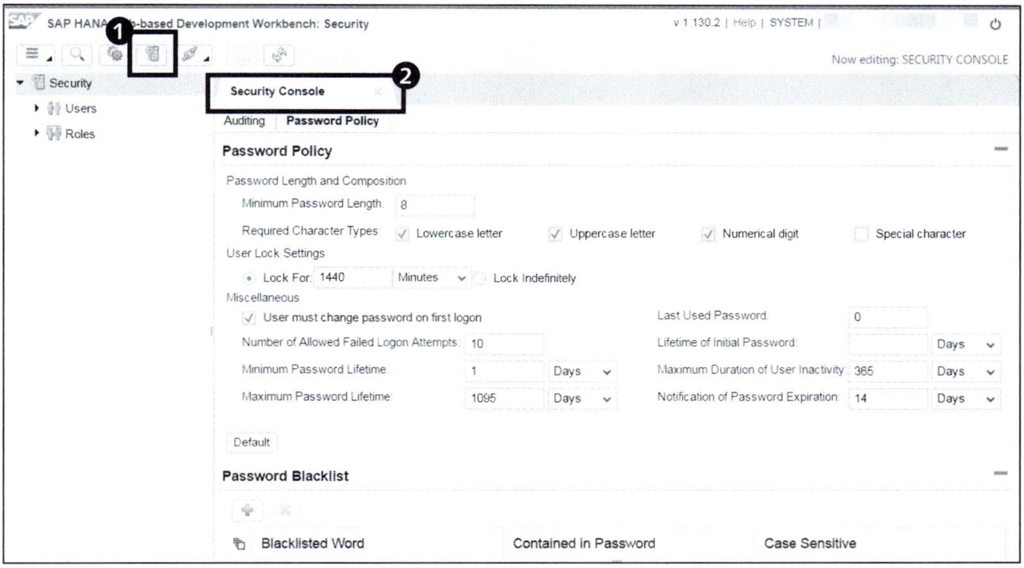

Figure 12.5 Password Policy Configuration in SAP HANA Web-Based Development Workbench

12.2 Supported Third-Party Authentication Providers

SAP HANA supports several well-established third-party authentication mechanisms for the purposes of SSO. This support will simplify the process of authentication within SAP HANA from trusted third-party applications. With third-party authentication, users aren't required to manually reenter their username and password each time they access resources within the SAP HANA platform. Instead, the SAP HANA system will trust that the external system has already properly authenticated the user and will therefore securely trust requests for the user from the external system. SAP HANA supports third-party system access via the HTTP, HTTPS, ODBC, and JDBC protocols, which allow for access to both web-based applications and data hosted in the SAP HANA platform. In this section, we'll discuss the third-party authentication mechanisms of Kerberos, SAML, X509, SAP logon tickets, and SAP assertion tickets, starting with Kerberos authentication.

12.2.1 Kerberos Authentication

Kerberos is a network authentication protocol based on work done at MIT dating back to the early days of networked computing. It's designed as a robust protocol that protects against many forms of unauthorized access. It uses strong cryptography, which makes it difficult to compromise. Because MIT released publicly available implementations of the protocol, and due to its robustness, Kerberos has been integrated into many computing systems over the years. One of the key integrations of Kerberos is its inclusion in Microsoft's popular Active Directory solution. This means that in almost every business environment using Microsoft Windows, when you log on to your desktop, you're likely using a form of Kerberos authentication.

Kerberos relies on the principals of public/private key cryptography to achieve its robust exchange of identity information and it relies on a central authority to manage credentials. This central system is known as a *key distribution center* (KDC). At a high level, supported client applications request tickets from the KDC and then send them to SAP HANA as a form of authentication. Figure 12.6 provides a high-level overview of the Kerberos ticket exchange process facilitating authentication via SSO. In this example, we can assume that the client is the SAP HANA Studio application running on a user's desktop.

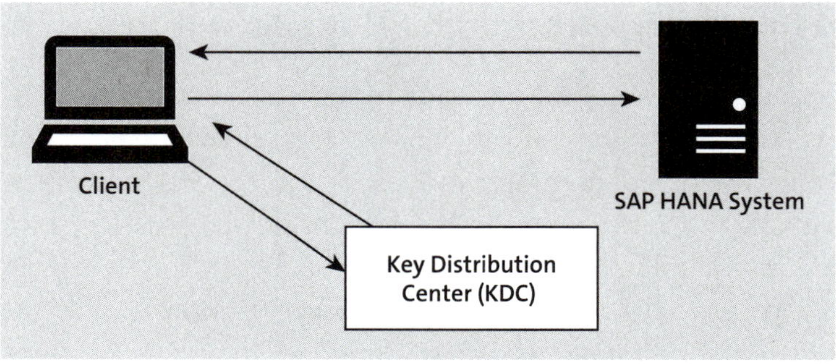

Figure 12.6 High-Level Kerberos Ticket Exchange among Client, KDC, and SAP HANA

We can assume that the client in Figure 12.6 has already authenticated with a master source that supports Kerberos authentication. When attempting to access SAP HANA resources, the client obtains an encrypted Kerberos ticket from the KDC. This ticket is then routed to the client, decrypted with client credentials, and sent to the SAP HANA system, along with other information, and used for authentication. The SAP HANA system accepts the ticket and locates an SAP HANA user with a matching Kerberos identity. All effective privileges assigned to this SAP HANA user account are then validated as the client interacts with the SAP HANA system.

In most implementations today, the KDC is provided by Microsoft Active Directory services. This reliance on an external central authority can make the configuration of an end-to-end Kerberos solution somewhat cumbersome. Kerberos was developed in the era of desktop software, so it works well in conjunction with desktop tools like SAP HANA Studio and protocols like ODBC and JDBC. However, it can be difficult to configure for Java-based applications and web-based applications.

Kerberos can also be used for web-based SSO by way of several additional standards that integrate Kerberos into web browsers. These were first introduced by Microsoft Internet Explorer and were later adopted by most modern web browsers. The XS engine and its web-based applications can leverage Kerberos with the *Simple and Protected GSSAPI Negotiation Mechanism* (SPNEGO) mechanism available in most modern browsers. For example, a client can log on to a personal computer, then, when the client accesses a trusted web application, the browser will use the initial logon credentials, obtain a ticket, and send the credentials to the web application for authentication.

Additional Resources and SAP Knowledge Base Articles (KBA)

For more technical details on Kerberos, we recommend the following resources:

- MIT's Kerberos project page (*http://web.mit.edu/kerberos/*)
- The Kerberos Consortium (*http://www.kerberos.org/*)
- Microsoft's Negotiate and SPNEGO protocols (*https://msdn.microsoft.com/en-us/library/ms995329.aspx*)

Information pertaining to the configuration of Kerberos within the SAP HANA platform can be found in the following notes and guides:

- SAP HANA Administration Guide (*http://help.sap.com/hana/SAP_HANA_Administration_Guide_en.pdf*)
- SAP Note 1837331: Detailed Instructions for Kerberos Configuration (*https://launchpad.support.sap.com/#/notes/0001837331*)
- SAP Note 1813724: Automation Tools to Assist with Kerberos Configuration (*https://launchpad.support.sap.com/#/notes/1813724/E*)
- SAP Note 2303807: Smart Data Access: SSO with Kerberos and Active Directory (*https://launchpad.support.sap.com/#/notes/2303807/E*)

Kerberos identities can be configured for a user via the SAP HANA user management options or via SQL commands. For example, to configure a Kerberos identity for a user in SAP HANA Studio, open the user management tab or window for a given user. The user management tab can be accessed by double-clicking a user account within the **Security** node found in the **Systems** tab of SAP HANA Studio after expanding the tree for a configured system.

In the user management tab (see Figure 12.7), to enable Kerberos SSO, select the **Kerberos** checkbox. Then, provide the external Kerberos identity in the **External ID** field. The format of this identity should match the *user principal name* (UPN) attribute of the external user Kerberos system user account. This is typically in the *user@domain.com* format, in which the user portion is replaced with the external system's username and domain.com is replaced with the external system's domain name.

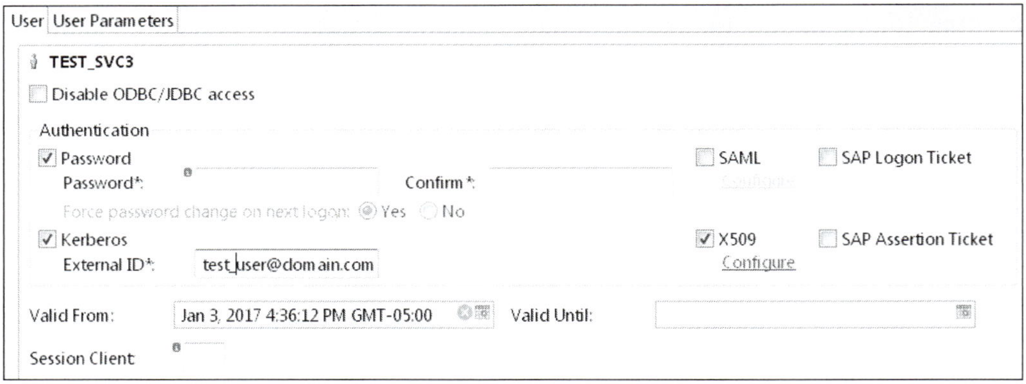

Figure 12.7 Configure Kerberos Identity for User Account

We can also use SQL statements to add a Kerberos identity to a user and to enable Kerberos support for a given user account, as follows:

```
ALTER USER <USER_NAME> ADD IDENTITY 'user@domain.com' FOR KERBEROS;
ALTER USER <USER_NAME> ENABLE KERBEROS;
```

The <USER_NAME> variable should be replaced with the name of an existing user account in the SAP HANA system. The string value following the `IDENTITY` statement should match the UPN from the external system; that is, the `'user@domain.com'` string value will contain a value specific to an individual user's UPN attribute in the external system. You should now have a basic understanding of the how Kerberos is supported within the SAP HANA system. Next, let's look at how SAML authentication can be leveraged in a similar fashion.

12.2.2 SAML Authentication

SAML is an authentication standard that comes from an open-source standards body called OASIS. One of SAML's key benefits is that transporting authentication and security data occurs via simple XML messages. This makes implementing SAML support in applications very straightforward.

SAML is somewhat different from Kerberos in that it has a much more decentralized architecture. This style of authentication solution is often referred to as a federated identity system. The solution is called federated because there is a loose coupling of multiple systems that have agreed to cooperate with each other for exchanging authentication and authorization data. Instead of a single central system that manages all identity information (as with Kerberos), SAML can support multiple identity providers that manage authentication of users for various parties.

In the SAP portfolio of products, the use of SAML is one example of SSO use between SAP BusinessObjects and SAP HANA. Although Kerberos is supported for SSO as well, the SAML configuration is significantly easier to implement and maintain. When using SAML with SAP BusinessObjects BI and SAP HANA as an end-to-end authentication solution, SAP BusinessObjects BI acts as the identity provider for the interaction. This means we don't need to configure anything beyond the SAP BusinessObjects BI and SAP HANA systems to get the solution working. In addition, because SAP BusinessObjects BI is the identity provider, any users that have successfully authenticated with SAP BusinessObjects can then access data in SAP HANA using their SAML identity. This offers a wide degree of flexibility. You could authenticate with the SAP BusinessObjects BI platform via Kerberos, LDAP, or SAP SSO and then access data in the SAP HANA system using SAML. Figure 12.8 provides an overview of the SAML authentication process.

The client in Figure 12.8 represents a user that authenticates with the SAP BusinessObjects BI system using assigned credentials. The SAP BI system, which is serving as the identity provider (IdP), manages and validates these credentials. The SAP HANA system is acting as the service provider (SP). If a trust relationship is defined between the two systems, a SAML identity is sent to the SAP HANA system and the authentication is accepted. The user in the SAP BusinessObjects BI system can query the SAP HANA system as an identified user based on the SAP HANA user's SAML identity. All effective privileges assigned to this SAP HANA user account are then validated as queries are issued by the SAP BusinessObjects BI system. This includes filter conditions required by any granted analytic privileges.

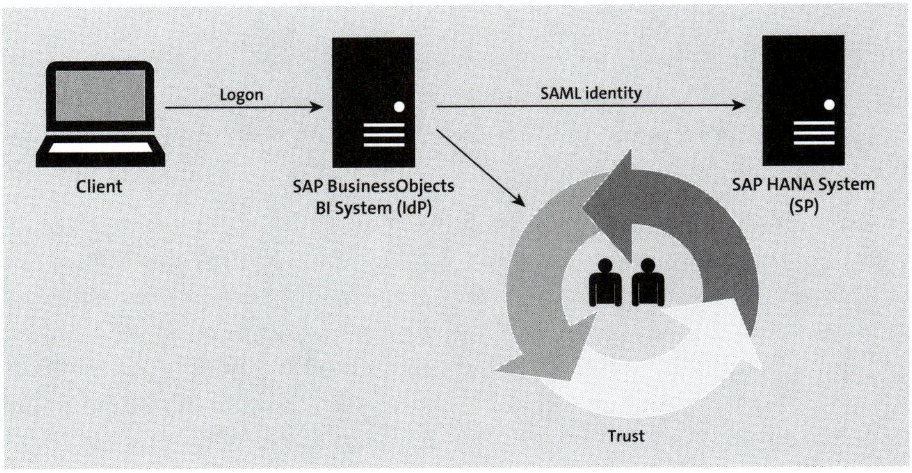

Figure 12.8 High-Level SAML Authentication Process

SAML is also a supported SSO mechanism for XS engine web applications. SAP HANA supports multiple SAML providers, allowing a variety of systems to perform SSO authentication for web-based applications hosted in SAP HANA. This also includes support for ODBC/JDBC connections used to interact with the SAP HANA RDBMS. In theory, any vendor's application has the potential to use SAML SSO when authenticating with SAP HANA. Keep in mind that it's the responsibility of each vendor to provide the integration between its application and SAP HANA's SAML provider configuration.

Additional SAML Resources and Configuration Guides

For more technical details on SAML, see the following resources:

- Technical overview of SAML (*https://www.oasis-open.org/committees/download.php/27819/sstc-saml-tech-overview-2.0-cd-02.pdf*)
- Complete SAML specification (*http://saml.xml.org/saml-specifications*)

For help configuring SAML SSO between SAP BusinessObjects and SAP HANA, review the following guides:

- SAP BusinessObjects BI Administration Guide, Section 18.1.3.14: Implementing SAML SSO from SAP BusinessObjects BI to SAP HANA (*http://help.sap.com/businessobject/product_guides/sbo42/en/sbo42sp3_bip_admin_en.pdf*)
- SAML SSO for BI Platform to HANA (*https://wiki.scn.sap.com/wiki/display/SAPHANA/SAML+SSO+for+BI+Platform+to+HANA*)

SAML identities can be configured for a user via SAP HANA's user management options or via SQL commands. For example, to configure a SAML identity for a user in SAP HANA Studio, first open the user management window for a given user by double-clicking a user account within the **Security** node found in the **Systems** tab of SAP HANA Studio after expanding the tree under a configured system.

In the user management window, select the **SAML** checkbox to enable SAML SSO. You must then provide the external SAML identity by clicking the **Configure** link below the **SAML** checkbox (see Figure 12.9).

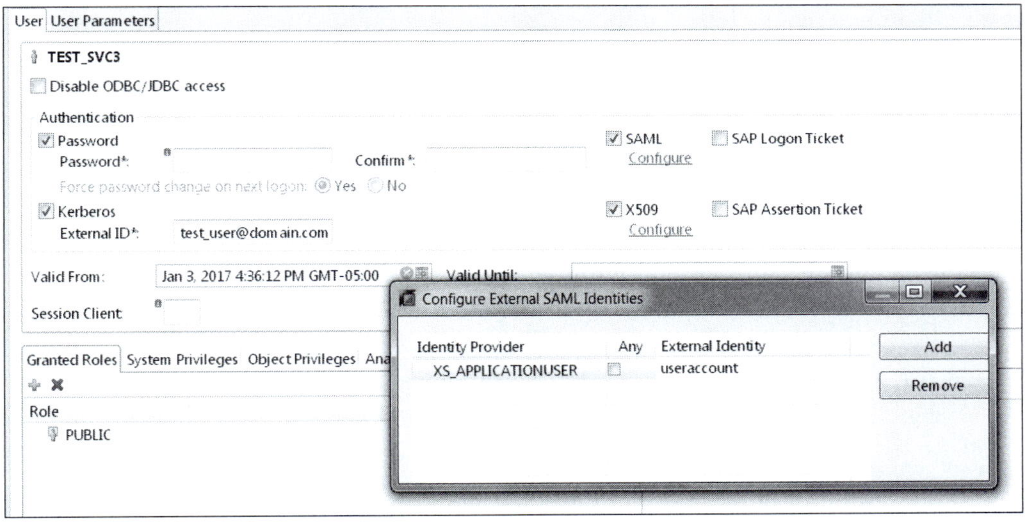

Figure 12.9 Configure SAML Identity for User Account

A window titled **Configure External SAML Identities** will appear (see Figure 12.9), allowing you to add one or more SAML identities to a user. Click **Add** to create a new identity. In the **Identity Provider** field, choose an existing SAML identity provider configured in the SAP HANA system. In the **External Identity** field, enter the name of the user in the external system.

If you prefer to have all external users mapped to a single SAP HANA user, place a check in the **Any** column. When the **Any** option is enabled, all external users will receive the permissions assigned to a single SAP HANA user. This option should only be implemented if you don't need to establish analytic privileges on an external system, user-by-user basis.

We can also use SQL statements to add a SAML identity to a user and to enable SAML support for a given user account—for example:

```
ALTER USER <USER NAME> ADD IDENTITY '<SAML IDENTITY STRING>' FOR SAML
PROVIDER <SAML PROVIDER>;
ALTER USER <USER NAME> ENABLE SAML;
```

The <USER NAME> variable should be replaced with the name of an existing user account in the SAP HANA system. The '<SAML IDENTITY STRING>' variable should match the user name found in the external system. The <SAML PROVIDER> should match the name of a SAML provider configured in the SAP HANA system.

As noted before, we can also configure a single SAP HANA account to support all users in an external system. For this, we need to use the IDENTITY ANY clause in our SQL statement—for example:

```
ALTER USER <USER NAME> ADD IDENTITY ANY FOR SAML PROVIDER <SAML PROVIDER>;
```

You should now have a basic understanding of the how SAML is supported within the SAP HANA system. Now, let's look at how X509 authentication can be leveraged in a similar fashion.

12.2.3 X509 Authentication

X.509 is the standard for the *public key infrastructure (PKI)* implemented to manage digital certificates for the purposes of verification, encryption, and authentication in some cases. SAP HANA supports the use of X.509 certificates for SSO access to XS engine applications.

Root certificates can be generated from a trusted certificate authority (CA) and imported into the XS engine trust store and the SAP Web Dispatcher trust store. When XS engine applications are deployed, the XS application administration tool can be used to configure X.509 SSO support for that specific web-based application.

SAP HANA users can be configured with a specific X.509 identity, which can be configured using SAP HANA user management options or with specific SQL commands that add external identities to user accounts. For example, the following SQL code will enable X.509 authentication for a user and add an X.509 identity to the same user account:

```
ALTER USER <USER_NAME> ENABLE X509;
ALTER USER <USER_NAME> ADD IDENTITY 'CN=MyUserName, O=ecorp, C=com'
ISSUER 'CN=ecert_so, O=ecorp, C=com' FOR X509;
```

The <USER_NAME> variable should be replaced with the name of an existing user account in the SAP HANA system. The string value in single quotes, following the

IDENTITY statement should match the string value specific to the generated certificate. For example, the string value CN=MyUserName will contain a value specific to an individual user.

To complete the process, a client certificate is generated, related to the SAP HANA user identity, and imported into a client's web browser. When a user attempts to access an XS engine application, the browser will ask the client to select a certificate for authentication. If the correct certificate is selected, the SAP HANA system will trust the client's certificate, locate the associated user account with the corresponding X.509 identity, and allow the client to interact with the XS application. Because the certificate was mapped to an existing user account, all granted privileges will be available during the session.

Additional Configuration Information

For additional configuration details, please see the section titled Maintaining Single Sign-On for SAP HANA XS Applications in the SAP HANA Administration Guide. You can download the guide at *http://help.sap.com/hana/SAP_HANA_Administration_Guide_en.pdf*.

12.2.4 SAP Logon Ticket

SAP logon tickets act as digital credentials that can be used to authenticate an SAP system user with supported external systems. In the case of SAP HANA, logon tickets can be used to provide SSO from SAP applications to XS engine web-based applications. For example, a user logs on to a web-based application hosted on an SAP NetWeaver Application Server. Within that application is a proxy link to an XS engine-based web application. The SAP NetWeaver–based application is configured to generate an SAP logon ticket and store it in the user's browser as a temporary session HTTP cookie. The XS engine application is configured to support SAP logon tickets. When the proxy link is clicked, the SAP HANA system finds the cookie in the browser and uses it to authenticate with the XS engine application.

Before the SAP HANA system will trust the SAP logon ticket, the external SAP application server certificates must be imported into the SAP HANA trust store. Once this trust is established, each SAP HANA user must be configured to support this authentication mechanism. It's assumed that the user ID found in the cookie will match that of a user configured in the SAP HANA system. Unlike Kerberos and SAML, there are no options to explicitly define the external identities of users with SAP logon ticket authentication enabled.

Additional Configuration Information

For additional configuration details, see the section titled Configure SSO with SAP Logon Tickets for SAP HANA XS Applications in the SAP HANA Administration Guide:

http://help.sap.com/hana/SAP_HANA_Administration_Guide_en.pdf

The SAP HANA Security Guide also provides a few additional details about the configuration process. Look for the section titled Single Sign-On Using SAP Logon and Assertion Tickets:

http://help.sap.com/hana/SAP_HANA_Security_Guide_en.pdf

Each SAP HANA user account must be configured to support SAP logon tickets. We can enable support for a user within the user management options in SAP HANA Studio or with SQL commands.

To enable SAP logon tickets for a user in SAP HANA Studio, open the user management window by double-clicking a user account within the **Security** node found in the **Systems** tab after expanding the tree for a configured system. In the user management window, select the **SAP Logon Ticket** checkbox (see Figure 12.10).

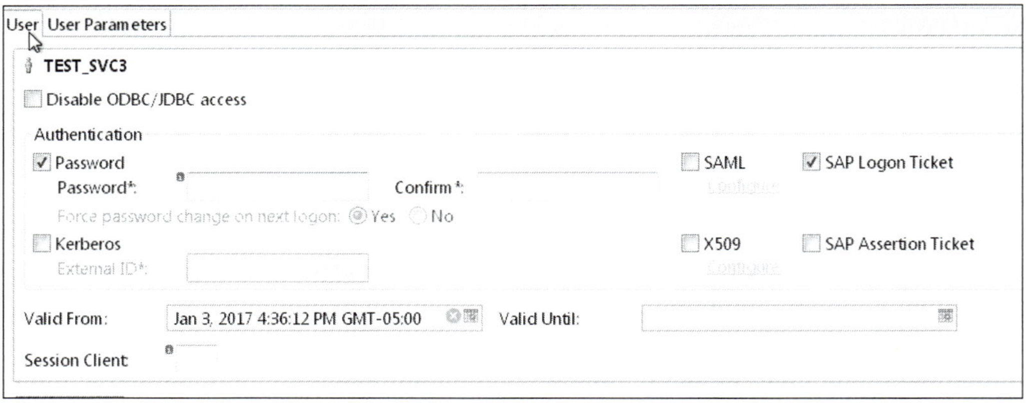

Figure 12.10 Enable SAP Logon Ticket in SAP HANA Studio

To perform the same operation using SQL, execute the following command in the SQL console, replacing the <USER_NAME> variable with an SAP HANA user:

```
ALTER USER <USER_NAME> ENABLE SAP LOGON TICKET;
```

12.2.5 SAP Assertion Ticket

SAP assertion tickets work like SAP logon tickets, with a few exceptions. The main difference is that SAP assertion tickets are transmitted in an HTTP header from one application server to the next. In the case of SAP HANA, the SAP credentials are obtained from the HTTP header, not from a session cookie. They're configured to work with only one specific target system and have a fixed lifetime of two minutes. Once an assertion ticket is used, it's deleted. Most experts would argue that they're somewhat more secure because of these factors. Outside of these differences, the SAP assertion ticket process is like the SAP logon ticket process.

An SAP HANA user account must be configured to support SAP assertion tickets. We can enable support for a user with the user management options in SAP HANA Studio or with SQL commands.

To enable SAP assertion tickets for a user in SAP HANA Studio, open the user management window by double-clicking a user account within the **Security** node found in the **Systems** tab after expanding the tree for a configured system. In the user management window, select the **SAP Assertion Ticket** checkbox (see Figure 12.11).

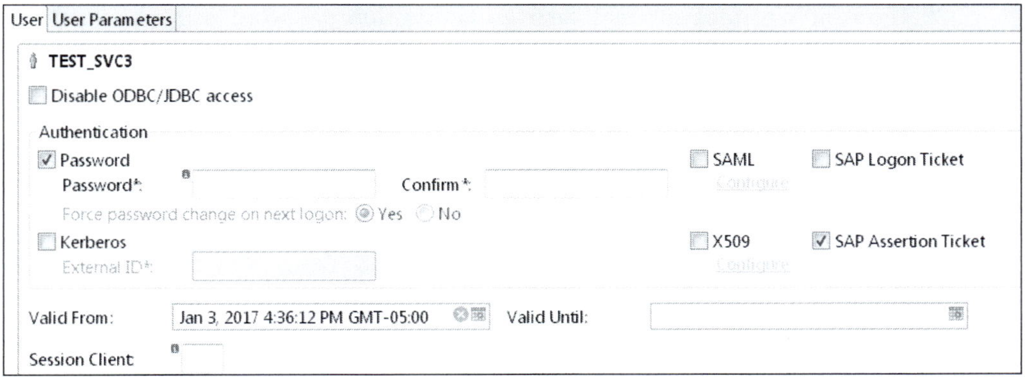

Figure 12.11 Enable SAP Assertion Ticket in SAP HANA Studio

To perform the same operation using SQL, execute the following command in the SQL console, replacing the <USER_NAME> variable with an SAP HANA user:

```
ALTER USER <USER_NAME> ENABLE SAP ASSERTION TICKET;
```

12.3 Case Study: Adding SAML Identity User Accounts

When E-Corporation originally implemented SAP HANA, it created several hundred user accounts before deciding to implement SAML authentication. Now, the company needs a script that will update existing user accounts and add the appropriate SAML identities. In Chapter 4, we discussed how E-Corporation imported user data from a file and used stored procedures to provision users. The procedure used there could create new users and add their SAML identities, but it wouldn't perform the same action on existing user accounts. To remedy this situation, E-Corporation has decided to create a new stored procedure that will add SAML identities to existing accounts. The procedure will only add SAML identities for users that are listed in the `Security.Tables::adusers` table and don't already have SAML identities.

The company has the following additional requirements for the stored procedure and the process needed to update user accounts programmatically:

1. User accounts will only be updated with a SAML identity if they have a record in table `Security.Tables::adusers`. This table is populated with user attributes obtained from an external system.
2. The user account's internal basis authentication password won't be changed; users can continue to use internal basis authentication and SAML authentication for SSO.
3. The user account's internal basis authentication password lifetime will comply with the configured password policy at E-Corporation.

To create the repository-based stored procedure in SAP HANA Studio, open the development perspective and go to the **Repositories** tab. Then, right-click the **Security. Provisioning** package and choose **New • Other.** Search for the object using the key word "procedure". In the search results, choose **SAP HANA • Database Development**, then **Stored Procedure**, and click **Next.**

A window named **New Stored Procedure** will appear. Near the bottom of the window, enter "ADD_SAML_TO_EXISTING_USERS", using uppercase letters, in the **File Name** entry field. In the **File Format** field, choose **Text (.hdbprocedure)** from the dropdown menu. In the **Target Schema** field, enter "security_tables", all in lowercase letters. Click **Finish** to save the file and open the **ADD_SAML_TO_EXISTING_USERS.hdbtable** configuration file on the right.

To define the `ADD_SAML_TO_EXISTING_USERS` repository-based stored procedure in SQL, use the syntax in Listing 12.2. Activate the design-time script by pressing [Ctrl]+[F3].

```
PROCEDURE "security_tables"."Security.Provisioning::ADD_SAML_TO_EXISTING_
USERS" ( )
  LANGUAGE SQLSCRIPT
  /* Procedure invoker must have privileges to create users */
  SQL SECURITY INVOKER
  AS
   BEGIN
/*Use a Cursor for future use. The following only
loops one time based on each record from SQL statement */

 DECLARE CURSOR c_users_list FOR
/* Find Active Users in SAP HANA that have no SAML Identity. If the
User is listed in the security table, add SAML Identity */
/* We need to escape the single quote mark around
SAMUSER and EMAILADDRESS with three single quote
marks ''' a total of 4 are needed */

SELECT
UT.AD_USER_NAME,
upper(UT.USER_NAME) as HANAUSER,
'''' || UT.AD_USER_NAME || '''' as SAMUSER
FROM  "security_tables"."Security.Tables::adusers" UT
WHERE upper(UT.USER_NAME) IN
    (SELECT upper(USER_NAME) FROM "SYS"."USERS" WHERE USER_NAME NOT IN
       (SELECT USER_NAME FROM "SYS"."SAML_USER_MAPPINGS") )
and UT.ACCOUNT_STATUS = 'A';

 FOR cur_row as c_users_list DO
    --- Add SAML identity to user
    EXEC 'ALTER USER ' || cur_row.HANAUSER || ' ADD IDENTITY '
        || cur_row.SAMUSER || ' FOR SAML PROVIDER TEST_SAML_PROVIDER';
    --- Enable SAML Authentication for the user account
    EXEC 'ALTER USER ' || cur_row.HANAUSER ||' ENABLE SAML';

 END FOR;

END;
```

Listing 12.2 Syntax for Stored Procedure to Create Users

The script uses a cursor to generate a list of users based on existing user accounts in the system with matching active records in table `Security.Tables::adusers`. The cursor query also validates that the users don't already have SAML identities. After it's validated, the script loops through the user list, executing two `ALTER USER` statements: The first `ALTER USER` statement adds the SAML identity listed in table `Security.Tables::adusers`. The second `ALTER USER` statement enables the SAML identity for the user. The script can be executed in the SQL console as needed using the following SQL command:

```
call "security_tables"."Security.Provisioning::ADD_SAML_TO_EXISTING_USERS"();
```

12.4 Summary

Authorization through the granting of privileges allows the SAP HANA system to determine permissible actions for a given user. However, before the system determines authorizations, the user must authenticate with SAP HANA. SAP HANA provides a basic internal authentication mechanism that supports password authentication. SAP HANA also supports external authentication providers, such as Kerberos, SAML, and X.509 certificates. External providers can only be used for the purposes of SSO with the JDBC, ODBC, or HTTP protocols.

Chapter 13
Certificate Management and Encryption

It's important to protect the data transmitted to and from SAP HANA and consider the data that is stored in SAP HANA. In this chapter, we discuss SAP HANA's offerings for stronger security: communication and data-level encryption to prevent unauthorized access to the system and its data.

In addition to authorization and authentication, we also need to use encryption to protect our SAP HANA systems. Encryption starts with the management of SSL certificates. We then must enable communication encryption between clients and the SAP HANA system. Finally, we must also encrypt the persistent storage volumes that contain a copy of the in-memory data. In this chapter, we'll discuss these encryption stages. Using and enabling encryption is an excellent way to protect data within SAP HANA.

13.1 SSL Certificates

X.509 is the standard for the *public key infrastructure (PKI)* implemented to manage digital certificates for the purposes of verification, encryption, and in some cases authentication. SAP HANA supports the use of X.509 certificates for securing both internal and external communication protocols.

In general, we refer to communication protocol security as *Transport Layer Security (TLS)* or, historically, *Secure Sockets Layer (SSL)*. You'll often hear both referred to as SSL protocols. The goal of SSL protocols within SAP HANA is to secure the communication channel between a client and the SAP HANA platform. Client communications occur via JDBC, ODBC, or HTTP within the SAP HANA platform.

When these communication channels are encrypted with SSL certificates, the individual TCP/IP application layer packets can't be intercepted and deciphered easily. For example, if we're using SAP HANA Studio to execute queries and return datasets, then enabling SSL in our system connection properties will ensure that the datasets are transmitted in an encrypted format. They're then decrypted by SAP HANA Studio, allowing them to be deciphered by users.

When SAP HANA is deployed, some of the client communication certificates are configured during the installation. This allows items such as HTTPS communication and JDBC/ODBC to support encryption out of the box. In SAP HANA, some X.509 certificates can be stored either in the database itself or within the file system of the operating system managing the SAP HANA instance. In Section 13.1.1, we'll review the list of certificates that can be managed within the SAP HANA database. In Section 13.1.2, we'll review the list of certificates that can be managed in the file system.

13.1.1 In-Database Certificate Management

SAP HANA allows X.509 certificates to be stored within the database itself, which means that certificate administrators don't need access to the OS or filesystem hosting the SAP HANA instance. Certificate information can be directly imported into the SAP HANA system using the SQL console and specific SQL commands. Once imported, they are assigned to a *certificate collection*, also called an internal *personal security environment (PSE)*. The internal PSE is a secure location within an SAP HANA database where both public and private key certificates are stored. The PSE can also contain trusted public key certificates and trusted root certificates.

Certificates can be used within SAP HANA for the purposes of both authentication and secure communication with TLS. Figure 13.1 depicts the mechanisms and purposes of the certificates that can be stored within the internal SAP HANA database.

For the purposes of authentication, SAP HANA can store certificates used for SAML, SAP assertion tickets, and X.509 certificates. To secure client communications at the TLS layer, SAP HANA system replication packets and client communication protocols can be encrypted. Client protocols such as ODBC and JDBC, including SAP HANA Studio communications, can all be encrypted using TLS security.

In-database certificate management is accomplished using SQL commands or, in some cases, the SAP HANA Cockpit. There are four categories of commands to discuss: those for adding certificates to the system, managing the certificate collection, managing certificates in the PSE, and defining the purpose of the certificate.

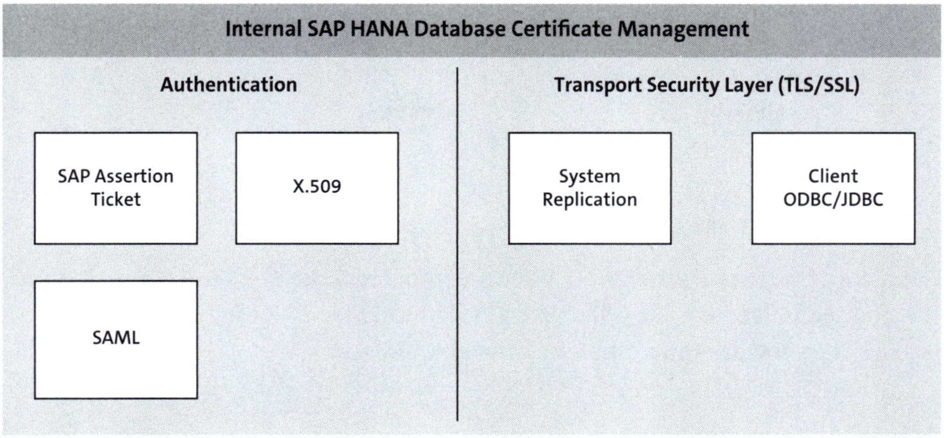

Figure 13.1 Items Supported in Internal Database Certificate Collections

Add a Certificate to the In-Database Store

To add a certificate to the in-database certificate store, use the CREATE CERTIFICATE FROM SQL command. To execute this statement, grantees will need the CERTIFICATE ADMIN system privilege. The SQL statement in Listing 13.1 illustrates importing a certificate.

```
CREATE CERTIFICATE FROM
'-----BEGIN CERTIFICATE-----
ERGJKjCCAz6gAwIDGDddtJHdfDFVmGMA0666*GSIb3DQEBBQUAMHkx89SDFGfV
cvdfSFGydfgDGGjgh5$5DSFghghdsdfs4%^SDfsdgfdgsdf++dffYTFTDFDSd
2FFgtDSFSDFdsfds==
-----END CERTIFICATE-----'
COMMENT 'E-Corp Certificate CA Client Communications';
```

Listing 13.1 SQL Code to Add Certificate to SAP HANA Database Store

To drop a certificate that hasn't already been added to a certificate collection, use the DROP CERTIFICATE SQL statement. For example, execute the following SQL statement to drop the certificate with the certificate ID of 123454:

```
DROP CERTIFICATE 123454;
```

You can query the system view to determine the certificate ID of a previously imported certificate. The following SQL statement will return all certificates currently imported into the system:

```
SELECT * FROM SYS.CERTIFICATES;
```

Next, we need to assign the certificate to a certificate collection.

Create/Delete a Certificate Collection or PSE

Certificates must be associated with a PSE, so we need to create one before we can assign the purpose of the certificate.

To create a PSE, execute the CREATE PSE SQL command. To execute this SQL command, the grantee must have the TRUST ADMIN system privilege. The following statements provide the general syntax and an example:

```
CREATE PSE <PSE_NAME>;
CREATE PSE "BI_SSO_SAM_CERT";
```

To view a list of certificates by PSE, we can query the PSE_CERTIFICATES system view. For example, to view all the certificate collections or PSEs within an SAP HANA system, use the following SQL query:

```
SELECT * FROM PSE_CERTIFICATES;
```

To view a list of PSEs defined in the system, execute the following SQL statement:

```
SELECT * FROM PSES;
```

To delete a PSE, use the following SQL command; the first provides the syntax and the second an example:

```
DROP PSE <PSE_NAME>;
DROP PSE "BI_SSO_SAM_CERT";
```

Next, we need to assign a certificate to the PSE.

Manage Certificates within the PSE

We can use SQL commands to add and remove certificates from a PSE. To add a certificate to the PSE, use the ALTER PSE SQL command. To alter the PSE, you must be the owner of the PSE. Alternatively, the grantee must have the ALTER object privilege on the certificate collection or PSE. For example, the following SQL will grant access to a PSE:

```
GRANT ALTER ON PSE "BI_SSO_SAM_CERT" TO SECURITY_ADMINS;
```

To add an existing certificate to the PSE, use the following SQL statement:

```
ALTER PSE <PSE> ADD CERTIFICATE <CERTIFICATE ID>
```

In the example, replace the `<PSE>` variable with the name of your PSE and the `<CERTIFICATE ID>` variable with the ID of the certificate that was previously imported into the SAP HANA system.

To remove a certificate from a PSE, use the following SQL command:

```
ALTER PSE <PSE> DROP CERTIFICATE <CERTIFICATE ID>
```

In the example, replace the `<PSE>` variable with the name of your PSE. Replace the `<CERTIFICATE ID>` variable with the ID of the certificate associated with the PSE.

Next, we need to define the purpose of the PSE.

Define the Purpose of the PSE

The final step in in-database certificate management is to define the purpose of the PSE and its certificates. The purpose of the PSE indicates how it will be used. We can use in-database PSEs for the purposes of authentication or TLS secure communications. For example, if we're using the PSE for SSO with SAML, we must define the purpose of the PSE as `SAML`. The system allows the purposes listed in Table 13.1 to be assigned.

Purpose	Use
SAML	If the PSE is used for SAML SSO authentication
SAP LOGON	If the PSE is used for SAP assertion ticket authentication
X509	If the PSE is used for X.509 certificate-based authentication
SSL/TLS	If the PSE is used to secure communications with JDBC, ODBC, or SAP HANA Studio connections
DATABASE REPLICATION	If the PSE is used to secure the network data packets communicated during system replication
JWT	If the PSE is used for JSON web token authentication

Table 13.1 Supported PSE Purposes for In-Database Certificate Management

There are two possible system privileges that a grantee must have when assigning the purpose of a PSE. First, if the PSE purpose is related to authentication, the grantee must have access to the PSE and the USER ADMIN system privilege. Second, if the PSE purpose is related to client communications or system replication, the grantee must have access to the PSE and the SSL ADMIN system privilege.

If a grantee doesn't have access to the PSE or isn't the owner of the PSE, the REFERENCES object privileges must be assigned to the grantee. For example, the following SQL command will grant REFERENCES to the CERT_ADMINS role:

```
GRANT REFERENCES ON PSE "BI_SSO_SAM_CERT" TO CERT_ADMINS;
```

To define the purpose of the PSE, execute the SET PSE SQL command, as follows:

```
SET PSE <PSE Name> PURPOSE <Purpose>;
SET PSE "BI_SSO_SAM_CERT" PURPOSE SAML;
```

In the first example, replace the <PSE Name> variable with the name of the PSE. Replace the <Purpose> variable with one of the purposes listed in Table 13.1.

To remove the purpose, use the UNSET PSE SQL command. For example, to remove the SAML purpose from PSE BI_SSO_SAM_CERT, execute the following SQL command:

```
UNSET PSE "BI_SSO_SAM_CERT" PURPOSE SAML;
```

The internal certificate store doesn't include all possible certificates. Let's look at how we can also use files within the OS to store certificates.

13.1.2 External SAP HANA PSE File and Certificate Management

Certificates can also be stored and managed within files located in the file system of the SAP HANA instance. By default, they're stored in the following path:

/hana/shared/<SID>/HDB<instance number>/<host name>/sec

The <SID> variable must be replaced with the SID of the SAP HANA system. A two-digit instance number should replace the <instance number> variable. The <host name> variable represents the configured host name of the SAP HANA system. The following example shows the path for an example SAP HANA system with a SID of PJ5, instance of 25, and host name of w4-hana-05:

/hana/shared/PJ5/HDB25/w4-hana-05/sec

Within this path, you'll find several files with a .pse extension. For example, the *sapsrv.pse*, *saplogon.pse*, *sapsslc.pse*, *sapssls.pse*, *sap_system_pki_instance.pse*, *sapsrv_internal.pse*, and *sapsrv_internal_*.pse* files. Each file has an intended purpose. They're used to store the public and private certificate keys used for either authentication or TLS secure communication. Figure 13.2 provides an overview of the files and how they relate to a given purpose.

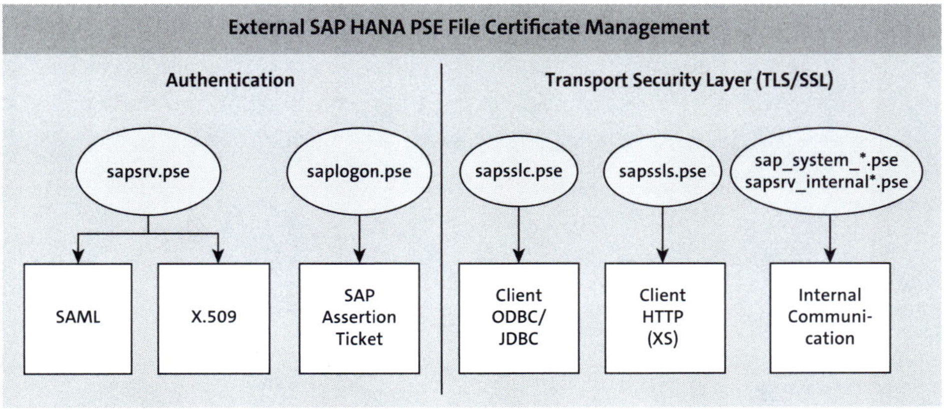

Figure 13.2 Items Supported with External PSE Files

Items in the **Authentication** section are related to supported external authentication providers. Items in the **Transport Security Layer (TLS/SSL)** section are related to client communication protocols, the XS engine's web application SSL protocols, and internal sever communication protocols. In Section 13.1.1, we identified several supported purposes for in-database managed certificates. Some of those same purposes can also be implemented using the PSE files on the file system. However, the PSE files in the file system are the only items in which internal server communication encryption and HTTP communication encryption can be configured.

There are two main ways to configure the PSE files. First, we can use the SAPGENPSE tool. This command-line interface tool can be used to manage SAP HANA PSE files. Second, we can use the web-based SAP Web Dispatcher administration GUI hosted in the XS engine. Most will find it much easier to manage PSE files using this second option. For the purposes of this chapter, we'll only explore the options available using SAP Web Dispatcher.

To access the SAP Web Dispatcher administration GUI, a grantee must have the role sap.hana.xs.wdisp.admin::WebDispatcherAdmin. Use the following URL with your host and instance details added to access this web-based GUI:

http://<SAP_HANA_XS_HOST>:80<Instance #>/sap/hana/xs/wdisp/admin/

For example:

http://w4-db4-hana19.e-corp.root.internal.com:8000/sap/hana/xs/wdisp/admin

When accessing SAP Web Dispatcher, you'll need to authenticate using a mechanism set up within your environment. In most environments, we're presented with a logon form in which we provide an SAP HANA internal user name and password. The landing page will default to the **SAP Web Dispatcher Monitor** (see Figure 13.3).

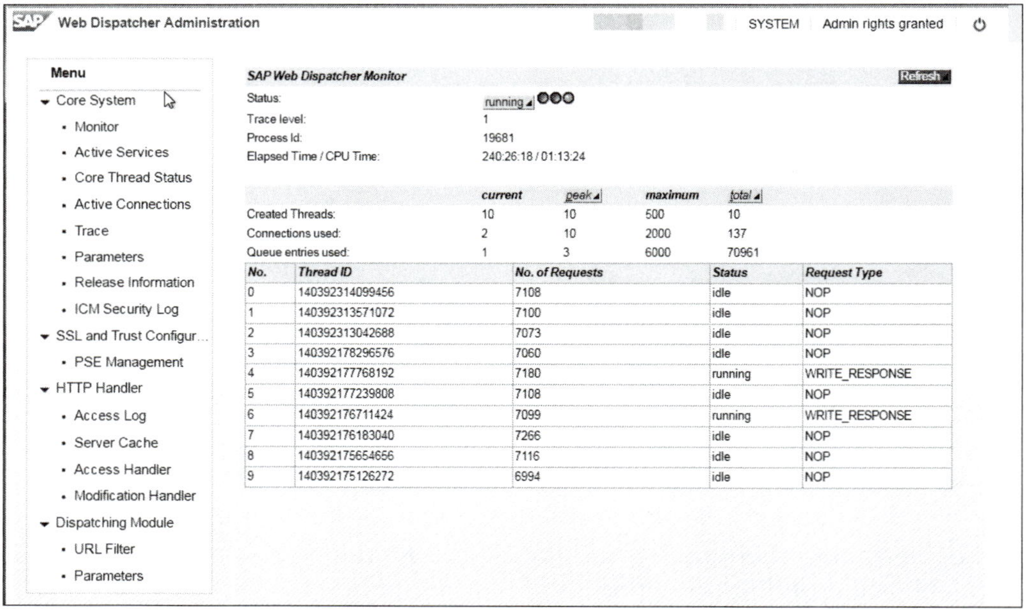

Figure 13.3 SAP Web Dispatcher Monitor

On the left side, you'll see a frame titled **Menu** containing several hierarchically oriented options. Look for the option in the menu titled **PSE Management** just under the **SSL and Trust Configuration** menu list item. Figure 13.4 provides an example of the interface that will appear when you click **PSE Management.**

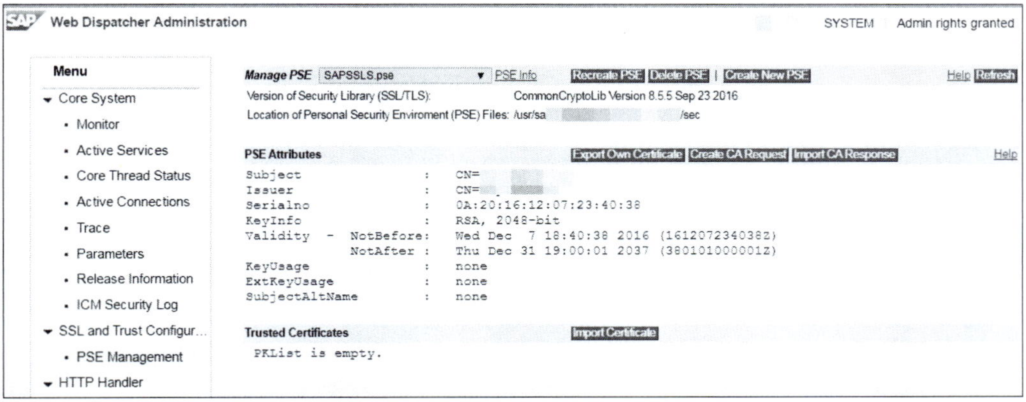

Figure 13.4 PSE Management Area in SAP Web Dispatcher

In the interface, there's a **Manage PSE** dropdown menu located on the top left, to the right of the **Menu** frame. Use this dropdown to select the PSE file that you want to manage. With the PSE file selected, you can perform several actions, as listed in Table 13.2.

Interface Option	Description
Recreate PSE	When selected, the active PSE file will be reset to a default state. All certificates will also be removed from the trust store.
Delete PSE	To delete a PSE from the file system, select the PSE file in the **Manage PSE** dropdown menu, then select this option.
Create New PSE	Used to create a new PSE. When clicked, a new window will appear, allowing you to define the PSE encryption algorithm, key length, distinguished name, and file name.
Export Own Certificate	When selected, a new window will appear containing the certificate of the selected PSE file.
Create CA Request	When selected, a new window will appear containing the certificate request text. Copy this text to a certificate authority to generate a new certificate response.
Import CA Response	When selected, a new window will appear containing a text entry block in which the certificate response text can be pasted or entered.
Import Certificate	When selected, a new window will appear containing a test entry block in which a trusted certificate's text can be pasted or entered.

Table 13.2 SAP Web Dispatcher PSE Management Options

Configuring and Managing Certificates

The processes and workflows required to configure certificates for the purposes of authentication and secure communications seem to change with each new version of SAP HANA. For example, we expect most of certificate management to be available via the SAP HANA 2.0 Cockpit in the near future. With this in mind, please consult the documentation for your version of SAP HANA. In most cases, you'll find the configuration steps in the SAP HANA Administration Guide:

http://help.sap.com/hana/SAP_HANA_Administration_Guide_en.pdf

The SAP HANA Security Guide also provides a few additional details about the configuration process:

http://help.sap.com/hana/SAP_HANA_Security_Guide_en.pdf

Using the SAP Web Dispatcher administration GUI will greatly simplify the process of managing PSE files and their certificates. Most would argue that it's best to use the in-database PSE management options when applicable. However, there are still items such as HTTP SSL and internal server encryption that must be managed in the PSE files found on the file system. In the next section, we'll explore the options used to enable encryption for clients connecting to SAP HANA.

13.2 Client Encryption Settings

In this section, we'll review the process for enabling TLS or SSL settings for SAP HANA Studio, the XS engine applications, and JDBC/ODBC clients. It's important that organizations understand how to configure these options to secure the communications or transmissions of data between clients and SAP HANA.

13.2.1 SAP HANA Studio

When configuring a system connection within SAP HANA Studio, there are several options we can select to enable SSL-based communication. Enabling SSL-based communication encryption is important when accessing SAP HANA using untrusted or unrestricted networks. For example, if you're access an SAP HANA cloud-based instance from you desktop at home, the communication channel between your desktop and SAP HANA will likely traverse a number of network hops. Each hop introduces the likelihood that someone or some organization might be monitoring and capturing your TCP/IP packets. Without encryption, these packets could be reconstructed and the information within them exposed to unauthorized individuals. The same can happen even on a private corporate network. Therefore, it's important that organizations try to encrypt communications with SAP HANA that could potentially contain sensitive data.

To enable SSL encryption for an existing system connection within SAP HANA Studio, right-click the system listed in the **Systems** tab. A **Properties** window will appear, with three properties tabs in the right-hand frame. The first tab, **General** (see Figure 13.5), contains a checkbox labeled **Connect Using SSL**. To force the connection to use SSL encryption, select this checkbox.

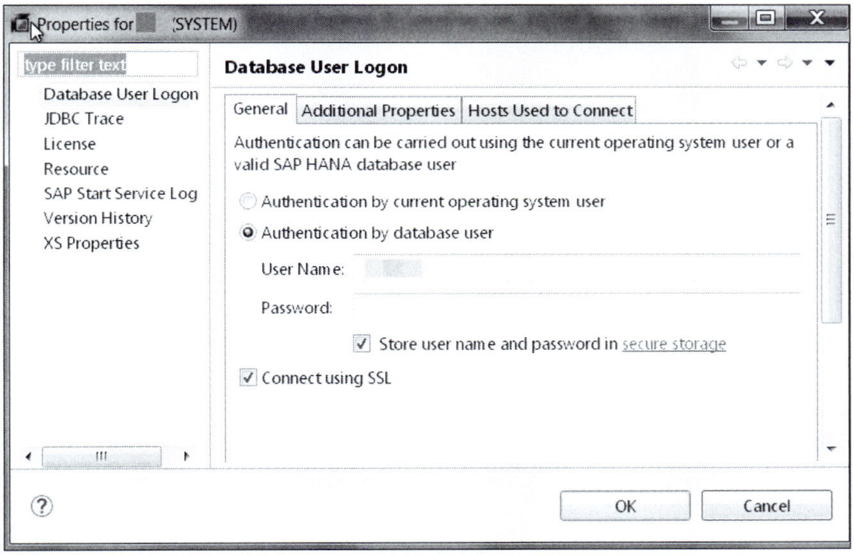

Figure 13.5 Configuring SAP HANA Studio Connection for SSL Communication

If you're using a self-signed certificate or a certificate not trusted in the SAP HANA Studio keystore, select the **Additional Properties** tab to configure a few additional options. On this tab, uncheck the **Validate the SSL Certificate** option to ignore certificate issues (see Figure 13.6).

SAP HANA systems are deployed with self-signed certificates usable for TLS communications. However, such certificates will be untrusted by clients such as SAP HANA Studio. Untrusted or self-signed certificates can still provide encrypted communications, however. If SAP HANA Studio is unable to validate a certificate, organizations can still rely on the certificate to encrypt communications between client and server, and SAP HANA Studio does provide an option to ignore issues with such certificates.

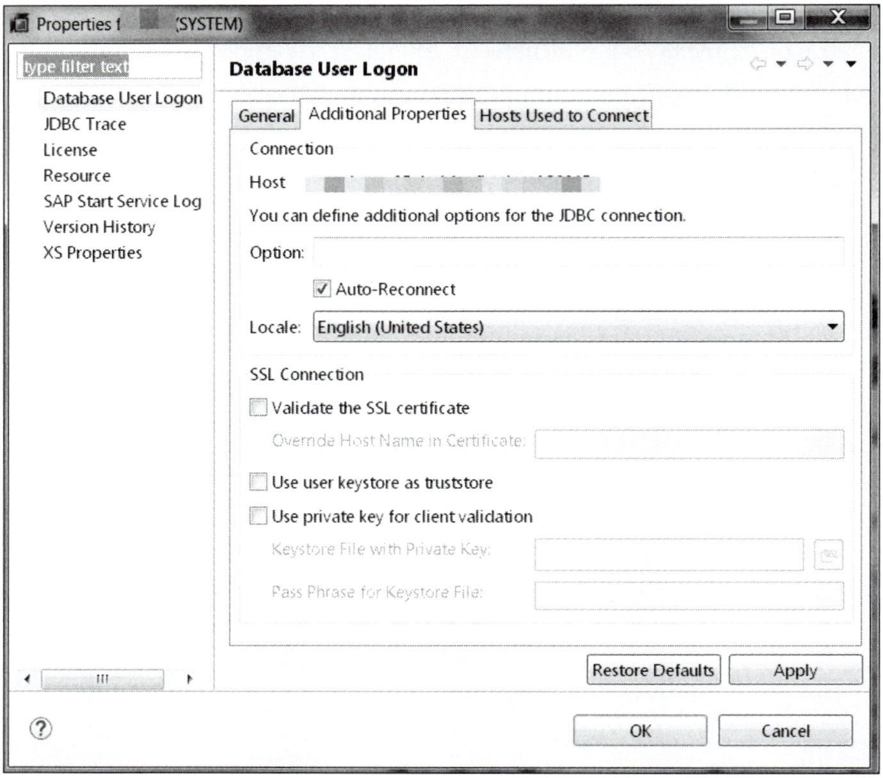

Figure 13.6 Configuring SAP HANA Studio Connection to Ignore Untrusted SSL Certificate Issues

Click **OK** to enable the new SSL settings. Your system, listed in the **Systems** tab, should now show an icon with a closed yellow padlock on the right side, indicating that the connection between the client and server is encrypted.

In the next section, we'll review the options required to secure communications with web-based applications hosted in the XS engine.

13.2.2 XS Engine Web-Based Applications

By default, SSL access to web-based XS applications is configured during installation using a self-signed certificate. Organizations also have the option to deploy a new certificate from a public trusted certificate authority. The default SSL listening port for web-based XS applications is 43XX, where XX represents the two-digit SAP HANA instance number. Although SSL access is available by default, it isn't mandatory for XS engine applications.

To properly secure an XS engine web-based application, the use of SSL should be forced. This enforcement is enabled on a per-package basis. Repository packages in SAP HANA have a direct relationship to the website folder structure. Therefore, we can enforce SSL access by subweb or website folder structure.

To force SSL, we must access the web-based XS Artifact Administration application, hosted in the XS engine for each SAP HANA instance. To access this administration portal, use the following URL with your details included; the second URL provides a complete example:

- *http://<HANA HOST>:80<INSTANCE NUMBER>/sap/hana/xs/admin*
- *http://w4-db-hana.e-corp.internal.net:8000/sap/hana/xs/admin/*

The landing page (see Figure 13.7) will start with the **Application Objects** frame on the left side of the window. The **Runtime Configuration Details** for each selected application object are located on the right side.

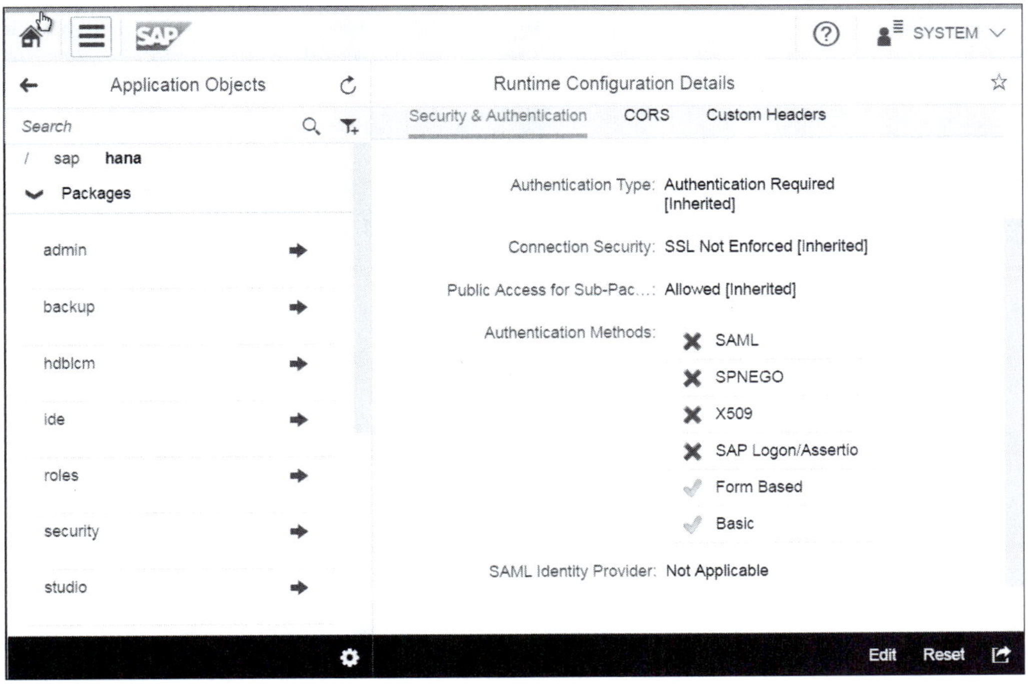

Figure 13.7 XS Artifact Administration Landing Page

To edit a package, select the package hierarchy level within the **Application Objects** frame. In the **Runtime Configuration Details** frame on the right side, look for the large **Edit** button at the bottom of the page and click it to open the package configuration options. Within the **Security & Authentication** section, select the checkbox titled **Force SSL** (see Figure 13.8).

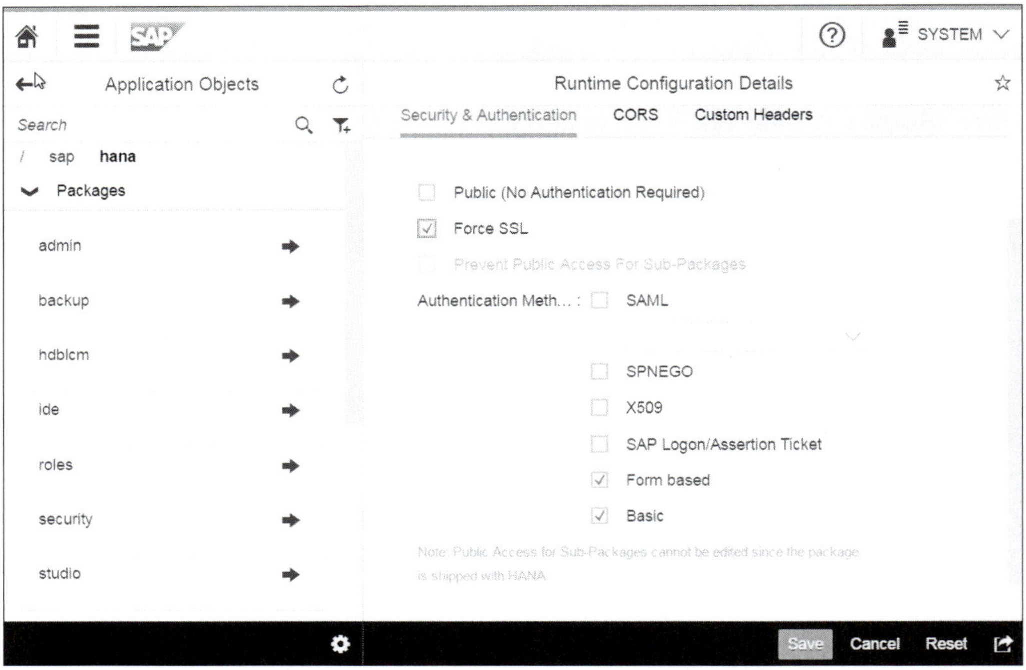

Figure 13.8 Forcing SSL Access

Selecting this checkbox will force the package or corresponding website tree structure to use SSL encryption. Click **Save** at the bottom of the window to activate the new configuration options. Once this option is enabled, users will have no choice but to interact with the web-based application using encryption.

13.2.3 JDBC and ODBC Drivers

JDBC and *ODBC* are industry-standard *APIs* used by software applications to interact with SAP HANA. These APIs are included with the SAP HANA client application. The SAP HANA client is application code that contains multiple industry-standard programming interfaces that can be used to access SAP HANA. For example, some organizations use these APIs to grant their software applications query access to the data hosted in SAP HANA. Because the communications between the client application and SAP HANA have the potential to contain sensitive data, it's recommended that these communication channels be encrypted.

When configuring an ODBC data source name (DSN) on the Windows OS, you'll find options for configuring an SSL-based connection. Just like in SAP HANA Studio, we can choose to bypass the validation of the SSL certificate.

For example, on a Windows OS with the SAP HANA client installed, we can use the ODBC data source administrator to configure an SAP HANA ODBC DNS. Search for the ODBC manager within the Windows **Start** menu. With the ODBC manager open, select the **System DNS** tab. Click **Add** to set up a new DSN. In the pop-up window, scroll through the list of data source drivers installed on your system. Look for the driver named **HDBODBC32** or **HDBODBC** (depending on the version of the DSN you're configuring). Select the driver and click **Finish**. A new window will appear, allowing you to define the **Data Source Name** and SAP HANA **Server and Port**. To configure SSL, click the **Settings** button at the bottom right. The **SAP HDB Advanced Setup** window will now appear (see Figure 13.9).

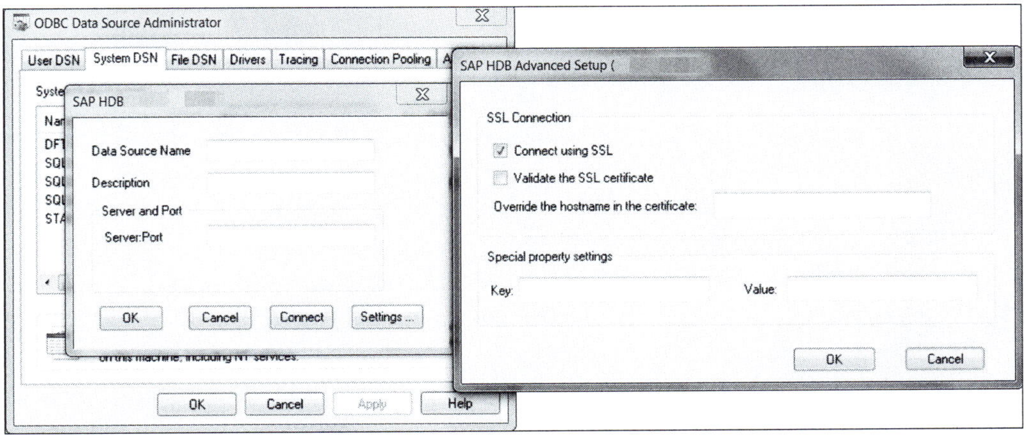

Figure 13.9 Configuring Windows ODBC DNS for SSL Communications

To enable SSL communications, select the **Connect using SSL** checkbox. If you're using an SSL certificate that isn't automatically trusted, leave the **Validate the SSL certificate** option unchecked. If you need to override the common name of the host listed in the

SSL certificate, enter the alternative hostname in the **Override the Hostname in the Certificate** field. Click **OK** to save the advanced settings and **OK** again to save the DSN.

Most JDBC connection strings will provide similar options. JDBC drivers can't be used in the Windows ODBC manager. Most Java-based applications will provide their own SAP HANA JDBC connection configuration interfaces. Given its proprietary nature, we won't provide a step-by-step configuration example for the JDBC driver, but note that the same SSL options available for ODBC drivers are also available for JDBC drivers. Application vendors have the API available, even if they choose not to incorporate SSL options into their configuration GUIs. For example, the code in Listing 13.2 was taken from the Java-based SAP HANA Studio trace file. In the connection string, you can see that the `encrypt=true` and `validateCertificate=false` options were listed in the trace file results.

```
new Connection 'jdbc:sap://w3-hanan01.e-corp.internal.root:30015;
10.54.240.31:30015'
locale=en_US
user=SYSTEM
password=***
reconnect=true
timeout=0
encrypt=true
validateCertificate=false
```

Listing 13.2 SAP HANA Studio Trace File Showing Secure JDBC Connection to SAP HANA

Enabling SSL communications for the JDBC or ODBC connection layers is a good practice. It ensures that the information exchanged with the client and server is well protected from unauthorized access. However, configuring this setting is optional unless the SAP HANA system itself requires an SSL connection. Fortunately, SAP HANA offers an option to force clients to use an SSL secured connection, found in the **Configuration** tab under the path **global.ini • communication • sslenforce**. Figure 13.10 provides an overview of this option in the SAP HANA Studio INI configuration interface.

This option defaults to **False**, meaning that clients can choose how to configure the connection. When the option is set to **True**, clients must enable the **Connect Using SSL** option. Instead of using SAP HANA Studio, we can also issue the following SQL statement to enable the option:

```
ALTER SYSTEM ALTER CONFIGURATION
('global.ini','SYSTEM')
SET ('communication','sslenforce') ='true' WITH RECONFIGURE;
```

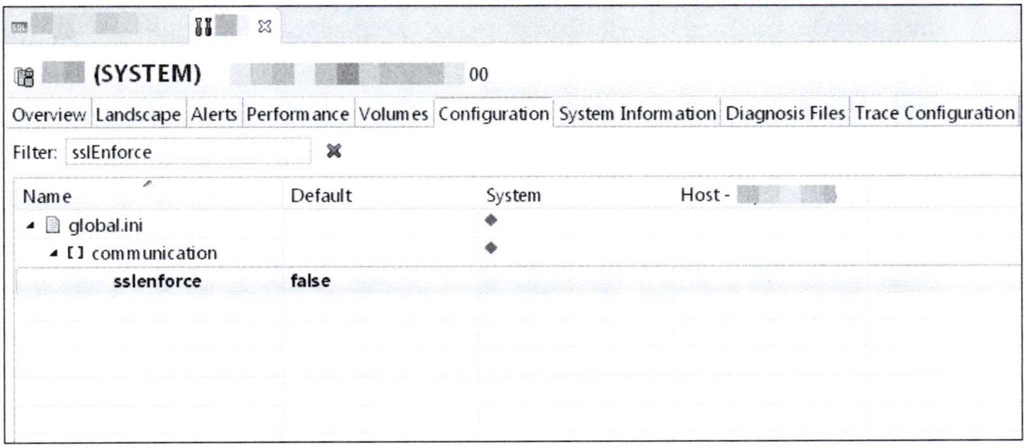

Figure 13.10 Communication Setting for global.ini to Force SSL Client Connections

To disable the option, issue the following SQL statement:

```
ALTER SYSTEM ALTER CONFIGURATION
('global.ini','SYSTEM')
SET ('communication','sslenforce') ='false' WITH RECONFIGURE;
```

SAP HANA offers several options to manage certificates and to encrypt communications between clients and the SAP HANA server. In the next section, we'll review how to use encryption to secure SAP HANA persistent storage layers.

13.3 Encrypting Data

Encrypting communications with SAP HANA is very important. However, encryption can also be used to secure the data stored on the SAP HANA server's persistent layers. Although SAP HANA is an in-memory database, its data is not exclusively stored in-memory. SAP HANA will periodically create savepoints to mirror the in-memory data to disk. The savepoint process saves the data to the */hana/data/<SID>* volume hosted on each SAP HANA server node.

In addition to these data savepoints, each committed transaction is simultaneously written to the */hana/log/<SID>* volumes and memory on each SAP HANA server node. In the event of a power failure, the SAP HANA system will recreate the in-memory data using a combination of the persistent data snapshots stored in the /data volume and the transaction redo logs stored in the /log volume of each SAP HANA server node. Because these storage areas contain a binary version of the data hosted in SAP HANA, it's often important that we encrypt that data.

Users with access to the SAP HANA OS can potentially access unencrypted data hosted in the data or log volumes. Most organizations vigorously restrict access to the OS of on-premise implementations of SAP HANA, but organizations leveraging hosted or cloud-based SAP HANA implementations might have limited control over users with OS-level access or physical access to the storage drives. When access to the OS can't be properly validated, it's highly recommended that data and log volume encryption be used. The same is true when individuals with physical access to the disk drives aren't properly managed.

Now, let's review how SAP HANA manages the root keys used for encryption.

13.3.1 Server-Side Data Encryption

SAP HANA has a built-in encryption service to help manage the encryption of data hosted in the data and log volumes. This service uses a *secure store in the file system* (SSFS) to protect the encryption root keys. Encryption root keys are the basis for all public or private keys used to encrypt data or communications within the SAP HANA system. SAP HANA has two secure stores in the file system. The first SSFS is the SAP HANA *instance SSFS*, which protects the root keys used to encrypt information stored in the data and log volumes. The second SSFS is the *system PKI SSFS*, which protects root certificates used to secure internal communications.

The instance SSFS key is stored on the OS in the following location by default:

/usr/sap/<SID>/SYS/global/hdb/security/ssfs

Replace the <SID> variable in the example with the SID of your SAP HANA system. Within the folder location, you'll find two files: *SSFS_<SID>.DAT* and *SSFS_<SID>.KEY*.

The system PKI SSFS key is stored on the OS in the following location by default:

/usr/sap/<SID>/SYS/global/security/rsecssfs/data

Replace the <SID> variable in the example with the SID of your SAP HANA system. Within the folder location, you'll find two files: *SSFS_<SID>.DAT* and *SSFS_<SID>.KEY*.

Given the importance of these keys, they should be backed up and stored in a root key backup file. This backup file and its location must be accessible by the administrator during a recovery situation for a new SAP HANA host or a host with a new key generated after the backup file's creation date. When data or log volume encryption is enabled, the SSFS will need to be restored from backup prior to a database recovery. However, if you're restoring a backup to the same database used to generate the backup files and the SSFS keys weren't changed following the backup, SSFS recovery is not necessary.

Next, we'll provide more details about the processes used to backup and restore SSFS keys. It's very important that organizations maintain backups of the SSFS keys each time they're changed and prior to enabling data or log volume encryption.

13.3.2 Changing New Root Keys within the SSFS

A unique root key is generated during the standard installation or upgrade of each SAP HANA instance. A standard installation is one in which a documented SAP HANA installation method is followed. However, because SAP HANA is often delivered as an appliance, it's possible that the appliance vendor used a copy of the same encryption root keys within each of its appliance builds. For example, the vendor might deploy a copied image of the SAP HANA appliance's file system. Using an image provides a quick and consistent deployment of the SAP HANA software, but it results in each default instance using the same root keys and SSFS. Organizations also must consider the security of the SSFS and its keys during installation. SAP HANA currently must be deployed by a certified vendor or certified individual. That individual could make a copy of the root keys and store them insecurely outside of the organization's control. As a result, there is no guarantee that a copy of the encryption root keys doesn't exist outside the organization. These keys should therefore be changed after the vendor has completed the installation.

Therefore, it's often necessary for an organization to generate new encryption root keys following the initial deployment of the SAP HANA system. Starting with SAP HANA 2.0, when new root keys are generated the SSFS should be backed up. To generate new keys, organizations can execute a series of SQL statements. To perform a backup of the SSFS, command-line access to the operating system is required. The process used to generate new root keys in SAP HANA 2.0 is as follows:

1. Generate new root keys using SQL commands.
2. Backup the new keys and store them in a secure file location.
3. Activate the new keys using SQL commands.

To properly perform these activities, grantees will need the <sid>adm operating system credentials to execute the command line utility hdbnsutil. The grantee will need the `ENCRYPTION ROOT KEY ADMIN` system privilege. We also need to establish a password for the root key backup file. To establish this password, execute the following SQL statement:

```
ALTER SYSTEM SET ENCRYPTION ROOT KEYS BACKUP PASSWORD "<Password>";
```

To generate new root keys for the SAP HANA data volume, execute the following SQL command:

```
ALTER SYSTEM PERSISTENCE ENCRYPTION CREATE NEW ROOT KEY WITHOUT ACTIVATE;
```

To generate new root keys for the SAP HANA log volume, execute the following SQL command:

```
ALTER SYSTEM LOG ENCRYPTION CREATE NEW ROOT KEY WITHOUT ACTIVATE;
```

To generate new root keys for SAP HANA's internal application encryption, execute the following SQL command:

```
ALTER SYSTEM APPLICATION ENCRYPTION CREATE NEW ROOT KEY WITHOUT ACTIVATE;
```

With all three of these SQL statements, the `WITHOUT ACTIVATE` option was specified. This allows new keys to be generated without making them active within the system. It's important that you back up the root keys prior to their activation. To do so, we can use the hdbnsutil command line utility. To use this utility, log on to the SAP HANA operating system with the <sid>adm credentials. Alternately, we can execute a SQL statement that returns a `CLOB` field containing an encrypted text message. We can copy the text message to a file and save it with the .rkb extension.

To use the hdbnsutil command-line utility, log on to the SAP HANA system using your Secure Shell (SSH) service of choice. Log on to the shell using the `<sid>adm` credentials. This utility is stored in */usr/sap/<sid>/HDB<instance_number>/exe*. Execute the following command to back up the root keys:

```
./hdbnsutil -backupRootKeys <file path and name>.rkb --dbid=<dbid> --type='ALL'
```

If SAP HANA is a single-container system, you can omit the `-dbid=<dbid>` portion of the command. The variable `<dbid>` should be replaced with the tenant database ID.

If you're unable to gain access to the operating system shell, you can also execute a SQL statement to return a `CLOB` field containing the contents of the RKB file. Copy the contents of the `CLOB` field and save them to a file with an .rkb extension. To return the `CLOB` field, execute the following SQL:

```
SELECT ENCRYPTION_ROOT_KEYS_EXTRACT_KEYS
('PERSISTENCE, APPLICATION, LOG') FROM DUMMY
```

Before activating the new root keys, it's important to validate that you have the correct password required to restore the root keys. To do so, execute the following command from the SAP HANA OS shell:

```
./hdbnsutil -validateRootKeysBackup <path to filename> --password="<password>"
```

When a backup is created with data and log volume encryption enabled, that backup can only be restored to a system with the same SSFS and root keys. In the event that we need to restore a backup to a system with different root keys, we must first restore the root keys from the RKB file. To recover root keys, execute the following command from the operating system shell; you must be authenticated as the <sid>adm user to restore the root keys:


```
./hdbnsutil -recoverRootKeys <path to filename>.rkb --dbid=<dbid>
--password="<password>" --type=ALL
```

If SAP HANA is a single-container system, you can omit the `-dbid=<dbid>` portion of the command. The variable `<dbid>` should be replaced with the tenant database ID.

Once the backup file is generated and validated, we can activate the new keys within the system. To activate the keys for all three areas, execute the following three statements:

```
ALTER SYSTEM PERSISTENCE ENCRYPTION ACTIVATE NEW ROOT KEY;
ALTER SYSTEM LOG ENCRYPTION ACTIVATE NEW ROOT KEY;
ALTER SYSTEM APPLICATION ENCRYPTION ACTIVATE NEW ROOT KEY;
```

To view the current and historical status of root keys generated within the system, query the `ENCRYPTION_ROOT_KEYS` system view. To query this view, execute the following SQL statement from the SQL console:

```
SELECT * FROM SYS.ENCRYPTION_ROOT_KEYS;
```

Generating new root keys within the SSFS is an important step that all organizations should consider after receiving a new SAP HANA appliance. In the next sections, we'll explore the requirements and commands necessary to enable data and log volume encryption.

13.3.3 Encrypting the Data Volume

There are two main ways to enable data volume encryption in SAP HANA: via a specialized SQL statement or via the security management options in SAP HANA Studio.

Using SQL

Note that you can't enable data volume encryption if extended storage has already been enabled within the system; you'll need to move extended storage tables back to in-memory and disable extended storage prior to executing the command successfully. Users will also need the `ENCRYPTION ROOT KEY ADMIN` system privilege to enable /data volume encryption. To enable data volume encryption, execute the following SQL command:

```
ALTER SYSTEM PERSISTENCE ENCRYPTION ON;
```

To monitor the status of data volume encryption, execute the following SQL statement:

```
SELECT * FROM SYS.M_ENCRYPTION_OVERVIEW
```

Using SAP HANA Studio

SAP HANA Studio also provides a way to enable data volume encryption. Log on to your system and expand the **System** node within the **Systems** tab. Expand the **Security** folder and double-click the **Security** icon. The security manager will appear on the right, as shown in Figure 13.11.

Within the security manager, click the **Data Volume Encryption** tab. On that tab, select the checkbox titled **Encrypt data volumes**. Press [F8] to deploy the changes. The **Status** of each service within the list will change to **Encrypted** once the encryption process is complete.

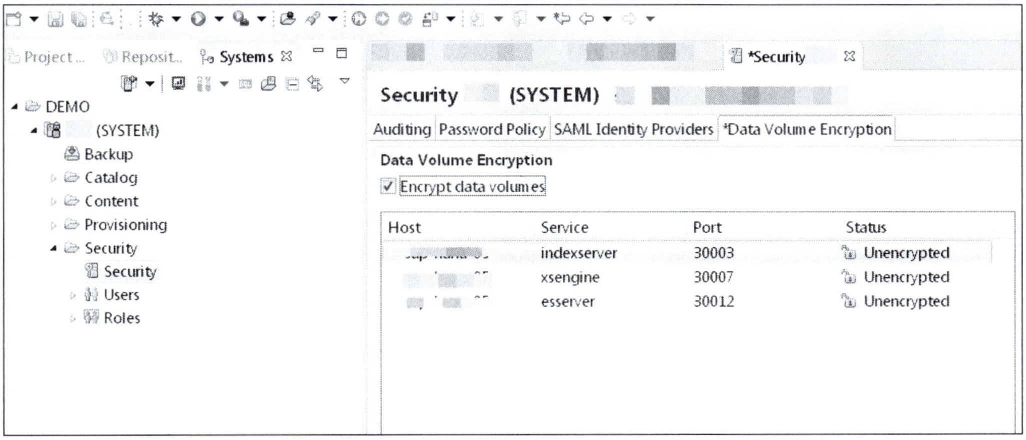

Figure 13.11 Using SAP HANA Studio to Enable Data Volume Encryption

Future Versions of SAP HANA

Although SAP hasn't made an official announcement, we expect that SSFS root key management, data volume encryption, and log volume encryption will be manageable from the SAP HANA 2.0 Cockpit's management application in future versions of SAP HANA. With that said, we also expect that such options will continue to be manageable using the SQL statements listed in this section.

For more information about the SAP HANA 2.0 Cockpit, please review SAP Note 2380291, available at *https://launchpad.support.sap.com/#/notes/0002380291*.

13.3.4 Encrypting the Log Volume

Encrypting the log volume is a feature that was first made available in SAP HANA 2.0 SPS 00. As of the time of writing, the log volume encryption can only be enabled using SQL commands. To enable log volume encryption, execute the following SQL command:

```
ALTER SYSTEM LOG ENCRYPTION ON;
```

To monitor the status of log volume encryption, execute the following SQL statement:

```
SELECT * FROM SYS.M_ENCRYPTION_OVERVIEW
```

13.4 Summary

To properly protect an SAP HANA system, communication and data volume encryption must be enabled. Without encryption, it's possible for individuals to gain unauthorized access to your SAP HANA system. SAP HANA offers options to protect communications using X.509 certificates, and it provides a root key system to protect data and log volumes.

Chapter 14
Security Lifecycle Management

Implementing a security model is just the beginning. In this chapter, we'll discuss the need to create processes and procedures to govern changes and to promote those changes to other environments.

As mentioned before, SAP HANA is a development platform, which makes it more than just a database. Because it's a development platform, security administrators will discover that security-related development artifacts can be easily transported between different SAP HANA instances. In this chapter, we'll outline the best practices and options available to use this transportation mechanism, helping to maintain a consistent security model between SAP HANA instances. We'll start by discussing ways to maintain a consistent security model. Then, we'll review the steps necessary to define a delivery unit containing security-related artifacts. The delivery unit will be used to transport a security model between systems. We'll then review the steps necessary to access the SAP HANA application lifecycle management tool. Finally, we'll discuss additional features in SAP HANA application lifecycle management that can benefit the lifecycle management of security artifacts.

14.1 Maintaining a Consistent Security Model

Most organizations will maintain more than one instance of SAP HANA within their landscapes. Some will need multiple instances to support multiple SAP application solutions, and some will need multiple instances to support lifecycle management within the same solution. Given the likelihood that organizations will have multiple unique or related instances, it isn't practical to expect a security administrator to manually create a security model for each unique environment. Fortunately, SAP HANA offers capabilities to easily transport repository-based content, including repository roles, between environments.

There are three set of guidelines we should follow to ensure that our security models are both consistent and secure. The first practice involves lifecycle management best practices. The second governs how we make changes to the security model and conduct testing. The final practice centers on policies and procedures required to maintain a consistent security model in each environment.

14.1.1 Best Practices

Security model lifecycle management encompasses the process, procedures, and tasks we follow to ensure that our security model is secure and consistent in all environments. Because SAP HANA is also a development platform, it has built-in tools to aid in the management and promotion of software code stored within its repository. Fortunately, many of our security artifacts, such as repository roles, are stored in this repository. To facilitate the management and promotion of the software code and security artifacts within SAP HANA, a tool called *SAP HANA application lifecycle management* is available to aid in the process; it's a web-based application hosted in the XS engine.

SAP HANA application lifecycle management allows organizations to both manage changes within the SAP HANA repository and promote those changes to other SAP HANA environments. In Section 14.2 and Section 14.3, we'll discuss SAP HANA application lifecycle management in more detail, but in this section we'll discuss a few basic security model lifecycle management best practices. Securing an SAP HANA environment is only the first step. Once it's secured, we need to follow strict policies and procedures to help maintain the security of the environment. Specifically, organizations should maintain multiple environments, create content in development, organize content effectively, cleanup unused content, have a rollback plan, and manage content dependencies. These best practices will help you formulate policies and procedures to aid in security model and content lifecycle management. To further your understanding, let's look at each of these items in more detail.

Maintain Multiple Environments

A key dependency in the development, validation, testing, and implementation of a security model requires that organizations maintain multiple unique SAP HANA instances. Most organizations will deploy a *development* (DEV) environment in which they create content, security models, and other dependent content; a *quality assurance* (QA) environment in which they validate the promotion process and test content changes to application code; and a production (PROD) environment, which serves as the active environment in which user work and execute business related transactions.

The purpose of maintaining multiple environments is to identify issues with developed content or identify issues related to configuration changes before they are implemented in Production. As depicted in Figure 14.1, the lifecycle management process for SAP HANA security follows a strict path from DEV to QA to PROD.

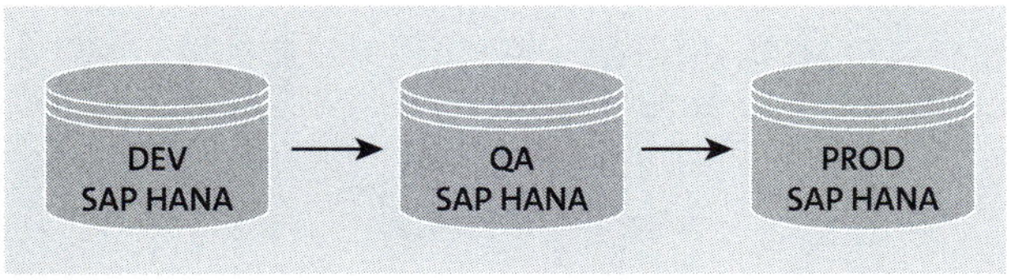

Figure 14.1 Lifecycle Management Process for SAP HANA Security

Create Content in Development

It's best to generate repository roles and their dependencies in a DEV environment. After the content is validated, it should then be transported to a QA environment for further testing. It's never wise to make security changes directly in production. Changes in production are untested and can lead to elevation of privileges or exposure of sensitive data.

Organize Content in Packages

SAP HANA development and security artifacts are both stored in the logical SAP HANA repository or package hierarchy. How we organize packages, subpackages, and their dependencies plays a key role in how we promote content to other environments. For example, let's assume that all content, both development-related and security-related, is stored in a single package. Packages and their subordinate objects are assigned to a delivery unit within SAP HANA. (Remember that delivery units are the objects transported between environments.) If all content is organized in a single package, an organization will have no choice but to promote everything in a single delivery unit each time it promotes code to production. This can lead to the promotion of content that is incomplete and not validated. Therefore, it's best to organize content into packages based on their relationship. Unrelated objects should be in their own independent packages and delivery units.

Clean Up Test and Validation Content

Development environments often become the application code testing grounds. The same can happen with security artifacts. For example, user accounts, repository roles, catalog objects, and other items can be created to test a scenario before changes to permanent objects are implemented. We should encourage this type of validation in development. However, we should also discourage the permanent proliferation of objects that won't be promoted to QA or PROD. Such objects should be deleted from the system when they're no longer used. Too often, these objects are mistaken for permanent objects and promoted to the QA or PROD environment. The most effective way to prevent validation content from an accidental promotion is to delete it from the system once the validation is competed.

Rollback Plan

When promoting content between environments, make sure that you always have a rollback plan. SAP HANA offers several features to help with these requirements. For example, we can restore the system from backup, catalog exports of content, and restore individual items from the repository activation history.

Promote Repository Role Dependencies

Repository roles often reference other repository-based objects or runtime catalog objects. These referenced objects are dependencies for a repository role. When we promote a repository role, we must ensure that all the referenced repository objects are included with the promotion delivery unit. If the repository role references a runtime catalog object, that object must exist in all environments. This is one of many reasons we highly recommend using repository-based objects for both security and database development.

14.1.2 Testing Security Model Changes

One outcome of security model lifecycle management is that it facilitates the testing and validation of changes. Special attention should be given to testing practices, given the amount of risk introduced when testing isn't emphasized. To ensure that organizations approach testing properly, there are a few best practices they should follow. They should track changes, validate code, socialize with their peers, test content in an environment identical to production, and define test plans based on the type of change. Let's look at each of these items in more detail.

Track Changes

Tracking security model changes in an external software application is very important for lifecycle management, compliance, and auditing purposes. Such systems should contain information pertaining to the purpose of the change and the specifics of the change itself. Retaining this information is helpful when organizations have multiple individuals implementing changes. It grants others access to information about a change in case contradictions or overlaps are introduced. More importantly, this information is often useful in communicating the intent of changes for future internal and external security administrators.

Validate the Security Model in Development

Security model developers and administrators should validate their own changes before they're promoted. Organizations often overlook the importance of emphasizing this within their security model lifecycle management process. We highly recommend that organizations require security model developers to validate their own work using test cases specific to their changes. Adding this extra requirement to the process further reduces the likelihood of security vulnerabilities and inaccurate changes. In addition, it isn't efficient to frequently promote content from DEV to QA because of development-related defects. Establishing a process and procedure that includes developer validation will help to reduce the frequency of content promotions.

Discuss Security Changes with Other Administrators

Security model changes should be discussed with the broader SAP HANA administration team. This line of communication can be socialized using meetings, emails, or other forms of communication. It's important to grant everyone access to open dialog about the change. In most situations, socializing about changes can help to identify unexpected issues, mitigating contingencies related to the change.

Test Security Changes in an Identical Environment

As we stated before, security administrators and developers should validate their work before promoting changes to a QA environment. However, once the content is transported to QA, it should be thoroughly tested. To make these tests more useful, the QA environment should be a mirror of the production environment. This isn't to say that we need the same data in QA, but we do need to make sure that the content, metadata, and configurations are similar, if not exact. If we use sound testing processes, using a near-identical environment will help to mitigate potential issues in production.

Define Test Plans Based on Change Types

When testing content in QA, make sure that you execute different levels of testing. There should be a series of standard tests always executed. However, you should also devise a test specific to the most recent change. For example, if the change was to a repository role that grants access to a new SAP HANA information view, testing should include a procedure to test access to this new information view.

14.1.3 Keeping Repository Roles in Sync

In most cases, we identify several repository roles that can exist in all environments within the organization. With some exceptions, these roles are predominantly related to administration-level access. In addition, repository roles used by SAP HANA instances within the same solution might host the same security content. For example, if we have a DEV, QA, and PROD SAP HANA instance each operating an equivalent SAP S/4HANA application server, we should strive to have the same repository roles in each environment. In short, we might have repository roles that exist in all SAP HANA instances and some that only exist in instances hosted in the same solution.

One way to ensure that administrators have the same level of access in each environment is by using the same administrative repository roles in each environment. For example, all SAP HANA instances can have the same base security administration role. We aren't suggesting that all repository roles exist the same in all environment, but it's quite possible that base-level administrative repository roles will be the same in each environment. For SAP HANA instances that share the same solution, we should assume that nonadministrative repository roles will be the same in each solution-based instance.

Therefore, we need to devise a procedure that ensures that repository roles remain consistent throughout the SAP HANA landscape. The most effective way to accomplish consistency is via a process in which changes are tracked and monitored until they're moved into production. For example, an incident-management system can be used to track a process from beginning to end. Such systems often provide alerts and reports for incomplete incidents. Similar solutions might work as well. In addition to the use of a tracking system, we can also follow a few guidelines to help keep content in harmony. Specifically, we can transport and test changes quickly, eliminate changes in production, design roles that work in multiple environments, document repository roles, schedule changes, and audit the environment often. Let's look at each of these items in more detail.

Transport and Test Quickly

One way to ensure that content remains in sync is to expedite the transportation process and subsequent testing. The longer content remains untested and un-transported, the more likely the organization is to experience inconsistency issues.

Eliminate Manual Changes in Production

When organizations make changes to repository roles directly in production, they run the risk of those changes being overwritten by subsequent transports. When this happens, such changes might be lost forever. We should strive to eliminate the need to make changes in production by using transports and predominantly using repository-based content for development objects and security objects. Using transports ensures that the same content is implemented in each target instance. Repository-based objects all can be transported between systems, which helps keep them consistent.

Design Repository Roles That Work in Other Environments

We need to design our repository roles so that they work in multiple environments. Strive to design a base set of repository roles that are universally applicable. We should also consider that users aren't automatically granted access to new repository roles; these roles must be manually assigned to users or other roles. Therefore, it's OK to have the same repository roles in each environment, even though the same user might have different roles granted to in each environment.

Document Repository Roles

It's important that each repository role have its configuration documented in an external master source location. Ideally, all security model changes would be updated in the documentation and in the SAP HANA instances during each change incident. This documentation can be used during periodic audits of the system or to determine inconsistencies within SAP HANA instances.

Schedule Changes

An organization should schedule changes to occur on a weekly basis. Set aside time each week to address transporting content and testing changes. If no changes are needed, these events can be skipped until the next week. Maintaining a consistent schedule helps keep instances in harmony.

Audit Security Often

Using resources external to the group that normally manages the lifecycle process, routine audits of the security model should be conducted. Such audits will help to ensure consistency within the SAP HANA landscape.

With these key principals in mind, let's now look at how to use SAP HANA's built-in tools to manage the transportation of development and security artifacts between systems.

14.2 Create Delivery Units for Security-Related Packages

Delivery units play a role in the lifecycle management of packages. Before we can export content to a file or transport development content from one SAP HANA system to another, we must first assign a package or package hierarchy to a delivery unit. A DU should contain packages and development artifacts that are associated with each other. For example, a web-based application developed in the XS engine and its associated package hierarchy can be assigned to a single DU. Using a DU allows the content to be transported in an organized and consistent manor.

Once content is organized into a DU, we can export it to a compressed file. This file can subsequently be imported into another SAP HANA system for the purposes of transporting the code. Using SAP HANA application lifecycle management, we can also transport DUs between systems. DUs can also serve as external backups of code and subsequently be imported back into the originating SAP HANA system if content needs to be restored.

Note that the administrator must define the vendor ID or content vendor within the system configuration before content can be assigned to a DU. This is configured in the indexserver.ini file under the **repository** option and **content_vendor** key. Specify a value that will identify your organization. For example, you can enter a domain name such as e-corp.com.

The user creating the DU must have privileges similar to those assigned to the sap.hana.xs.lm.roles::Administrator default role. Note that the `INIFile Admin` system privilege, found in this default role, is only necessary to define the content vendor. A custom role should be created for developers that create DUs to avoid granting them access to make configuration changes to the SAP HANA system.

There are two main GUIs we can use to create and manage DUs: SAP HANA Studio (Section 14.2.1) and the web-based SAP HANA application lifecycle management application (Section 14.2.2).

14.2.1 Creating a Delivery Unit with SAP HANA Studio

SAP HANA Studio provides an interface to manage DUs. To access this interface, open the default modeler perspective. Then, go to the **Quick View** area on the right. The **Quick View** area provides several buttons that act as shortcuts to interfaces used when managing development artifacts. The first item in the list of shortcuts is the **Delivery Units** shortcut. Click this shortcut to manage DUs within the system. When you first click the shortcut, a new window will appear named **Select System**. From the list of systems configured within SAP HANA Studio, select the system related to the DUs you need to manage. Click **Next** to open the **Delivery Units** management window (see Figure 14.2).

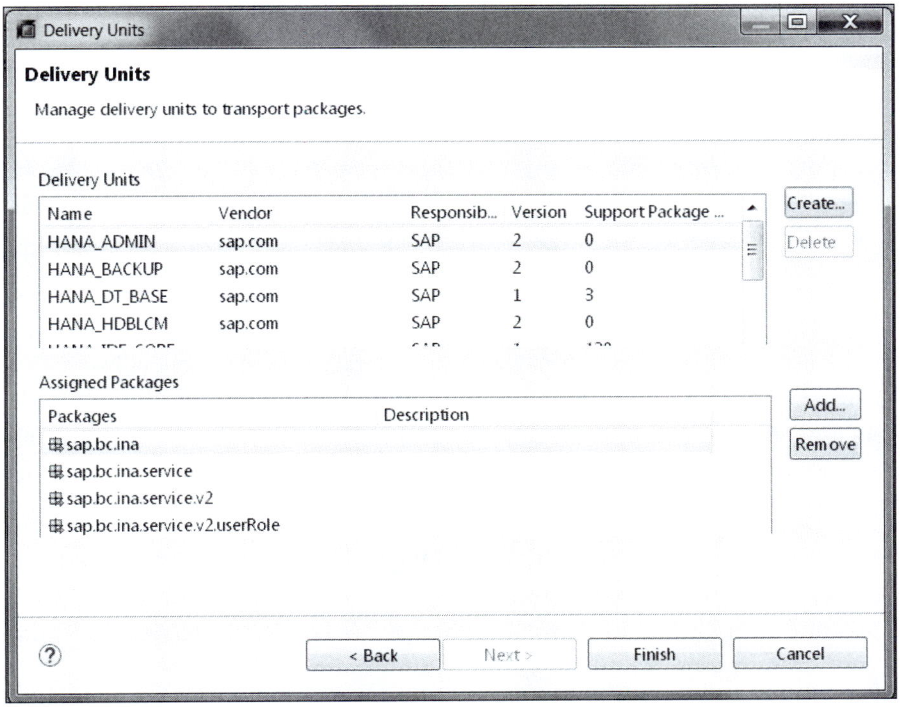

Figure 14.2 Delivery Units Management Window in SAP HANA Studio

Minimum Privileges to Manage Delivery Units in SAP HANA Studio

A grantee will need at least a few privileges to manage a DU for a given package. The following examples use SQL statements for demonstration purposes only. We recommend that you apply the same privileges within a repository-based role when developing a security model.

The grantee must be able to execute the REPOSITORY_REST stored procedure. The following SQL example demonstrates how this catalog object privilege can be granted:

```
GRANT EXECUTE ON "_SYS_REPO"."REPOSITORY_REST" TO <GRANTEE>;
```

The grantee must have a system privilege to maintain delivery units. The following SQL example demonstrates how this system privilege can be granted:

```
GRANT REPO.MAINTAIN_DELIVERY_UNITS TO <GRANTEE>;
```

The grantee must have privileges to read and maintain imported packages on the packages referenced by the DU. The following SQL example demonstrates how these package privileges can be granted:

```
GRANT REPO.READ, REPO.MAINTAIN_IMPORTED_PACKAGES on "<Package>" TO <GRANTEE>;
```

The DU management window is divided into two main sections. The top half of the window is titled **Delivery Units**. In this section, we can create and delete DUs within the system. To create a DU, click the **Create** button located to the right of the section. A new window will appear, titled **New Delivery Unit** (see Figure 14.3).

In this window, enter the **Name** of the DU. The **Vendor** field should be pre-populated with the content vendor ID configured in the indexserver.ini configuration file. All other configuration fields are optional. **Version**, **Support Package Version**, **Patch Version**, **Caption**, and other fields are typically used by SAP or other vendors that provide plug-ins for the XS engine. Click **OK** to create the DU. To delete a DU, remove all assigned packages, highlight the DU in the **Delivery Unit** list, then click the **Delete** button.

At the bottom of Figure 14.2, you can see the **Assigned Packages** section. We use this section to add or remove packages from the DU. To add a package to the selected DU, click the **Add** button. A new window will appear named **Assign Packages** (see Figure 14.4).

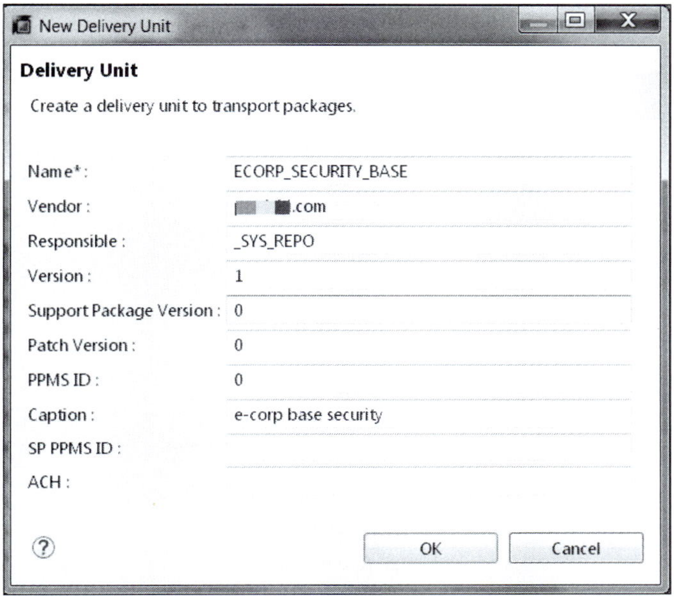

Figure 14.3 New Delivery Unit Window in SAP HANA Studio

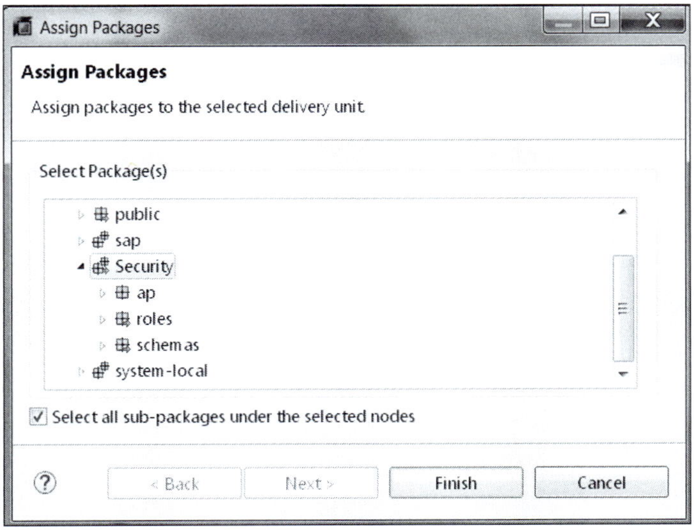

Figure 14.4 Assign Packages Window in SAP HANA Studio

Repository Role Dependencies

In the example, we've packaged all the security-related development artifacts into a single DU. We included dependent subpackage items, such as schemas and analytic privileges. Although this methodology will capture most of the dependent items, the DC likely won't contain all dependent items. All dependent items will need to be packaged into their own respective DUs and transported into target systems before the security-specific DUs are imported.

To select a package, click the top-level package node within the package hierarchy using the **Select Package(s)** section of the window. To include all subpackages with the top-level package node, select the checkbox next to the option titled **Selects all sub-packages under the selected nodes**. Click **Finish** to add the packages to the DU. To remove a package or subpackage from the **Assigned Packages** section, select it in the list and click the **Remove** button. A confirmation pop-up will appear. Click **OK** to confirm that you want to remove the selected package from the DU.

14.2.2 Creating a DU with SAP HANA Application Lifecycle Management

In Section 14.3 and Section 14.4, we'll discuss SAP HANA application lifecycle management in more detail. In this section, we'll look specifically at DU management in SAP HANA application lifecycle management. To access SAP HANA application lifecycle management, we must use a web browser. Customize the following URLs for your system.

For secure SSL access to SAP HANA application lifecycle management, use the following URL:

https://<HOST_NAME>:43<INSTANCE NUMBER>/sap/hana/xs/lm

For example:

https://w5-3db-hana01.e-corp.root.local:4300/sap/hana/xs/lm

If SSL isn't configured, use the following URL:

http://<HOST_NAME>:80<INSTANCE NUMBER>/sap/hana/xs/lm

For example:

http://w5-3db-hana01.e-corp.root.local:8000/sap/hana/xs/lm

In these examples, replace the <HOST_NAME> variable with the host name of your SAP HANA instance and the <INSTANCE NUMBER> variable with the two-digit instance number of your SAP HANA instance.

To access SAP HANA application lifecycle management and manage DUs, you must have the sap.hana.xs.lm.roles::Administrator role. During our testing, we found that this role is required even if the grantee has the privileges necessary to perform the same actions using SAP HANA Studio. Once you have access to SAP HANA application lifecycle management and log on using the configured method for your environment, the home page shown in Figure 14.5 will appear.

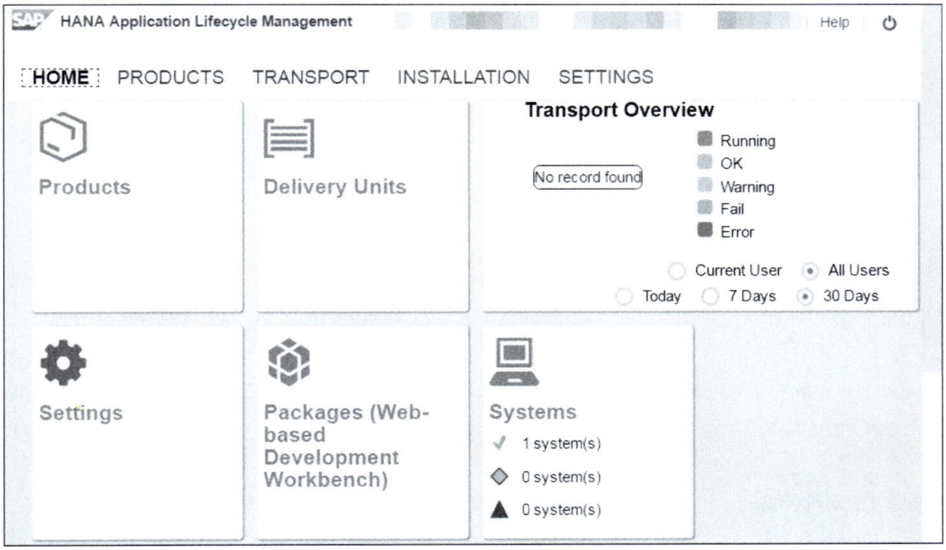

Figure 14.5 Home Page of SAP HANA Application Lifecycle Management

On the **Home** page, click the tile labeled **Delivery Units**. A new window will appear and the navigation path **Products • Delivery Units** will be preselected. Within this **Delivery Units** window, you'll see a list of DUs on the left side. On the right side, you'll find configuration options for the selected DU. Figure 14.6 provides an example of the DU management window in SAP HANA application lifecycle management.

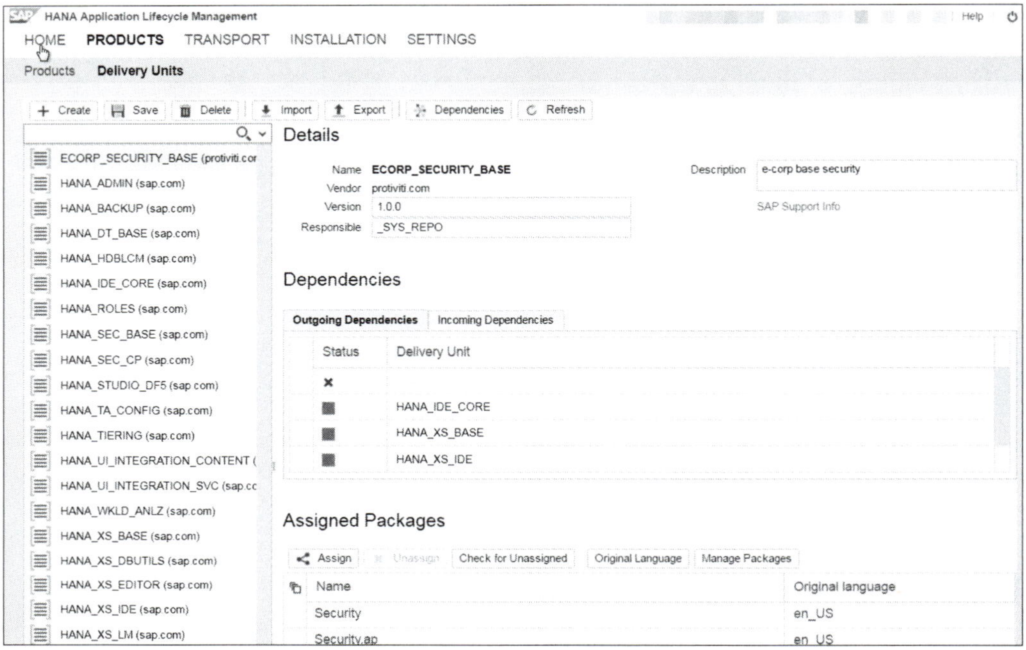

Figure 14.6 DU Management Window in SAP HANA Application Lifecycle Management

To create a new DU, click the button at the top left labeled **+ Create**. A new window will appear titled **New Delivery Unit** (see Figure 14.7).

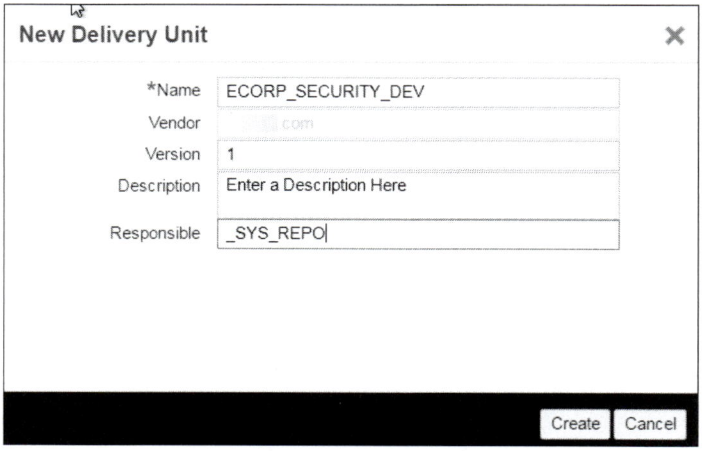

Figure 14.7 New Delivery Unit Window in SAP HANA Application Lifecycle Management

The **Name** field is mandatory and must be filled. The **Vendor** field will contain the name of the content vendor configured within your environment. All remaining fields are optional. Click **Create** once you've entered the required information.

To assign packages to the DU, select the DU on the left, then, on the right side of the window, scroll down until the **Assigned Packages** section is visible. In this section, click the **Assign** button to add packages to the DU. A new window will appear titled **Assign Packages** (see Figure 14.8).

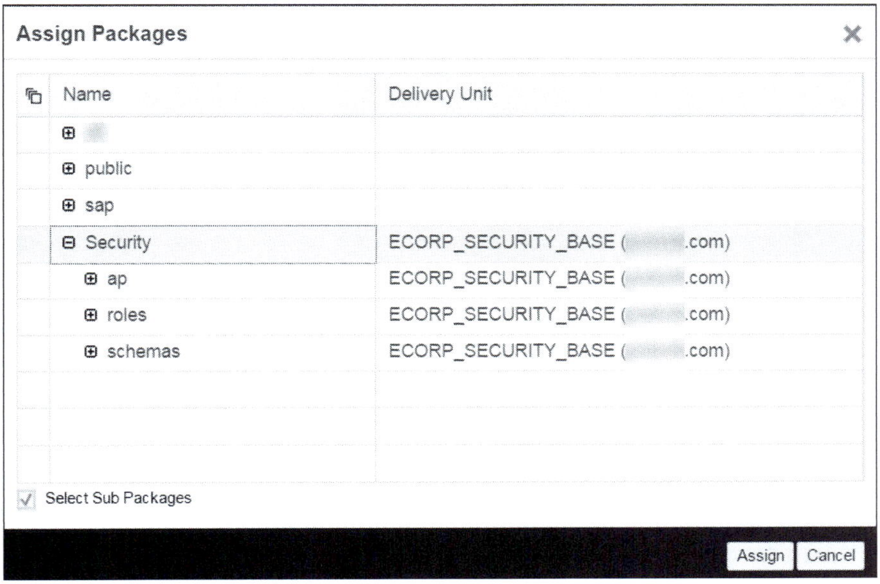

Figure 14.8 Assign Packages Window in SAP HANA Application Lifecycle Management

Click the package node level that you want to assign to the DU. Choose the **Select Sub Packages** option to include all subpackages within the DU. Click the **Assign** button to assign the packages.

To remove packages from the DU, select the DU on the left, then, on the right, scroll down to the **Assigned Packages** section. Select the package to remove and click **Unassign**. To save changes made to the DU, click the **Save** icon just to the right of the **+ Create** button.

Additional Information

For additional information pertaining to SAP HANA application lifecycle management, please download and review the SAP HANA Application Lifecycle Management Guide:

http://help.sap.com/hana/SAP_HANA_Application_Lifecycle_Management_en.pdf

In the guide, you'll find information on the following topics discussed briefly in this chapter:

- Maintaining Delivery Units (this section)
- Register a System for a Transport Route (Section 14.3.1)
- Create a Transport Route and Start the Transport (Section 14.3.1)
- Maintaining SAP HANA Change Recording (Section 14.4.1 and Section 14.4.2)

In the next section, we'll explore the options necessary to transport or promote content between SAP HANA systems. We'll also review the processes necessary to export a DU to a file.

14.3 Transport Security Packages to Other SAP HANA Systems

As we stated earlier in this chapter, transporting our security model between systems leads to a more consistent implementation of the security model within the overall SAP HANA landscape. To use the SAP HANA transport system and achieve this goal, we must define repository-based roles within our security model. If our security model is based on standard roles created using SQL statements, we can't transport it between SAP HANA instances.

When we transport DUs between systems, all packages and development artifacts within the DU are imported and activated within the target system. If existing objects with the same name exist, they're overwritten. If objects exist in the target but not in the DU, they're marked for deletion. If objects exist in the DU but not in the target, they're created in the target. When a DU is imported, that same DU is created in the target, including all the packages and development artifacts associated with the DU. This is an excellent way to ensure that repository roles remain consistent.

SAP HANA provides two tools to aid in the promotion of security-related DUs between instances. The first tool is SAP HANA application lifecycle management, which you were introduced to in Section 14.2.2. The second tool is SAP HANA Studio, which provides options to both export and import a DU to a compressed file. The file generated can be imported into an SAP HANA system operating on a similar software version.

In this section, we'll explore the process used to transport a DU using SAP HANA application lifecycle management. We'll also review the process used to export and import a DU using SAP HANA Studio.

14.3.1 Transport a DU with SAP HANA Application Lifecycle Management

To manage transporting or migrating content between systems, SAP developed the SAP HANA application lifecycle management web-based application. This application is hosted in the XS engine. When transporting objects to a new system, we must access the SAP HANA application lifecycle management instance on the target SAP HANA instance. SAP HANA application lifecycle management uses a pull methodology, meaning that the target SAP HANA application lifecycle management instance accesses the source SAP HANA application lifecycle management instance and pulls the DU into the target's local repository. Figure 14.9 provides an overview of this process.

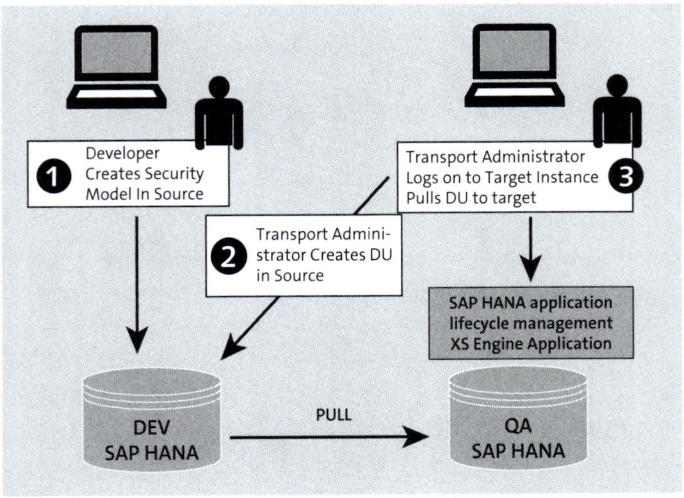

Figure 14.9 High-Level SAP HANA Application Lifecycle Management Transport Process

Based on Figure 14.9, step one in the process requires that a developer or security administrator create content in the DEV SAP HANA instance. Step two of the process requires that the transport administrator assign the content to a DU within the source instance. Step three of the process requires that the transport administrator access the target SAP HANA application lifecycle management instance and pull the DU from the source to the target.

As a reminder, you access SAP HANA application lifecycle management using a URL specific to each instance, as follows:

- *https://<HOST_NAME>:43<INSTANCE NUMBER>/sap/hana/xs/lm*
- *https://w5-3db-hana01.e-corp.root.local:4300/sap/hana/xs/lm*

Or, if SSL isn't configured:

- *http://<HOST_NAME>:80<INSTANCE NUMBER>/sap/hana/xs/lm*
- *http://w5-3db-hana01.e-corp.root.local:8000/sap/hana/xs/lm*

On the home page of the SAP HANA application lifecycle management instance, you'll see a series of tiles. Just above the tiles is a menu bar (see Figure 14.10). The third option in that menu bar is titled **Transport**; click it to start the transport process.

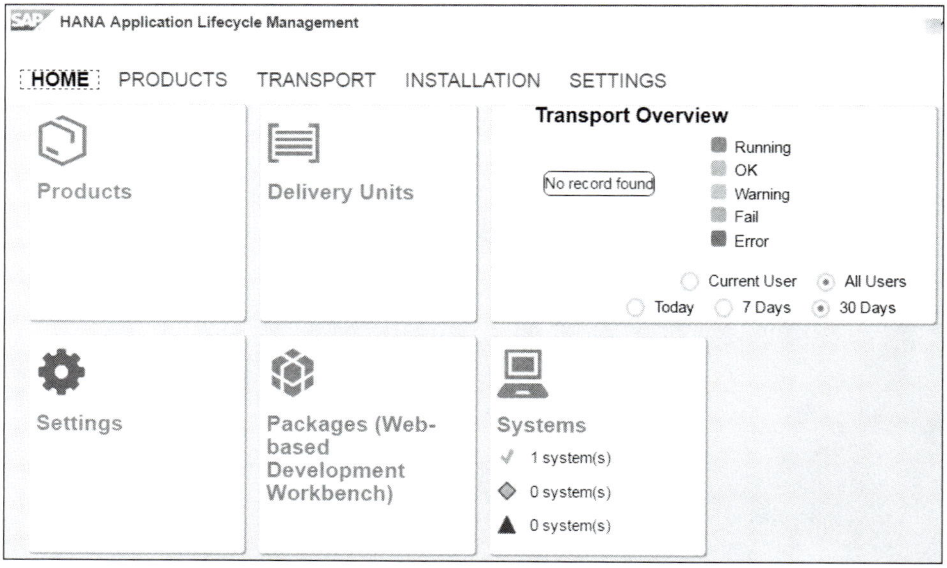

Figure 14.10 SAP HANA Application Lifecycle Management Home Page

The transport management window has three main tabs or menu options just under the main menu bar. The **System** option is selected by default, and the **Transports** and **Logs** options are available as well (see Figure 14.11).

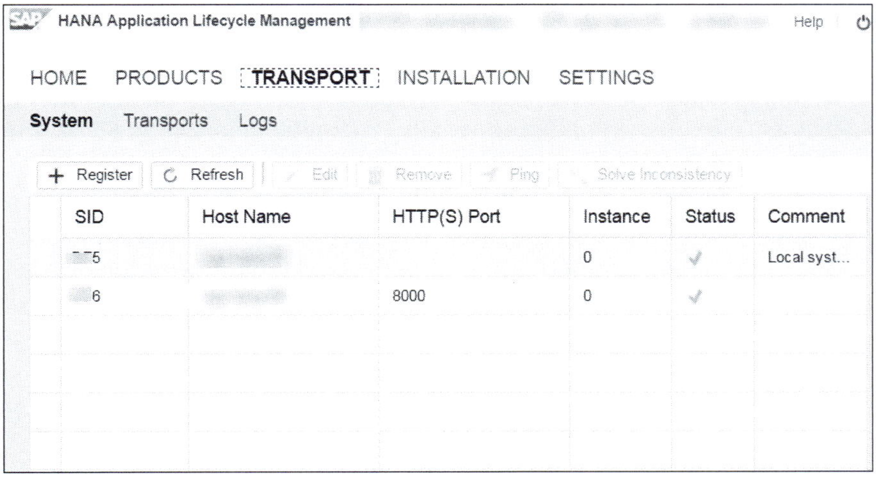

Figure 14.11 Transport Management Window and System Option

Before the transport process can begin, we must register a source system in the target system's SAP HANA application lifecycle management instance. To register a new system, click the **+ Register** button just below the submenu bar. A new window will appear named **Register System** (see Figure 14.12).

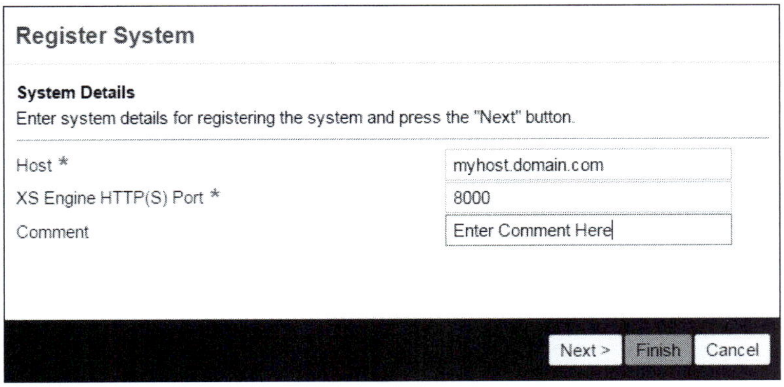

Figure 14.12 Register System Window in SAP HANA Application Lifecycle Management

In this window, enter the **Host** of the source SAP HANA instance. Enter the TCP/IP port for the source SAP HANA instance's XS engine in the **XS Engine HTTP(S) Port** field. The **Comment** field is optional. Click **Next** once you've entered the correct information. A new window will appear labeled **Configure Destination**. This window explains that you must configure the connection and authentication details specific to the source SAP HANA instance. To configure these details, click the **Maintain Destination** button to open a new window titled **HTTP Destination Details**.

In this window, specify the connection details for the source system. Click the **Authentication Details** menu option to open its configuration page.. On the **Authentication Details** page, click the **Edit** button at the bottom right. Now, you can specify the authentication details for the source. The most common option is to select the **Authentication type** of **Basic**. You can then use the **User** and **Password** fields to specify the logon credentials for the source system. The source system service account used will need the sap.hana.xs.lm.roles::Transport role granted at a minimum. Once the credentials are entered, click the **Save** button located at the bottom right. Close the **HTTP Destination Details** window using the **X** located at the top-right-hand corner of the window. Click **Finish** on the **Register System** window. Your source system should now be registered in the transport system list.

The next step in the process is to define a transport route. To create the transport route, click the submenu item titled **Transports** (see Figure 14.13).

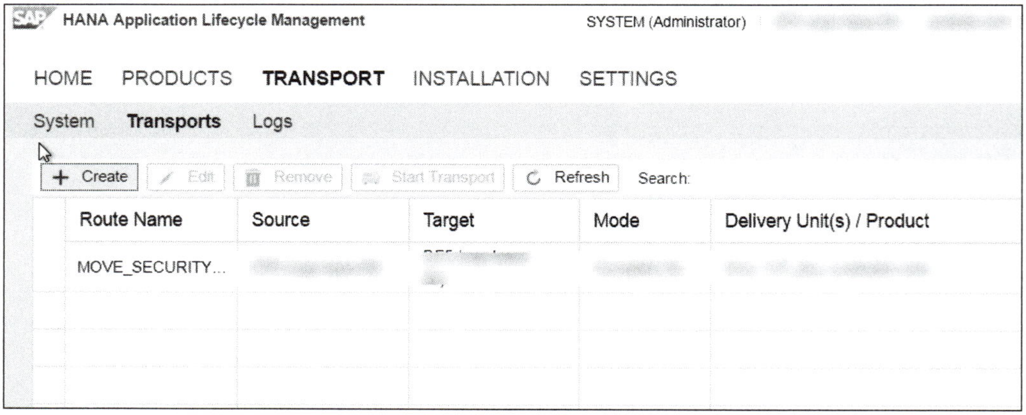

Figure 14.13 Transport Management Window and Transport Option

To create a new transport route, click the button titled **+ Create**. A new window will appear titled **Create Transport Route** (see Figure 14.14).

Enter the **Name** of the transport route and choose the **Source System**. The **Source System** dropdown will only contain registered systems. The target system value is fixed and can't be changed. In the **Content** section, select the **Delivery Units** radio button and then select one or more source system DUs to transport. Click the **Create** button at the bottom right.

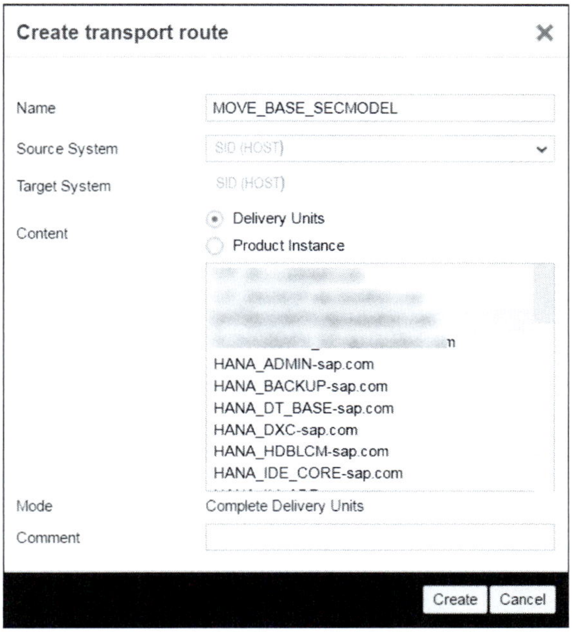

Figure 14.14 Create Transport Route Window

With the transport route defined, we can now start the transport process (see Figure 14.15). To transport a DU, select the transport route in the list ❶. Once selected, start the transport process by clicking the **Start Transport** button ❷.

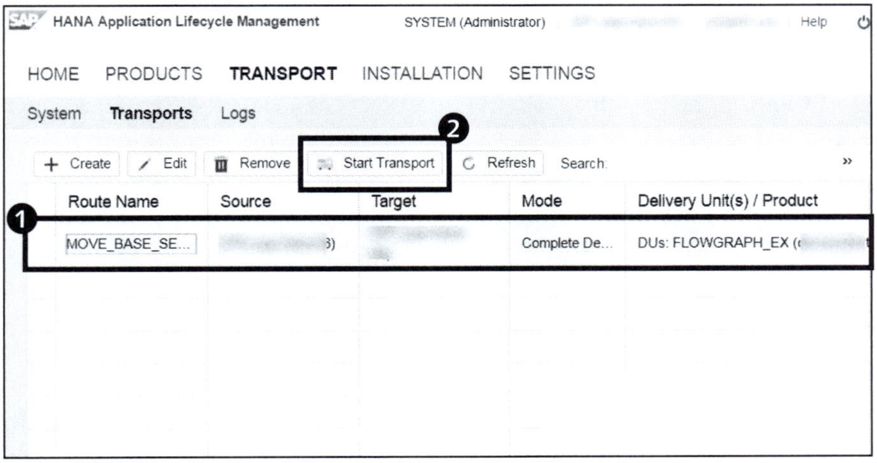

Figure 14.15 Selecting Tranport Package and Starting Transport Process

Once the **Start Transport** button is clicked, a new window titled **Start the Transport** will appear to confirm the start action. Click the **OK** button to start the transport process. The window will disappear, and you'll return to the transport route-listing page.

To view the status of the transport request, click the submenu item labeled **Logs**. Here, you can see the current and historical status of transports initiated within the system. If there are any issues, the **Status** column will show a red triangle. If the transport is complete, the **Status** column will show a green square.

14.3.2 Export a DU to a File

SAP HANA Studio provides an interface to export a delivery unit to a compressed file. This compressed file can be imported back into the SAP HANA repository later. Developers often use this export process to serve as a backup of their code. However, it also can be used for lifecycle management, even though SAP HANA application lifecycle management is the preferred tool to manage transports between SAP HANA instances.

To start the process, switch to the administration console perspective within SAP HANA Studio. From the menu bar, choose **File • Export**. A new pop-up window will appear titled **Export**. Within the **Select an Export Wizard** section, expand **SAP HANA Content** and then choose **Delivery Unit**. Click **Next** to continue. A new pop-up window will appear titled **Select Source System**. In the list of systems, select the system that will serve as the source of the DU. Click **Next** to continue. A new pop-up window will appear titled **Export Through Delivery Unit** with a subtitle of **Select Delivery Unit**. This window is used to specify the DU export options (see Figure 14.16).

In this window, use the **Delivery Unit** dropdown menu to choose the DU for export. The export tool will include all development artifacts associated with the packages listed in the section labeled **List of Packages**. However, there's an option to export development artifacts based on their activation date. Use the **Filter by time** checkbox to enable the time-based filters. With the box checked, choose a **Time Internal** using the provided dropdown list. The dropdown list provides the following intervals: **Last Week**, **Last Month**, and **Time Range**. Choose **Time Range** to specify custom **From** and **To** dates.

When exporting the DU file, we can choose to place it on the server or download it to SAP HANA Studio's client system. Typically, we export to the client system, because most developers don't have access to the SAP HANA server's file system. Choose **Export to Client** in the **Export Location** section. In the **Location** field, specify the local file path where the DU file will be downloaded. The **File Name** field will be prepopulated with a file name based on the current time, system, and DU name. You can change the name, but be sure to retain the file extension .tgz. Click **Next** to continue. A **Summary** page will appear with an overview of the export settings. Click **Finish** to start the export process. Once completed, a file will appear in the configured path. Once the file is created, it can be used as a backup or as an import source.

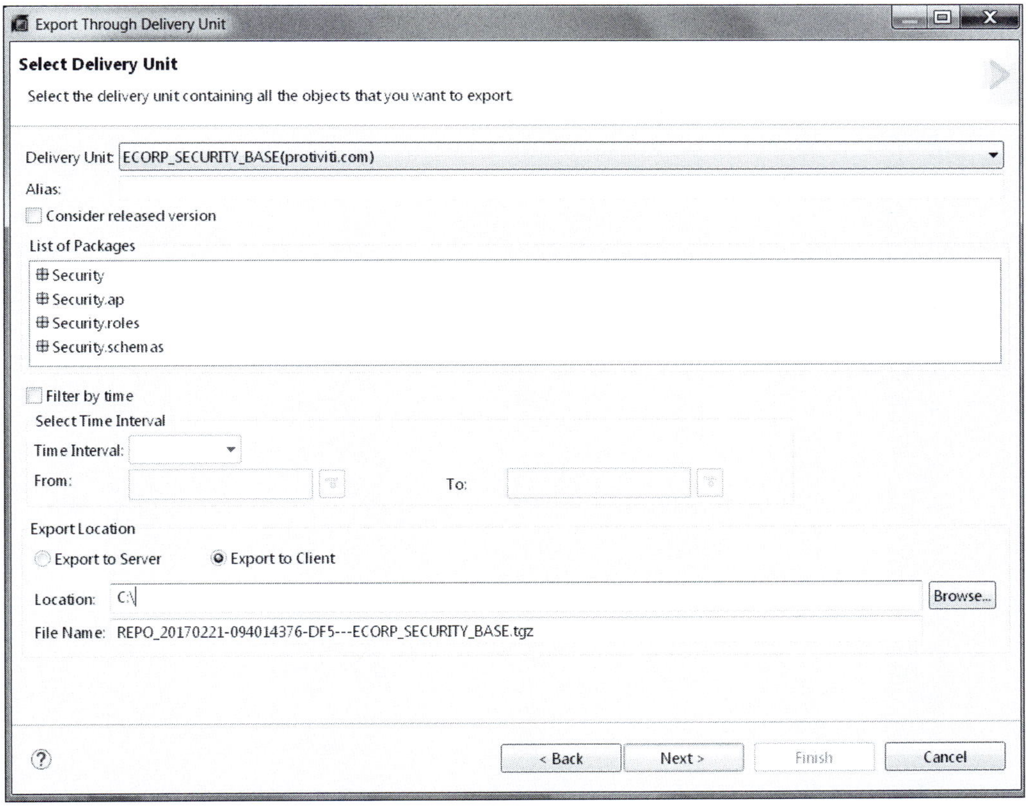

Figure 14.16 Export Options in SAP HANA Studio

14.3.3 Import a DU from a File

SAP HANA Studio provides an interface to import a DU file into a package repository. The tool will import all development artifacts found in the file and active them within the repository. The file can be imported into an SAP HANA instance, assuming that the export source and import source share a similar SAP HANA software version.

To start the import process, switch to the administration console perspective in SAP HANA Studio. From the menu bar, choose **File • Import**. A new popup window will appear titled **Import**. Within the **Select an Import Wizard** section, expand **SAP HANA Content** and then choose **Delivery Unit**. Click **Next** to continue. A new pop-up window will appear titled **Target System**. In the list of systems, select the system that will serve as the import target for the DU file. Click **Next** to continue. A new window will appear titled **Import Through Delivery Unit** (see Figure 14.17).

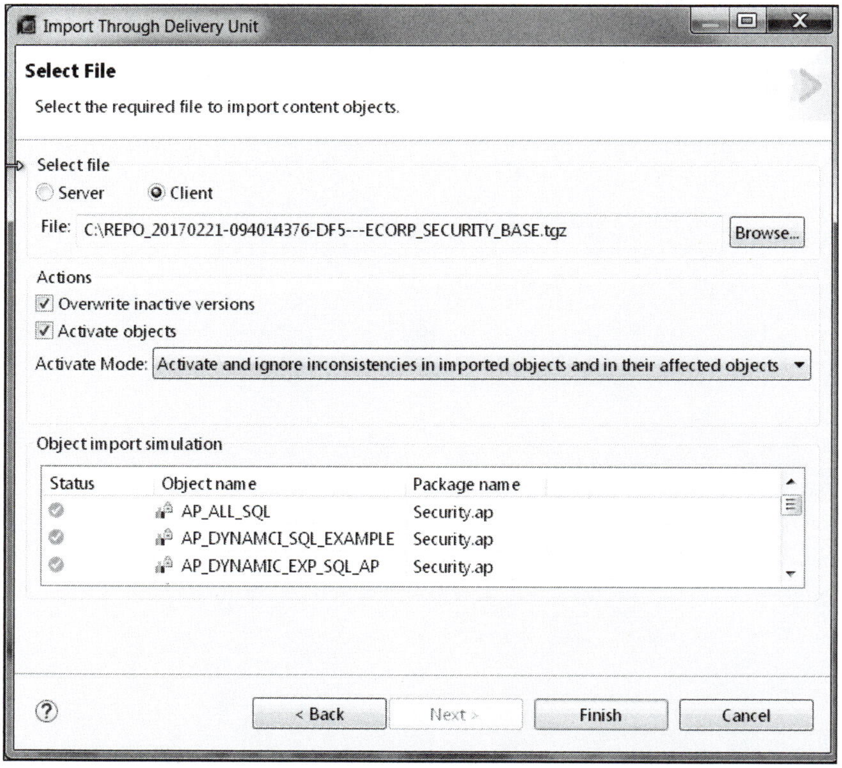

Figure 14.17 Import Options in SAP HANA Studio

To configure the import options, start by choosing the import file location. Choose the **Client** location for files stored on the SAP HANA Studio client system. Click the **Browse** button to specify the path of the file. In the **Actions** section, choose from the following options: Choose **Overwrite inactive versions** to import the DU content even if another version of the content already exists in the target. Choose **Activate**

objects to have the import wizard activate the newly imported development artifacts. If this option isn't selected, the objects will be imported without activation.

In the **Activate Mode** dropdown list, choose how the wizard should handle inconsistencies. The **Activate and ignore the inconsistencies in affected objects** mode will activate the objects directly found in the DU file even if their activation causes existing development artifacts to become inconsistent. The **Stop activation in case of inconsistencies in affected objects** option will stop the activation process if any inconsistencies are detected during import. The default option is to **Activate and ignore the inconsistencies in imported objects and in their affected objects**. With this option selected, the import wizard will attempt to activate development artifacts found in the DU file even if some of the artifacts and their affected objects fail to import.

The **Object import simulation** section contains a listing of the development artifacts that will be imported. In addition, it provides an anticipated activation status based on a review of the target repository. Please note that objects might fail to import even if the simulation indicates that there will be no errors. Click **Finish** to import the objects.

To monitor the status of the import job, locate the **Job Log** tab (see Figure 14.18), which will appear at the bottom of the perspective once the import process is started. Within the **Job Log** tab, the import job type name will be listed as **Import (Delivery Unit)**. Use the **Status** column to determine the import status.

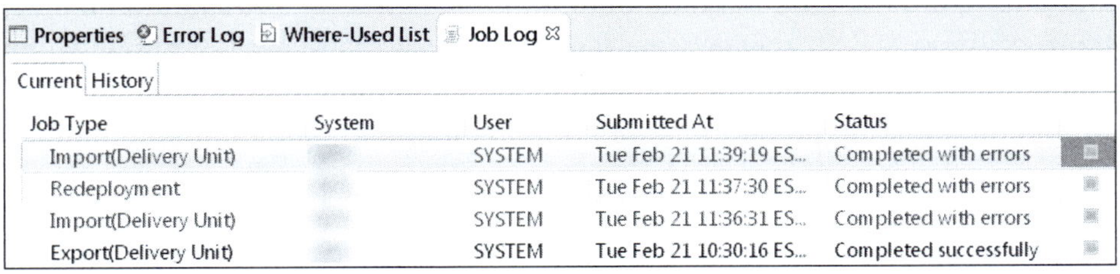

Figure 14.18 Job Log Tab in SAP HANA Studio

If there are errors, double-click the **Job Status** row to open the **Job Details** window, which will provide a detailed import status for each development artifact included in the DU. Identified issues will need to be resolved, and the import process will need to be repeated until they are.

14.4 Additional Options in SAP HANA Application Lifecycle Management

In addition to the management of DUs and transportation of DUs between systems, SAP HANA application lifecycle management offers a few other features that might benefit the lifecycle management of security-related artifacts. SAP HANA application lifecycle management provides the ability to use a change recording mechanism. It also supports the SAP Change and Transport System (SAP CTS). Let's take a closer look at each of these options.

14.4.1 Change Recording

Change recording is an option that can be enabled in the SAP HANA repository. When enabled, the initial activation of a development artifact will need to be assigned to a change list or change ID until the change list is released. The purpose of the change list is to keep track of changes within a development artifact. As you recall, artifacts are assigned to a package and packages are assigned to a DU. When change recording is enabled, DU changes aren't available for transport until they're confirmed and released within SAP HANA application lifecycle management's change management interface. This means that we can't transport a change until its individual revision is confirmed and the change list is released using the change management area of SAP HANA application lifecycle management.

When change recording is enabled, organizations will have a middle layer within the transport process. This middle layer requires that all changes be approved before they're transported or even exported to a DU file. Without change tracking, a DU would be composed of the most recent changes each time the transport process executes or each time a DU file exports from SAP HANA Studio. All objects within the DU and package would need to be transported even if they weren't ready. Change tracking allows the transport manager to reassign changes to different change lists. For example, let's assume that a DU contains five development artifacts. One of the five artifacts needs to be promoted to QA as soon as possible. However, the remaining four artifacts haven't been validated. The transport manager can reassign the one artifact needed in QA to a new change list and then approve and release the change list for transport. This eventually allows the transport manager the option to transport individual development artifacts within a package and DU.

14.4.2 Using SAP CTS

SAP CTS is a utility that organizations often use to manage the lifecycle of traditional SAP Application Servers. It helps facilitate the promotion of development projects in ABAP Workbench. SAP CTS and SAP HANA application lifecycle management are independent applications, but SAP HANA application lifecycle management offers integration with SAP CTS. When this integration is enabled, organizations can use the tools and processes within SAP CTS to manage the promotion of native SAP HANA development artifacts between SAP HANA instances.

14.5 Summary

Managing the full lifecycle of a security model is important because it helps to eliminate potential security vulnerabilities within the landscape. For an SAP HANA security model, the lifecycle management process involves the use of software tools, adherence to policies, and adherence to procedures. We use tools such as SAP HANA application lifecycle management to ensure consistency within the model between environments. We develop policies and procedures to properly test and audit our security design.

Chapter 15
Auditing

Implementing a security model is just the beginning. We also need to set up rules to record and track select changes made within the SAP HANA system. In this chapter, we'll discuss SAP HANA's internal auditing mechanism for recording and tracking changes by user name, client address, and other attributes.

Auditing allows organizations to configure rules that record important activities conducted within the SAP HANA system. For example, administrators can record any SQL statement issued containing the `ALTER ROLE` or `GRANT ROLE` syntax. These details are recorded to a log that can be reviewed as needed. In this chapter, we'll discuss why we need auditing within SAP HANA. We'll also discuss the steps required to enable auditing and define policies to record critical activities. Finally, we'll walk you through a case study in which we create auditing rules to track important changes within the SAP HANA landscape.

15.1 Why Do We Need Auditing?

From a technical standpoint, auditing on its own doesn't protect the SAP HANA system from unauthorized access. However, it can, in many instances, be used to determine the source of unauthorized access. In addition, it can be a deterrent to users who want to fraudulently change the data or maliciously harm the system's integrity. There are many reasons that we need to implement auditing with SAP HANA, such as the following:

- **Provide accountability**
  When auditing is enabled, organizations will have accountability for the configuration, security, and object changes made within the SAP HANA system. This information can be used for a variety of purposes. Most importantly, it grants the organization insight into the events that lead to changes within the SAP HANA system. Organizations often must grant administrators significant access to the

SAP HANA system. When auditing is enabled and set up properly, users understand that their actions are being recorded, making them accountable for any changes they implement.

- **Regulatory compliance**
  Many organizations are subject to several regulatory compliance measures. These measures often require that systems like SAP HANA not only remain secure but also have specific auditing measures in place. Audit logs and audit rules are a principal requirement for most regulations. Auditing doesn't prevent a security breach, but it does help authorities identify the source of the breach.
- **Discourage incongruous actions**
  When auditing is enabled, it discourages others from performing unauthorized or malicious actions within the system. The auditing mechanism records actions taken by user name and records information about the computer used to make the change, such as IP address, host name, and operating system user name. This information can help identify the true source of actions executed within the SAP HANA system.
- **Monitor suspicious activity**
  When auditing is enabled, organizations can set up monitors that probe the audit log data for suspicious activities. For example, monitors can be developed to search for multiple sequential failed logon events. Multiple consecutive failed logons from a single source could indicate that someone is attempting to gain unauthorized access to the SAP HANA system. Monitoring the logs might be an organization's only mechanism to stop a breach before sensitive data is stolen or the system is compromised.
- **Improve processes and procedures**
  Audit log data can be reviewed to ensure that administrators are following proper procedures. For example, we can set up events to track instances in which privileges are assigned directly to a user account. If policy states that a user account should only be granted roles, we can query the audit logs to make sure administrators follow this procedure.
- **Gauge system utilization and concurrency**
  Audit log data can be queried to determine the frequency and concurrency of user actions. This data is helpful from a system sizing and maintenance standpoint. For example, we can use the audit log data to determine the number of concurrent users querying the system. We can also use it to determine the best time for system maintenance.

- **Database forensics**
  In the event of a security breach or fraud, audit log data can provide forensic information related to the source and scope of the breach. In the event of fraud, a properly configured audit system can identify the source and scope of changes that were made to the SAP HANA system.
- **Chronological audit trail**
  When auditing is enabled and configured properly, organizations will have a means to chronologically review changes made by users. This level of information is critical to investigations of fraud and malicious activities. Without this level of detail, suspicious and fraudulent activities can be conducted without accountability.

15.2 Configuring Auditing

By default, SAP HANA auditing is not enabled, nor are systems configured to capture specific events within SAP HANA. To enable and configure auditing, SAP HANA offers several interfaces. The most commonly used interfaces are within SAP HANA Studio and the SAP HANA Web-Based Development Workbench security manager. Future versions of SAP HANA will likely rely on the SAP HANA 2.0 Cockpit for this configuration, but until that functionality matures, let's look at the workflow used to enable auditing using SAP HANA Studio, the SAP HANA Web-Based Development Workbench security manager, and SQL statements.

15.2.1 Enable Auditing with SAP HANA Studio

SAP HANA Studio has an embedded security manager. To access the security manager, log on to your system and expand the **System** node within the **Systems** tab. Expand the **Security** folder and double-click the **Security** icon. The **Security** manager tab will open. Within this tab, there is a subtab labeled **Auditing**. Select this tab to display the auditing settings (see Figure 15.1).

On the **Auditing** tab, there is a section titled **System Settings for Auditing**. To enable auditing, change the **Auditing Status:** dropdown option to **Enabled**. In the **Audit Trail Target:** dropdown, choose **Syslog (Default)**, **Database Table**, or **CSV Text File**. In the following sections, we'll look at each of these target options in detail before moving on to a discussion of auditing levels.

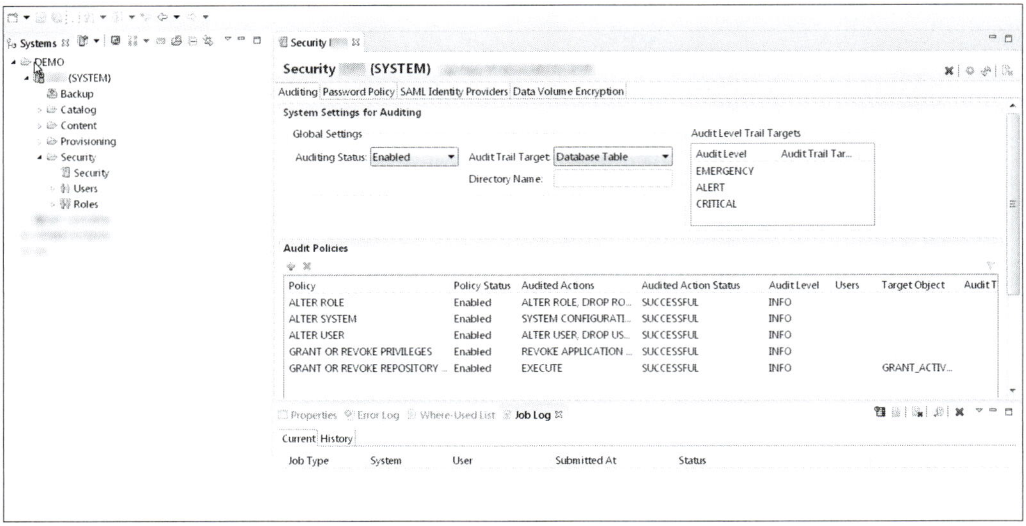

Figure 15.1 Managing Auditing in SAP HANA Studio

Linux Syslog

The operating systems that run SAP HANA have a secure central location to which events can be written, called a syslog. This location can contain audit logs and other event data from software packages running on the Linux OS. When the **Syslog (Default)** option is chosen, configured audit event rules will record activity within the operating system syslog. Organizations should use this option when events need to be collected in the syslog, but they must also ensure that the syslog is configured and operational. SAP HANA will discard events if they can't be written to the OS level syslog. It's also possible to tamper with the syslog outside the knowledge of the SAP HANA system. For example, the log can be cleared by an operating system with access to the syslog files.

Internal Database Table

Events can also be written to a table hosted within the SAP HANA instance. In most cases, it's best to use the internal **Database Table** option for SAP HANA audit logging. When this option is selected, audit events are reordered to the system table `SYS.AUDIT_LOG`. Because the data is written to a database table, SQL `SELECT` statements can be crafted to analyze the data. For example, we can use the following SQL statement to query the audit log table for actions executed for a specific user within SAP HANA:

```
SELECT * FROM SYS.AUDIT_LOG WHERE USER_NAME = 'ADMIN_JHAUN';
```

This table only allows SELECT statements. For example, users cannot insert, update, or delete audit log records regardless of their privileges. To clear the audit log, a user must have the AUDIT OPERATOR system privilege. They must also issue a specific SQL command to delete entries within the audit log. The following example will clear the audit log of all records before the specified date:

```
ALTER SYSTEM CLEAR AUDIT LOG UNTIL '2016-01-01 23:59:59';
```

When this statement is executed, a mandatory system-generated event is recorded in the audit log, indicating the source and user account that issued the statement. This event is recorded after the log is truncated. It's important for this event to be recorded, because it can be used as evidence that a particular user attempted to delete suspicious activity.

CSV File

Events can also be written temporarily to a CSV file. When this option is selected, the events are written to a file using the directory specified in the **Directory Name:** field. This field is found just below the **Audit Trail Target:** field. The specified path is local to the SAP HANA host operating system. This option should only be used temporarily for testing purposes, because these CSV files are not secure. If a directory name isn't specified, the audit logs are written to the default trace file path in SAP HANA. Users with access to the trace files will also have access to this audit log CSV file.

Audit Level Trail Targets

When defining an audit rule, its audit level can be classified as **Emergency**, **Critical**, **Alert**, **Warning**, or **Info**. We will discuss this further in Section 15.3.1. However, event classified as **Emergency**, **Critical**, or **Alert** can be directed to one or more targets. To configure these alternative target locations, we need to configure the options found in the **Audit Level Trail Targets** section of the **Auditing** tab. Figure 15.2 shows these options, located at the top right when the **Auditing** tab is selected.

In the **Audit Level Trail Targets** section, we can configure one or more targets using the table. To do so, configure the options within the **Audit Trail Target** field. Based on the **Audit Level** column on the left side of the table, chose one or more **Audit Trail Target** locations from the dropdown menu activated when clicking within the cell. If no targets are configured for a given audit level, the events will be recorded to the master **Audit Trail Target Option:** setting found to the left of the **Audit Level Trail Targets** section.

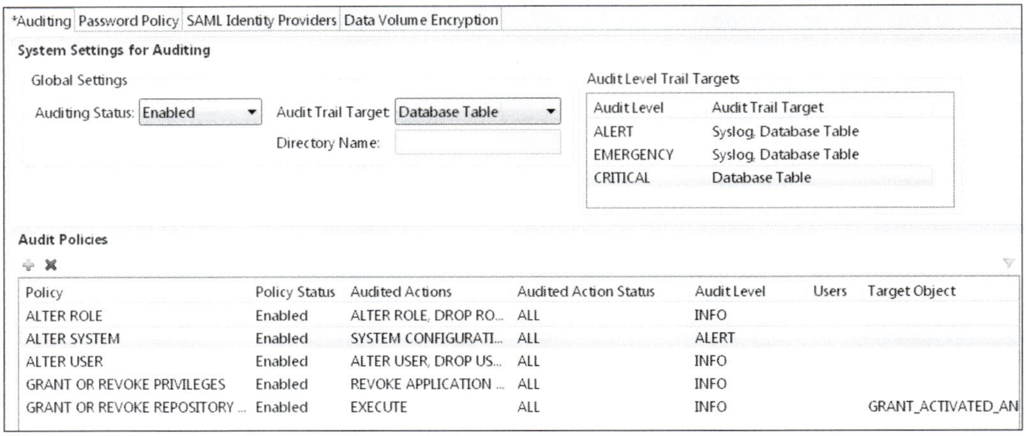

Figure 15.2 Audit Level Trail Targets Configured in Auditing Tab

This option is particularly useful when we need to record important events to multiple target locations. For example, some organizations might want to record events to the audit table and the syslog because they use third-party software to monitor the Linux syslog. We can configure alert, emergency, and critical events for all three possible target locations. For example, we can configure emergency alerts to be written to the audit table, the syslog, and a CSV file on the operating system.

Another advanced option uses a special icon found within SAP HANA Studio to truncate the audit log database table. This icon is not easily found within the interface. It's located at the top right side of the security manager. The icon is depicted as a large red **X** ❶, as shown in Figure 15.3. If you hover over the icon, the tooltip reads **Truncate the Database Table Audit Trail**.

When we click this icon, a new calendar-based pop-up window ❷ will appear, as shown in Figure 15.3. To truncate the audit table, we must specify a date and time. All entries before the specified date and time will be deleted. Click **OK** to truncate the events. Note that a user must be granted the AUDIT OPERATOR system privilege to perform this action.

Once you've specified the desired options, press F8 or click the **Deploy** icon at the top right to save and activate the options within the SAP HANA system.

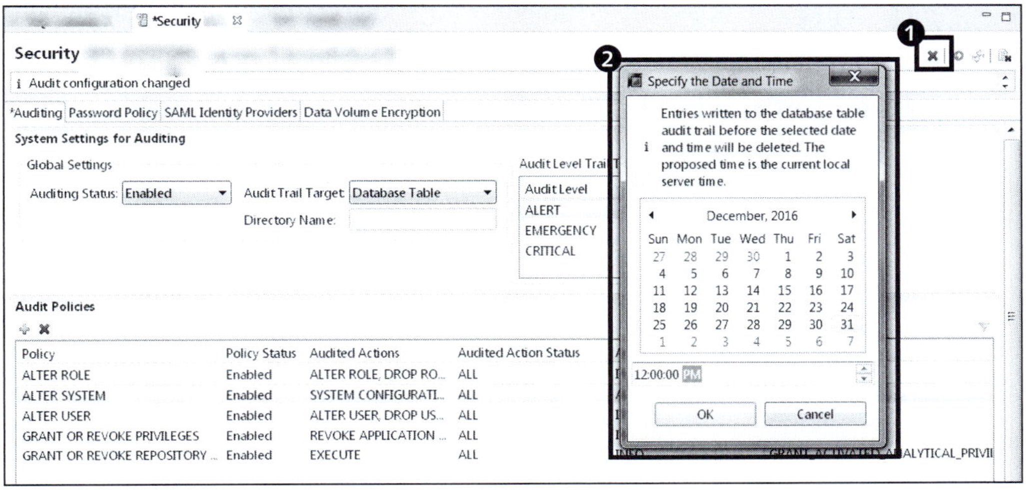

Figure 15.3 Truncating Audit Events in Audit Table in SAP HANA Studio

Now that we've reviewed the options and workflows necessary to enable auditing and define audit targets within SAP HANA Studio, let's briefly review how these options can be configured in the SAP HANA Web-Based Development Workbench security manager, hosted within the XS engine.

15.2.2 Enable Auditing with SAP HANA Web-Based Development Workbench

The SAP HANA Web-Based Development Workbench security manager, hosted within the XS engine, provides an interface to configure SAP HANA auditing.

You can access SAP HANA Web-Based Development Workbench via a supported Internet browser. To use this tool, a user must have the sap.hana.xs.ide.roles::SecurityAdmin role at a minimum. The following two URLs can be customized to match the details of your environment:

- *http://sap-hana.myhost.com:8000/sap/hana/ide/security*
- *http://<sap_hana_host>: 80<instance_number>/sap/hana/ide/security*

In the last example, replace <sap_hana_host> with the hostname of the SAP HANA system in your environment and <instance_number> with the two-digit instance number corresponding to your SAP HANA system.

For secure access, the following examples should help you construct the correct URL:

- *https://<sap_hana_host>: 43<instance_number>/sap/hana/ide/security*
- *https://sap-hana.myhost.com:4300/sap/hana/ide/security*

Once you have access to the SAP HANA Web-Based Development Workbench security manager, you'll see a series of buttons located at the top-left side of the GUI's ribbon. The icon depicting a vertical key and server opens the security console; click it to open the **Security Console** tab on the right side. Click the **Auditing** tab to reveal audit configuration options. The options and interface are nearly identical to those found in SAP HANA Studio, with a few exceptions. Figure 15.4 provides an example of the security console with the auditing options visible.

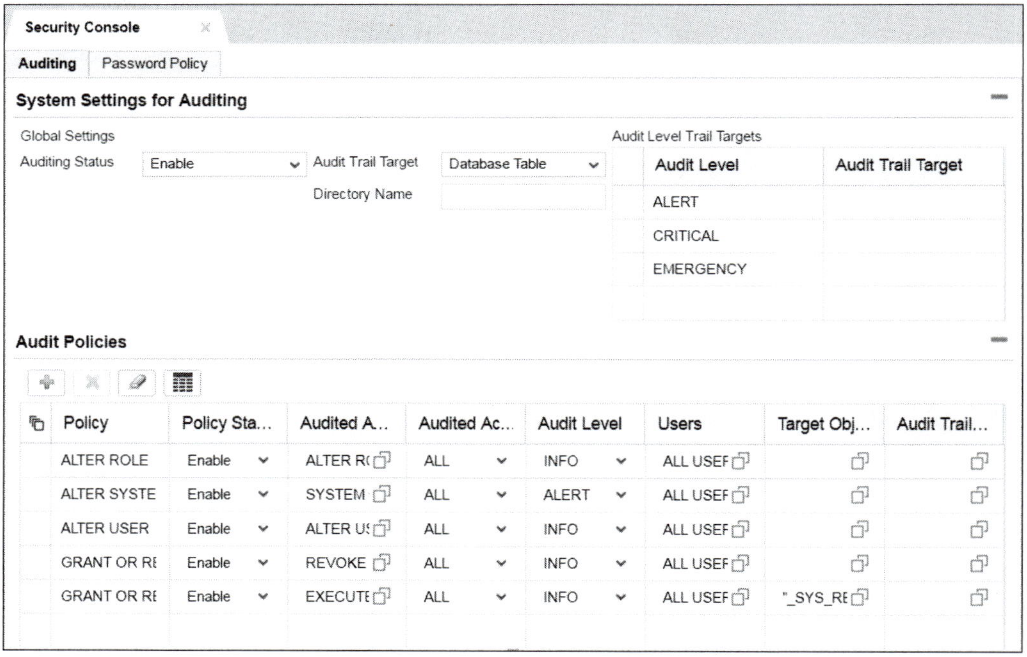

Figure 15.4 Managing Auditing Settings in SAP HANA Web-Based Development Workbench

To enable auditing, use the **Auditing Status** dropdown and choose **Enable**. Specify the **Audit Trail Target** using the dropdown menu. Based on our testing using SAP HANA 1.0 SPS 12 and SAP HANA 2.0 SP 00, the **Audit Level Trail Target** settings aren't working in SAP HANA Web-Based Development Workbench; they will have to be viewed and established using SAP HANA Studio (see Section 15.2.1).

SAP HANA Web-Based Development Workbench has a few differences from SAP HANA Studio. First, the **Truncate the Database Table Audit Trail** icon is in the icon bar just below the **Audit Policy** settings and shows a pink eraser. Click the icon to open a pop-up window in which you can specify the end date for the audit event truncation. Also in this icon bar, note the icon depicted as a table to the right of the log truncation button. When clicked, this icon will open a new window that launches the web-based development workbench catalog interface and its web-based SQL console. The console will be prepopulated with a SQL statement that queries the audit log table. Note that this option, though available, was not working in SAP HANA 2.0 SP 00In Section 15.3.1, we'll also discuss how audit policies can be individually configured with a specific audit trail target. For example, we can specify that a particular audit policy outputs information to a CSV file.

SAP HANA 2.0 Cockpit

The SAP HANA 2.0 Cockpit was introduced during the development of this book and therefore was not included as an available tool in the sections above. However, we can confirm that all the auditing options can be configured using the SAP HANA 2.0 Cockpit, a web-based interface.

For more information about the SAP HANA 2.0 Cockpit, please visit the following links:

- *https://wiki.scn.sap.com/wiki/display/SAPHANA/SAP+HANA+2.0+Cockpit+FAQ*
- *https://help.sap.com/viewer/1fc5d914096f4ef6929735be88f91f97/2.0.00/en-US*

15

15.2.3 Enable Auditing with SQL

In addition to using the GUIs, users with `INIFILE ADMIN` system privileges can also use `ALTER SYSTEM ALTER CONFIGURATION` SQL scripts to configure the auditing mechanism within SAP HANA. Using a script is helpful when we need to ensure that all SAP HANA systems within our landscape use the same settings.

To enable auditing, we need to update the global.ini file setting for the auditing configuration. The setting name is `global_auditing_state`. Execute the following SQL code to set the value to `true`:

```
ALTER SYSTEM ALTER CONFIGURATION ('global.ini', 'SYSTEM')
   SET ('auditing configuration', 'global_auditing_state') =
'TRUE' WITH RECONFIGURE ;
```

To specify the audit trail type, we need to update the global.ini file setting for the auditing configuration. The setting name is default_audit_trail_type, and we can choose the CSTABLE, SYSLOGPROTOCOL, or CSVTEXTFILE option. To use the system database table, execute the following SQL code:

```
ALTER SYSTEM ALTER CONFIGURATION ('global.ini', 'SYSTEM')
   SET ('auditing configuration', 'default_audit_trail_type') =
'CSTABLE' WITH RECONFIGURE ;
```

To write events to the Linux syslog, specify the SYSLOGPROTOCOL option, and to use a CSV file as the target, specify the CSVTEXTFILE option.

When using the CSV file option, we should also specify a secure path where the CSV file will be stored. To specify the path, update the global.ini file setting for the auditing configuration. The setting name is default_audit_trail_path. For example, we can execute the following SQL code to specify that the audit log CSV file use the path */usr/sap/HDB/HDB00/auditlog*:

```
ALTER SYSTEM ALTER CONFIGURATION ('global.ini', 'SYSTEM')
   SET ('auditing configuration', 'default_audit_trail_path') =
'/usr/sap/HDB/HDB00/auditlog' WITH RECONFIGURE ;
```

We can also use SQL to define custom audit log targets based on levels. We can choose from among alert, emergency, and critical audit levels. There are three specific global.ini file settings for the auditing configuration: emergency_audit_trail_type, critical_audit_trail_type, and alert_audit_trail_type. For example, execute the three SQL statements in Listing 15.1 to specify custom audit targets for the alert, emergency, and critical audit levels.

```
ALTER SYSTEM ALTER CONFIGURATION ('global.ini', 'SYSTEM')
   SET ('auditing configuration', 'emergency_audit_trail_type') =
'CSTABLE, SYSLOGPROTOCOL, CSVTEXTFILE' WITH RECONFIGURE ;

ALTER SYSTEM ALTER CONFIGURATION ('global.ini', 'SYSTEM')
   SET ('auditing configuration', 'critical_audit_trail_type') =
'CSTABLE, SYSLOGPROTOCOL' WITH RECONFIGURE ;

ALTER SYSTEM ALTER CONFIGURATION ('global.ini', 'SYSTEM')
   SET ('auditing configuration', 'alert_audit_trail_type') =
'CSTABLE, SYSLOGPROTOCOL' WITH RECONFIGURE ;
```

Listing 15.1 SQL Statements for Configuring Custom Audit Targets

Simply enabling auditing isn't sufficient. We must also define audit policies to track specific events within the SAP HANA system. In the next section, we'll discuss how audit polices are configured.

15.3 Creating Audit Policies

As stated earlier, auditing is disabled by default within the SAP HANA system. In addition, no custom *audit policies* are included out of the box. Audit polices can be defined to track specific events based on specific conditions. They're defined by an audit administrator based on the requirements of the organization. In an ideal situation, an organization would record every event within its SAP HANA system. However, recording all events to an in-memory database is costly, both financially and architecturally. Therefore, an organization must configure specific audit policies to record only the events that are critical to the security and stability of the system.

Even after auditing is enabled globally, most events won't be recorded until specific audit policies are defined, though SAP HANA does have several *mandatory audit policies* that cover events specific to the audit mechanism itself. For example, if we disable auditing, change auditing settings, or truncate the audit logs, such events will be recorded in the default target location even if no polices are defined. A user must have the `AUDIT ADMIN` system privilege to define audit policies.

Most actions within the SAP HANA system can be audited. Audit policies are comprised of a combination of specific actions, an action status, and a user performing the action. The action status is based on one of three status options: successful, unsuccessful, or all.

Some actions can only be activated if they reference one or more user accounts. In addition, policies can also be enacted for all users except specified users. If an action doesn't require a referenced user, it's assumed to apply to all users within the system. Furthermore, some actions also require a referenced catalog object. For example, we must reference a user and a catalog object when defining audit policies with data manipulation actions.

Before we review the makeup of the audit policy and the various tools used to define it, let's look at the 16 different categories of actions that can be audited. In the following section, we've outlined these categories and provided a few examples of the specific actions they encompass.

15.3.1 Components of the Audit Policy

Audit policy is comprised of an audit action, audit action status, audit level, target object, target user, and trail target. In the following sections, we'll look closer at each of these items.

Actions Available for Auditing

There are 16 different categories of actions that can be monitored within SAP HANA. Most of the actions within these categories directly correspond to SQL statements executed to perform actions related to the category. Within each category, we'll find a variety of actions that can be configured and selected. Most audit policies can only be defined using actions from the same actions category. In addition, some actions within each category can range from broad to very specific. To better understand the types of actions that can be audited, let's review the sixteen categories:

1. **All actions**
   The *all actions* category includes a single audit action by the same name. This action must be mapped to specific users or excluded from specific users. When enabled, all actions within the system will be audited based on the configured audit action status and selected user. In general, we don't want to enable this rule for many users, because it can negatively influence the performance of the system. Its use should be limited to events that don't occur often. For example, it can be used as a universal policy to capture all unsuccessful events for all users except the system accounts. In this case, it would record any action by a user when he isn't authorized to perform the action. The policy referencing all actions must be mapped to specific users or it must be mapped to a list of excluded users. It can't be universally applied to all users in the system.
2. **Backup deletion**
   The *backup deletion* category includes only the `BACKUP CATALOG DELETE` action. This action is useful when an organization needs to monitor users that delete backup catalog entries and files. Policies with this action do not have to be assigned to specific users.
3. **Certificate and PSE store**
   The *certificate and PSE store* category includes all `ALTER`, `CREATE`, and `DROP` SQL actions related to the management of the PSE or certificates within the SAP HANA system. Policies with this action do not have to be assigned to specific users.
4. **Data definition**
   The *data definition* category includes almost all `CREATE`, `ALTER`, `DROP`, and `RENAME`

SQL actions that can be performed against a catalog object. Catalog objects include tables, views, schemas, indexes, and triggers, among others. The actions listed in this category are specific to particular catalog objects. For example, you'll find CREATE TABLE, CREATE VIEW, CREATE PROCEDURE, and CREATE actions for most catalog objects in this category. Policies with these actions do not have to be assigned to specific users.

5. **Data provisioning**
   The *data provisioning* category includes ALTER, CREATE, DROP, and PROCESS REMOTE SUBSCRIPTION EXCEPTION commands related to external adapters, agents, and remote subscriptions. Policies with these actions do not have to be assigned to specific users.
6. **Data query and manipulation**
   The *data query and manipulation* category includes all SQL actions performed against a specific target catalog object. These actions are related to SQL commands such as DELETE, EXECUTE, INSERT, SELECT, and UPDATE. For example, we can record actions when a user issues a SELECT statement against a specific table or all objects in a schema. Basing the rules on a schema is beneficial when an organization wants to audit all catalog objects within the schema. The actions selected are not specific to any particular catalog object type, but you must specify the target object and target user when defining the policy. To avoid any negative performance impacts, audit policies based on these rules should be limited.
7. **Data volume encryption**
   The *data volume encryption* category includes all SQL actions related to the ALTER command against application, data, and log encryption. It also includes the ALTER command used to change the root key backup password. Policies with these actions do not have to be assigned to specific users.
8. **Granting and revoking authorizations**
   The *granting and revoking authorizations* category contains actions specific to the use of SQL commands such as GRANT and REVOKE. Such commands are used to grant or revoke privileges to users or roles. They will only capture instances in which a user is the grantee of the privilege. Policies with these actions do not have to be assigned to specific users or target objects.

   Note that most organizations will use repository-based roles within their security model. It's important to mention that the actions in this category won't capture granting and revoking repository-based roles. Organizations will need to set up polices that monitor the execution of the stored procedures within the _SYS_REPO schema. For example, a *data and query manipulation* action will need to be set up to monitor the execution of the `_SYS_REPO.GRANT_ACTIVATED_ROLE` stored procedure.

9. **LDAP provider management**
   The *LDAP provider manager* category contains actions specific to the management of LDAP providers. This functionality is unique to SAP HANA 2.0. Policies with these actions do not have to be assigned to specific users or target objects.

10. **License deletion**
    The *license deletion* category contains one action, which can be used to audit instances in which the SAP HANA license key is removed from the system. For example, if a user executes the SQL statement `UNSET SYSTEM LICENSE` within a SQL console or uses the SAP HANA Studio GUI to delete the license key, this action will be used to record such events. Policies with this action do not have to be assigned to specific users or target objects.

11. **License installation**
    The *license installation* category contains one action, which can be used to audit instances in which an SAP HANA system license key is added to the system. For example, if a user executes the SQL statement `SET SYSTEM LICENSE` within a SQL console or uses the SAP HANA Studio GUI to install a new license key, this action will be used to record such events. Policies with this action do not have to be assigned to specific users or target objects.

12. **Repository content operations**
    The *repository content operations* category contains actions specific to importing, exporting, and activating development artifacts within the SAP HANA repository. Policies using these actions must specify one or more user accounts to either include or exclude from the policy. It's important to limit the scope of these actions, because they might negatively affect the performance of the system.

13. **SAP HANA dynamic tiering**
    The *SAP HANA dynamic tiering* category contains actions specific to the management of dynamic tiering. These policies are only necessary when dynamic tiering is installed and enabled within the SAP HANA cluster. Policies with these actions do not have to be assigned to specific users or target objects.

14. **Session management and system configuration**
    The *session management and system configuration* category contains actions related to session management, stopping services, and system configuration changes. In most cases, it's important that these actions be included in any audit policy. For example, we need to record any system configuration changes and

need to record any instances in which a user's session is terminated. Note that configuration changes related to auditing do not require a policy defined with these actions. Audit changes are system-mandatory and always will be recorded. Policies with these actions do not have to be assigned to specific users or target objects.

15. **Structured privileges management**

    The *structured privileges management* category contains actions specific to the management of repository analytic privileges and catalog structured privileges. Structured privileges are catalog objects used to restrict access to information views and catalog views. When restricting an SAP HANA information view, they are called analytic privileges, but they are still technically structured privileges.

    It's important to note that the system account _SYS_REPO will be recorded in the audit logs as the action user when a repository analytic privilege is changed or created. To properly audit repository-based analytic privileges, you will also need to enable actions within the *repository content operations* category using a separate policy rule. Both actions will have the same timestamp, which can be used to correlate the two events. Policies with these actions do not have to be assigned to specific users or target objects.

16. **User and role management**

    The *user and role management* category contains actions specific to actions that alter, drop, or create a user account or standard role. For example, when a user is created, these events can be included in a policy to capture the action within the audit logs.

    Note that these actions do not audit repository-based roles. Organizations will need to enable actions within the *repository content operations* category using a separate policy rule to monitor the creation of repository-based roles. Policies with this action do not have to be assigned to specific users or target objects.

Audited Action Status

In an ideal scenario, organizations would audit all actions within the SAP HANA system. Unfortunately, auditing all actions can affect the performance of the system negatively and can lead to a significant increase in memory consumption based on the growth of the audit log table. Therefore, audit rules must be defined based on necessity. Fortunately, we can specify several conditions when defining audit policies; one such condition is the audit action status.

When defining an audit policy, we can choose from one of three status options. When a user is authorized to perform an action, the status of the action will be successful. Audit polices can be defined to capture only successful actions, or we can define an audit policy based on instances in which a user was prevented from performing an action. In these instances, the status of the account would be labeled unsuccessful. We can use this status to capture only actions carried out by users that are not authorized to perform them. It's important that we monitor unauthorized access, because it's often a leading indicator that someone is attempting to compromise the system or data. As a third option, we can also choose to audit both successful and unsuccessful audit status with the all audit status.

Audit Levels

When defining an audit policy, we can choose to assign our audit policies to one of the following audit levels: **Emergency**, **Critical**, **Alert**, **Warning**, or **Info**. As mentioned in Section 15.2.1, the first three levels are useful when **Audit Level Trail Targets** are implemented. Overall, they can also be used to classify the severity of the action that was audited. For example, we can establish a policy configured with an audit level of **Emergency**. Because this value is written to the audit log, the audit event can be easily identified.

Target Objects

When defining an audit policy that uses actions from the data query and manipulation and procedure execution categories, we must also choose a target object. Target objects are catalog objects within the SAP HANA system. If we choose a schema object, all objects within the schema will be subject to the audit rule. If we choose an individual table, view, index, sequence, or procedure, only changes to the selected object will trigger an audit policy. Within each individual audit policy, we can specify one or more target catalog objects.

Target User

When defining an audit policy, we have the option to specify one or more users. When a user is selected, the audit policy will only be triggered for the selected users. Some policies require that target users be specified before they are activated. However, all policies can be configured based one or more users. The policy also supports the use of rules by which all users are audited except those selected. This is helpful when we want to ignore activity created by system user accounts. Note that some policy actions support all users. If a user isn't included or excluded from the policy, the policy assumes that it applies to that user.

Audit Trail Target

On a per audit policy basis, we can override the global audit target settings. This is helpful when we need to capture specific events to a particular target. For example, we can capture all SELECT statements issued to a schema and store them in a CSV file, which can be loaded to a database and analyzed for capacity planning or load analysis purposes.

15.3.2 Managing Policies with SAP HANA Web-Based Development Workbench

The SAP HANA Web-Based Development Workbench security manager, hosted within the XS engine, provides an interface to define audit policies.

You can access SAP HANA Web-Based Development Workbench via a supported Internet browser. To use this tool, a user must have the sap.hana.xs.ide.roles::SecurityAdmin role at a minimum. The following two URLs can be customized to match the details of your environment:

- *http://sap-hana.myhost.com:8000/sap/hana/ide/security*
- *http://<sap_hana_host>:80<instance_number>/sap/hana/ide/security*

In the last example, replace <sap_hana_host> with the hostname of the SAP HANA system in your environment and <instance_number> with the two-digit instance number corresponding to your SAP HANA system.

For secure access, the following examples should help you construct the correct URL:

- *https://<sap_hana_host>:43<instance_number>/sap/hana/ide/security*
- *https://sap-hana.myhost.com:4300/sap/hana/ide/security*

Once you have access to the SAP HANA Web-Based Development Workbench security manager, you'll see a series of buttons located at the top left, in the ribbon. The icon depicting a vertical key and server opens the **Security Console** tab on the right side. Click the **Auditing** tab to open the audit policy management interface.

At the bottom of the **Auditing** tab, you'll see a section titled **Audit Policies** (see Figure 15.5).

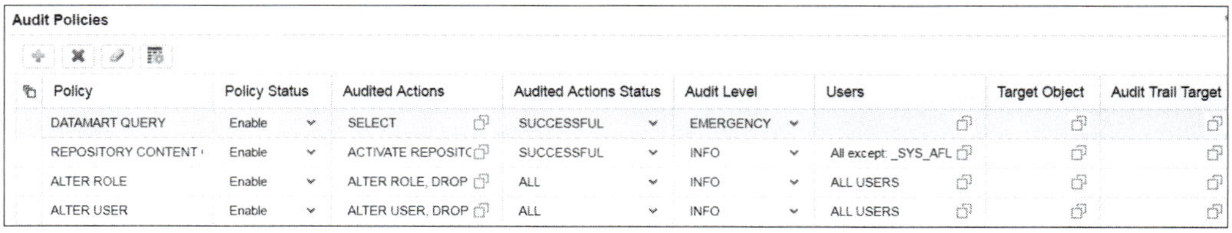

Figure 15.5 Interface to Define One or More Audit Policies

Under the **Audit Policies** label, you'll see four icons. The first icon, **+**, lets you define a new audit policy. The second is an **X**, used to delete a selected audit policy. The third icon is a pink eraser, used to delete audit events from the audit log. The final icon shows a table with a green gear overlay. We can use this icon to open a SQL console in which we can query the audit log table or execute SQL commands.

To define a new audit policy, click **+**. A new row will appear in the audit policy table. To begin the process, enter a unique name for the policy within the **Policy** column using the cell titled **Enter Name**. In the **Policy Status** column, click the down arrow within the cell and select **Enable** from the options. In the **Audited Actions** column, click the icon within the cell that contains two stacked boxes to open a new window, **Edit Actions Audited by Policy**. In this window, we can choose from some of the available audit actions by category. Select the actions that need to be audited; remember that the selected actions must be from the same category. When finished, click the **OK** button located at the bottom right.

Within the **Audited Actions Status** column, click the down arrow located to the right of the cell. Choose **Successful**, **Unsuccessful**, or **All**. Within the **Audit Level** column, click the down arrow located to the right of the cell. Choose **Emergency**, **Critical**, **Alert**, **Warning**, or **Info.**

In the **Users** column, click the icon within the cell that contains two stacked boxes. A new window titled **Select Users** will appear. Use the options in the window to search for one or more existing users. Once the users are located, use the **Add** button located between the **Matching Items** list and **Selected Items** list to add the selected users to the right side of the window. Choose **Include Selected Users** in policy or **Exclude Selected Users** from policy above the **Selected Items** area. Click **OK** once you've selected users to include or exclude. Note that most actions don't require that you select a user. When the field is left blank, the system assumes that it should apply the policy to all users. If the policy won't activate without a user, you can assume that the policy action requires a referenced user.

If the audit policy uses actions from the data query and manipulation and procedure execution categories, we must also choose a target object. Within the **Target Object** cell, click the icon that contains two stacked boxes. A new window titled **Target Object** will appear. Within the search box, enter the name of the catalog object that will serve as the target for the audit policy. Click the **OK** button found in the bottom right once you've completed your selections.

If you want to define specific audit targets for the audit policy, use the **Audit Trail Target** column and cell to define additional targets. Within the **Audit Trail Target** cell, click the icon that contains two stacked boxes. A new window titled **Select Targets** will appear. Select each audit target location's checkbox. Click the **OK** button to continue.

Once the audit policy is defined, click the large disk icon on the main icon bar to save the changes or press Ctrl+S to save the audit policy settings.

In addition to defining audit policies this way, we can also use SQL commands, as we'll discuss in the next section.

15.3.3 Managing Audit Policies with SQL

We can also use SQL statements to define SAP HANA audit policies. Using SQL isn't as easy, but it does provide a scripting option that can apply a consistent audit policy throughout the SAP HANA landscape. SQL script can be executed with the SAP HANA SQL console found in most management tools. We've found that the GUI-based tools are inconsistent at times and don't support all audit policy options, but the SQL options support all possible audit configurations.

When creating an audit policy, use the generic SQL syntax in Listing 15.2.

```
CREATE AUDIT POLICY <POLICY NAME>
AUDITING <STATUS> <ACTIONS>
ON <CATALOG OBJECTS>
FOR | EXCEP FOR <USER LIST>
LEVEL <LEVEL>
TRAIL TYPE <TRAIL>;
```

Listing 15.2 SQL Template for Defining Audit Policy

The `<POLICY NAME>` variable will be replaced with the name of the policy. The `<STATUS>` variable should be replaced with `SUCCESSFUL`, `UNSUCCESSFUL`, or `ALL`. The `<ACTIONS>` variable should be replaced with the syntax specific to the action being audited; for example, we can specify one or more actions, such as CREATE USER, ALTER USER, or ALTER ROLE. The syntax of all possible actions is quite extensive and can be found in the SAP HANA SQL and System View Reference Guide, under the *CREATE AUDIT POLICY Statement* reference section.

The ON clause and <CATALOG OBJECTS> variable are required for data manipulation actions. The <CATALOG OBJECTS> variable should be replaced with the fully qualified name of the catalog object.

The <USER LIST> variable can contain a comma-separated list of user accounts in the system. The FOR and EXCEPT FOR syntax is optional for most audit actions.

The <LEVEL> variable can be replaced with EMERGENCY, ALERT, CRITICAL, WARNING, or INFO. The <TRAIL> variable can be replaced with TABLE, SYSLOG, or CSV.

To better understand the SQL syntax, let's review a few complete SQL examples.

To audit the management of standard roles, we can create an audit policy titled MANAGE ROLE as follows:

```
CREATE AUDIT POLICY "MANAGE ROLE"
AUDITING ALL CREATE ROLE, ALTER ROLE, DROP ROLE
LEVEL INFO;
```

To audit the management of user accounts, we can create an audit policy titled MANAGE USER as follows:

```
CREATE AUDIT POLICY "MANAGE USER"
AUDITING ALL CREATE USER, ALTER USER, DROP USER
LEVEL INFO;
```

To monitor instances in which the stored procedures in the _SYS_REPO schema are executed, we can create an audit policy using the SQL code in Listing 15.3.

```
CREATE AUDIT POLICY "GRANT OR REVOKE REPOSITORY OBJECTS"
AUDITING ALL
EXECUTE ON
"_SYS_REPO"."*"
LEVEL INFO;
```

Listing 15.3 Create Policy Named GRANT OR REVOKE REPOSITORY OBJECTS

To monitor all unsuccessful actions for all users except system account users, we can create a policy using the SQL code in Listing 15.4.

```
CREATE AUDIT POLICY "ALL ACTIONS"
AUDITING UNSUCCESSFUL ACTIONS
EXCEPT FOR
_SYS_DI, _SYS_AFL, _SYS_XB, _SYS_WORKLOAD_REPLAY,
_SYS_TASK, _SYS_STATISTICS, _SYS_SQL_ANALYZER,
_SYS_REPO, _SYS_ES, _SYS_EPM, _SYS_DI_TO, _SYS_DI_SU,
_SYS_DI_SEARCH_CATALOG, _SYS_DI_CDS_CATALOG, _SYS_DI_CATALOG,
_SYS_DI_BI_CATALOG
LEVEL INFO;
```

Listing 15.4 Create Policy Named ALL ACTIONS

When an audit policy is created using SQL, it's disabled by default. To activate the policy, we need to issue an ALTER AUDIT POLICY SQL statement. For example, we can issue the following SQL statement to enable an audit policy named ALL ACTIONS:

```
ALTER AUDIT POLICY "ALL ACTIONS" ENABLE;
```

To disable an audit policy, we can issue the following SQL statement:

```
ALTER AUDIT POLICY "ALL ACTIONS" DISABLE;
```


To delete an audit policy, we must use the DROP AUDIT POLICY SQL statement. For example, we can delete the ALL ACTIONS policy as follows:

```
DROP AUDIT POLICY "ALL ACTIONS";
```

SAP HANA SQL and System View Reference Guide

The complete syntax used to drop and alter audit polices can be found online in the SAP HANA SQL and System View Reference Guide or in the SAP HANA Studio help. Look for the sections titled ALTER AUDIT POLICY Statement (Access Control) and DROP AUDIT POLICY Statement (Access Control).

The complete syntax used to create audit polices can be also be found in this guide or in the SAP HANA Studio help. Look for the section titled CREATE AUDIT POLICY Statement (Access Control).

You can download the guide from *https://help.sap.com/doc/9b40bf74f8644b898fb07dabdd2a36ad/2.0.00/en-US/SAP_HANA_SQL_and_System_Views_Reference_en.pdf.*

Using SQL to define and manage audit polices is helpful when organizations need to apply a consistent audit policy through the SAP HANA landscape. In the next section, we'll briefly review how audit policies can be created in SAP HANA Studio.

15.3.4 Creating Policies with SAP HANA Studio

SAP HANA Studio has an embedded security manager in which audit policies can be defined. To access the security manager, log on to your system and expand the **System** node within the **Systems** tab. Expand the **Security** folder and double-click the **Security** icon. The **Security** manager tab will open. Within this tab, select the subtab labeled **Auditing** and locate the **Audit Policy** area near the bottom (see Figure 15.6).

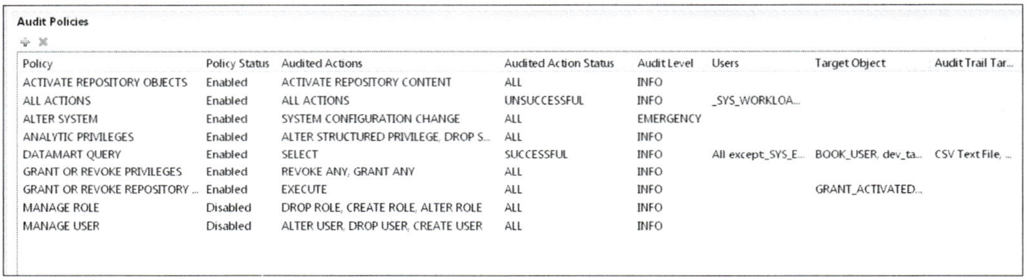
Audit Policies

Policy	Policy Status	Audited Actions	Audited Action Status	Audit Level	Users	Target Object	Audit Trail Tar...
ACTIVATE REPOSITORY OBJECTS	Enabled	ACTIVATE REPOSITORY CONTENT	ALL	INFO			
ALL ACTIONS	Enabled	ALL ACTIONS	UNSUCCESSFUL	INFO	_SYS_WORKLOA...		
ALTER SYSTEM	Enabled	SYSTEM CONFIGURATION CHANGE	ALL	EMERGENCY			
ANALYTIC PRIVILEGES	Enabled	ALTER STRUCTURED PRIVILEGE, DROP S...	ALL	INFO			
DATAMART QUERY	Enabled	SELECT	SUCCESSFUL	INFO	All except_SYS_E...	BOOK_USER, dev_ta...	CSV Text File, ...
GRANT OR REVOKE PRIVILEGES	Enabled	REVOKE ANY, GRANT ANY	ALL	INFO			
GRANT OR REVOKE REPOSITORY ...	Enabled	EXECUTE	ALL	INFO		GRANT_ACTIVATED...	
MANAGE ROLE	Disabled	DROP ROLE, CREATE ROLE, ALTER ROLE	ALL	INFO			
MANAGE USER	Disabled	ALTER USER, DROP USER, CREATE USER	ALL	INFO			

Figure 15.6 Audit Policy Area in SAP HANA Studio

To define a new audit policy, click **+**. A new row will appear in the audit policy table. Now, enter a unique name for the policy in the **Policy** column. In the **Policy Status** column, click the cell and a down arrow will appear. Select **Enable** for policies that you need to activate. In the **Audited Actions** column, click the cell to reveal an ellipsis icon (...) to the right of the cell. Click the ellipsis to open a new window, titled **Edit Actions Audited by Policy**. In this window, we can choose from all available audit actions by category. Select the actions that need to be audited. Remember that you can only select one or more actions from the same category. When finished, click the **OK** button at the bottom right.

Within the **Audited Actions Status** column, click the cell to reveal a down arrow located to the right. Choose from **Successful**, **Unsuccessful**, and **All**. Within the **Audit Level** column, click the cell to reveal a down arrow located to the right. Choose from **Emergency**, **Critical**, **Alert**, **Warning**, and **Info.**

In the **Users** column, click the cell to reveal an ellipsis icon to the right of the cell. Click the ellipsis, and a new window titled **Select Users** will appear. Use the options in the window to search for one or more existing users. Once the users are located, use the **Add** button located between the **Matching Items** list and **Selected Items** list to add the selected users to the right side of the window. Choose from **Include Selected Users** in policy or **Exclude Selected Users** from policy above the **Selected Items** area. Click **OK** once you've selected users to include or exclude. Note that most actions don't require that you select a user. When this field is left blank, the system assumes that it should apply the policy to all users. If the policy won't activate without a user, you can assume that the policy action requires a referenced user.

If the audit policy uses actions from the data query and manipulation and procedure execution categories, we must also choose a target object. Within the **Target Object** cell, click to reveal an ellipsis icon to the right of the cell. Click the ellipsis, and a new window titled **Select Target Object** will appear. Within the search box, enter the name of the catalog object that will serve as the target for the audit policy. Click the **OK** button at the bottom right once you've completed your selection.

If you want to define specific audit targets for the audit policy, use the **Audit Trail Target** column and cell to define additional targets. Within the **Audit Trail Target** cell, click to reveal a dropdown menu, containing the **Syslog**, **CSV Test File**, and **Database Table** options. Select the checkbox beside each audit target location. Click the **OK** button to continue.

Once the audit policy is defined, click the large disk icon on the icon bar to save the changes, or press F8 to save and deploy the audit policy.

You should now have a strong understanding of the components that make up an audit policy. In addition, you should have a strong understanding of how policies are configured using the SAP HANA Web-Based Development Workbench security console, SAP HANA Studio, and SQL statements. In the next section, we'll review various system views that contain audit-specific data.

15.4 Querying Audit Data

There are three main system views that we can query related to audit data and the auditing configuration within SAP HANA. These views are useful for a variety of purposes. The three views are `AUDIT_ACTIONS`, `AUDIT_LOG`, and `AUDIT_POLICIES` and are all located in the SYS schema.

15.4.1 AUDIT_ACTIONS

The *audit actions view* provides access to a listing of all possible auditable actions within the SAP HANA system. This view provides a listing of audit actions and flags to indicate actions that require a user or catalog object reference. It's useful when we need to see a listing of supported audit actions. For an overview of the columns within this system view, see the SAP HANA SQL and System View Reference Guide: *https://help.sap.com/doc/9b40bf74f8644b898fb07dabdd2a36ad/2.0.00/en-US/SAP_HANA_SQL_and_System_Views_Reference_en.pdf.*

To query the view, issue the following SQL statement:

```
SELECT * FROM SYS.AUDIT_ACTIONS;
```

15.4.2 AUDIT_LOG

The *audit log view* provides access to all recorded actions based on enabled audit polices. When an audit policy is enabled, events are written to the hidden system table `_SYS_AUDIT.CS_AUDIT_LOG_`. The audit log view references this system table.

Administrators can create a variety of audit-related queries referencing this system view, and the view contains several columns. For a list of the important columns available within this view, see the SAP HANA SQL and System View Reference Guide: *https://help.sap.com/doc/9b40bf74f8644b898fb07dabdd2a36ad/2.0.00/en-US/SAP_HANA_SQL_and_System_Views_Reference_en.pdf.*

To query the view, issue the following SQL statement:

```
SELECT * FROM SYS.AUDIT_LOG;
```

15.4.3 AUDIT_POLICIES

The audit policies view provides a complete listing of all audit policies defined within the system. It can be queried to determine the quantity and scope of audit policies defined within the SAP HANA system. It's important to note that a single policy might have multiple records within the view; each record represents a unique configuration option. For example, if we reference multiple users in the policy, a record for each user will be represented in this view. For a list of the important columns available within this view, see the SAP HANA SQL and System View Reference Guide: *https://help.sap.com/doc/9b40bf74f8644b898fb07dabdd2a36ad/2.0.00/en-US/SAP_HANA_SQL_and_System_Views_Reference_en.pdf.*

To query the view, issue the following SQL statement:

```
SELECT * FROM SYS.AUDIT_POLICIES;
```

The views listed in this section are useful when organizations need to examine the data that is collected from auditing and the configuration of the auditing mechanism itself. In the next section, we'll walk you through a case study that outlines the decision-making process E-Corporation used when defining its audit policies. We'll also list the SQL the company used to define its audit policies.

15.5 Case Study: Defining Audit Policies

E-Corporation recently enabled auditing within the SAP HANA landscape. Its internal audit group determined that it was necessary to capture audit events for the purposes of regulatory compliance and best practices. E-Corporation contacted its SAP HANA security consultant and requested help to review and implement proposed audit policies. In the following sections, E-Corporation has listed its requirements followed by its consultant's recommendations. The consultant will use SQL statements to define the exact policy recommended.

E-Corporation requires that an audit policy be configured to facilitate proactive event monitoring, audit reporting, authentication actions, unauthorized access, system change, security management, and super user events.

15.5.1 Proactive Event Monitoring

Requirements

E-Corporation requires that the SAP HANA audit system support external tools that are capable of proactively mining the system's audit logs. Such tools require ODBC and JDBC access to the audit log tables.

Solution

Audit policies should be configured to support events that can be proactively monitored. This includes, but is not limited to, failed logon events, unauthorized actions, excessive query access to the system, and other activities. In addition, the events will need to be recorded to the internal SAP HANA database table to allow such events to be available via a JDBC or ODBC connection and SQL query. Most monitoring tools support this type of access.

15.5.2 Audit Reporting

Requirements

E-Corporation requires that all audit log data be accessible using the ODBC and JDBC protocols.

Solution

Audit events will need to be recorded to the internal SAP HANA database table. This will allow such events to be available via a JDBC or ODBC connection and SQL query. Most reporting tools support this type of access.

15.5.3 Authentication Auditing

Requirements

E-Corporation requires that all connection and disconnection attempts are recorded within the audit logs. However, the company does not want to see authentication attempts made by internal system accounts.

Solution

The security consultant recommends that an audit policy be created to record this activity to table `AUDIT_LOG` within SAP HANA. An audit policy titled `USER CONNECT AND DISCONNECT` will be created to monitor all `SUCCESSFUL` connections and subsequent disconnection actions performed by standard users. There is no need to audit unsuccessful attempts, because they'll be captured in a subsequent audit policy. The policy won't record events for system-generated accounts.

The policy will be defined using the SQL code in Listing 15.5.

```
CREATE AUDIT POLICY "USER CONNECT AND DISCONNECT"
AUDITING SUCCESSFUL CONNECT, DISCONNECT SESSION
EXCEPT FOR
     _SYS_AFL,
     _SYS_DI,
     _SYS_DI_BI_CATALOG,
     _SYS_DI_CATALOG,
     _SYS_DI_CDS_CATALOG,
     _SYS_DI_SEARCH_CATALOG,
     _SYS_DI_SU,
     _SYS_DI_TO,
```

```
    _SYS_EPM,
    _SYS_ES,
    _SYS_REPO,
    _SYS_SQL_ANALYZER,
    _SYS_STATISTICS,
    _SYS_TASK,
    _SYS_WORKLOAD_REPLAY,
    _SYS_XB,
    SYS_XS_SBSS
LEVEL INFO;
```

Listing 15.5 SQL Code to Create Policy Named USER CONNECT AND DISCONNECT

To activate the policy, the following SQL statement must be executed:

```
ALTER AUDIT POLICY "USER CONNECT AND DISCONNECT" ENABLE;
```

15.5.4 Unauthorized Action Auditing

Requirements

E-Corporation requires that all unsuccessful actions be recorded to the audit logs. Users with a high number of unsuccessful actions within a given day are to be questioned ASAP. A high number of unsuccessful actions often indicates that someone is attempting to compromise the system's security using their account or someone else's account.

Solution

The security consultant recommends that an audit policy named ALL FAILED ACTIONS be created to record this activity to table AUDIT_LOG within SAP HANA. The policy will be configured to record all UNSUCCESSFUL actions performed within the system.

The policy will be defined using the SQL code in Listing 15.6.

```
CREATE AUDIT POLICY "ALL FAILED ACTIONS"
AUDITING UNSUCCESSFUL ACTIONS
EXCEPT FOR
_SYS_DI, _SYS_AFL, _SYS_XB, _SYS_WORKLOAD_REPLAY,
_SYS_TASK, _SYS_STATISTICS, _SYS_SQL_ANALYZER,
_SYS_REPO, _SYS_ES, _SYS_EPM, _SYS_DI_TO, _SYS_DI_SU,
```

```
_SYS_DI_SEARCH_CATALOG, _SYS_DI_CDS_CATALOG, _SYS_DI_CATALOG,
_SYS_DI_BI_CATALOG
LEVEL INFO;
```

Listing 15.6 SQL Code to Create Policy Named ALL FAILED ACTIONS

To activate the policy, the following SQL statement must be executed:

```
ALTER AUDIT POLICY "ALL FAILED ACTIONS" ENABLE;
```

15.5.5 System Change Auditing

Requirements

E-Corporation requires that all system configuration changes be recorded to the audit logs. Such events should also be set up using the `EMERGENCY` level so that they're easily identified within the audit logs. In addition, they should be written to a CSV file stored in a secure directory in the operating system.

Solution

The security consultant recommends that an audit policy titled `ALTER SYSTEM` be created to record this activity to table `AUDIT_LOG` table and a CSV file within SAP HANA. The policy will be defined using the following SQL code:

```
CREATE AUDIT POLICY "ALTER SYSTEM"
AUDITING ALL SYSTEM CONFIGURATION CHANGE
LEVEL EMERGENCY
TRAIL TYPE CSV, TABLE;
```

Note that the SQL code uses a `LEVEL` of `EMERGENCY` and a `TRAIL TYPE` of both `CSV` and `TABLE`. To activate the policy, the following SQL statement must be executed:

```
ALTER AUDIT POLICY "ALTER SYSTEM" ENABLE;
```

Because the policy will record such events to a CSV file, the system needs to be configured with a new default audit trail CSV file path. A directory was created within the path */usr/sap/HB5/HDB00/auditlog/*, which will store audit trail files containing system configuration changes. No other audit rules within the system will use the CSV file option. To configure the CSV file path within SAP HANA, the following SQL statement must be executed:

```
ALTER SYSTEM ALTER CONFIGURATION ('global.ini', 'SYSTEM')
   SET ('auditing configuration', 'default_audit_trail_path') =
'/usr/sap/HB5/HDB00/auditlog/' WITH RECONFIGURE ;
```

15.5.6 Security Management Task Auditing

Requirements

E-Corporation requires that all security-related activities be recorded to the audit log. This includes the management of users, roles, and repository roles, as well as granting and revoking privileges and roles to other users.

Solution

The security consultant recommends that a series of audit policies be created to record this activity to table `AUDIT_LOG` within SAP HANA. The audit policies titled `MANAGE ROLE`, `MANAGE USER`, `GRANT OR REVOKE REPOSITORY OBJECTS`, `GRANT OR REVOKE PRIVILEGES`, `ANALYTIC PRIVILEGES`, and `ACTIVATE REPOSITORY OBJECTS` will be created.

The `MANAGE ROLE` policy will record all attempts to create, alter, or drop roles within the SAP HANA system. E-Corporation's standard policy is to create repository-based roles, and such roles would not be covered using this policy. However, this policy will identify security administrators that are not following policy. In addition, it will record their actions related to standard roles. To create the policy, the following SQL code must be executed:

```
CREATE AUDIT POLICY "MANAGE ROLE"
AUDITING ALL CREATE ROLE, ALTER ROLE, DROP ROLE
LEVEL INFO;
```

The `MANAGE USER` policy will record all attempts to create, alter, or drop users within the SAP HANA system. E-Corporation allows security administrators to create users within the system. To create the policy, the following SQL code must be executed:

```
CREATE AUDIT POLICY "MANAGE USER"
AUDITING ALL CREATE USER, ALTER USER, DROP USER
LEVEL INFO;
```

The `GRANT OR REVOKE REPOSITORY OBJECTS` policy is designed to record the use of the stored procedures within the _SYS_REPO schema. These procedures are used by security administrators and give them the ability to grant privileges to repository-based objects, including repository-based roles. They should be closely monitored, because repository object privileges are always granted by _SYS_REPO regardless of the user executing these procedures. To create the policy, the SQL code in Listing 15.7 must be executed.

```
CREATE AUDIT POLICY "GRANT OR REVOKE REPOSITORY OBJECTS"
AUDITING ALL
EXECUTE ON
"_SYS_REPO"."*"
LEVEL INFO;
```

Listing 15.7 SQL Code to Create Policy Named GRANT OR REVOKE REPOSITORY OBJECTS

The `GRANT OR REVOKE PRIVILEGES` policy will record all attempts to grant or revoke privileges within the SAP HANA system. E-Corporation's standard policy is to create repository-based roles, and privileges within repository-based roles are granted or revoked by the system account _SYS_REPO. However, this policy will identify security administrators that are not following policy. In addition, it will record their actions related to the granting and revoking of privileges. To create the policy, the following SQL code must be executed:

```
CREATE AUDIT POLICY "GRANT OR REVOKE PRIVILEGES"
AUDITING ALL GRANT ANY, REVOKE ANY
LEVEL INFO;
```

The `ANALYTIC PRIVILEGES` policy will record any attempts to create, alter, or drop structured privileges within the SAP HANA system. Because these privileges provide data-level security, it's important that they be audited. Note that classic repository-based analytic privileges will be created, altered, and dropped by the system account _SYS_REPO. To create the policy, the SQL code in Listing 15.8 must be executed.

```
CREATE AUDIT POLICY "ANALYTIC PRIVILEGES"
AUDITING ALL
ALTER STRUCTURED PRIVILEGE,
CREATE STRUCTURED PRIVILEGE,
DROP STRUCTURED PRIVILEGE
LEVEL INFO;
CREATE AUDIT POLICY "ACTIVATE REPOSITORY OBJECTS"
AUDITING ALL ACTIVATE REPOSITORY CONTENT
LEVEL INFO;
```

Listing 15.8 Two SQL Statements to Create ACTIVATE REPOSITORY OBJECTS and ANALYTIC PRIVILEGES Policies

The ACTIVATE REPOSITORY OBJECTS policy is required to capture the true source of changes related to repository roles and other repository-based objects. When a repository object is activated, many auditing events will record that the _SYS_REPO user performed a series of actions. To properly correlate those actions to an actual user, we must ensure that all repository activations are also audited. In this way, we can know the identity of the user that initiated the actions carried out by the _SYS_REPO user. To create the policy, the following SQL code must be executed:

```
CREATE AUDIT POLICY "ACTIVATE REPOSITORY OBJECTS"
AUDITING ALL ACTIVATE REPOSITORY CONTENT
LEVEL INFO;
```

Once the policies are created, they need to be activated. To activate these policies, the SQL in Listing 15.9 must be executed.

```
ALTER AUDIT POLICY "MANAGE ROLE" ENABLE;
ALTER AUDIT POLICY "ANALYTIC PRIVILEGES" ENABLE;
ALTER AUDIT POLICY "ACTIVATE REPOSITORY OBJECTS" ENABLE;
ALTER AUDIT POLICY "GRANT OR REVOKE PRIVILEGES" ENABLE;
ALTER AUDIT POLICY "MANAGE USER" ENABLE;
ALTER AUDIT POLICY "GRANT OR REVOKE REPOSITORY OBJECTS" ENABLE;
ALTER AUDIT POLICY "ACTIVATE REPOSITORY OBJECTS" ENABLE;
```

Listing 15.9 Seven SQL Statements to Activate Seven Audit Policies

15.5.7 Super User Event Auditing

Requirements

E-Corporation requires that all users with elevated privileges have all their actions recorded. Super users at E-Corporation have user names prefixed with ADMIN_. Monthly, the audit team will query the audit logs to make sure super user activities fall within the acceptable usage requirements for their given responsibilities.

In addition to super users, E-Corporation requests that all actions performed using the SYSTEM user account be recorded. This account is typically disabled and only used when necessary.

Solution

The SUPER USER AUDIT policy is required to record the SUCCESSFUL actions of all super users set up within the SAP HANA system. UNSUCCESSFUL actions will be recorded by the ALL FAILED ACTIONS policy. To create the policy, the following SQL code must be executed:

```
CREATE AUDIT POLICY "SUPER USER AUDIT"
AUDITING SUCCESSFUL ACTIONS
FOR SYSTEM, ADMIN_JHAUN, ADMIN_PETER, ADMIN_BOB
LEVEL INFO;
```

Once the policy is created, the following SQL must be executed to activate the policy:

```
ALTER AUDIT POLICY " SUPER USER AUDIT " ENABLE;
```

The policies recommended by the SAP HANA security consultant will grant E-Corporation better insight into the critical actions within its SAP HANA system, help E-Corporation remain compliant with many of its regulations, and help E-Corporation manage compliance with its own internal policies.

15.6 Summary

Auditing is a critical component of any SAP HANA security model. It allows an organization to keep users accountable to the policies and procedures related to security and system changes. Auditing can help an organization proactively identify unauthorized access attempts. Finally, auditing can help an organization reconstruct events after it has experienced a security breach.

Within an SAP HANA landscape, auditing should be enabled, and specific audit policies should be implemented to protect the security and stability of the system.

Chapter 16
Security Tracing and Troubleshooting

Implementing a security model can be a complex endeavor, and it's common for security administrators to find gaps within their security model. In this chapter, we'll discuss security tracing and effective privileges views, which can help a security administrator identify these gaps.

In the real world, most security models are quite complex. In instances in which it's difficult to traverse the complex lineage of roles and their privileges, SAP HANA offers a security trace option that will capture and list many of the privileges missing from users attempting to interact with SAP HANA. This chapter will outline the steps required to enable a security-related authorization trace and review the trace file results.

In addition to security tracing, we'll also review the various system views that provide details about the effective rights granted to individual users, and we'll provide example queries to help bolster your understanding of how these system views can be leveraged.

16.1 Authorization Tracing

An *authorization trace* is a type of *user-specific trace* that's limited by tracing detailed actions conducted by an individual user account. User-specific traces can be configured to record detailed information about a variety of activities within the SAP HANA system. Just about every component of SAP HANA can be traced, and trace information can be leveraged to provide specific information related to activity within the SAP HANA system. Security administrators can use this trace mechanism to focus on the authorization component.

Tracing the authorization component provides detailed information related to actions that are both allowed and denied for a given user. For example, an authorization trace will record instances in which a user is not authorized to perform an action. In addition, it often records the privileges a user is missing when attempting to conduct the unauthorized action.

Tracing is different from auditing (discussed in Chapter 15). Tracing provides significantly more details concerning the internal processing of a user's actions. Because of its level of detail, tracing should only be enabled for a short time and should be coordinated only with troubleshooting activities. An authorization trace not only records the actions of a user but also in many cases provides suggestions as to the permissions required when actions are denied. Tracing activities are also recorded only to trace files; the information recorded to the trace file is semistructured and not easily recorded to a database table. Therefore, it's difficult to query the trace data.

In contrast, auditing records the specific actions performed, including the action status. Audit data can be queried easily when recorded to a database table, but it doesn't provide the same level of detail that tracing can provide. In addition, audit polices typically remain active all the time and aren't intended to troubleshoot security-related gaps.

In general, there are two ways to enable a security trace for an individual user: SAP HANA Studio provides a GUI in which an authorization trace can be enabled quickly, and administrators can also use `ALTER SYSTEM ALTER CONFIGURATION` SQL statements to configure and enable an authorization trace. In the following sections, we'll explore these options in detail.

16.1.1 Enable Tracing with SAP HANA Studio

Within SAP HANA Studio, we can use the *administration editor* to configure trace settings. To open the administration editor, launch SAP HANA Studio and switch to the administration console perspective. In the **Systems** tab, located on the far left, connect to the system in question. Once connected, right-click the system and choose **Configuration And Monitoring • Open Administration**. The **Administration Editor** will appear in a new tab to the right of the **Systems** tab and will contain several tabs at the top of the window. Locate the **Trace Configuration** tab to configure a user-specific trace (see Figure 16.1).

Locate the section within the **Trace Configuration** tab titled **User-Specific Trace**. On the right side of that section, you'll see a very small icon that looks like a page with a yellow plus sign and clock hovering over it. Click this icon to configure the trace settings. A new window will appear titled **Trace Configuration** (see Figure 16.2).

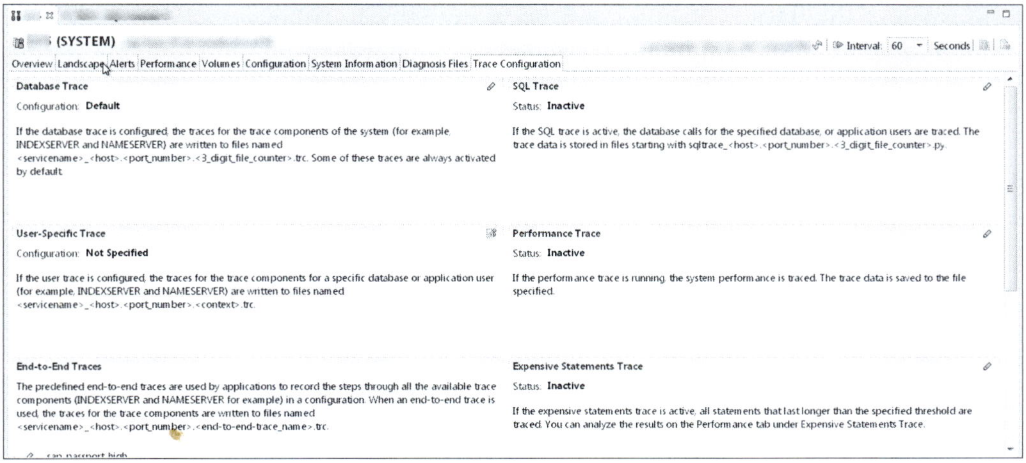

Figure 16.1 Trace Configuration Tab in SAP HANA Studio

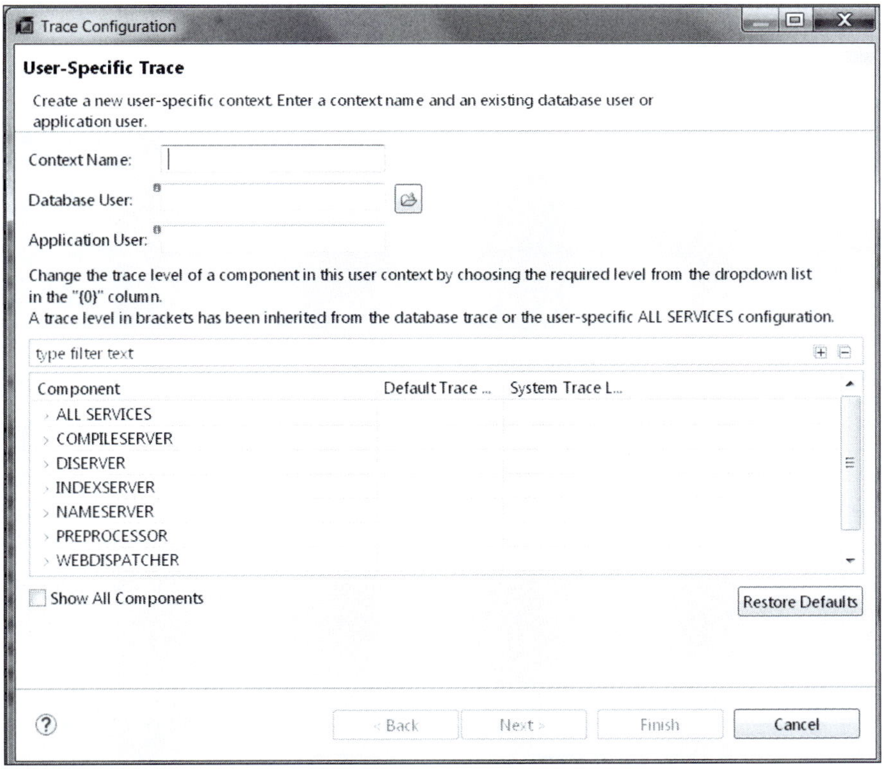

Figure 16.2 User-Specific Trace Configuration Window in SAP HANA Studio

Within the trace configuration window, we need to configure several options to enable the trace. In the **Context Name:** field, enter the custom name you want to use for a portion of the trace file that will be generated. For example, "USERAUTHTRACE". In the **Database User:** field, enter the name of a single database user within the system; you can also click the folder icon to the right of this field to search for an existing user within the system. The **Application User:** field isn't necessary to fill when performing an authorization trace.

To configure the trace as an authorization trace, set the trace level for authorization. To begin this process, select the checkbox next to the **Show All Components** option. In the section just above this option, you'll see a table with three columns. The first column is titled **Component**, the second is **Default Trace Level**, and the third is **System Trace Level** (see Figure 16.3).

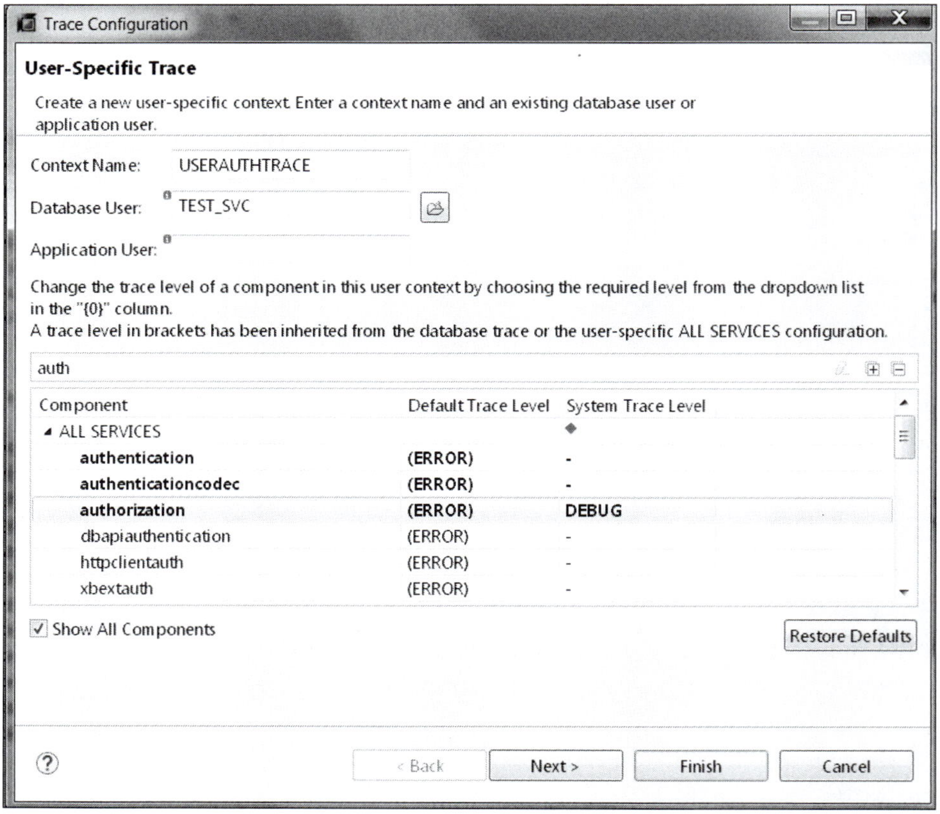

Figure 16.3 Setting Authorization Trace Level for User-Specific Trace

To configure an authorization trace, first locate the **Authorization** option under **All Services** within the **Component** column. In the field just above the table, enter the search phrase "auth" to narrow the results. In the results, locate the row in which **Authorization Component** is visible. Using the **System Trace Level** column for the same row, click the cell to reveal a dropdown menu. In the dropdown menu, choose **Debug**. Click **Finish** in the window to activate the authorization trace. The **User-Specific Trace** section should now display **User Configured** to the right of the **Configuration:** option, and the **User Traces** area will list the specific trace you just configured, with a pencil and red **X** icon to its left (see Figure 16.4).

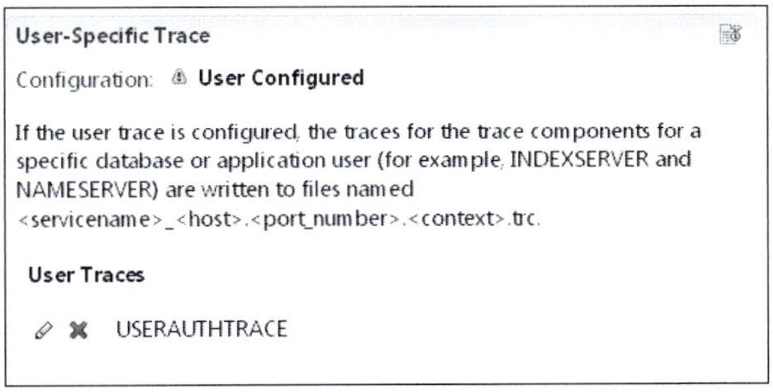

Figure 16.4 User-Specific Trace Configuration Section with Active Trace Enabled

It's important to remember to delete a trace when you've completed collecting trace data. To delete the trace, click the red **X** icon next to the trace profile name (**USERAUTHTRACE** in Figure 16.4).

16.1.2 Enable Tracing with SQL

User traces also can be configured using specific SQL statements. The trace configuration is stored in the global.ini configuration file. Using the `ALTER SYSTEM ALTER CONFIGURATION` SQL syntax, we can make configuration changes to this file and enable a user-specific trace.

The first configuration option that must be specified is the trace user name. To configure the specific user, we must create a *trace profile* with the `sql_user` option. The trace profile name is a concatenation of the static term `traceprofile_` followed by the user-specific profile name. The profile name will be used with other settings and will be appended to the trace file name. The following SQL syntax can be used to construct the required SQL code for your environment:

```
alter system alter configuration ('global.ini','SYSTEM')
SET ('traceprofile_<Profile Name>', 'sql_user') = '<User Name>'
with reconfigure;
```

The <Profile Name> variable must be replaced with the name of the trace profile, and the <User Name> variable must be replaced with the name of a user within the SAP HANA system. The following example demonstrates the SQL for the trace profile named USERAUTHTRACE for the user TEST_SVC:

```
alter system alter configuration ('global.ini','SYSTEM')
SET ('traceprofile_USERAUTHTRACE', 'sql_user') = 'TEST_SVC'
with reconfigure;
```

Next, we must specify the trace level. The following SQL syntax can be used to construct the required SQL for your environment:

```
alter system alter configuration ('global.ini','SYSTEM')
SET ('traceprofile_<Profile Name>', 'authorization') = 'debug'
with reconfigure;
```

The <Profile Name> variable must be replaced with the name of the trace profile; this is the same profile name used in the previous example. The profile name must match that used in other settings. The following example demonstrates the SQL code for the trace profile named USERAUTHTRACE:

```
alter system alter configuration ('global.ini','SYSTEM')
SET ('traceprofile_USERAUTHTRACE', 'authorization') = 'debug'
with reconfigure;
```

It's important to remember to disable the trace when you've finished collecting the trace details. To disable the trace profile with the name USERAUTHTRACE, unset the trace using the following two SQL statements. The first statement removes the setting for a specific user:

```
alter system alter configuration ('global.ini', 'SYSTEM')
unset ('traceprofile_USERAUTHTRACE', 'sql_user') with reconfigure;
```

The second statement removes the trace-level setting:

```
alter system alter configuration ('global.ini', 'SYSTEM')
unset ('traceprofile_USERAUTHTRACE', 'authorization') with reconfigure;
```

Using SQL is a quick and easy way to enable an authorization trace within the SAP HANA system. In the following section, we'll explore the process used to locate and review the trace files generated when the trace is active.

16.1.3 Viewing the Trace File in SAP HANA Studio

Once the trace is enabled, we need to perform a test using the user specified within the trace configuration. For example, we can log on as the user and attempt to recreate the action being denied. It's important to conduct the troubleshooting exercise again to guarantee that the denied actions will be recovered in the trace file. Once we've concluded the troubleshooting, we can view the contents of the generated trace files.

Within SAP HANA Studio, we can also use the *administration editor* to view trace files. To open the administration editor, launch SAP HANA Studio and switch to the administration console perspective. In the **Systems** tab, located on the far left, connect to the system in question. Once connected, right-click the system and choose **Configuration and Monitoring • Open Administration**. The **Administration Editor** will appear within a new tab to the right of the **Systems** tab. The **Administration Editor** contains several tabs at the top of the window. Locate the **Diagnosis Files** tab to configure a view of all trace files generated within the SAP HANA system (see Figure 16.5).

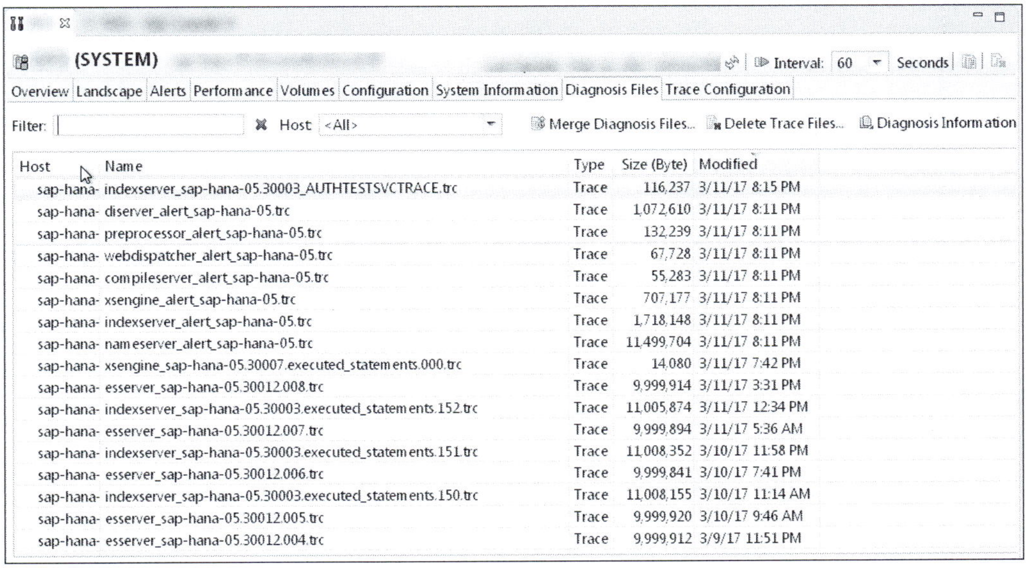

Figure 16.5 Viewing Trace Files within Diagnostic Files Tab in SAP HANA Studio

Using the **Filter:** field, we can narrow the list of trace files to those generated by the authorization trace. Fortunately, the trace profile name we used during the trace configuration also can be used to locate the files. For example, we can enter "USERAUTH-TRACE" to narrow the list of files to those containing our authorization trace details.

Trace files use a file extension of .trc, which stands for trace. Once you've located the trace file in the results, double-click it to open it within a text viewer tab. A new tab will appear, titled with the name of the trace file. The file will default to the last lines generated. Figure 16.6 provides an example of the data that can be found within the trace file.

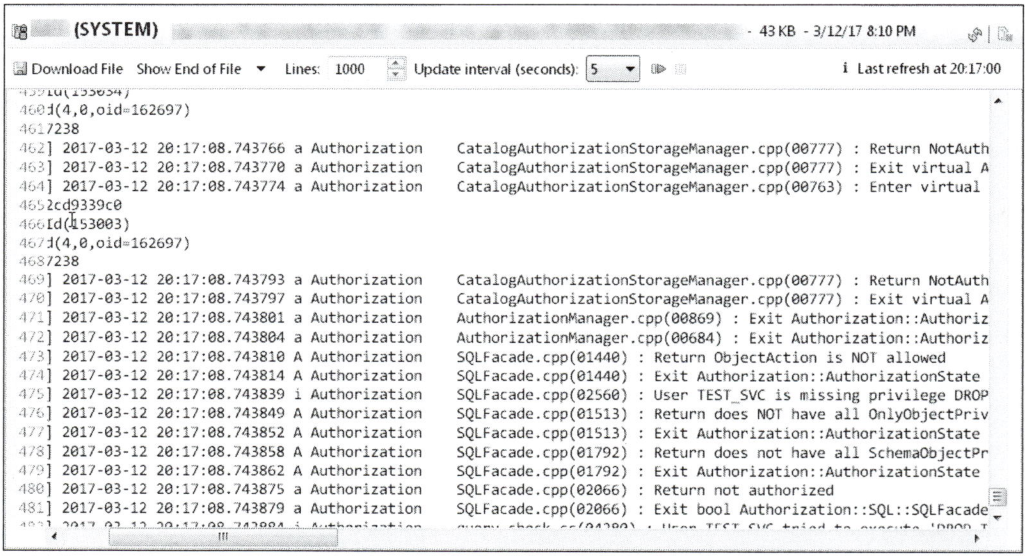

Figure 16.6 Detailed Data within Authorization Trace File

Once the file is open, click the **Refresh** button at the top right of the tab to load the most recent data written to the file. The detailed data within the file isn't always easy to decipher when the **Debug** trace level is specified, but typically you can press [Ctrl]+[F] to open a **Find/Replace** dialog window within the text viewer.

Using the **Find/Replace** dialog window, we can try to locate the trace details related to our security model troubleshooting. In many cases, the phrases **Return Not Authorized** and **Missing** are located near the exact action and privilege being denied. We can also search for the specific SQL we executed, the name of the object we interacted with, or the privileges that we expect to be missing.

Remember that the trace file viewer is limited to one thousand lines of text by default, though the value can be increased to 100,000. Using the **Debug** trace level can result in hundreds of thousands of lines during troubleshooting. Therefore, it's important to increase the number of lines. Figure 16.6 shows the **Lines:** setting; change the value to 100,000 to broaden the search range. If your trace file has more than 100,000 lines, use the **Download File** button located at the top of the trace file viewer to download the file. Once downloaded, you can open the file within a text-viewing application that offers search functionality for more than 100,000 rows.

When you're done, don't forget to disable the user-specific trace using the options described earlier in Section 16.1.

Tracing alone doesn't always provide all the information we need. In addition to tracing, SAP HANA offers several system-managed catalog views that provide the effective privileges for a grantee. These views can be queried using SQL statements and filter conditioning within the `WHERE` clause. In the next section, we'll look at each of these views in more detail.

16.2 Query the System to Review Effective Privileges

It's often difficult to determine the exact privileges that a user will inherit given the layers produced within our security models. User accounts can be granted roles that themselves are granted an additional layer of nested roles. It's also often difficult to determine the exact number of grantees with specific privileges granted for a given object. To help security administrators understand the effective or net result of privileges, several system views have been provided.

There are eight different views available to help security administrators. These views provide access in the areas of granted privileges, granted roles, accessible views, effective privilege grantees, effective structured privileges, effective privileges, effective role grantees, and effective roles. In the following sections, we'll explore how each of these view types can aid a security administrator in the management of an SAP HANA security model.

16.2.1 Granted Privileges

When an administrator needs to view the privileges explicitly granted to an individual user or runtime role, the `GRANTED_PRIVILEGES` system view can be queried to list the privileges. This view doesn't recursively check the privileges of roles granted to the grantee. To see the effective privileges assigned to a grantee, use the `EFFECTIVE_PRIVILEGES` system view, which we'll discuss in Section 16.2.6.

Use the following SQL syntax to query the GRANTED_PRIVILEGES system view:

```
SELECT * FROM "SYS"."GRANTED_PRIVILEGES"
WHERE GRANTEE = '<USER OR ROLE NAME>';
```

Note that the GRANTED_PRIVILEGES view doesn't require a filter condition or statement within the WHERE clause. If executed without a filter, all grantees and their privileges will be returned. All columns within the view can be used to filter, sort, and group the data. Table 16.1 provides a list of each available column and a description of the values that each column can return.

Column Name	Column Value Description
GRANTEE_SCHEMA_NAME	The grantee's schema
GRANTEE	A runtime role or user account
GRANTEE_TYPE	Static value of either USER or ROLE
GRANTOR	User that granted the privilege
OBJECT_TYPE	Type of object granted
SCHEMA_NAME	The owning schema of the object
OBJECT_NAME	Object's name
COLUMN_NAME	Column name
PRIVILEGE	Name of the granted privileges
IS_GRANTABLE	TRUE or FALSE: Was the privilege granted using WITH GRANT OPTION or WITH ADMIN OPTION?
IS_VALID	TRUE or FALSE: Is the privilege valid?

Table 16.1 Columns in GRANTED_PRIVILEGES View

16.2.2 Granted Roles

If an administrator needs to view the roles explicitly granted to an individual user or runtime role, the GRANTED_ROLES system view can be queried. This view doesn't recursively check nested or effective roles granted to the grantee. To see the effective roles assigned to a grantee, use the EFFECTIVE_ROLES system view, which is discussed in Section 16.2.8.

Use the following SQL syntax to query the GRANTED_ROLES system view:

```
SELECT * FROM "SYS"."GRANTED_ROLES"
WHERE GRANTEE = '<USER OR ROLE NAME>';
```

Note that the GRANTED_ROLES view doesn't require a filter condition or statement within the WHERE clause. If executed without a filter, all grantees and their roles will be returned. All columns within the view can be used to filter, sort, and group the data. Table 16.2 provides a list of each available column and a description of the values that each column can return.

Column Name	Column Value Description
GRANTEE_SCHEMA_NAME	The grantee's schema
GRANTEE	A runtime role or user account
GRANTEE_TYPE	Static value of either USER or ROLE
ROLE_SCHEMA_NAME	The role's schema
ROLE_NAME	The name of the granted role
GRANTOR	Name of the user account that granted the role
IS_GRANTABLE	TRUE or FALSE: Was the privilege granted using WITH GRANT OPTION or WITH ADMIN OPTION?
IS_GRANTED_BY_LDAP	TRUE or FALSE: Was the role granted by an LDAP group?

Table 16.2 Columns in GRANTED_ROLES View

16.2.3 Accessible Views

To list all catalog and column views that can be accessed by a given user, the ACCESSIBLE_VIEWS system view can be queried. The view must be filtered with the condition USER_NAME = 'Some User'. To return the accessible views for multiple users, use multiple USER_NAME = 'Some User' conditions, with an OR operator separating each condition clause. For example, the following SQL code will return the views that can be accessed by User Name 1 and User Name 2.

```
SELECT * from "SYS"."ACCESSIBLE_VIEWS"
WHERE (USER_NAME = '<User Name 1>'
OR USER_NAME = '<User Name 2>');
```

All columns within the view can be used to filter, sort, and group the data. Table 16.3 provides a list of each available column and a description of the values that each column can return.

Column Name	Column Value Description
USER_NAME	Name of the user with access to the catalog or column view
SCHEMA_NAME	The view's schema
VIEW_NAME	Name of the catalog or column view
ANALYTICAL_PRIVILEGE_NEEDED	TRUE or FALSE: Is an analytic privilege needed to query this view?

Table 16.3 Columns in ACCESSIBLE_VIEWS System View

16.2.4 Effective Privilege Grantees

When an administrator needs to view a list of grantees with assigned privileges, the EFFECTIVE_PRIVILEGE_GRANTEES system view can be queried. This view is designed to list grantees that have the specified access to a particular catalog object, system privilege, or analytic privilege. This view can be queried using a variety of different filter values. At a minimum, the OBJECT_TYPE and PRIVILEGES columns must be included within the filter condition WHERE clause. Depending on the value specified in the OBJECT_TYPE column, additional columns must also be included in the WHERE clause.

When you need to list grantees with a specific level of access to a schema, use the SQL syntax in Listing 16.1.

```
SELECT * FROM EFFECTIVE_PRIVILEGE_GRANTEES
WHERE OBJECT_TYPE = 'SCHEMA'
AND SCHEMA_NAME = '<schema_name>'
AND PRIVILEGE = '<privilege>';
```

Listing 16.1 Example SQL Syntax Used to Identify Users with Specific Privileges Granted to a Specific Schema

The filter conditions in the SQL code must include OBJECT_TYPE = 'SCHEMA', with additional filter conditions on the SCHEMA_NAME and PRIVILEGES columns.

When you need to list grantees with a specific level of access to a given catalog object, use the SQL syntax in Listing 16.2.

```
SELECT * FROM EFFECTIVE_PRIVILEGE_GRANTEES
WHERE OBJECT_TYPE = '<object_type>'
AND SCHEMA_NAME = '<schema_name>'
AND OBJECT_NAME = '<object_name>'
AND PRIVILEGE = '<privilege>';
```

Listing 16.2 Example SQL Syntax Used to Identify Users with Specific Privileges Granted to a Specific Catalog Object

In Listing 16.2, the four filter conditions must be satisfied to identify users with the specified privileges on the specified catalog object. The filter must include the OBJECT_TYPE filter condition. For example, condition values TABLE, VIEW, PROCEDURE, INDEX, or other catalog objects are possible. The condition for the SCHEMA_NAME column must contain the object's schema name. The condition for the OBJECT_NAME column must include the name of the object in question. The PRIVILEGE condition must include the object privileges. For example, SELECT, EXECUTE, DELETE, ALTER, INSERT, UPDATE, or DELETE can be included with this condition. A grantee will only be listed if the privileges are explicitly granted to the object. As a result, you should always check the object's schema for the given permission in addition to the object itself. As you recall, objects inherit privileges from their schemas; however, inherited privileges will not be calculated with the SQL statement in this section.

When you need to list grantees with a specific system privilege, use the following SQL syntax:

```
SELECT * FROM EFFECTIVE_PRIVILEGE_GRANTEES
WHERE OBJECT_TYPE = 'SYSTEMPRIVILEGE'
AND PRIVILEGE = '<privilege>';
```

The OBJECT_TYPE = 'SYSTEMPRIVILEGE' filter condition must be included, and the PRIVILEGES column must be included within the WHERE clause.

16.2.5 Effective Structured Privileges

To view the effective filter conditions applied for a given user and view, the EFFECTIVE_STRUCTURED_PRIVILEGES view can be queried. When queried, three columns must be included in the WHERE clause: ROOT_OBJECT_NAME, ROOT_SCHEMA_NAME, and USER_NAME. The ROOT_OBJECT_NAME column filter must reference the name of the catalog or column view, the ROOT_SCHEMA_NAME column filter must reference the root object's schema, and the USER_NAME column filter must reference the user that will query the view specified in the root object filter condition.

The SQL code in Listing 16.3 can be customized to match objects within your environment.

```
SELECT *
FROM "SYS"."EFFECTIVE_STRUCTURED_PRIVILEGES"
WHERE ROOT_SCHEMA_NAME = '_SYS_BIC' AND
ROOT_OBJECT_NAME = '<Column View Name>'
AND USER_NAME = '<User Name>';
```

Listing 16.3 Example SQL Statement Template for Querying the EFFECTIVE_STRUCTURED_PRIVILEGES View

The SQL code in Listing 16.4 presents an example in which we can identify restrictions applied to the TEST_SVC user when querying the `dft.infoview/CV_INTERNET_SALES` column view.

```
SELECT *
FROM "SYS"."EFFECTIVE_STRUCTURED_PRIVILEGES"
WHERE ROOT_SCHEMA_NAME = '_SYS_BIC' AND
ROOT_OBJECT_NAME = 'dft.infoview/CV_INTERNET_SALES'
AND USER_NAME = 'TEST_SVC3';
```

Listing 16.4 SQL Code to Query EFFECTIVE_PRIVILEGE_GRANTEES View

All columns within the view can be used to filter, sort, and group the data. Table 16.4 provides a list of each available column and a description of the values that each column can return.

Column Name	Column Value Description
ROOT_SCHEMA_NAME	The column or catalog view's schema. This column must be included in the filter.
ROOT_OBJECT_NAME	The column or catalog view's name. This column must be included in the filter.
USER_NAME	The name of the user account we're testing. The view will return the effective restrictions applicable for the user.
USER_ID	The numeric user ID of the user account we're testing. The view will return the effective restrictions applicable for the user.

Table 16.4 Columns in EFFECTIVE_STRUCTURED_PRIVILEGES View

Column Name	Column Value Description
EFFECTIVE_FILTER	All effective filter conditions combined into a single statement.
STRUCTURED_PRIVILEGE_NAME	Name of the structured privileges.
STRUCTURED_PRIVILEGE_ID	Numeric ID of the structured privileges.
STRUCTURED_PRIVILEGE_FILTER	Single filter condition applied by the given structured privilege's name.
STRUCTURED_PRIVILEGE_STATUS	Indicates the status of the structured privileges. Possible values are APPLIED, NOT GRANTED, NO MATCHING ATTRIBUTE, or NO FILTER VALUES FOUND.

Table 16.4 Columns in EFFECTIVE_STRUCTURED_PRIVILEGES View (Cont.)

16.2.6 Effective Privileges

To see a complete listing of privileges that have been granted directly and indirectly, the EFFECTIVE_PRIVILEGES view can be queried. This view returns the net effective privileges, even if they're granted from roles. The view provides the source of the privileges and a list of objects related to the granted privileges.

The following example SQL statement can be used to list all of the privileges granted to a particular user account:

```
SELECT * FROM "SYS"."EFFECTIVE_PRIVILEGES"
WHERE USER_NAME = '<USER_NAME>';
```

Replace the <USER_NAME> variable with the user account in question. This view provides access to several columns that can be used to sort, group, and filter the view. Table 16.5 provides a listing of the key columns available in this view.

Column Name	Column Value Description
USER_NAME	The name of the user related to the privileges.
GRANTEE_SCHEMA_NAME	The grantee schema name.
GRANTEE	The name of the user or role that provided the privilege.
GRANTEE_TYPE	The type of grantee; outputs either USER or ROLE.

Table 16.5 Columns in EFFECTIVE_PRIVILEGES View

Column Name	Column Value Description
GRANTOR	The name of the user or role that granted the privilege.
GRANTOR_TYPE	The type of grantor; outputs either USER or ROLE.
OBJECT_TYPE	The catalog object type or the type of privilege.
SCHEMA_NAME	If object type is schema, the name of the schema is returned.
OBJECT_NAME	When applicable, the name of the object, for which the privileges is applied, is returned.
COLUMN_NAME	The column name.
PRIVILEGE	The name of the privileges that has been granted.
IS_GRANTABLE	When TRUE, the column indicates that the WITH GRANT OPTION, WITH ADMIN OPTION has been granted.
IS_VALID	Returns TRUE or FALSE; when TRUE, the privilege is currently active and valid.

Table 16.5 Columns in EFFECTIVE_PRIVILEGES View (Cont.)

16.2.7 Effective Role Grantees

To generate a list of users and roles that have been granted a role, the EFFECTIVE_ROLE_GRANTEES view can be used. This view requires that the ROLE_NAME column be included in the WHERE clause as a filter condition. To query this view, use the following SQL syntax:

```
SELECT * FROM "SYS"."EFFECTIVE_ROLE_GRANTEES"
WHERE ROLE_NAME = '<role_name>';
```

The view must be queried with a WHERE clause containing a filter condition on the ROLE_NAME column. There are also other columns within the view that can be used for sorting, filtering, and grouping. Table 16.6 provides a list of the available columns.

Column Name	Column Value Description
ROLE_SCHEMA_NAME	The role's schema name.
ROLE_NAME	The name of the role in question.

Table 16.6 Columns in EFFECTIVE_ROLE_GRANTEES View

Column Name	Column Value Description
GRANTEE	The name of the user or role that has been granted the role in question.
GRANTEE_TYPE	The type of grantee in question. Choose USER or ROLE.
GRANTOR	The name of the user that granted the role.
GRANTED_ROLE_NAME	The name of the role that provided the granted role. When the granted role name and role are the same value, the role is directly granted. When the granted role name is different, the role was inherited from another role.
IS_GRANTABLE	When TRUE, this column indicates that the WITH GRANT OPTION or WITH ADMIN OPTION has been granted, and the user can grant this role to other users or roles.

Table 16.6 Columns in EFFECTIVE_ROLE_GRANTEES View (Cont.)

16.2.8 Effective Roles

To view a complete list of roles that have been directly and indirectly granted to a given user, the EFFECTIVE_ROLES view can be used. This view is very useful in listing the roles that a user has been granted, both directly and through role inheritance. To query this view, use the following SQL syntax:

```
SELECT * FROM "SYS"."EFFECTIVE_ROLES"
WHERE USER_NAME = '<USER_NAME>';
```

The USER_NAME column must be used in the WHERE clause as a filter condition. Table 16.7 provides a list of the available columns.

Column Name	Column Value Description
USER_NAME	Name of the given user related to the roles that are listed.
GRANTEE	Lists the user name when the role is directly granted to the user. A role name is listed when the role is granted from the listed role name.
GRANTEE_TYPE	Indicates the type of grantee. The USER or ROLE option will be listed.

Table 16.7 Columns in EFFECTIVE_ROLES View

Column Name	Column Value Description
GRANTOR	The user that granted the role.
ROLE_SCHEMA_NAME	The role's schema name.
ROLE_NAME	The name of the role.
IS_GRANTABLE	When TRUE, this column indicates that the WITH ADMIN OPTION has been granted, and the user can grant this role to other users or roles.

Table 16.7 Columns in EFFECTIVE_ROLES View (Cont.)

16.3 Case Study: Identifying Deficiencies in Information View Access

E-Corporation has developed numerous information views within its SAP HANA environment. E-Corporation also has several users complaining that they can't query the views. The E-Corporation security team members believe that they have set up the privileges properly; they're unable to determine why users are unable to access information views. To help E-Corporation identify the missing privileges, the company has contracted a security consultant.

E-Corporation has provided the following information to the security consultant to help him properly identify the problem with the missing privileges:

1. HAUNJON is the name of one of the user accounts experiencing the access issue.
2. The name of the information view is `ecorp.sales.view/CV_SALES`.
3. In the following sections, we'll walk through the steps the security consultant will take to identify the issue.

16.3.1 Troubleshooting the Problem

To start the troubleshooting process, the security consultant has requested that E-Corporation execute the SQL statements in Listing 16.5 and Listing 16.6 to help identify why the user can't query the information view.

```
SELECT *
FROM "SYS"."EFFECTIVE_PRIVILEGES"
WHERE
```

```
USER_NAME = 'HAUNJON'
AND SCHEMA_NAME = '_SYS_BIC'
AND PRIVILEGE = 'SELECT'
AND IS_VALID = 'TRUE'
AND (OBJECT_NAME IS NULL OR OBJECT_NAME = 'ecorp.sales.view/CV_SALES');
```

Listing 16.5 SQL Code to Query EFFECTIVE_PRIVILEGES System View

Listing 16.5 will validate that the user has SELECT privileges on the SYS_BIC schema. Information views are published as column views into the _SYS_BIC schema, so users must have the SELECT privilege on the schema or on the column views containing the ecorp.sales.view/CV_SALES prefix. If the user has access to the schema or to the individual column view, records will appear when the view is queried.

```
SELECT *
FROM "SYS"."EFFECTIVE_STRUCTURED_PRIVILEGES"
WHERE ROOT_SCHEMA_NAME = '_SYS_BIC'
AND ROOT_OBJECT_NAME = 'ecorp.sales.view/CV_SALES'
AND USER_NAME = 'HAUNJON';
```

Listing 16.6 Example SQL Used to Query the EFFECTIVE-STRUCTURED_PRIVILEGES System View

Listing 16.6 will validate that the user has the appropriate analytic privileges for the information view. In addition to requiring the SELECT object privilege on the _SYS_BIC schema, the user must also have an analytic privilege. In the SQL output, the STRUCTURED_PRIVILEGES_STATUS column will indicate the status as either NOT AUTHORIZED or APPLIED. When the status is APPLIED, we can assume that the user has an analytic privilege.

16.3.2 Reviewing the Results

E-Corporation's SAP HANA security administrators executed the two SQL statements. When executing the first statement, written against the EFFECTIVE_PRIVILEGES view, several records were returned. Based on the results, the user does have SELECT privileges on the _SYS_BIC schema and should be able to query the information view. However, the results of the second SQL statement, written against the EFFECTIVE_STRUCTURED_PRIVILEGES view, indicated that the user wasn't authorized to access the view.

16.3.3 Reviewing the Solution

After the security consultant reviewed the results, he provided a solution. Because the EFFECTIVE_STRUCTURED_PRIVILEGES view indicated that the user account wasn't authorized, it was apparent that the user doesn't have the required analytic privileges. The consultant recommended that E-Corporation grant the required analytic privileges to a role that's also granted to the user.

When the E-Corporation security team members received the recommendation from the security consultant, they didn't initially agree with the recommendations. The security team was under the impression that users only need analytic privileges when the data requires row-level restrictions. The security consultant explained that all users must have an analytic privilege that references the information view they need, even if they don't require restrictions. SAP HANA requires that each user have both an object privilege and analytic privilege when querying an information view.

The E-Corporation security team now understands the issue. To resolve the issue, the team members created a new analytic privilege that references the information view. After granting this analytic privilege to one of the user's roles, the user successfully queried the information view.

16.4 Summary

Using a user-specific trace to record authorization debug information is an excellent way to determine the permissions that a user is lacking when attempting to perform an action that isn't authorized. In addition to security tracing, security administrators can also use several security-related views within the SYS schema to list the explicit and effective security for a given user, role, or grantee.

Chapter 17
Security Recommendations

Knowing how to configure and implement security within SAP HANA is vital, and we often need guidelines based on established best practices. In this chapter, we'll provide several recommendations for securing an SAP HANA system based on the principals covered in this book.

Throughout this chapter, we'll identify several important security configuration options within SAP HANA. This is by no means a complete list, and organizations should consult their security teams when adopting any recommendations within this chapter. We'll include recommendations related to password authentication, encryption, high-level privileges, the SYSTEM account, escalation vulnerabilities, appliance handover, and audit policies.

17.1 Password Authentication Settings

SAP HANA provides an internal user and password authentication mechanism. Any user with an enabled password should comply with industry and organization password standards, so now, let's review recommendations related to standard user password policies and service accounts.

17.1.1 Standard User Password Policies

Standard users are those related to actual people that log on to the SAP HANA system using an SAP HANA–managed user name and password. Out of the box, SAP password authentication requires only a single token for authentication: That token comes in the form of a password. Therefore, it's important that security administrators implement measures to strengthen the passwords used by users.

There are six key password policy items that need to be addressed with any SAP HANA system: password lifetime, complexity, number of reused passwords, lockout policy, initial password policy, and password disabled option.

Password Lifetime

Passwords should be configured so that they expire after a specified number of days; in SAP HANA, the default is 182 days. Depending on the required password complexity and length, this number might need to be lowered. For example, many organizations require passwords to expire every 90 days, because they only require eight characters and limited complexity. Consult with your organization's security team for a policy appropriate for your situation.

In addition to the maximum password lifetime, a minimum password lifetime should be implemented to prevent the user from conducting frequent, consecutive password changes. For example, a user might try to change his password several consecutive times, attempting to circumvent the password reuse policy. The default value of one day will generally discourage users from circumventing the reuse policy, but the value should be increased if users frequently abuse the policy.

Password Complexity

Passwords should require a minimum number of character types to decrease the likelihood that both software programs and other users might guess them. By default, passwords require an uppercase letter, lowercase letter, and numeric digit in SAP HANA. They also default to a minimum of eight characters in length. Organizations can increase the complexity requirement for passwords by requiring a special character in addition to the other character types. They can also increase the complexity by increasing the minimum number of required characters and preventing use of common dictionary words in passwords.

Number of Reused Passwords

When changing passwords, based on the maximum lifetime, organizations should prevent users from reusing passwords for a time. The default value for SAP HANA is the five previous passwords. Multiply five times 182 days, and you'll see that passwords can't be reused for about 2.5 years by default in SAP HANA. This assumes that users don't change their passwords before the expiration date.

Organizations should review this setting and increase as needed based on the configured minimum and maximum password lifetime. For example, many organizations increase this value to 12 previous passwords to reduce the likelihood that a password is compromised.

Lockout Policy

When a password is entered incorrectly a specified number of times, the account should be locked out or restricted from use until the owner and administrator can review the cause. SAP HANA defaults to a value of six invalid passwords before an account is locked out. In addition, SAP HANA defaults to 1440 minutes or one day until the system automatically removes the lockout.

Organizations should review these default settings and implement a policy based on their security team's requirements. For example, many organizations will increase the number of failed attempts from six to 10 but also force an account to remain locked out indefinitely. When locked out indefinitely, only the administrator can remove the account lockout condition. This forces the user and administrator to communicate about the cause of the lockout, helping identify instances in which someone else might be trying to guess the account password.

Initial Password

When an administrator creates an account for a user, she establishes an initial password. SAP HANA defaults to forcing a user to change this initial password the first time they log on. An administrator should never know a user's password in the long term. Therefore, it's important that users change this password as soon as possible. SAP HANA also disables an account if this initial password isn't changed within sevent days of its creation.

These settings are very important, and the default values within SAP HANA are typically acceptable. However, organizations should consult their security policy team about their own required settings. For example, some organizations might increase the initial password lifetime if new users typically don't access the system within the first 30 days of the account creation. However, when increasing this policy setting, security administrators should choose an initial password that is unique for each user. This will reduce the likelihood of a new user account being compromised.

Disable Password Authentication

Organizations that use third-party authentication and SSO with SAP HANA accounts don't necessarily need password authentication enabled for a given user. The following SQL code will disable password authentication for a given user:

```
ALTER USER <USER_NAME> DISABLE PASSWORD;
```

Users configured with a SAML or Kerberos identity can still authenticate using a third-party authentication mechanism without the need to authenticate with SAP HANA via a password managed by SAP HANA. This methodology eliminates the need to manage passwords for a user.

17.1.2 Service Accounts

It's likely that service accounts or technical user accounts will need to be created within your SAP HANA system. Such accounts are used by software applications to authenticate with the SAP HANA system. For example, a service account is set up to allow SAP NetWeaver to manage the SAP HANA RDBMS. It's also common for the password lifetime limit for such accounts to be disabled, which helps to ensure that the password doesn't expire and thus stop the external application from functioning. When establishing service accounts, we recommend the following guidelines:

- Generate a 64-character or longer password using a secure random password generator. This makes it very difficult for the password to be compromised by software applications designed to decrypt a password store.
- Limit the overall privileges assigned to service accounts. Only grant what's absolutely necessary for the account to service the application's use within SAP HANA.
- Plan to generate a new password every year—and remember that applications using the service account must also support changes to the password. It's important to change this password, because it can become compromised due to human error. For example, media containing the password might be unencrypted and easy to compromise.
- Use a secure password manager application to store the password. Such applications typically have their own internal security mechanisms and auditing to help organizations manage service account passwords that are accessible by multiple users. For example, the password can be checked out for testing. When checked out, SAP HANA security administrators can correlate the use of the account with SAP HANA audit logs.
- SAP HANA audit policies should be created to monitor service account activity, especially for critical actions. It's not necessary to monitor all actions, but it's highly recommended that important actions be audited.
- An acceptable use policy for service accounts should be drafted. Such policies should limit how these accounts are used within the organization and should establish guidelines for password policies, limitations for use, and limitations of individuals with access to the accounts' passwords.

17.2 Encryption Settings

SAP HANA 2.0 supports communication encryption, data volume encryption, and log volume encryption. SAP HANA 1.0 only supports communication and data volume encryption. Encrypting communication protocols helps to protect information as it's transmitted between a client application and the SAP HANA server. Data and log volume encryption protects the data from individuals with physical access to the SAP HANA file systems. When data and log volume encryption is enabled, data can only be accessed through SAP HANA's supported authentication and internal authorization mechanism.

Communication encryption should be used anytime information travels over untrusted and insecure networks, which might include an organization's internal network and definitely includes access over a public network. For example, if your SAP HANA system is hosted by a cloud provider, the communications protocols should be encrypted using Transport Layer Security (TLS), and clients should be required to connect using TLS.

Data and log volume encryption should be used if absolute control over the physical access to the SAP HANA server or storage is in question. For example, if the server's data center is shared by multiple organizations or hosted with a cloud provider, then data and log volume encryption is highly recommended.

17.3 Identifying Users with Elevated Privileges

When implementing a security model, organizations should maintain a list of users that have been granted a high level of access to the SAP HANA system. The term high-level access loosely describes having privileges that are inherently risky for a user to possess. Many of the system privileges within SAP HANA are inherently risky to grant to other users, and other types of privileges can also be risky.

Organizations using SAP HANA can't entirely avoid granting these privileges to some of their users. However, they should scrutinize and frequently audit their system to ensure that users have the appropriate privileges based on their established job functions and based on the organization's defined division of duties.

In this section, we'll identify system, package, and analytic privileges that are inherently risky, and we'll also list default roles that are inherently risky. In addition, we'll help you identify user accounts with these privileges using SQL statements.

17.3.1 System Privileges

With a few exceptions, most system privileges are inherently risky, because they allow a user to make changes to the system. However, the data admin, user admin, role admin, audit operator, and INIFILE admin system privileges, in our opinion, are some of the riskiest privileges that can be granted. Users with these system privileges should be limited, and their actions should be routinely audited. Let's look at each of these system privileges in more detail.

Data Admin

Grantees with the *data admin* system privilege can query all system views. They can also execute Data Definition Language (DDL) SQL commands against any table in any schema. The DDL commands include items such as `ALTER`, `DROP`, and `CREATE`. This privilege should only be granted when necessary. To identify grantees with this privilege, execute the SQL code in Listing 17.1.

```
SELECT *
FROM SYS.EFFECTIVE_PRIVILEGE_GRANTEES
WHERE OBJECT_TYPE = 'SYSTEMPRIVILEGE'
AND PRIVILEGE = 'DATA ADMIN'
AND GRANTEE NOT IN ('SYSTEM','_SYS_REPO');
```

Listing 17.1 SQL Code to Identify Grantees with DATA ADMIN System Privilege

Note that Listing 17.1 excludes the SYSTEM and _SYS_REPO default accounts from the results.

User Admin

The *user admin* system privilege allows a grantee to `CREATE`, `ALTER`, or `DROP` any user within the system. This includes actions such as passwords resets, third-party identity management, and the deletion of users. In most cases, this privilege should only be granted to users tasked with the administration of user accounts.

To identify grantees with this privilege, execute the SQL code in Listing 17.2.

```
SELECT *
FROM SYS.EFFECTIVE_PRIVILEGE_GRANTEES
WHERE OBJECT_TYPE = 'SYSTEMPRIVILEGE'
AND PRIVILEGE = 'USER ADMIN'
AND GRANTEE NOT IN ('SYSTEM','_SYS_REPO');
```

Listing 17.2 SQL Code to Identify Grantees with USER ADMIN System Privilege

Note that Listing 17.2 excludes the SYSTEM and _SYS_REPO default accounts from the results.

Role Admin

The *role admin* system privilege allows a grantee to CREATE and DROP standard roles. It also allows the grantee to grant an existing standard role to another grantee, even if the role admin privilege holder is not explicitly assigned the WITH ADMIN option. Therefore, organizations can't limit which roles can be granted if a user possess the role admin system privileges. In addition, organizations should limit their use of standard roles in favor of repository-based roles. With these risks in mind, this privilege should be granted only when necessary.

To identify grantees with this privilege, execute the SQL code in Listing 17.3.

```
SELECT *
FROM SYS.EFFECTIVE_PRIVILEGE_GRANTEES
WHERE OBJECT_TYPE = 'SYSTEMPRIVILEGE'
AND PRIVILEGE = 'ROLE ADMIN'
AND GRANTEE NOT IN ('SYSTEM','_SYS_REPO');
```

Listing 17.3 SQL Code to Identify Grantees with ROLE ADMIN System Privilege

Note that Listing 17.3 excludes the SYSTEM and _SYS_REPO default accounts from the results.

Audit Operator

The *audit operator* system privilege allows a grantee to clear the audit logs. Therefore, it should only be granted when necessary. Typically, audit log–related system privileges are never assigned to security administrators. This ensures that the security administrator can't change an audit policy or clear the audit logs in an attempt to cover his tracks.

To identify grantees with this privilege, execute the SQL code in Listing 17.4.

```
SELECT *
FROM SYS.EFFECTIVE_PRIVILEGE_GRANTEES
WHERE OBJECT_TYPE = 'SYSTEMPRIVILEGE'
AND PRIVILEGE = 'AUDIT OPERATOR'
AND GRANTEE NOT IN ('SYSTEM','_SYS_REPO');
```

Listing 17.4 SQL Code to Identify Grantees with AUDIT OPERATOR System Privilege

Note that Listing 17.4 excludes the SYSTEM and _SYS_REPO default accounts from the results.

INIFILE Admin

The *INIFILE admin* system privilege allows a grantee to change any SAP HANA configuration setting. Changes to the system configurations are extremely risky within a production landscape, and they can also affect operations in nonproduction landscapes. Therefore, this system privilege should only be granted to administrators responsible for implementing system configuration changes.

To identify grantees with this privilege, execute the SQL code in Listing 17.5.

```
SELECT *
FROM SYS.EFFECTIVE_PRIVILEGE_GRANTEES
WHERE OBJECT_TYPE = 'SYSTEMPRIVILEGE'
AND PRIVILEGE = 'INIFILE ADMIN'
AND GRANTEE NOT IN ('SYSTEM','_SYS_REPO');
```

Listing 17.5 SQL Code to Identify Grantees with INIFILE ADMIN System Privilege

Note that Listing 17.5 excludes the SYSTEM and _SYS_REPO default accounts from the results.

17.3.2 Root Package Privileges

When a grantee has root package privileges, he is assumed to have the granted privileges on all packages within the repository. It's important to identify users with root package privileges that allow changes to the repository. The following package privileges allow for changes to the repository:

- `REPO.EDIT_NATIVE_OBJECTS`
- `REPO.ACTIVATE_NATIVE_OBJECTS`
- `REPO.MAINTAIN_NATIVE_PACKAGES`

The `REPO.READ` privilege allows a user to view all repository objects without making changes. At the root level, it should be limited to only grantees that need to view all repository objects. It's best to limit who can see everything, because such information can be used to construct more sophisticated hacks.

When a grantee has been granted root package privileges, those privileges will be assigned to a special package object named .REPO_PACKAGE_ROOT. Privileges assigned to this object will be inherited by all packages and development artifacts within the repository. We advise that you limit root package access, because the repository often contains repository roles, and users can potentially elevate their own privileges if they can modify a repository role that they're granted.

To identify grantees with risky root package privileges, execute the SQL code in Listing 17.6.

```
SELECT *
FROM SYS.EFFECTIVE_PRIVILEGE_GRANTEES
WHERE OBJECT_TYPE = 'REPO'
AND (PRIVILEGE = 'REPO.EDIT_NATIVE_OBJECTS'
 OR PRIVILEGE = 'REPO.ACTIVATE_NATIVE_OBJECTS'
 OR PRIVILEGE = 'REPO.MAINTAIN_NATIVE_PACKAGES')
AND OBJECT_NAME = '.REPO_PACKAGE_ROOT'
AND GRANTEE NOT IN ('SYSTEM','_SYS_REPO')
ORDER BY GRANTEE;
```

Listing 17.6 SQL Code to Identify Grantees with Risky Root Package Privileges

To identify grantees with the root package REPO.READ privilege, execute the SQL code in Listing 17.7.


```
SELECT *
FROM SYS.EFFECTIVE_PRIVILEGE_GRANTEES
WHERE OBJECT_TYPE = 'REPO'
AND (PRIVILEGE = 'REPO.READ')
AND OBJECT_NAME = '.REPO_PACKAGE_ROOT'
AND GRANTEE NOT IN ('SYSTEM','_SYS_REPO')
ORDER BY GRANTEE;
```

Listing 17.7 SQL Code to Identify Grantees with Read-Only Root Package Privilege

17.3.3 Bypass Analytic Privileges

In SAP HANA, there are two ways to bypass an analytic privilege check. Analytic privileges protect data within the SAP HANA system. To ensure that they haven't been bypassed, we need to review grantees with the _SYS_BI_CP_ALL analytic privilege and identify information views that have disabled analytic privilege checks.

SYS_BI_CP_ALL

Information views require that all grantees have analytic privileges before the view can be queried. Information views, configured using the classic XML-based analytic privilege model, are automatically assigned to a special system of managed analytic privileges named _SYS_BI_CP_ALL. This analytic privilege provides unrestricted access to all information views using the classic XML-based analytic privilege check.

Grantees with this privilege won't be subject to any data-level restrictions, even if they're assigned custom analytic privileges that have restrictions. When a grantee has multiple analytic privileges, they're effectively combined using an OR condition. For example, if a grantee has an analytic privilege where REGION = 'North' and the _SYS_BI_CP_ALL analytic privilege, the system will generate the effective filter restriction of (1=1) OR (REGION = 'North'). Because the first condition (1=1) is always TRUE, the system ignores the remaining restrictions. Therefore, the _SYS_BI_CP_ALL analytic privileges will always grant access to all data and all information views with a classic XML-based check.

It's important to note that this doesn't apply to information views that use SQL-based analytic privileges; that is, the _SYS_BI_CP_ALL analytic privilege doesn't apply to information views with the SQL-based check.

To identify grantees with the _SYS_BI_CP_ALL analytic privilege, execute the SQL code in Listing 17.8.

```
SELECT *
FROM EFFECTIVE_PRIVILEGE_GRANTEES
WHERE OBJECT_TYPE = 'ANALYTICALPRIVILEGE'
AND OBJECT_NAME = '_SYS_BI_CP_ALL'
AND PRIVILEGE = 'EXECUTE'
AND GRANTEE NOT IN ('SYSTEM','MODELING', 'CONTENT_ADMIN');
```

Listing 17.8 SQL Code to Identify Grantees with Risky Analytic Privileges

There are two default roles that also grant the SYS_BI_CP_ALL analytic privilege: MODELING and CONTENT_ADMIN. These roles should never be used within a security model because of their inherent risk. To identify grantees with these roles, execute the SQL code in Listing 17.9.

```
SELECT *
FROM EFFECTIVE_PRIVILEGE_GRANTEES
WHERE OBJECT_TYPE = 'ANALYTICALPRIVILEGE'
```

```
AND OBJECT_NAME = '_SYS_BI_CP_ALL'
AND PRIVILEGE = 'EXECUTE'
AND GRANTEE NOT IN ('SYSTEM')
AND GRANTOR IN ('MODELING', 'CONTENT_ADMIN')
AND GRANTOR_TYPE = 'ROLE';
```

Listing 17.9 SQL Code to Identify Grantees with Risky Default Roles

Information Views with No Analytic Privilege Checks

To identify information views with no analytic privilege checks enabled, we must query table ACTIVE_OBJECT in the _SYS_REPO schema. For example, to identify information views with disabled analytic privilege checks, we can execute the SQL code in Listing 17.10.

```
SELECT *
FROM "_SYS_REPO"."ACTIVE_OBJECT"
WHERE
( UPPER("CDATA") LIKE  UPPER('%checkAnalyticPrivileges="false"%')
AND
"OBJECT_SUFFIX"
IN ('analyticview', 'calculationview', 'attributeview'));
```

Listing 17.10 SQL Code to Identify Information Views with Risky Analytic Privilege Check Settings

Any information view with its analytic privilege check disabled can be queried by any grantee with the SELECT privilege on the _SYS_BIC schema or the SELECT privilege on the associated column view. In addition, no filter restrictions can be applied to the information view. Therefore, it's important that organizations maintain a listing of insecure information views and document the reasons for their configured states.

In addition to listing information views without an analytic privilege checks, we can also list those with different analytic privilege check types. To list all information views with either classic XML-based analytic privilege checks or with SQL-based analytic privilege checks, execute the SQL code in Listing 17.11.

```
SELECT 'XML BASED AP CHECK' AS AP_TYPE, *
FROM "_SYS_REPO"."ACTIVE_OBJECT"
WHERE
( UPPER("CDATA") LIKE UPPER('%applyPrivilegeType="ANALYTIC_PRIVILEGE"%'))
AND "OBJECT_SUFFIX"
```

```
IN ('analyticview', 'calculationview', 'attributeview')

UNION ALL

SELECT 'SQL BASED AP CHECK' AS AP_TYPE, *
FROM "_SYS_REPO"."ACTIVE_OBJECT"
WHERE
( UPPER("CDATA") LIKE UPPER('%applyPrivilegeType="SQL_ANALYTIC_PRIVILEGE"%'))
AND "OBJECT_SUFFIX"
IN ('analyticview', 'calculationview', 'attributeview');
```

Listing 17.11 SQL Code to List All Information Views by Analytic Privilege Type

17.3.4 Default Standard Roles

In general, standard users shouldn't be granted the default roles included with the SAP HANA installation, some of which grant very high privilege levels. In this section, we'll discuss two of these roles, CONTENT_ADMIN and MODELING.

Content Admin

The CONTENT_ADMIN role is intended for grantees that manage the development repository and related areas of the system. Given the following risks associated with granting this role, we recommend that organizations do not use it:

- Many of its system, object, and package privileges are granted with the **Grantable to Others** option enabled. This allows a grantee with the `CONTENT_ADMIN` privilege to grant many privileges to other grantees. Such actions are typically reserved for security administrators, not lead developers.
- It grants the `_SYS_BI_CP_ALL` analytic privilege, which bypasses all data security implemented on applicable information views. Organizations should use caution when granting this privilege to any user.
- It grants full root package privileges and the ability to grant those privileges to other grantees. This is risky in most scenarios, but especially so when repository-based roles have been implemented. Users with the CONTENT_ADMIN role could elevate their privileges by modifying existing repository-based roles.

To identify grantees with this role, execute the SQL code in Listing 17.12.

```
SELECT * FROM
SYS.GRANTED_ROLES
WHERE
ROLE_NAME = 'CONTENT_ADMIN'
AND GRANTEE NOT IN ('SYSTEM');
```

Listing 17.12 SQL Code to Identify Grantees with CONTENT_ADMIN Role

Modeling

The MODELING role is intended for grantees that work within the development repository and related areas of the system. Given the following risks associated with granting this role, we recommend that organizations do not use it:

- It grants the `_SYS_BI_CP_ALL` analytic privilege, which bypasses all data security implemented on applicable information views. Organizations should use caution when granting this privilege to any user.
- It grants root package privileges for native objects. This is risky in most scenarios, but especially so when repository-based roles have been implemented. Users with the MODELING role could elevate their privileges by modifying existing repository-based roles.

To identify grantees with this role, execute the SQL code in Listing 17.13.


```
SELECT * FROM
SYS.GRANTED_ROLES
WHERE
ROLE_NAME = 'MODELING'
AND GRANTEE NOT IN ('SYSTEM');
```

Listing 17.13 SQL Code to Identify Grantees with MODELING Role

17.3.5 WITH GRANT or WITH ADMIN

When a grantee is granted a privilege, there is an additional option that allows that grantee to also grant the same privilege to another user or role. The option is named `WITH GRANT` or `WITH ADMIN` when using SQL to grant privileges. When using a GUI, the option is named **Grantable to Others**. Only grantees that manage security should have this additional privilege option.

To identify grantees with this additional capability, execute the SQL code in Listing 17.14.

```
SELECT DISTINCT "GRANTEE", "GRANTEE_TYPE", "PRIVILEGE", "IS_GRANTABLE"
FROM "SYS"."GRANTED_PRIVILEGES"
WHERE "IS_GRANTABLE" = 'TRUE'
AND GRANTEE
NOT IN ('PUBLIC','SYSTEM','_SYS_REPO','SYS','_SYS_AFL','_SYS_DI_SU')
AND GRANTEE NOT LIKE '_SYS%'
AND GRANTEE NOT LIKE 'SYS_%'
AND GRANTEE NOT LIKE 'USR_%'
AND GRANTEE NOT LIKE 'AFL__%'
AND GRANTEE NOT LIKE 'SBSS_%'
AND GRANTEE NOT LIKE 'XSSQLCC_%'
ORDER BY 1 DESC;
```

Listing 17.14 SQL Code to Identify Grantees Who Can Grant Privileges

Note that Listing 17.14 attempts to remove many of the internal system-generated accounts, because SAP controls the privileges for these accounts. However, if your organization creates users based on a naming convention that is like the one SAP uses, then the code in Listing 17.14 will need to be modified.

In newer versions of SAP HANA, there are also multiple grantees generated with a name that appears to be a random combination of letters and numbers. Such accounts should be ignored; they're managed by the system or are disabled.

17.4 Disabling the SYSTEM Account

After the system has been set up and a security model is established, we recommend that organizations disable the SYSTEM account. This account should only be enabled under extreme circumstances. When it's enabled, its actions should be fully audited by a member of the security team.

Disabling the SYSTEM account is important for the following reasons:

- The account has almost complete access to all aspects of the system. It's very high risk because of its default capabilities.
- It is a well-known administrative account that's often exploited by hackers inside and outside the organization. If it's disabled, then it can't be exploited.

- The SAP HANA auditing mechanism can't always identify the actual user executing actions as the SYSTEM account. Therefore, there's little or no accountability when this account is used.
- The account offers no division of duties.

To disable the SYSTEM account, execute the following SQL code while logged in as a different user:

```
ALTER USER SYSTEM DEACTIVATE;
```

To validate that the SYSTEM account has been disabled, execute the following SQL code:

```
SELECT * FROM USERS
WHERE USER_NAME = 'SYSTEM'
AND USER_DEACTIVATED = 'TRUE';
```

If a record is returned containing the SYSTEM account details, you can assume that it's been disabled. If you need to reactivate the SYSTEM account, execute the following SQL code:

```
ALTER USER SYSTEM ACTIVATE;
```


17.5 Identify Privilege Escalation Vulnerabilities

When an organization uses repository-based roles, it's important to restrict access to the areas of the package hierarchy that contain the repository-based roles. Only grantees authorized to manage the repository roles should have edit access to the package containing those roles.

To identify grantees with access to repository roles, we must create a SQL query that checks each level of the package hierarchy. For example, let's assume that our repository roles are stored in the package `Security.roles`. To list users with potential access to the repository roles, we must check the `root` package, the `Security` package and the `Security.roles` package for package privileges, as in Listing 17.15.

```
SELECT *
FROM SYS.EFFECTIVE_PRIVILEGE_GRANTEES
WHERE OBJECT_TYPE = 'REPO'
AND (PRIVILEGE = 'REPO.EDIT_NATIVE_OBJECTS'
 OR PRIVILEGE = 'REPO.ACTIVATE_NATIVE_OBJECTS'
```

```
 OR PRIVILEGE = 'REPO.MAINTAIN_NATIVE_PACKAGES')
AND (OBJECT_NAME = 'Security'
OR OBJECT_NAME = 'Security.roles'
OR OBJECT_NAME = '.REPO_PACKAGE_ROOT')
AND GRANTEE NOT IN ('SYSTEM','_SYS_REPO')
ORDER BY GRANTEE;
```

Listing 17.15 SQL Code to Identify Grantees with Access to Change Repository Roles

Listing 17.15 excludes the SYSTEM and _SYS_REPO accounts from the validation check, because it's assumed that they'll always have access to all packages. Any grantee listed in the results can potentially access the repository and escalate their own privileges. Therefore, only authorized users or roles should be listed.

17.6 Handover from Hardware Vendors

Under the SAP HANA appliance or *Tailored Datacenter Integration* (TDI) delivery models, SAP HANA is often deployed by a hardware vendor or certified individual. Because individuals outside your organization often deploy the SAP HANA system, it's important that several key user account passwords and encryption keys be changed after the appliance has been handed over to an organization:

- **Operating system users**
  During the installation of SAP HANA, the operating system user root, sapadm, and <sid>adm are created. The <sid> portion of the <sid>adm account will be the three-character *SAP system identification* (SID) chosen during the installation. For example, if the instance SID is HDB, then the operating system user will be named hdbadm. There can be more than one SID on the SAP HANA operating system, and each SID will have a dedicated user account.

  Once the system has been handed over from the vendor, the password for each of these accounts should be changed. In addition, any additional vendor accounts created should be disabled or deleted from the system.

- **Database accounts**
  During installation, the vendor must establish a password for the SYSTEM user account. Once the handover is complete, the SYSTEM account password should be changed. As noted in Section 17.4, this account also should be disabled once the system is in full operation. If the vendor created any additional accounts, those should also be disabled or dropped from the system.

- **Encryption root keys**
  Hardware vendors often use a disk image when deploying SAP HANA. Because this image might be used at multiple client sites, it's important that all encryption root keys be changed. Even if the vendor doesn't use a disk image, they have access to copy the encryption root keys, and therefore, they should all be changed.

17.7 Create Audit Policies

Auditing is disabled by default, and no audit policies are included with the system. The auditing mechanism should be enabled and audit policies should be created.

To validate that auditing is enabled, execute the following SQL code:

```
SELECT * FROM "SYS"."M_INIFILE_CONTENTS"
WHERE SECTION = 'auditing configuration'
AND KEY = 'global_auditing_state';
```

If the column value returns `TRUE`, then the audit mechanism is enabled.

In addition to enabling auditing, we must also ensure that specific policies have been defined. Without any active policies, most events aren't recorded. To validate that active audit polies exists, execute the following SQL code:

```
SELECT *
FROM "SYS"."AUDIT_POLICIES"
WHERE "IS_AUDIT_POLICY_ACTIVE" = 'TRUE';
```

If any polices are listed, we can assume that the listed audit actions are being captured.

17.8 Summary

To properly secure an SAP HANA system, we must first understand the mechanics of the SAP HANA security model. The relationships among users, roles, and privileges are key to this understanding. However, we must also take advice from others when defining a model based on best practices. This chapter introduced many of those best practices, and we offered SQL statements to help you check your organization's adherence to those standards.

Chapter 18
SAP HANA 2.0 Security

SAP HANA 2.0 has incorporated several changes to SAP HANA security. In this chapter, we'll provide an overview of these changes.

SAP HANA 2.0 was released in November 2016, during the writing of this book. Because not all organizations will be upgrading immediately, not all SAP HANA 2.0 changes are discussed explicitly in this book. The goal of this chapter is to highlight the key changes in SAP HANA 2.0 related to security. We expect that the migration from SAP HANA 1.0 to SAP HANA 2.0 will take some time for organizations to complete. SAP HANA 2.0 has strict operating system and hardware requirements that some organizations won't be able to facilitate without a reinvestment into their SAP HANA hardware. Therefore, we fully expect the information in this book to be applicable to most organizations that are still running SAP HANA 1.0 SPS 11 and SPS 12.

With that said, several key changes to security in SAP HANA 2.0 are outlined in this chapter. These key changes are related to authorization, encryption, classic XS engine applications, and the new SAP HANA 2.0 Cockpit.

18.1 Authorizations

There are three key changes to authorization in SAP HANA 2.0, marking options that weren't possible in SAP HANA 1.0. In this section, we will discuss the PUBLIC role, allowing or disallowing a user access to his/her own schema, and LDAP group mappings.

18.1.1 Granting or Revoking the PUBLIC Role

In SAP HANA 1.0, it wasn't possible for an administrator to grant or revoke the PUBLIC role. Users were created as either standard users or restricted users. For standard users, the SYS account automatically granted the PUBLIC role. Restricted users were created without the ability to connect using ODBC/JDBC and without the PUBLIC role.

Starting with SAP HANA 2.0, an administrator can now use SQL statements to grant or revoke the PUBLIC role on behalf of the SYS account. To revoke the PUBLIC role and to disable ODBC/JDBC connectivity, use the following SQL syntax:

```
ALTER USER <USER_NAME> REVOKE ROLE PUBLIC;
ALTER USER <USER_NAME> DISABLE CLIENT CONNECT;
```

Replace the `<USER_NAME>` variable with the user account name defined within your system. The first statement revokes the PUBLIC role, and the second statement disables client connectivity using ODBC/JDBC. This effectively converts a standard user to a restricted user within SAP HANA.

To convert a restricted user to a standard user, use the following SQL syntax:

```
ALTER USER <USER_NAME> GRANT  ROLE PUBLIC;
ALTER USER <USER_NAME> ENALBLE CLIENT CONNECT;
```

Replace the `<USER_NAME>` variable with the user account name defined within your system. The first statement grants the PUBLIC role on behalf of the SYS user, and the second statement enables client connectivity using ODBC/JDBC. This effectively converts a restricted user to a standard user within SAP HANA.

18.1.2 Granting or Revoking Access to a User's Own Schema

In SAP HANA 1.0, it wasn't possible to prevent a user from accessing his own schema unless that user was set up as a restricted user. With SAP HANA 2.0, we can now grant or revoke a standard user's access to his own schema. An admin can use the following SQL syntax to prevent a user from creating objects within his own schema:

```
ALTER USER <USER_NAME> REVOKE CREATE ANY ON OWN SCHEMA;
```

Replace the `<USER_NAME>` variable with the user account name defined within your system. To allow a user to create objects within his own user schema, use the following syntax:

```
ALTER USER <USER_NAME> GRANT  CREATE ANY ON OWN SCHEMA;
```

Replace the `<USER_NAME>` variable with the user account name defined within your system.

18.1.3 Map LDAP Groups to SAP HANA Roles

SAP HANA 2.0 supports integration with an LDAP sever to effectively map LDAP group membership to specific roles within SAP HANA. This feature doesn't provision LDAP users within SAP HANA, but it does allow SAP HANA to look up LDAP group memberships for users. LDAP groups can then be assigned one or more SAP HANA roles.

This feature is useful when existing LDAP groups align with SAP HANA roles. SAP HANA 2.0 administrators don't need to explicitly grant roles to users when this LDAP feature is enabled. SAP HANA will look up a user's LDAP group and automatically grant SAP HANA roles that are mapped to the LDAP group. This will simplify the user administration process by eliminating the need to assign roles that are mapped to specific LDAP groups.

18.2 Encryption

In SAP HANA 2.0, there are several key changes to encryption: Log volume encryption, a root key backup process, and SQL for managing encryption have been introduced.

18.2.1 Log Volume Encryption

In SAP HANA 1.0, only persistent data in the */hana/data* partition could be encrypted. Starting with SAP HANA 2.0, both the */hana/data* and */hana/log* volumes can be encrypted. Before enabling log volume encryption, be sure to back up the root keys. To enable log volume encryption, execute the following SQL statement:

```
ALTER SYSTEM LOG ENCRYPTION ON;
```

To disable log volume encryption, execute the following SQL statement:

```
ALTER SYSTEM LOG ENCRYPTION OFF;
```

18.2.2 Root Key Backup and Password

In some scenarios, we can't restore an SAP HANA backup with the original root encryption key. SAP HANA 2.0 offers new options for creating a root key backup.

Before we can generate the root encryption key, we must specify a password for the *root key backup* (RKB) file. Specify this password using the following SQL syntax:

```
ALTER SYSTEM SET ENCRYPTION ROOT KEYS BACKUP PASSWORD <PASSOWRD_PHRASE>;
```

Replace the variable `<PASSWORD_PHRASE>` with a complex password. This password should be securely retained, because it will be needed when restoring root keys. After the SQL statement is executed, any time an RKB file is generated, it will be secured using this password.

We can also use SQL to generate the root key backup file content or use the `hdbsutil` command to generate an RKB file. See Chapter 13 for more details.

18.2.3 Using SQL to Update All Encryption Keys

SAP HANA 2.0 also supports the use of SQL to update all encryption root keys. This includes the persistence key, log keys, and application keys. See Chapter 13 for more details.

18.3 XS Engine Applications and Roles

The SAP HANA 1.0 Cockpit was removed from the classic XS engine in SAP HANA 2.0. As a result, this web-based application is no longer accessible. In addition to the application being removed, its supporting repository-based roles were also removed. When upgrading to SAP HANA 2.0, the following roles no longer exist:

- sap.hana.admin.roles::*
- sap.hana.admin.cockpit.sysrep.roles::SysRepAdmin
- sap.hana.backup.roles::*
- sap.hana.security.base.roles::*
- sap.hana.security.cockpit.roles::*
- sap.hana.admin.cockpit.sysdb.roles::SysDBAdmin

If you referenced these roles within your existing security model, you'll need to update your model; these roles are no longer referenceable.

18.4 SAP HANA 2.0 Cockpit

The SAP HANA 2.0 Cockpit runs within the XS engine or XSA engine. It fully replaces the functionality of the SAP HANA 1.0 Cockpit. In addition, it also offers a few new features. With SAP HANA 2.0 SPS 00, the cockpit doesn't provide all the functionality of SAP HANA Studio or the SAP HANA Web-Based Development Workbench hosted within the XS engine. Therefore, organizations will continue to use SAP HANA Studio, SAP HANA Web-Based Development Workbench, and SQL to manage most security aspects within SAP HANA 2.0 SPS 00.

Based on information from SAP, future versions of the SAP HANA 2.0 Cockpit will eventually provide all the security-related functions found in SAP HANA Studio and SQL. Although SAP hasn't released an official roadmap, we fully expect the cockpit eventually to replace SAP HANA Studio and other XS engine applications used to manage security.

18.5 Summary

SAP HANA 2.0 offers several key changes related to authorization and encryption. It offers the ability to convert standard users to restricted users and log volume encryption, and the new SAP HANA 2.0 Cockpit will eventually be the replacement for SAP HANA Studio and other XS engine applications prevalent in SAP HANA 1.0.

The Author

Jonathan Haun currently serves as a director within Protiviti's Data and Analytics group. Over the past several years, he has helped several clients implement solutions using SAP HANA. In addition to being certified in multiple SAP BusinessObjects BI tools, he also holds the certifications of SAP Certified Application Associate—SAP HANA 1.0, SAP Certified Technology Associate—SAP HANA 1.0, and SAP Certified Technology Specialist—SAP HANA Installations.

Jonathan has worked in the field of business intelligence and database administration for more than 14 years. During this time, he has gained invaluable experience helping customers implement solutions using the tools from the SAP BusinessObjects BI and SAP HANA product lines. Before working as a full-time SAP consultant, he worked in a variety of information technology management and administrative roles. His combination of experience and wealth of technical knowledge make him an ideal source of information pertaining to SAP BusinessObjects BI and SAP HANA. You can follow Jonathan on Twitter at *@jdh2n* or visit his blog at *http://sapbi.blog*.

Index

A

E

F

G

H

I

J

K

L

M

N

O

P

Q

R

S

T

U

V

W

X